MAKING
MANAGEMENT
WORK

MAKING MANAGEMENT WORK

A Practical Approach

Kenneth Stott
Nanyang Technological University
Allan Walker
Northern Territory University

PRENTICE HALL

New York London Toronto Sydney Tokyo Singapore

First published 1992 by
Prentice Hall
Simon & Schuster (Asia) Pte Ltd
Alexandra Distripark
Block 4 #04-31
Pasir Panjang Road
Singapore 0511

© 1992 by Simon & Schuster (Asia) Pte Ltd
A division of Simon & Schuster International Group

Published in co-operation with
Singapore Institute of Management

Printed in Singapore

1   2   3   4   5   96   95   94   93   92

ISBN   0-13-544693-7

Cover design : Oracle Design
Cover photo : Apa Photo Agency
'Humphrey' cartoons : Sam Cheah

Prentice-Hall International (UK) Limited, *London*
Prentice-Hall of Australia Pty. Limited, *Sydney*
Prentice-Hall Canada Inc., *Toronto*
Prentice-Hall Hispanoamericana, S.A., *Mexico*
Prentice-Hall of India Private Limited, *New Delhi*
Prentice-Hall of Japan, Inc., *Tokyo*
Editora Prentice-Hall do Brasil, Ltda., *Rio de Janeiro*
Prentice Hall, Inc., *Englewood Cliffs, New Jersey*

Contents

A Few Introductory Words from a Multinational Company Chairman   xi

Foreword   xiii

Preface   xvii

Introduction   **1**

Chapter 1   Leading People   **14**

What Is Leadership?   16
Some Theories of Leadership   17
A Comprehensive Approach   23
A Framework for Leadership Action   31
Leader Style and Decision-Making   36
Conclusion   53
References   53

Chapter 2   Motivating   **55**

Motivation   56
Understand   58
Accept   75
Identify   78
Act   84
Conclusion   92
References   98

Chapter 3   Developing Effective Teams   **99**

Successful Teams   102
Why Have Teams?   110
From Birth to Maturity: Phases of Development   115
Phased Team Development: How the Team Leader Can Help   118
Improving Teamwork: Guidelines   124
Team Performance Inhibitors   128
Conclusion   130
References   130

Chapter 4   Planning Team Action   **136**

Planning   139
A Scheme for Getting Things Done   140
Conclusion   158
References   162

Chapter 5   Developing Team Roles   163

The Winning Team   164
Team Behaviour Roles: The Basics   165
Team Roles: Descriptions   169
Personal Assessment Analysis   181
The 'Ideal' Team   187
Constructing the Team   190
Helping Your Team Members   191
Some Notes on Teams   198
Conclusion   200
References   201

Chapter 6   Solving Problems and Making Decisions   202

Making Decisions   202
Types of Decisions   203
Steps in Making Decisions   206
Identify   207
Isolate   210
Involve   216
Investigate   234
Implement   245
Inquire   250
Conclusion   251
References   256

Chapter 7   Interviewing   257

Purpose   261
Poor Practice   264
Making Interviews Work   265
Conducting the Interview   272
Some Common Problems   278
Asking Questions   280
Pressure Tactics   284
Interview Structure   285
Organisation of Interviews   289
What to Cover in Selection Interviews   292
Gathering Information   294
Avoid These . . .   295
Conclusion   303
References   304

Chapter 8   Developing Staff   305

Training and Development   305
Why Have a Staff Development Programme?   307

Methods of Staff Development 309
Identifying Needs 315
Staff Development Model – How to Do It 317
Guidelines for Improving Staff Development 329
Do Not Forget – They Are All Adults 331
Conclusion 335
References 335

Chapter 9   Adaptive Supervision 336

Supervision 338
Judgemental and Developmental Supervision 338
Supervisory Responsibilities 341
Adaptive Supervision 341
The Developmental Options 345
The Judgemental Mandates 351
Flexibility, Matching and Planning 354
Conclusion 357
References 361

Chapter 10   Developmental Appraisal 362

Develop or Stagnate 366
Benefits 368
Purposes 369
The Approach 370
The Scheme 371
Principles 372
Problems 375
The Process 377
Conclusion 407
References 408

Chapter 11   Setting Targets 410

The Simple Steps of Target Management 412
Advantages 421
Problems (or Why Target Management Sometimes Fails) 423
Guidelines for Writing Specific Target Statements 425
Conclusion 429
References 429

Chapter 12   Dealing with Conflict 430

Conflict: Is It All Bad? 430
Types of Conflict 433
Conflict Initiators 434
Dealing with Conflicts 442

People Conflicts   442
A Little about Intergroup Conflict   468
Dealing with Organisationally Initiated Conflict   470
When Conflict Has Been 'Resolved'   470
Conclusion   471
References   472

Chapter 13   Influencing   **473**

Influence   473
Influencing People: Behaviour Strategies   479
Influencing People: Behaviour   488
Successful Influencing   500
Conclusion   503
References   504

Chapter 14   Negotiating   **505**

The Way Negotiation Works   508
You Do Not Have to Negotiate   510
Towards Agreement   511
Preparing to Negotiate   516
How Negotiation Proceeds   524
Some Negotiation Skills   534
Style   542
Conclusion   544
References   545

Chapter 15   Managing Time   **546**

Managing Time   549
The Five A's   549
Aware   551
Analyse   557
Assign   563
Attack   568
Arrange   584
Conclusion   589
References   590

Chapter 16   Running Productive Meetings   **592**

Meetings, Meetings!   592
Poor Meetings   596
Effective Meetings   599
Conducting the Meeting   603
After the Meeting   608
Setting the Right Conditions   610

Conclusion   619
References   620

Chapter 17   Delegation   **621**

What Is Delegation?   623
What Can Delegation Do for Me?   626
'I Couldn't Possibly Delegate'   628
Increasing Delegation   634
Successful Delegation   637
Prepare   640
Select   642
Meet   645
The Contract   647
Monitor   651
Review   652
Conclusion   656
References   656

Chapter 18   Writing Reports   **657**

Report Preparation   660
Getting the Message Across   663
Writing the Report   679
Writing Your Next Report   690
When It Is Finished   692
Conclusion   694
References   701

Chapter 19   Making Presentations   **702**

Making Presentations   703
Preparation   708
Essential Features   717
Getting Ready for the Presentation   718
Giving It Shape   720
Delivery   729
Visual Aids   738
Conclusion   740
References   741

Conclusion   **743**

The Authors   **747**

Index   **749**

A Few Introductory Words From a Multinational Company Chairman

In our unabating quest for quality and productivity improvement, against the background of an increasingly competitive business environment, outstanding leadership and sound, contemporary management are indispensable prerequisites. In the present phase of development in my company's part of the world, for example, the need for Singapore enterprises to internationalise is a compelling one. This need has been repeatedly expressed by representatives of government as well as the business community. A recent research project conducted at one of our universities, looking at the implications of globalisation, concluded that the most significant problem and obstacle, as claimed by the majority of the companies surveyed, is the lack of managerial skills and talent.

Solving the problem of scarce managerial resources will require meticulous attention to management development as well as promotion and support of the education and training facilities across the whole gamut of the management sciences.

The academic institutions and the various business schools can only partially satisfy the demands for managerial expertise and it is thus evident that business and industry will have to organise their own in-house management training and create their own possibilities for their staff to acquire on-the-job management experience. Extensive use could also be made of the various training schemes and the recognised providers of management training.

Under this approach a pool of management capacity could be developed, which is not only theoretically qualified but also thoroughly practical in application and experience. What is needed in such a training infrastructure is the required mindset, the will to succeed and the appropriate training material for this 'practitioner's' approach.

Under the title *Making Management Work*, Kenneth Stott and Allan Walker have set out to provide a pragmatic application manual about managerial topics ranging from the esoteric issues of leadership and motivation, through down-to-earth responsibilities like decision-making and target-setting, to the seemingly peripheral activities of writing reports and making presentations. It is to their credit that they have not tried to reinvent the wheel, but have based themselves on established conceptual frameworks and sound, proven theories in combination with examples of successful practice.

It is my firm belief that management, which is tantamount to 'getting things done through people', will be successful only if it complies with three basic conditions:

- Managers must be able to lead and motivate their people.
- Managers must be able to mould their people into a team with common objectives and targets.
- Above all, managers must be able to make use of the most valuable assets of a company, i.e. the human resources, in a mutually satisfactory way.

In this context, Stott and Walker have written a book which, I believe, will go a long way in contributing to the management development of public and private companies, and which may claim a part of the credit if success is attained in *Making Management Work*.

Bonno H. Hylkema
Chairman/Managing Director
Philips Singapore Pte Ltd

Foreword

Over the last ninety years (since the days of Fayol and Taylor) there seems to have grown an ever-widening gap between those who would *teach* management, and those who of necessity have to *practise* it. Despite the praiseworthy – and often fiercely resisted – efforts of thinkers/practitioners such as Urwick, Drucker, Mintzberg, Bennis, Revans and, more recently, Handy, the mainstream of management educators has frustrated attempts to bridge that gap. These educators, more often than not research-driven, have endeavoured to 'prove' that there are 'true' theories of management and organisational behaviour. Moreover, to parallel Einstein's General Theory, management researchers have attempted to identify panaceas for all functional ills in all types of organisation. The gap was probably at its widest in the 1970s when the plethora of hard-hitting enquiries was triggered by the discrepancies between managerial effectiveness in the United Kingdom and that in the Far East and Western Europe. These reports were exemplified then by the enquiries of Rose and Mant; since that time there have been the reports of the Handy and Constable/McCormick investigations. Each of these highlighted the deficiencies of modern management education in the United Kingdom, and advocated moves to bring theory and practice side by side, if not fully integrated. However, the old myths remained and the sturdy dividing walls continued to resist change and to obscure the increasingly self-evident truths of modern management.

'A manager is a manager is a manager . . .': A manager in a public service has to achieve results by obtaining controlled work from other human beings, as does a manager of a production unit, or a manager of an educational establishment. Much disservice has been done to the course of management education by pigeon-holing *Marketing Managers*, *Production Managers*, *Education Managers* and, specifically, *Public Sector Managers*. That is not to say such managers do not exist, but that the educationalists have prioritised the contexts of management above the processes of management. One immediately evident strength of Stott and Walker's book is that the management processes are treated as endemic to any organisation.

To a certain extent the deficiencies criticised above are now being recognised and partially counteracted by the work of the MCI, the Management Charter Initiative, in the United Kingdom. A developing national plan, with much political support, and which will have repercussions over the world of business, seeks to identify the competences needed for effective management. Once they are fully defined, as appropriate to the context of the situation being managed, they may then be developed in an individual. This approach does not throw theory out of the window, rather the concepts of competence place theory into its proper perspective.

In the past much has been made of *management education,* and from this perhaps there has arisen a tainted aura around *management training,* so it is as well to consider what is meant by these terms. Education inevitably refers to the process of acquiring knowledge and thereby – often hopefully – achieving an understanding of what and why things happen. Training identifies what skills are needed to perform tasks and generates ways and means of practising those skills to achieve better performance and increased confidence. Both are obviously necessary to an individual who has to develop and control a situation; but over-emphasis on education could produce a lot of understanding but insufficient action. Too much concentration on training on the other hand, could well result in inappropriate, albeit consistent responses to changing situations. As Marx affirmed: 'Theory without practice may well be futile, but practice without theory is definitely sterile.' Each cannot be pursued comfortably without the other; management theory and practice must go together, which is where the concepts of appropriate competence come in.

This is also where the Stott and Walker book enters the arena with considerable impact. Managerial situations tend to be dynamic, and require considerable sensitivity on the part of the manager if he or she is to exert influence over those situations. Inescapably other human beings will be involved (otherwise the individual is not a true manager!), and will contribute further uncertainty to the situation. The manager has to bring to bear on the situation knowledge and understanding of a broad range of possible influences. The expression *heuristic eclecticism,* albeit near-jargon, admirably fits the processes of managerial decision-making. Stott and Walker provide an adequate and broad basis of knowledge, and, through their self-testing exercises, the media via which the reader may be developed in analytical skills.

The effective manager recognises at the outset that most managerial difficulties arise from human influence, and correspondingly human influence is necessary to resolve them. Throwing money at problems, or increasing automation, or creating computer-controlled systems, rarely solve basic managerial problems. The good manager, however, recognises that it is not the person, the human individual, that is the problem, but the set of traits, characteristics or attitudes that mould it. Accordingly, management problems are generally soluble in the long term through better education, training and personal development, leading to better, more coherent teamwork. This book deals with these ideas throughout, but Chapter 14 is excellent for those who wish to gain a deep understanding of the processes involved. Stott and Walker admirably integrate theory and practice; each in its proper perspective, without subjecting the reader to unnecessary research findings and without lessening the advantages of the self-learning exercises. Because of this the book is especially suited to the MCI mode of management development, and meets the requirements of the core module of *The Effective*

Manager. In this respect it is also worth noting the importance of 'mentors' in an organisation. Stott and Walker not only highlight the need for mentors but also the resource commitment associated with the correct use of them. Again the MCI schemes demand mentoring as part of their concentration on the human relationships aspect of managerial competences.

The authors additionally develop two aspects of the management process that are essentially personal to the individual manager, whether he or she be at directorate, general, or sectional level. The management of available time to the benefit of all is dealt with exceptionally well in Chapter 15, and deserves reading for the first time before the main thrust of the book is tackled. The format of the text lends itself to this approach, which is of advantage to the average manager. Also, the abilities necessary for managers to express themselves adequately, and to present their cases and judgements convincingly, are treated in an excellent manner in the final chapter.

This book, then, is an excellent and practical text for all levels of management, and an unparalleled medium for use in any form of management development course, whether it be for a formal qualification via tuition, in-house work or for distance-learning. The reader will find it an exciting book, full of interest, stimulus and challenge, regardless of his or her position in the organisation.

I defy anyone not to find it so!

Charles J. Sammonds
Head of Postgraduate and Professional Studies
Wolverhampton Business School

Preface

We are concerned in this book with a practical approach to manager development. We try to draw on appropriate theory to inform effective practice and then to encourage the reader to consider how this learning might be applied in the real setting for managerial activity.

Because we believe that skills must be practised and applied, we describe our exercises as **Application Tasks** rather than simply exercises, which invariably give the impression of detachment from the real context. In our work we have indeed often been frustrated by such exercises, games and simulations which may be somewhat removed from the realities of the job. We have been equally disappointed by many exercises available which demand reference to experience (which may not be present anyway) and then which leave the matter without any attempt to tie it in with appropriate management concepts. Experience is valuable, but on its own it can be quite misleading. We do in fact draw on experience, but we use it as a basis for reflection. So you will notice, for example, that we use a number of self-analysis exercises. This is because it is difficult to move along the never-ending path to development unless we know where the starting point is. The tasks, which are used as analytical tools therefore to obtain information about preferred behaviours, attitudes and actions, should be seen as starting points for reflection and discussion, not as statements of fact or as ends in themselves. They do give interesting and useful information, but they need to be plugged into the other developmental activities if they are to have utility.

We apologise to our female colleagues and readers for our inability to cope successfully with the difficulties of the English language. After several clumsy attempts at trying to accommodate both genders throughout, we eventually followed the lead of most writers and opted for the male pronoun. This is not intended in any way other than for linguistic convenience.

Our debt of gratitude goes to those colleagues who over the years have shared their knowledge and experience with one or other of us. In particular, we would mention Vernon Trafford, Peter Smith and John Davies of Danbury Park Conference Centre; John Moss-Jones, Bob Peck, Betty Bell, Andrea Burnage, Terry O'Mahoney and other staff of the Centre for Management Studies at Luton College of Higher Education; Ian Meadows of the Australian Management College Mt Eliza for his helpful review; Joseph Murphy of Vanderbilt University; James G. Ward of the University of Illinois; the late William Walker, former principal of the Australian Management College Mt Eliza and professorial fellow of the Graduate School of Management at Monash and Deakin University; Michael Shoefield, principal of Harlow College and Michael Mann, senior lecturer in the same institution; colleagues in the division at Nanyang Technological University; Jerene Tan, editor at Prentice-Hall and her colleague, Helene D'Cruz, who were both models of help and guidance; Bryan Stonehouse for giving insights into the life of a managing director; Sam Cheah for helping us create 'Humphrey'; Andrea for her patience and support throughout the project; and Teh Mui Kim for her invaluable help in typing and commenting on our imperfect use of language as a communication tool. To all these we express our sincerest thanks.

We must however reserve a special paragraph for Charles Sammonds, former Head of Postgraduate Studies at Wolverhampton Business School, who, in his initial review of our raw text, gave us the support and encouragement to continue writing. In his detailed review of the finished work, his meticulous attention to detail and skilful use of the question mark provided a stimulating challenge to our thinking, and we are particularly grateful to him for enabling us to complete a text which can give us at least a fair degree of satisfaction.

Kenneth Stott
Allan Walker

Introduction

Success is a journey, not a destination.

(Ben Sweetland)

Many managers have an increasingly complex role to play. They are accountable to multiple constituencies and the tensions created can be difficult to reconcile. Those at the top of the organisation provide a link with the outside world, but in some situations there are also considerable expectations of them as technical experts. Indeed, many actually found their way into their senior roles, not through management expertise, but through their superior abilities in the job. Many nurses, for example, who had exemplary ward skills now find themselves behind desks running the hospital's administrative systems. Similarly, some of the most competent teachers now occupy the principal's office.

Middle managers face similar problems through their dual roles. On the one hand they are managers and provide the link with the senior administration; on the other hand they are an integral part of the workforce and are expected to offer effective leadership in this capacity.

This book recognises the complexity of these roles and focuses on the skills which will help managers cope with their diverse expectations and which will contribute most significantly to managerial effectiveness. It is not easy to define in simple terms what effectiveness is, but Stewart (1986 : 189), in discussing the process of becoming a better manager, helps to draw the distinction between effectiveness and efficiency:

> The manager has to learn to manage himself or herself. Any manager who is in charge of other people has to learn how to get their commitment. All managers have to work with people other than their subordinates and have to learn the skills required to get their co-operation. . .
>
> Managers who want to improve should review both their effectiveness and their efficiency. Effectiveness is doing the right things. Efficiency is making the most economical use of the resources. Effectiveness is more important than efficiency, because one must be doing the right kind of work. Only then does it matter whether the work is done efficiently.

Learning how to get commitment is indeed central to effective management. We mention the word 'commitment' frequently in this book and highlight the need to look beyond the superficial acceptance of directives to something which is much deeper, durable and productive in terms of people's behaviour. This naturally relates to an ability to get the best out of those with whom you work, and indeed much of the material in this text is about the skills required to manage other people. This is central to our thinking on management. Management is often described as getting things done through other people. Yet there are many who seem uncomfortable with their roles as delegators, motivators, team leaders and influencers, all facets of the job which involve a productive relationship with people.

Those with management responsibility are often highly competent workers with great capabilities. They are, however, frequently unaware of how they can improve their skills and thus simplify their jobs. In the first place, they have to be aware of their own shortcomings and rid themselves of the blindness which is caused by a 'self-righteousness' syndrome. With this in mind, we challenge you to examine your own performance and assumptions. We provide the opportunity for self-analysis through questions, questionnaires and application tasks. To gain maximum benefit from this book therefore, we urge you to take time to answer the questions and complete the tasks in an attempt to discover more about yourself. This can then form the springboard for future development as a manager, sometimes through a recognition of your personal strengths and preferences, and sometimes through an acceptance that there may be better ways of doing things.

We consider our text both innovative and conventional. We have not tried to reinvent the wheel and write new things for the sake of it, especially where relevant theory has stood the test of time. In this respect, we are conventional and the reader will find many of the fundamental concepts outlined here available in other texts. At the same time, we have introduced our own ideas and interpretations, and these may represent a departure from what is usually found elsewhere. Our models for supervision, developmental appraisal and planning team action, for example, may not have been explained precisely in this form before, but they are based on established conceptual frameworks. Our reason for introducing them in our way is because we have applied them in several contexts, and they work. We have also adopted a practical approach through the use of application tasks and questions as a form of challenge: a way of encouraging you to think about the way you do things. And our title chapters demonstrate the mix between convention and innovation. We have included such familiar topics as time management, running meetings and delegating because we feel they are important skills for the manager. We have also included some areas which are not familiar territory for most books about management practice, but areas which we felt we had a responsibility to address because they are both neglected and important. This is the reason we have written about influencing, adaptive supervision and the developmental aspect of appraisal.

All the material in this book is concerned with what you can do as an individual manager. Although we are predominantly concerned with skill development, the so-called 'how-to' of your management life, we also suggest some new ways of organising activities in your sphere of work. When we look, for example, at 'developmental appraisal', we propose a scheme which you can introduce, alongside the skills required to identify and discuss employees' development needs. Similarly, when discussing 'adaptive supervision', we encourage you to examine your supervision processes and, if appropriate in your context, implement a new way of approaching the issue. Obviously, some of these topics encroach on what might be considered organisation territory, but we explain our rationale in the relevant chapters for placing these issues at least partly in the individual manager's domain.

Our book though is mainly about people; about those who have responsibility for managing other people. Our approach considers managers at all levels as a source of great potential which has to be nurtured. Those who are prepared to develop these skills can have a considerable impact on their organisations and subunits, with higher levels of motivation, productivity and general satisfaction with the working environment.

We are both experienced in sport, one of us being a former sports coach on the international scene, so you may notice the occasional use of sport as an analogy in this book. There are certainly distinct similarities between the way in which skill development is managed for effective sports performance and the processes involved in acquiring a range of managerial skills. There are of course also substantial differences, but the word which seems to have common applicability is *skill*. Skill is not something we are born with; it is sought, acquired and developed. It is our belief that managers can develop and become *skilful*. We refute any suggestion that if a young person has not got the requisite qualities when he leaves school, he will never make a manager or leader. This would remove the whole notion of development from the scene, and it is this on which our book is based.

We work on the premise that the manager can become skilful through appropriate practice. The Chinese have an idiom which literally translated means 'familiarity enables quick growth'. This familiarity might best be acquired through realistic practice. This of course suggests that most of the learning takes place on the job, and our material is intended to be related to the work place, the site of real managerial action. But it is more than simple action. True, you learn by actually doing things. But we add another dimension which we believe is critical, and that is the process of reflection.

We cannot learn by simply repeating experiences. We often tell the story to groups of managers about the head of a public sector organisation who proudly claimed he had forty years' experience behind him. A colleague who had worked with him for some time whispered that he had not really had forty years' experience, but one year's experience forty times! Development can only come about by preparing, acting and reflecting.

We believe that managers can develop and must develop. Because of this, we have written for the practising manager. We ask many questions which relate to the real job, and these issues only become real when you can apply them to situations with which you are familiar. We have also written with the management student in mind, since most of those who attend management programmes are already practising managers. They have a situation which they can relate to.

When working with managers on postgraduate programmes, we searched the market for books to use ourselves, but found there was very little which dealt with the skills of management and which approached them in a practical way. There were some simple texts which were helpful in condensing important ideas, but many of them were superficial and failed to explain the conceptual bases of the management practice they advocated.

We attempted therefore to put this right. Having undergone rigorous training as students of management, but both having experienced the difficulties of converting theory to practice, we set out to provide a solid conceptual base for our material and to use that to inform good practice. This does not mean that we are constrained by theory, but rather use it to support our beliefs about what really works in the real world of managing. Not surprisingly though, there is a consistency between our experience of successful practice and good theory. One of the first things we ever learnt in our management education was that 'there is nothing so practical as good theory'.

Our preferences and assertions are probably evident from the chapter headings and focus simply on the importance of people to get the job done. That is of course a common sense statement. It is also a belief which is widely ignored, although we have found considerable lip service paid to the importance of good human relationship skills. Unfortunately, we have worked with many managers who, in reality, abide by the principle that people do not really matter so long as the job gets done. They believe that employees are dispensable commodities who can be bullied, coerced and generally treated very badly in order to complete assignments. In our minds, that is a very short-term perspective which may prove a barrier to longer-term success.

With this in mind, it is appropriate that we start our book with a chapter on 'leading people' which demonstrates the balance which must be struck between task and people. In its simplest form, it says that if, as a manager, you do not look after your people, tasks will not get done very well. Similarly, if you do not do tasks well, your employees are not going to gain much satisfaction from their work, and that is obviously going to affect their performance. From this it is easy to see that the text applies to all managers, regardless of function or specialist contribution to the organisation.

There are some areas which we would like to have included and these may be considered for future editions. We believe however we have addressed some of the central issues and these form a sound basis for effective management. Most of the chapters address issues concerned with managing and developing people, although the final two chapters are a slight departure, covering the specialised skills of management report writing and making presentations. We included these because, in our work, we have found them to be widely used activities and ones which are either done badly or which give rise to concern. We have avoided areas which have particular relevance only to a single group of management personnel. The areas included probably have applicability to managers across the board, although we accept our knowledgeable reviewers' comments that middle and junior managers might best benefit from the reading of this book. We still maintain that most senior managers cannot escape the need to consider such issues as managing time, developing effective teams and delegating effectively.

Although it is not intended as a conventional textbook we hope that managers undertaking award-bearing courses will find it useful in their studies. Theory has been included, but we have not tried to cover the entire field under each chapter heading. We have often selected theoretical frameworks which we find convincing, attractive and of practical utility. Conventional management textbooks explain theories and generally stop there. We use them to inform practice and to give you guidelines on how you can improve the way you manage. It is with this purpose in mind that our text is immediately relatable to the philosophy of the Management Charter Initiative.

We have tried to write the text in such a way that the chapters stand up on their own. You do not have to read the chapters in any particular sequence either, although there are some obvious groupings of topics. Chapters 3, 4 and 5, for example, are all concerned with team development and they follow a logical progression. If you are particularly interested in 'team roles', however, there is no reason why you should not read that chapter before the other two. It is probably best not to read the book at one go. There is a great deal of material to assimilate and this is best done over time. By completing the application tasks and answering the questions which are asked, you will gain a deeper understanding of the topics and you will find this a more beneficial approach than simply reading it like a normal textbook. There is also the question of application. If you are a practising manager and are keen to improve and develop, you will know it is impossible to implement a whole new range of activities with immediate effect. You have to make your changes, both in personal behaviour and systems, on an incremental basis. So it is advisable to take one or two topics and consider what you can do with those before attempting to cover the full spectrum.

We hope that our text will be a developmental experience for you. Writing the book has been an educational experience for us, as we have reflected on many of the things which have happened to us in our working lives. We have thought of the times when we have been on the receiving end of less than perfect management practice and we have reflected with disbelief on some of the things we have done in the past. We think back to some of the times when we have 'delegated' work and wondered whether our former colleagues will ever forgive us for the imperfections in our influencing skills! Similarly, we have not always been as systematic as we advocate in our chapter on 'planning team action'. We have nevertheless learnt the importance of an open mind and a willingness, not necessarily to accept, but to listen critically to different ideas. In reading this book, you too have to forget the in-built assumptions about what will work and what will not and allow yourself to at least consider the possibilities of doing things differently. As the saying goes: 'We are continually faced by great opportunities brilliantly disguised as insoluble problems.'

Sometimes we have written about some of the worst examples of bad practice and then, with some amusement, actually seen them happen! Just after the chapters on 'managing time and delegating tasks' had been written, we saw the newly appointed chief executive of a large public sector organisation spending valuable time doing what must be considered as one of the less critical tasks of top management – approving and signing junior employees' leave forms, a job which should have been delegated right down the line! We also witnessed examples of getting policy totally out of line with objectives. An institution of higher learning was quite articulate about the need for its academic staff to be involved in professional development and thoroughly up-to-date in their specialist areas, but was quite obstructive about conference leave! You will find more examples of dubious practices in the book.

We were also able to reflect on some of the better experiences we have enjoyed and appreciate some of the excellent people we have worked with. Often unappreciated at the time and even held in contempt, they have provided fine examples of being able to apply the skills of management in difficult settings.

The first chapter looks at the subject of *Leading People*, a topic which receives an enormous amount of coverage in traditional management texts but which is missing from the writing of some of the eminent authors on management skills. Very little of what is written focuses on what leaders do and the actions they take. In other words, we believe that leadership can be developed and we go along with much of John Adair's work, which supports the developmental notion and gives clear guidelines for effective leadership action. In some ways we were impelled to deal with the subject in an attempt to correct much of the incoherent rhetoric we read in the daily press about leadership qualities. It is also our experience that many managers are not significantly clear about the leadership role and the way it might be manifested in practice. We start off with an examination of some of the more important theories, and then present a framework for developing leadership performance. We also look at some activities and suggest specific actions which can be applied to each of these. Some of the latest trends in leadership research are examined briefly, and then, finally, we consider leader style and the degree of participation which a leader might afford subordinates. The chapter, in summary, examines how you might practise leadership skills in terms of completing tasks, maintaining group cohesion and looking after the needs of individual members.

The performance of these individual members is determined by three central factors, namely, ability, work environment and motivation. The employee must obviously know how to do the job, there must be an environment which provides a supportive framework for his work, and he must want to do the job. It is this last issue which provides the greatest difficulty for the manager. All managers need to be effective at motivating those in their charge. Employees are motivated by various factors and they are not necessarily the same for all. After a brief explanation of some major motivation theories, we suggest in the chapter *Motivating* some methods for identifying how your individual staff members are motivated and provide some strategies which might be adopted to increase their motivation levels. There is also an examination of whether the manager is contributing in a positive manner to the motivation of employees and then some guidelines are provided on how to develop a short practical plan for improving the motivation process. Motivation represents a long-term commitment for the manager, but it is vital to organisational productivity, employee satisfaction and consequently your success as a manager.

Managers frequently talk about teams in their organisations: departmental teams, senior management teams and so forth. But do they really act like teams or more like groups of disparate individuals? Through a series of short exercises, the chapter *Developing Effective Teams* looks at the ingredients of successful teams and the purposes they serve for the organisation. It also examines the phases through which teams might go on the path to development and suggests specific actions you can take to move your work teams through their early superficial stage to one which enables effective performance to take place.

There is no doubt that when teams perform well, they can produce outstanding results. Unfortunately, it is often the case that interesting ideas are not converted into action, or action ensues but is not based on idea generation and the critical scrutiny of solutions to problems. In *Planning Team Action* we advance a scheme which enables the team to work systematically through a series of stages from the initial presentation of the problem or project through to implementation and review. It is called the '7D' scheme and covers the processes of defining, drawing, discussing, deciding, detailing, discharging and dissecting. Under each heading is a checklist of actions which you can engage to ensure that the stage is covered thoroughly.

Still on the theme of teams, many people wonder why you can put the very best technical experts together and yet their work is not particularly stunning. Spending considerable sums on assembling the best players for a football team does not guarantee success. *Developing Team Roles* attempts to address the problem and examines how winning teams can be built through the contributions of individual members. Apart from the functional expertise which individuals bring to the team, they also have different roles to play, and if these roles are not enacted well, the team generally fails to perform optimally. We provide a way of helping you discover your naturally preferred roles and how these can be used to enhance the work of the teams you lead or of which you are a member. Without a complementary mix of roles, the team may indeed fail, and so it is vital to understand how to strengthen existing roles and adopt secondary ones to improve team effectiveness. We then look at the important question of what constitutes an effective mix of roles within a team and give practical guidelines on how you can help your members improve their contributions and thus elevate team performance.

In looking at the way teams might be propelled more systematically towards effective action, we draw attention to some of the processes involved in reaching and making incisive decisions. In *Solving Problems and Making Decisions* this issue is taken up in more detail as we examine the skills involved in these two important areas of managing. Managing is about making decisions. It is a substantial part of the manager's job. Some decisions can be dealt with by groups, some only by the manager and some delegated to others. Different types of decisions are identified and a set of factors for determining who should be involved in specific decisions is provided. The relative advantages and disadvantages of various decision-making strategies are considered, and the trend towards more participative approaches is discussed. Without some involvement in decision-making, managers may find themselves overworked, isolated and ineffective. We provide a framework which might act as a practical guide to solving problems and making decisions, and we promote the idea of sensible involvement.

We then consider an activity most managers are involved in for at least part of the time, that of interviewing. It may be a selection interview, an appraisal discussion, a disciplinary interview or simply a face-to-face meeting to gain information. They are all important in their own way and need to be conducted well. In *Interviewing*, we look therefore at the skills involved and the actions you can take to make your interviews effective. The right environment is important and adequate preparation is critical. We examine each of these alongside the skills of listening and questioning, which are central to the interviewer's conduct. We also consider the relative advantages and disadvantages of the different ways in which interviews might be organised.

We then turn our attention to a group of topics which are concerned with improvement through the process of development. Good human resources management demands an investment in human potential through staff development. This is much more than sending people on the ubiquitous courses. It must also include a range of other structured activities and involve also those whose main work is in management or administration. In *Developing Staff* we provide some background information on the issue and suggest that the manager has a central role to play in development and training, regardless of what the larger organisation is doing. We propose a model for the building of a coherent staff development programme which meets both organisational and individual needs. Experiences are then explored which help employees become more effective in their jobs and these experiences are translated into staff development policy concepts.

Few managerial concepts give rise to more intense feelings than the supervision of staff. It is a sensitive subject which is frequently ignored by managers until things start to go wrong. In some organisations, managers often face substantial opposition to any form of supervision, yet are expected both to develop and evaluate their staff. In these situations, supervision is inevitably more than the observation of a routine activity. It is more commonly about the oversight of such complex activities as managerial work and performance. This chapter suggests that supervision should be a systematic process involving everyone in the organisation. At the same time however, individual differences should be recognised, especially where those individuals are involved in complex work. In our scheme of *Adaptive Supervision* these differences are accounted for and conditions are established which might lead to effectiveness and satisfaction. The scheme emphasises the importance of developmental supervision but recognises that not all employees need to be supervised through any single approach.

Much of the information required for staff development and supervision purposes might arguably best be acquired through the appraisal process. We propose that, apart from any formal scheme which might exist in the organisation, there should be an ongoing process of examining the work of employees and their development. Most of what we see in organisations is judgemental and fails to answer key questions about progress and how the individual can improve performance. We see little evidence of schemes which encourage self-evaluation, and the summative systems in operation are seldom based on a partnership between manager and employee. If anything, we detect a polarisation of positions between the two. Our informal scheme of *Developmental Appraisal* is based on manager and employee working together, and is designed to help the employee grow in both the job and his career. It is based on structured discussions, conducted in an atmosphere of openness and trust, which look at the job, the aspects which are going well and the steps which might be taken to effect improvement.

Partnership also needs to be extended to formulating direction and goals. Many managers now realise that they need to involve their staff in setting certain organisational targets. Involvement in setting targets can provide ownership and a greater commitment and motivation among employees. It is therefore based on a very positive philosophy about people and what makes them work well. It assumes a willingness and desire to be involved. Target management can be useful at all levels of the hierarchy. It focuses and formalises both personal and organisational targets. The chapter on *Setting Targets* presents the steps involved in the concept and its usefulness to managers. Guidelines for writing specific targets are supported by practical activities for target-setting in both a simulated and a real situation.

We then address one of the realities of management. For most managers we have worked with, conflict is an ugly word. It is also an inevitable fact of organisational life. The more people you are responsible for, the more conflicts will occur. To be effective as a manager, you have to develop competence at dealing with conflict and at least try to transform potentially destructive episodes into constructive experiences. Conflict can have positive or negative outcomes, and it is the former for which we should strive. In the chapter *Dealing with Conflict* we discuss the different types of conflict you might face and identify their possible sources or causes. We then examine in detail a set of strategies which might have relevance to particular situations. We emphasise the advantages of a collaborative approach, where people can work together positively towards the sort of constructive outcomes which are characterised by increased adaptability, creativity and improved productivity.

Managers are involved in influencing people all the time but this is a subject which is seldom addressed in texts which deal with the 'how-to' of management. Some strategies are more effective than others. Some people are good at determining the behaviour of others, whether superiors, subordinates or peers, whilst other managers experience little success. *Influencing* examines a range of influence strategies and shows in what situations they might be appropriately used. In outlining the advantages and disadvantages of each strategy, we reach conclusions on which strategies have potential for success and which can best be described as 'high risk'. We also give a profile of the 'tactician manager', probably the ideal example to follow in terms of the appropriate and flexible use of influencing strategies, and the one who enjoys most success in getting what he wants, whilst at the same time maintaining good relationships.

One conclusion we reach in looking at influence is that coercive approaches have severe limitations. There seems to be a growing realisation that simply telling people what to do is unlikely to secure long-term commitment from employees. There are many occasions where negotiating has a role to play. Conducted properly, negotiation enables both sides to gain satisfaction and be committed to the outcome. The chapter *Negotiating* explains the basic sequence involved and a structure for even the simplest negotiation episode. It then goes through the steps involved in preparing for negotiation. The skills of listening and questioning are considered. The strength of the negotiation process lies in the 'agreement' of the parties involved, and this integration of interests, arrived at through a skilled approach to bargaining, seems to have considerable potential for many situations a manager might face and which are characterised by differences of perspective.

Before managers can expect to run an organisation effectively, they must be able to manage themselves. We examine a vital component of this in *Managing Time.* Time is often considered as the most important resource to the manager. He must be able to identify therefore those activities which steal his time and stifle productivity. This chapter helps you do this and presents a practical system for effective and efficient time utilisation. We emphasise the importance of prioritising tasks and setting goals. We also advocate the analysis of your current time expenditure as a basis for action and improvement. We look at some strategies for combatting some of the most common time 'thieves' and we suggest a time-planning system which can be used on a permanent basis.

Ask any manager for a list of his major time thieves and the word 'meetings' will appear sooner or later. Meetings are an accepted fact of organisational life. They are also a regular source of complaint. As management systems seek to become more democratic and decision-making more participative, the pressures on people's time and concentration become more acute. Despite the questionable worth of meetings, they have tended to proliferate in most organisations. It follows therefore that meetings have to be handled well if they are to serve their purposes. Great skill is required, both on the part of participants and that of the leader, to ensure that meetings are clearly focused and productive. In *Running Productive Meetings* we cover some of the central issues in making these events effective. We examine the preparation which must take place, including agenda item selection, prioritising items, allocating time and assembling the necessary materials. We then look at the conduct of the meeting and at the ways in which the discussion might be focused and members encouraged to participate. Actions to be taken after the meeting are identified and we examine the conditions which best contribute to the event's success in an attempt to ensure that meetings become worth the considerable organisational time they consume.

Another important facet of managing time is the ability to get things done effectively by other people. Regrettably, delegating tasks is a skill which is so generally practised poorly and there are many tales of managers distributing trivial tasks or burning themselves out by attempting to do everything themselves. The chapter on *Delegating Tasks* provides a framework for successful delegation which will enable colleagues to gain thorough developmental experiences. It looks at some of the reasons we avoid delegating and asks some critical questions which are central to the manager's organisation of work. The benefits of skilful delegation are identified and a systematic process is laid out which can be used when a potential task first appears. The partnership between manager and delegate is emphasised and essential support actions on the part of the manager are listed. Done well, delegation will enable both the manager and the organisation to be more productive, and the delegate to enjoy more satisfaction through true responsibility and development.

We then address two topics which we believe are important to managers and which are concerned with particular forms of communication. Managers at all levels have to write concise and accurate documents. With so much paperwork finding its way into organisations, it is important that reports have the impact which is intended, and this is best achieved through a systematic approach. *Writing Reports* gives you a simple and suitable structure for conveying the message, and goes through the preparation which must take place. We examine some important considerations relating to layout, style and checking the document when it has been finished.

The second communication topic again involves managers at all levels to varying degrees. Making presentations, either to groups of colleagues at departmental meetings or to larger gatherings at special events, is a part of the job which superiors expect to be done well, especially the higher up the ladder you go. The skill displayed in this form of communication determines whether the message is put across accurately. In the chapter *Making Presentations* we look at three key aspects of making oral presentations, namely, preparation, shape and delivery. We see preparation as the key to effective delivery. We explain how thinking about the purpose, the presentation's content, and the way in which you are going to transmit the message, is important to quality delivery. We examine a basic structure which is suitable for most situations and we look at the factors which might support successful delivery of the presentation.

The success of our text can be judged only by its transferability from the written page to the real world. We are committed to the skills approach, that, as a manager, you have to actually practise management skills to develop your competence. It is our intention therefore that this book is used as a guide for action, and not so much read as a book about management. Like Whetten and Cameron (1984 : 2) '... we emphasize *practicing* management skills, rather than merely reading about what managers do, or what researchers surmise managers ought to do.'

We have also focused very much on 'people' management. We accept that other skills are important, and it is useful to be able to interpret balance sheets, decipher graphics and analyse management information system data. But being able to work effectively with others and get the best out of people seems to us to be at the centre of management. There are many in the highest echelons who recognise this fact and are incorporating ability in working with other people into their major selection decisions.

This book is addressed to practising managers, whether hospital administrators, school principals, church leaders, owners of small companies, local authority superintendents, department heads or managers in industrial and commercial concerns. It is written for those who have responsibility for the work of other people. It is also written for managers who face more difficult conditions than ever before. A more articulate and demanding workforce, pressures of accountability and the pervasive new technologies all place extensive demands on managers. Under these pressures, it seems more important than ever that skills are developed which will enable the highest levels of performance to take place and which will make it possible for both employees and managers to be satisfied with their working lives.

One final note: take things gradually, and do not expect everything to work at once. The Chinese have a story about an old woman who was grinding a large iron pestle on a stone by the roadside. She explained to an inquisitive youngster that she was grinding it to a needle to sew cloth with. When the child laughed, she explained that if she persevered day after day, it would eventually become a needle. We believe much of what we have to offer in this book is worth persevering with, whether in terms of your behaviour or the way you do things. And do remember the quotation at the beginning, that success is a journey, not an immediate certainty. We wish you a pleasant journey through the book.

References

Stewart, R. (1986) *The Reality of Management,* Pan : London.
Whetten, D. and Cameron, K. (1984) *Developing Management Skills,* Scott Foresman : Illinois.

Chapter 1

Leading People

Leadership is many things. It is patient, usually boring coalition building. It is the purposeful seeding of cabals that one hopes will result in the appropriate ferment in the bowels of the organization. It is meticulously shifting the attention of the institution through the mundane language of management systems. It is altering agendas so that new priorities get enough attention. It is being visible when things are going awry, and invisible when they are working well. It's building a loyal team at the top that speaks more or less with one voice. It's listening carefully much of the time, frequently speaking with encouragement, and reinforcing words with believable action. It's being tough when necessary, and it's the occasional use of naked power – or the 'subtle accumulation of nuances, a hundred things done a little better,' as Henry Kissinger once put it.

(Peters and Waterman, 1982 : 82)

Leadership is indeed many things. It is also one of the most elusive concepts in the world of management. It is a word which is often used very loosely and with little apparent understanding of what it means. The quotation from Sir Michael Edwardes, 'Success is about leadership and leadership is about success' (Goldsmith and Clutterbuck, 1984 : 13), is typical of the sort of statement which does little to enhance our understanding of leadership, but which nevertheless has a ring of truth about it. Try asking a friend or colleague what he thinks leadership is. The usual answer includes an example of some high-profile leader or a list of qualities rather than an explanation of the concept of leadership.

To further complicate matters, *leadership* is often used interchangeably with *management* and although some writers have tried to draw the distinction, there seems to be a general acceptance amongst practising managers that they are very much the same thing. In the USA for example, leadership is preferred to management, whereas in Britain it is the other way round. Some progressive organisations in the latter country however have tried to capture the spirit of the 'out front' role of management and incorporate the expression 'leader' in job titles. A college which was redesigning its management structure, for example, chose to call its middle managers 'leaders of division' rather than 'heads of department'. It was hoping these 'leaders' would take a traditionally minded workforce with them down innovative paths. The expression could also have been used because it is often fashionable to be different!

One writer who has successfully drawn the distinction is Kotter (1990: 104): 'Management is about coping with complexity....Good management brings a degree of order and consistency to key dimensions like the quality and profitability of products. Leadership, by contrast, is about coping with change.' He goes on to highlight the need for leadership as managers have to cope with increased amounts of change. The environment is more competitive (and that applies not only to the world of business) and there is faster technological change. The activities of management are planning and budgeting, organising, controlling and problem-solving. In contrast, the activities of leadership are giving direction, aligning the workforce and motivating people.

This is a useful way of viewing leadership and one which is incorporated in this chapter as we attempt to grasp the concept. Most managers who read this text will be involved in change to a greater or lesser extent, and on this premise it seems that effective leadership skills will be needed. At the same time, we are concerned with managers as leaders and it is very difficult to separate the two elements of the job in practice. We have therefore brought the two together in a fundamental concept of leadership and management where people have to be led towards task completion and the meeting of organisational goals.

Let us now look at the word **leadership** and the images it conjures up. We may visualise someone walking in front of a group of followers, with the leader choosing the direction and pace. When we think of some of the great leaders from the international stage, they appear to choose and others appear to follow in obedient compliance. We may have an image of someone with a great concern for arriving at a destination and inspiring the troops to get there. 'What "leaders" meant was managers who had the ability to point the way and to get people committed to going that way' (Stewart, 1986 : 61).

But is this what leadership is really about? Is it simply about guiding groups of subordinate employees to the destination of task completion? Many studies have indeed gone down this road by supposedly linking successful leadership with the capacity to encourage others to follow towards the goal of economic success. Goldsmith and Clutterbuck (1984), in their well-known book *The Winning Streak*, identify three elements of leadership: the visibility of the leader; the provision of a clear statement of direction to which they themselves are committed and to which they can get others to commit themselves; and the provision of clear objectives with adequate resources. These authors go on to draw attention to the importance of the individual and the need to display a caring attitude.

With all this in mind, we think the clue lies in the title to this chapter: leadership is about leading people. We did not refer to leading *machines* but leading *human beings*, people with feelings, aspirations and reasons for complying. Therein lies our mandate for developing leadership skills: if you are going to increase your effectiveness as a leader, you must complete tasks and lead human beings who have very complex sets of needs.

In this chapter, we shall be presenting an overview of some of the major developments in leadership theory and seeking to help you understand how your preferences and situational influences fit into the picture. In particular, we examine the contribution which *trait, behavioural* and *contingency* approaches have made to the understanding and development of leadership. We then present a model which focuses on the actions you can take and which will help you to achieve the purposes you have been set, whilst at the same time ensuring that your team is working cohesively and that the individuals involved are receiving the sort of support they demand in the satisfaction of their personal needs to operate effectively. The issue of management style is a common theme in the leadership literature and we shall be presenting a framework of styles which are available to the leader as he makes managerial decisions. We shall also try to show how it is important to understand the key factors of the situation in which you operate and give you the opportunity to consider your own particular context for management. Finally, we shall take a brief look at what is currently happening in leadership research and comment on some of the more significant developments.

What Is Leadership?

APPLICATION TASK 1.1

Think of someone you have worked for who you consider to be a good leader. Write three reasons why you think he or she is a good leader. Try to be specific: Give examples of things he or she might have done which demonstrated effective leadership.

Name of leader:

Reason 1:

Reason 2:

Reason 3:

In Application Task 1.1, you are encouraged to consider your experiences of leading and being led. You are putting together your own thoughts on what effective leadership is.

If you were to do this task with a group of colleagues, you would probably emerge with many different answers. If you summarised all the answers on a large sheet of paper, you would be surprised at the differences in responses.

We have done this exercise many times with groups of managers. We are usually able to write between twenty and thirty items on the flipchart. What is particularly surprising is the number of people who actually believe you have to meet all the listed requirements to be an excellent leader. Of course, many of the items listed are qualities or personality characteristics which in themselves may be quite elusive. If you really do have to acquire all these attributes, there does not seem to be much hope for most of us as leaders!

But the message from all this is clear: people expect an enormous amount from leaders. The pursuit of twenty or thirty 'essential' qualities is not realistic of course, but we believe it is possible to develop the skills to lead people effectively. Much of this chapter is about the ways in which you can extend your skills in three key areas in order to meet the requirements of productive leadership.

Some Theories of Leadership

We have to bite our tongues when we hear the expression *leadership qualities*. There is nothing wrong in the notion of leaders possessing some qualities, but it seems to us that many indulge in rhetoric about 'developing the qualities of leadership' without much understanding of the nature of leadership and its potential for development.

Leadership is a subject which is very close to the hearts of most organisations and it is not surprising that there is a wealth of literature on this key facet of organisational life. Some of it is based on extensive research and some is largely intuitive, based on the experiences of figures who have enjoyed considerable success in their respective fields. One of the more traditional approaches is that of *Trait Theory* and we shall briefly examine this explanation which still enjoys support in some quarters.

Trait Theory is essentially about personal qualities. The basis is that leaders are born and not made. There are certain qualities therefore which make a good leader. In order to identify a good leader, you measure whether the appropriate characteristics are present. Stogdill (1948) for example listed: *intelligence, scholarship, dependability, responsibility, social participation* and *socio-economic status* as characteristics of leaders, whilst other researchers listed *intelligence, supervisory ability, initiative, self-assurance,* and a host of other desirable qualities.

One major problem of Trait Theory was the fact that there was little agreement on which qualities were relevant. Another failing was that the notion favoured *selection* rather than *development*. We are always amused by John Adair's little story about the senior manager who wrote on a junior's report: 'Smith is not a born leader yet' (Adair, 1973 : 5). At least there seems to be some concession that Smith might some day acquire the attributes with which he should have been born! Yet there is good evidence to show that leaders can be developed. This is the basis of many management development programmes where leadership is an integral component.

Apart from the seemingly insurmountable problem of arriving at a set of traits which could be universally applicable, the approach did not account for the different contexts in which leadership is practised. Situations can be vastly different. Owens (1987 : 126) makes this very point:

> The characteristics of the group being led (for example, maturity level, level of trust, cohesiveness), the nature of the group's tasks or mission (for example, clarity of goals, complexity of tasks), and the psychological environment in which leadership is attempted (for example, levels of ambiguity, uncertainty, threat and conflict), are illustrative of variables that differ from situation to situation and that have an impact on the ability of individuals to lead effectively.

This takes us on to a consideration of leadership from a more contextual perspective, and we shall be looking later at an approach which expressed leadership as being 'contingent' on the situation in which it was applied. We return briefly however to the traits or personal characteristics approach.

There are still many who subscribe to Trait Theory in its entirety. You will hear people talk about 'born leaders' or people who possess the 'qualities' to be leaders. It largely depends, though, on which qualities, because if the list is too demanding, that might disqualify people who have proved themselves to be highly effective in the leadership role.

Despite the faults of the approach, there are undoubtedly one or two qualities which may be expected of all leaders. It seems difficult to endure as a leader without *courage*. Similarly, we have seen several leaders suffer severe setbacks because of lack of *integrity*. Whilst we are tempted to include *intelligence* in this short list, we feel it may be misinterpreted as a call for educational qualifications as a prerequisite for leadership positions. What we would expect however is that a leader should be able to grasp the intricacies of a situation. This does not need qualifications, but many situations will demand a modicum of brainpower! We use the word *expectations* advisedly. We are NOT saying that possession of these qualities will actually make an effective leader.

It would be all too easy to add to this list and dream up an array of desirable attributes. It is probably expedient to accept that many excellent leaders have had their faults in terms of characteristics but still managed to fulfil their roles successfully. Despite this, those two qualities, above all others, seem to be essential.

Think of your own experience. If you have been facing change in your area of work, what is it like to work for a boss who has no courage to stand up for what he believes to be right? We are reminded of one chief executive whose public sector organisation was facing major change, as the central agency sought to restructure provision. The organisation was under-resourced and held in generally low esteem. As the workforce was kept completely in the dark about the changes taking place and treated badly, despite their substantial contribution to the service, he could only shrug his shoulders and say it was not his fault, because no one told him what was happening. He agreed that his staff deserved recognition, but he was simply lacking in the courage necessary to stand up for his organisation and lead it through the change with an increased level of esteem.

Again, integrity seems to be a prerequisite for leadership. We draw an example from the education service. Wilma became the head of a school which had suffered a decline in recent years. She was appointed to lead the school to renewal, to review practices and inspire the workforce to improve performance. She found it difficult to win the support of her staff however because her integrity was constantly in question. She claimed she had not said things when she obviously had. Then one day an important incident underlined her problem. She assured one of her staff she would be recommending her for promotion, but immediately after the interview, wrote in her confidential report a statement which expressed complete opposition to promotion. It was some time later that Wilma's staff member discovered what had been written after seeking an appointment with the inspectorate.

If people are going to be behind you and support you through difficult episodes of change, they have to trust you, that what you say is the truth and that you keep your word. And bear in mind that it takes only one mistake like Wilma's to give you a reputation you can well do without.

Another popular concept of leadership relates to knowledge and competence, and indicates that a leader in one situation may well be a follower in another, because of the authority (or lack of it) of knowledge. Apart from the obvious problems of shifting leadership round the group as situations vary, there are other difficulties. Even though someone may have all the knowledge and qualifications in a given situation, he may still not be a leader. You can probably provide real life examples of this. There are many instances of experts in particular skills or knowledge areas who are given such a position of authority because of that ability. You may know someone who has been 'rewarded' with a leadership position because of his technical knowledge in his area of work. He may be the best technician. He may be the best teacher.

He may have the best qualifications, but they do not necessarily make him the best leader. It is not usually practicable though to pass leadership round the group. There has to be someone who is accountable for achieving the task set. One only needs to think about finding the person responsible for making a particular decision in a large government department or a similar organisation to understand why sharing leadership in this way can be problematic!

It is tempting to be dismissive of this shifting-leadership approach, but it is nevertheless widely practised in many spheres, especially in terms of leadership selection decisions. It presents however a very limited view of how the situation might impact on leadership. Situational elements may in fact be very important in determining leader behaviour and the style emphases he might adopt in order to be effective. We shall look at the importance of these elements a little later.

It is generally accepted that leadership theory has passed through three key stages. The first of these, the *trait* stage, was highly influential and lasted until about the middle of the century, although, as we have indicated above, it may still be exerting an influence even now in some quarters. The second stage is usually referred to as *behavioural* and was largely concerned with leadership style in an attempt to draw conclusions about which style is most effective across the board. The third stage, known as the *contingency* approach, looked at the interrelationship of three factors: the leader, the subordinates (or followers) and the situation. Whereas behavioural theories tend to emphasise the effectiveness of leader behaviours characterised by high concerns for task and for relationships, contingency views propose that there is no best style which works in all situations and that leadership effectiveness is evaluated in the unit's success in achieving its objectives.

One of the most famous episodes of leadership research was undertaken at Ohio State University where leadership was defined in terms, not of characteristics, but of performance. Two basic functions were defined: *consideration* or *human relations* which relates to the extent of care and concern for the staff, and *initiating structure* which was associated with the task. The latter related to defined relationships, roles and patterns of working. The general basis of the work was that effective leaders were those who gave evidence of behaviour high on both dimensions.

Blake and Mouton (1964), famous for *The Managerial Grid*, advanced the notion that good leaders are those who can develop good relations with their staff and initiate new ways to solve problems. You may hear some advocates of this approach describing effective leaders as 'high on task, and high on people'. It simply means that they get things done well and at the same time care for the needs of people. The grid has been a highly popular tool for analysis and for identifying the alternative emphases available to the leader.

There is often a problem with this. A tension may exist between task accomplishment and looking after the welfare of staff. There may even be different expectations. For example, middle managers in particular suffer from the tension created by conflicting demands. They are part of the management of the organisation, responsible to the executive for productivity and task completion, but at the same time their subordinates want their interests protected and demand that their bosses are considerate to them.

It may be unrealistic in some situations to expect a single individual to reconcile these two tensions. Some would argue that it may be more realistic to look to team leadership as the answer. Where the boss is obviously task-centred and focuses on achieving organisational goals, for example, the deputy might concentrate more on the social and emotional needs of the subordinates. The leadership role then can be shared, and this has been done very effectively in many organisations.

It does seem, however, that both needs have to be met. Whilst success in achieving results is important, how it is done is equally important. We have seen many leaders using their formal authority to push things through, supervising closely, checking repeatedly, and interfering in everything. Effective leaders in contrast have a concern for their charges' needs and lead by consent.

Despite the persuasive attractions of such behavioural theories, there is no consistency of relationship between the leader's effectiveness and the two measures of consideration and initiating structure. Situational Leadership Theory (Hersey and Blanchard, 1977) is an attempt to account for the inconsistency. It extends the managerial grid and draws on Reddin's (1970) 3-D Management Style Theory. Before we outline Hersey and Blanchard's notable contribution to the understanding of leadership, let us look briefly at Reddin's work. He was responsible for providing an effectiveness dimension as an additional component to the dimensions of task and relationships. He defined effectiveness as the extent to which the manager achieves the goals for which he is responsible. He identified four basic styles (related to task and relationships) and five key situational factors or pressures:

1. The superior.
2. The subordinates.
3. The fellow workers.
4. The nature of the work, tools of the job, and their influence.
5. The fundamental beliefs or the culture of the organisation.

His four basic leadership styles are essentially the same as those expressed in *The Managerial Grid*, and are called *separated, related, integrated* and *dedicated*. The key to Reddin's work, though, is the notion that the effectiveness of any given style is dependent on the situation in which it is employed. This of course is a substantially different approach to the more traditional views of leadership where personal qualities are the key factors or where one style is seen as universally effective. The basic grid was extended into a three-dimensional model, adding the dimension of effectiveness, and provided a framework in which style can be assessed. To the basic styles were added four effective and four ineffective styles. Appropriateness is the key, each style being effective or ineffective according to the situation.

Hersey and Blanchard's work has two categories of behaviour: the first, *task behaviour*, is closely related to *initiating structure*; the second, *relationship behaviour*, corresponds largely with *consideration*. Task behaviour is concerned with the leader's arrangement and definition of group members' roles. It is characterised by delineating the what, when, where, how and with whom of each task. Things are clearly laid down, including whose permission should be sought and so forth, and there is generally little ambiguity. Relationship behaviour on the other hand is concerned with the extent to which personal relationships between leader and members are maintained. There is scope for contribution through open communication, and the provision of emotional support is important.

Hersey and Blanchard's theory is useful to the understanding of leadership by dwelling on the importance of follower characteristics in determining the appropriateness of leadership style. The situational factor of *maturity* is considered one task at a time. In terms of the member's capacity to set challenging goals, the willingness to accept responsibility, and his education or experience, he may be considered very mature on one task, but comparatively immature on another. Maturity in this model has two components: job maturity, which is concerned with the skills and knowledge to do the job; and psychological maturity, which is to do with self-confidence and self-respect.

The way that Hersey and Blanchard's model addresses the problem of effectiveness is by prescribing appropriate leadership behaviour for the situation. As a subordinate's level of maturity increases (up to a moderate level) the leader should use more relationship and less task behaviour. As maturity continues to increase, there should be less relationship (and still less task) behaviour. A description of the basic tenets of the prescription is given in Yukl (1981 : 141–142).

The same author also highlights the inadequacies of the model, pointing to the weak conceptual basis and the lack of a coherent rationale for the assumed relationships. Situational variables which may be relevant to leader behaviour are also ignored, and maturity is defined too broadly. On a positive note, however, the work has made an important contribution to the field. People have to be treated differently and according to their situations. Leaders can also actively change the situation by building the maturity of subordinates. Finally, the prescription for effective leadership behaviour in a given situation may be advanced, but the leader has to have the skill in employing that behaviour (Yukl, 1981 : 144). Owens (1987 : 152) also draws attention to some possible problems. Some leaders for instance may actually force immaturity on subordinates by being inappropriately directive and failing to provide the opportunities and conditions in which growth and development can take place; and again, some leaders may give responsibilities to followers who are not ready, and who have neither the job nor the psychological maturity. Despite any drawbacks, the theory demonstrates a useful incremental approach for taking the organisation through a series of steps to a high level of maturity.

Fiedler (1967) was one of the earlier proponents of contingency leadership, considering critical contextual factors for the practice of leadership. He classified situations in terms of their *favourableness* to the leader, and identified three key factors which would determine this:

1. The quality of the relationship between the leader and his followers.
2. The extent to which the task has clarity.
3. The powers which the leader has.

Whilst there may be differences about which situational factors are the most influential, there has been increasing agreement that leader behaviour is difficult to separate from contextual considerations. Despite the absence of a firm and proven prescription for leadership in any given situation, as Yukl (1981) indicated, there are skills which must be acquired before any choices about behaviour can be made. This is the way forward and the key to our contribution. We believe a number of important actions can be identified for leaders and that skill must be attained in using these actions. This forms the basis of our comprehensive approach.

A Comprehensive Approach

The focus in this chapter takes up the theme of needs, in moving to a state where effectiveness is achieved in three key areas. It lays the emphasis not on what leadership is, but what the leader does. It takes into account not only the leader, but the demands of the job, the groups being led and the individuals who form that group. It also goes a step further by considering these demands against three activities: planning, controlling and reviewing.

At this stage it will be useful to you to obtain some preliminary opinions about the way in which you behave as a leader. There are two things you should do. First, complete the questionnaire My Typical Leader Actions. Consider how you normally behave and try to answer as accurately as possible. We shall refer to your answers later.

Questionnaire

MY TYPICAL LEADER ACTIONS

Think of the way you lead your work team. Where the words work group, staff or individuals are used, they refer to the people for whom you are normally responsible. It may help you to think of particular situations such as meetings or projects. Try to answer, however, according to how you normally behave.

For each of the statements below, circle the appropriate number.

4 = I invariably do this
3 = I sometimes do this
2 = I seldom do this
1 = I never do this

1. I explain tasks and make sure they are understood.   1 2 3 4

2. I outline the importance of each individual contribution   1 2 3 4
    to the task.

3. I keep my discussions with staff to the point and avoid   1 2 3 4
    irrelevant chit-chat.

4. In meetings I ask for ideas on how to solve problems.   1 2 3 4

5. I give a fixed time scale for tasks.   1 2 3 4

6. I consider how well my staff are doing and give them   1 2 3 4
    regular feedback.

7. I try to develop a pleasant working atmosphere in my   1 2 3 4
    work team.

8. I unravel the difficulties of tasks before distributing work. 1 2 3 4

9. If things are not going well, I tell staff they must   1 2 3 4
    shape up, or else!

10. I build on individual suggestions in trying to arrive at a 1 2 3 4
    group solution.

11. I spell out the constraints of tasks.   1 2 3 4

12. I encourage my work group to be self-critical and   1 2 3 4
    evaluate their work.

13. I ensure that I have all relevant information before embarking on a job.   1 2 3 4

14. With a new and complex task, I draw on people's relevant experiences.   1 2 3 4

15. If differences of opinion emerge, I explore them.   1 2 3 4

16. I get expert help to ensure a quality job.   1 2 3 4

17. I willingly give individuals help when they need it.   1 2 3 4

18. When there are several things to think about, I set priorities.   1 2 3 4

19. I find out about and use people's skills.   1 2 3 4

20. From individual ideas, I identify options which can be discussed.   1 2 3 4

21. I work out the possible consequences of different courses of action.   1 2 3 4

22. I congratulate my work group when we do something successfully.   1 2 3 4

23. I arrange back-up plans in case things go wrong.   1 2 3 4

24. I ask staff members individually for their ideas.   1 2 3 4

25. I make sure my staff know their roles and responsibilities.   1 2 3 4

26. I lay out the standards I expect from my staff.   1 2 3 4

27. I listen to everyone's ideas, regardless of their worth.   1 2 3 4

28. I make myself available to help in any way I can.   1 2 3 4

29. I push staff into making decisions to avoid time-wasting.   1 2 3 4

30. I make helpful suggestions to people engaged in a task.   1 2 3 4

31. I give individuals specific tasks to do which fit into the big job.   1 2 3 4

32.	I keep a close watch on jobs in progress.	1 2 3 4
33.	If personal disputes emerge, I reconcile them for the sake of group harmony.	1 2 3 4
34.	I check up to make sure people are doing what they should.	1 2 3 4
35.	I ensure the group has the resources to do the job.	1 2 3 4
36.	I tell staff to 'get a move on' to ensure deadlines are met.	1 2 3 4
37.	I plan guidance and appropriate training.	1 2 3 4
38.	I inspect work to make sure it is up to scratch.	1 2 3 4
39.	I keep my staff informed about what is going on.	1 2 3 4
40.	If necessary, I replan tasks which have deviated from expectations.	1 2 3 4
41.	When things are not going well, I give them reassurance.	1 2 3 4
42.	I review work objectives and assess whether they are being met.	1 2 3 4
43.	If we don't do something well, I work with them to analyse mistakes.	1 2 3 4
44.	If they don't perform to expectations, I admonish them.	1 2 3 4
45.	I arrange for social meetings to build the work team's spirit.	1 2 3 4

Second, you will need to gain the help of some of your colleagues. Ideally, they will be your subordinates, but if you prefer you can seek the co-operation of managers at the same level as yourself. Ask them to complete the Leadership Analysis Form below, considering the way you normally lead. If you want them to give you honest answers, you will have to be very open to criticism and avoid making any counter-criticisms, otherwise you may find it difficult to secure co-operation in the future.

Questionnaire

LEADERSHIP ANALYSIS FORM

Think about the working situation involving the manager and his staff. If you agree with the statement, please tick the box. Please do this carefully in order to provide accurate and helpful feedback to the manager.

1. There is often little leadership of any kind in the work group.   X   ☐
2. The manager usually gives most attention to those who talk the most.   I   ☐
3. The manager regularly compliments people on their contributions.   I   ☐
4. The manager attempts to draw all people into discussions.   G   ☐
5. The manager is always anxious about getting the job done.   T   ☐
6. The manager is always checking on the time available to complete jobs.   T   ☐
7. The manager constantly asks whether we are going about it the best way.   T   ☐
8. The manager listens to work group members attentively.   I   ☐
9. The manager usually attempts to do most of the work himself.   T   ☐
10. The manager frequently tries to deal with differences of opinion.   G   ☐
11. The manager tries to involve everyone in the task and to share ideas.   G   ☐

Write down the things the manager does which make the work group successful:

Write down the things the manager does which make life difficult for the work group:

Stott, K. and Walker, A., *Making Management Work.* © 1992 Simon & Schuster (Asia) Pte Ltd.

Take all the completed forms (the more, the better) and total the responses for each statement. Then add up the scores for each code (letter) category. For this, you will need to use the form Analysis Scores.

ANALYSIS SCORES

Statement	Code	Score
1.	X	☐
2.	I	☐
3.	I	☐
4.	G	☐
5.	T	☐
6.	T	☐
7.	T	☐
8.	I	☐
9.	T	☐
10.	G	☐
11.	G	☐

Totals

T ◯   G ◯   I ◯   X ◯

Stott, K. and Walker, A., *Making Management Work*. © 1992 Simon & Schuster (Asia) Pte Ltd.

The letter codes refer to the following:

T = Task
G = Group
I = Individual
X = General point

These all refer to the particular focus. You can therefore explore whether you tend to emphasise one particular aspect. If you have high scores in the T category, you may be task-centred. If you have scored highly in the I box, it could indicate that you are strong on personal relationships and see these as very important. High scores in the G box may show a concern for team cohesion, that everyone should be pulling together. These of course are only indicative and need supporting through discussion with those who gave the scores and who work with you. If you have any scores at all in the X category, this must be explored, because your colleagues may feel they are without a leader. Those unfortunate people in the public sector organisation we mentioned earlier probably felt their ineffectual chief executive was not providing any leadership.

In the spaces at the bottom of the form, your colleagues may have written about the things you do which help them in their work and the actions you take (or fail to take) which are less than helpful. You should take notice of these and be prepared to discuss them, because you may not be aware that you are hindering your colleagues in some ways.

It is useful to explore any differences of scoring or perception amongst your participants. It is equally helpful to you to open up about the way you feel regarding your emphases. Do you see yourself as very much task-centred, keen to get work done well and on time, or are you more a 'people' manager? You can learn so much about yourself and how others see you by discussing your performance in this way.

You can now check the information you derived from this exercise with colleagues with your answers on the questionnaire you completed earlier. Using the scoring chart, calculate your scores for each of the three areas. These indicate your possible emphases in terms of orientation. A high score on task, for example, may indicate that the actions you generally take reveal a preference for getting the task done over and above other considerations. Again, like the other items of information, it is not definitive, and is best used as a basis for personal reflection and discussion with those who know your work.

QUESTIONNAIRE SCORING CHART

Look at the scores you have given to each statement on the questionnaire. Enter them on the chart below. The numbers on the chart refer to the statement numbers.

Task		**Group**		**Individual**	
1.	◯	4.	◯	2.	◯
3.	◯	7.	◯	6.	◯
5.	◯	10.	◯	14.	◯
8.	◯	12.	◯	17.	◯
9.	◯	15.	◯	19.	◯
11.	◯	20.	◯	24.	◯
13.	◯	22.	◯	27.	◯
16.	◯	25.	◯	30.	◯
18.	◯	28.	◯	37.	◯
21.	◯	31.	◯	41.	◯
23.	◯	33.	◯		
26.	◯	35.	◯		
29.	◯	39.	◯		
32.	◯	43.	◯		
34.	◯	45.	◯		

Individual

Total = [   ] X 6 ◯

Group

Total = [   ] X 4 ◯

36.	◯
38.	◯
40.	◯
42.	◯
44.	◯

Task

Total = [   ] X 3 ◯

A Framework for Leadership Action

John Adair's (1973) work on team-building and leadership is well known in management circles and seems to make a great deal of sense in providing a coherent analysis of the leadership role. The *action-centred leadership* approach has been successfully adopted by many major companies who have put their managers through programmes based on the model.

The essence of action-centred leadership is the move away from what leaders *are* and more towards what they *do* . You will recall that the quotation from the book *In Search of Excellence* at the beginning of this chapter spoke of things the leader does, and had very little to say about what he is. By focusing on the actions which leaders take, Adair is clearly indicating that leaders can develop. Qualities therefore assume little relevance and the accent is on identifying key actions in three interrelated areas which will ensure that leadership is effective. These areas are shown in Figure 1.1.

Figure 1.1
The Three Interrelated Demands

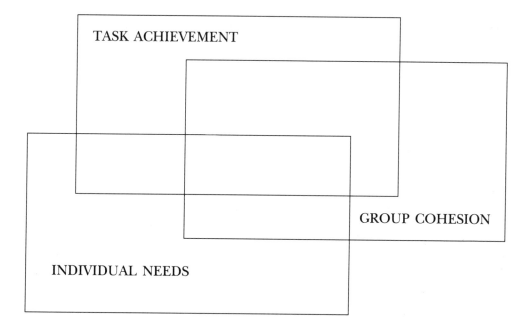

Firstly, there is a demand to achieve the task, the purpose for which the group exists. Secondly, there is a need to attain group cohesion. Thirdly, there are the needs and demands which individuals bring with them into the group. These are important considerations. Highlighting the importance of the group and the individuals in it, Hemphill (1949) tied in leadership with the degree of cohesion felt amongst group members and their satisfaction as individuals derived from their membership. Being 'together' and taking pride and pleasure in membership is therefore associated with the group's leadership.

Task

Achievement of the task is crucial to the team's success. Your job is about completing tasks and assignments, and the chances are that if you do not get them done, you will not have a job! Although it is true that this is the key need, some managers fail to acknowledge the other needs and team performance suffers as a result.

Group Needs

If the group is to achieve the task, it must be held together. This may be a difficult challenge for the leader. If everyone decides to do his own thing, the sum of the individual, disparate efforts is unlikely to add up to the required amount. For example, the football team must function as a unit – this does not mean everyone has to do the same thing, but the roles have to be complementary, and it is part of the leader's brief to achieve a high level of cohesion. We shall see in Chapter 5, Developing Team Roles, how the leader may have to harness the preferred behaviours of team members so that effective task completion can be attained.

Individual Needs

The needs which individuals bring to the group are very complex. This is tied in very much with motivation. Herzberg (1959) proposed the theory that if you want to influence satisfaction, you have to provide possibilities for achievement, recognition, responsibility and job interest.

Probably the most well-known work in motivation is that of Maslow (1954) who arranged a hierarchy of human needs. He proposed that once certain needs are satisfied, other areas of need are sought. When you can satisfy the basic needs of thirst and hunger, you then need to look to security needs like pensions, job security, and so on. As far as the leader is concerned, such needs as acceptance by the group (social), status (self-esteem) and the opportunity to use one's ability (self-actualisation) are examples of those which must be satisfied. Motivation is a key aspect of the manager's job and we discuss the subject in detail in the next chapter.

Getting it Together

If you achieve the task, the effect will be to create a sense of unity in the group and satisfy individuals for the reasons already mentioned. If individuals are fully involved and motivated, they will contribute much more to the team and the team is much more likely to achieve the task.

By contrast, if there is failure in any one of the rectangles, it affects the other two. A lack of group cohesion, for example, affects the achievement of the task and need fulfilment of individuals. The leader therefore has to be aware of task, group and individual needs, and he has to perform activities to satisfy those needs. In other words, he has to *do* things.

Activities

Although there are many variations on the theme of management or leadership activities, we prefer to think of them under three umbrella headings of *planning, controlling* and *reviewing*. Of course there are many subactivities within these areas, but the main activities give us some idea of our particular leadership action emphases. Figure 1.2 is a summary of what each activity-grouping entails.

Under each of the activities listed in Figure 1.3 are some actions which the leader can take. As a rough guide, these are further subdivided into task actions, group actions and individual-centred actions.

You can use the list to assess whether you tend to concentrate on any one activity or orientation within that activity. Also, by looking at the lists, you may see some actions which you tend to neglect and which you ought to consider including when you take your work team through tasks. Bear in mind though, that this is only an attempt to delineate actions to facilitate understanding of your behavioural emphases. It cannot be seen as categoric. You will see that many of the actions are not exclusive to any one orientation (task, group, individual) or to a particular activity-grouping (planning, controlling, reviewing). Furthermore, not all actions are relevant to all situations.

The framework has been presented to show the actions which might be relevant to certain orientations and activities, and you can identify whether there are any areas which you neglect or which might need attention. We have covered these actions only briefly, and for a more detailed and systematic account of how to take teams through tasks, you are advised to see Chapter 4, Planning Team Action, which examines the whole process in seven stages and gives details of the actions a leader and team can take to reach an effective conclusion.

The responsibilities of the leader have been distilled into three interrelated areas. He must outline and achieve the task; must build up and coordinate a group of people; must satisfy and develop individuals. This model demands a recognition of all three dimensions to achieve prolonged success.

Figure 1.2
Leadership Activities

ACTIVITIES

Planning

    Explaining the job
    Asking for ideas
    Assessing skills
    Distributing work and responsibilities
    Setting targets

Controlling

    Supervision
    Monitoring
    Co-ordinating work
    Giving help and support

Reviewing

    Reflection
    Assessment of performance
    Rethinking plans

Figure 1.3
Leadership Actions

PLANNING TASK ACTIONS

Explaining the task to colleagues
Specifying the time available
Unravelling the difficulties
Listing the various constraints
Asking for relevant supporting information
Obtaining expert advice
Checking resource availability
Setting priorities
Considering consequences of actions
Specifying standards of performance
Explaining contingencies

PLANNING GROUP ACTIONS

Explaining the reasons underlying the task
Asking for ideas
Building on suggestions
Generating options
Developing group solutions
Assigning responsibilities
Allocating specific tasks
Giving out resources
Summarising comments for the group

PLANNING INDIVIDUAL ACTIONS

Taking audit of relevant skills
Asking individuals for ideas
Asking for relevant experiences
Listening to all contributions
Optimising individuals' skills
Specifying roles and standards

CONTROLLING TASK ACTIONS

Keeping discussions on line
Prodding members to decisions
Observing the task in progress
Checking that actions are related to goals
Inspecting performance standards
Influencing work tempo

CONTROLLING GROUP ACTIONS

Exploring differences of opinion
Intervening or helping
Reconciling conflicts
Maintaining group atmosphere

CONTROLLING INDIVIDUAL ACTIONS

Making supporting suggestions to individuals
Giving individual help
Guiding and training
Giving reassurance

REVIEWING TASK ACTIONS

Summarising progress
Reviewing objectives
Asking for replanning
Challenging preferred solutions

REVIEWING GROUP ACTIONS

Identifying and commenting on successes
Getting group to learn from failure
Persuading group to be self-evaluative

REVIEWING INDIVIDUAL ACTIONS

Assessing value of individual contributions
Assessing individual performance
Giving feedback to individuals

Leader Style and Decision-Making

In our brief review of some of the major theories underlying the development of leadership understanding, we mentioned the subject of *style* in connection with several theories. Managerial work demands that decisions are made, but one of the key questions relates to the degree of involvement which the leader affords to subordinates. From the contingency perspective, it depends largely on the circumstances surrounding the decision. A style appropriate in one set of conditions will not necessarily be appropriate in another, and very different, situation. We shall present a framework of styles available to the leader a little later which is based approximately on other more established frameworks. You will recall that we discussed earlier the contingency approach to the subject of leadership. Vroom and Yetton's (1973) contribution to this approach was in proposing the degree of participation in decision-making as the central issue of leadership. They specified how leaders ought to behave to achieve effectiveness according to the contingencies. Their taxonomy of five different styles has provided the basis for several subsequent frameworks.

For ease of understanding, we have tried to simplify the conceptual material about style and provide five 'discrete' categories. They are not really discrete of course, since they are best thought of as on a continuum and there are spaces between the categories. They do help, however, to illuminate our preferred approaches and thereby heighten our understanding of how we typically choose to behave.

Before we look at the style emphases which leaders might adopt, try doing this short exercise to obtain an initial impression of your particular preferences. Read the outline case study and then decide how you would deal with the situation, given the five options available. These options do not relate perfectly to styles, but they are an approximate explanation of some key differences in the way managers prefer to make decisions.

Caldex Manufacturing Company is in a small rural town. It makes toiletry bags and several related products. It is not easy to get workers because the nearest large town is some 25 miles away. Most of the eighty workers are female and quite young, some fresh out of school. There are some older ones, but they are mostly employed on a part-time basis.

Until now, the company has supplied chemists shops with its products. The orders have been quite small but regular. It has been necessary to raise prices because of the increased costs of labour and materials, which has led to a drop in demand. The company has now been offered a three-year contract to supply a major chain of stores, but the products will have to be substantially reduced in price. Nevertheless, a large and certain order like this would not only offer short-term security, but also provide some much needed finance to update the equip-

ment.

Getting new employees is virtually impossible. If the contract is accepted, it will mean the present workers having to do new jobs. They are quite set in their ways, and the last time a change such as this was discussed, they demanded more money and some key people even quit.

You are the manager of this company. You know it makes sense to accept the contract, otherwise the company could go under within the next couple of years, especially in view of the high interest rates. What would be your approach with the workers? Complete Application Task 1.2.

APPLICATION TASK 1.2

Look at the five alternatives below and rank them in order of your preference. If you think solution 4 is the best approach, then you will put a 1 in the box beside it, and so on.

1.   You send a letter to all employees informing them you have accepted the contract for the good of the company.

2.   You arrange ten short meetings over three days, meeting eight workers at a time, and discuss the issue with them. You keep a fairly open mind.

3.   You hold a meeting with the entire workforce and explain to them that your job description demands you make the decision, but you are allowed to accept comments in writing so long as they are sent through, and approved by, the supervisors.

4.   You try to meet socially with as many of the workers as possible and use your pleasant personality to get the message across about the advantages to them of accepting the contract. You try to get them to agree with you.

5.   You get the supervisors together and tell them to go and persuade the workers to accept the necessary changes to their jobs, and then only report back in five days' time which is when the contract has to be signed.

Stott, K. and Walker, A., *Making Management Work.* © 1992 Simon & Schuster (Asia) Pte Ltd.

As you read the next section, you will understand the differences between these responses to such a situation. So that you can relate your ranking to the framework which will be used, the possible solutions in Application Task 1.2 relate to the styles as follows:

Solution 1 : Solo

Solution 2 : Sharer

Solution 3 : Rules and regulations

Solution 4 : Sweet-talker

Solution 5 : Opt-out

As far as the task is concerned, how far should the leader share decisions with other members of the work group? Should he take them on his own? Figure 1.4 shows some of the options.

The trend in today's management world is to go for more involvement in decision-making. Advocates of this approach maintain the more you share in decisions, the more motivated and committed you are to carrying them out. Of course, things are not always quite as simple as that. Although a participative sort of operation may be desirable, the right conditions may have to be present. If the organisation is not performing well, the leader may

Figure 1.4
Freedom and Involvement

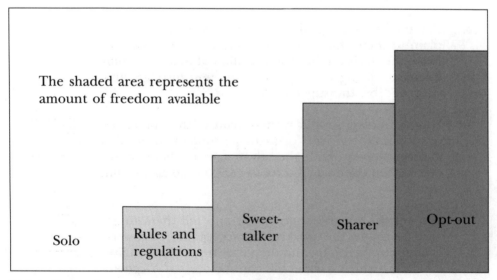

This indicates the amount of relative freedom subordinates might have to participate in decision-making under different leadership styles.

not be able to employ participative methods. In fact, he may have to be directive as he tries to move his organisation or subunit to a point where it is relatively effective and where participation can be sustained. The options shown are generally referred to as *styles*. It is probably true that many leaders operate predominantly in a given style. Below is just one framework of leadership styles.

Solo

The *solo* leader gives directions, tends to operate on his own and keeps away from subordinates. This person often communicates by memorandum and you will usually find him in his office. He will have low visibility but obviously his influence is pervasive. Subordinates are often frightened of doing things without his approval, so most affairs have to be referred upward.

He is clearly the boss and his authority is unchallenged. Whilst it seems to work well in some situations, there are some groups of employees who will react against this sort of domination and will fail to perform optimally.

There is also the question of time. Where it is available for considered decision-making, it may be possible to extend involvement, but where time is short, the more directive approach may be necessary. In an emergency situation, for example, such as a fire or a machine breakdown, it is not practicable to throw the decision open to discussion. The officer in charge has to act as a solo leader so that action can be taken immediately.

Rules and Regulations

The *rules and regulations* leader may also be fairly directive, but instructions are based on rules and laid-down guidelines. Everything is done by the book. There is little room for initiative, but this leader can always blame someone else or the system for any imperfections.

Of course, the style has its advantages. The rules and regulations leader is seen to be fair and impartial, so you may feel that any rewards are not the result of partial judgements or friendships.

There is a set way of doing things, so you know where you stand and the style is good for those who have a low tolerance for ambiguity and need everything laid out neatly for them. You have to be aware though that the style can be intensely frustrating: when you want something done quickly or you would like to use your initiative in making a decision, you will probably find the rules and regulations leader holding you back because it is not being done 'by the book'.

Sweet-Talking

The *sweet-talking* leader usually has a persuasive disposition. He has the skill of making things sound attractive to individuals although they are related to organisational goals. He does not like to use his authority, so that he can retain his popularity. Of course though, he has the authority. After all, he is the boss, but he believes that it is not productive to simply tell people what to do. At the same time, he knows what he wants, and uses his personality and political skills to succeed. He is sometimes described as 'charismatic', a 'born leader', and so forth. It is unlikely he is a born leader – he is just using his personal attributes and skills to support a strategy designed to get things done with little personal damage.

Sharing

The *sharing* leader is broad in outlook and socially inclined. He encourages sharing in decision-making and gives people latitude in determining their own job structure. He looks after the interests of his charges and shows concern. He will work hard to achieve a congenial atmosphere.

It is the trend these days to see this democratically inclined leadership as the best style. When people are asked to describe their style, they invariably opt for democratic and sharing, even if they are really quite autocratic. They generally perceive that it is good to be seen as a sharing leader.

It is true that the style is in vogue and that there is an increasing recognition that extended involvement leads to wider commitment on the part of participants. We have already hinted at the problems associated with assumptions that a participative style is appropriate across the board. It also has to be recognised that the leader is still accountable and cannot put important issues 'to the vote'. This would be inappropriately democratic. But the sharing leader can do so much to enhance the partnership with the work team, and an inevitable consequence of such an approach seems to be improved quality decision-making, as more people are involved and able to contribute their knowledge, expertise and experience.

Like all the styles in this framework however, the sharing leader has his problems and this is best illustrated by the general manager of a small manufacturing company who decided to share the decision about diversification with the workforce. A market opportunity had been identified and the question was whether to take the risk of committing resources to a relatively new field of operation. Although he knew it made economic sense to diversify, he set up a series of meetings at different levels to gauge opinion, to discuss problems and to secure commitment to the idea of expansion, not a difficult thing to do, since employees would see the benefits of increased profitability. It took nearly five months to complete the process. By the time a decision had been reached, a rival company had already established operations and failing to be the first in the field seriously impaired any chance of success. The idea had to be abandoned.

From this rather extreme case can be seen that sharing tends to take time, and although the sharing leader generally gets support from colleagues and develops a good working climate as people feel they share some ownership of major decisions, the time has to be available to take this approach. With this in mind, the leader has to be very skilful in deciding what should be shared and what should be decided by him (or simply delegated). It is a waste of valuable organisational time, for example, to impose a democratic process on simple administrative decisions which can best be described as trivial.

Opt-Out

The *opt-out* leader is very active at first in setting guidelines and deadlines. He then withdraws from the scene and lets everyone get on with the job without monitoring or evaluation.

He is similar to the solo leader in one respect: he tends to hide away and not make himself very visible to subordinates. But he lets them get on with things. In this way, he can divorce himself from the problems which crop up and save himself the attendant worry and stress. He runs into difficulties though when things start to go wrong. Take the case of the services manager of a company who asked a subordinate to improve the canteen facilities for employees and told him to get on with the job and let him know when it was finished. He was the sort of person who did not like to be bothered. The subordinate ran into a problem with one of the canteen staff and dismissed her. There was a reaction amongst union members which resulted in the canteen being closed. The services manager was furious he had not been consulted about such serious action, and was of course answerable to the chief executive for the difficulties. He only had himself to blame however, since he made no attempt to monitor the task nor keep any link with it once it had been assigned.

This sort of event may happen from time to time with many leaders, whatever predominant style they adopt. What we are looking at here though is the leader who permanently opts out and chooses to abdicate his responsibilities. It could even be suggested he is not doing his job properly. He has little control and his staff get the general impression he has no care or concern for what takes place.

There is a major advantage. In some situations, colleagues may thrive on having almost complete freedom to tackle assignments without any sort of interference. These people are usually highly skilled (probably professionals) and experienced, and have the political know-how to understand when matters should be referred upwards. Nevertheless, they still prefer to have some interest from the leader, even if it is simply an acknowledgement at the end of the task.

SUMMARY

- The *solo* leader gives directions and makes his own decisions.
- The *rules and regulations* leader bases decisions and directives on laid-down guidelines and procedures.
- The *sweet-talking* leader uses his persuasive disposition and personality attributes to secure agreement.
- The *sharing* leader involves others and keeps an open mind. He tries to develop a congenial working climate and tries to share decisions in an effort to gain commitment.
- The *opt-out* leader may set guidelines and deadlines, but generally removes himself from the scene while others make decisions and get on with the job.

Which style do you prefer? More importantly, which style do you think you commonly adopt? Perhaps you use more than one style. You should now complete Application Task 1.3.

It is not so simple to say one style is better than another. There are advantages and disadvantages with each – even the solo or autocratic styles. We have already acknowledged the desirability in many circles of pursuing a sharing approach, with greater recognition of (if not undue emphasis on) the needs of people, and with supervision which is not too close. Sometimes, however, leaders can be too 'people-centred', leading to inadequate task performance and resultant low morale amongst members. Furthermore, not all employees can cope with a sharing approach; some may thrive only in conditions where they are told in clear terms what to do and how to do it.

This hints at the need to consider several issues before reaching conclusions on which is the 'best' style. You will recall that Reddin posited that the effectiveness of any style is dependent on the situation, and that pressures from five potential sources will determine the context in which leadership style has to be employed. You will find it useful to attempt to understand your own context for leadership. So apart from knowing your preferred style emphases, you may also need to understand the ways in which your superiors, subordinates, fellow workers, the nature of your work, and the culture of the organisation affect your situation. Some of these sources of demand were accounted for earlier by Tannenbaum and Schmidt (1958) who identified three sets of characteristics: those of the manager, the subordinates and the situation. Amongst the manager's characteristics are his personal values, his confidence in his workers, his style preferences in terms of the desired

APPLICATION TASK 1.3

Write down the leadership styles you adopt in rank order. If you feel you are mostly the *rules and regulations* leader, but occasionally employ a *sharing* style, you will put rules and regulations first and sharing second. Under each style, give one example of how you have displayed this style.

1.

Example:

2.

Example:

3.

Example:

Stott, K. and Walker, A., *Making Management Work.* © 1992 Simon & Schuster (Asia) Pte Ltd.

amount of sharing and his ability to cope with the uncertainty which arises when work is shared. The subordinates' characteristics include the level of their independence, their tolerance for ambiguity, their knowledge and experience, and their expectations of participation. Amongst the situation characteristics are the culture of the organisation (in other words, how things are customarily done), the nature of the problem (whether it is relatively simple or complex), and the amount of time available. These correspond approximately to Reddin's, since the demands from superiors and peers, and the nature of the work may be incorporated in the situational characteristics.

In an attempt to understand your impacting characteristics better, it will be helpful to undertake a short audit in the three areas listed above. We have raised several issues which may have an important bearing on the style which may be appropriate. They are not exhaustive, and you may be able to think of several other factors which might have an impact on potential style. When you answer the questions in Application Task 1.4, relate your responses to your job and its context.

The best leaders are probably flexible, operating up and down the scale according to a number of influencing factors. These may include the maturity levels and knowledge base of employees. With experienced and knowledgeable employees, for example, a directive style may be counter-productive. Other factors which have already been identified above might also include the capacity of people to cope with ambiguity which would enable them to operate with considerable freedom, the way things are generally done in the organisation and the time available to complete a task. In this particular situation time is not on the sharing leader's side, which may necessitate a move to a more directive style. This need for flexibility is confirmed by Tannenbaum and Schmidt (1958) in stating that strong leadership is called for in some situations and a more permissive style in others.

SUMMARY

The best leaders are probably flexible, applying the best style to cope with a particular situation. This means they have to develop skills in more than one style.

APPLICATION TASK 1.4

1. You as the Leader:

    How much say should your subordinates have in decisions?
    How important to you is the personal and career development of
    your subordinates?
    How important is efficiency and profitability as opposed to indi-
    vidual needs?
    How confident are you of your subordinates' abilities?
    Do you enjoy telling people what to do, or do you prefer to share?
    How do you feel about entrusting your subordinates with impor-
    tant responsibilities?

2. Your Staff:

    How good are they at working without supervision?
    Do they call out for clear guidelines or can they work in ambiguous
    situations?
    What is the level of their knowledge and experience?
    Do they like to share in decision-making or would they prefer to be
    directed?

3. Your Situation at Work:

    Is there scope for participation or is it simply unrealistic?
    Does your organisation expect bosses to be bosses, or does it pro-
    mote sharing?
    What sort of problems do you get: would they benefit from wider
    involvement in their solutions?
    How much time do you generally have for decisions?

Stott, K. and Walker, A., *Making Management Work*. © 1992 Simon & Schuster (Asia) Pte Ltd.

Leadership: A Problem Case

When you read the case below you can consider whether a good balance
between the task, group and individual dimensions was achieved, and identify
specific examples of observed behaviours and actions. You may find it useful
to note these down. Consider the new director's style and her possible
reasons for behaving as she did.

Preamble

A new director takes over the helm of a large public service department. She has her own ideas and expectations but these are not shared by the staff. The assistant director is the most affected by her aggressive management style. In a short space of time, she manages to antagonise a large part of the workforce. A series of events following the new chief's statement of her plans for the department leads to strong feelings amongst staff and a direct confrontation with her second-in-command.

The Case

The former director of the Parks and Recreation Department had asked for early retirement at the age of 50. He had been unwell for several years. The assistant director had expected to take over his place and the former director had supported his case. They had been friends and colleagues for some time. The Public Service Board decided, however, to advertise and appoint from outside.

The new director came into a department where there was little cohesion in the planning. The previous incumbent had set policies without much consultation, but had more or less abdicated his responsibilities of following them through. Area supervisors tended to do things their own way without a great deal of monitoring. Many of the junior supervisors had only recently completed their horticultural training.

Basically, the department had become run down. Development plans needed revamping and employees needed lifting out of the doldrums. Supervisor motivation was a priority. Furthermore, better communication with the public was needed in order to gain its support for improved leisure and recreation amenities.

The new director was proud of her achievements in her former department. She insisted on taking the assistant director to that department to demonstrate the way she had developed innovative planting schemes and a more efficient way of producing plant materials. She had also set up a work environment which could only be described as dynamic. She was very much concerned with public attitudes and employees' attitudes towards the public. The new director also asked several of her senior colleagues to visit her former department in a neighbouring authority.

On her first day in work, the director, accompanied by her immediate boss, made a brief visit to each section in the department. She introduced herself to the section supervisor but did not speak with the other employees. She did not call a meeting of staff nor did she have any informal contacts with people in the department that day. This approach led to many staff being apprehensive about the new leadership and the clerical staff were decidedly uneasy.

The second day saw a major incident between the director and assistant director. The latter was informed that his office was to be used as an interview room when new appointments were to be made. On these occasions, the assistant direc-

tor would be expected to vacate his office and use a small desk which would be put in the typists' office for him. In view of the director's intention to extend the department's work and therefore take on new staff, it was quite probable that his office would be required frequently. On the previous day, the director had stayed behind and personally rearranged the furniture in his office to make it more appropriate as an interviewing room.

She did similar things in other places. She had items of furniture moved and started a massive clean-up operation. Where offices had any litter or were untidy, the person responsible was admonished and given twenty-four hours to clean up.

The director entered the social lounge and drew the staff's attention to a duty roster which she pinned on the notice board. The original roster had been drawn up during the holidays by the area supervisors. She had made several changes to it and introduced an element of flexitime, albeit on a small scale. Nevertheless, it changed lunch time arrangements and added thirty minutes onto each end of the day. It was apparent that she had overlooked some problems in terms of the domestic arrangements for those with families and had interfered with social ties because of staggered lunch breaks. The staff who spotted these, however, were unwilling to point them out.

She then took the unprecedented step of calling staff meetings each day either early in the morning or at the end of the day. These were very short meetings, seldom lasting more than ten minutes, and on some occasions she had nothing at all to say, which meant that the staff dispersed within one minute of meeting.

She was very purposeful and clear about her intentions for the department. Despite the antagonism she created, employees felt they had now got strong leadership after a rather ineffectual former director.

On the third day, the new director demonstrated her intention to have an effect on the work in the department. She visited Mr Low's section and explained that a different furniture arrangement would facilitate work. She then proceeded to direct the clerks as they lifted the desks and chairs to different places whilst Mr Low looked on in silence. During his next lunch break, Mr Low spoke angrily to the assistant director, complaining bitterly about the interference.

Another incident highlighted the director's attitude to discipline and the supervisors' handling of it. A junior supervisor had been having difficulty with a young employee who had used insulting behaviour and on one occasion had threatened to throw a trowel at the supervisor. When this was drawn to the director's attention, it was apparent that she took the employee's side and hinted that supervisors who are unable to control employees properly are incompetent. In the next staff meeting she stated this position and said that she would not tolerate any retaliatory action against young employees who were 'learning the ropes' and trying to cope with 'a whole new world of work'.

Several supervisors (probably representative of many more) took exception to this stance by the director and raised the matter with the assistant director. Although he had the opportunity in the next management meeting he failed to *raise the matter.*

Generally the discipline in the department became worse as it was obvious that the director would show no support for the supervisors. Many of them became very unhappy with their jobs as the younger gardening staff began to take advantage of a situation where they knew they would not be dealt with strictly.

Several weeks later, matters came to a head when the director made a spot inspection of the work records. Some of them were distinctly untidy with alterations and missing data. Several staff and the clerical assistants were present when the director reprimanded the assistant director for the state of the records. He protested that he had spent considerable time and effort in trying to persuade supervisors to improve the condition of their work records but claimed that he could not be held responsible for those who failed to comply. The director disagreed and reiterated her displeasure.

Two weeks later, the director asked the assistant director to see her at lunch time. She left her door open and the conversation could be heard in the administrative office and by a few employees who were in there at that time. She spoke harshly and made the following assertions about the assistant director's work and attitude:

1. *He had failed to show any initiative.*
2. *He had failed to have any impact on the quality of work in the department.*
3. *The staff were generally too friendly with him.*
4. *He had failed to call sufficient meetings.*
5. *He allowed too much autonomy to the supervisors.*
6. *He had left before the end of the department dinner and social evening.*
7. *He had failed to be present at several staff meetings.*
8. *He was attending an evening badminton session which was distracting him from his work.*
9. *He was not contributing sufficiently to the department.*
10. *He was listening to supervisors' complaints behind her back.*
11. *He showed favouritism to several employees who happened to be females.*
12. *She (the director) would not support his application for a promotion.*

Before reading the discussion, it will be helpful to you to fill in the boxes in Application Task 1.5. Your analysis should give some clear ideas about how you would behave in a similar situation. It is not important that this study is about a local authority amenities department; it could relate to any situation where people have to be managed through a process of change. The question is: how would you do it?

APPLICATION TASK 1.5

1. Refer to the theory outlined in this chapter and describe the new director's orientation. What was the balance between task, group and people emphases?

2. How would you describe her leadership style? Was it appropriate for the situation?

3. What lessons are to be learnt for anyone taking on a new leadership responsibility in a situation where change is necessary? How would you handle a similar situation?

Stott, K. and Walker, A., *Making Management Work.* © 1992 Simon & Schuster (Asia) Pte Ltd.

Discussion

Prior to the director's arrival, the department had deteriorated. The former director may have known that he was soon to leave the job and was content to play out time. During this period it is probably true that the assistant director could have had an impact on the department and that the retiring director, in view of their friendship, would have been willing to let him take the initiative. As it was, the assistant director chose to let matters ride. He kept things going fairly efficiently, but so obviously failed to provide the leadership which the department needed during this holding phase. This did not endear him to the new director who was intolerant of any sort of *laissez-faire* attitude.

The whole staff became affected by the new director's actions and several in particular felt the brunt of her incisive tongue. There were acrimonious exchanges between director and assistant director and her position on most matters was clearly laid out to the workforce.

She was concerned about two major issues: the level of apathy among staff, and the state of untidiness in the department. The latter resulted in a clean-up operation and a rearrangement of furniture. The former led to an unsettling of staff and their ingrained attitudes.

She obviously knew what she wanted for the department and was uncompromising in her attempts to reach these objectives. Most of her efforts were directed towards task completion and there seemed to be little recognition of individual or group needs. However, her appointment was almost certainly made to shake up the department and she had the single-mindedness and confidence to carry this out.

The effects on the really important matters, like those related to the development of leisure and recreation amenities, were minimal at this stage. What she managed to achieve was probably a reduction in the amount of complacency and an acceptance amongst staff that changes would be inevitable.

But at what cost was all this achieved? There were many upsets and some of the interventions and displays of displeasure seemed unnecessary. There was no flexibility in leadership style and all situations seemed to be treated in the same way. Her behaviour therefore was hardly contingent on the situation she found herself in. Indeed, she made little effort to analyse her context and consider the key impacting factors. Although it may have been her eventual intention to develop teamwork and team approaches, there was little evidence in the early episodes to suggest that she was interested in building cohesive work units. Furthermore, her treatment of individuals seemed questionable. Although the task facing her was a daunting one it is difficult to understand how she could possibly win the long-term commitment and support of the workforce if she consistently failed to recognise their individual needs.

In your analysis, you probably indicated that you would take a more cautious approach to change and that you would take time to get to know your new colleagues. This may be expedient in most circumstances, but here was a need for radical change. Having read the discussion, what fresh thoughts have you about the leadership role in this type of situation? How can you make a rapid impact on the work and at the same time consider the needs of individuals and group cohesion? It is also worth considering the key situational factors in terms of the new boss, her subordinates, the expectations of her superiors, the nature of the work, and the culture of the organisation. There is no doubt that the situation should have had a considerable influence on appropriate style and action emphases, although there were obvious tensions and difficulties.

You have had the opportunity to reflect on a number of issues related to the role of the leader. You have completed several analyses, both of your own performance and that of others. You may have involved some of your colleagues in analysing your leadership behaviour. All this is of immense use to you, but it means little unless you convert your learning to action. Rather than simply identify your weaknesses in terms of orientation (task, group, individual) or activity (planning, controlling, reviewing), you will find it helpful to specify some actions you can take which will improve your leadership performance. For example, if you have concluded that you do not give sufficient emphasis to individual needs when you are leading your work group in a task, then you should list a few positive actions you can take to improve your performance in this dimension. You will find it helpful to refer to the checklist earlier in the chapter.

APPLICATION TASK 1.6

List several ways in which you feel you can improve your leadership of people at work:

Despite the fact that we have tried to examine some of the more recent developments in the conceptualisation of leadership, this is unlikely to be the final word. Even today things are happening which could have a profound impact on furthering our understanding of leadership effectiveness. Schriesheim and Neider (1989 : 19) draw attention to the fact that behavioural and situational theories have not really accounted for the broad managerial roles which are generally carried out and that style has been treated in a simplified way. They indicate that current research is more managerial in its emphasis, with leadership as a part of the job. The authors also identify influence processes and the conceptualisations of style as topics for investigation. In terms of the broader managerial role, delegation is an issue central to leadership, and they indicate (Schriesheim and Neider, 1989 : 21) that preliminary data is pointing to the effectiveness of middle-ground delegational strategies. This means that the leader neither retires completely from the scene having delegated a task, nor indulges in excessive interference by checking up and having the subordinate request permission for every move. The data is showing subordinate job satisfaction and organisational commitment if this approach is practised. We cover the topic of delegation in detail in Chapter 17.

The second focus, influence processes, we also cover in a separate chapter. Schriesheim and Neider (1989 : 21) advocate the integration of such processes (with special attention being given to 'rational' strategies) into leadership development, and suggest 'investigating other influence styles to determine more effectively which styles are most appropriate under varying situational and subordinate characteristics. Ultimately, such research should lead to a set of prescriptions for new managers concerning how best to achieve organizational goals.'

Finally, in addition to the two strands just outlined, leadership is being looked at as a 'multidimensional, dynamic interpersonal process'. Fiedler, previously associated with pioneering work in contingency approaches, has more recently been developing the process by which leaders achieve effective group performance (Fiedler and Garcia, 1987). 'To achieve high performance, these authors now contend that organizations must enhance group support for managers, select experienced managers for high-stress positions and train intelligent leaders to be more directive in their interactions with subordinates' (Schriesheim and Neider, 1989 : 22).

It is worth mentioning a few other developments which have been gathering momentum. Still in relation to the broader perspective of style, *transactional* leadership, which may be thought of almost as a trading agreement or a bargaining approach, is a way of helping people understand the behaviours they must employ to receive the intended outcomes. The wants and needs of the leader are traded for the wants and needs of followers (Sergiovanni, 1990). *Transformative* leadership speaks of leaders and subordinates pursuing common goals. The leader has charisma and can call on loyalty and commitment from the band of followers. The approach involves satisfying higher-order needs, having high expectations, motivating, building employees and bonding them in the pursuit of common ideals.

Conclusion

This chapter has attempted to help you improve your skills as a leader. It is not easy to lay down a prescription and expect your performance to be transformed. What you have to do is to reflect on the way you behave. Consider on a regular basis the three interrelated needs – task, group and individual. Look back at the checklist of actions and see whether you are carrying them out. Also look at the activities. Are you as good at controlling as you are at planning, for example? Consider also the factors present in your situation and whether you are accounting for them as you select your style of operation. And whilst your self-assessment is a productive lead-in to development as a leader, you will only understand how you are seen by others if you ask them and discuss your emphases with them. In an era of constant change and development we believe there has never been a greater need for skilled and reflective leaders of people.

References

Adair, J. (1973) *Action Centred Leadership*, Gower : England.

Blake, R. and Mouton, J. (1964) *The Managerial Grid*, Gulf : Houston.

Fiedler, F. (1967) *A Theory of Leadership Effectiveness*, McGraw-Hill : New York.

Fiedler, F. and Garcia, J. (1987) *New Approaches to Effective Leadership: Cognitive Resources and Organizational Performance*, Wiley : New York.

Goldsmith, W. and Clutterbuck, D. (1984) *The Winning Streak*, Penguin : England.

Hemphill, J. (1949) *Situational Factors in Leadership*, Columbus OH, Bureau of Business Research, College of Commerce and Administration : Ohio State University.

Hersey, P. and Blanchard, K. (1977) *Management of Organization Behaviour: Utilising Human Resources*, Prentice Hall : New Jersey.

Herzberg, F. (1959) *The Motivation to Work*, Wiley : New York.

Kotter, J. (1990) 'What leaders really do', *Harvard Business Review*, May–June, pp. 103–111.

Maslow, A. (1954) *Motivation and Personality*, Harper Brothers : New York.

Owens, R. (1987) *Organizational Behaviour in Education*, Prentice Hall : New Jersey.

Peters, T. and Waterman, R. (1982) *In Search of Excellence*, Harper and Row : New York.

Reddin, W. (1970) *Managerial Effectiveness*, McGraw-Hill : New York.

Schriesheim, C. and Neider, L. (1989) 'Leadership theory and development', *Leadership and Organization Development Journal*, **10**, 6, pp. 17–25.

Sergiovanni, T. (1990) *Value Added Leadership*, Harcourt Brace Jovanovich : New York.

Stewart, R. (1986) *The Reality of Management*, PanT: London.

Stogdill, R. (1948) 'Personal factors associated with leadership: a survey of the literature', *Journal of Psychology*, **25**, pp. 35–71.

Tannenbaum, R. and Schmidt, W. (1958) 'How to choose a leadership pattern', *Harvard Business Review*, **36**, pp. 95–101.

Vroom, V. and Yetton, P. (1973) *Leadership and Decisionmaking*, University of Pittsburgh Press : Pittsburgh.

Yukl, G. (1981) *Leadership in Organizations*, Prentice Hall : New Jersey.

Chapter 2

Motivating

We were having lunch with Sue, a senior manager in a large transportation firm. She had a record of innovation and success, substantially increasing both productivity and profitability over the last two years. However, she had recently encountered a problem in one of her key units and it was threatening to detract from her recent gains. She told us her story.

> *I recruited Larry because everyone told me what a good manager he was. When I checked I found his track record at TACBAM (the company he worked for previously) to be very impressive. Upon reflection I realise that I did not do my homework properly. At TACBAM Larry had a very small staff performing fairly routine duties – production stability was the only requirement. In his work with us I have no complaints about his expertise in managerial procedures. He has developed strategies to redesign existing programmes and implemented new ones. He has established checkpoints for staff productivity and to track their progress. He has a system for everything, even for protecting his staff from too much 'red tape'. Larry is also a very nice person.*
>
> *Despite all these talents, he still has a lot of trouble in getting his staff to reach organisational targets. He definitely works harder than any other manager under me, but his staff seem listless and don't respond to his leadership.*

Sue summed the problem up in one sentence, 'Larry doesn't seem to be able to *motivate* his staff.'

As Larry's case implies, even if you have the most highly qualified employee in the business, and provide the most up-to-date support, if that employee is not motivated himself, or, in the case of a manager, cannot motivate his staff, effective performance will not result.

Your employees' performance is basically determined by three factors: ability, work environment and motivation. For an employee to perform effectively he must know how to do the job, must want to do the job and must have a conducive, well-supported environment. If any one of these factors is absent it is unlikely your employees will be truly effective (Griffin, 1984). In this chapter we will deal with the 'want to do the job', in short, **motivation**.

The chapter aims to provide you with an understanding of the basics of motivation. We will summarise some of the major motivation theories, challenge you to accept your role as a motivator and help you to identify how your staff are motivated. Finally, we will explore some avenues through which employees can be motivated.

Motivation

Motivation basically involves looking at why people do the things they do or why they behave the way they do. It relates to your ability to excite and move your employees to action and achievement while satisfying their needs. Before we begin the 'know-how' we must clarify a fundamental concept. Motivation is not a thing that we do or give to our subordinates like a pill. Employees are self-motivated and do things for their own reasons, not yours. We can certainly offer rewards and so forth, but unless these are viewed as desirable by the employee they will have little effect. Whether such rewards are desirable to the employee depends on the needs, values and priorities he, as an individual, brings to the work place with him (O'Mahoney, 1984).

This, of course, does not mean that you cannot work towards motivating your employees; but it does mean that to do so effectively you must attempt to identify *your* employees' needs, values and priorities and work towards helping them attain them.

Employees can be motivated by three generic types of needs or forces (some call them drives): *personal forces, push forces* and *pull forces.* Personal forces come from within ourselves. For example, if we hold strong religious or political views, these can influence our behaviour. If something is, or becomes, a matter of personal importance it becomes a motivational force. Push forces come from other people such as family, colleagues, superiors or subordinates. If either or all of these groups make you feel pressured to do something, this becomes a push force. In a work situation these forces usually come from either your boss or your employees, or both. Pull forces come from external factors, those which exist outside of yourself and which attract you. Items such as a car, a house or a holiday usually involve you in either earning or saving more money. Perhaps these 'pull' you to make more money or get a promotion to meet an external need.

Motivation then, from a manager's perspective, involves you in helping your employees to satisfy their needs or 'forces' so they will work towards the organisation's goals. Figure 2.1 explains the basic rationale behind motivation.

Each of your employees has certain *needs*. For example, Jose has a need to be recognised by you, the boss, for his accomplishments. These needs create certain *wants* : Jose wants you to acknowledge his special contributions to the department. Wants then initiate *actions* or behaviours in order to achieve certain *goals* : Jose sets a goal to refine the system for tracking 'out-of-country' stock, a problem in the department. The achievement of these goals results

Figure 2.1
Motivation: How It Works

in *accomplishments*: Jose refines the system to be more accurate and efficient for the department. You praise Jose in the staff newsletter and at a meeting (perhaps you even attach another reward). Jose feels good because his need has been satisfied and this motivates him to continue the good work. This simple example serves as a basic explanation of the motivation cycle.

We now examine a practical motivation framework. It is designed to increase your understanding of motivation and to assist you in developing strategies for motivating employees. The framework comprises four stages and is shown in Figure 2.2.

The stages are:

- Understanding some of the basic concepts of motivation.
- Accepting that you play a vital role in motivating employees.
- Identifying the needs of your staff, or finding out how they are motivated.
- Acting to consciously motivate staff.

Figure 2.2
Motivation: A Practical Framework

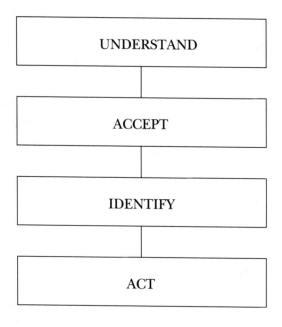

Understand

The first step in improving the motivation of your employees is to acquire a basic understanding of some major motivation theories. In the following pages we present a brief summary of some theories which have influenced management thinking. Our coverage is not intended to be exhaustive. We have attempted simply to draw out the fundamental tenets of each and provide the information which you can put to use in your management role.

Maslow: Needs Hierarchy

One of the most influential motivation theories was advanced by Abraham Maslow. Maslow's theory asserts that human beings have certain needs and that these needs are arranged in a hierarchy of importance. This is shown in Figure 2.3.

He suggested that our needs can be viewed as being in five categories and that they all have the potential to act as motivators. Firstly, our most basic needs, such as those for food, water, sex and air, were labelled *physiological* needs – in short, basic survival needs. His second category, which he called *security* or *safety* needs, includes needs such as a secure emotional and physical environment. *Social* or *belongingness* needs, related to social processes such as love, affection and acceptance comprised the third category. The fourth category he labelled *esteem* needs, referring to our need for self-respect and recognition from others. Maslow's final category, *self-actualisation* needs, encompasses our needs for reaching our full potential and continued growth. These needs focus on individual development.

Maslow arranged these needs in the form of a hierarchy. His theory stated that once lower-order needs, such as food and security were satisfied, other higher-level needs, such as those for self-esteem become dominant motivators. Once lower-order needs have been satisfied they no longer act as motivators. If lower-order needs are not satisfied it is unlikely that higher-order

Figure 2.3
Maslow's Needs Hierarchy

SELF-ACTUALISATION	
Maximise own skills	RISK-TAKING
Ability and potential	AUTONOMY
ESTEEM	
Self-esteem	SOCIAL
Esteem from others	PROFESSIONAL
	REWARDS
BELONGINGNESS	
Acceptance	FAMILY
Appreciation	FRIENDS
	SOCIAL GROUPS
SAFETY	
Safe, secure	SALARY
Order, rules	INSURANCE
	LAW
BASIC	
Food, water	GIVEN FOR
Shelter, clothing, sex	MOST TODAY

needs such as self-actualisation will dominate. A very basic example: if you live in abject poverty and expend all your energy acquiring food and shelter you are unlikely to be too concerned about whether or not you are being challenged in your job.

In modern, developed societies, physiological, security and social needs are usually met by a combination of work, family and community factors. In an organisational sense, employees have adequate wages and work conditions, job continuity and friendship; however, managers still need to be aware of their responsibility for meeting these needs and also cater to esteem needs by providing rewards such as job titles and promotional opportunities. This is relatively easy. Understandably, management still struggles most in attempting to satisfy self-actualisation needs. Probably the most effective way to do this is to ensure you provide adequate challenges and opportunities for employees to develop their abilities and skills.

To aid your understanding of Maslow's theory and how it applies to your work situation, try completing Application Task 2.1.

APPLICATION TASK 2.1

We have listed the five needs categories developed by Maslow. In each category we have listed two examples of how you can help your employees satisfy their needs through their job. Your task is to add to our examples by using your intimate knowledge of your own work place (start from the bottom). When you have done this, you may want to discuss your ideas with some colleagues.

1. Self-actualisation Needs:
   Staff development opportunities; Challenging assignments

2. Esteem Needs:
   Clear and fair reward system; Promotions

3. Belongingness Needs:
   Group projects; Social gatherings

4. Safety Needs:
   Pension schemes; Trade union membership; Medical insurance

5. Physiological Needs:
   Adequate salary; Rest breaks

Now ask yourself: What level of needs satisfaction do I provide for my employees?

Stott, K. and Walker, A., *Making Management Work.* © 1992 Simon & Schuster (Asia) Pte Ltd.

Although Maslow's theory has received criticism, it has still had a major impact on management thinking over the last fifty years. It carries certain implications for managers. It has helped us realise that our employees are motivated in a variety of ways. Managers must provide opportunities for higher-order needs, not just simply lower-order items such as a reasonable salary. Of course, you must provide for these basic needs, but it may not be enough if you are aiming for maximum productivity. You need to think about which factors in your work place can be altered and those which cannot.

Herzberg: Two-Factor Theory

Another influential motivation theory was advanced by Frederick Herzberg (1959). Herzberg developed his theory by asking a group of professionals to list what satisfied them at work and made them highly motivated. He also asked them to list occasions when they had been unmotivated and dissatisfied. His findings were quite surprising.

Herzberg discovered that there were certain factors associated with job satisfaction (motivation factors) and a completely different set of factors associated with dissatisfaction (maintenance or hygiene factors). He discovered, for example, that an inadequate salary could cause dissatisfaction at work, but that a high salary would not necessarily cause job satisfaction.

Herzberg's work challenged the assumption that job satisfaction was one-dimensional, ranging along a continuum from satisfaction to the opposite end, dissatisfaction. Instead, he found motivation to be two-dimensional. His theory, which has been labelled the Two-Factor Theory, is summarised in Figure 2.4

Figure 2.4
Herzberg's Two-Factor Theory

MAINTENANCE FACTORS	MOTIVATION FACTORS
Supervisory methods	Challenge of work
Salary	Promotional opportunities
Relationships with colleagues	Sense of achievement
Working conditions	Recognition of job done
Company policy and administration	Sense of responsibility
Personal life	
Status	
Interpersonal relations	

Herzberg claimed that maintenance factors, if correct, did not cause dissatisfaction, but neither did they motivate workers. However, when they were not right, they led to dissatisfaction and exerted negative impact. Hence, Herzberg believed that we had to look elsewhere for motivators. When motivating factors such as *recognition, acceptance* and *responsibility* are provided by management, job satisfaction is obtained and motivation increased. If such factors are not right, job satisfaction and hence motivation is lacking. This is true even if the worker is not dissatisfied with his job. The basic ideas proposed by Herzberg are presented in Figure 2.5.

Figure 2.5
Maintenance and Motivation

MAINTENANCE FACTORS		MOTIVATION FACTORS	
EFFECT OF FACTORS			
WHEN RIGHT	WHEN WRONG	WHEN RIGHT	WHEN WRONG
No dissatisfaction	Dissatisfaction	Job satisfaction	No job satisfaction
Do not motivate	Negative impact	Increased motivation	No dissatisfaction

Herzberg's theory has implications for you as a practising manager.

1. Factors which make workers happy on the job are apparently not the opposite of factors which make them unhappy. Hence, you cannot expect to satisfy your employees by simply removing the cause of their dissatisfaction.
2. Attempts to motivate employees by concentrating on maintenance factors alone are not effective. You must also ensure that the motivation factors are right.

In short, your role, according to Herzberg, is quite complicated. Not only must you remove causes of dissatisfaction, but you must also ensure that opportunities for satisfaction are provided to motivate staff.

Like Maslow, Herzberg has his share of critics, but his theory has served the purpose of increasing managerial awareness of the importance of motivation.

You may have thought of several factors under each heading: a reliable, decent boss; understandable, reasonable organisational policies; opportunities for working with people you relate to; taking responsibility for others (maintenance factors); challenging assignments; recognition of achievement, responsibility for target attainment (motivation factors).

APPLICATION TASK 2.2

To apply Herzberg's theory to your work, think about motivation and maintenance factors in your work place. At the same time, try to think of some demotivating factors: examples of factors which may actually demotivate your employees. Try to list practical examples in the correct categories (we have started you off with two examples). Think about whether you are providing both sets for your employees.

1. Maintenance Factors :
    Fair remuneration; Comfortable canteen

2. Motivation Factors :
    'Employee of the Month' Scheme; Proper delegation

3. Demotivating Factors :
    Favouritism shown to one employee

Stott, K. and Walker, A., *Making Management Work.* © 1992 Simon & Schuster (Asia) Pte Ltd.

Achievement/Affiliation and Power Theories

Herzberg and Maslow attempted to identify individual needs associated with motivation and to arrange them in some type of hierarchical importance. Other researchers have examined the needs themselves without attempting to order them.

Perhaps the most influential of these researchers was David McClelland. McClelland (1961) isolated three basic needs, *achievement, affiliation* and *power* as the most influential motivation-influencing needs.

The best known is perhaps the need for achievement. Put simply, workers are motivated to do well in their jobs by a need to achieve. McClelland found that workers with high achievement needs had:

- A desire to assume personal responsibility.
- A tendency to set difficult targets for themselves.
- A need for specific and immediate feedback.
- A preoccupation with their task (Griffin, 1984).

The need for affiliation is similar to Maslow's need for belongingness – a need for acceptance and companionship. Workers in which such needs are dominant work best in jobs which provide social interaction and friendship.

The third need involves a demand for power, i.e. a need to control and influence one's environment. People who have a strong need for power and achievement tend to become the managers and superior performers. Some would contend that the most successful managers tend to have a pattern of a high need for power, a moderate need for achievement and relatively low affiliation needs.

To consolidate this theory in your own mind, try the following exercise. Think of a manager or supervisor who works for you or with you. Keep him or her in mind and fill in the following questionnaire. Ask yourself what statements most accurately describe him or her. Remember, this is only a guide. Do not judge the person you selected on the outcome. The question-naire is designed only to give you some idea of how different people are driven by different needs.

The A box and column in the questionnaire approximately identify your employee's need for *affiliation.* The B box and column identify his need for *power*, and the C his need for *achievement.* If an employee's dominant need seems to be for affiliation he will be best motivated to work by being placed in a team or more social situation. If he is driven mainly by needs for achievement, he may best be motivated by setting and working towards his own targets and being left to achieve these targets. If he is pushed by power needs, he may be motivated by being placed in a position which suits his desires to be up front in many situations.

Questionnaire

MOTIVES

Instructions: Read each of the following statements.

1. If you believe the statement *accurately describes the employee* you selected, write a 10 in the corresponding box.
2. If you believe the statement *partly describes the employee* you selected, write a 5 in the corresponding box.
3. If you believe the statement is *nothing like the employee* you selected, write a 2 in the corresponding box.
4. You must record a number in every box.

The employee:

1. Empathises with other people's problems. ☐

2. Likes his work to be challenging. ☐

3. Likes to be popular with his work mates. ☐

4. Always wants to lead the group. ☐

5. Likes to look neat and tidy. ☐

6. Will assume personal responsibility for task completion. ☐

7. Is often argumentative. ☐

8. Goes out of his way to help work mates. ☐

9. Is often forceful and outspoken. ☐

10. Likes to set and achieve his own targets. ☐

11. Always shouts rather than talks. ☐

12. Never misses a social gathering. ☐

13. Seems to enjoy controlling other people. ☐

14. Often argues with others about how to do things. ☐

15. Always chats with others at breaks. ☐

16. Likes to receive prompt feedback on his actions. ☐

17. Always runs to you with his problems. ☐

18. Becomes upset if forced to work on his own. ☐

19. Works very long hours. ☐

20. Tends to become bored when doing routine jobs. ☐

21. Will gamble at the organisation's expense. ☐

22. Tends to perform best when working in a team. ☐

23. Enjoys speaking to large groups. ☐

24. Often tries to demand his own way. ☐

25. Carefully analyses and assesses problems. ☐

MOTIVES SCORING CHART

When you have finished, total the numbers as shown below:

A.   1 + 3 + 8 + 12 + 15 + 18 + 22

     __ + __ + __ + __ + __ + __ + __ = ☐

B.   4 + 7 + 9 + 13 + 14 + 23 + 24

     __ + __ + __ + __ + __ + __ + __ = ☐

C.   2 + 6 + 10 + 16 + 19 + 20 + 25

___ + ___ + ___ + ___ + ___ + ___ + ___ = □

Disregard numbers 5, 11, 17 and 21.

When you have added the numbers for A, B and C, place them in the corresponding boxes below and graph the final figure.

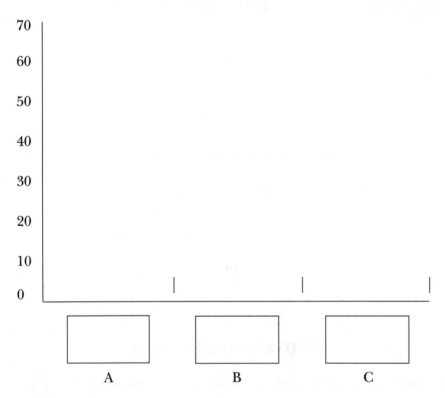

Although needs theories have been very influential they have been criticised because they fail to look at the process of motivation. Two well-known theories that try to address this process perspective are *expectancy* and *equity* theories.

Expectancy Theories

Expectancy Theory proposes that motivation is a function of an individual's expectations. It suggests that a worker's motivation depends on two things: how much he actually wants to do something, and how likely he thinks it is that he will get it. Let us take a simple example.

Assume you are the manager of a sales department in a medium-sized firm that specialises in providing office furniture. You see a call for three tenders for office furniture. The first wants furniture for an entire office block. You would like the contract but realise that you could not possibly meet the order. The second call is from a small three-office company for six chairs and desks. You know you could get the contract but it is not worth your time. The third call is for about 100 desks, chairs and other fixtures. You apply for the third tender because you want the contract and believe you have a reasonable chance of getting it. You are motivated to apply for the third tender but not the other two.

There are various forms of Expectancy Theory available, with perhaps the most famous being developed by Victor Vroom (1964), and Lyman Porter and Edward Lawler (1968). O'Mahoney (1984 : 62) provides a good summary of its essence and how it expands needs theories.

In addition to the individual's needs (using whatever classification or model you prefer) and the reward available in a situation, we need to consider the individual's *perceptions* and *expectations* (however arrived at) of:

1. The situation.
2. The rewards.
3. The likelihood of being able to perform in ways that will ensure secure rewards.
4. The likelihood of actually being 'paid' – even if satisfactory performance is achieved (O'Mahoney, 1984).

Expectancy Theory expands needs theories by going beyond, or expanding, their content perspective. They acknowledge that different workers have different needs and will try to satisfy these needs in various ways. Let us use an example to illustrate the theory in a little more detail.

I Want a Promotion – I Think!

Scene One

> *A young manager has been with the same firm for more than a year and wants to be promoted to a more senior position. If she believes she will get the promotion*

from performing well, and believes that this performance will result from her efforts, she will be motivated to exert this effort. If, however, she believes that her effort will have little or no bearing on her performance she will be less or not motivated towards effort. This is labelled 'effort-to-performance expectancy', i.e. the manager's perception of the likelihood that her effort will lead to high performance.

Scene Two

If the manager believes that her performance will almost certainly lead to promotion she will be motivated to perform. However, if she believes that despite her good performance she may not or will not get the promotion she will once again be less motivated to perform, or not motivated at all. This is called 'performance-to-outcome expectancy' and refers to the manager's perception that her performance will result in a promotion.

Scene Three

The manager realises that if she gets the promotion she faces a number of outcomes from the organisation. She realises that her effort and subsequent performance could lead to promotion and reward, but may also subject her to more stress and even the resentment of her colleagues. To her, each of these possible outcomes have a certain value (or 'valence') which will shape how much she desires the promotion. If she really wants the promotion she will be extremely motivated. If she definitely does not want it she will be unmotivated. If she can 'take it or leave it' she may be only moderately motivated.

For the manager in our example to be motivated she must believe that her effort will lead to performance and that this performance will lead to a good chance of promotion. Additionally, she must believe that the value of the promotion, status, more pay and boss's admiration, are more important to her than more work, more stress and possible peer resentment. If all these conditions are met, Expectancy Theory tells us our manager will be motivated to work hard.

Porter and Lawler (1968) expanded Expectancy Theory by including an intrinsic addition. They stated that values or outcomes could be intrinsic (accomplishment, recognition, self-concept), as well as extrinsic (promotion, pay rises). In our previous example, the manager would consider intrinsic rewards and outcomes as well as the extrinsic outcomes she already took into account.

How then can a knowledge of Expectancy Theory help you to improve the motivation of your subordinates? Nadler and Lawler (1983) recommend the following:

1. Work out the outcomes each employee may want.
2. Decide on the performance necessary to meet organisational goals.
3. Ensure desired performance levels are attainable.
4. Tie desired outcomes and desired performance.
5. Examine the situation for varying expectations.
6. Ensure rewards are tempting enough.
7. Make sure the system is fair to all employees.

Expectancy Theory contributes to our understanding of motivation by building on earlier needs theories by examining the *process* of motivation.

Equity Theories

Another important consideration in 'managing' motivation is whether workers believe the organisational reward system is fair. This issue is addressed through yet another group of motivation theories labelled *equity* theories. Equity Theory assumes that people in organisations want to be treated fairly and that they tend to compare their contributions and rewards to those received by others.

J. Stacy Adams (1963) is largely credited with developing Equity (or Inequity) Theory. The theory basically states that people need to perceive equal outcomes for perceived equal circumstances.

Equity Theory, as its name implies, is based on the following principles:

1. If employees perceive that they are not properly rewarded by the organisation they will be dissatisfied and not work to their full ability. They may even quit.
2. If employees believe they are adequately rewarded for what they do they will maintain the same level of output.
3. If employees perceive the rewards as more than they consider fair they will probably work harder. However, they may also discount the reward (Koontz and Weihrich, 1988).

One obvious problem with this is that the employee may overestimate his own contribution and the rewards other employees receive. Most people will tolerate some inequities but if they feel something is unfair, and are faced with this for long periods of time, they may overreact to apparently minor events. You need to stay in touch with your employees' perceptions of inequities and try to control them to avoid this. We experienced an example of an organisation lacking this control.

Kal worked as a manager in a major overseas office for a large corporation. From the first week he arrived he did not feel comfortable in the organisation and wondered if it may have been because he came from another country. Some of the local managers seemed to resent his presence. As the months went by his feelings of being treated differently seemed to be reinforced. Even though he worked hard and was a productive, effective manager he did not appear to be considered for promotion and was even prevented from going to some major overseas conventions.

Things got worse and worse for Kal. The regional office he worked in merged with a branch (from the same company) from a nearby country which was forced to relocate for political reasons. Even though he knew he was more productive than many of his colleagues who were promoted in the 'absorption', he was, in real terms, demoted and asked to take a reduction in benefits.

Even though Kal was angry, he stayed on because he saw his fellow overseas workers being treated the same way and did not really have any other concrete job offers. Kal put up with his lot for another six months, and then it happened. His boss called him to his office and told him he was not completely satisfied with a report he had just compiled and wanted Kal to make a few minor adjustments. To his boss's surprise, Kal stood up and said 'Do it yourself, I quit' and stormed out of the office. His boss was totally bemused. It was only one report and he only wanted a few changes; he wondered what had got into Kal.

What Kal's boss did not realise was that Kal did not resign because of the report. He left the firm because he felt that he had been unfairly treated over a period of time by the organisation. The report was merely the catalyst for his leaving. He did not see the organisational reward system as equitable.

McGregor: X and Y (and Ouchi: Z) Theory

McGregor's X and Y Theory (1960) was not developed as a theory of motivation like the others we have discussed. It relates the manager's assumptions about his employees to the style of management used. We discuss this under motivation because your managerial assumptions influence your own motivation for doing things and how you believe other people are motivated.

The incentives that you provide for your employees will depend in many instances on your views of why people work and what they want out of work. The basic tenets of Theory X and Y are shown in Figure 2.6. Be aware that these are not prescriptions or managerial strategies; they are simply assumptions against which you can test reality. Nor should they be viewed as being on a continuum, but should be seen as completely different views of employees.

Figure 2.6
McGregor's Theory X and Y

THEORY X MANAGERS ASSUME:	THEORY Y MANAGERS ASSUME:
■ Employees are fundamentally lazy.	■ Employees enjoy work and achievement.
■ Employees are interested only in their own benefits.	■ Employees like to help others.
■ Punishment gets results.	■ Punishment is counter-productive.
■ Employees have no real interest in the work they do.	■ Most employees are basically interested in their work.
■ Employees are basically dishonest.	■ Employees are basically honest.
■ Employees are basically sly.	■ Employees are basically open in their dealings with others.
■ Discipline and control produce the best results.	■ Employees respond best when given freedom of action.
■ Employees are not really interested in the goals of the organisation they work for.	■ Employees are interested in the goals of the organisation they work for.
■ Employees avoid responsibility.	■ Employees enjoy responsibility.

Which assumptions do you think dominate your own thinking? Can you see how your assumptions can influence how you approach your employees?

Let us say that you believe that your employees dislike work and must be coerced, controlled, directed and threatened to put in effort, then your motivational techniques will probably be limited to bullying, telling and bribing employees. You believe that you are a Theory X person, and will probably agree with a statement made by Henry Ford, a typical Theory X manager:

The average worker, I am sorry to say, wants a job in which he does not have to put forth much physical energy – above all, he wants a job at which he does not have to think.

On the other hand, if you believe that your employees will exercise self-direction and self-control in the service of objectives to which they are committed, you will approach motivation differently. You will probably involve employees in decision-making, believing this will motivate them to work harder.

Theory Z was expounded by William Ouchi (1981). The theory was developed at a time when Japanese companies were making deep inroads into the American market. This was of great concern to many American businesses since they realised that Japanese organisations were managed differently from their own.

Ouchi attempted to integrate common management practices from both the USA and Japan into a 'middle-of-the-road' framework. He identified three theoretical types of organisations. Type A (American), Type J (Japanese) and Type Z (his middle-ground framework). He identified seven basic differences between Type A and Type J organisations. These are shown in Figure 2.7.

Figure 2.7
Theory Z

CHARACTERISTICS OF TYPE A ORGANISATIONS	7 DIFFERENCES	CHARACTERISTICS OF TYPE J ORGANISATIONS
Short term	EMPLOYMENT	Long term
Individual	DECISION-MAKING	Collective
Individual	RESPONSIBILITY	Collective
Rapid	EVALUATION AND PROMOTION	Slow
Explicit	CONTROL MECHANISMS	Implicit
Specialised	CAREER PATH	Non-specialised
Segmented	CONCERN FOR EMPLOYEE	Holistic

Source: Summarised from Ouchi (1981)

He developed an ideal, hybrid-type organisation (Type Z) which he believed was appropriate for American organisations. It included the boxed characteristics in the above chart as well as 'implicit, informal control with explicit, formalised measure, moderately specialised career paths and a holistic concern for the employee, including family' (Ouchi, 1981 : 58).

The implications for motivation are fairly obvious. Ouchi's findings imply that companies who aim to be productive through their workers can motivate staff in a number of ways, They can, for example, provide long-term employment, open communication, implement participative decision-making and show they are concerned for their employees and their families.

Although there has been a great deal of controversy surrounding Ouchi's study, mainly over methodological issues, there is little doubt that he significantly influenced how large numbers of US corporations operated in the 1980s.

You should now have a basic understanding of some of the major motivation or motivation-related theories. We have not attempted to cover all the available theories but to select those which we consider to have most relevance to you as a manager. We now move on to stage two of our framework for motivating staff – *accepting.*

Accept

After reading the descriptions of the various motivation theories you should now be convinced that motivation is a major part of your job as a manager. Can you accept that your role as a motivator is vital? Obviously you want your employees to be motivated. If they are motivated they will work harder, be more agreeable, and enjoy their jobs more. The logical result of these is that they will get more work done and make your job much easier.

You need to motivate staff for many reasons. The end result of motivated employees should be increased organisational productivity. Motivation actually represents your employee's commitment and desire to work, which is manifested as effort. Your job is to try to obtain this commitment to effort. This point was emphasised by John Harvey-Jones, CEO of ICI, Britain's largest chemical company [as cited in Stewart (1985 : 56)] when he stated: 'The real purpose of management is motivation of the group to use its energy to achieve objectives.' Of course, employees must also have some ability to perform their jobs but this is not the purpose of motivation. This ability angle will be dealt with in Chapter 8, Developing Staff.

Kotter (1990 : 73) describes motivated or inspired employees as 'a group of people who exhibit a level of energy, intensity and determination far above what is considered normal.' He also expounds their possible impact as being 'able to overcome major economic, bureaucratic and political obstacles that stand in its (their) way.' If you want employees or teams of employees, and the accompanying results, as described by Kotter, you must accept your vital, inescapable role as a *motivator*.

It is easy of course to motivate people for a short time and in our experience this is what many managers do. They become enthusiastic about motivating their staff , and do all the right things – for about a month or less.

Motivating people for a short time is fairly easy. Even a crisis can do it, or a specially contrived event. Rumours of a corporate takeover from a hostile source, for example, which has a reputation for 'culling' staff will motivate employees to work harder for the company in order to stave off the foe. A once-a-year visit from the dynamic CEO can fire up and inspire your employees. However, motivating employees over long periods of time is much more difficult – it is also far more important.

When you have accepted the importance of your responsibility as a motivator, you should be able to concur with the following statements:

- I am motivated myself.
- I can develop my staff.
- Motivating employees is my long-term commitment.
- Appropriate motivation will increase productivity.

If you subscribe to these statements, you have accepted your role in motivating staff. You are ready to move on to the next stage.

Before you do this complete the following questionnaire: How Good a Motivator Am I? Score the questionnaire to gain some idea of where you stand as a motivator at present.

Questionnaire

HOW GOOD A MOTIVATOR AM I?

Test your motivational practices by rating yourself on the questions below.

	Usually	Sometimes	Never
1. I believe my employees are competent and trustworthy.	☐	☐	☐
2. I avoid stereotyping employees.	☐	☐	☐
3. I avoid sarcasm, put-downs and ridicule of employees.	☐	☐	☐

	Usually	Sometimes	Never
4. I provide adequate opportunities for staff development.	☐	☐	☐
5. I listen to what employees really say.	☐	☐	☐
6. I let employees know they are missed when they are away.	☐	☐	☐
7. I allow employees to use their expertise.	☐	☐	☐
8. I delegate responsibility and authority with tasks.	☐	☐	☐
9. I encourage employees to better themselves and go for promotion.	☐	☐	☐
10. I avoid overemphasis on competition, rewards and winning within my organisation.	☐	☐	☐
11. I help groups of employees to evaluate their effectiveness in group processes.	☐	☐	☐
12. I give time, attention, and support to all employees.	☐	☐	☐
13. I communicate my high expectations to my employees.	☐	☐	☐
14. I focus on my employees' future successes rather than past failures.	☐	☐	☐
15. I look for what is positive in my employees' work and behaviour.	☐	☐	☐
16. I jointly set and communicate targets for and with my employees.	☐	☐	☐
17. I provide constructive feedback in the event of setbacks.	☐	☐	☐
18. I realise each employee has his own strengths and weaknesses.	☐	☐	☐
19. I involve employees and teams when searching for solutions to problems.	☐	☐	☐
20. I provide rewards in the form of praise and more tangible benefits.	☐	☐	☐
21. I ask low-risk, open-ended questions when asking employees' advice.	☐	☐	☐
22. I regularly review individual performance.	☐	☐	☐
23. I suspend judgement of employees until I get all the facts.	☐	☐	☐

	Usually	**Sometimes**	**Never**
24. I recognise the contributions of both individuals and teams.	☐	☐	☐
25. I acknowledge and build on success.	☐	☐	☐

Total your scores by adding all the numbers in the boxes and enter the total in the box below. For any statement where you ticked 'usually' score 4, for any ticked 'sometimes' give yourself 2. Where you ticked 'never', you do not score any points.

Total = [ ]

If you got 90–100 rate yourself as excellent.
If you got 80–90 rate yourself as very good.
If you got 70–80 rate yourself as good.
If you got less than 70 rate yourself as poor.

Identify

Your first action is to identify the needs or desires of your employees. The question must be asked: What makes them want to commit themselves to achieving organisational goals? To do this effectively you must know your staff. To begin this process, you will find it helpful to complete Application Task 2.3 followed by the questions in Application Task 2.4.

Identifying why employees work is not easy, mainly because different employees have different needs. Managers are often under some misconception about what is really important to employees. A study conducted in 1980 highlighted some of these discrepancies. (See Figure 2.8.)

You can see at a glance that there are substantial discrepancies in the rankings. What does this mean? It appears that managers may be spending time, effort and resources in motivating employees in unproductive ways. At the same time, they may be neglecting the things which are really important to employees.

One common misconception held by many managers is that *money* is the most powerful, or even sole, motivator. This is not the case. Certainly money is important to employees for providing the essentials which meet people's most basic needs, but it is wrong to assume that money is the vital ingredient or that it will always make people work harder. Money will get your employees to come to work but is unlikely to make them work more efficiently or effectively when they arrive.

APPLICATION TASK 2.3

Think of two of your keenest and most effective employees who you consider to be very motivated. Using the list of possible motivation points presented below, identify the *six factors* which you think are most influential in affecting the employee's motivation. Rank the points you identify 1 to 6. For example, if you feel job security is the most important to employee A, you will put a figure 1 against that point, and so on.

Motivation points: Employee A   Employee B

1. Pay scale
2. Promotion prospects
3. Participation in decision-making
4. Supportive manager/supervisor
5. Clear organisational direction
6. Comfortable working conditions
7. Managerial support
8. Holidays/fringe benefits
9. Recognition of achievements
10. Job challenge
11. Job security
12. Respect of colleagues
13. Flexibility of rules
14. Position in organisation
15. Love of job
16. Collegial support
17. Freedom of action
18. Involvement in target-setting
19. Development opportunities
20. Trust in superior

Stott, K. and Walker, A., *Making Management Work.* © 1992 Simon & Schuster (Asia) Pte Ltd.

APPLICATION TASK 2.4

Having considered what motivates some of your staff try to answer the following questions. They are intended to stimulate your thinking about motivation and challenge your assumptions.

1.   What prompted you to select the motivation points and subsequent rankings?

2.   What do you consider to be the most influential motivators for your employees as a group?

3.   If asked to identify the motivation points that you consider were *least* influential in motivating staff which would you select? Why would you select these?

4.   How can you as a manager identify the factors which influence the motivation of staff?

Stott, K. and Walker, A., *Making Management Work.* © 1992 Simon & Schuster (Asia) Pte Ltd.

Figure 2.8
Order of Importance of Various Job Factors

JOB FACTORS	SURVEY OF EMPLOYEES	SURVEY OF BOSSES
Full appreciation of work done	1	8
Feeling of being in on things	2	10
Sympathetic help with personal problems	3	9
Job security	4	2
Good wages	5	1
Interesting work	6	5
Promotional growth in organisation	7	3
Personal loyalty to employees	8	6
Good working conditions	9	4
Tactful discipline	10	7

Source: Le Due (1980)

You may have to accept then that your perceptions of what motivates employees may not be accurate. To discover what does motivate them you should do three things: *read, ask, watch.*

1. **Read:** Be aware of what research tells you about motivation and how employees are motivated. By reading you will discover how the assumptions you hold of your employees can affect how you treat and motivate them. You started this process when you read the earlier sections of this chapter.
2. **Ask:** Ask your subordinates what is important to them, what they would like to achieve, how they feel they can help the organisation, and what makes them feel good about coming to work.

     It is also a good idea to become at least somewhat familiar with their personal circumstances away from the job. This can provide valuable insights into what makes them 'tick'.

You can gather the information through group or private discussions in formal or informal situations. Perhaps you could use the developmental appraisal session to gather information. You can also collect information by using a simple questionnaire like the one shown in Figure 2.9.

Figure 2.9
An Employee Questionnaire

To the employee: Complete these sentences in your own words, without pausing for much thought. Try to be as spontaneous as possible.

I go to work because _____

_____

Work to me means _____

_____

_____

The best part of work is _____

_____

_____

My job is _____

_____

_____

I work harder and smarter when _____

_____

_____

The worst part of my work is _____

_____

_____

If I could make one change to make my work more interesting I would

_____

_____

_____

My motivation would improve if _____

_____

_____

My motivation would decline if _____

_____

_____

My ambition is _____

_____

_____

_____

Stott, K. and Walker, A., *Making Management Work.* © 1992 Simon & Schuster (Asia) Pte Ltd.

3. Watch: Observe your employees on the job to try and identify when and under what conditions they work best. Which processes seem to bring out the best in them? Do they appear to need some say in decision-making in order to really be committed to a course of action? Do they prefer to have concrete targets to aim for?

You can also identify how employees are motivated or 'excited to work' through analysing results of their work and by pinpointing the situations under which it was produced. For example, we recently spoke to the head of department in a polytechnic institution who was somewhat distressed by the fact that one of her staff members produced work of distinctly varying standards. Sometimes it was outstanding and at other times it was just short of abysmal. She decided she needed to look into this. She consciously observed her subordinate in meetings and then compared his work outputs with how he was 'given' the task. She discovered that the tasks in which he performed well were those in which she allowed some input about 'how to do it'. Conversely, his worst work almost inevitably came when she simply told him what to do. She claimed this discovery helped her motivate the staff member and get work of a consistently high quality.

Act

The starting point for motivating employees is to recognise that your job is to obtain their commitment, not to exercise control. You have already accepted that motivation is a long-term commitment on your and the organisation's behalf.

Kotter (1990:72) provides a straightforward example of what motivation at the organisational level involves.

1. Communicate visions and strategies on a regular basis.
2. Communicate beyond simply informing; it should excite employees by connecting to their values.
3. Involve employees in deciding how to implement the vision – make the involvement real, not manipulative.
4. Provide support so employees can succeed in making progress towards the vision.
5. Ensure that rewards and recognition are sincere.

Think of your own organisation and your role within it. As we go through methods of motivation think about whether they can be useful to you. We will discuss the major motivation strategies under the following headings.

- Job enrichment/Enlargement.
- Participation/Involvement.
- Achievement.
- Recognition/Reward.
- Responsibility.
- Promotion/Advancement.
- Support/Environment.
- Money.

Remember, staff are not all motivated in the same way. It is impractical, therefore, to provide a finite list of motivators. Differences are inherent in each employee. An effective manager is one who attempts to recognise these differences and to influence the motivation on both a team and individual basis. As you consider these suggestions you will notice that they draw on various motivation theories.

Job Enrichment/Enlargement

It is important to provide jobs which are both challenging and meaningful. Research has shown that these two factors act as very powerful motivators. Job enrichment attempts to build an increased sense of challenge and achievement into a job. You can enrich your employees' jobs in a number of ways.

1. By providing more discretion in areas such as work methods, sequencing of tasks and work pace. (Flexitime is one example of this.)
2. By encouraging employee participation.
3. By providing personal responsibility for tasks.
4. By encouraging employee interaction.
5. By showing employees that their roles are valuable.
6. By showing employees how their jobs fit in with the overall organisation.
7. By providing prompt feedback on performance.
8. By giving employees a say in the physical conditions in the work place.

Quality of Working Life (QWL), which uses management–labour committees to come up with ways of enhancing the job, is a form of job enrichment.

Job-enrichment strategies have been criticised in a number of ways, especially in relation to rapidly improving specialised technology. It has also been questioned in terms of cost and whether workers really want it. It has had a marked impact however on motivational techniques. Automakers Volvo and Saab have found that job-enrichment strategies have increased the motivation of their workers and claim that such strategies make the companies more productive. Some of the more specific motivational strategies we discuss in this section relate to job enrichment.

Job enlargement proposes that jobs need to be made more varied and interesting by eliminating many of the tedious aspects often present while performing repetitive operations. The rationale is that workers who have more varied and exciting jobs will be more motivated. Secretaries in a typing pool, for example, may be encouraged to take on a different, if related task, one day a week. Try to think of some ways that you could make some of your employees' jobs more interesting.

Participation/Involvement

Your employees are more likely to be committed to their work if they have a say in it. They are more inclined to believe in, and support decisions into which they have had some input. This tends to make the job more meaningful to both teams and individuals. One excellent method to extend staff involvement is that of target-setting (see Chapter 11). Employees have a major input into the targets and how they will be achieved.

Participation can be encouraged in a number of ways. You can ask for opinions in formal meetings or during short informal talks. Questions such as: 'Have you any ideas on how we can improve the system?' are useful for promoting participation if directed at individuals. It takes very little effort on your part to ask an employee for an opinion or advice on how to solve a problem. But it can mean a lot to an employee to be consulted. If you ask for suggestions you must consider the responses seriously. If you always ask, but never act, you will receive little response in the future.

Many employees want to be involved in decisions, especially when they impact their jobs. If you can ask for their participation in a real sense, and they cannot help, you have lost nothing. If they can be helpful they will feel good about their contribution and be more committed to carrying it out.

Achievement

Employees will be motivated by successfully achieving a specific target such as completing a job, solving a problem, making a successful sale or meeting a deadline. This feeling of achievement is akin to the satisfaction you derive when you finish a race, or stand back and admire the house extension you have just built, all by yourself. We all feel good when we finish something and achieve something tangible.

Unfortunately, a sense of achievement in completing a specific task does not last very long. As soon as we start the next task the sense of achievement we felt quickly disappears. In this respect it is your job to ensure that you provide opportunities for employees to experience achievement regularly.

The feeling or sense of achievement is related to the size of the challenge. Would you feel more satisfaction after finishing a 100 metre jog or after completing a marathon? The greater the challenge the greater the sense of achievement. On the other hand, we are not doubting the importance of minor tasks and achievements. These keep them motivated on a regular basis and are an important feature of the whole achievement process.

Recognition/Reward

Recognition is a strong need in most people. Recognition is simply acknowledgement and appreciation of a person's or a team's contribution to the organisation. We all like to be recognised when we have done something worthwhile. Think about young children: how do we encourage them to learn how to walk, speak or even eat? We may clap when they do something special or say a few words of encouragement.

A pat on the back recognising a job well done has similar motivational effects for an employee. You may be surprised how infrequently many managers even think to acknowledge an achievement. If an employee has achieved something special and does not get any recognition, do not be surprised if he does not try as hard the next time. Contributions from either individuals or teams that go unrecognised breed unhappiness, discontent and act as demotivators – 'nobody cares that I did a good job, I certainly won't put in so much effort next time.' Consider how you feel in the same circumstances.

As a motivating manager you must recognise other people's achievements. Some managers are tempted to take the credit for what their employees achieve. You cannot do this as a leader of people. Your leadership role includes using rewards or recognition to motivate people. This can be difficult because you are being asked to share the credit for successful achievements when you know you are the one who has to take the blame if things go wrong – this is one of the difficulties of effective management. If you wish to encourage employees who are not doing their job to maximum potential you can use positive or negative reinforcement techniques.

How can you reward and recognise contributions within your organisation? In the military they give medals for special achievements; many shops have an 'employee of the month' board; and some companies give bonuses as a form of recognition for a good job. Other companies may provide certain perks such as a name on a desk, business cards, or personal telephones.

It would be a good idea to think about how you can recognise or reward employee contributions in your own organisation. In Application Task 2.5 you should think of appropriate rewards that can be given at both an individual and team level. Write down everything you think of, even the little things such as 'a pat on the back' or 'you can leave early today'. Remember to be realistic. When you have completed your list, you may wish to discuss it with some colleagues to obtain more ideas.

Remember, only give recognition when it is due. You can use it sometimes for encouragement, but if you reward inappropriate or sloppy work you will be sending the wrong message. For example, if you gave everyone precisely the same rewards, regardless of their contribution, those who have put in that bit extra may question whether they should bother next time. If you can get your colleagues to recognise each other's contributions they will be even more motivated.

APPLICATION TASK 2.5

Rewards and recognition: What can I do?	
INDIVIDUAL	TEAM

Stott, K. and Walker, A., *Making Management Work.* © 1992 Simon & Schuster (Asia) Pte Ltd.

Responsibility

You are responsible and accountable for the results produced by your organisation. Is that a commitment you accept readily? Those who seek management positions generally thrive on the responsibility (despite the occasional protests). Many of your employees are no different from you. They also like to have responsibilities. They perceive this as being important.

The keys to developing responsibility are risk-taking and trust. Delegating an employee to do a job is an expression of trust and the means of creating responsibility.

Think about how giving someone responsibility can bring out dedication and effort. As a student, I once worked in a hospital on the 'graveyard shift' (10p.m. to 7a.m.), and the only person I could really interact with was Ross, the night janitor. Ross was basically in charge during the night. He was responsible for locking doors, cleaning floors and keeping everything in shape. He took his responsibility very seriously. He was often still there when I left, making sure everything was in order, including the things he did not have to do. The point is, Ross was given his responsibility and was proud of the fact that people depended on him and trusted him to do a good job. He was not paid much but the responsibilities he held kept him going. We all know people like Ross.

Responsibility, surprisingly, is often relatively easy to give. It is often a matter of perception. You do not necessarily have to alter someone's job for him to feel he has responsibility. If someone came to the hospital at night and asked for something (other than medical advice) I referred them to Ross, indicating it was his responsibility. This was quite motivating to him since his responsibility was recognised. The good thing about responsibility is that it is an ongoing motivator.

Of course you should also give employees responsibility for new or major tasks. This often involves you in taking a risk but it is also a way of showing recognition of an employee's ability and competence. Delegation is an excellent way of dealing with this and you will find detailed guidelines in Chapter 17.

Responsibility involves allowing employees to use their discretion in completing tasks or assignments and granting them the responsibility to make decisions. It always involves trust. You are trusted enough to be made accountable for the work of your employees.

Can you think of the ways that you can give your employees more responsibility? Think about how responsibility will motivate them.

Promotion/Advancement

Promotions and advancement are rewards and a recognition that you can handle responsibility. Promotion to a higher-level job or the delegation of extra duties is a form of reward and a powerful motivator. Part of your role may be to promote people. Whether they concede the fact or not, many employees like to think they will be promoted. Few want to stand still for too long. Your influence in suggesting or giving promotions allows you to motivate employees, especially if they are ambitious and able. The prospect for advancement is undoubtedly a potential motivator.

We think the way forward is to ensure that advancement is based on merit and results rather than other factors, such as knowing the right people or indulging in flattery. We know these latter conditions exist and are widespread but organisations which have inadequate or unfair promotion systems often run into difficulties. Promotion offers increased status and benefits, and should go to the employees who contribute the most to the organisation. Do not use promotions as motivators if no such positions exist – the consequences will be demotivating throughout the organisation.

Support/Environment

Employees want adequate support so they can do their jobs properly. If you do not provide them with the necessary resources, whether time, materials, money or personnel, they can quickly lose interest in their jobs. Imagine how motivated a worker would remain if his team where short-staffed and had to carry extra loads? Well-supported and equipped employees are freed from having to 'make do' and so can concentrate more on their jobs. A lack of support can be demotivating but adequate support in itself is not necessarily motivating. Support in the form of management interest is discussed in other sections, such as in 'recognition'.

Employees may also be motivated or demotivated by their everyday working environment. We use the term to include such things as work hours, hygienic conditions and temperature. Work environments are so varied that it is impossible to give advice on what can be done. You and your employees are in the best position to do that.

Beware: If your employees are complaining about the work environment and you *know* it is at least reasonable, look for other reasons for dissatisfaction. Employees do not usually complain about work conditions if they are committed to and like their jobs. However, treat the environment as important. Few people can work optimally if they are too hot or too cold. Highly congested and untidy offices also have a considerable impact on an employee's attitude towards his work.

APPLICATION TASK 2.6

An improved work environment; List some ideas on how you can realistically enhance the work environment for your employees:

Money

We cannot leave this section without mentioning money as a motivator. It is foolish to assume that money is not. Most of us want money, and usually more than we presently have. But more money will not act as a lasting motivator. For pure motivation the other strategies we have mentioned are more effective. Remember the statement we made earlier in the chapter. Money will certainly get people to work but it will not necessarily make them work hard when they arrive.

In Figure 2.10 are some hints for motivating staff. You may wish to keep these close to hand.

Figure 2.10
Some Hints For Motivating Staff

- Clearly *define* expectations and goals.

- *Recognise* achievements with rewards.

- Keep staff *informed* of decisions and changes.

- *Involve* staff in decision-making.

- *Provide* a sense of ownership in the organisation mission.

- Attempt to *understand* the needs and goals of your employees; be careful of your own assumptions.

- *Support* and *encourage* employees to develop both personally and professionally.

- *Establish* and *maintain* an open, *co-operative* climate in your organisation.

- *Set* realistic targets with your staff.

- *Challenge* your employees.

- *Establish* an employee welfare policy.

- *Allow groups* to work on organisational projects to encourage motivation.

- Use continuous *positive reinforcement* – do not reinforce inappropriate behaviours.

- *Do not* depend on money or punishment as effective motivators.

Remember:

- If job satisfaction is to be good employees should experience a sense of personal satisfaction in what they are doing in the job.
- They should feel that their contributions are worthwhile and valued by the organisation.
- They should be challenged by their jobs and feel they have the responsibility to match their expertise and capabilities.
- They should feel that they are growing and developing professionally in both experience and ability.
- They should receive adequate compensation for what they do. This includes financial remuneration and other forms of recognitions and rewards.

Employees should feel that they have a certain amount of control over aspects of the job that have been delegated to them. In Application Task 2.7 add any thoughts of your own.

APPLICATION TASK 2.7

Your own hints for job motivation:

Stott, K. and Walker, A., *Making Management Work*. © 1992 Simon & Schuster (Asia) Pte Ltd.

Conclusion

The job that a person does is not, by itself, a motivator; it is what people want and expect to get out of the job that affects how they behave. A good manager plans situations which enable his staff to reach their own goals through meeting organisational goals. To create these situations managers must be motivated themselves, believe they can develop the best in their staff, role-model their beliefs and support and trust their staff.

Adair (1988 : 140) provides a useful summary of how employees should feel if motivation and job satisfaction are to be good and not just adequate or weak. Each employee must:

1. Feel a sense of personal achievement in the job he is doing, and that the contributions he makes to team or organisational attainment are considered worthwhile.
2. Feel that his job is challenging and demands his best effort. He must feel that the job provides him with the responsibility to match his capabilities.
3. Receive adequate reward and recognition for his achievements.
4. Have considerable control over aspects of the job which have been delegated to him.
5. Feel that he is developing as a person and that he is advancing his ability and experience.

We have emphasised throughout the chapter that motivation is a long-term commitment for the manager. In fact, it is a never-ending process. In Application Task 2.8, which is to help you deal with the problem of motivation systematically, we have included a planning outline for you to use. The action plan aims to help you think about how you will motivate individuals and a permanent work team.

APPLICATION TASK 2.8

MOTIVATING YOUR EMPLOYEES: AN ACTION PLAN

Phase I: Directions

1. Identify a group of employees whose motivation you want to increase.
2. Develop an individual profile of each staff member.
3. At the same time, develop a team profile of the group or team as a whole.
4. Identify the needs, or how your employees are motivated. Perhaps you can use some of the instruments and ideas presented in the chapter.

5.   Reread the theories of motivation (you can go to other sources to do this in more detail if you wish) and the possible strategies of motivation and decide which of these may be appropriate for use with your employees. Ask yourself what benefits should they provide for the individual employees or the team? Do you have to change your management style in any way to implement the strategies?

6.   If you wish, use the following forms: Phase I: Employees and Phase I: Team.

Phase II: Directions

1.   After your plan has been in operation for approximately six months, review its success in motivating your individual employee or your team. Note any aspects which indicate to you that motivation has increased. Ask yourself what worked and what did not.

2.   Change or refine the action plan in line with your findings.

3.   If you wish, use the following forms, Phase II: Employees and Phase II: Team.

Phase I : Employees

Employee	Elements of Motivation to be Increased	Expected Benefits		Strategies Employed	Expected Time frame
		Employee	Org.		

Phase I : Team

Team: _____

Team Targets: _____

Desired Team Outcomes	Elements of Motivation to be Increased	Expected Benefits		Strategies Employed	Time frame
		Team	Org.		

Phase II : Employees

Employee	Strategies Employed		WHY	Indicators of Success	Next Step
	Succeeded	Failed			

Phase II : Team

Desired Team Outcome	Strategies Employed		WHY	Indicators of Success	Next Step
	Succeeded	Failed			

Stott, K. and Walker, A., *Making Management Work.* © 1992 Simon & Schuster (Asia) Pte Ltd.

If you decide to employ this or a similar plan it is essential that you do both phases. You must assess whether your plan worked, and continually update it. Before we leave the topic of motivation we want you to gauge your own understanding of its intricacies and methods. To help in this, you should read and consider carefully the two short case studies below. There are no right or wrong answers but it would be useful if you could discuss your thoughts with some colleagues.

Case One: Mike Neville

Mike Neville has just had his 60th birthday and has been with the company for almost seventeen years. He is one of four supervisors in your unit. He is looking forward to retirement in five years' time and wants a quiet end to his reasonably successful career.

Recently he has started arriving late for work and you even suspect he has been falsifying his time sheets. You have spent a lot of time in the last month or so in going over production figures. Mike's team's output does not compare well with the other three teams in your unit. It has been making a lot of errors and you can see that the quality of its finished product is not up to what you or the company expected.

Your boss has delegated to you the responsibility for introducing a new productivity drive in your unit as a trial run for other units. You know it will only succeed if your supervisors are committed to it and accept the slightly higher workload that comes with any innovation.

In the past, when you were a supervisor yourself, you saw Mike Neville effectively sabotage many changes that required him to commit extra effort or hours. For example, he often uses negative comments such as 'I remember we tried something like this in 1985, or was it 1987; anyway it didn't work', in front of other supervisors and his team members.

You really want the new productivity drive to work. A promotion might depend on it. As the manager of your department, are you going to do or say anything to Mike about his behaviour and about the introduction of the innovation. If so, what and how?

Case Two: Caroline Tay

Caroline Tay joined your managerial team last year. It was her first managerial appointment. She came to you with very good academic results and is currently working on her MBA. Evidently she is an outstanding student. She has always been a very quiet, shy person who sometimes has trouble communicating with her staff but is generally liked and respected by other managers.

You have observed that recently she has not been very visible, failing to go into the canteen and spending much of her spare time alone. Although she never volunteers for extra duties and does not speak up in team meetings unless asked a question, she never refuses a job if you ask her to do it. Because of this she seems to end up with the jobs that no one else wants. Still, what can you do if she does not come forward?

This morning while you were doing your regular 'walk-around' you were surprised by the amount of noise coming out of the meeting room. Finally you thought you had better go and investigate because you were expecting an important client to arrive in half an hour. When you went in, to your surprise, you saw Caroline close to tears and one of her team members shouting: 'Well, how can you expect us to do it if you won't tell us what you want, and let us have some input.' Caroline saw you and abruptly left in the direction of her office. The team members just looked at you and shook their heads.

What can you do to motivate Caroline and to help her motivate her team members? List your ideas and discuss them with your colleagues.

In this chapter we have attempted to guide you towards a basic understanding of the fundamental concepts of motivation. We have summarised some major motivation theories and challenged you to accept the importance of your role as a motivator. We have suggested some methods for identifying how your staff are motivated and provided some strategies you could employ to motivate your staff. We strongly believe that motivation is a central aspect of your job as a manager. There is no doubt that the motivation level of your employees is related to your organisation's productivity. In other words, effective motivation leads to good business. If you fail to give attention to the motivation of your employees you run the risk of being a very ordinary manager. By evaluating your employees' motivation levels, you will be serving the interests of your employees, the organisation and yourself as a highly successful manager.

References

Adair, J. (1988) *Effective Leadership*, Gower : England.

Adams, S. (1963) 'Towards an understanding of inequity', *Journal of Abnormal and Social Psychology*, **67**, pp. 422–436.

Griffin R. (1984) *Management*, Houghton Mifflin : Boston.

Herzberg, F., Mausner, B. and Snyderman, B. (1959) *The Motivation to Work*, Wiley : New York.

Koontz, H. and Weihrich, H. (1988) *Management*, 9th edn, McGraw-Hill : Singapore.

Kotter, J. (1990) *A Force for Change: How Leadership Differs From Management*, The Free Press : New York.

Le Due, A. (1980) 'Motivation of programmers', *Data Base*, Summer, pp. 4–12.

Maslow, A. (1954) *Motivation and Personality*, Harper and Row : New York.

McClelland, D. (1961) *The Achieving Society*, Van Nostrand : Princeton.

McGregor, D. (1960) *The Human Side of Enterprise*, McGraw-Hill : New York.

Nadler, D. and Lawler, E. (1983) 'Motivation: a diagnostic approach', in Hackman, R., Lawler, E. and Porter, L. (eds.), *Perspectives on Behaviour in Organisations*, 2nd edn, pp. 67–78, McGraw-Hill : New York.

O'Mahoney, T. (1984) *Human Motivation: A Review of Theories and an Attempted Integration*, unpublished paper, Luton College of Higher Education : Luton, UK.

Ouchi, W. (1981) *Theory Z: How American Business Can Meet the Japanese Challenge*, Addison-Wesley : Reading, Massachusetts.

Porter, L. and Lawler, E. (1968) *Managerial Attitudes and Performance*, Dorsey Press : Homewood, IL.

Stewart, R. (1985) *The Reality of Management*, Pan : London.

Vroom, V. (1964) *Work and Motivation*, Wiley : New York.

Chapter 3

Developing Effective Teams

I remember many years ago watching a professional football match involving the team which enjoyed my loyal support and the one which was currently topping the league. The latter had no notable names in it nor did its play look particularly exciting. Yet it won the match with consummate ease. It was difficult to understand why that team was so effective.

Perhaps you have seen groups of people, either in work or in social situations, who just seem to knit together in a mysterious way. Perhaps you have also wondered what the formula is for this particular chemistry. In the majority of cases there is no magic. The success of teams has to be worked at. There are usually no short cuts.

Most of us are involved in teams. As managers we are usually in charge of them. As you go through this chapter, we shall try to dispel some of the myths surrounding teamwork and leave you with some clear guidelines on what you can do to improve effectiveness.

This is the first of three chapters which address key issues regarding the ways teams behave and perform. In this chapter we set the scene by looking at the ingredients of successful units and the purpose they serve for the organisation or subunit. We also look at the development of teams and suggest ways in which you can take them towards a stage which is characterised by competence and achievement. In Chapter 4 we then look specifically at a way of getting things done effectively through teams. Despite the willingness and enthusiasm of team members it appears that many teams fail to perform very well because tasks and projects are not approached systematically. Our '7D' scheme is an attempt to deal with this problem. Chapter 5 draws on the work of Meredith Belbin and his associates, and examines how individuals can improve their contributions to team effectiveness by developing the roles they play. This is a fascinating topic and one which receives little attention when considering the membership of teams.

Application Task 3.1 encourages you to think about teams and to complete a preliminary analysis of what you believe are the key factors.

Later we shall examine the key characteristics of successful teams in a brief summary of the research in the field. First it will be helpful to think back to a recent project which your work group had to undertake as a **team** and then use that as a basis for analysis. You will have to recall accurately what happened if your observations are going to be realistic. Complete Application

Task 3.2 which raises some initial thoughts about team performance.

APPLICATION TASK 3.1

Think about any successful teams which you have either worked in or know. What characteristics do they have in common? List your answers below:

1.

2.

3.

4.

5.

APPLICATION TASK 3.2

EVALUATION FORM

This is to get you thinking about team performance. Think about your work team and a project on which you have recently worked together.

1. What behaviour was helpful?

2. What behaviour made task completion difficult?

3. Who participated most?

4. Who took part the least?

5. Who took on the leader's role and how?

6. What could you do to improve the way you worked?

These questions are important in elevating team performance. You can relate your observations to what you actually do in the work situation. Consider these questions:

- Do you promote the helpful behaviours in your work teams or do you support or tolerate the sorts of behaviours which hinder task completion?
- Do you endure one person taking part to the extent that others are excluded, or do you actively draw on contributions from everyone?
- What do you do about the person who participates least? Do you treat it as a sign of non-cooperation, or do you treat the individual as one who needs to be positively asked to contribute?
- The final question is probably the critical one. There is no point in being complacent: all teams can improve. The question is : 'How?' What are the actions which can be taken which will enhance effectiveness?

As you go through the chapter, you will understand what your role is in moving towards improvement and increased chances of successful outcomes as you work with people in teams.

Successful Teams

Earlier you were asked to think about successful teams in which you had been involved and to consider the common features. We have distilled much of what has been written on effective teams into four areas:

- Shared targets.
- Quality relationships.
- Pulling together.
- Balanced leadership.

Shared Target

The most important characteristic of successful teams is that they are working toward a shared target. They know precisely what they want to achieve. This is the same as Goldsmith and Clutterbuck's (1984) 'clear mission' outlined in *The Winning Streak*. In the successful companies the top management team knew where it was going. Everyone pulls in the same direction.

Probably one of the main faults of organisations is that they fail to clarify goals. Management 'down the line' does not understand what 'mission' is – the real purpose for which the organisation exists. Furthermore, personal or subgroup goals may appear which are at variance with the true mission.

In teams then, whether senior management teams at the apex of the organisation or teams of workers at operational level, it is vital to know what the goals, aims and targets are. If as a manager you have formulated such goals with your team members they are probably more aware of them than those who have had no say. In any event, you must constantly refresh people's memories; it is so easy to become distracted from central purposes by the day-to-day activities.

A consultant, working with the senior management team of a small manufacturing company, interviewed members of the team individually and asked them a question which had never been addressed before. He asked them: 'What do you understand to be the key purpose of this company?' One response was 'to expand distribution to other parts of the region'; another 'to add another two product lines before the end of next year'; yet another who had very strong social inclinations 'to provide jobs for this area which has high unemployment.' The managing director's response was 'to make as much brass (money) as possible!'

It is difficult to see how a team can work well together if it is not sure where it is going. Imagine a football team with different perspectives about purpose; it is highly unlikely they would move together in the same direction towards the opponents' goal. A common sense of direction and purpose, alongside clearly defined targets, is essential.

Quality Relationships

Relationships between members of the group are of a high quality. They need to support the group interaction processes which are critical to success. People not only get on well together, but they are conscious of each other's moods and feelings, and they treat everything which is said as valuable. They are very skilful at getting the message across and they know how to read body language. Generally they are experts in the art of communication.

We shall touch on the subject of relationships when we look at the development levels of teams later in this chapter. But it has to be made clear now that high-quality relationships do not mean people are simply nice to one another. You may be nice to your neighbours but it does not mean you have the makings of a successful team. Quality relationships are only present when people are fairly close to each other. That means they can argue without disintegrating, that they can disagree without resentment setting in.

That does not mean they are insensitive; on the contrary, they just seem to understand what makes each other tick. They know the things to say and the things not to say. They share happiness together and they sense when something is wrong. They do not really need to ask 'How are you?' They tend to know instinctively.

Those who keep themselves at a 'respectable' distance from team members are probably failing to contribute towards the relationships which are almost certainly essential for effective team development. How do you rate the quality of relationships amongst your team members? Look at Figure 3.1. Can you locate each member of your team and his relationship with you? How many of your colleagues are in the inner ring?

Figure 3.1
The Relationships Circle

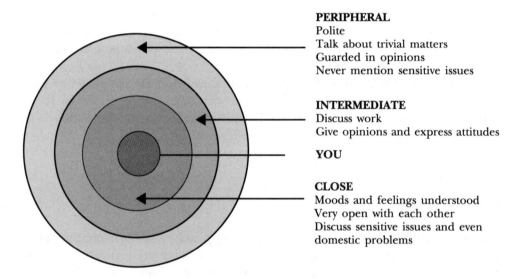

PERIPHERAL
Polite
Talk about trivial matters
Guarded in opinions
Never mention sensitive issues

INTERMEDIATE
Discuss work
Give opinions and express attitudes

YOU

CLOSE
Moods and feelings understood
Very open with each other
Discuss sensitive issues and even domestic problems

Pulling Together

Pulling together is another feature of success and ensures that people behave as a team rather than as a group of disparate individuals. They recognise that the team is there to complete a task and it is more than an individual can manage. They each bring with them their individual differences in terms of personality make-up and a set of skills and experiences. The respective contributions therefore have to be co-ordinated.

Let us take the football analogy again. Each player has a respective contribution to make. Some players are goal scorers, others are goal preventers and some are adept at transferring the ball from defence to attack. Some are creative and some are fierce tacklers. All these abilities have to be co-ordinated. Imagine what it would be like taking the field with eleven goalkeepers. There would be no skills to co-ordinate!

When you assemble a team it is almost certainly because the job is beyond you alone. Although you are working with individuals, they have to understand that their separate efforts are part of an overall effort leading to the team's product.

In our work in organisations we often hear leaders say they have 'a good team of staff'. They are usually referring to the entire workforce and we recognise such supportive remarks for what they are. It does not, however, really mean they have a single unit which is united in purpose and which displays high levels of cohesion. They may have effective teams, but once a certain number has been exceeded, a high degree of co-ordination is very difficult to maintain. What usually happens is that large groups of people split up into several teams (perhaps departments or units) and the aim should be to make these cohesive.

We think it is better to keep teams small. In a previous job I was a member of the organisation's marketing team. When it was newly formed it already had a membership of twelve, comprising people with a range of skills, knowledge and status across the organisation. It was probably already too large. The first thing members did, though, was to suggest other people who might have a contribution to make and to intimate that it would be unfortunate to exclude them. The size of the group expanded to such an extent that the only real work which got done was in subcommittees and project teams.

It may be true that George is an expert in 'mystorrheopic destabilisers' and has a contribution to make, but the more of these suggestions you accede to, the more unwieldy the team becomes. You can always draw on expertise on an occasional basis, but if you want your teams to be effective, the message is clear: keep them small! Francis and Young (1979) suggest that 'nine' is the limit but qualify this by indicating that teamwork characteristics can be cultivated in larger groups.

Team membership is an issue which has raised much debate. The right combination of members can ensure that the pulling together is effective. There are two dimensions which must be examined when assessing membership. Some people have clear functional roles which are directly related to task accomplishment. Others may have roles which might be called *process roles*; they are concerned with keeping the team together as a harmonious unit and with making it effective in its transactions. We shall be looking at this latter set of roles in detail in Chapter 6 on Developing Team Roles.

We believe that you can facilitate 'pulling together' by developing and supporting a common language and culture. In effective teams this happens naturally to a certain extent. There is a code of behaviour which seems to appear over a period of time. Team members are expected to abide by this set of 'unwritten laws', and the use of inappropriate language or dress, and such behaviours as airing certain grievances, may be looked upon with disapproval.

Balanced Leadership

Successful teams usually have skilful leadership and this means a leader who is able to balance the demands of task completion, team cohesion and individual needs. Effective leadership is an enhancer of team performance rather than a substitute for what is there already.

In Chapter 1, on Leading People, we examined the demands of the job, of the group with which the leader works and the individuals within that group. The successful team leader has to reconcile these demands and ensure that high-quality results are achieved through cohesive team effort, and that individual members feel their contributions have been worthwhile and recognised. You have to understand your team members as individuals, that although there is a common goal, each one has a set of personal goals. Each member is motivated by different factors and comes with a different set of experiences. In Chapter 2 we encouraged you to identify these motivational factors for your individual staff. You need to invest time in getting to know your team members and the sorts of influencing strategies which are most likely to work.

We must not lose sight of the fact that people are important. The need to consider issues other than the task alone is the theme for many management writers: 'We need to accept that teams do need managing, and that the social and professional needs of team members have to be recognised' (Brennan, 1988 : 29).

The issue of style also has to be addressed. The very notion of teamwork suggests that the leader has to adopt a participative approach and if he is unable to cope with this he is likely to run into difficulties. Under these circumstances it is unlikely that much team development can take place.

You have a vital role to play as the manager. You cannot simply trust to chance that your teams will be successful. And teams are not a management 'fad'. They have proved to be a valuable asset to those organisations which have discovered how to build them and then to look after them. Your job then is an important one: 'We need to recognise that teams need to be deliberately created, effectively encouraged and professionally sustained, or as the Japanese say "nurtured and stroked"' (Brennan, 1988 : 29).

Complete Application Task 3.3, Team Characteristics Chart. It will help you to think about the prevalent conditions in your team or teams at work. This short exercise, which uses bipolar statements, can also be used with team members if you want to seek their opinions on team characteristics. You can then have a graphic representation of perceived conditions in the team. We like to do this exercise with a management team and then put all the 'profiles' on one sheet, but using different colours for each team member's profile. We then explore any big differences in item scores. This is invariably a highly productive exercise.

APPLICATION TASK 3.3

TEAM CHARACTERISTICS CHART

Read the bipolar statements and circle the number which approximates to the condition in your team. Join the circles together with lines. This presents a profile of team characteristics.

Members have their own ideas about team goals.	1 2 3 4 5 6 7	Everyone knows precisely what the team's goals are and they could state them without hesitation.
Top management lets lower management formulate its own ideas about organisational goals so long as things are going well.	1 2 3 4 5 6 7	Top management knows exactly where the organisation is going and tells everyone regularly.
Members have their own agendas and are negative towards team goals.	1 2 3 4 5 6 7	Everyone pulls together and all efforts are directed at the team's stated goal. There is commitment.
People are polite to each other and avoid discussing sensitive issues.	1 2 3 4 5 6 7	Members are entirely open and honest with each other and are willing to reveal how they feel.

Team members do not understand each other very well.	1 2 3 4 5 6 7	Team members seem to have a sixth sense. They can almost communicate telepathically.
Distinctive abilities are seldom used, and experience and knowledge are not really recognised.	1 2 3 4 5 6 7	Abilities are used and harnessed for a successful outcome.
The manager achieves tasks satisfactorily and is not concerned whether people enjoy their work.	1 2 3 4 5 6 7	Tasks are done well and members enjoy their participation.
There is pressure on team members to conform and some practices are restrictive.	1 2 3 4 5 6 7	There is a recognition that individuals are different and these differences are used to advantage.

Stott, K. and Walker, A., *Making Management Work.* © 1992 Simon & Schuster (Asia) Pte Ltd.

If the pattern is one which is fairly central or, better still, having several points marked to the right of centre, then it is likely that several criteria of successful teams are being met satisfactorily. If the pattern is very much to the left of centre you may have to review your actions in several areas.

Completing this chart gives you an initial impression of your team's characteristics. In Application Task 3.4, think of your team at work and consider whether things are in good shape, OK, or in need of attention. You will find it helpful to write a few notes beside the item if it needs attention and to indicate what you can do.

If you perceive there are deficiencies in the 'shared target' section, you may have to look at the ways in which goals and targets are formulated, and whether more involvement is called for. This may not be necessary of course, because the objectives may be set already and generally accepted. In this case, organisational or departmental intentions may have to be clarified on a more frequent basis.

The building of quality relationships takes time but does not happen on its own. Strategies have to be employed to develop the depth of relationships which enhance teamwork. We shall look at this in a little more detail later.

APPLICATION TASK 3.4

IN GOOD SHAPE?

	In good shape	OK	In need of attention	Notes
Shared target	☐	☐	☐	
Quality relationships	☐	☐	☐	
Pulling together	☐	☐	☐	
Balanced leadership	☐	☐	☐	

Team cohesion can be improved by ensuring that people's abilities are being used and that their part in the overall task is clearly delineated. The opportunity to meet together to discuss the way the overall task is progressing is helpful from the team cohesion standpoint.

Balanced leadership can be improved through constant reappraisal of performance in the areas of task, group and individual (see Chapter 1 on Leading People). The leader must employ actions which encourage and support individuals, and actions which draw out contributions from the team and co-ordinate them so that performance is not simply the sum of disparate parts.

SUMMARY

The Characteristics of Effective Teams Are:

- Shared target.
- Quality relationships.
- Pulling together.
- Balanced leadership.

Why Have Teams?

So far we have looked at the key features of successful teams and you have been encouraged to look at teams with which you have been involved with these criteria in mind. We now ask a question which is central to our whole discussion: Why have teams?

Sometimes, when things are not going well, many ask this question; and it is true that teams are often formed without adequate reason. It may even be on a directive from higher management. It is worth noting at this point that there must be support from top management since team-building efforts may 'create a change in the relationship between the team and the organization which would require the sanction of higher-level management' (Baker, 1979 : 369).

In some quarters it seems fashionable to form teams in order to tackle specific tasks, but there are many circumstances which do not necessitate them. In the same way that some managers call meetings because it is the done thing, some form teams for the same reason. Forming a team to complete a simple project which could be comfortably handled by one person is expensive and a questionable policy. Where they are necessary, however, they should fulfil several purposes which are central to their existence.

There seem to be several obvious benefits, two of which were identified in a survey conducted by Francis and Young (1979 : 6). The first is of key importance and sufficient to separate the approach from other forms of intervention. 'Effective teams produce outstanding results and succeed in achieving despite difficulties. Members feel responsible for the output of their team and act to clear difficulties standing in their way.' The critical benefit is that teams can produce results of considerable quality.

The management of modern organisations can be a complicated business. The conditions they encounter can be highly complex and unpredictable. In recent years the demands of changing technology have had a considerable impact on many organisations across the board. Furthermore, competition has increased, matched by competitive responses. Some writers describe the environment as complex and turbulent. The response internally seems to have been the appearance of increased interdependencies amongst employees. Consequently there appears to be an expanding need to employ a team approach to management, a response which emphasises the interdependencies and interrelationships amongst organisational members (Baker, 1979). Organisational goal structures further combine with environmental complexity to create a need for effective teamwork and associated team-building processes.

We actually use the word *teams* quite loosely: we talk about senior management teams and so forth. Sometimes we use the word team when the word *group* would be more appropriate. But where a group works cohesively to process complex information leading to effective task performance, developing a level of morale amongst members, we may consider using the word *team*. We accept that if the work is too much for one person, teams are necessary to complete the task. But what are the specific purposes of teams? By answering this question we can do something as managers to develop the way in which they fulfil these purposes.

We have identified four purposes which are central to all management teams in varying degrees:

- They give support.
- They handle complexity.
- They create.
- They choose the optimum solution.

They Give Support

Traditional motivation theories tell us we need to be valued and recognised by our colleagues. Teams can fulfil that need. In an effective team there is care and compassion. People are close to one another. They notice when things are wrong.

Teams value the contributions of members and give firm support when individuals need it. Sometimes people run into difficulties and need the support of colleagues. Sometimes they face insecurity as major changes take place and again need the firm emotional support of colleagues to see them through the difficult phase.

This type of relationship encourages the sort of openness which *must* exist for teams to develop. There must be depth to discussions. Those who restrict themselves to superficialities are likely to inhibit teamwork since relationships will tend to remain shallow and, in some cases, false. Many managers we come into contact with state that communication in the management team is completely open. It is our experience, however, that relationships are fairly shallow and openness is seldom practised to the extent that managers would have you believe.

They Handle Complexity

This relates to the task and is central to the issue of team formation. Teams are formed to deal with complex information and to co-ordinate it. In other words, the task is beyond the reasonable capabilities of just one person. If a task is so simple, repetitive or mechanistic that one person could manage it, there is no point in wasting time and money forming a team. In many organisations, though, the complexity of information and task structure is such that teams are essential to quality task accomplishment.

They Create

Teams probably have a greater capacity for creating and developing ideas than individuals. It is true that individuals can produce stunning ideas, but teams add the component of rigour – they put ideas to the test and bring a note of objectivity into the arena. The output of a well-organised team can be remarkable in terms of ideas. It uses the talents of its members to produce something which is far more than the sum of the individual parts. Members feed on each other's strengths leading to what many call *synergy*, best expressed in the equation $2 + 3 = 6$. What this means is that the final outcome is greater than the simple sum of each individual's potential contribution. It is also true that $2 + 3$ may add up to 4 if some factors are not handled well.

They Choose the Optimum Solution

Wiser decisions are usually reached. This comes through having all the relevant information, and going through an appropriate decision-making process. The success of this may depend to a large extent on team members having the right abilities. Apart from those with the appropriate knowledge and information, the team needs someone who Belbin (1981) called a *monitor–evaluator:* someone who has the capacity to assimilate complex data and interpret it. The same person can also listen to ideas and challenge their validity through an intellectual approach. There is, of course, the danger of being over-critical, a tendency which must be avoided if ideas are not to be stifled.

Wiser decisions naturally improve task accomplishment and this is achieved through the actions of team members. The behaviours of individuals will have a considerable impact on the effectiveness of team performance and it seems appropriate therefore to pay great attention to those behaviours which are dysfunctional and which are likely to harm the successful operation of the team.

Perhaps one of the reasons teams are able to select the best options is because of their collective strength, and this applies not only to the combination of abilities, but to the confidence created by being able to make an impact which could not be achieved in the organisation on an individual basis.

Consider a work team in which you are involved. It may be one you lead, or it may be one in which you are a member, perhaps a management team. Ask yourself these questions:

- Does it give support to individuals and help members through difficulties?
- Does it manage to break down complex issues and unravel difficulties?
- Does it support creativity and look for new ways to solve problems?
- Does it encourage conflicting views in an attempt to choose the best and tested solution?

Having considered these questions you will find it helpful to complete Application Task 3.5, Team Purposes, which asks you to identify the things which the team does well and the areas which are less than satisfactory. It also asks you what you can do (either as leader or member) to effect improvement.

APPLICATION TASK 3.5

TEAM PURPOSES

Think of a work team of which you are a member or which you lead. Complete the form below:

1.   The team performs these purposes well:

2.   The team does not perform these purposes well:

3.   Indicate some of the things you can do to bring about improvement:

Stott, K. and Walker, A., *Making Management Work.* © 1992 Simon & Schuster (Asia) Pte Ltd.

SUMMARY

Purposes of Effective Teams:

- They give support.
- They handle complexity.
- They create.
- They choose the optimum solution.

From Birth to Maturity: Phases of Development

Teams begin as a collection of individuals without much concern for the unit's success. It is possible however for them to go through a series of phases leading to a high degree of ability. The relationships can develop to such an extent that people become friends for life. Tuckman and Jensen (1977) call the development phases: *forming, storming, norming, performing* and *mourning*. Our framework covers the growth stages in four phases and we call these:

- Polite niceties.
- Politicking.
- Achieving.
- Competence.

Polite Niceties

Think of the first time you met your colleagues. It is hardly likely you opened up your innermost thoughts or revealed your emotions; you probably talked about work, your previous job or the weather. At this stage people are weighing each other up and deciding where they stand in the group. Some like to show off whilst others prefer to see how disruptive they can be. Some prefer to stay in the background and watch what is going on. The fact is that people are different and respond in vastly different ways to the new setting for their efforts.

People do not really know each other well and they seem to have little care for each other, although many will deny this. They will not reveal their weaknesses and there is little openness. They tend to be extremely polite to one another which acts as a convenient defence mechanism. In this phase the team (if it can be called such) is at its most ineffective. Unfortunately some groups of colleagues in organisations never get past the stage of polite niceties and never achieve very much as a consequence.

Sometimes the organisational situation is responsible for the lack of openness. The system may wish to keep emotion out of the frame and keep communication on a rational footing. This is probably misplaced optimism, but it has to be acknowledged that the prevalent rituals do have a great impact on what can take place and what cannot.

We visited an educational establishment and, after a tour of the facilities, the principal told us what a happy workforce he had. There were no problems. A visit to the staff room found everyone addressing each other very formally, Mr This and Miss That, and everyone was very polite. Staff confirmed they had good relationships and always avoided discussing anything which could start an argument! This sort of behaviour merely conceals what is going on below the surface. There seems to be little possibility of development unless these barriers are broken down. The truth is that the principal had as many problems with his staff as anyone else but they were never allowed to see fresh air.

Politicking

Eventually people get to know each other for what they really are. Positions in the team emerge and there may be an element of conflict as rivals vie for the leadership, each with their band of supporters. There may be differences of opinion and difficulties may affect relationships. Interest or splinter groups may form and there is a great deal of micropolitical activity. The more complex or dangerous the task, the more the chance of ill-feeling and arguments surfacing.

We are all familiar with the micropolitical activity which is characteristic of this phase. Think of those who try to develop a relationship with influential people at work. They often make themselves very influential since they have the boss's 'ear'. Other people develop coalitions on the basis that there is strength in numbers. Those who are skilful at coalition-building will join forces with the important people, those who provide an important link in the chain, and who can be quite influential.

Sometimes we naively believe that organisational life will be better without such activities which represent a striving for power or position, but the organisational underworld is a reality and we may be better advised to learn to use it to our advantage rather than try to fight its existence. Although the world of organisational politics and micropolitical activity is more relevant to the concern as a whole, there is no doubt that similar experiences on a smaller scale occur frequently in teams, and particularly those which are ongoing such as management teams.

Some research has focused on the problems of mixed-gender teams. There is often a great deal of competitiveness, just as there may be in single-gender teams, but things are done more subtly. Members are sometimes attracted to a member of the opposite sex and this can produce quite irrational behaviours which may compromise team effectiveness.

Achieving

Again, many teams in organisations fail to get past the political phase. If individuals can achieve a degree of tolerance and temper their own satisfactions, they can then experiment with new ways of doing things and learn to accommodate the members' strengths and weaknesses.

As the team experiences success it may be prepared to reduce its insularity and attempt to relate with other teams. People are proud to be members of the team. Relationships are good and people are able to combine their distinctive contributions to work together effectively. They like to spend social time together and their families may even share holidays.

Very few teams seem to reach this stage where members have an amazing knowledge of how each other will behave in any given situation. Some sports teams display this attribute and it results in performance at the highest level. Relationships are deep and people do not have to pretend.

Competence

There is a problem, though, if the team feels unable to be challenged and that everything it does is right. Some political units and organisation committees seem to demonstrate this dysfunctional effect. In your organisation for example, you may find a management team which is so confident of its own superiority that it does not analyse information adequately and engage appropriate decision-making mechanisms. It may get rid of people with alternative views and insulate members from information which represents contrasting opinions.

Despite the dangers, teams which reach this competence phase can achieve a vast amount and are capable of dealing with tasks which are complex, dangerous or need excessive efforts on the part of members.

SUMMARY

Phases of Development:

- Polite niceties.
- Politicking.
- Achieving.
- Competence.

Phased Team Development:
How the Team Leader Can Help

If your team seems to be stuck at one phase even after a period of time, what can you do in an attempt to facilitate its development? Knowing about the phases through which teams might progress is only of value to the manager if he can do something about it. Team leaders can help their teams through each phase and you are asked to consider this in Application Task 3.6.

APPLICATION TASK 3.6

Try to think of some ways in which you can help the process through each stage. Indicate specific things you can do which are quite simple to implement.

Phase 1.   Polite niceties:

Phase 2.   Politicking:

Phase 3.   Achievement:

Phase 4.   Competence:

Stott, K. and Walker, A., *Making Management Work.* © 1992 Simon & Schuster (Asia) Pte Ltd.

In the task, you were asked to think of ways in which you could help teams of which you are a member or which you lead to progress through phases. You may have thought of some useful and practical ideas. Below are some of our ideas which we have found helpful. A word of caution though: do not be too impatient; it may take some time before you notice changes. Also bear in mind you may have to examine your own behaviour. If you want people in your team to express their feelings about certain issues you too will have to be quite open.

Phase 1

Get to Know Each Other in Different Settings

One of the problems with teams in the early stages of development is that they only meet in the work situation and, depending on the nature of the task, there may be little opportunity for relationships to develop. Try organising the occasional lunch for team members or have a party where they can bring their families along.

Providing the opportunity to take the team away for a few days in a residential setting is a form of team development which should be looked at very seriously. At this stage of development (or lack of it) in particular, it is very important to get people together for a more 'intensive' experience than that which is available in the daily work routine. The advantages are considerable. They can develop self-awareness, a greater understanding of the way in which their behaviour affects other team members, and they may then be able to modify their behavioural patterns if this is thought necessary. If you are the leader you too need to develop an increased level of self-awareness, for by asking other members about their perceptions of your behaviour, you may discover that your 'participative' style of management is actually seen as relatively autocratic!

Working together in a different setting can often reveal to people that there are different ways of doing things, often better, and that we are generally constrained by our own assumptions and preferences. Developing a more flexible attitude can release a great deal of team energy.

Have Fun Together

Work is often very serious. It is surprising how quickly people can get to know each other when the situation is more relaxed and members can let their hair down. This can obviously be achieved through organising activities like social events and the occasional outing.

Express How You Really Feel

As we said earlier you need to let people know how you honestly feel about things. Similarly you can ask them to express their feelings. You may for example say something such as: 'I was very angry when the marketing manager did not produce the figures on time.' You can ask questions like: 'How did you feel about not being asked to take part in that project?'

Being able to express feelings may also lead to increased control of them. Feelings of hostility or aggression, for example, can become dysfunctional if they are not coped with adequately. Similarly, the drive towards intense competitiveness can have adverse effects on teamwork.

Ask People to State Their Honest Concerns

For the good of team performance, you want people to express their concerns. If they are worried, for example, that a particular course of action might affect them personally, they need to bring this into the open, otherwise it may interfere with the work. This problem of insecurity is identified by Baker (1979 : 369) as a potential dysfunction: 'If team members are highly insecure, they may be unable or unwilling to discuss problems which seriously need to be examined.'

Ask People to Reveal Their Strong Points

In some situations members may be shy about revealing the skills and experiences they bring with them into the team. They consider it immodest to 'sing their own praises'. Would it have helped the Brazilian football team to perform so well if no one knew what Pele's strengths were, so decided to play him as a goalkeeper? You may know in advance what people are good at, but there may be other strengths which are relevant to task performance, and it is useful to ask members individually (addressing them by name) whether they have any knowledge, skill or experience in a particular area.

Encourage People to Share Some Details of Their Life Away from Work

This is a way of trying to develop the relationship and move it from the 'peripheral' towards the inner circle. You are not likely to get members talking about domestic problems at this stage in the team's life, but by sharing some conversation about life outside work, you are showing interest in the person as an individual rather than just a contributor to a group.

Build Up Trust and Confidence: Do Not Talk about People Behind Their Backs

If you are the team leader the development of trust and confidence in your integrity is essential if the team is to progress. You need to set an example which team members must be constantly encouraged to follow. If they have anything to say they should be able to say it to people's faces, even if it is critical. If it is not appropriate to say it in the presence of others it is probably destructive and best not said at all. Bear in mind that trust is built up through actions rather than words. You can say to people that they can trust you, but they will judge you by your actions.

As leader you need to try to remove the superior–subordinate feeling for effective teamworking. You can have confidence that fellow adults will not take advantage of a situation in which you are creating a team of equals for more effective task accomplishment. It can be destructive to talk down to team members.

Phase 2

Encourage People to Be Open about Their Feelings

We have already mentioned this as a strategy for progressing beyond the first phase of a team's life. It is something which needs to be progressively developed. Members need to be encouraged to become more and more open, and when they have developed trust in you, they will realise the benefits of adopting this approach. The leader too needs to be open. If you can be open in your relationships with the team they are more likely to be responsive to you.

Ask People to Discuss Their Ideas on How to Tackle the Task

In examining the purposes of teams we have mentioned the area of creativity. If you are going to listen to just one person's ideas, there may be little point in having a team. You need to listen to others and although some suggestions may seem impractical, they may contain the fragment of an idea which is useful and on which a solution might be built. Furthermore, you will support your team members by giving them firm involvement in the generation of potential options.

Always allow sufficient time for adequate discussion to take place and for everyone to be able to participate. Also, try to avoid leaving issues before they have been fully discussed. Rather than let one or two dominate discussions, say something like: 'We have only a short time to go through this issue; let us each keep our comments to five minutes and then everyone can speak.' Elicit comments from reluctant individuals by addressing them by name and asking what they think.

Try to Achieve Success, However Small, and Celebrate It

We have a friend who keeps telling us we should celebrate at every opportunity! When we have completed an article together we might go out for a meal, and it does have a beneficial effect. It is advantageous for teams to celebrate success because it shows that it is the *team* which has achieved something and it helps to bind it together.

Identify and Expose Conflicts and Achieve Compromise or Reconciliation

There is no greater hindrance to team development than festering conflicts and ill-feeling. Whether you are leader or member, you can act as 'healer' by exposing differences and discussing ways in which these might be reconciled. You should move the focus away from personal differences and on to conflicting views about the task. This sort of conflict is beneficial. There is a saying which sums it up: 'When two men in a business always agree, one of them is unnecessary.' But members so often fall out because they see things in different ways and these then turn into personal disputes which can be quite injurious to the team and its effective functioning. You have a responsibility to do something about the situation if you want your team to move beyond this phase to that of 'achievement'.

Phase 3

Do a Strengths and Weaknesses Analysis

If your team has reached this phase of development you are very fortunate in having what must be an effective unit. There is still room for improvement though. Members need to re-examine their own strengths and weaknesses alongside those of the team. During this phase, therefore, you need to ask the questions: 'What are we good at?' and 'Where do we need to improve our performance?'

Try out New Ways of Doing Things

Do not get stuck in a rut. It is best to assume that the way in which you do things can be improved on. Now is an opportunity to try out new ways.

We mentioned earlier the advantages of the team undergoing some form of residential experience together in an attempt to expose supportive and dysfunctional behaviours. Whilst the early phases of development may be inappropriate for some of the more searching forms of self-disclosure, at this stage members should know each other well enough not to feel threatened by such techniques. Many organisations who have seen the advantages of building teams have engaged the services of specialist consultants to handle this sort of interpersonal development.

The differences which individual members bring to the team with them can be an enormous asset and can be used in a creative way. However, there is a tendency in many situations to try to exercise greater control than that which is necessary and to lay down group norms of conformity. This phenomenon has been witnessed in some sports teams which have failed to capitalise on the creative talents of some individuals and opted for a more systematic conformity which has done little to aid team performance. It is often conflict which has led to the suppression of different skills and talents, but this reaction is more likely to lead to mediocrity than innovative solutions to complex problems. The management of this aspect of teamwork has to be skilful because it is too easy to achieve compromise by restraining talent. Furthermore, a great deal of individual resentment can build up if individual creative abilities are not used and fostered.

Assess the Individual Skills Which Are Required and Develop Them

Because things tend to be going very well when a team has reached this stage of development, there is now the opportunity to provide for the extension of team members' skills. Such development will bring in new ideas and provide refreshing experiences for the members.

Clarify Each Individual's Role in the Task

It may be easy to lose sight of the overall task as individuals become involved in their own activities. Roles need to be clarified and responsibilities reassessed, and then individuals need to be reminded of the whole picture so that there is no loss of cohesion.

Link Up with Other Teams

One of the dangers of successful teams is that they become very insular and detach themselves from other teams or people doing similar work. The most effective teams always recognise that there is room for improvement and prefer to draw on the successful experiences of other units in order to enhance their own performance.

Celebrate Team Success (Rather Than Individual)

Recognising success is just as vital in this phase as in the previous one. Celebrating does not need to be a spectacular affair; it can be a get-together at coffee time and a few words of encouragement and congratulation from the boss.

Review the Team's Operation and Ask How Things Could Be Done Better

Review is a key process in development so that the information can be used to realign some activities. A constant search for better ways of doing things, by internal evaluation or looking at other teams' performance, can only elevate the chances of team success.

Phase 4

Allow Others to Assume the Leader's Role

At this stage of development the team has reached a high level of competence and it can now afford to look towards the development of individuals in order to support the longer-term needs of the organisation. It may be productive to give others the opportunity to head up various aspects of the work, and this can prove to be of benefit to both the individual and the organisation or department.

Include Opposing Views and Treat Them Seriously

We have seen that one of the biggest dangers is that of infallibility. You need to expose your team constantly to rival views lest it becomes completely insulated from the real world. There are many examples of organisations which are operating in the past with the most ridiculous constraints because the senior management team has not exposed itself to the conflicting views of others.

Change the Routine Occasionally

One way of avoiding staleness is to change the routine. The occasional change of venue for a meeting or to bring in an outsider can help to avoid the staleness which can depress performance.

Ask Someone from Outside the Team to Comment on Its Performance

It is useful to employ an outsider who can comment on the team's performance without the constraining factor of personal involvement. Some senior management teams obtain the services of consultants to examine their work and this can be useful if the team has been together for a long time and with little change of membership.

Figure 3.2 is a summary of the actions you can take for teamwork improvement.

Improving Teamwork: Guidelines

It is helpful to have methods of improving the effectiveness of our teams and you will find many of these in the literature. Below is a technique which is aimed at improving the performance of a team which is already formed and operating. If you are involved a great deal in team projects you are strongly advised to read the next chapter on Planning Team Action which delineates a system for completing tasks effectively through the use of teams. Below is a system which looks at some general issues which are applicable to all kinds of teams, whether small project teams or permanent groups such as management teams.

Improving Teamwork

The result of a team's efforts should be a well-completed task and a satisfied group of team members whose individual needs have been met through working together cohesively. All of us at some time or another have probably been part of a team where this just does not happen – discussions go round

Figure 3.2
Phased Team Development: How The Team Leader Can Help

Phase 1

Get to know each other in different settings.

Have fun together.

Express how you really feel.

Ask people to state their honest concerns.

Ask people to reveal their strong points.

Encourage people to share some details of their life away from work.

Build up trust and confidence: Do not talk about people behind their backs.

Phase 2

Encourage people to be open about their feelings.

Ask people to discuss their ideas on how to tackle the task.

Try to achieve success, however small, and celebrate it.

Identify and expose conflicts and achieve compromise or reconciliation.

Phase 3

Do a strengths and weaknesses analysis.

Try out new ways of doing things.

Assess the individual skills which are required and develop them.

Clarify each individual's role in the task.

Link up with other teams.

Celebrate team success (rather than individual).

Review the team's operation and ask how things could be done better.

Phase 4

Allow others to assume the leader's role.

Include opposing views and treat them seriously.

Change the routine occasionally.

Ask someone from outside the team to comment on its performance.

---

in circles, efforts and contributions are disjointed, and there is either no outcome or one that is less than satisfactory. Some teams are obviously better than others at achieving tasks.

Below is a system of getting things done.

1. *Define the task.*
   Tell your team members in clear terms what the job is and when it has to be completed.

2. *Obtain appropriate and relevant information.*
   You may have to obtain the advice of experts or acquire some statistical information. It will be very difficult to proceed unless you possess the important items of information.

3. *Discuss ideas.*
   Hold full and frank discussions of problems, tasks and processes. Focus the discussion. Give everyone in the team a chance to have a say and, as leader of the team, make sure you summarise all the contributions.

4. *Reach consensus on the optimum course of action and make an incisive decision.*
   Try to avoid vote-taking because this tends to split your team into winners and losers. Although not everyone may agree on the optimal course of action, through discussion you should be able to secure agreement to go along with one solution.

5. *Break down the task into bite-sized chunks and decide how to co-ordinate them.*

6. *Negotiate targets.*
   Give individuals specific tasks and ensure there is understanding. You should have a clear idea of your team members' abilities so you can distribute appropriate responsibilities. Communicate high expectations of quality work.

7. *Set indicators to measure progress.*
   Discuss appropriate measures and agree on a time scale.

8. *Implement.*
   Convert the plans into action. Plan rapid and productive task performance. Do not allow too much time; people will lay things aside.

9. *Think about how the team performed the task.*
   What can be improved? Give feedback to team and members. This feedback is important to development. Sometimes it may not be possible to have much effect on the current task, but you can have an impact on future related operations. In this case it is desirable to generalise the experience, so that relationships between the present and future problems can be identified.

Now, having looked at a systematic approach for processing work in teams, you should consider how the teams in which you are involved perform in relation to each of the steps. Consider whether the particular step is generally dealt with very well, whether it is merely adequate or whether it is dealt with badly, in which case you will have to determine what you can do to improve it. Complete Application Task 3.7, ticking the appropriate box for each of the nine steps.

APPLICATION TASK 3.7

IMPROVING TEAMWORK : STEPS

Tick the appropriate box:

	Handled very well	OK	Done badly
1. Defining the task.	☐	☐	☐
2. Obtaining appropriate and relevant information.	☐	☐	☐
3. Discussing ideas: Holding full and frank discussion of problems, task and processes. Focusing the discussion.	☐	☐	☐
4. Reaching consensus on the optimum course of action and making an incisive decision.	☐	☐	☐
5. Breaking down the task into bite-sized chunks and deciding how to co-ordinate them.	☐	☐	☐
6. Setting targets: Giving individuals specific tasks and ensuring there is understanding. Communicating high expectations of quality work.	☐	☐	☐
7. Setting indicators to measure progress.	☐	☐	☐
8. Implementing: Converting the plans into action. Planning rapid and productive task performance.	☐	☐	☐
9. Giving feedback to team and members.	☐	☐	☐

Stott, K. and Walker, A., *Making Management Work.* © 1992 Simon & Schuster (Asia) Pte Ltd.

In this chapter we have looked at the characteristics of successful teams and asked you to examine the characteristics of your teams at work. We have suggested some key purposes of teams and asked whether your teams fulfil these purposes. We then looked at a framework of development phases, asked you to assess where your teams were in relation to these stages, and then provided some actions you can take in order to move your team on to the next phase and thereby to a higher level of performance.

On a lighter note, we now provide some ideas on how to inhibit team performance. Nevertheless, perhaps some of the items may have to be taken seriously if they have a ring of truth about them for you. If you recognise something which you are doing regularly ask yourself whether it is really helpful to the team.

Team Performance Inhibitors

1. *Waiting for others to initiate.* As a member of the team, you probably have some good ideas, but you do not bother to voice them. Something needs doing but you might as well wait for someone else to make the first move.
2. *Lack of accurate and comprehensive data.* It really is a lot of trouble to obtain information and the team can probably do just as well without it.
3. *Feelings and opinions taking precedence over facts.* You can sense when something is wrong. Facts, such as declining sales figures, are not that important.
4. *Inadequate discussion of separate ideas.* It gets too confusing if there are too many ideas, so it is best to take just one and see what can be done with that.
5. *Closed minds.* The team has worked together for some time. There is only one way of doing things.
6. *Indulgence in politeness to mask open feelings.* People expressing their feelings can be a dangerous business. It may even lead to differences of opinion.
7. *Unrealistic plans.* The team may get complacent if it actually achieves anything, so it is better to be unrealistic.
8. *Forgetting everything after the meeting: no follow-up.* Meetings are simply for discussing things amongst the team. They are not intended to lead to anything.
9. *Only considering immediate concerns.* You look only at pressing issues and do not consider the future; it is too far away.
10. *Unwillingness to try the unfamiliar.* It is safer to stay with what team members know.

11. *Unwillingness to accommodate dissent.* Everyone should agree with what you say, especially if you are the leader. Dissent is likely to lead to breakdowns in relationships.

12. *Badly prepared meetings.* Team meetings do not have to be prepared; they would become too rigid and inflexible.

13. *Woolly meetings.* Team meetings are an opportunity to talk in general terms in order to avoid the specifics; that might lead to having to do things.

14. *'We've always done it this way!'* And it has always been OK so why change things now?

15. *'New ideas won't work!'* You cannot beat an old idea, tried and tested over time.

16. *Unwillingness to tread on toes.* It is best not to do this as it might offend Fred. The fact that it could double profits is of no concern.

17. *Lack of co-ordination between the task subdivisions.* You let everyone go away with a bit of the task and hope that they will fit together when they return. You probably find that some activities are being duplicated, which means they are probably done twice as well!

18. *Lack of rigorous reviews of team performance and progress.* There is no point in reviewing what has happened. That is now history.

19. *Wrong people doing tasks because of tradition or position.* Bill always takes charge of this job because he is senior to Fred. The fact that he does it badly is irrelevant.

20. *Protocol.* If it does not meet the protocol criteria, it cannot be done. It is far more important than effectiveness and productivity.

21. *Withdrawing.* Forget what is going on in the team and hold your own private conversation with the person sitting next to you. If he won't talk, try day-dreaming.

22. *Competition.* Have a private competition to see if you can talk more than anyone else or come up with the most suggestions, regardless of whether they are relevant.

23. *Blame others.* If things are not going well, blame everyone else.

24. *Personal gain.* Ignore the needs of the team and look after your own interests and those of your section or department.

25. *Become excessively formal.* This effectively cools the atmosphere and destroys team climate.

As we said before this short section on performance inhibitors, do not simply dismiss them if some of the items can be identified with your behaviour or that of your team members. Do something about such behaviours otherwise you may find them blocking the effectiveness of your team for some considerable time.

Conclusion

We have stated that we believe many organisations face the sorts of environmental (both external and internal) conditions which necessitate a team approach for organisational effectiveness. But we also believe that team-building strategies should be employed only where the right conditions exist. We do not see it as a productive strategy in all circumstances. Top management has to be convinced that it is appropriate, and that the time and resources are available to make it work.

Team-building methods practised by specialists in the field tend to focus on one of three areas: the role of the individual in the team; the interpersonal relationships; the establishing of goals and action plans. We have attempted to incorporate a number of facets from each of these models to provide a broad and comprehensive framework for teamwork development.

To support this comprehensive approach, we have provided in Application Task 3.8 a fifty-item instrument which can help you undertake a detailed assessment of the prevalent conditions in your management team. Because it deals with a wide range of factors concerned with effective team performance, it can be applied only to a team which operates on a permanent or semi-permanent basis. It would be unrealistic to use it with a team formed only for a short-term project, since the time is not available for the sort of development which the instrument tests. If you are seriously concerned about your management team's performance and its effective operation, we suggest you use a few minutes at the beginning or end of a team meeting for all your members to complete the form. You can then aggregate the scores, divide them by the number of people in the team to arrive at an average score, and then compare your overall score with the index given at the bottom of the instrument.

References

Baker, H. K. (1979) 'The hows and whys of team building', *Personnel Journal*, June.

Belbin, R. M. (1981) *Management Teams: Why They Succeed or Fail*, Heinemann : London.

Brennan, J. (1988) 'Teams in education', *Management in Education*, **2**, 1, p. 29.

Francis, D. and Young, D. (1979) *Improving Work Groups: A Practical Manual for Team Building*, University Associates : San Diego.

Goldsmith, W. and Clutterbuck, D. (1984) *The Winning Streak*, Penguin : England.

Tuckman, B. and Jensen, M. (1977) 'Stages of small group development revisited', *Group and Organizational Studies*, **2**, pp. 419–427.

APPLICATION TASK 3.8

TEAM CONDITION ASSESSMENT

Tick the appropriate box for each statement. Do not write anything in the circles yet.

	Strongly disagree	Disagree	Agree	Strongly agree	SCORE
1. We are prepared to air differences of opinion.	☐	☐	☐	☐	◯
2. Our meetings are focused and do not waste time.	☐	☐	☐	☐	◯
3. The team leader draws contributions from all members.	☐	☐	☐	☐	◯
4. If we need an input from outside, we willingly bring in someone who can help us.	☐	☐	☐	☐	◯
5. We show concern for fellow members who are experiencing personal problems.	☐	☐	☐	☐	◯
6. We like to dream up new ways of doing things.	☐	☐	☐	☐	◯
7. The leader understands what influences us.	☐	☐	☐	☐	◯
8. We are confident we can overcome problems and difficulties.	☐	☐	☐	☐	◯
9. We are made to feel equal despite status and experience differences.	☐	☐	☐	☐	◯
10. We encourage problem redefinition and creative solutions.	☐	☐	☐	☐	◯

	Strongly disagree	Disagree	Agree	Strongly agree	SCORE
11. We painstakingly search for all relevant information.	☐	☐	☐	☐	○
12. All suggestions are treated seriously, even if later discarded.	☐	☐	☐	☐	○
13. Each team member is brought into discussions.	☐	☐	☐	☐	○
14. We constantly measure our accomplishments against goals.	☐	☐	☐	☐	○
15. We encourage members to play 'devil's advocate' so that we can test ideas rigorously.	☐	☐	☐	☐	○
16. Conflicts are defused and differences reconciled.	☐	☐	☐	☐	○
17. We set high standards for our team.	☐	☐	☐	☐	○
18. Our respective skills, knowledge and abilities are utilised appropriately and productively.	☐	☐	☐	☐	○
19. We are prepared to take risks when necessary.	☐	☐	☐	☐	○
20. Members communicate effectively with each other.	☐	☐	☐	☐	○
21. Members are open enough to deal with sensitive issues.	☐	☐	☐	☐	○
22. All necessary talents and abilities are available in the team for effective task completion.	☐	☐	☐	☐	○

	Strongly disagree	Disagree	Agree	Strongly agree	SCORE
23. We are open and honest with each other.	☐	☐	☐	☐	◯
24. We know what we are supposed to be doing.	☐	☐	☐	☐	◯
25. We understand perfectly what our contributions to the team are.	☐	☐	☐	☐	◯
26. The leader is committed to a participative approach.	☐	☐	☐	☐	◯
27. We can work well with other teams and share ideas.	☐	☐	☐	☐	◯
28. Team members enjoy being part of the team.	☐	☐	☐	☐	◯
29. We often ask whether our actions and procedures are the best.	☐	☐	☐	☐	◯
30. We enjoy our successes.	☐	☐	☐	☐	◯
31. We have a good mix of people in terms of personal characteristics.	☐	☐	☐	☐	◯
32. We help each other when difficulties are experienced.	☐	☐	☐	☐	◯
33. Our meetings have clear intentions and productive outcomes.	☐	☐	☐	☐	◯
34. We can all state our prime goal clearly.	☐	☐	☐	☐	◯
35. We feel we gain personally through being involved in the team.	☐	☐	☐	☐	◯

	Strongly disagree	Disagree	Agree	Strongly agree	SCORE
36. We do not rest on our laurels, but constantly review our operation.	☐	☐	☐	☐	◯
37. We celebrate even small successes.	☐	☐	☐	☐	◯
38. We are enthusiastic.	☐	☐	☐	☐	◯
39. Our meetings invariably end up with people having to take action.	☐	☐	☐	☐	◯
40. We work well together.	☐	☐	☐	☐	◯
41. The team leader is supportive.	☐	☐	☐	☐	◯
42. We evaluate the way we work and rectify matters.	☐	☐	☐	☐	◯
43. We produce quality results.	☐	☐	☐	☐	◯
44. Members seem to understand each other's moods and feelings.	☐	☐	☐	☐	◯
45. Individual efforts are well co-ordinated towards the team effort.	☐	☐	☐	☐	◯
46. Individual differences are recognised and used to effect.	☐	☐	☐	☐	◯
47. Complex information is deciphered by the team and difficulties are unravelled.	☐	☐	☐	☐	◯
48. Individual suggestions are taken and developed towards a solution.	☐	☐	☐	☐	◯

	Strongly disagree	Disagree	Agree	Strongly agree	SCORE
49. Various options are considered in arriving at a team decision.	☐	☐	☐	☐	◯
50. There is trust and confidence in the leader.	☐	☐	☐	☐	◯

Now you can write points in the circles. Award points as follows:

Strongly agree	:	4 points
Agree	:	3 points
Disagree	:	2 points
Strongly disagree	:	1 point

140–200	You probably have a management team which is in good shape. Try to identify any obvious weaknesses from the statements.
100–140	The team is probably proficient in some areas and not so good in others. Look at the low-scoring statements and see if there is a common link. Performance may have to be reviewed in these areas.
Less than 100	The team may not be fulfilling its role in key areas. If some areas are scored highly and others with one's or two's, then examine the latter for linkages. If the team is going to achieve anything, a serious effort will have to be made to assess and improve the way it develops targets, its interpersonal relationships between members, the level of cohesion and the way in which the leader reconciles the demands of task, team and individuals.

Chapter 4

Planning Team Action

Good planning is incredibly important in organisations today... Without it organisations have a tendency to lurch from one crisis to the next exhausting people, resources and money in the process.

(Kotter, 1990 : 36)

You will appreciate that the complexities of your modern organisation and the world it operates in require more than one or two dynamic personalities to enable it to be successful... The team has to work together to arrive at the best pattern of organisation.

(Watts, 1988 : 104)

We were running a management exercise for a group of senior managers from the education service. These were people who are used to working in complex organisations where working together and planning as a team is necessary for a successful operation. We gave them the exercise brief and informed them they had two hours to complete the task. Within five minutes several groups (we could not call them teams) had started the task which involved them splitting up and dealing individually with information. In fact, within fifteen minutes all the groups were working. To the outsider it may have looked as if they were people of action, not wasting time talking, but actually doing things. They attacked the task with a great deal of vigour and several observers commented on what keen and active managers they were.

However, the exercise ended in failure. Not one of the groups achieved more than a quarter of the task. They used excuses like 'the task was too difficult for those without technical knowledge' or 'there was insufficient time'. In the review, speaking openly about what had gone wrong, many of them admitted that they often did things at work without considering all the issues and implications involved. It was simply not part of their work pattern to sit down and think! Thinking was perceived as avoiding action and did not go down well with their superiors who always wanted immediate action, or so they thought!

There is action for the sake of it and there is a more considered form of action where results can be fairly confidently predicted. These managers found that by omitting to consider in detail the answers to a number of questions, they failed in the purpose for which they had been formed as teams. Even if they had achieved some success, it was unlikely they could ever have performed optimally without adequate thought or planning. They also failed to work as a team, each individual tending to 'do his own thing'.

A couple of weeks later, we ran the same exercise with another group of senior managers. This time we purposely built a *planning period* into the schedule. We insisted that they stay together and actually plan for one whole hour and then spend only one hour converting the plans into action. At first they complained that they would not have sufficient time to carry out the implementation. Furthermore, we gave them some guidelines on some of the issues they should consider. As it turned out several groups spent an extra few minutes planning when they could have left the room, because they found one hour slightly less than they needed.

And the result? The least successful of the teams did 300 per cent better than the best group from the previous exercise! By considering precisely how to go about the task and who was responsible for what, they were able to make up for the lack of time by ensuring that all their efforts were well directed, co-ordinated and productive. Members of the first group in contrast spent their time running round in circles, unclear about their objectives and unsure what to do when things started to go wrong.

This serves to illustrate the importance of **planning** as a team and how much we tend to undervalue it. Planning makes us proactive rather than reactive. Yet it is the latter state which characterises many organisations: running out of stock and trying to pacify an irate customer who expects immediate delivery; waiting for the electrical system to break down instead of servicing the wiring; suddenly realising that product demand has increased and the organisation is short-staffed.

Numerous Mintzberg-type (1973) studies (Kotter,1982) have shown that, despite the folklore that managers spend their time carefully planning, staffing and organising, reality is different. Managers' work is actually characterised by pace, brevity and variety of activities, and fragmentation. In the real world of management managers are reactive and spend little time planning. And teams are often little different, being less than systematic when confronted with new tasks.

This chapter presents a scheme for getting things done by using your team to maximum potential. It is concerned with effective task completion, where that task is sufficiently complex to require the contribution of more than one person (a team) and where these contributions have to be co-ordinated . The scheme, called the *7D Scheme for Planning Team Action*, covers several phases of short-term planning activity followed by the phases of implementation and review. The scheme is presented in detail later in the chapter and follows the seven phases shown in Figure 4.1.

Figure 4.1
The 7D Scheme

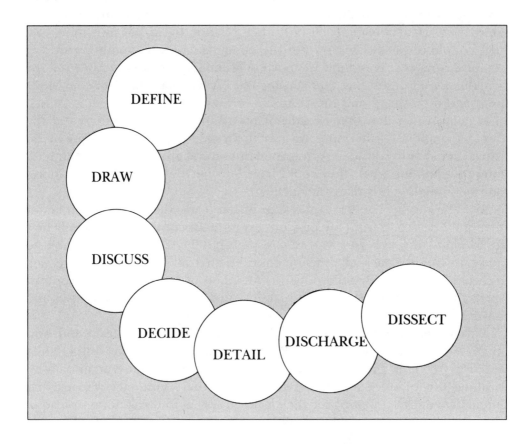

We have developed the scheme with three basic ideas in mind. For a team to successfully complete a task members must:

1. Carefully plan what they are going to do and how they will do it.
2. Ensure that the plan is implemented as far as possible in accordance with its original design.
3. Evaluate the plan and the process itself to see how it can be improved, either while it is in action or after the task is completed.

In reality, the seven steps which comprise the scheme should not be viewed as discrete steps, and it may be necessary on occasions to modify the sequence. By sticking loosely to the order of steps, however, you will increase your chances of successful task completion.

The scheme does not assume complete rationality. We acknowledge that micropolitical factors, human nature and other unforeseen circumstances can affect task completion. The scheme, however, does provide a sound framework for effective team action. With this in mind, we provide an explanation of each of the seven phases and a checklist of practical actions which can aid their application following a brief discussion of planning.

Planning

Planning is the process of looking into the future: deciding what you want to achieve and then determining how to achieve it. 'It is a process that precedes everything we do either on our own or with others' (Watson, 1981). Managers often know what they want but fail to formulate the optimal strategies for reaching their desired targets. So the planning process involves decisions on how to do things. However, it has to be more precise than that. You have to know exactly what has to be done and make a number of statements which relate to the method, the time, the location and the people involved.

In some environments planning may be a relatively simple affair, even to the point of mechanisation. In many others though, life is considerably more complex and unpredictable, and lack of sufficient planning can have a major impact on success or failure. Much planning is inadequate because managers try to do it all themselves and do not draw on the power and expertise of the team.

Planning for some managers even seems to be an activity to be avoided. This is because it is often perceived as being separate from action. We put money in the bank, for example, or we contribute to pension schemes. We are giving something of our resources away without feeling the benefits. We know though, that it is right because we want to enjoy those benefits in the future. Plans also bear their fruits in the future and the investment in time and brainpower is just as vital as our personal financial investments.

Short-Term Planning

The 7D scheme is concerned essentially with tactical or short-term plans. Long-term planning is vital for continued organisational success, but if it is not operationalised through shorter-term processes, long-term goals may remain unattainable. The fact is we are more likely to be concerned with shorter-term planning on a more frequent basis. Short-term plans are highly specific and relate to the intended outcomes for organisational subunits. They tend to cover all eventualities (as far as is realistically possible), are quantifiable in terms of performance and time scale and have checkpoints so that performance can be evaluated along the way.

PLANNING

- Plan your time so you have time to plan.
- Make sure you can measure progress.
- Set time limits.
- Make individuals responsible.

In our scheme for Planning Team Action we are concerned with the essential ingredients of shorter-term planning. This forms the largest part of our seven-point framework. But it also includes actions for ensuring that plans are implemented and that their processes and outcomes are adequately reviewed. We base the 7D scheme on the belief that planning should be a continuous process; ensuring that it is implemented, and that its degree of success is reviewed, are inseparable parts of the overall model.

A Scheme for Getting Things Done

The 7D scheme for planning team action can be used in those situations where task completion requires the combined effort of several individuals. We have found that it can be successfully applied to most situations.

The scheme covers all the key phases leading from the initial task assignment to the analysis and review of what happened. Fundamental to effective task performance is detailed planning and the success of control mechanisms hinges on the way such control processes have been determined during the planning phase. So whilst the two final phases, *discharge* and *dissect*, stand alone as the implementation and evaluation elements, what has gone on before largely determines the specific activities which take place in these two parts of the scheme.

The scheme assumes that important task completion is best approached through teams. We believe a team can be more creative, innovative and productive than any one individual, regardless of how capable that person may be. We also suggest that the most important tasks for today's managers are often too complex for one person. We now look at each of the phases in detail. Before we provide the explanations of the key activities, we follow the progress of a management team as it tackles a new project. Hazel, Tom, Duncan and Janet all work at Brookfield Leisure Centre which is situated on the outskirts of a large industrial town and near an expanding housing estate. They form the centre's management team.

They demonstrate the practical application of the 7D scheme, using many of the key actions to ensure that appropriate decisions ensue, that ideas are put to the test, that actions are monitored and that performance is reviewed. They do not do everything perfectly – few teams do – but they follow a neat progression. When you read the descriptions of each phase, you might go back to the relevant scene and pick out the points which have been handled well and those which may have been omitted and which would have enhanced the process for them.

> *The cast:* *Hazel – manager of the centre. She is also responsible for two other much smaller facilities in the area.*
> *Tom – Hazel's assistant, mainly responsible for programming facilities usage. He is 50 years old.*
> *Duncan – senior supervisor, in charge of plant, equipment and maintenance staff.*
> *Janice – supervisor, responsible for swimming pool operation and some coaching in 'dry' activities. She is in her early twenties.*

1. Define

Scene One

> *Hazel has called a meeting to discuss an issue which she has been asked to address with her management team. She begins the meeting by explaining that the deputy director for Recreation and Leisure Services (her boss) has instructed all the leisure centres in the area to attempt to increase the number of women taking part in the centre's activities. She goes on to say that no firm targets have been fixed, but that an upward trend should be detectable in the near future, and that this is likely to result in improved funding for the centre.*
>
> *Hazel asks for the commitment of her colleagues, which they willingly give. They decide to give themselves six months to see some noticeable effects. After a few questions requesting clarification about details of finance, time and likely problems, Hazel explains that the deputy director has agreed to provide some limited funding for additional equipment and an initial sum of $1,000 for advertising.*

In this phase you define or explain succinctly the basic task to those who will be undertaking it (Stott and Walker, 1991). The emphasis is on achieving clarity so that efforts can be appropriately directed. You may, for example, explain to several colleagues involved in a small assignment that the task is to draw up job descriptions for two new secretarial posts. The job descriptions should specify the major responsibilities, the reporting relationships, qualifications and experience required. The task does not involve placing advertisements or interviewing candidates.

The task in this example is clearly delineated. The participants know what it is and what it is not. The terms of reference have been laid out and that helps the focus to be maintained throughout the rest of the planning phase.

This first stage sets the scene for the success or otherwise of your team's subsequent action. It is not enough to simply explain the task. You must also explain *why* the task needs to be done. It is unlikely that you will be able to gain commitment from your team members unless they understand the value and relevance of the task.

Commitment to effective task completion will also encourage the team to unravel the difficulties involved in its successful completion. Few tasks are as simple or as difficult as they first appear.

You must also specify the time which is available for task completion and for specific phases of planning. All tasks must be completed within a certain time frame. It is a risky strategy to leave the outcome date open : 'Let's see if we can finish this one sometime around Christmas?'

The team also needs to be made aware of the other constraints to task completion that you are aware of. Of course, it is impossible to know about all constraints at this stage but some will be obvious: 'We have $100,000 to develop a prototype; it must be functional by 23 October this year and we will have to use Workshop Number Three.'

You cannot afford to ignore political constraints: 'You should be aware that Boulton in Marketing is against this project and has stated quite clearly that, at best, he will stay away from it.' Be practical, it can be counter-productive to get too enthusiastic if actions have little chance of working.

The *define* phase, like most of your job, requires exact communication. You must be able to clarify the nature of the task to all team members. The defining stage 'gets the ball rolling' for the team by defining its direction and purpose.

SUMMARY

Action Points : Define

- Explain the task.
- Explain why the task needs doing.
- Gain commitment to the task.
- Unravel the difficulties.
- Specify the time available.
- Spell out the known constraints.

2.   Draw

Scene Two

> *Hazel asks her colleagues whether there is any information already available on the number of women involved in the centre's activities. Tom agrees to liaise with reception about the possibility of taking an activity tally count for the next couple of weeks. He also agrees to conduct a membership analysis in the next few days. Hazel then asks each of her colleagues in turn what experience they have had in promotional drives such as this. She also asks them for ideas on what expert advice they can get. Each team member makes some comments about additional resources which may be required to make such an effort worthwhile. They all agree that they will probably need to discuss the matter with, and gain the support of, other staff at the centre.*

The second phase involves the drawing in of information and all the available data necessary to make informed choices. Poor planning often results from failing to acquire all relevant knowledge which is available. It is recognised however that it is unlikely that all the necessary data can be collected. Nevertheless, that which is available should be acquired. Information can be gathered by individual team members in specific areas: technical information, market information, the competition.

Some of the key questions once again relate to time. It is necessary to know, for example, how much time there is to complete the task. When this is known, the time to be allocated to planning can be planned. This should be adequate. Try not to leave yourself short. In the example given at the beginning of the chapter it was shown how one hour's planning was needed to tackle a task successfully, the total amount of time for which was only two hours.

Other questions relate to resources and what is available to the team for task completion. Relevant resources which may be available include people, equipment and facilities, materials, services and energy, money, and information. You may also consider how you can acquire or generate additional resources if you feel they are necessary for effective task completion.

It is important to ask what human resources are available; this might entail bringing others into the team. The task, for example, may require certain resource people to be consulted and may even demand that specialist advice be sought. During this phase then, these people will be identified. Do not be afraid to co-opt expert advice; it should not be perceived as a threat to you or your team.

Team members should declare the skills and expertise they can contribute towards task completion. Although you will no doubt be aware of most of the strengths and weaknesses of your employees, they may surprise you. Expertise offered can vary from situation to situation and can often be related to the commitment of the member to a task.

While it may be necessary to recruit additional expertise, do not forget that as a manager you are responsible for developing team members as well as achieving the task. If you continually provide development opportunities for your employees they will obviously be of more value to the team when future tasks arise.

When nearing the end of the *draw* stage, you and your team should have as much information as is available. Do not become complacent. Remember to gather all relevant information. You must however reach a point when you decide that you have most of what you can acquire. Once again time frames should be set regarding how long you have to collect information.

When you have isolated all the available information you are ready to discuss how you will proceed.

SUMMARY

Action Points : Draw

- Ask for relevant information.
- Check the resources available.
- Consider whether additional resources can be acquired.
- Ask members what related skills and expertise they offer.
- Ask for knowledge and expert advice.
- Allow for developmental needs.

---

3. Discuss

Scene Three

Hazel states that they have to get moving on the project straight away, even whilst some of the information is being gathered. She then invites ideas from each of her colleagues in turn and writes them on the whiteboard. She encourages them to chip in anything they wish, however ridiculous it may sound. During this time Janice and Duncan start to offer realistic criticisms of some of the ideas. Hazel asks them to refrain from this until later. The ideas include providing more team activities, more individual activities such as weight training and aerobics sessions, starting a leaflet campaign, asking members to bring friends, providing discounts for families, having women-only swimming sessions, running some special competitions in women's activities, and several other ideas.

Tom's suggestion is simply to 'find out'. He explains that if they are going to make the right decision they have to know what potential customers really expect. It is no use asking only existing customers since they are already supporting the centre, suggests Tom.

Hazel goes through each of the ideas in turn. Some are discussed and some discarded with the agreement of all the team members. During the discussion, which includes a fair amount of friendly criticism, Hazel summarises regularly and comments that some useful ideas have emerged.

She in fact groups them together to form three main options. One is to plan activities for which they have good resources and which would in theory attract the female population to the centre; another is to rely on an effective publicity campaign, possibly keeping the present activity offer; the remaining one is to delay any decisions until they have discovered what potential customers indicate would be attractive. They thrash out the pros and cons of each and give their different views of what could work best. For each option Hazel asks them what they would need in terms of resources and what could go wrong. Through the arguments and discussions they are moving towards an acceptance of adopting the market research option. At this point Hazel is able to draw the options together by suggesting that if they first do some finding out, they could reach more appropriate decisions on programming and publicity. She asks her colleagues individually for their reactions to this suggestion and they all agree.

By this stage you should be starting to formulate priorities for task completion. You may need to clarify or even redefine the purpose of the project so that everyone is reminded what the task is intended to achieve.

This is obviously the longest phase of the planning scheme and it is appropriate so long as discussions are kept strictly on line. Ideas, methods and possible solutions will all be aired and opportunities should be given for all members of the team to contribute to this phase. Depending on personality and distinctive capability factors, individuals may contribute by advancing ideas, applying critical analysis processes or by co-ordinating separate ideas and putting them together into a coherent whole.

The strength of the team's contribution to task accomplishment or problem solution usually hinges on the quality of the discussion phase. An important aspect is that of creativity. It is a facet which separates outstanding teams from mediocre ones. If creativity is to be fostered in the planning scheme, constraining assumptions must be avoided. However ridiculous some suggestions might sound, they must be encouraged (if not used) since they may contain the nucleus of an idea. It is a great weakness of many teams that they tend to become bound by their assumptions, and creative ideas are seen as impractical. Brainstorming is a worthwhile method for eliciting creative ideas. For more detail on this technique see Chapter 6 on Solving Problems and Making Decisions.

Another strategy which can be used is what we call the Clean Sheet Method. Give team members a clean sheet and explain that if there were no constraints at all, an ideal solution would be possible. They can be asked to identify their ideal solutions and then to examine how constraints can be broken down or accommodated.

It is essential that team members feel free to contribute and even argue openly. If you have no disagreement it is unlikely that you will generate creative or worthwhile suggestions.

> Alfred P. Sloan, when President of General Motors, is reported to have said at a meeting of one of his top committees: 'Gentlemen, I take it we are all in agreement on the decision here.' Everyone around the table nodded assent. 'Then', continued Sloan, 'I propose we postpone further discussion of this matter until our next meeting to give ourselves time to develop disagreement and perhaps gain some understanding of what the decision is all about.' (from Adair, 1988 : 88)

The following steps are involved in building up this approach which provides for creativity: firstly, individuals should be asked for experiences and ideas; secondly, they should be allowed to start with a clean sheet to avoid the negative effect of constraints; thirdly, build on individuals' suggestions and put ideas together.

- Ask for experiences and ideas.
- Start with a clean sheet.
- Put ideas together.

During the discussion phase it is necessary to generate options or alternative solutions. Whilst a fairly free approach can be adopted for option generation (such as brainstorming), the evaluation of options must be systematic and based on sound critical judgement. It is advisable to record against each option the resources needed, the resources available, the possible outcomes and the estimated chances of success. For this last item it is a useful technique to make a numeric assessment out of ten. In this way participants have to state preferences quantitatively and explain the reasons for their judgements. You can use a form similar to that shown in Figure 4.2 for this purpose.

During the option-evaluation stage the team considers the consequences of different courses of action and rejects inappropriate ideas. Finally you should test the 'shortlisted' options for consensus. Can all team members agree on their applicability?

As the team leader during the discussion phase you have a vital role to play. First you must promote and encourage open discussion and allow ideas

Figure 4.2
Evaluation Form

OPTION:		
RESOURCES AVAILABLE	RESOURCES NEEDED	PREDICTED OUTCOMES

	Chance of Success	WHY?
10		

Stott, K. and Walker, A., *Making Management Work.* © 1992 Simon & Schuster (Asia) Pte Ltd.

to be challenged [after the brainstorming session(s)]. You should listen carefully to the discussion and pull it back on line if necessary.

You will be called upon to use all your technical, interpersonal, synthesising and summarising skills. Technical skills refer to your knowledge of the task at hand. Interpersonal skills are those skills you use when dealing with team members. Synthesising skills: 'allow you to take things that appear separate and see a unifying pattern to them... You have to take the separate individuals and skills (and ideas) in your work group and pull them together' (Carr, 1989 : 208). You must also be able to halt the discussion at appropriate stages and summarise where it has been and where it should be going.

The discussion phase is not complete without an answer to two questions: 'What could go wrong?' and 'What actions are to be taken in that eventuality?' A discussion of these questions will take you into the next phase.

SUMMARY

Action Points : Discuss

- Set the priorities.
- Ask for ideas: Brainstorm alternative solutions.
- Resist premature judgements.
- Generate options.
- Explore different viewpoints.
- Challenge ideas.
- Listen carefully and summarise contributions.
- Synthesise: Build on suggestions, co-ordinate contributions.
- Consider consequences of different courses of action.
- Reject inappropriate ideas after considering.
- Keep discussions on line.
- Test for consensus.

---

4.   Decide

Scene Four

> *Members of the management team start to discuss in more detail what sort of market research should be carried out. After much discussion, some of it un-productive and going back over old ground about activities which will work and those which will not, Hazel gets them to agree on a simple survey amongst existing customers. The reason for this is that she sees the opportunity to use the services of existing customers in handing questionnaires to their friends. A time scale of three weeks is set, and if this does not prove feasible it is agreed that they person-ally should conduct a survey of women in neighbouring districts. This is the general plan; the finer points of detail now need to be discussed.*

A decision or several decisions have to be reached at some point. Having clarified the task, sought supporting information, discussed ideas, generated options and evaluated them, the decision-making process should be on a sound footing. Because of the number of people involved in the discussion phase, it is likely that decisions will emerge which are at least of acceptable quality.

The main problem which is encountered in this phase is an unwillingness to reach a decision, and instead to return to old ground covered in the discussion phase. Once this stage has been reached – the team must be incisive and this is where the leader has an important part to play, not necessarily in making the decision but moving the group quickly towards a firm and decisive outcome. It is probably advisable to avoid anything which resembles vote-taking, but reach agreement on consensus principles, with all sharing in the acceptance of a particular decision and being prepared to go along with it. Consensus is discussed in greater detail in Chapter 6.

Consensus of course is easy to talk about but difficult to achieve. We are convinced though, that it is worth the effort.

> It is frequently easier to get managers to agree that consensus is desirable than it is to obtain it. The additional time and effort more than compensate for the reduction in time and effort required to implement the decision it produces and the increase in the effectiveness of that implementation., (Ackoff, 1986 : 160)

So the role of the team is to try to reach consensus. It is possible however that time constraints will inhibit this process. If this is a consideration it is your role as the team leader to 'prod the team' to a decision. Do this gently; do not push or demand. If you do, commitment and effective implementation might be threatened. Come as close to consensus as possible.

Once the decision is made – *Stick to it* : *Be incisive.* Convert the decision into a simple, workable plan. Make sure it is understood by everybody. Do not assume your plan will automatically work; the best-made plans of mice and men sometimes go astray.

Be psychologically and practically prepared to adjust the plan as you go along. We are certainly not advocating 'sloppy' plans and urge that you plan as carefully as possible, but we do believe that plans need to be organic: changing and adapting with and to the environment. The best way to accept this is to develop contingency plans, should some of your 'possible problems' eventuate. These plans should also be fairly specific and clear to all team members.

Your team is now almost ready to discuss the specific details and move towards implementation.

SUMMARY

Action Points : Decide

- Try for consensus.
- Prod members to an incisive decision.
- Make a simple and workable plan.
- Make contingency plans.

5.   Detail

Scene Five

> *Fortunately, Janice offers to design a questionnaire because, although she learned how to do this on a recent supervisory course, she has yet to put her skills into action in a real situation. Tom agrees to gather other items of information about membership, and Duncan, because he has friends in other centres, agrees to find out what is happening in similar areas elsewhere. Hazel says that she will meet with the Sports Council officer who is responsible for promoting this type of programme.*
>
> *After checking that each member is clear about his or her contribution, and then writing everything down, Hazel also discusses any finance they need for resources, such as photocopying and travel allowances. She tells them how their normal duties might be covered when they are involved in the project. She also specifies precisely what they should have in time for the next meeting three weeks later and even gets them to specify some targets for themselves after one week and two weeks. Each of them should meet with her briefly each intervening week just to discuss progress. If anything serious should go wrong she sets a date for an emergency meeting.*

This phase covers the dimensions of task division and briefing the team on the way the task will be carried out, along with the ways in which performance will be measured.

Assuming the task is sufficiently complex to need the combined efforts of several or more people, it is often wise to break it up into several pieces for action by individual team members. This action can take many forms depending on the nature of the task: acquiring information, undertaking research, drafting advertisements, and so on. It is usually more productive to do this than waste time involving the whole group in subsidiary task completion which only needs individuals or smaller groups of members.

This is one way of applying the division principle. Another way is to divide up the task so that the team can deal with one part at a time. This is applicable to those situations which require that the entire team is involved throughout the task. In this case, the division is done in such a way that the parts are manageable and logically sequential. It would, for example, be necessary to devise a job specification before drafting an advertisement, since the latter would be constructed from the former.

Carr (1989 : 44) provides some sound advice for assigning tasks. Write down every task that has to be done. Besides each task, write the name of the person who will do it. If more than one person, identify the person with overall responsibility. Then brief the team.

In the next part of the phase, the whole task or the subsets of it are specified and members of the team are thoroughly briefed. Briefing team members should not be taken lightly. For your plan to be effective all team members must understand what part they must play in achieving the task. Briefing, or sending effective messages to people, is a communication skill which is essential for managers or team leaders of any kind.

It is vital therefore that you are sure every team member understands and is committed to his role in the task. Full explanations are essential to all involved, as is the opportunity for clarifying questions in preparation for implementation. With expectations outlined, members should be in little doubt as to their precise part in the process.

Part of the briefing process involves determining how performance will be measured. The group needs 'performance markers' and these form an important part of the controlling process. The markers have to be clearly specified so that the group knows whether it is on course, below expectations or exceeding the planned levels.

In addition to setting performance standards for the group, it is necessary to define requirements for individuals or subunits. At various points ('progress checkpoints') in the task completion process, individuals should be able to answer the simple question: 'How well am I doing?' Times therefore must be specified when members carrying out specific duties will be asked to comment both on their progress towards the targets and on the standards of performance.

Probably the best way to encourage adherence to these 'progress checkpoints' and 'performance markers' is to set individual or subteam targets. A full explanation of the target-setting process is given in Chapter 11.

In traditional management terms you have now built in some controls: mechanisms for ensuring that your plan progresses as closely as possible to your original intentions. You are now ready to *discharge* or implement your plan.

SUMMARY

Action Points : Detail

- Assign responsibilities and ensure individual work is challenging.
- Brief thoroughly: Give careful explanation to the group.
- Allocate specific tasks.
- Check that members understand their individual contributions.

- Distribute resources.
- Explain contingencies.
- Set 'progress checkpoints'.
- Specify 'performance markers'.
- Specify individual targets.

6.   Discharge

Scene Six

Not everything goes according to plan. Janice finds that when she tries out her questionnaire on a few of her friends among the regular customers, one or two items are ambiguous. She puts this right but then finds that she is several days behind schedule. Tom's analysis goes smoothly but Duncan finds it difficult to contact his friends who never seem to return his calls. After meeting with Hazel, Duncan makes arrangements to visit several other centres and Tom agrees to help him with this. Tom also agrees to help Janice with the distribution of her questionnaire.

Hazel spends a fair amount of time out of the centre but still keeps herself and her colleagues informed. Janice is worried when, after two weeks, she still has less than a third of her questionnaires returned. Hazel reassures her and gives her some helpful advice on how she can chase up the remainder. Despite the difficulties, Hazel is conscious that they are getting a lot of useful information that will help them make a reasonably good decision in this phase of the project.

Discharging the task means setting everything in motion. All the planning is now transposed into action. If the planning process has been accurate and accounted for the likely consequences of different courses of action, this implementation phase should run smoothly and lead to an eventual degree of success in task completion.

An element of discipline is required in this phase so that activities are those which are planned. The mechanisms for ensuring the plan stays on target, which have been designed during the preceding process, should take care of this. They should also ensure that the intermediate measures of performance and progress are responded to appropriately. For example, both Janice and Duncan were getting behind schedule, but because intermediate markers had been set, Tom was able to give them some much needed help. Furthermore, it was appropriately decided that there should be some modification to the original intentions.

Your job is to ensure that team members are working satisfactorily towards their predetermined targets. Only check progress formally at the previously agreed-upon intervals. As leader you should 'keep your finger on the pulse' by observing progress towards specific targets. You must also keep an eye on the 'big picture'; that is, constantly placing the various pieces together so you can see progress towards the task as a whole, and not simply as a collection of disparate pieces.

Once plans have been converted into action, it is necessary for you to check and direct the action. Sometimes it is possible to escape the consequences of inadequate 'ensuring' mechanisms, but where the activity can cause damage to successful task completion it is unwise to ignore your role in this area.

In reality the discharging process is totally integrated with the other phases. By regularly comparing plans to actual events, it is possible to spot and correct problems. Controlling then involves replanning and taking corrective actions (Watson, 1981).

Monitoring is an essential activity for checking progress towards task completion. This involves ensuring everything is 'on course'. As a team, you have already planned what should be happening. Now it is necessary to observe what is *actually* happening . The gap (if there is one) is called a discrepancy.

It should be clear to everyone in the team what should be happening, when it should take place, who is in charge or involved, and how it will be done. All these items of information will have been discussed, specifically communicated and understood during the *discuss, decide* and *detail* phases. In this phase you are checking what is actually happening against planned performance or targets and then taking corrective action if it is deemed necessary or worthwhile to make performance conform to that which was originally planned. This process, of course, does not always involve a third party, but can be effected by a more self-regulated system, characteristic of many professional groups.

If you do discover a discrepancy between intended and actual, the next question is whether any action should be taken. What is an important deviation from the planned action? The answer depends on the activity itself. If it is crucial to the organisation's performance then something must be done about even small deviations. If it is of little or no significance then larger deviations may be tolerated. Put simply, the benefits of actions must justify their costs.

If you discover a discrepancy, you can:

1. Put things right.
2. Do nothing.
3. Scrap the plan.

If you intend to do something about the discrepancy, the reason needs to be correctly identified and understood by the team and this will obviously affect their preferred solution. What are the courses of action open to you if this happens? It largely depends on what has been discovered. The manager, for example, may have found no discrepancy, meaning that everything is going according to plan. On the other hand, there could have been discrepancies of varying degrees, but they could have been on either the good or the bad side. Making changes to the original plan is one option. If performance is better than expected, plan revisions can be made which increase targets. If Janice, Duncan and Tom had been going really well after the first week they could have agreed to bring their completion dates one week forward. This sort of change should be handled with care however since individuals may modify their standards of performance to account for new measures. In other words, they may sacrifice quality for quantity.

Another option, and a very positive one in the right circumstances, is to do nothing. Quite often, where there is minimal discrepancy, the wise option is to leave things alone. If it costs more to solve a problem, either in human or resource terms, than the benefits it would reap, it may be expedient to take no action.

A final option, and a radical one, is to scrap the plan altogether. This, of course, should only be done in extreme cases. If, for example, you discover that the final outcome can be nothing but disastrous, you may be advised to cut your losses and start again.

In this phase you must take care with how closely you monitor team members and interfere with their roles. Too much control can be seen as interference and may have adverse effects, whereas too little may lead to inadequate direction and the attendant problems which that might cause.

If action needs to be taken, it must be a speedy process. Problems have to be dealt with quickly and actions have to be effected soon after the event. There is little point in acquiring information and then finding discrepancies long after critical events have happened. Feedback and action need to take place immediately.

Plans converted to action should be controlled. It is not possible to evaluate the plan unless you have knowledge about what is happening. At the same time, though, you should take a facilitative rather than a 'watchdog' role. Mechanisms for ensuring that the plan is working must not become more important than the activity itself.

A public sector organisation, for example, was recently concerned about the quantity of photocopying which employees were doing, so it set up an elaborate control system of form completion, rubber-stamping by superiors and logging copies in a book. It managed to reduce the number of photocopies. It also reduced the amount of information to workers, the quality of materials, and produced a great deal of dissatisfaction among people who then spent three times the amount of organisational time completing forms. So it is best not to take matters to extremes during this phase. Use your position instead to ensure efficient and quality work is taking place in accordance with tactical plans.

In Chapter 1, we examined leadership actions which reflected particular emphases on task completion, group cohesion or the satisfaction of individual needs. The actions involved in discharging can similarly be considered in these three interrelated areas. The task-centred actions include keeping discussions on course, observations, influencing work tempo and inspecting standards of performance. If you find that things are falling behind schedule for ultimate task completion, you must 'hurry' the team along. Of course you will do this in as diplomatic a way as possible. Those which relate to group cohesion include co-ordination, intervention and maintenance of a suitable working atmosphere. Individual actions involve giving help, guiding and training, and providing reassurance.

You must utilise your human skills during this phase. Keep in mind your developmental role. You may help junior team members in certain areas with the idea of upgrading their skills and confidence. It is vital that you keep all team members informed of progress. This should be done on a 'whole-team' basis and not with separate work groups. Everyone must keep the overall task in view.

You should also encourage, motivate and reassure team members. Acknowledge teamwork, small successes and staying on time. If you do this your team should stay motivated. Although we are emphasising the positive, be aware that it may also be necessary for you to discipline certain members if they are not playing their part. This might involve reminding them of agreed targets, appealing to their team spirit, or even reassigning them elsewhere.

During this phase then you actually implement the plan and do all that you can to ensure it is progressing to your satisfaction in line with agreed targets.

SUMMARY

Action Points : Discharge

- Check that actions are related to targets.
- Look for discrepancies between actual and planned.
- Observe where necessary.
- Intervene and help where necessary.
- Guide and train where necessary.
- Inspect standards of performance.
- Monitor progress towards targets.

- Keep members informed of progress.
- Keep discipline.
- Give reassurance and encouragement.
- Continually motivate.
- Keep overall task in view.

7. Dissect

Scene Seven

At the next meeting, Hazel gives a detailed summary of the information that each of them has gathered and congratulates them on their efforts. They have not achieved everything they originally planned and she asks them where they could improve next time they do this. Both Janice and Duncan say they would like to start the process again, but settled for the useful information they have acquired. Hazel comments on the teamwork displayed in the way that Tom had helped the other two and they had willingly accepted his help.

The successes are that they have managed to acquire information which they were not aware of, and in some cases, surprised by, and that they now have a much clearer picture of the sort of programme development which they should be discussing.

The failures are that not enough potential customers' opinions have been tapped, and that they failed to clarify which age group they should have targeted. Hazel, Tom and Duncan all assumed that they were trying to attract housewives and mothers, whilst Janice was under the impression that they were trying to catch school leavers in particular. This issue is now sorted out and they plan some continued information-gathering as they progress through the next stage.

This final phase is not really a separate stage in the scheme, but something which is applied throughout several of the other phases. It involves constant review and asking questions such as: 'Have we covered everything relevant?' and 'Have we reached the right conclusion?' A performance discrepancy, for example, may be identified through the controlling actions and this may require immediate replanning. Similarly, reviewing is not something which takes place when everything else has been finished. Reviews should take place on a regular basis and the information derived needs to be fed back into the other processes. Plans, for example, need to be reviewed whilst they are being formulated; objectives need to be checked and the feasibility of pre-ferred options must be reviewed.

In the *defining* phase, for example, it can be asked whether the definition of the task is appropriate, whereas in the second phase, the question may be raised as to whether the information acquired is sufficient and relevant. The process can be applied effectively to the other phases and then finally, the whole task performance can be improved.

Despite the continuous nature of this *dissecting* process, it is also necessary to review everything at the end of a project to determine the degree of success in terms of task completion, group cohesion and satisfying experiences at an individual level.

So *dissecting* can be seen as operational at two levels: the single individual actions which guide the progress of the scheme, and the overall evaluation of performance following task completion. Whereas the initial phases involved looking into the future, and *detailing* and *discharging* were concerned with the present, *dissecting* is both a backward and a forward-looking process to see what has happened and what should happen. It involves making some judgements about the course of events and it should lead to learning. This learning will either impact on future related operations or will lead to a reappraisal and replanned action with present operations.

The sorts of activities which characterise this phase include regular summaries, asking for close scrutiny of plans and testing possible consequences. These are related to task completion, whereas learning from failure, assessing the value of individual contributions and giving appropriate feedback are associated with the human resource emphasis.

Dissecting also involves giving and receiving feedback. This is best done in a team meeting. Go through each of the phases and ask team members to give their opinions on the effectiveness of actions in the various phases. As in the option-generation stage, the discussion must be open, with members feeling free to openly criticise. You must solicit feedback on your own skills and performance. It is unlikely that you will learn anything of value if you do not allow or take note of feedback. Feedback, of course, should be a regular feature of all phases.

Your job as team leader requires that you assess individual performance and the value of individual contributions. Praise and reward productive, worthwhile contributions and discuss how inadequate effects or results can be improved next time. It is preferable if these points can be identified through monitoring and corrected in the earlier phases of the scheme. Telling a team member that his performance was substandard after task completion is much less powerful than catching it and trying to correct it during the process itself.

Finally, identify the team's successes and learn from the failures. *Reward* success, use it as a motivational tool, openly acknowledging a job well done. Attempt to stay positive about failures (this can be very difficult). Once again try to identify them during the process, not just after task completion. If you do face some failures in some areas of the process heed the words of Henry Ford: 'Failure is the opportunity to begin again more intelligently.'

SUMMARY

Action Points : Dissect

- Summarise progress.
- Replan where necessary.
- Ask for feedback on the process and outcome.
- Give feedback to the team and individuals.
- Get feedback on your own performance.
- Assess value of individual contributions.
- Assess individual performance.
- Identify successes.
- Learn from failure.

The process and actions described are designed to help you and your team successfully complete tasks. It is more than likely that you will be working on more than one task at a time, perhaps with different teams. To begin with you may find it difficult to follow the phases and action points but the more your teams learn to follow a systematic process, the easier it should become for you. Develop your teams to the stage where they approximately follow such a scheme and you should be rewarded with improved performance, more cohesive efforts, and individuals who feel they have a useful part to play. Successful task completion will breed confident, competent teams.

In Figure 4.3 we have included a checklist of all the action points in their various phases. Remember our original caution, this is not an exhaustive list nor is it necessary to apply all the items, but it gives some guidelines for action and may serve as a checklist when the planning of a complex task commences.

Conclusion

The 7D scheme is a way of planning team action for effective task completion. It sets a framework in which the dimensions of planning can be considered. If performance does not match up to expectations it may be useful to look back at the scheme and assess whether any one of the phases was omitted or under-emphasised.

Whatever the size of the task, provided it is complex enough to require a team-coordinated approach (and most tasks in modern organisations are like that) this scheme will help members plan more effectively and ensure that their efforts and skills are appropriately harnessed for successful task completion.

Figure 4.3
The 7D Scheme for Planning Team Action: A Checklist

Explain the task.	DEFINE	
Explain why the task needs doing.		
Gain commitment to the task.		
Unravel the difficulties.		
Specify the time available.		
Spell out the known constraints.		
Ask for relevant information.	DRAW	
Check the resources available.		
Consider whether additional resources can be acquired.		
Ask members what related skills and expertise they offer.		
Ask for knowledge and expert advice.		
Allow for developmental needs.		
Set the priorities.	DISCUSS	
Ask for ideas: Brainstorm alternative solutions.		
Resist premature judgements.		
Generate options.		

Explore different viewpoints.	
Challenge ideas.	
Listen carefully and summarise contributions.	
Synthesise: Build on suggestions, co-ordinate contributions.	
Consider consequences of different courses of action.	
Reject inappropriate ideas after considering.	
Keep discussions on line.	
Test for consensus.	
Try for consensus. DECIDE	
Prod members to an incisive decision.	
Make a simple and workable plan.	
Make contingency plans.	
Assign responsibilities and ensure DETAIL individual work is challenging.	
Brief thoroughly: Give careful explanation to the group.	
Allocate specific tasks.	
Check that members understand their individual contributions.	
Distribute resources.	
Explain contingencies.	
Set 'progress checkpoints'.	
Specify 'performance markers'.	
Specify individual targets.	

Check that actions are related to targets. DISCHARGE	
Look for discrepancies between actual and planned.	
Observe where necessary.	
Intervene and help where necessary.	

Guide and train where necessary.	
Inspect standards of performance.	
Monitor progress towards targets.	
Keep members informed of progress.	
Keep discipline.	
Give reassurance and encouragement.	
Continually motivate.	
Keep overall task in view.	

Summarise progress. DISSECT	
Replan where necessary.	
Ask for feedback on the process and outcome.	
Give feedback to the team and individuals.	
Get feedback on your own performance.	
Assess value of individual contributions.	
Assess individual performance.	
Identify successes.	
Learn from failure.	

References

Ackoff, R. (1986) *Management in Small Doses*, Wiley : New York.

Adair, J. (1988) *Effective Leadership*, Pan : England.

Carr, C. (1989) *New Manager's Survival Guide*, Wiley : New York.

Kotter, J. (1982) *The General Managers*, The Free Press : New York.

Kotter, J. (1990) *A Force for Change*, The Free Press : New York.

Mintzberg, H. (1973) *The Nature of Managerial Work*, Harper and Row : New York.

Stott, K. and Walker, A. (1991) 'Effective task completion: the 7D model of planning', *The MPractising Administrator*, **1**, 13, pp. 45–48.

Watson, C. (1981) *Results-Oriented Management: The Key to Effective Performance*, Addison–Wesley : Massachusetts.

Watts, B. (1988) *Creating the Hands-On Manager*, Mercury : London.

Chapter 5

Developing Team Roles

It is now fairly well recognised that many organisations can best operate with management teams rather than 'solo' go-it-alone leaders. Whilst there are examples of good practice, the general picture may be one of hard-working and well-intentioned groups of people enjoying less than excellent achievements. Our proposition is that if teams are carefully selected or coached, the performance of organisations and their subunits can be considerably elevated.

You will recall that in our last chapter, which looked at how teamwork might be improved, we drew attention to two perspectives on the contributions which members bring to teams in which they participate. On the one hand they have a functional role; in other words, they are there for the specific expertise they offer. They may, for example, be experts in marketing, information systems or any other aspect which is related to the task in hand. The contribution which they are expected to make is relatively straightforward.

Members also have another part to play in the team and that is related to their behaviour. How they behave has a considerable impact on the effectiveness of the team's operation. The behaviour can influence not only performance but also the satisfactions which members derive from the team. The two are linked of course. If members do not feel happy about the team and its work, they become ineffective in carrying out their assignments, and this leads to further dysfunctional behaviours (Dyer, 1980). The team's success therefore might be thought of as the product of a combination of the functional skills and the behaviours which members typically employ in the team setting. We call these behaviours **roles** and we argue that they are critical to team effectiveness. This second dimension is hinted at by several writers in emphasising the contributions which members bring to the team: 'They contribute a much wider range of acquired know-how and in-built qualities many of them paradoxically opposites which they balance and apply with fluid ease' (Hastings, Bixby and Chaudhry-Lawton, 1986 : 95).

Our aims then in this chapter are:

- To understand the significance of individual roles to team performance.
- To identify your own team roles and how to use them to best

effect.

- To help you analyse your colleagues' preferred roles and help them develop their contribution.
- To use this knowledge to learn how to build an effective team.

The Winning Team

The work of Meredith Belbin (1981) is possibly the most significant piece of research into team effectiveness undertaken to date. Previously, common wisdom had dictated that if you put the best people together you would automatically have the best team. Traditionally, the most skilled people therefore would be selected for the team. You can probably think of examples of this: a committee which comprises distribution experts; an urban redevelopment task force which comprises the best architects in the field. Even chequebook-waving football managers tend to believe that top performance comes from acquiring the best individual players available. As many have found out to their cost, things are never so simple, and Belbin discovered that factors other than technical ability were more important in determining the success of a team.

It was originally thought that there may be a personal characteristics mix which produced the right formula. This was a reasonable assumption; most of us talk about teams in which we have taken part and which had some sort of 'chemistry'. It is this chemistry which Belbin tried to investigate by conducting a series of psychometric tests on people working in teams. He found that you could put some combinations of personality mix together and the team would be successful all the time. Other combinations were less than successful and, in some cases, doomed to failure.

What has this to do with the management of organisations and subunits within those organisations? It seems that many are under the mistaken belief that if you have people who are sufficiently intelligent, any teams you form will be successful. Surprisingly however, a group of intelligent professionals is likely to fail due to members' high critical analysis capacities. Everard and Morris (1985) draw attention to this phenomenon in groups of secondary school heads and teams of higher-education academics in the United Kingdom. Whilst it may be necessary that a team should comprise people who have a relevant knowledge of the task area, there are other factors which determine the extent of the team's success.

Central to current management thinking is the notion of team management, where the task of managing complex issues and extensive information inputs is too much for one person. Skills and abilities need to be complementary, not duplicated. If teams are seen as desirable features of organisation and subunit management, then factors concerning individuals' behaviours need to be considered if these teams are to perform to optimum capacity, otherwise the results could be less than satisfactory, as Everard and Morris found. This is not a plea to avoid team management. On the contrary, in today's context, with rapid change, increased uncertainty and constantly expanding demands on many managers, it may be a necessity rather than a trendy response to the current vogue.

Desirable as it is, team management looks destined to fail in some sectors of organisational life unless it is taken beyond the mere selection of *capable* colleagues. In most cases though, even selection does not enter the equation. This is a fact of life in most organisations where people are already in positions and assume team membership on this basis. Whilst this may be less than ideal in forming the winning team, it is a situation which has to be lived with and more complex strategies are required to weld a diverse group of people into a unit which becomes substantially more than the sum of the individual parts.

As a starting point, it will be useful for you to find out something about yourself. We have included the application tasks below so that you can formulate some initial impressions about your personality characteristics and the way you typically behave in teams. It does not matter whether you are normally a team leader or a participant. When you do these tasks, you should try and assess yourself as you think you *are*, not as you *would like to be*. In the case of Application Task 5.2, you should reach some conclusions about your typical preferences and behaviours: do not represent what you think is desirable behaviour or how you think your colleagues see you. We shall be dealing with this issue later.

We shall be interpreting your scores in the tasks a little later. First we look at some general tenets of team roles theory, followed by a description of each of eight team roles.

Team Behaviour Roles: The Basics

The premise on which the team roles theory is built is that individuals are seldom good at everything. They also have much more to contribute than their professional skills or expertise. The task then is to discover what the team member is good at and try to build on that. What this means is that strengths are emphasised and weaknesses recognised and accommodated.

Some basic premises:

1.   People working in teams tend to adopt particular roles.
2.   They tend to prefer these roles and stick with them.
3.   Certain combinations lead to more effective teams.

APPLICATION TASK 5.1

CONTRIBUTION TO THE TEAM
SELF-DESCRIPTION: WORDS

Look at each of the boxes below. Select a maximum of *three* boxes which come *closest* to describing you as you see yourself. You have 25 points to award. If you feel one box describes you perfectly, you may write the whole 25 points in it. On the other hand, you may wish to spread the 25 points out over two or three boxes, but ensure that the points you award relate to the amount of applicability of the box to you. At this stage do not concern yourself with the letters at the left of each box.

TW Sociable / Mild / Sensitive	*CF* Orderly / Conscientious / Anxious
SH Energetic / Outgoing / Dynamic	*CW* Conservative / Dutiful / Predictable
ME Sober / Unemotional / Wise	*CH* Calm / Self-confident / Controlled
RI Extrovert / Enthusiastic / Curious	*PL* Individualistic / Serious / Unorthodox

Stott, K. and Walker, A., *Making Management Work*. © 1992 Simon & Schuster (Asia) Pte Ltd.

APPLICATION TASK 5.2

SELF-DESCRIPTION: STATEMENTS

Award marks to these statements according to their applicability to you. You have 25 points to use which may be distributed amongst a maximum of *three* boxes. You may want to give all the 25 points to one statement or you may wish to spread your points out over two or three boxes. Think carefully about it and try to be as accurate as possible.

Award points

1. You like to lead the group. You want to involve others and you are democratic, but you know when you have to take control. You keep an eye on the targets your group is supposed to achieve and you ensure the group stays on course. You like to prioritise decisions and to have clear role definitions. You are concerned with practicalities and you cope well with pressure. You like to do things properly.

2. You like to lead the group from the front. You like quick results and willing team members who will do what you say. You make incisive, no-nonsense decisions and push your own ideas. You are not particularly popular, but popularity does not get results. You hate the rules and regulations which prevent you from achieving your objectives. You call a spade 'a spade' and you tell people if they are not doing things right. You are impatient but people respect your drive and enthusiasm.

3. You are an ideas person. You make creative suggestions in new ways. You are fairly self-confident and not too diplomatic at times. You have a clever mind which discovers innovative strategies when others are constrained by their rigid thinking. You have a strong belief in your own ideas and are not too concerned about other team members. You are not exactly delighted when someone criticises your ideas. Sometimes you feel it is best to opt out of the team rather than stay there and antagonise others.

4. You have an analytical mind. You like to examine ideas and suggestions critically and relate their practical worth to the team's objectives. You are serious and shrewd. You enjoy finding the flaws which others overlook and you may be accused of being negative, of knocking things down, but at least, you prevent the team from doing things which are ill-advised. You have the knack of interpreting very complex information and can pinpoint the best decision.

5. You are a practical person. You are able to buckle down to the real job of doing the work. You look for clear goals, practical work routines and tangible results. You are not too concerned with exciting ideas. You work with care and determination. You are more concerned with thoroughness than speed. You wish those above you would stop changing things and allow you to do a good solid job with present tasks.

6. Your first concern is for people, their feelings and needs. You can spot their strengths and weaknesses and you like to put your colleagues in the limelight. You hate friction and you will step in to console those who are upset. Achieving tasks is important only so long as people are happy. You do not see why people should compete with each other. You are skilful at delegating and concerned with employees' development. You want to be part of a happy family unit at work. You help others and draw reticent colleagues into discussions.

7. You have a very enquiring mind. You explore ideas outside the team, so you like to visit other institutions and agencies to see what they are doing. You develop a wide range of contacts. When you are working with colleagues, you use their talents well and try out their ideas. You need variety in life and constant stimulation, otherwise you get easily bored. At times, you may be a bit impulsive. You are really good at exploring new possibilities and you have the ability to persuade and motivate colleagues.

8. You are an anxious sort of person and you have considerable nervous energy. You want to see jobs finished and finished well. You are also anxious to see they are completed on time. You nag colleagues, never allowing them to become complacent. You breathe urgency into discussions and keep people on their toes. You spot mistakes in detail and prevent urgent matters being put aside. At times, you may irritate people, but you stop them from becoming careless, over-confident or lazy.

Stott, K. and Walker, A., *Making Management Work*. © 1992 Simon & Schuster (Asia) Pte Ltd.

In order to develop effective teams, therefore, it is necessary for individuals to be given opportunities to:

- Become aware of their role preferences.
- Understand how they can use these role preferences for the good of the team.
- Develop their role preferences so they are more effective.

Team Roles: Descriptions

The descriptions below are our interpretation of the roles delineated by Dr Meredith Belbin (1981) in his well-known research at Henley. This interpretation has also taken into account the work of Belbin's co-researchers, and our experience of conducting experiments with teams of managers from the public sector. Below each description we have included a summary of the key points of the particular role.

The Chairman

This role is one of the two team leadership roles. It is substantially different from that of the more directive leader, called the Shaper, and described below. The Chairman likes to identify people's skills and abilities, and use them. He will involve colleagues in decision-making and will genuinely share whenever possible. However, he does not lose control and things do get done, because he retains a focus on the task. He politely brings discussions back on line and ensures that contributions are relevant to the matter at hand. In a management meeting, for example, a manager who enacts the

Chairman role will give colleagues the feeling that their contributions are important and that their skills are there to be recognised and utilised. He will seldom announce decisions but·seek an input from interested parties.

He is quite bright, but this can be problematic if his intellect far exceeds that of other team members. He is emotionally stable, not showing much concern for the problem of others taking on leading roles, because he is basically secure. He can be assertive and is quite realistic, with his feet firmly on the ground. The Chairman has faith in his colleagues to do a good job.

SUMMARY

The Chairman:

- Involves others in decision-making.
- Still retains control.
- Uses people's abilities.
- Retains focus on task.
- Quite bright.
- Emotionally stable.
- Assertive but not domineering.
- Shows faith in colleagues.
- Pragmatic.

The Shaper

The Shaper is a direct contrast to the Chairman. He is brash and has a sharp, sometimes uncontrolled, tongue. He makes rapid, incisive decisions and gives direct orders, which he would probably argue are more productive and less time-consuming than participative episodes. Essentially, he is an action man and wants to see quick results. He likes 'yes men' and has no time for those who question his decisions. He is extremely task-centred and people's needs tend to take a poor second place. He is not very popular with colleagues, but he has the advantage of making sure that things get done promptly.

His no-nonsense approach gives rise to impatience, intolerance and competitiveness. He is emotionally insecure and seems to have boundless energy. He is often critical of others but is incapable of accepting criticism himself.

Some people can accept this, but some team members may have their own ways of reacting to what may be seen as a bullying style. It is unlikely that the Shaper heading a professional organisation or unit will get lasting commitment and co-operation from colleagues, unless another colleague adopts a more conciliatory role. There are situations however where the Shaper role may be necessary to shake things up and make rapid changes.

SUMMARY

The Shaper:

- Brash with sharp tongue.
- Direct orders.
- Wants action, quick results and likes 'yes' men.
- Makes incisive decisions.
- Not popular.
- Quite task-centred.
- Emotionally insecure.
- Assertive.
- Impatient.
- Competitive.
- Intolerant.
- Critical.

The Innovator or Plant

He is the ideas person and can take a team out of dull mediocrity into new realms of performance, if only other team members would listen to him. He has a highly creative mind and likes to search for new ways of doing things. This does not always go down too well though with the Shaper, the Monitor–Evaluator and the Company Worker. As a result, the Innovator is quite likely to disappear into the background unless there is a skilful team leader who can draw on his creativity and at the same time direct it into activity which is on line with the task objectives. Rejecting the Innovator is injurious to the team, since it will almost certainly lack that vital spark which is the hallmark of high performance.

The Innovator is a loner who does not like to be bound by group norms nor restricted by petty rules and procedures. In systems which are largely bureaucratic, it seems difficult to provide the conditions in which Innovators can be nurtured. Our experience is that, in these circumstances, Innovators are few and far between. It is also interesting to note that Innovators may be in short supply in systems which promote a narrow focus in their educational systems and provide little support for activities which might be described as 'creative'.

The Innovator can be a nuisance to the rest of the team, is often undiplomatic and his radical ideas seem to be divorced from reality. He is also intensely sensitive to criticism, which suggests that the team may have to pay a high price in terms of tolerance if it is to enjoy the benefits which the Innovator inevitably·brings.

As many teams seem to survive in mediocrity, the role of the Innovator may be of crucial importance in feeding new ideas to both senior management and other organisational teams. Managers at all levels therefore may be well advised to seek out those colleagues who provide this role preference and make full use of their special skills. These special skills are highlighted by Watts (1988 : 121):

> If you have a Plant on your team you have probably already experienced both the benefits and disadvantages they can offer. A strong innovative disposition and an effective thinking ability of a high order are considerable assets to any management team but they must be managed with great skill if negative side-effects are to be avoided. There may, for example, be long periods of non- or low contribution. The Plant is a talented midfield player who is always one step ahead of the others. Once your team learns to match the Plant's attributes with its collective efforts and stops demanding a continuous work rate, you are on your way to success.

SUMMARY

The Innovator or Plant

- Puts in new ideas and ways of doing things.
- Can transform a team.
- Loner.
- Undiplomatic.
- Radical.
- Sometimes divorced from reality.
- Sensitive to criticism.
- If rejected, opts out.
- The manager must know how to work with this person.
- Without the Innovator, the team will lack spark.

The Monitor–Evaluator

If the Innovator is the one who creates the ideas, the Monitor–Evaluator is the one who breaks them down and often discards them. He provides a quality control mechanism, meticulously finding the faults in everything and rejecting any idea which has not accommodated the necessary constraints and limitations. As a result he is no friend of the Innovator and can indeed incur the wrath of the rest of the team by an over-critical and negative attitude. This is not always the case of course, but the role demands a sort of filtering mechanism so that only the ideas which meet rigorous criteria are allowed to pass through.

The Monitor–Evaluator has a great capacity for interpreting complex data and more often than not chooses the best decision from a range of alternatives. He deals with confusing information in the same way children tackle game puzzles: it is a stimulating challenge. He is an excellent planner and he invariably keeps team goals in mind. He is not a risk taker, but errs on the cautious side, which can be infuriating for the Innovator. He can actually start to enjoy antagonising 'ideas people' and this type of behaviour can become destructive.

We have found many Monitor–Evaluators in teams of professionals, which is not surprising in view of the fact that the role demands intellect and analytical capacities. Whilst the worst picture has been painted of the role in its more destructive form, the Monitor–Evaluator is of great value to teams in all spheres, but particularly to those organisations which face considerable complexity and uncertainty, since he will probably prevent colleagues from taking on projects which are inadvisable and which are not aligned to company mission. At operational rather than strategic levels, he will certainly have a clear idea of what will work and what will not.

SUMMARY

The Monitor–Evaluator

* Puts ideas to rigorous test.
* Keeps team goals in mind.
* Cautious.
* Good planner and assessor of ideas.
* Interprets complex data.
* Reaches best decisions from confusing information.
* Over-critical.
* Sometimes negative.
* Can lower morale.
* Can enjoy antagonising ideas people.

The Company Worker

The Company Worker is a solid, reliable individual who thrives in a stable, little-changing environment, so he is not particularly well disposed towards the Innovator. He is down to earth, conscientious and disciplined, and as such, can easily accept rules and procedures, seeing them as necessary constraints. Totally unlike the Innovator who can thrive on ambiguity, the Company Worker likes to be told what to do. In return, he will get on with the job and work carefully for good results. He is also meticulous about quality and quite determined, which means that he does not like to be pushed into doing a quick job, which may bring him into conflict with the Shaper who does not share the same concern for quality.

He is considered essential to the effective functioning of the team, but despite his admirable qualities, his limitations can be frustrating for the team. He lacks vision and reacts badly to situations which may involve ambiguous information and change. He may also react against new ideas, which can make the atmosphere uncomfortable if several team members are pressing for change.

Like the Monitor–Evaluator, there are many Company Workers to be found in management teams. They are seen as good, reliable people who will get jobs done. The team must be careful, though, unless it settles for maintaining the status quo. Development can only take place if the Company Worker is shielded from the ambiguity and given specific meaningful tasks to carry out. The most difficult situation occurs where this person becomes the team leader because leadership, by its very nature, demands vision and the capacity to look beyond the immediate. There are many organisations which put Company Workers in charge because it is part of their culture to reward experience and a declared willingness to toe the company line. This is probably detrimental as far as team effectiveness is concerned. At the top of the organisation it can be disastrous if a Company Worker takes a strong hold, and for this reason, it is critical that senior management team members recognise the relevance of roles to their work so that they can modify their behaviours if the situation dictates it.

SUMMARY

The Company Worker:

- Accepts rules, procedures and constraints.
- Gets on with the job.
- Likes to be told what to do.
- Meticulous and determined.
- Works carefully for good results.
- Likes a stable environment.
- Down to earth.
- Conscientious.
- Disciplined.
- Solid and reliable.
- Lacks vision.
- Reacts badly to ambiguity and change.
- Reacts against new ideas.

The Teamworker

The Teamworker is everyone's friend but may be less concerned about getting the task completed than other colleagues. He has interpersonal skills and is adept at developing team cohesion. He is good at 'reading' people, being able to understand their moods and feelings. He works quietly to achieve harmony and will address discord if it threatens to surface.

He is emotionally stable and without a strong competitive streak. He is sometimes seen as being too soft, which may be true in some situations where a much harder line and a bit of discomfort are required. A department, for example, may need shaking out of its complacency, but the Teamworker is not the person to do this, preferring to emphasise harmony. This is all very well, but harmony may fail to get things done.

His complementary role has to be used well so that he can help build team spirit and heal the wounds, whilst Shapers and Innovators stir things up.

It is good to have a Teamworker in management teams, especially where they (the teams) are predominantly task-centred. Apart from their ability to build and maintain relationships between people, they are good at promoting development and, when in senior positions, they are usually effective delegators, providing the sorts of opportunities for colleagues to gain development experiences which are valuable to their careers. They are not worried about others being able to do their job.

SUMMARY

The Teamworker:

- Interpersonal and team cohesion skills.
- Promotes team spirit.
- Good at 'reading' people.
- Works quietly to achieve harmony.
- Will address discord.
- Emotionally stable.
- Not competitive.
- Sometimes seen as too soft.
- Good at developing colleagues.
- May over-emphasise harmony.

The Resource Investigator

This role provides the link with the outside world as the Resource Investigator seeks ideas and develops contacts with other units and organisations. The purpose of this is to ensure that the team is getting the best ideas and that it does not wither through insularity.

The Resource Investigator, like the Chairman, likes to develop people's talents, but is not quite so stable as the latter. He is impulsive and can lose interest quickly. He needs lots of variety in his work, challenge and constant stimulation. He also needs people around to maintain his interest, because he is certainly not one to become involved in long tedious paperwork tasks which demand perseverence and attention to detail.

It is this tendency to become bored quickly which can be problematic, alongside a failure to stay closely focused on the relevant issues. Despite this, the team needs his outward-looking orientation and the capacity to keep in touch with life outside the team.

In a competitive environment, the person who adopts this role may look for examples of good practice in other organisations, either by visiting them or by being constantly in social contact with colleagues outside. He may hold membership of professional associations and is usually enthusiastic about introducing ideas acquired from conferences and development sessions outside the place of work. He is also the person who may devise innovative ways of linking up with the outside world for the benefit of the team and the organisation by, for example, inviting customers to make an input into new product development or by getting recipients of goods or services to meet with the team to offer advice.

SUMMARY

The Resource Investigator:

- Link with the world outside.
- Develops contacts.
- Seeks ideas.
- May lose interest quickly.
- Can be impulsive.
- Needs variety, challenge, people and constant stimulation.
- May focus on irrelevant issues.

The Completer

The Completer is one of life's 'naggers'. He can be infuriating, often turning up at the wrong time and pestering for work to be completed. In fact, his boundless nervous energy is used to this end. He invariably meets deadlines and makes sure others do so. He communicates urgency and many colleagues learn to dread his frequent appearances as time deadlines approach. He can easily upset people with his persistence. He certainly prevents complacency and poor work.

Some aspects of organisational life can be highly complex and there may be many initiatives which teams at all levels have to deal with. Whilst intentions are good, it is understandable that some things either fall behind schedule or fade completely into the background. Where the Completer has a part in a project, however, this is unlikely to happen, since he will ensure colleagues are constantly reminded of the task's status and what they must do to reach a satisfactory conclusion.

His influence extends beyond time deadlines, however. He has great attention to detail and will often take on the task of checking everything himself so that mistakes do not pass through unnoticed. With a Completer in the team, it is more than likely that the output will be accurate and on schedule, and that nothing important has been omitted. It does not mean that the work is necessarily creative or that it incorporates particularly stunning ideas. That is not part of his role.

Apart from his nagging, which can easily lower morale amongst team members, he is likely to be at loggerheads with those who are casual, clumsy or fail to meet his expectations of urgency and meticulous accuracy.

SUMMARY

The Completer:

- Nervous energy is used for getting jobs completed.
- Meets deadlines.
- Nags colleagues.
- Communicates urgency.
- Prevents complacency and poor work.
- May upset people.

Personal Assessment Analysis

Earlier you completed two forms. The one entitled Self-Description: Words is an attempt to describe some basic characteristics of each of the team roles, whilst Self-Description: Statements aims to examine your preferred behaviours in the team. By entering your scores on the analysis form in Application Task 5.3, you should obtain an idea of how you perceive your own contribution to the effective performance of the team. The initials at the side of each box represent the eight team roles. Read off your scores, and pay particular attention to your two highest scores in the column on the right, the 'statements' scores. These two figures are your perceived primary and secondary roles. You can then look back at the descriptions in the text above to see how closely your perceived behaviour relates to the 'pure' role.

Now is the time for you to assess the roles which the members of your management team prefer to play. By doing this role preference analysis, when we look at team composition and balance later, you will be able to relate the particular preferences of your team to the 'ideal'. You should complete Application Task 5.4, Members' Role Preferences, and make entries for each of your management team colleagues. Do it carefully, because it may release new insights into the relationship between team performance and behaviour and thus enable you to make some constructive adjustments at a later stage to either team membership or role preferences.

If you have time to spare and a supportive group of fellow workers, you can subject yourself to the views of your colleagues. At the same time, they may be interested in knowing what their preferred roles are in the team. If you choose to do this with colleagues from your management team, you should give them the form Other Members' Perceptions shown in Figure 5.1, and ask them to complete it for each member of the management team. Do not forget you will have to explain what each of the roles means and possibly give them the descriptions above. This can be an interesting exercise and one which can form a productive development session for the management team. We have found that managers generally appreciate finding out about themselves and being exposed to the perceptions of colleagues, especially if there is a good *esprit de corps* in the team.

When you have each completed the form for each other, you can then enter all the scores on the form Team Roles : Perception Scores shown in Figure 5.2. By totalling the scores awarded for each role and then dividing by the number of people in the team, you will arrive at an average score for each role. You should then turn to Personal Role Profile in Figure 5.3 and shade in the appropriate amount for each role. This will give you a graphic representation of your team role as perceived by those who work with you. If you do this for each member of the team, you can enter all the information (perhaps using different colours) onto one profile form. This will give you a

APPLICATION TASK 5.3

TEAM BEHAVIOUR ROLES : PRELIMINARY ANALYSIS

Look at the self-description forms you completed earlier. Complete the key below by entering the three scores you gave yourself for each.

WORDS		STATEMENTS	
CH	☐	CH (1)	☐
SH	☐	SH (2)	☐
PL	☐	PL (3)	☐
ME	☐	ME (4)	☐
CW	☐	CW (5)	☐
TW	☐	TW (6)	☐
RI	☐	RI (7)	☐
CF	☐	CF (8)	☐

The initials refer to the behaviour roles. The numbers in brackets refer to the statement numbers on Self-Description: Statements. By referring to the descriptions of each of the team roles, you will now be able to see how your initial perceptions relate to your revised assessment after reading the detailed information above.

picture of how balanced your management team is, and we shall be discussing this issue of composition in more detail below.

APPLICATION TASK 5.4

MEMBERS' ROLE PREFERENCES

Think of your management team. Try to assess each member's team role by awarding scores. You have 25 points to award to each person (including yourself), and you may distribute these points over a maximum of three boxes. If you are unhesitating about a person's team role, you can enter all 25 points in one box. Otherwise, spread the 25 points according to the individual's preferred behaviours as you see them.

Enter the names of team members in the boxes across the top of the grid.

CH							
SH							
PL							
ME							
CW							
TW							
RI							
CF							

Figure 5.1
Other Perceptions

TEAM BEHAVIOUR ROLES: OTHER MEMBERS' PERCEPTIONS

Think of your management team. Try to assess each member's team role by awarding scores. You have 25 points to award to each person, and you may distribute these points over a maximum of three boxes. If you are unhesitating about a person's team role, you can enter all 25 points in one box. Otherwise, spread the 25 points according to the individual's preferred behaviours as you see them.

Enter the names of team members in the boxes across the top of the grid.

CH	☐	☐	☐	☐	☐	☐
SH	☐	☐	☐	☐	☐	☐
PL	☐	☐	☐	☐	☐	☐
ME	☐	☐	☐	☐	☐	☐
CW	☐	☐	☐	☐	☐	☐
TW	☐	☐	☐	☐	☐	☐
RI	☐	☐	☐	☐	☐	☐
CF	☐	☐	☐	☐	☐	☐

Figure 5.2
Perception Scores

TEAM ROLES: PERCEPTION SCORES

Use the form below to write the scores which your colleagues have awarded you.

Role	Scores							Total	Average
CHAIRMAN	□	□	□	□	□	□	□	□	○
SHAPER	□	□	□	□	□	□	□	□	○
INNOVATOR	□	□	□	□	□	□	□	□	○
MONITOR–EVALUATOR	□	□	□	□	□	□	□	□	○
COMPANY WORKER	□	□	□	□	□	□	□	□	○
TEAMWORKER	□	□	□	□	□	□	□	□	○
RESOURCE INVESTIGATOR	□	□	□	□	□	□	□	□	○
COMPLETER	□	□	□	□	□	□	□	□	○

You obtain the average by dividing the total for each role by the number of people in the team.

Discuss your scores with the rest of the team, asking for clarification where your perceptions are at variance with theirs.

Figure 5.3
Personal Role Profile

Take your average score for each role and complete the profile chart below by filling in the grid to the appropriate level.

The longest bar represents your primary preferred role, whilst the next longest is your secondary role.

	0.5	1.0	1.5	2.0	2.5	3.0	3.5	4.0	4.5	5.0	5.5	6.0
CHAIRMAN												
SHAPER												
INNOVATOR												
MONITOR–EVALUATOR												
COMPANY WORKER												
TEAMWORKER												
RESOURCE INVESTIGATOR												
COMPLETER												

We have to stress at this point that few people are completely identifiable with one category. Our work has shown that managers may have two or three scores quite close together and this tends to indicate some merging of roles. At the same time, we seldom encounter individuals who score uniformly across the board, which would indicate that there are behavioural preferences, even if they are not clear-cut. In our reviews, we have often found it useful to look at what people are *not*: in other words, to eliminate the very low-scoring categories. Sometimes, individuals may have been assigned responsibilities demanding role strengths which are not present. Many of the senior managers we have worked with, for example, score very highly on Company Worker and lowly on the two leadership categories, which suggests an inconsistency between team responsibility and role preference.

The 'Ideal' Team

First of all, is there such a thing as an 'ideal' team? There probably is, but it may only be ideal for a particular situation. Where, for example, a team is operating in an uncertain environment, facing competition and having to move quickly, an active Resource Investigator may be essential if the team is to be 'ideal'. In other circumstances, his presence may not be quite so important and he may even be a liability if he becomes bored with the lack of action.

Most of us, of course, are unlikely to encounter a team which is perfect in every respect. We know a great deal about the technical skills which our teams require, and the team roles research presented here is sufficiently persuasive to lead us to believe we could construct the ideal team, but reality tends to be different. If we had a clean slate and were to apply some of the principles of team composition outlined in this chapter, we could possibly form teams which approach the ideal. We cannot go round sacking everyone who does not fit into prescribed team roles however, so we have to make do with the people we have. Despite this there are situations where it may be wise to move one or two people in or out of teams, because their presence (or absence) may be critical to organisational or subunit success.

What can we do about the team which is already formed and operating, and which could not be disbanded in any way? The first task you may have done already, and that is to analyse the individual team members' preferred roles. This is the starting point. The next step is to assess the balance of the team and see whether it contains the requisite roles. Consider therefore your management team and complete Application Task 5.5, Team Balance. This will give you an indication of how balanced your team probably is. It is only a rough guide and should not be used for any purpose other than gaining an initial impression of how appropriate the membership is.

APPLICATION TASK 5.5

TEAM BALANCE

In the table below, enter the names of your team members alongside their preferred roles. Their highest-scoring one will go under primary role, the second highest under secondary role, and so on. You can have more than one name in any box.

TEAM ROLE	PRIMARY	SECONDARY	TERTIARY
CHAIRMAN			
SHAPER			
INNOVATOR			
MONITOR–EVALUATOR			
COMPANY WORKER			
TEAMWORKER			
RESOURCE INVESTIGATOR			
COMPLETER			

Add up the number of completed boxes in the primary column ☐ x 2 ☐

Add up the number of completed boxes in the secondary column which were not already filled in the primary column. ☐

Add a bonus point each if you have Innovator or Monitor–Evaluator in the primary column. ☐

TOTAL ☐

If your score is greater than 10, you may have a reasonably balanced team, although a score approaching 15 indicates a more extensive range of roles.

The notion of balance would suggest that the presence of all eight roles would make the perfect team. Belbin's experiments supported the view that it is desirable to have most of the roles represented. The exception to this relates to the leadership of the team. The presence of both Chairman *and* Shaper is not desirable, since it may create unproductive tension in the team's leadership. Whilst the ideal may point to everyone having different roles, role duplication may be acceptable in some circumstances, although you have to be careful of confusion and competition. It largely depends on which role it is. There are some people (Chairmen are probably good examples) who can use their role characteristics to good effect in other parts of the team, but there are some which seem very limited in the extent to which they can sever their role affiliations.

As you review your membership list, you may have several people occupying the same role slot and some blank boxes alongside several of the other roles. Whilst this is not ideal, it is still possible to overcome the difficulties by assigning people to secondary (or even tertiary) roles. This means that a role 'gap' appears in the team. It is obvious it has to be filled because it is important to team success. An individual who is already duplicating another role is asked to adopt his secondary role more prominently in order to fill the gap. Some can do this. Chairmen, as we have mentioned, are very adaptable creatures and can often fill in the missing spaces. Teamworkers too have adaptive capabilities and can often take on the task of discovering what is going on in the outside world (Resource Investigator), being the friendly people they are and generally good at interaction.

Just in case you think you can move anyone to any role however, a note of caution must be entered here. Shapers seldom become Teamworkers overnight, if ever; so do not try for unrealistic maneuvers. Some roles require the sort of ability which is not easily acquired. Innovators are very creative people and you cannot expect people to take on this role responsibility if they do not have the ability in the first place. Similarly, the Monitor–Evaluator is clever and can make sense of complicated information, a capacity which is not acquired very easily. If you have people like these in your team, you are very fortunate and you need to leave them in their primary roles. In fact, there are many teams who have never possessed any creative talent and have suffered from the curse of mediocrity as a result. If you have an Innovator therefore, treasure him!

Obviously it makes sense to utilise individuals' primary roles, which are the result of particular abilities and behavioural preferences. This is where the main contribution to the team's effectiveness will come from. Learning a secondary role can be a difficult and time-consuming business, but one which may be necessary in some circumstances.

Constructing the Team

We have already said that an ideal team will have all the roles represented, although they may not all be primary roles. Indeed, if we have the optimum team size of six, which Belbin found to be the best compromise figure, it will not be possible to have the eight roles all in primary slots. There are some roles which are critical though and these are shown in the outline of the ideal team composition in Figure 5.4.

Figure 5.4
Outline Team Composition

Chairman Innovator Monitor–Evaluator
Company Worker(s) Teamworker(s) Resource Investigator(s) Completer(s)

Those in the top box are probably vital to real effectiveness. We have opted for the ideal of a Chairman rather than a Shaper, although we accept that, in some circumstances, the directive approach of the Shaper may be useful. In most cases though, we have found the Chairman type to be more satisfactory and supportive to the effective functioning of the team. We have found too many problems with the leader who expects submissive behaviour:

> Some leaders like people to be dependent and encourage this; some leaders are so task oriented they do not see the counterreactions to them that drain off the energies and creativity and emotional well-being of the members. Hopefully we in leadership positions center our focus on the people and their needs and try to create conditions which allow us to work *with* them rather than over them. (Dyer, 1980 : 184)

We have found a further but related problem with Shaper-type leadership and that relates to team climate. It is best expressed in Dyer's discourse on group behaviour:

> In a defensive climate people usually spend their time trying to defend themselves against the authority persons. They do not have time or emotional energy to be creative – to grow and mature – for their energies are dissipated in trying to protect themselves from the punishment, censoring, telling, controlling efforts of others. (Dyer, 1980 : 185)

This group reaction is often expressed in statements such as: 'If a leader does not lead, he is not doing his job.' But this may hide poor attitudes towards a highly directive leader. Because of the relationship which exists between leader and 'followers', the latter may push all responsibility onto the leader, and this may give rise to a relationship which is wary and antagonistic (Hastings *et al.*, 1986). There are situations however, where expectations on the part of team members of a leader's directive stance are realistic and desirable. Where time is short and the team has a 'firefighting' mission, firm central guidance may be critical to success. But in other settings, this sort of behaviour may hinder effective teamwork.

There are many situations in management where the creative person may be critical to success. Belbin found that, when 'planted' in an ordinary team (hence the alternative name 'plant'), he could transform the team from a state of mediocrity to one of high achievement. That is assuming, of course, that the team will listen to his ideas and use his creative talents. In all the management teams we have seen and worked with, we are convinced there has been a place for the Innovator. Sad to say, they are in short supply, and although we may have been unfortunate, most of the teams we have seen have been no more than average performers. Not surprisingly, their perceptions of performance have been unrealistically high. That has usually been because they have compared themselves with equally mediocre teams.

We have already outlined the key contribution which the Monitor–Evaluator makes. We rate his presence as being as essential as that of the Innovator. He indeed may be what teams are formed for: processing complex information, sifting ideas for flaws and relevance to the key purpose, and selecting the optimum solution. These attributes all fall within the Monitor–Evaluator's domain. With this person in the team, and provided he possesses the necessary critical analysis capabilities, high-quality decisions should emerge.

Helping Your Team Members

So you have got your team and you have analysed their roles. You have decided where the 'gaps' are and you are going to slot some of your people into secondary roles in order to fill the missing spaces. It can work, but your members have to first of all understand what the roles involve. If, for example, you have more than one Chairman and you want one of them to take on his secondary role of Resource Investigator, he has to know that the role involves exploration work, that he has to set up contacts outside the team. Secondly, you have to help all your team members develop their contributions in their preferred or determined roles.

As a manager, you may want to take on this responsibility to effect team improvement by helping each of your members become more skilful in using role preferences to enhance the work of the team. Even if you are not in a position to do this, you can still improve your contribution by developing your own role preferences. With these two purposes in mind, we have provided some notes below on how performance in each of the eight team roles might be improved.

Chairman

If you are a Chairman, you have a responsibility to be well organised and to co-ordinate the contributions of others. Try to limit your talking to paraphrasing, summaries and the occasional personal contribution, which should be skilfully timed. Spend long periods of time listening and then summarise what has been said. Keep an open mind (even though you may have strong personal opinions) and accept that some people may have unusual, even eccentric, ideas. One of your key duties is to ensure that you find out what each individual can offer and then to use those abilities. You must say things like: 'John, tell us about the experience you have had in office relocation.' By using people's abilities, you will be able to delegate effectively. Note however that you should delegate real responsibilities which offer a challenge to the individuals concerned, and not merely dish out work as a way of off-loading tedious chores. Delegation and the acceptance of responsibility in this context is not necessarily a structured process; in teamworking situations, any authority delegated tends to be more sapiential and acquiescent than structured. You should learn to be incisive: when you think the discussion has gone on for long enough, and all relevant issues have been covered, you should move towards a decision, and be firm about it. You should build up your skills of gaining consensus for the decision and try to avoid vote-taking.

If you are the leader of the team, there may be a tendency for you to dominate. The problem can be exacerbated if you are also the 'ideas' person. Meetings can become solo performances and this will do little to support the effectiveness of your team. Sometimes you will have to bite your tongue and make a conscious effort to let others speak for 80 per cent of the time available.

Chairman, learn to:

- Organise well.
- Listen and summarise.
- Discover others' abilities and use them.
- Delegate responsibilities.
- Make incisive decisions.
- Gain consensus.

Shaper

You are a directive leader and you are responsible for giving drive, enthusiasm and clear direction to the team. Like the Chairman though, you should try to be more of a co-ordinator. Recognise how each individual can contribute to team success and avoid at all costs treading all over people in your enthusiasm. You can be quite objective and can stop people getting carried away with their ideas which may become detached from the real purpose. You should use target-setting techniques to ensure that tasks stay on line. Although it may be difficult for you, try to listen to others and to thank them for their contributions. Make your members feel they are important to the team's success.

Shaper, learn to:

- Give clear direction to the team.
- Co-ordinate members' contributions.
- Set up appropriate control mechanisms.
- Use members' abilities.
- Keep discussions on line.
- Employ target-setting.
- Listen to others and support them.

Innovator

You are the 'ideas person'. Keep your creativity going because that is your enormous contribution to the team and your colleagues depend on you. Try to focus your ideas though and do not get carried away. If you are in a team which seems to you over-critical, do not let them put you off, because without you they will suffer. Try to concentrate your attention on problems which the team is having real difficulties in solving. Do not be too dejected if colleagues seem unreceptive to your contributions: some of the great composers could not get audiences for their early works! Your time will come and colleagues will learn to appreciate you.

If you lead the group as well as bring creative approaches to it, you will have to do a fair amount of listening. Do not let your organisational duties detract you from your key contribution. In some ways it is better that you are not the leader, but that is not always possible. Some football teams make the mistake of electing the most creative player in the team as captain. The responsibilities sometimes provide an unnecessary burden which hinders the creative input which is so essential.

Innovator, learn to:

- Focus your ideas on relevant issues.
- Concentrate on problems which are hard to solve.
- Become thick-skinned – not to be put off by critical colleagues.
- Listen to other views.

Monitor–Evaluator

You are the brains of the team and it is your job to simplify complex issues for your colleagues and to analyse ideas to ensure they are related to the team's primary task and that they are workable. You will also evaluate potential solutions to problems and ensure that the best option is selected. Do not be too critical though, otherwise your colleagues will either become inhibited or they will compete with you. Try to be constructive by listening to members' suggestions and then building on them rather than knocking them down. You will become quickly appreciated if you follow this course. Try to keep an open mind and consider each contribution on its merits. If there is a creative person in the team, try to become friendly with him, even though he might come up with the most outrageous suggestions at times! The two of you working collaboratively will probably be worth more than the rest of the team put together. Do not forget your key intellectual role; do not let unsound ideas get through the net.

If you are the team leader, be careful that you do not put team members off by being too critical. Show that you are prepared to consider all suggestions fairly by addressing members by name and asking for their comments, ideas and so forth. If you can get someone else to point out the flaws, so much the better. It does not matter that you saw them five minutes earlier! You can say something like: 'Peter, you are suggesting we introduce more flexible lunch time arrangements. You have outlined the very persuasive advantages. What do you think are the problems that might occur?' That is far better than saying: 'It can't possibly work. When you want typing done, the secretary will be on lunch. When she is there, you will be out on your lunch.'

Monitor–Evaluator, learn to:

- Make sense of complicated issues.
- Put ideas in simple language to aid understanding.
- Look for weaknesses in ideas and assess practicability.
- Put problem solutions in rank order.
- Listen to your colleagues and make constructive remarks.
- Keep an open mind until discussions have finished.
- Make friends with the 'ideas person'.
- Use questioning technique to help others identify weaknesses.

Company Worker

You are the hard-working, reliable colleague, very down to earth and practical. Although you like things neatly laid out and with clear targets, do not knock the 'ideas people' in your team. They may have their heads in the clouds, but your team is aiming for the skies! Try to be flexible and accept that there is more than one way of doing things. Help your colleagues with the practicalities and keep their feet on the ground as far as quality and meeting targets are concerned. Ensure that by the end of team meetings, targets have been clearly stated and that people know what they are supposed to be doing. Your colleagues are going to rely on you for the job going well.

Company Worker, learn to:

- Be flexible and accept different ways of working.
- Listen to new ideas.
- Help colleagues with practicalities.
- Prepare good target statements.
- Outline what has to be done and by what time.

Teamworker

You are the 'people' person in the team, the harmoniser and relationship healer. Ensure you stay fair-minded and do not take sides. Be friendly and supportive, and try to listen to people carefully and then compliment them on their contributions. Just little comments are enough to lift the spirit in the team: 'That's a useful idea' and 'Jane's suggestion seems to build nicely on what Peter said earlier.' If anyone starts to make comments which are personal, such as: 'You never come up with anything that is practical...' divert the focus of the comment immediately before it causes too much damage. You quickly interject with something like: 'Andrew, I think that might be a little unfair. What you are saying is that there may be difficulties in trying to get Phil's idea off the ground. Is that right?' If there are real breakdowns in relationships, where people do not talk to one another, or even avoid each other, you can do a worthwhile job in trying to heal the wounds. Perhaps you can meet the people concerned outside the team setting and talk things through over a cup of coffee. You may find you have effective counselling skills and you would do well to develop your questioning technique.

You can also be supportive to the team by taking an interest in individuals, something which is seldom done very well. You can find out what interests and abilities people have and do your best to promote these in the team's working. You may also be prepared to help individuals in various ways, by making contacts for them (not the exclusive domain of the Resource Investigator) and by seeking resources.

As a Teamworker, the chances are that you will be keeping a low profile and doing a very effective 'unseen' job, but if you are the leader, you must learn to play on your members' strengths and to help them develop as individuals. This may be achieved through skilful delegation.

Teamworker, learn to:

- Stay fair-minded and impartial.
- Be friendly and supportive.
- Nip destructive comments in the bud.
- Heal relationship breakdowns.
- Discover members' interests and abilities.
- Help individuals.
- Consider individual development needs.

Resource Investigator

You are the link with the world outside the team. Try to build up a good network of contacts and find out how teams doing similar work operate. Find out whether there are any examples of good practice that you can observe. Read appropriate materials and keep yourself up-to-date. If you find anything interesting in your travels, tell your team about it and let them decide if it is useful. Ensure your contributions are related to the team's purpose and that you do not get too locked into the social world, which can be a source of distraction. At the same time, do not let your talent for establishing friend-ship and productive contacts be wasted through over-regulated time con-straints. Since you are good on the relationships front, you are probably good at maintaining harmony in the team also. You should use this skill and try to be supportive and encouraging to your colleagues.

Hastings *et al.* (1986 : 98), in referring to the role which technical special-ists might play, seem to identify such members with the typical Resource Investigator's activities. The following description is also apt advice for you or your colleagues who have this role:

> . . . the members who are technical specialists value their contacts with other specialists and those who use their services. Not only that, they go out and talk to people. They have the skills to develop relationships and build mutual respect and confidence by translating and explaining their specialism to others. They are also eager to find out in broad terms the expertise that other specialists have to offer. They see all the other specialists in their team not as boffins or blockages, but as resources that may help them or the team do the job better. These members' attitude is to 'find out – not keep out'.

Team leaders may often be Resource Investigators and the items of advice above apply to both leaders and team members who possess this external orientation.

Resource Investigator, learn to:

- Build up friendships and contacts.
- Find out what other teams are doing.
- Discover good practice and investigate it.
- Keep up-to-date in the team's area of concern.
- Keep your team informed.
- Focus on the team's purpose.
- Be supportive and encouraging to your team colleagues.

Completer

You are the perfectionist, but so is the Company Worker to a certain extent. The difference is that you make sure everything is finished on time. You should act as the team's major control mechanism by keeping an eye on progress and standards of performance. Do not accept shoddy work, and although you may be under pressure from some quarters to make sure dead-lines are met, do not accept anything less than optimum quality. You can encourage people to keep up to targets but do not nag them to the point of annoyance. Watch out for mistakes. Although you are concerned about quality and deadlines, do not 'nit-pick' to the extent that the finer points of detail become more important than the overall task. And do try to smile occasionally, giving people the sort of encouragement they need.

If you are the leader you will keep your team well focused on the task and you will be purposeful in seeing things through to completion. Although you are tempted to check everything yourself and even involve yourself in correcting errors, try to apply some good delegation principles and trust others to do the work, otherwise you may damage your team's morale.

Completer, learn to:

- Keep an eye on progress and standards.
- Communicate expectations about quality work.
- Spot mistakes.
- Give encouragement to your colleagues.
- Avoid being submerged in trivial details.
- Delegate well.
- Share your exhilaration about successful task completion.

Some Notes on Teams

Thinking of teams we have worked with or observed, there are some themes which emerge quite often, and you may recognise some of these characteristics in your team. Even if you do you may still not be able to do much about the composition, but at least you will be alerted to the dangers of inappropriate membership. If you are fortunate enough to have some say in the selection of team members, you should note that 'their ability to contribute to the workings of the team needs to be considered just as much as their specialist technical skills' (Hastings *et al.*, 1986 : 99).

A government department decided some radical changes were needed in the higher-education provision. A team was set up to restructure the service. It comprised some of the leading 'brains' in the land with no one holding less than professorial status. They were all very clever but no one was particularly creative. The outcome was disappointing and in no way radical. It involved calling one institution a different name and moving a few departments round, but failed to deal with the fundamental manpower problems and the in-built access problems to the higher-education service.

The team in the above example may have all been Monitor–Evaluators – we do not know – but there seemed to be insufficient balance to produce anything like a worthwhile outcome. Had there been an Innovator in the team, the result of their work may have been somewhat different.

Putting people all of one type, whether technical skills or role denomination, can be problematic. The specialist problem raises particular concerns about protective behaviours: 'those very specialisms provide problems for teams because the members' attitudes to their own and other specialisms often prevent the team from performing to its full potential' (Hastings *et al.*, 1986 : 98). We suggest that you try to avoid this situation and do not assume that putting the best experts together will necessarily produce the best results. Many wealthy football clubs have found this out to their cost.

Whilst we have pointed to the need for creativity in the team, it seems that there can be too much of it. We gave an example in the previous chapter of the team of top architects who failed to produce anything astounding. There are many situations where creative people are formed into teams and the results are less than satisfactory. There tends to be much confusion as they struggle to find their niche. Some delight in having other creative people around (like a group of ensemble musicians), whilst others see themselves in competition and engage in seemingly irrational behaviours. You could have a team like this in, say, a research and development department. One useful strategy may be to give each person clearly defined areas of responsibility.

The team which is most well known to us is the one which comprises people who are there because of their specialist knowledge, experience or status. That could describe most teams in organisations. They have credibility. No one disputes their right to be there. Their achievements are generally acceptable. It is invariably impossible to break them up to any degree. Even when one person leaves, he is replaced by someone who meets similar membership criteria. They seldom achieve anything exceptional, and that is probably because they have neither an Innovator nor a Monitor–Evaluator. They seldom have winning ideas and the ones they do think of are not put to the test of critical scrutiny. They are neither creative nor clever people, but are possibly seen as 'good chaps' who have worked their way through the system, always avoiding rocking the boat and generally being good 'organisation people'. The problem of conformity is identified by Dyer (1980): 'we find that if a person is to get along best in these situations he remains submissive, obedient and conforming, dependent, and is encouraged to use only a few of his skills' (Dyer, 1980 : 181).

Although we have conducted only limited research in one professional field, our preliminary findings lead us to suggest there may be management teams around in organisations such as these which comprise almost solely Company Workers. It is hardly surprising that the output is mediocre. Individuals are caught in the involvement/submission trap. On the one hand, they may want to be involved in planning their actions, but if they do, conflicts may arise about goals, targets and procedures. They then resort to being told what to do and put the onus of responsibility on someone else. Such conformity hardly supports elevated team performance (Dyer, 1980). This tendency of conformity is identified by other writers, who observe 'a tendency towards this passivity in certain team members who see their contribution as "not stirring things up" or "going along with others" ' (Hastings *et al.*, 1986 : 96).

We have already outlined a balanced team which is likely to be successful because it has the presence of key roles. Intuitively we feel that a good Chairman who is skilled in most aspects of the Chairman's role, an Innovator and a Monitor–Evaluator can go a good way to ensuring a team's success. What we are saying is that we believe these roles are central. We encountered one senior management team in an educational establishment where the principal was a Chairman/Monitor–Evaluator and one of the heads of department was an Innovator. When the rest completed their role analyses, there were few with clear primary roles (two or three scores were very close together). It did not seem to matter very much. The team was highly successful, taking the lead in many initiatives and being about a year ahead of other schools. We discovered that the principal and the creative head of department were close friends outside school, both members of the same club. The three key roles were covered between them.

We have also done some small-scale experiments on management development courses which have resulted in some teams being a puzzle to us. The analysis of roles has suggested that creativity is not present and that there is little balance. Yet in our exercises a few of these teams have performed in an outstanding way. We cannot describe the reasons in role terms, but the participants usually explain their success as being due to their capacity to get on well with each other and to gain 'excitement' from being part of a team. They often say there is no leader and that they start off the complex tasks we set by brainstorming. They then plan and break up the work in a well-co-ordinated way. Whether their effectiveness in simulated contexts is transposed to the real situation is not known. The nature of the situations we set up could of course be an important factor. The reverse side of the coin is that there are many teams with similar membership which perform disastrously, so success in this case·may have to be a phenomenon which remains unexplained.

Conclusion

As a manager you are advised to treat the issue of team roles seriously. Belbin's research has suggested that team composition has a considerable impact on performance, and the more critical the team is to organisational success, the more economic sense it makes to do something about getting the role balance right.

First of all, you can analyse your role and do something about improving your role contribution to the team, either as leader or member. The real benefits will be felt, however, when you are able to work with your management team at analysing and improving individual performance in the members' roles. You can effect some role redistribution where necessary, and if the membership is likely to change in the near future, you have got something else other than technical expertise to consider when selecting new members. You can review the types of management team we have outlined above and assess where your team fits in. Have you got a team of people who are simply there because of status or experience? Is your team composed of members who all have analytical minds or who are high on creativity? Or have you got a nicely balanced team, with at least a Chairman, an Innovator and a Monitor–Evaluator? Are you part of a reasonably successful team but which seems to be missing that 'spark' characteristic of great teams? Answers to these questions will help you in your attempts to build up a team which is high achieving and successful in meeting the needs of the organisation and the satisfaction of its members.

References

Belbin, R. M. (1981) *Management Teams: Why They Succeed or Fail,* Heinemann : London.
Dyer, W. (1980) 'Group behaviour', in Ritchie, J. and Thompson, P. (eds.), *Organization and People,* West : Minnesota.
Everard, K. and Morris, G. (1985) *Effective School Management,* Harper and Row : London.
Hastings, C., Bixby, P. and Chaudhry–Lawton, R. (1986) *The Superteam Solution: Successful Teamworking in Organisations,* Gower : England.
Watts, B. (1988) *Creating the Hands-On Manager,* Mercury : London.

Chapter 6

Solving Problems and Making Decisions

Driving home after a busy day at work, I was thinking: What shall I have for dinner? Which reports to write? When shall I take my annual leave? It is amazing how many decisions we have to make in a day.

Think back to the last couple of hours and the decisions you had to make or think about. You will find it helpful to make a quick list of these decisions.

If you look at your list, you will probably see the following points:

- Not all decisions are of equal importance.
- Some decisions you could make on your own, others you could not.
- All decisions seem to have more than one solution.
- Most decisions involve a consideration of factors other than yourself.
- Some decision situations seem to occur each day, others are unique.

Making decisions involves solving problems and solving problems involves making decisions. You do not need to separate the two terms. In this chapter we shall look at the points presented above in greater detail. We shall present a framework which we believe will assist you in making better quality decisions. It is essential when making decisions to follow a sequence of steps to guide you towards the 'optimum' decision.

Making Decisions

Managers are always **making decisions**, and decision-making is one of the essential skills of management. You are constantly called upon to make and implement decisions. The quality or outcomes of your decisions have the potential to positively or negatively affect your employees and your organisation. It is essential that you maximise your decision-making ability if you are to become a truly effective manager.

Types of Decisions

As you will have discovered, not all decisions are of equal importance. This determines such factors as how much time you will commit to the decision, who else you will involve and what resources will be required. When you are faced with a decision, ask yourself: how important is the final outcome of the decision I make? We have found it useful to categorise three levels or types of decisions. Each of these necessitates the utilisation of distinctive management skills. The three types of decisions are:

- Standard decisions.
- Crisis decisions.
- Deep decisions.

Standard Decisions

Standard decisions include those everyday routine decisions which tend to be repetitive. The solutions to these types of decisions are normally dictated by set procedures, rules and policies. They are relatively simple because of their repetitive nature. You tend to deal with these decisions using logic and by referring to set procedure. Problems can arise if you do not make them according to set rules.

Of course, there are standard-type decisions which are not directly covered by organisational procedures. You still tend to deal with these almost automatically. Problems will normally only occur if you are insensitive or fail to act at the right time. One word of warning: do not allow standard decisions to become an excuse for 'sloppy' or evasive decisions.

Ted is the manager of a chain-store furniture outlet and has a fairly simple job. All outlets have standard procedures for dealing with almost all situations, including overtime, customer complaints, ordering, returned products and accounting. Ted's job is to work within the procedures while looking after and motivating his staff. Major problems which sometimes occur are referred to a senior manager. Although mainly working on routine matters, he does occasionally have to make major decisions to try to make his outlet competitive with others. Most of his decisions are however standard.

Crisis Decisions

Crisis decisions are those which require quick, precise action and need to be made almost immediately. These are the types of decisions which usually crop up without any advance notice and demand your immediate, undivided attention. Crisis decision situations allow very little time for planning or involving other people.

> *3 p.m. Tuesday: 'What do you mean they can't do it? I promised Zinload's we'd deliver tomorrow morning. They're our best customers.' Jane slammed down the phone and thought quickly. She could hold up the regular Maline order and use those trucks, call Bob and hire his fleet: 'I'll put Maline on hold but I'll have to do it now. Hope the boss doesn't mind' she said. Sue has just made a decision in a crisis situation.*

Deep Decisions

Deep decisions are usually not straightforward and require concentrated planning, discussion and reflection. These are the types of decisions which often involve setting direction or implementing change. They are also the decisions which involve the most debate, disagreement and conflict. Deep decisions often involve substantial time and specialised input. A variety of options or potential plans to choose from can be advantageous.

Deep decisions can involve selective, adaptive and creative or innovative processes (Woodcock and Francis, 1982). Selection from decision alternatives allows the best fit between the decision to be made and a number of 'field-tested' solutions. Your effectiveness depends on your choosing the decision which will be the most acceptable, productive and effective.

Adaptive processes involve you in combining some field-tested solutions with some new, more creative answers. You must be able to control and draw on past experience of what works and combine this with a touch of innovation.

Innovative processes involve you in complex and creative insights into decision-making. You will need to use these skills in major, often poorly understood, unpredictable situations which require novel solutions.

Most of this chapter will deal with deep-type decisions: the type that can enhance (or detract from) your managerial image and effectiveness. Before we take you through a decision-making framework, complete Application Task 6.1.

APPLICATION TASK 6.1

Develop a list of decision situations you face which fit into the categories *standard* decisions, *crisis* decisions and *deep* decisions. List possible decisions in column I. When you have done this write the name or names of the person (including yourself) who you believe should be involved in making the decision. The reason for this will become apparent later in the chapter.

Types of decisions:

I	II
Standard:	
Crisis:	
Deep:	

Stott, K. and Walker, A., *Making Management Work.* © 1992 Simon & Schuster (Asia) Pte Ltd.

Steps in Making Decisions

The framework or system suggested for making decisions has six stages:

1. Identify and understand the problem and its causes.
2. Isolate the details of the problem and further define your understanding and desired outcome criteria.
3. Involve those people whom it is advantageous or necessary to involve.
4. Investigate various possible solutions and then evaluate these alternatives for decision applicability.
5. Implement and communicate your decision.
6. Inquire into the effectiveness of your decision, review results and think how the decision can be improved next time.

The key words are shown in Figure 6.1.

Figure 6.1

THE SIX I'S : A PROBLEM–SOLVING/DECISION–MAKING FRAMEWORK

IDENTIFY
ISOLATE
INVOLVE
INVESTIGATE
IMPLEMENT
INQUIRE

Limits of a Rational Approach to Decision-Making

Before we discuss the system we must draw attention to a few cautions. The above system, on the surface, seems to assume rationality. That is, it assumes that you as a decision maker have clear, unconflicting objectives, a perfect knowledge of the decision situation and can gather all possible alternatives and predict all consequences. Put simply, it assumes you can accurately foresee the outcomes of your decision. We all know this is not true.

Classical decision-making theory approached decision-making as a purely rational process. It assumed that decision makers think and act completely objectively. It also assumed that decision makers know all the alternatives and possible consequences of a situation. In the 1950s several scholars began to challenge this notion and developed so-called *limited rational models*. Perhaps the most famous of these was Herbert Simon (1951) who proposed the concept of *bounded rationality*. He stated that decisions were made through a 'satisficing' rather than an 'optimising' mode. In simple terms, Simon believed that decision makers usually settled for the best available decision under the circumstances they faced. You will probably agree that this is a much more realistic view.

Lindbloom (1959) maintained that decisions were made through an incremental process. He characterised the decision process as a method of successive limited comparisons, proposing that decisions were made in 'fits and starts' and 'bits and pieces', rather than by any great design (Jones, 1970).

A more in-depth analysis of decision-making over the years has shown us that decision-making is affected by a number of factors, such as political considerations, organisational constraints, ideological beliefs and market forces.

Whereas the decision framework we present obviously assumes rationality, we have attempted to take care when making definitive statements about what will happen. We do not believe you can possibly predict all outcomes or consequences. Nor do we believe it is possible to collect all relevant information involved in a problem. We do believe however that you need some type of structured format for approaching decision-making. We have provided this structure but tried to frame it in as realistic a way as possible.

Identify

> It isn't that they can't see the solution.
> It is that they can't see the problem.
> G.K. Chesterton, *The Scandal of Father Brown*

The first stage in decision-making is recognising that a problem exists which requires a decision. Before you proceed with the decision-making process, make sure the decision you are about to make is actually yours to make. If it is not – leave it alone. You will often find as a manager that people are very generous at sharing problems, and if they can, they will off-load them!

You must try to anticipate problems and identify them when they occur. Make sure you know what the problem is before you set out to make a decision. As Peter Drucker once said: 'There're few things as useless – if not as dangerous – as the right answer to the wrong question.'

When most people are faced with a decision situation they tend to 'attack' what they perceive as the problem without understanding what causes it.

Think of what could happen if a doctor treated the surface symptoms of a sickness rather than trying to ascertain and treat the causes. He would probably spend most of his time prescribing pain-killers to relieve the symptoms, but few of his patients would be cured. The causes of the pain would remain. Read the case in Application Task 6.2 and then answer the questions which necessitate a correct identification of the problem.

APPLICATION TASK 6.2

MARK'S CASE

Mark Tain owned a small business which manufactured and marketed specialised bathroom fixtures. He had two outlets with a manager and five staff in each. His small factory was managed by his cousin Lynn and employed thirty-two people. Recently his profits had fallen sharply – he had to do something about it. He had been thinking about the problem for almost a week, and had decided on his own that the falling profits must be due to inefficient staff. He had noticed that the staff at one of his outlets seemed lazy and listless. After all, Louis's store in Fairdale Shopping Centre, which sold similar products to his, seemed to be doing better than ever. Mark decided to cut staff from all three work sites, believing this would restore his profitability. He had made his decision and would inform his employees forthwith.

Did Mark examine his problem closely enough? Was he treating the symptom or the cause? Did he really know the cause of his problem? He assumed, apparently without referring to his managers or anyone else, that his staff were inefficient – he did not look deeper. Perhaps you can be more insightful than Mark. Use the space below to identify some of the possible causes of his problem.

Possible causes:

1.

2.

3.

Stott, K. and Walker, A., *Making Management Work.* © 1992 Simon & Schuster (Asia) Pte Ltd.

We do not think Mark examined his problem carefully enough. Some reasons for his slump in profitability which he did not consider may have been:

1.   Increased competition from other firms.
2.   Over-priced products.
3.   High costs such as rent, raw materials, overtime, power.
4.   Unmotivated, bored employees.
5.   Inadequate marketing strategies.
6.   Dishonest or inefficient management.
7.   Change in shopping patterns.
8.   Depressed local economy.
9.   Outlet policies on credit for tradesman.
10.   Poorly trained staff.

Mark may have jumped the gun with his decision to retrench employees. If he had looked closer he would have discovered that Louis's, one of his competitors, had reduced the price of their products and embarked on an aggressive marketing campaign – *that* may have been closer to the reason Mark's profits were suffering.

Thankfully, most of us are not as careless or reactive as Mark, but his case should serve as a reminder. The decision situation, or problem, is not always as it appears on the surface. You must delve into the apparent symptoms to identify the causes. Sometimes you will have to look very deeply to really understand the problem and what is causing it.

You can use a number of strategies to enhance your problem identification skills.

1.   Look for discrepancies between what exists and what you would consider 'typical'.
2.   Examine cause–effect relationships.
3.   Consult those who are in a position to offer insights or different perspectives into a decision situation.
4.   Examine the situation from different angles.
5.   Be open, accepting that even you may be part of the cause of the problem.
6.   Consciously monitor performance to uncover when things are not going according to plan.
7.   Look out for problems that keep recurring. This usually indicates they have not been fully understood.

Additionally, you can try to anticipate problems or identify them when they first occur. They can be identified earlier by:

- Listening to and observing employees in order to stay in touch with concerns involving their job, the company and their feelings toward colleagues and management.
- Keeping your eye out for unusual or inconsistent behaviour; this may reflect some underlying problem.
- If appropriate, stay informed about what the 'opposition' is doing.

Once you have identified the 'real' problem or situation, and understand its causes you must make one of your first decisions. Decide whether to:

- Do nothing (a decision not to make a decision is a decision).
- Place the problem on hold but under observation and return to it at a later date.
- Attempt to control the problem.
- Move ahead to find a solution and make more decisions.

Your initial identification and understanding of the problem will allow you to decide on the type of decision you need to make. If it can be decided by routine procedures it will require little further clarification. Remember, not all problems require the same depth of analysis. Part of your skills as a decision maker involves identifying the different types of problems and how then to proceed with your analysis.

In business, many decisions involve more than one decision. When you have identified the problem, and decided to search for a solution, or make a decision, you should attempt to isolate further details and decisions within decisions.

> *Identify causes not symptoms.*

Isolate

You understand the decision situation, you have identified the cause, but still need to isolate or diagnose other relevant, related details. In other words, you must define the problem more clearly and discover the specific challenges it offers. Does it, for example, relate to a group? If so, team members need to understand the problem and decide on its intricacies.

Your isolation analysis will involve:

Gathering Data about the Situation

This involves being able to distinguish between fact and opinion. Especially in interpersonal problems, people's opinions can be powerful and affected by emotion. You need to collect and organise data relevant to the problem. Realistically you will not be able to gather all the information you would like, so you must prioritise what is most important.

Defining the Scope of the Problem

Consider who and what is involved. Is it a problem with the potential to affect the whole organisation or only a few members? Is it an interpersonal, systems or team problem? Such factors can have an impact on the resources you allocate to solution-searching. If, for example, the problem threatens the competitiveness of your organisation and costs money, you will obviously commit considerable resources to the cause. The scope will also help determine who should be involved. This issue is dealt with in the next section. It needs to be mentioned here however because wide-ranging problems are best analysed by a group of people, not an individual.

Determining the Consequences of the Problem

Decide on the possible consequences of the problem to see if it provides further analysis and commitment of resources (Lewis and Kelly, 1986).

Considering Possible Constraints to Problem Solution

Are there any factors which may prevent a satisfactory solution? Such factors are often difficult to detect. They often stem from political sources. If the boss instituted a specific programme and initial analysis points to its ineffectiveness, it may not be worth your time, resources and energy (or job) in trying to solve the problem.

Gathering data to isolate intricacies of your problems can be hard work. It is a good idea to solicit the help of others. You can analyse and diagnose official records, interview employees or superiors and conduct surveys. Defining the scope can also be complicated. It involves you (and often your team) in deciding the importance and complexity of the situation. Consequences and constraints which can affect problem solution also require thoughtful diagnosing. Isolating these details helps you determine the problem's importance and provides useful details of the problem's intricacies and challenges. This in turn can increase the chance of your arriving at a worthwhile decision. Application Tasks 6.3 and 6.4 present one method for practising some of these skills.

The isolation stage involves analysing or diagnosing the problem you identified in the first stage: delving deeper into the real causes of the problem and attempting to detail why it is a problem. You also consider who is involved and what possible consequences or constraints could block its solution.

APPLICATION TASK 6.3

CONSTRAINTS

1.   Think of a problem you currently face at work. This will of course require some type of decision. Write the problem below:

2.   Write the problem in the centre rectangle of the Considering Constraints form (CCF1).
3.   Think about the constraints which may influence the problem and write them in the surrounding boxes.
4.   When you have completed the boxes think about how the constraints identified provide useful details which can maximise the potential for a 'right' decision.

CONSIDERING CONSTRAINTS (CCF1)

Constraint

PROBLEM

Notes: How can these constraints influence you in making a 'right' decision?

At this stage, you may wish to formalise what you intend to achieve through the decision process. This involves setting targets or objectives and perhaps establishing criteria which can be used to judge decision outcome effectiveness. Targets should be 'set in terms of reducing or eliminating the root causes of the problem' (Leong, 1990 : 36). At this stage the targets should take into account the information presently available. Targets and outcome criteria may have to be altered during the later stages of the decision-making process.

You may also decide that the problem is so complex that it needs to be broken up into smaller segments. Different teams can work on the different 'bits' and meet regularly to keep each other informed.

You have now completed some of the important tasks involved in decision-making and are ready to move onto actually solving the problem and making a decision. Before you do this however it is vital that you decide (yes, another decision) who should be involved in making the actual decision.

APPLICATION TASK 6.4

CONSEQUENCES

1. Think of a problem you currently face at work. This will of course require some type of decision. Write the problem below:

2. Write the problem in the centre rectangle of the Considering Constraints form (CCF2).
3. Think about the consequences which may influence the problem and write them in the surrounding boxes.
4. When you have completed the boxes think about how the constraints identified provide useful details which can maximise the potential for a 'right' decision.

CONSIDERING CONSEQUENCES (CCF2)

Consequence

PROBLEM

Notes: How can these consequences influence you in making a 'right' decision?

Stott, K. and Walker, A., *Making Management Work.* © 1992 Simon & Schuster (Asia) Pte Ltd.

SUMMARY

Isolate Relevant Details By:

- Gathering data about the situation.
- Defining the scope of the problem.
- Determining the consequences of the problem.
- Determining possible constraints to problem solution.

Involve

> There are differences in who should be involved in reaching a decision, in the process by which this should be done and whether it is recorded.
>
> (Stewart, 1985 : 26)

Much has been written about when, if and how to involve others in the decision-making process. Over the last decade or so, organisations have moved toward participative decision-making. In doing so many have encountered difficulties when they have tried to involve groups in all decisions. There is now a realisation that although participative decision-making is valuable in many situations, in others it can actually be counter-productive. We will briefly explain some of the thinking related to when to involve employees. This coverage is not intended to be comprehensive.

When to Involve Others

Expertise and Relevance

When, and how much, to involve employees in decision-making has been the focus of much investigation. Edwin Bridges (1967) researched this area and developed what he called the *zone of acceptance*. The zone of acceptance refers to an invisible area of decision acceptance perceived by employees. If employees are likely to accept your decision without being involved, it is considered to be inside their zone of acceptance. If they are unlikely to accept your decision, it is outside their zone of acceptance.

Bridges proposes two tests to identify situations that fall within the employees' zone of acceptance. He labels these:

1. *The test of relevance*: Do your employees have a personal stake in the decision outcome?

2. *The test of expertise*: Do your employees have any expertise which could assist in making a quality decision?

If your employees have a personal stake and can contribute some expert knowledge to a decision situation, then the decision falls *outside* their zone of acceptance. In such cases the employees should be involved in the decision-making process. Conversely, if employees have no personal stake in a decision and have no expertise to offer, the decision falls *within* their zone of acceptance. In such decision situations, employees should not be involved in the decision process. Involving employees in decisions which are within their zone of acceptance is pointless, and can even be counter-productive and cause resentment. Some examples may assist understanding.

1. You are considering extending the hours that your reception facility stays open to deal with customers. Your main purpose for doing this is because you believe evenings are more convenient for many of your customers.

    Obviously your employees have a stake in this decision. They will be the ones who will have to rearrange their time to work the extended hours. You must know whether they would be willing to do this. Additionally, their expert advice on whether or not their customers will be more disposed to use the extended hours is needed. The decision falls *outside* their zone of acceptance. It would certainly be advantageous, if not vital, to seek their involvement in the decision.

2. You want to alter the format of your annual executive report to the CEO to make it more readable.

    Your employees probably have little interest in how the executive report is presented. Few if any employees have any expertise in writing or presenting such reports. Your decision on how to proceed clearly falls *inside* their zone of acceptance, so you do not need to involve them.

An expanded version of Bridges' proposal by Hoy and Miskel (1987) is presented in Figure 6.2.

Bridges expanded his ideas by also commenting on the possible extent of involvement of employees in decision-making. Situations where employees have both a stake and expertise are labelled Type I situations. In these circumstances employees should be involved in decision-making from the early stages. On the other hand, if employees have no stake in the problem, they do not need to be involved at all. This is called a Type IV situation.

Type II and III situations fall somewhere between the two extremes and relate to when employees have either, but not both, a stake in or expertise related to the decision.

Quality and Acceptance

Other considerations about when to involve employees concerns the quality of the decision and, once again, the acceptance by employees of the decision (Maier, 1963). The amount of time available for making the decision also influences who can or should be involved (Morris and Sashkin, 1976).

When considering whether to involve others or not you should think about how important the quality of the decision is to you and your organisation. You should also think about how important the acceptance of your employees is to the effective implementation of the decision. Maier (1963) produced four 'either/or' conditions to guide group involvement in decision-making. These are shown in Figure 6.3.

Figure 6.2
When to Involve Employees: The Zone of Acceptance

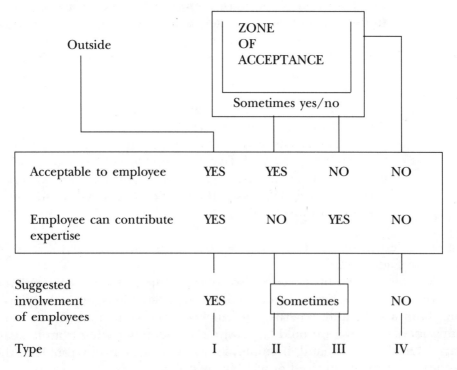

Source: Adapted from Hoy and Miskel (1987 : 340).

Figure 6.3
Quality and Acceptance

CONDITION 1 : Neither quality nor acceptance is important.

Involvement : No involvement is required; you might as well flip a coin.

CONDITION 2 : Acceptance is important, quality is not.

Involvement : Involvement is appropriate and necessary. These type of situations usually involve 'people' decisions, such as work conditions, overtime rates or holiday schedules.

CONDITION 3 : Quality is important, acceptance is not.

Involvement : Although involvement of employees is not vital for acceptance, it may be wise to involve others whose expertise can assist in making a quality decision.

CONDITION 4 : Both quality and acceptance are important.

Involvement : These situations are best dealt with through participative processes.

APPLICATION TASK 6.5

Think of some situations at work which would fit into the four situations and write them in below. We have provided an example in each category to help you. When you have finished each section think about whether you agree with the involvement level suggested in the text.

1. Quality – NO, Acceptance – NO
   Whether to hold a meeting in the morning or the afternoon.

2.   Acceptance – YES,   Quality – NO
     Which employees will be able to take time off over the Christmas holidays and who will have to work?

3.   Quality – YES,   Acceptance – NO
     Where to get the best deal on components for a new product.

4.   Quality – YES,   Acceptance – YES
     The design of a new system to streamline production and maximise work time.

Stott, K. and Walker, A., *Making Management Work*. © 1992 Simon & Schuster (Asia) Pte Ltd.

Time

Time pressures can also influence the intensity of employee involvement in decision-making. There are two major considerations:

1.   How much time is available and required to reach a decision?
2.   How much time is needed to develop an understanding of the decision outcome by those expected to implement the decision?

Often you would like more time to make a decision, but this is not always possible. Organisational or market forces, for example, can make a quick decision critical. Take the case of a young doctor in an inner-city hospital when he was presented with a gunshot victim. He had little experience and would have liked to consult some of his more experienced colleagues, but obviously did not have the time – it was a matter of life or death. He had to make a decision and carry it out regardless of the consequences.

Hopefully you will not be faced with too many decisions as critical as the young doctor's, but you will often face time constraints. This can increase the time required to gain employee commitment to implementation of the decision.

If you are faced with time restrictions you will find it difficult to involve others in the decision process. Quite simply, if you make the decision your-self it may not take you very long but it will take longer to explain, gain employee commitment and implement. Conversely, the more people you involve, the longer the decision will take to make, but then it will be quicker and easier to implement and commitment will be more forthcoming. This is shown graphically in Figure 6.4.

Figure 6.4
Time and Decisions

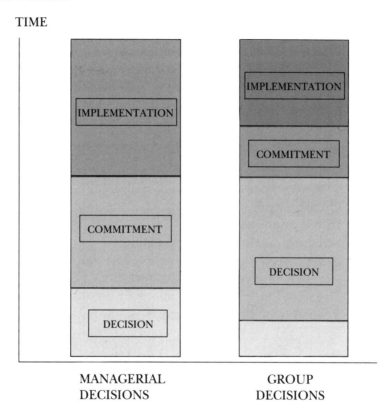

TIME

IMPLEMENTATION

IMPLEMENTATION

COMMITMENT

COMMITMENT

DECISION

DECISION

MANAGERIAL
DECISIONS

GROUP
DECISIONS

SUMMARY

When Involving Others Consider:

*   Expertise and relevance.
*   Quality and acceptance.
*   Time.

Vroom and Decision-Making

Perhaps the best-known practical model developed to determine the most
effective level and manner of subordinate involvement in managerial decisions was proposed by Vroom and Yetton (1973). Vroom followed earlier
researchers and suggested three considerations which have a bearing on
decision effectiveness – *quality, acceptance* and *time*. We have seen these before.
What made Vroom's model more comprehensive was that he identified five
distinct styles or options for making decisions. These were:

1. Make the decision yourself.
2. Obtain information from others, then make the decision.
3. Ask for individual advice, then decide whether to use it.
4. Ask for advice from a group, then decide whether to use it.
5. Share the problem with others and read comments.

Vroom also listed what he considered the key characteristics of a decision
situation:

1. Quality required.
2. Information necessary.
3. Structure of the decision situation.
4. Acceptance by employee for effective implementation.
5. Acceptance if made by manager.
6. Degree of employee acceptance of organisational goals.
7. Possibility of conflict caused by solution.

Vroom and Yetton developed a '*Decision Tree Approach*' for identifying the
optimum decision style that the manager would find suitable in a particular
situation.

When thinking about who and how much to involve others in decisions
you should also consider how you work best. You need to be aware of your
own values and assumptions and how much you trust your employees. If you
do not trust them to contribute to decisions it is pointless going through the
process of involving them. Of course, you should be willing to accept any
consequences of this. You should also be aware of any organisational preference for decision-making styles; this can influence the extent of involvement.
In Figure 6.5 is a list of questions you should ask yourself when considering
who to involve in a decision. The list can also be used as a checklist for
ensuring you have considered all relevant factors.

Figure 6.5
Factors to Consider: Involvement of Others

ASK YOURSELF: HAVE I CONSIDERED?

TASK	
The complexity of the decision which needs to be made?	
What constraints we may be faced with?	
The expertise necessary for making the decision?	
The possible consequences of various solutions?	
ORGANISATION	
How much time is available?	
Whether the organisation prefers a particular DM style?	
Whether any political considerations may be involved?	
The resources we have available?	
How the organisation usually responds to change?	
EMPLOYEES	
The expertise the employees can contribute?	
Whether the implementation of the solution depends on employee acceptance?	
The expectations of my employees?	
The needs (developmental) of my employees?	
The relevance of the problem to my employees?	
ME	
My own values which may affect the decision?	
How much I trust employees to be involved?	
My own assumptions regarding my employees?	

Stott, K. and Walker, A., *Making Management Work.* © 1992 Simon & Schuster (Asia) Pte Ltd.

Decision-Making Styles or Methods

It is not enough to consider when to involve others in a decision, you must also think about how much involvement they should have. The involvement may be formal or informal, such as simply asking for ideas. You may involve other employees at any stage in the decision process, or throughout the process. Whereas we believe different decisions require different methods, we would suggest that when you are faced with complex problems the involvement of others is essential. You can get much richer, more innovative ideas from a group than from one person.

The type of decision affects who should be involved in making the decision. This in turn determines which method can be used. You have a number of decision-making strategies at your disposal. Each has its inherent advantages and disadvantages. Individual managers need to assess the individual decision needed before deciding which method is the most suitable. You have at least six decision methods available to you. Each of these methods involves others to a greater or lesser degree. Think of the methods which are discussed as being along a continuum with many variations in between: from *autocratic* to *consensus.*

Figure 6.6
The Methods Continuum

Autocratic   Consensus

The *Autocratic Method* is when you make the decision completely on your own and then announce it to your employees. When you make an unpopular decision you may try to sell it to the staff, but will not invite conversation or challenge.

In the *Final Say Method* you allow other employees to discuss and suggest solutions to a problem. You may or may not take these suggestions into account when making the decision. You can allow situations to be discussed by staff in an open manner but at the end of the discussion you make the decision by yourself.

The *Elite Group Method* involves you and at least one other person in making the decision without consulting others. You discuss and generate solutions, make the decision and present it to the remainder of the staff. You may even discuss the basis of your decision in front of other employees.

The *Consultancy Method* places you in the position of a consultant. You may make an initial, tentative decision and present it to the group for discussion and input. You carefully and openly consider the group's opinions before making the decision. Often you will arrive at an initial decision and then present it to the group for discussion. You must keep an open mind and allow yourself to be swayed by arguments put forward by other employees. You also allow others to refine your initial decisions or, conversely, offer suggestions and support for other points of view. The final decision is made by you, carefully and openly considering other points of view.

The *Majority Rules Method* is a democratic method which involves all group members in the decision process by allowing each member an equal vote. The group votes on what decision to take. The decision which receives the most votes wins and becomes *the* decision.

The *Consensus Method* involves all staff members in making the decision. A decision cannot be reached until all staff agree on a specific decision. This method can produce high-quality decisions because of the intense and varied input, but can be very time-consuming. Consensus is a decision method for making full use of available staff resources, and for resolving conflicts and major problems creatively.

Consensus is difficult to reach as all group members must agree on the final decision. Complete unanimity is not the goal as it is rarely achieved, but each group member should be able to accept the group ranking on the basis of logic and feasibility. When all group members feel this way you have reached consensus, and the judgement may be entered as a team decision. This means, in effect, that a single person can block the team if he thinks it is necessary. It is unlikely that every detail will meet with everyone's complete approval. Voting is *not* allowed. In consensus decision-making you must be personally convinced that the decision is the right one and agree to go along with it.

Each of these decision-making methods have certain advantages and disadvantages. These are related to the considerations we discussed earlier in this section. Table 6.1 outlines the strengths and weaknesses of each approach. When you have read the table, complete Application Task 6.6.

Your selection of a particular decision-making method or style will depend on factors such as those you were asked to consider (see Factors to Consider: Involvement of Others). In the previous application task you listed a decision situation and described why you believed it was suitable. Now let us try to tie those considerations in a structured way to your selection of a decision-making method. Here are two methods for doing this. Read the following

Table 6.1
Methods of Decision-Making: Some Strengths and Weaknesses

METHOD	STRENGTH	WEAKNESS
AUTOCRATIC	Time-saving Good for standard decisions Leadership expertise	Little commitment Resentment One person's trade

FINAL SAY	Uses some group
	    resources
	Allows for some
	    innovation
		Little commitment
		Conflict remains
		Increases competition

ELITE GROUP	Time-saving Open discussion Ideas generated	Little commitment Conflict remains Little interaction
CONSULTANCY	Group input Open discussion Ideas generated	Who is expert? Openness of leader
MAJORITY RULES	Time-saving Closes discussion	Alienated minority Not full commitment Easy way out
CONSENSUS	Innovative Commitment All abilities utilised Serious decisions	Very time-consuming High degree of teamwork skill needed

decision situation and the two examples shown in Figures 6.7 and 6.8 which show how a particular method was selected.

Decision situation

Jenny is the manager of a personnel department. Her department has grown to such an extent that she has been told she can hire an assistant manager. This manager will be responsible for dealing with all staff matters within the department.

APPLICATION TASK 6.6

Try to write one decision you have faced in the last few weeks, or are facing now which may be suited to each of the methods. Also write a short sentence which justifies why this method is appropriate.

1. Autocratic Method:

Decision Situation:

Why this method?

2. Final Say Method:

Decision Situation:

Why this method?

3. Elite Group Method:

Decision Situation:

Why this method?

4.   Consultancy Method:

Decision Situation:

Why this method?

5.   Majority Rules Method:

Decision Situation:

Why this method?

6.   Consensus Method:

Decision Situation:

Why this method?

Stott, K. and Walker, A., *Making Management Work.* © 1992 Simon & Schuster (Asia) Pte Ltd.

Why: Since the person selected must be accepted by other employees and Jenny has three months to select the person, she can and should consult others. Jenny cannot select anyone already on staff and realises that choosing the wrong person could damage her department. She must make a careful decision. She wants a person in the job, however, who is a college graduate and has a similar management style to her own. She will probably shortlist a few candidates and present her suggestions to the staff. She will allow them some input and even let them meet the candidates. She will genuinely consider their opinions when final selection is necessary.

Figure 6.7
Example 1: Consideration Factors

TASK	ORGANISATION	EMPLOYEES	YOU
Not too complex Cannot select a person already on staff Wrong selection could damage department harmony	Have three months to hire Selection style up to me	Must accept new person Must be able to relate to people and meet this expectation Staff used to being responsible Final choice very relevant to staff Staff know this job well	You want someone with good HR skills. A college graduate would be best Should have same style as me

Decision-making method selected: consultancy method.

Why: We now follow this system and see what Jenny may decide. Firstly, she is concerned about the quality of the decision. She is also concerned about her employees accepting the decision. She has a reasonable amount of time (three months) in which to make the decision so there is no urgency. She may decide therefore to utilise either the consultative or the consensus approach. If she had less time, or was not concerned about her employees' acceptance of the new assistant manager, she may have arrived at a different decision method.

Figure 6.8
Deciding on a Method: Quality, Acceptance, Time

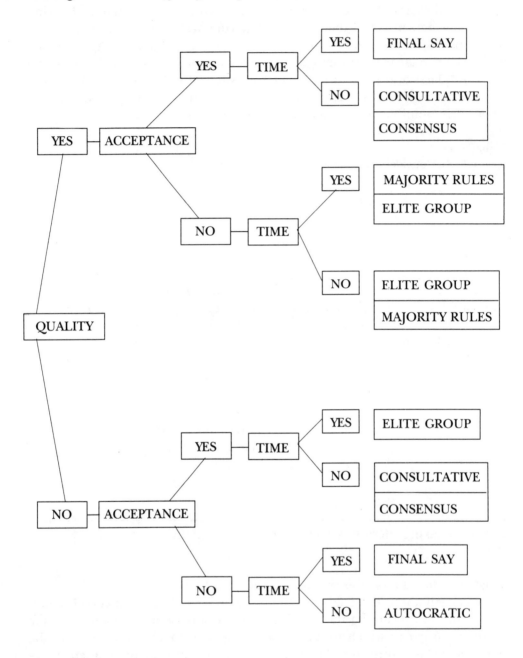

Decision-making method selected: consultative or consensus.

Disadvantages of Participative Decision-Making

The two methods shown are only suggestions. Once you have developed your decision-making skills, similar processes will become automatic. Remember, participative decision-making is not applicable in all situations and its advantages are somewhat negated, depending on the problem. Participative decision-making takes much time, and involves discussion, conflict and debate. As the group grows, co-ordination becomes more difficult and efficiency can suffer.

Another major problem is labelled *groupthink*. We looked at this problem briefly in Chapter 3 on Developing Effective Teams. It occurs when a team has reached a high level of maturity.

Groups who work together can often become too complacent. Strong cohesiveness can promote uniformity in the group. This uniformity can produce a sameness in the group which causes them to easily agree with each other. Groups can also become arrogant about their decisions, believing they are always correct. This can be extremely detrimental to the group's creativity and competitiveness. This is called groupthink. Watch out for these signs:

- The group ignores dangers, takes too many risks and assumes everything will work as planned.
- The group rationalises its decisions so it can ignore outside opportunities.
- The group believes its decisions are morally correct, regardless of ethical considerations.
- The group negatively stereotypes rivals outside the group.
- The group pressures any members who disagree with the group, accusing them of disloyalty.
- Group members do not express reservations or arguments with the group's decisions.
- The group believes all members agree with the decision made; silence is agreement.
- Some group members believe it is their role to protect the group from advance information that may threaten its 'togetherness'.

(Janis, 1982)

You may have observed this in several situations: an established sports club committee; the board of directors; the cabinet team in some political systems. It is obvious that groupthink is a threat to effective, creative decisions. It is important to recognise its presence. Janis (1982) recommends a set of prescriptions for counteracting situations which can foster groupthink.

Battling Groupthink

1. Be aware that groupthink exists.
2. You as leader should remain neutral when allocating decision-making tasks.
3. Accept and encourage objections, doubts and criticisms.
4. Always consider unpopular alternatives; encourage 'innovators' or 'plants' in the group (see Chapter 5, Developing Team Roles).
5. Divide the group in half to consider alternatives.
6. Be alert for warning signals from rival organisations.
7. After reaching agreement, solicit comments on remaining doubts.
8. Include outside experts when making vital decisions.
9. Test tentative decisions with trusted colleagues outside the group.
10. Establish a number of groups to work on the same problem if it is really important.

Before we leave this important section try to apply some of what you have read to Application Task 6.7, Consensual Anita. Read the case carefully and then attempt the accompanying questions. If possible, discuss your answers with a colleague.

Anita probably should have used a decision method other than the consensus approach. She had some ideas about where she wanted the targets to be but did not communicate these to her employees. She may have been better off using the consultancy method, presenting her ideas and then asking for input. This way she could at least have guided the decision and retained some discretion over its outcome. She made the mistake of trying to involve her employees in every decision. This problem simply was not suited to this method. By trying to change decision methods 'mid-stream' she further confused her employees and alienated a number of them (the minority). At this stage Anita should probably submit her own projections and then sell the idea to her employees. This is not an ideal solution but she has left herself few options. This, of course, is not the only interpretation of Anita's case.

In this section we have discussed the how, when and why of involving others in the decision processes. Involvement can come in any stage of the decision process, or throughout. It is essential however that if you face a complex decision, you involve others in the next stage of the decision-making framework: *investigate.*

APPLICATION TASK 6.7

CONSENSUAL ANITA

Anita Lopez had been appointed to her first managerial position two months ago. She was now facing her first really major decision: what output targets to set for next year. She knew that if she did a good job she would really be noticed by senior management. She felt she was quite used to making decisions and had recently completed a course in 'Decision-Making Strategies'. She had a full month to submit her figures so did not feel she was pressed for time. Anita was convinced that her employees should be involved in all decisions. Anita strongly believed in a consensus-type approach.

She called a meeting with all twelve of her staff and presented them with the decision which needed to be made:
'What should our target figures be for next year?'

Of course she had some ideas of her own but believed the employees' figures could be more realistic. She announced at the meeting: 'We all know that we have to decide. I want you to make a decision on our targets for next year. Let's talk about it.'

She was surprised at the comments which then emanated.

'Well, they're too high now, definitely should stay the same.'

'We can double our output if you follow my suggestions to ...'

'I am already overworked.'

'Five per cent tops.'

'I need new equipment if you want increases.'

'What do the other units have to do?'

'Do we get any extra money?'

'We could produce more if Brian pulled his weight.'

The whole meeting went on like this and broke up with no decision at all. Anita met her staff twice more before she realised that the deadline was getting awfully close. She had to have her targets submitted by next Tuesday, only eight days away. She could see that consensus was not going to work and decided to get the men to vote on the proposed targets.

On Friday she asked for the vote and was forced to insist that the projection be higher than this year. She said she would go along with the majority. The team voted. Seven of the twelve employees voted for a 7 per cent increase over last year's targets. Almost half her employees walked out of the meeting mumbling 'too low' or 'too high'.

Anita was dumbfounded. All the other units had set targets of at least 15 per cent over this year's. She had hoped for at least a 20 per cent increase on existing output. Anita did not know what to do. She was faced with another major decision. She could either impose the targets on her unit, which involved disregarding the involvement she had vigorously encouraged, or tell the boss that she was only going for a 7 per cent increase. Either way she would lose.

Questions:

1. Which decision method do you think Anita should have used?
2. Why would you suggest another method?
3. Did Anita make any mistakes when trying to involve her employees? If so, what were they?
4. Can you give Anita any advice on what she should do now?

Stott, K. and Walker, A., *Making Management Work.* © 1992 Simon & Schuster (Asia) Pte Ltd.

Investigate

Once you understand the intricacies of the problem, you need to 'get down to the business' of making the decision. The *investigate* stage involves the generation of alternatives, evaluation or analysis of alternatives, and the selection of alternatives: a decision. This is the stage in which creativity is essential.

When faced with problems there are almost always a number of possible solutions. In some cases there are many alternatives. If there is no choice of alternatives, there is no decision to be made. Your job is to use your team to identify as many alternatives as possible. Some books will tell you to consider *all* alternatives and *all* their possible consequences. We all know that this is impossible in most situations. We do not have clairvoyancy skills. What you must do is consider all the *available* alternatives, and then decide which offers the most practical solution. In other words you will select the best solution, the one which meets your objectives and which accounts for the constraints of the situation. Finding solutions to problems involves two processes: *creative thinking* and *analytical thinking*.

Creativity in Decision-Making

To begin, complete the questionnaire How Creative a Manager Am I? It will provide a starting point for understanding creativity by giving you a rough measure of your own managerial creativity. Tick the statements which best describe you, leaving any others blank. At this stage only complete the *first* column. Leave the second column (score) completely blank.

Questionnaire

HOW CREATIVE A MANAGER AM I?

		Tick	Score
1.	I like to play with ideas.	☐	☐
2.	I am uncomfortable with innovative employees.	☐	☐
3.	I am bound by organisation traditions.	☐	☐
4.	I am afraid of change.	☐	☐
5.	I often feel the need for change.	☐	☐
6.	I like an ordered environment and do not want it disturbed.	☐	☐
7.	I allow my staff to express themselves freely.	☐	☐
8.	I encourage staff to take risks.	☐	☐
9.	I value creativity among my staff.	☐	☐
10.	I tend to be complacent.	☐	☐
11.	I am willing to take risks.	☐	☐
12.	Other people seem to be more creative than I.	☐	☐
13.	I often miss opportunities.	☐	☐
14.	I feel embarrassed when I make mistakes.	☐	☐
15.	I give up easily when solutions to problems are not obvious.	☐	☐
16.	I persist with tasks.	☐	☐
17.	I have trouble generating ideas.	☐	☐
18.	I encourage novel solutions to problems.	☐	☐
19.	I try to learn from my mistakes.	☐	☐
20.	I dislike uncertainty.	☐	☐

Give yourself 5 points for each statement if you ticked numbers 1, 4, 5, 7, 8, 9, 11, 16, 18 and 19. Place your scores in the 'score boxes'. Then, total your scores. Place your score on the graph below.

```
0      10      20      30      40      50
```

If you have a high score, 35+, you have fairly high creativity, and tend to encourage creativity among your staff. The lower the score, the lower your creativity.

Everyone has the capacity to be creative. Creativity does not necessarily mean coming up with a unique, novel approach. More often than not it involves combining a number of ideas already tried in an imaginative fashion. If you wish to encourage creativity and generate more creative solutions, you need to be willing to meet four criteria. These are:

> - Have an open mind.
> - Take a risk.
> - Involve others.
> - Resist judgements.

Have an Open Mind

Treat each problem as a new and different problem. Do not simply apply existing solutions to any problem which arises. Be willing to listen to different ideas, no matter how bizarre they may sound. Some of the most innovative and powerful decisions have come from such 'seeds'. Encourage your staff to be open-minded by allowing them to comment on or criticise the 'status quo'.

Take a Risk

Many of us do not speak up because we are afraid of feeling foolish in front of others. Some managers actually accentuate these feelings among their employees by ridiculing their suggestions. This discourages them from contributing their ideas. Do not let the fact that something has never been done before stop you from trying it out. Although the saying 'risk takers go places' is often true, you must be prepared for some ideas to fail. You should treat these 'failures' as learning experiences. The extent of your risk must be calculated in relation to its possible costs, benefits and consequences to the organisation, and to you.

Involve Others

Run your ideas by employees and colleagues who are not involved in the decision process. These 'others' can often provide a perspective very different from your own. It is true that we often become too close to our problems and cannot see beyond certain boundaries. Involving others often also helps negate the dangers of groupthink, which we discussed earlier.

Resist Judgement

Try not to react to problems where the solution appears obvious. Encourage the generation of as many alternatives as possible before you judge their merit or otherwise. If you judge too quickly you will discourage open contribution and risk 'missing' creative decisions. I remember a meeting I attended where the manager chairing the meeting instantaneously judged every possible solution or alternative. His reply to suggestions included: 'tried that, didn't work', 'let's be sensible about this' and 'you're joking'. As the meeting went on, most members stopped offering solutions; the manager could not understand it. In frustration he mumbled: 'I give you a chance to contribute and this is what happens.' Whose fault was it that members stopped participating?

You can find some more tactics which are commonly used to stifle ideas in Chapter 16, Running Productive Meetings.

Generating Alternatives

All forms of creativity necessitate the generation of a large number of ideas. Often the best source of ideas comes from those employees who are somewhat unconventional. As you are probably aware, managing or leading such individuals can be troublesome, but, if you want insightful, innovative ideas, it is well worth it. One of the best techniques for the generation of alternatives is that of brainstorming.

Brainstorming proposes that ideas are best generated before they are evaluated. They require that you, and others included in the process, are open-minded, willing to take a risk, and suspend judgement. We now look at this process.

How to Use It

It would be advantageous if you could do Application Task 6.8 with a group of people. The brainstorming technique is more effective in group decision-making situations. You can also do it on your own (but it is more fun with someone else). First of all read the rules for brainstorming and then commence the task.

Nine rules for brainstorming (Sashkin and Morris, 1984 : 197):

1. Ask each participant explicitly to contribute an idea: 'Jane, what do you think?'
2. List every idea mentioned, even if it repeats a previous suggestion.
3. Record ideas making them visible to everyone. A flipchart or whiteboard is ideal.

4. Constantly encourage participants to contribute more ideas when they seem to 'run out'.

5. Ensure that before you stop, *all* ideas have been posted. You may even say:'Let's get one more idea from everyone.'

6. Encourage silly, amusing and even apparently 'crazy' ideas. These suggestions can often be creative and eventually tailored to reality. Brainstorming should be fun.

7. Contribute and record your own ideas. This can be done to energise the group when they have slowed down.

8. Encourage participants to expand and add to ideas already posted. This should not involve discussing or judging the ideas in any way.

9. No one must evaluate their ideas during the brainstorming period. If this happens in either a negative or a positive way, your job is to ignore it and ask the 'culprit' to add another idea, thereby channelling participation into a contribution.

APPLICATION TASK 6.8

Try to brainstorm alternative solutions to the following situation:

Your department has been charged with increasing the sales of one of your company's least-known items, 'Animal Glasses'. Your job is to develop an advertising campaign to attract buyers.

Alternatives:

If you did the task with others you probably thought of some novel solutions. Did you adhere to the rules? Brainstorming is a very time-consuming activity. If you have time constraints you may not be able to conduct as thorough a session as is necessary.

The ability to generate alternatives is just as important as selecting the correct alternative. Many of these alternatives however will be impractical or cannot be properly evaluated.

Evaluating or Analysing Alternatives

There are a number of ways of evaluating suggestions, alternatives or ideas. You can eliminate some through asking the following questions:

1. Do my organisation's physical facilities make the alternatives impractical?
2. Does the cost of the alternative make it impossible for the organisation?
3. Have your bosses indicated that certain alternatives are not acceptable?

Asking these questions will often eliminate a number of alternatives, but, if you have 'generated' correctly, there will be many remaining. When evaluating these you have the difficult job of attempting to predict the consequences of all possible outcomes. As mentioned earlier, it is impossible to foresee all consequences, but by careful thinking and analysis you can identify many. Once again a group approach to this may be more advantageous.

Drucker (1955) recommends four timeless criteria for evaluating possible alternatives:

1. The risk in relation to the expected outcome.
2. The effort required.
3. The desired rate of change.
4. Availability of resources (human and material).

Consider the following problem, possible alternatives and consequences.

John's Big Dilemma

> *John is the owner and manager of a company which markets fitness equipment to health clubs and hotels throughout Southeast Asia. Lately business has been good, in fact, too good. His company has been flooded with orders. John can meet*

the equipment orders without any problems. However, it is impossible for him to provide staff to install and service the equipment, or to train the client's instructors in its use. The 'service angle' has been one of his major marketing strategies. If he reneges on his commitments, his reputation and consequently his profitability could suffer.

John realises the problem and has a brainstorming session with five of his employees. They have suggested the following list of alternatives:

Alternatives:

1. Cancel orders to small or less important customers.
2. Train extra employees to service the extra equipment.
3. Just give basic service and hope nothing major goes wrong.
4. Contract companies in the client's own countries to provide the service.
5. Slow down or stagger delivery so service commitments will not be all needed at the same time.
6. Merge with a rival company to draw on their resources.

The group sat down to analyse the various alternatives and their possible consequences.

Possible Consequences of Alternatives:

1. The small companies were still important to John. They were his 'bread and butter' and had always supported him. If he cancelled their orders they would probably go elsewhere – for good. John is not sure how they would react. If they did leave him, he could lose a source of steady profit and valued clients who, in many cases, had become friends.
2. The training of new employees has to be done in the United Kingdom and is a very expensive business. Frankly, the company could not afford to train more than three people. This would not relieve the situation significantly for some time.
3. Doing very basic service might be the answer, but John had to be prepared to take the risk that major breakdowns would not occur. He knew that this was not realistic. Furthermore, misuse could damage the equipment. John would also be responsible for this under warranty conditions. Personal injuries resulting from misuse could cost John dearly.
4. There were companies in the various countries which could fulfil the service and they were reasonably priced. The repu-

tation of some of the companies was, however, to put it mildly, 'unreliable'.

5.   Staggered delivery could be arranged, but since the company did not get paid until delivery, this could result in a serious cashflow problem which John could not afford with so many orders coming in.

6.   There were only two rival companies that could help with the service. They had both been trying to get a piece of John's 'action' for some time. They had much more to gain than him and he did not really like the way they did business.

What would you do if you were John? We will see what he decided to do a little later.

By considering consequences you may be conducting what has been labelled *marginal analysis*. The most commonly utilised forms of marginal analysis are *cost-effectiveness analysis* or *cost-benefit analysis*.

Whereas traditional marginal analysis dealt with 'dollars and cents', that is, comparing additional revenue to additional cost, cost-effectiveness and cost-benefit analyses attempt to deal with alternatives which cannot necessarily be captured in monetary or other specific measures.

Cost-effectiveness analysis is a technique for selecting the best alternative when objectives are not specifically related to sales costs or profits. It focuses on the results of a programme, helping you to weigh the potential benefits of each alternative against its potential cost, and then makes you compare the alternatives in terms of overall advantage (Koontz and Weihrich, 1988 : 139).

John conducted a type of cost-effectiveness analysis when considering alternative 1. Not only did he consider the possible costs in terms of money, but also in terms of human factors such as friendship and loyalty. He has to weigh the possible benefits of his new contracts to his company against his cost (financial and human).

Evaluation or analysis of alternatives can be very time-consuming but must be as thorough and systematic as possible if you are to make the best decision. You saw in John's example that each alternative has a number of possible outcomes. Analysing them forces you to narrow your options. It is now time to make a decision and decide on the 'best' alternative.

Making the Decision

We assume you have reduced the number of available alternatives. In most situations you will not be able to make a decision using complete information or predict all consequences. You also have little control over political factors within or outside of the organisation. Your final decision then is usually the one that is fairly good but not necessarily perfect.

You have to weigh the costs and consequences of your alternative. Remember, you may have to be creative. Let us return to John and see what decision his company made. Their solutions included aspects of two of their possible alternatives. John and his team sent a memo to all company employees informing them of the decision.

Figure 6.9
John's Solution

MEMO

From :   John
To   :   All Staff

You are all aware of the 'fortunate' predicament we are in and we have decided on a course of action. We will immediately hire three trainee service technicians and send Peter, Chris and Jenny to England for a 'crash' training course. In the meantime, we will contract service companies in all cities to install immediately and service the equipment and train staff (company names attached). As soon as Peter, Chris and Jenny return from England they will be sent to Bangkok, Kuala Lumpur and Brunei to take over from the local companies for as long as necessary. We hope this will solve our problem.

Thanks for your support.
Everything will be fine.

Do you agree with John's decision? Can you see how he made his decision? When you select an alternative you can draw on three strategies:

To select an alternative draw on:

- Your previous experience.
- A systematic analysis.
- Pilot-testing.

John drew on his experience to make the decision. He knew some firms had a bad reputation and that equipment was prone to breakdown if not serviced properly. If you want to 'try out' an alternative, you can, but be prepared for the expense it may involve. Obviously, you cannot do this with too many alternatives, but if the decision is vitally important, like deciding the future direction of your organisation, it may be worthwhile. Whereas both these methods are useful, they are no substitute for systematic analysis in most cases.

John conducted a systematic analysis when making his decision. He considered the potential positive and negative outcomes of each decision, and considered possible costs and benefits. He may have used a chart similar to the one in Figure 6.10. You can easily fill in his problem, alternatives and possible consequences from his story. He also used research to decide such things as cost of training, cost of contracts, reputation of companies, and time needed.

Figure 6.10
John's Decision: Example 1

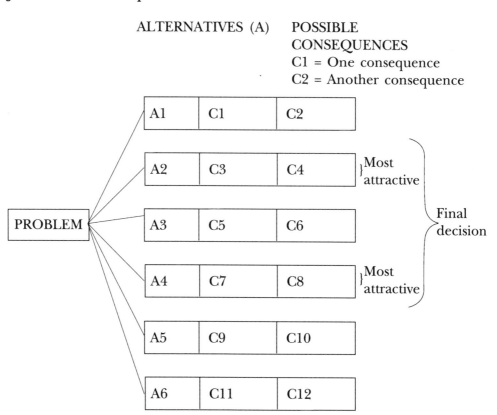

He may also have used a form such as the following alternative: Consequences for Decision Form (ACD), shown in Figure 6.11.

Figure 6.11
ACD Form: John's Decision: Example 2

ALTERNATIVE 3: GIVE BASIC SERVICE, HOPE NOTHING GOES WRONG		
POSSIBLE CONSEQUENCES	Positive	Negative
Basic service could meet the need	+	
Risk of breakdown (bad for reputation)		−
Risk of breakdown (cost of repair)		−
Personal injury from equipment (legal)		−
Decision on outcome: TOO RISKY		

When you have made the decision you should feel comfortable that you have done all within your power to give it the best chance of success. So when you have made the decision STICK TO IT. There are few things more frustrating to employees than to have their boss waiver, fence sit or change his mind. Quite simply, they will not be sure what to do, will lack direction, lose confidence in you and become demotivated.

There are no guarantees that the decision will be the right one. No one can guarantee success, but once you have made it, move confidently ahead. After all, you cannot act on what you do not know or cannot control.

Jan Polanski was the coach of a world-renowned acrobatic troop. His artists, known as 'Lighter Than Air' had just commenced a tour of Southeast Asia and Australia. The tour was an important one and to make it special Jan had coached the troop to execute a 'triple-flip, turn and catch'. This was an extremely difficult maneuver which few other troops had attempted. Jan had worked for three months on training his acrobats. They had perfected it.

Towards the end of the first, very successful performance, Boris, the number one acrobat, felt it was time for the new act. He looked over to Jan standing in the shadows of the tent to get his approval to commence. Jan smiled confidently and gave the 'thumbs up'. Boris swung from his trapeze, flew through the air twisting and flipping but as he reached to grab his partner's hands he missed and fell.

Although there was a net, he only managed to hit the side, tumbling off the edge and injuring himself. He would be out for the rest of the tour and everyone would suffer.

After the commotion had died down someone asked Jan if he had erred in giving permission to proceed. He replied: 'No, I did not make a mistake. If I were in the same position again I would make exactly the same decision. We'd been practising the act for three months and had perfected it. How was I to know the acrobats would misjudge the catch and fall? I did not make the wrong decision; I made the correct decision, but we failed to execute it properly.'

Implement

We have all heard the saying: 'There are four types of managers: those who wondered what happened, those who don't know what's happening, those who watch things happen, and those who make things happen.' Implementing a decision obviously involves you in being productive: making things happen. As we saw in the above example, it does not matter how creative or insightful your decision is, if you do not plan and implement efficiently, you will not achieve the desired result.

Getting a decision implemented is primarily your responsibility. It does not matter how many people have been involved up to this stage. If the outcome is not satisfactory through 'sloppy' implementation, you will be the one who is held accountable. You must therefore develop your skills and capacities for ensuring that the decision is implemented and produces the desired outcomes or changes.

If you are to be successful in this vital stage you will need to develop at least some of the following skills.

Effective implementation

- Clarifying.
- Establishing.
- Communicating.
- Drawing.
- Role-modelling.
- Risking.
- Believing.

Clarifying

You must be totally clear in your own mind about what has to be done. Make sure you know exactly where you are going before you set off. Ask yourself: What is the decision expected to achieve?

Establishing

You must establish clear targets and timeframes for the implementation process. As in target management, employees must know exactly where they are going and be aware of task completion dates.

Communicating

Communicate clearly to others what must be done to achieve the decision. If employees involved in implementing the decision do not understand the expected outcomes and the role they are to play, efficient implementation may be hampered.

Drawing

Be prepared to solicit the experience and assistance of others when you are planning how to implement a decision. Do not assume that you have all the answers and ideas. Implementation, especially of complex decisions, requires careful, often specialised, planning. Do not try and do it all by yourself.

Risking

Be prepared to take a calculated risk to make things happen. Be enthusiastic, decisive and committed when implementing a decision. A creative decision often requires creative implementation. Do not resort to 'typical' implementation procedures for every decision.

Role-Modelling

You have to 'role-model' standards for employees to emulate. Be prepared to work hard yourself. Set yourself high standards of performance. If you do this you can more reasonably set high standards for employees and expect them to achieve goals. Do not be like a manager I once worked for who was always telling us that we were expected to work long and hard for the organisation. Yet he was always the last to arrive and the first to leave. He was almost solely responsible for the high profits of the staff canteen!

Believing

Believe that you and your staff can always improve. Do not hold back on implementing a decision because you do not think you and your employees are capable. People will usually work to the level you believe they are capable of, so long as it is reasonable.

The quality of implementation will usually be congruent with the amount of preparation you commit to the task. You can improve your implementation skills by thinking about how you, and others, have approached it in the past. Now do Application Task 6.9. It is designed to help you identify how you and your staff either assisted or impeded successful implementation.

APPLICATION TASK 6.9

IMPLEMENTATION: WHAT HELPS, WHAT DOES NOT?

1. Describe a recent situation in your job where you were responsible for implementing a specific decision (or where you were involved in a team implementing a decision). If you cannot think of a suitable situation, consider a decision someone else implemented which you had the opportunity to observe.

   Decision situation:

2. In the appropriate columns, list:

   (a) Any of your behaviours that may have assisted successful implementation;
   (b) Any of your behaviours that may have impeded successful implementation;
   (c) Any behaviours of others that may have assisted in successful implementation;
   (d) Any behaviours of others that may have impeded successful implementation.

Assisting or impeding decision implementation:

BEHAVIOURS			
YOU		OTHERS	
ASSIST (1)	IMPEDE (2)	ASSIST (3)	IMPEDE (4)
e.g. *Involved others in generating solutions.*	*Did not allow staff to examine possible outcomes.*	*Generated very imaginative alternatives.*	*Could not agree on the best outcome.*

Stott, K. and Walker, A., *Making Management Work.* © 1992 Simon & Schuster (Asia) Pte Ltd.

When you have completed your lists, look at the points you have recorded which relate to how either you or other actors assisted implementation of the decision and continue by completing Application Task 6.10.

The systematic and imaginative implementation of a decision should produce outcomes which are relatively close to those you planned for. Try not to be disappointed if things do not always proceed exactly according to your plan; they rarely do. The best you can do is to be systematic and flexible enough to deal with unforeseen complications. If problems do arise, you should try to learn from them.

APPLICATION TASK 6.10

List the five behaviours which you consider to be most important or influential in promoting effective implementation. Then do the same for how you or others may have impeded the implementation of the decision.

When you have identified the five assisting and impeding behaviours think of the following: For the assisting behaviours, suggest some ways that they can be encouraged (for you and your staff). If, for example, you believe the careful communication of expectations is essential for effective implementation, give some ways that it can be encouraged: regular meetings, feedback mechanisms, timeframes posted.

Do the same for impeding behaviours: How can you improve the identified behaviour next time? If, for example, you believe you did too much of the planning yourself and that this may have hindered implementation, you may suggest: involving others during implementation-planning, running the plan past another expert, having others review your plan.

Assisting:

BEHAVIOURS	METHODS FOR ENCOURAGEMENT
1. *Communication*	*Regular meetings; Feedback mechanism; Time*
2.	
3.	
4.	
5.	

Impeding:

BEHAVIOURS	METHODS FOR IMPROVEMENT
1. *No creativity*	*Use brainstorming; Reward creative ideas*
2.	
3.	
4.	
5.	

If decision implementation goes according to plan, remember what you did. To learn from both success and failure you need to inquire into the problem-solving/decision-making process in order to identify where you can improve in the future.

Inquire

Inquiry into a decision's effectiveness requires a two-pronged approach. First, you must evaluate on an ongoing basis: Is the implementation proceeding according to plan? Are you achieving the desired outcomes? Second, you should inquire into the effectiveness of the overall decision and the decision-making process itself.

If your decision is not attaining its desired outcomes you may have to adjust your implementation approach, or even abandon the decision. Abandoning the decision can be very difficult, especially if you have committed considerable energy to the process. You must ask yourself whether it would be more advantageous professionally, financially or personally, to cut your losses. It takes a lot of courage to do this but it may be unavoidable. In some situations you may not have the 'abandonment' option. Some decisions are irreversible. If, for example, you have made a decision to send three employees to a specialised training course, and they have started the course, it would be very difficult to retract your decision. In such cases you must proceed with the decision and make the best of your circumstances.

On a less drastic note, let us assume that most of your decisions proceed relatively closely to what you have planned and only stray off path occasionally. The occasional small discrepancy may require you to refine aspects of the decision which deviate from your plan. A more in-depth explanation of how to do this is described in Chapter 4 dealing with our 7D scheme of planning team action.

Ongoing evaluation of your decision is best conducted at two levels: formal and informal. Formal reviews should be planned with firm dates which are built into the implementation process. This is shown in Figure 6.12. Formal review can be done through standard control mechanisms such as meetings, output checks, production records and reports.

Informal review is constant. It involves observing and talking to employees involved in the implementation process: 'How is it going?', 'Any problems so far?' These types of situations also present ideal opportunities for offering encouragement and keeping employees on task.

It is also important to evaluate the effectiveness of the decision as a whole. Here you examine the final outcome of the decision to ascertain whether the actual outcomes match the intended results. This can be done by comparing the outcomes or solutions to the targets and criteria you set yourself earlier

Figure 6.12
Decision Implementation (I) and Planned Reviews (R)

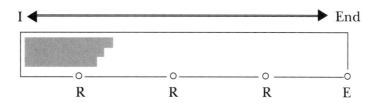

in the decision-making process.

If you are to become a more effective 'decision maker' you should also review the decision process itself. The purpose of this inquiry is to collect information to enable you to improve future performance. 'The way to become good at decision-making is to make lots of decisions' (Adair, 1985 : 105). We would expand this statement by suggesting that you can become an even better decision maker if you are willing to critically analyse your own and your team's performance. If you do not do this you risk repeating mistakes and missing valuable developmental opportunities. If you find you have made errors, try not to become too despondent; treat them as learning opportunities.

To get some idea of how thorough and systematic you have been when solving a problem and making a decision, you can use the checklist shown in Figure 6.13. It is designed to provide you or your team with some initial feedback on the decision process.

Using the checklist will help you identify possible weaknesses and strengths. These provide valuable feedback when you are evaluating the decision process itself.

Figure 6.14 displays a form, Making Decisions: A Summary Form, which you can use to identify the important factors at each stage in the decision-making framework.

Conclusion

You have now reached the end of the decision-making process. In reality there is no 'end'. You will always be making decisions and many of these will overlap. As soon as one decision is made there is another waiting in the wings.

As you have been reading you have no doubt realised that there are many situations which do not require conscious adherence to the steps. Standard

Figure 6.13
Inquiring Into the Process: Decision-Making/Problem-Solving

ASK YOURSELF: DID I (OR WE)?

	Yes	No
1. See the problem when it surfaced?	☐	☐
2. Check the facts before going any further?	☐	☐
3. Make the right assumptions about the problem?	☐	☐
4. State the problem so we could all understand it?	☐	☐
5. Set some targets or outcome criteria?	☐	☐
6. See the difference between causes and symptoms?	☐	☐
7. Try to see the possible effects of the problem?	☐	☐
8. Think about the assumptions I was making?	☐	☐
9. Recognise the size and complexity of the problem?	☐	☐
10. Break the problem into more manageable pieces?	☐	☐
11. Try to identify possible constraints?	☐	☐
12. Look for ways of overcoming these constraints?	☐	☐
13. Work out the resources I would need?	☐	☐
14. Think about which decision-making method to use?	☐	☐
15. Use a number of problem-solving techniques?	☐	☐
16. Think about how each method could help?	☐	☐
17. Ask others for suggestions?	☐	☐
18. Consider whether others wanted to be involved?	☐	☐
19. Identify a number of possible alternatives?	☐	☐
20. Analyse strengths and weaknesses of alternatives?	☐	☐
21. Think about why I selected an alternative?	☐	☐
22. Explain the decision to others?	☐	☐
23. Regularly review the implementation process?	☐	☐
24. Evaluate the decision's effectiveness?	☐	☐

Figure 6.14
Making Decisions: A Summary Form

IDENTIFY

_____

_____

_____

ISOLATE

_____

_____

_____

INVOLVE

_____

_____

_____

INVESTIGATE

_____

_____

_____

IMPLEMENT

_____

_____

_____

INQUIRE

_____

_____

_____

decisions can often be dealt with through organisational policies. Crisis decisions need to be made quickly. Many of the decisions you make however may best be set within the framework.

As stated at the outset, we recognise that many decisions do not lend themselves to a purely rational approach. The framework we have presented attempts to account for this fact and encourages you to consider the irrationality of many organisations and individuals (including yourself). We believe that any complex decision situation or problem must at least follow a sequence to guide its solution and progress.

In this chapter we have tried to provide a practical framework for solving problems and making decisions. We have suggested that managers are faced with a number of different types of decisions. We have promoted the 'sensible' involvement of employees in decision-making and emphasised the importance of being creative when searching for solutions. We have also emphasised the importance of analysing the what, the why, and the how of improving the quality of decision-making.

It is now up to you to make the decision of whether or not you want to improve your decision-making skills. We suggest you treat this as a *crisis* decision, and begin immediately to develop and improve your ability in this vital managerial skill.

Try now to transpose what you have read in this chapter into something you can use in your work situation. Identify a decision you have to make in the near future, fill in the appropriate boxes, and then use this as a practical guide as you go through the process.

APPLICATION TASK 6.11

DECISION TO BE MADE:	STANDARD CRISIS DEEP (delete as appropriate)
Objective (outcome criteria):	

Think about the decision in terms of:

QUALITY	ACCEPTANCE	EXPERTISE	TIME

Major Consideration Factors:
1.
2.
3.
4.

Decision-Making Method Selected

Possible Alternatives and
Possible Consequences

AUTOCRATIC	
FINAL SAY	
ELITE GROUP	
CONSULTANCY	
MAJORITY RULES	
CONSENSUS	
Why selected:	

Final decision:

Implementation Plan:

Informal Review: (dates)

Formal Review:

Process Review:

Lessons for next time:

Stott, K. and Walker, A., *Making Management Work.* © 1992 Simon & Schuster (Asia) Pte Ltd.

References

Adair, J. (1985) *Management Decision Making*, Gower : England.

Bridges, E. (1967) 'A model for shared decision making in the school principalship', *Educational Administration Quarterly*, **3**, pp. 49–61.

Drucker, P. (1955) *The Practice of Management*, Heinemann : London.

Hoy, W. and Miskel, C. (1987) *Educational Administration*, Random House : New York.

Janis, I. (1982) *Groupthink: Psychological Studies of Policy Decisions*, Houghton Mifflin : Boston.

Jones, C. (1970) *An Introduction to the Study of Public Policy*, Duxbury Press : California.

Koontz, H. and Weihrich, H. (1988) *Management*, 9th edn, McGraw-Hill : Singapore.

Leong, W. (1990) 'Problem solving simulation', in Low, G., Chong, K., Leong, W. and Walker, A. (eds.), *Developing Executive Skills*, pp. 34–51, Longman : Singapore.

Lewis, M. and Kelly, G. (1986) *20 Activities for Developing Managerial Reflectiveness*, Gower : England.

Lindbloom, C. (1959) 'The science of muddling through', *Public Administrative Review*, **19**, pp. 79–99.

Maier, N. (1963) *Problem Solving Discussions and Conferences*, McGraw-Hill : New York.

Morris, W. and Sashkin, M. (1976) *Organisation Behaviour in Action: Skill-building Experiences*, West : Minnesota.

Sashkin, M. and Morris, W. (1984) *Organisational Behaviour: Concepts and Experiences*, Reston : Reston, VA.

Simon, H. (1951) *Administrative Behaviour*, Macmillan : New York.

Stewart, R. (1985) *The Reality of Management*, Pan : London.

Vroom, V. and Yetton, P. (1973) *Leadership and Decision Making*, University of Pittsburgh Press : Pittsburgh.

Woodcock, M. and Francis, D. (1982) *The Unblocked Manager*, Gower : England.

Chapter 7

Interviewing

It was Monday morning. I was called in for a ninety-minute-information-gathering interview with the new boss. He wanted to discover more about the areas of work for which I was responsible and to seek my views on developments which should take place to improve the quality of our products. He sat on his executive chair behind his large desk and I on an uncomfortable upright chair. Within five minutes of the interview's start, the telephone rang, which it did another three times during the following hour or so. A secretary also walked in with some papers which caused a break in the conversation. Despite these interruptions and my physical discomfort, he displayed some good skills as an interviewer and managed to elicit most of the information he needed.

At what level are your skills? Are you an accomplished interviewer or do you often fail to utilise the full potential of this highly interactive process? To give yourself an initial impression of your ability, complete the questionnaire How Good an Interviewer Are You? It will not provide a definitive picture of your skill level, but it will help to draw attention to some of the areas in which you need to improve.

Questionnaire

HOW GOOD AN INTERVIEWER ARE YOU?

	Yes	No
1. Do you sit at the same level as the interviewee and away from your desk?	☐	☐
2. Do you let the interviewee talk for at least two-thirds of the time?	☐	☐
3. Do you arrange the furniture in a 'friendly' informal way?	☐	☐
4. Do you avoid asking questions which are already answered on forms and documents?	☐	☐
5. Do you ensure there are absolutely no interruptions?	☐	☐

	Yes	No
6. Do you identify the key areas to cover before the interview?	☐	☐
7. Do you explain the purpose of the interview at the beginning?	☐	☐
8. Do you explain to the interviewee how you have arranged the agenda?	☐	☐
9. Do you establish a good rapport at the beginning by asking friendly questions?	☐	☐
10. Do you read and assimilate the contents of relevant documents before the interview?	☐	☐
11. Do you write down some important questions beforehand?	☐	☐
12. Do you look at the interviewee most of the time he is talking?	☐	☐
13. Do you ask for clarification if you do not understand something he has said?	☐	☐
14. Do you plan out an ordered agenda?	☐	☐
15. Do you delve deeper into an area if you are not satisfied with the answer?	☐	☐
16. Do you use mostly open questions, allowing the interviewee to talk?	☐	☐
17. Do you keep your questions short and clear?	☐	☐
18. Do you ensure there are no audible or visual distractions?	☐	☐
19. Do you work out how you will interpret the responses in advance?	☐	☐
20. Do you adopt a friendly and unassuming approach?	☐	☐
21. Do you have the central purpose in mind throughout the interview?	☐	☐
22. Do you plan your time so that all important topics are covered?	☐	☐
23. Do you ensure the room is neither too hot nor too cold?	☐	☐
24. Do you summarise what the interviewee has said from time to time?	☐	☐
25. Do you take brief notes throughout the interview?	☐	☐
26. Do you watch for visual clues about such things as boredom, irritation, interest and disagreement?	☐	☐

	Yes	**No**
27. Do you avoid being unduly influenced by your prejudices about dress, speech, etc?	☐	☐
28. Do you conceal the fact that you might disagree with an answer to a question?	☐	☐
29. Do you use supportive gestures like nodding and smiling to encourage responses?	☐	☐
30. Do you avoid asking questions which already have the answer built into them?	☐	☐
31. Do you ask one question at a time?	☐	☐
32. Do you always let the respondent finish his reply?	☐	☐
33. Do you try to find out about such things as feelings and opinions as well as facts?	☐	☐
34. Do you know what you are looking for before the interview starts?	☐	☐
35. Do you avoid putting unnecessary pressure on interviewees?	☐	☐
36. Do you review what happened in the interview?	☐	☐
37. Do you try to understand things from the other person's point of view?	☐	☐
38. Do you allow sufficient time to conduct an interview without rushing responses?	☐	☐
39. Do you respond to unexpected responses flexibly?	☐	☐
40. Do you demonstrate you are comfortable even with awkward situations?	☐	☐

It would be difficult for even the most experienced and adept interviewer to say with honesty that he could answer 'yes' to all the questions, but at least we hope you managed to answer 'yes' to some! If you have a number of 'no' answers, see if they have a pattern. Do they relate to the physical setting for example? Or are they about the questions which are asked? Many people find difficulty in getting things right *before* the interview; in other words, they do not prepare properly. As you read on, you will see how all these points combine to provide a situation in which the central purpose can best be fulfilled.

When we watch a skilled interviewer in action, maybe on television, it can be made to look deceptively easy, but like all skilled exponents, much practice is involved in becoming accomplished. If we interview someone, unless we possess the necessary skills and have spent a great deal of time and thought in preparation, the sort of information we acquire may lack any depth, be irrelevant, inaccurate or even untruthful.

Interviewing is not easy. Even when we know the questions we should ask to break the barriers of superficiality, we have difficulty in phrasing them. It is only through thought and conscientious practice that we can build up a portfolio of skills which will ensure the data we elicit is comprehensive and meaningful.

Many people think of interviewing as simply the selection type when we hire people. We have tried to look at the interviewing situation and its associated skills in a more general way, although you will obviously relate the contents of this chapter to the context with which you are most familiar. We do not interview only because we need to fill a vacancy. The developmental appraisal discussion (see Chapter 10) is also a form of interview and much of what we have to say here can be applied to that situation. Similarly, we may wish to obtain information from someone and it is sufficiently important for us to meet face to face and ask a number of questions. This of course is a form of interview characteristic of the research situation. Equally you may have the misfortune to interview one of your employees about inadequate performance or even misbehaviour. You could interview staff about development ideas or projects. Whatever the situation, the skills are very much the same. We make frequent reference however to the particular situation of the employment interview, because it raises a number of issues with relevance to other structured discussion contexts through its intensity for the participants.

Most of us are aware of the shortcomings of such selection interviews. You can adopt the most elaborate and lengthy procedures, but there still seems to be little guarantee that you will get the best person available. Despite this, the use of interviews to serve this purpose is widespread. No one seems to have found anything that works better. For this situation then, and others, it makes sense that you develop your skills; that you become a more accomplished interviewer, so that if you are in the position of hiring people, appraising staff or gaining information, you can at least give yourself more than a sporting chance of getting it right.

In this chapter, after a brief examination of the purpose of interviews and some examples of practices that are less than effective, we look at the skills and processes involved in making interviews serve their purposes. We focus on preparation and the interview meeting, and consider the skills to be developed and the key issues involved. We then look at the advantages and disadvantages of different types of interview structure, followed by an explanation of how interviews might be organised. The final sections relate to what might be considered in selection interviews and the factors involved in making interviews designed to gather information successful.

Purpose

What is the purpose of interviewing? If you watch some exponents in action, you may be forgiven for seeing it as an attempt to give the poor interviewee as traumatic a time as possible. In some extreme circumstances, that may be a positive strategy, but the basic purpose of interviewing is to see things from the respondent's perspective. This seems like a difficult prescription, but interviewing has to involve something more than simply acquiring data, especially when it could be obtained using a more economical technique. So in skilled interviewing, we try to enter the mind of the interviewee and understand the way he sees the world.

The interview itself is just a framework, a structure for providing responses. How we conduct the event determines to a large extent the accuracy and depth of responses. One other point is worth mentioning. It is a two-way process in some situations. The job interview is a prime example. You are interviewing someone to reach a decision on whether he is suitable for a particular appointment. At the same time he is interviewing you to see whether your organisation matches his demands and expectations. Under these conditions, the structure has to accommodate his need for information.

SUMMARY

The basic purpose of interviewing is to understand things from the other person's perspective. The interview provides a framework in which this can take place.

At this point we want you to consider any interviews you may have been involved in, preferably as the interviewee. Try to recollect the good and the bad things that happened. Something may have annoyed or upset you; on the other hand, someone may have made you feel good. You need to reach some conclusions therefore on what you least like about interviews and the conditions that are most conducive. Think of it in a personal way: What are the things that affect you? Try completing Application Task 7.1, Interviewing: Good and Bad Practice. This will help you as you read on and identify the features and skills of effective interviews.

APPLICATION TASK 7.1

INTERVIEWING: GOOD AND BAD PRACTICE

What irritates you in an interview? In other words, as an interviewee, what can you identify as examples of bad practice? List three which stand out for you.

1.

2.

3.

What makes a good interview? Give three features which are important to you. Be very specific, avoiding generalisations like 'honesty', 'enthusiasm', etc.

1.

2.

3.

Both of us have had the experience (not very pleasurable in many cases) of being on the receiving end of interviews, mostly those of the selection variety. Some of the events we recollect are frustrating and a source of annoyance; others give us some humorous stories to tell. One occasion saw me being interviewed by a panel (about nine people altogether) and the chairman said to one of his colleagues on the panel: 'Have you any questions, Councillor Bloggs?' There was a silence for five seconds before everyone looked in his direction to see him fast asleep! The criterion for success in that interview may have been to keep the councillor awake!

Some of the things which turn us off are a feeling of aggression or antipathy from the beginning of the event, typified by interrogation-type techniques, interrupting you, failing to smile and putting you at a physical disadvantage. In a panel interview, for example, the members may sit behind a large table and you sit all alone in front of the 'firing squad'. We are less than open in that environment. Another thing which frustrates us is the wasting of time going over data which has already been provided on the ubiquitous application form: 'Right, you are Mr Jones and you went to Fairfield School and you obtained how many GCE subjects? What were they? And then you went into the sixth form? What did you do at the polytechnic? And which dates did you work for the computer company?' Before you get round to talking about the really important things, like yourself and the job, the interviewer says that time is up. You have probably only clarified your work history and he is expected to reach decisions on that! One other thing which we identified as a common problem was a lack of clarity in questions from the interviewer. Interviews are stressful enough without having to decipher the most complex and long-winded questions, usually about simple issues.

When we ask managers about the good interviewers who have influenced them, we often get a list of qualities. Pleasant, understanding, patient, good at listening, and jovial. All these tend to feature prominently in responses. It is not surprising, because when you are in the stressful situation of being interviewed, say, for a job, life is made so much easier if the behaviour of the interviewer actually puts those characteristics into operation.

You may have mentioned these same points and several others in the exercise. We shall be considering effective practice a little later. First though, we want to look at some of the behaviours and conditions which do little to enhance the success of interviews. Generally, examples of poor practice fall into the categories of poor preparation, failing to discover and stick to the main purpose, lack of anticipation and getting the roles mixed up. We discuss these briefly. There are of course others and we shall cover these from a different perspective, that of making interviews work effectively.

Poor Practice

The main reason for interviews failing to be as productive as they should be is the lack of adequate *preparation*. In some cases there should be at least as much time spent in preparing for the interview as there is in conducting it. We shall look at preparation shortly and give some pointers to effective practice.

Another common problem is deviating from the main purpose. The respondent may go off at a tangent and the interviewer may fail to bring the discussion back on line. This may mean that the information acquired is not related to the key purpose. Digression can be a good thing in some circumstances, but more often than not, it demonstrates a lack of skill on the part of the interviewer.

Lack of preparation often leads to surprises. This can be disastrous for the television interviewer and not too helpful for the interviewer in, say, the disciplinary situation. Some responses may not have been anticipated and this can lead to paralysis in the interview because it is not apparent where the line of questioning should lead. If you have thought about it in advance you should have a good idea of what the likely responses to your questions will be, and you will therefore know which are the appropriate follow-up questions.

Another problem is getting the roles mixed up. This is where the interviewer loses sight of the main role and almost becomes the respondent, asking lengthy questions, giving opinions and generally spending considerably more time talking than the interviewee. We were at a conference recently when the speaker invited questions from the audience. One person stood up and asked what was supposed to be a question – it lasted nine minutes! Not only was the respondent confused but the rest of the audience had lost interest. This sort of effect occurs similarly in one-to-one interviews when the interviewer fails to clarify his thinking. Short, carefully worded questions are necessary to retain the respondent's interest.

SUMMARY

Poor Interviews Are Often Caused By:

- Lack of adequate preparation.
- Deviating from the main purpose.
- Failing to identify possible responses to important questions.
- Getting the roles mixed up.

Making Interviews Work

We now look at ways in which you can use your skills and set up conditions so that interviews can work successfully. Much of what we have to say applies across the board to selection interviews, information-gathering interviews and those which are concerned with other matters such as discipline and performance. We examine the environment and the need to provide a conducive setting. Preparing for the interview is then considered with reference to some of the items which must be thought out in advance. We then look at the interview itself and give some guidelines on some of the things you can do (and some things you should not do) to ensure the meeting serves its purpose. Some common problems are examined, especially those which act as distractors and which may distort the information you receive. We then look at the skill of asking questions and identify different types of questions which are relevant to interviews. The development of a good questioning technique is critical to successful interviewing and we encourage you to give this part of the process your *careful* attention. We have included a short section on 'pressure tactics' which are sometimes applied, and we warn against their indiscriminate use.

The Right Environment

The importance of setting the right conditions for the interview should not be overlooked. If these are not right, the interview may falter through distractions.

First of all, the temperature should be right. Of course, if you are interviewing on someone else's territory, it is difficult to do anything about this, but you must be aware that a steamy room without ventilation or an area where frostbite is a potential hazard does not enhance the quality of the interview. Fortunately, most interviewers set reasonably comfortable conditions.

Interruptions are extremely problematic. Regardless of where the interview is held, it is necessary to do something about the possibility of telephone or casual caller interruptions. If the interview is the type which may be held at the interviewee's work place, it may need a polite request that the interview be free from interruptions for a given period, since the responses are of great importance and such interruptions would form a major distraction. Put this way, you will probably get co-operation. Where the session is on the interviewer's territory, it is a simple matter to divert calls or take the telephone off the hook, and, if necessary, lock the door. For interviews which do not have to be held in the work place, you can meet on neutral ground in, say, a quiet corner of a hotel lounge. This sort of setting can be quite conducive to information-gathering.

Any kind of noise is a distraction, including loud talking outside the room and roadworks outside the building. Keep doors and windows closed so that these distractions are minimised.

The furniture arrangement is of major importance. Wherever the interview is held, some attempt must be made to arrange furniture in such a way that it enhances two-way communication. Quite often if you interview someone of seniority in his office, he will choose to sit behind his desk, usually in a high-back chair, and you end up with a large physical barrier between you and the respondent. A useful strategy for dealing with this problem is to have a sheet of paper with information which you both need to view at the same time. You can then ask whether you can move your chair round to the respondent's side of the desk. The latter hopefully will not refuse and you end up with a much better arrangement for open and productive discussion.

As a manager you will generally have control over the furniture arrangement. Do not feel you have to'give confirmation of your authority by sitting in your executive chair protected by your desk. Wherever possible it is best to avoid barriers and those include square or rectangular tables, especially where the interviewer and interviewee sit directly opposite each other. Ideally it is considered most productive to dispense with tables and instead sit on comfortable chairs, reasonably close, and facing or alongside each other.

In the same way a client entering the organisation for the first time gets an initial (and lasting) impression from the physical appearance, an interviewee will receive messages from the furniture arrangement when he enters the interview room. He may feel warmly welcomed or like an intruder. He may feel that the interviewer is going to be interested in what he has to say, or that it is merely a necessary imposition on the interviewer's time. It seems that in many interviews, the interviewee is supposed to receive the message that the interviewer is superior and that he should be looked upon in awe!

Even outside the interview situation we have found it advantageous to move away from our desks to talk with visitors or colleagues, and to sit with them on a settee or easy chairs. We can still look at documents together and we find that we can discuss even contentious issues in a setting which is decidedly friendlier than the more formal arrangements commonly found.

SUMMARY

Set The Right Environment:

- Ensure there is a comfortable temperature.

- Avoid interruptions at all costs.
- Ensure there are no distractions.
- Arrange the furniture in a 'friendly' way.

Well Thought Out

> Chance favors the prepared mind.
> (Louis Pasteur)

The interview should be well planned. This does not mean it always has to be structured, but it should be thought about carefully in advance. The introduction needs to be planned carefully as does the line of questioning. By planning your agenda, you will have time in the interview for the really important activity: listening.

Questions

The types of questions chosen should be simple and easy to grasp, leaving no room for misunderstanding. It is also useful to list the key questions which should be asked, especially where inappropriate wording could lead to ambiguity. The quality of questions is of the utmost importance. This will determine whether the interviewer manages to reach the individual perspective of the respondent and develop the responses through skilful probing-type questions. Without in-depth questioning, only superficial and marginal data is likely to emerge, and this is particularly so where the substance is of a sensitive nature.

If you consider that there are such things as appropriate responses for your interview situation, you should prepare these in advance. If you do not know how to evaluate the answers, the corresponding questions may be of little use.

Read in Advance

Do your homework. Read and study documents in advance. If it is a job interview, read the *curriculum vitae* and any other materials thoroughly so that you have a good picture of the candidate and you do not need to waste time searching for data during the interview. Use a highlighter pen to indicate the statements you want to explore. It is useful to use two colours, one for the really important matters which you *must* ask about, and another for those of interest, but for which you may not have time. By doing this, you may find things which have been omitted, or possibly avoided, and you may wish to pursue these matters. The reasons for leaving a particular job, for example, may not be clear, so you will highlight this as an issue to be explored.

Identify Key Topics

A list of topics could be prepared in the form of a checklist and ticked off when they have been covered. These should be logically sequential so that the train of thought is not broken. Consider the relevance of the information sought. In preparing for the interview you have to be absolutely clear what is important to performance in the job and what is not (assuming that the decision is yours). Some high-level job interviews we have experienced, for example, have wasted time on issues like primary school performance and 'O' level results. For mature applicants, what happened ten, twenty or thirty years previously is hardly likely to have much effect on performance, so there is no reason to waste time on it. Interview time is valuable for both parties, so you should consider the degree of relevance of each matter you intend to cover.

Plan Your Time

Even if the interview is unstructured, you need to know the time you have available. Against each of the key areas to be covered, you should indicate the time allotted, and stick to it unless there are good reasons for doing otherwise. This way you will avoid the common problem of leaving key matters not discussed, and where you are interviewing several people, each will have roughly the same time on these important issues.

Where the interview is of a counselling nature (many managers are involved in such interviews) you must allow more time, because if emotional issues are being discussed, you cannot rush them. Such interviews involve helping people in their problem-solving. You are not doing the job for them, but rather helping them to define and frame the problem, so that they themselves can solve it.

SUMMARY

- Identify the central purpose of the interview and write it down.
- Prepare your key questions, making them easy to understand.
- Consider what appropriate responses might be.
- Read relevant materials in advance.
- Identify the important topics which *must* be covered.
- Plan your time carefully.

As a guide to your preparation, the next time you conduct an interview of any kind, we suggest you use the form Interview Preparation shown in Figure 7.1 which will help to ensure you have considered the important details. We explain structure and question formulation later in the chapter.

Figure 7.1
Interview Preparation

What is the purpose of the interview?

What structure is to be used: structured, unstructured, semi-structured?

How much time is available?

Main headings to be covered, with accompanying key questions:

1.

2.

3.

4.

To help you relate the central purpose of the interview to more specific objectives and then to the corresponding questions, you should complete Application Task 7.2. It will help you to identify your main purpose, specific objectives and the relevant questions.

There are a number of answers you could give and we have suggested some possibilities in Figure 7.2. Do not treat these as the 'right' answers; you may have come up with some suitable alternatives. The important thing is that you have related your objectives to the central purpose, and that the key

APPLICATION TASK 7.2

You are the chief executive of a manufacturing company. The manager of your Marketing and Sales Department has been pressing for some time to restructure his department and has indicated that, although it would involve a few additional posts being created, the benefits for the company would outweigh the increased resource costs. Although he has outlined the basic proposition in a memorandum, you have decided to conduct an interview with him so that you can gather information which will help you reach a wise decision and then make your recommendation to the board. You know that, through the interview, you can obtain information which might not be available through written documents.

As preparation, you should complete the form which will act as a guide, setting out your main purpose, the specific objectives and the questions which will best meet those objectives. For this task, limit yourself to three objectives and two questions under each. There will obviously be others you could ask, but at this stage, there is no need to go into too much detail; it is more important to understand the basic principle of objective-setting and key question formulation.

PURPOSE, OBJECTIVES AND QUESTIONS

Central Purpose:

Objective 1:

Key Question:

Key Question:

Objective 2:

Key Question:

Key Question:

Objective 3:

Key Question:

Key Question:

Stott, K. and Walker, A., *Making Management Work*. © 1992 Simon & Schuster (Asia) Pte Ltd.

questions you have chosen are tied in to the objectives and that they will begin to draw out the sort of information you need in order to make an informed decision.

Obviously there will be searching and follow-up questions to those listed, but the idea of writing key questions is to start the discussion moving in the right direction. Once you are under way you can adapt your questioning to the responses you get, but use the guide to keep you on line so that you meet your objectives.

Conducting the Interview

The Setting

Whereas some forms of interviews are like normal conversations, job interviews present a false situation and the interviewee is going to feel uncomfortable unless you make a positive effort to put him at ease. The environment

Figure 7.2
Preparation Sheet Example

Central Purpose:
  To reach a decision on whether to support a proposition to restructure the Marketing department.

Objective 1:   *To ascertain the problem with the present situation.*

  Key Question: *How do you see the current situation in the department?*

  Key Question: *What do you feel are the underlying causes of the problems?*

Objective 2:   *To discover the likely benefits and effects.*

  Key Question: *What are the probable benefits if we were to restructure?*

  Key Question: *How would your colleagues in the department react to it?*

Objective 3:   *To find out the resource implications involved.*

  Key Question: *Why would additional staff be needed?*

  Key Question: *How does this restructuring exercise fit into your long-term plans for the department?*

Stott, K. and Walker, A., *Making Management Work.* © 1992 Simon & Schuster (Asia) Pte Ltd.

will help in this respect and you are best advised to adopt an informal setting wherever possible. You do not need a large table or desk in order to write; you can use a clipboard or place a coffee table on which to lay documents at the side of your chair. Even the most confident and competent people can show up badly in interviews and if you set up the wrong conditions, you may be swayed against the individual who performs poorly, but he may just happen to be the best person for the job. You obviously need to avoid this.

The Early Part

Smile when you greet the interviewee and make your facial expressions supportive right from the beginning. Stand up when he comes into the room, unless of course you are close friends and can dispense with formalities. Standing up, though, is a welcoming gesture and displays respect for the interviewee. Have you ever been to a job interview where members of the panel stay seated, talking amongst themselves, and totally ignore you? Sometimes they do not even bother to introduce themselves, so you are never quite sure to whom you are talking or what his status or expertise is. Fortunately most interviews are not quite so bad as this, but many still fail to give the welcoming feeling which would get them off to a good start.

The introduction should set the tone and provide an explanation of the purpose. You could say something like: 'The purpose of this interview is for me to obtain the relevant information so that I can make a recommendation to the board about the establishment of a retail outlet.' You then need to give an agenda, an explanation of how the interview will be arranged: 'I shall be asking you about what is happening in other recreation centres in the area; then I shall need to examine the resource implications; finally, I shall be asking for your frank views on what we should do.'

Unless the respondent is a very close friend, it is not a wise strategy to lead off with a difficult or controversial question. You would find your respondent guarded and unlikely to divulge information of any depth or consequence. Like an athlete, the respondent has to be 'warmed up' gradually if peak performance is to be achieved, and in the case of the interview, that means eliciting data of high utility. Give looks of encouragement though when he opens up about himself, and when he obviously feels comfortable with the situation, you can start introducing your more searching questions.

Time

Some exploratory-type interviews have a mutually agreed time limit, usually because the interviewee is doing a favour by agreeing to be interviewed. In this case, if you have agreed with your respondent that it should last for one hour, then ensure you finish within that time, otherwise it may be difficult to secure co-operation in the future. On the other hand, if you realise you are running short of time and still have several areas to cover, it is not wise practice to cut the respondent off in mid-sentence, even if you do offer an explanation of the time problem. Avoid having too many questions and reach the important ones as soon as the respondent seems willing to co-operate fully. A good technique is to start with easy-to-answer questions which require relatively short responses, and then move on to the more searching variety progressively.

An Equal Relationship

Whatever the situation, we feel it is good practice to make the respondent feel important and that the information shared is going to be of worth. A friendly approach is usually appropriate and it is best to avoid giving either an impression of superiority or one of extreme servility. Give the feeling of an equal relationship and show respect for him and his views, regardless of his current status.

Take Notes

When the interviewee is talking, the interviewer will be taking notes and if anything is not clear, clarification should be sought. Take notes, but not extensive ones. You need them for a few reasons. You will demonstrate your interest in what the candidate is saying; you will be able to go back to expand on certain key points without interrupting him; you will be able to refer to the notes after you have interviewed all candidates and compare the respective responses. Furthermore, subsequent discussion may hinge on what has been said before. Just write a few words for each point because you want to also look at the other person and observe his body language. If you write throughout, he may feel as if he is giving dictation!

Visual Clues

The skilled and experienced interviewer not only listens to the words which are spoken but also watches the body language signals. These will either confirm what is being said or be incongruent. Where there is a mismatch between the spoken and visual signals, it can be problematic. The respondent may not be purposely trying to deceive and the visual signal can be misread.

If it is an important part of the interview it is expedient to pursue the matter and use probing questions in an attempt to reach the truth. Apart from confirming the veracity of what is being said, body language also gives clues about the level of interest of the respondent and about such feelings as irritation and disapproval.

Use Supportive Gestures

Body language works two ways: you receive signals and you also give signals. By making eye contact and nodding occasionally, you are giving the message that you are attentive. You can reinforce those by leaning forward occasionally to show keen interest in what is being said at that time. It is important to demonstrate that you are listening.

Listen

Do not dominate the interview. Let the respondent talk most of the time, and as a rough guide, you could aim to reduce your contribution to about a quarter or a third of the total time. Do not forget the purpose is to see things from the other person's perspective and this can only be achieved by listening to him. Whilst there are occasions where it is appropriate for you to give information, most interviews should be listening events for the interviewer, with constant stimulus coming from skilfully constructed and applied questions. Do not interrupt him when he is talking even though you may be somewhat impatient because of the time or the content of the response. Interrupting is rude and demonstrates a lack of interest.

If you are listening carefully you will spot when someone is purposely missing things out and trying to avoid issues. You can then use questions to search for the truth. Sometimes you do not even need questions; you can just keep quiet and let the silence tell the interviewee you are waiting to listen to his response.

By listening you will build up the interviewee's confidence and this will mean that the responses you obtain are more likely to be open. But he has to know you are listening. It is no good simply staring at him. Such prolonged eye contact gives little impression of listening, so try to avoid looking like a stuffed dummy, and use your facial expressions and your body movements, combined with the occasional 'I see' or 'yes' to tell the interviewee very clearly 'I am very interested in you and I am listening to everything you tell me.' The action which contradicts this statement more than any other is looking at your watch. As soon as the interviewee sees you do this, he will know that you have lost interest and it can have a devastating effect. If you have to know the time, put your watch on or near your papers, so that when you take any notes, you can check the time.

Related to the use of supportive remarks is the skill of reflecting or para-phrasing. This shows that you are listening and that you have understood the meaning. You will find that George uses this effectively in our case study near the end of the chapter. After the interviewee has answered your question, you might say something like: 'So what you are saying is that some of the tech-nicians are disappointed with the new arrangements?' He will then either agree or correct your interpretation.

Consider how you sit in interviews and put yourself in the position of the interviewee. Is it helpful or a hindrance? Do you sit bolt upright with your arms folded? Do you slump back in your chair? Do you fiddle with a pencil or rub your neck? All these may signify that you are not listening, whereas in fact you may be. One remarkable interviewer I met asked me a question and whilst I was answering, began to talk quietly to his co-interviewer. I was convinced that he had lost interest in me, and apart from the distraction which only helped me lose my train of thought, I was not too bothered about my response if he wasn't. To my amazement he summarised precisely what I had said and had even spotted a minor evasion! Few people can claim to have such a skill that they can hold a conversation and listen to someone else at the same time. Even if you are gifted like this, demonstrating that you are not listening is a major distraction and should be avoided.

There is more to the skill of listening than this of course. Some interview-ers accurately hear the words that come out and they know what has been said. They are not bad listeners. But the really skilled listener knows what is being said beyond the words. In Chapter 14, Negotiating, we say that you must listen for signals, for messages which are not being expressed directly in words. It is the same in interviewing; you have to read between the lines and look for hidden messages. If you listen in this way you will discover feelings about issues and you will spot when the truth is being concealed.

Final Remarks

It is a good idea at the end of the interview, not only to ask the interviewee if he has any questions, but also to invite his remarks. He may wish to em-phasise something which has been said earlier or he may wish to raise a matter which is important to him. In some types of interview, you will use the final phase for summarising everything which has been said (or decided). Ensure that you always finish on a positive note, whatever the issue. If it is an employment interview, you must put the candidate in the picture. You may tell him, for example, that he will definitely hear the result of the interview from you within seven days. He knows then where he stands. Even if it is simply a deferral, you must have a conclusion to the interview. If you can make the interviewee feel that the experience has been of value to you both, then so much the better. Finally, ensure you thank him and, if appropriate, shake hands.

SUMMARY

- Greet the interviewee by standing up and shaking hands.
- Put him at ease.
- Adopt an informal setting where possible.
- Explain the purpose of the interview.
- Use friendly, easy-to-answer questions at the beginning.
- Keep to time limits.
- Make him feel an equal.
- Take brief notes.
- Watch for visual clues.
- Show him that you are listening to him.
- Let him talk for about three-quarters of the time.
- Give him the opportunity to ask you questions.
- Tell him what the next step is and thank him.

Some Common Problems

Distractions

If we were giving advice to job candidates, we would tell them to dress and behave appropriately; in other words, play the interview 'game' according to the 'rules'. As an interviewer however, you have to ask yourself how important some of these game rule components are and how much they should sway you in your judgement. A major distraction for example is physical appearance. Most of us have biases and so long as we recognise them, we can reduce their distracting power. Some of us, for example, do not like particular forms of dress or may be intolerant of certain accents. Interviewing members of the opposite sex, people of different heights, and a host of other characteristics, also contribute to a situation in which we can easily lose our objectivity. This can be offset in good part by having the criteria laid out in the form of a checklist and assessing the merits of candidates against that.

Halo Effect

The *halo effect* is a commonly mentioned problem in interviewing. This is where someone is good on one dimension, so you assume he is good on other dimensions. The person may be well dressed, for example, and able to speak very well, answering your questions clearly. You may then assume him to be intelligent and capable of dealing with people at all levels in the organisation. You may of course be quite wrong. He is able to articulate clearly but he may not be able to grasp conceptual ideas and his relations with less articulate people may not be all that good. We knew a school principal who gave one of her staff all the intellectually demanding jobs because he had attended one of the country's top primary schools. His name being associated with that school was sufficient to convince her he *must* be a cut above everyone else when it came to intellect! The message is to be aware of this effect and to avoid inferring ability in many areas based on limited observations.

False Assumptions

We often jump to conclusions and sometimes it makes us look silly. Similarly, we often hear only what we want to hear, which is not very helpful in interviews. Unless the responses tie in with our preconceived notions we are quite likely to 'switch off'.

Another problem is the tendency to make false interpretations of events. You notice, for example, that the candidate spent only nine months in one job before moving to a company 100 miles away. You treat it dismissively as lack of loyalty, inability to fit in or an unwillingness to see a job through. Of course, it could be one of these, but at the same time it could be because his aging parents had been taken ill and he needed to move to employment nearer their home.

SUMMARY

Beware of:

- Your in-built prejudices about factors like physical appearance and dress.
- Assuming that ability in one area reflects ability in others.
- Making assumptions without securing accurate information.

Asking Questions

This is one of the key skills of interviewing and one to which a great deal of attention should be given. Apart from the skills of phrasing questions appropriately and deploying them at the right time, there are some types of questions which are particularly suited to certain interview situations. We shall look at these below and offer some advice on how to use them. There are a few general points which should be raised first.

Do not rush the interviewee into answers. Ask simple, well thought-out questions and allow him time to consider his response. A pause here and there may indicate that the candidate likes to think before saying something, which can be an asset!

If you get an answer you disagree with, do not expose your feelings, but accept it and note it. It is all too easy to become involved in differences of opinion, but the last thing you want is for an argument to ensue; this is the best way of losing your focus.

If you are not sure what he means when he responds, ask for clarification: 'I didn't understand what you meant by "referring the matter"; could you please go over that again for me', is a friendly enough way of saying: 'You are not explaining your ideas very clearly!' And do listen – your questions may be linked in some way to the quality of responses you get.

'What Would You Do?' Questions

If you want to find out how well a person might do a particular job, you may need to ask situational questions. We prefer to call them 'What would you do?' questions. You give him a situation with a problem which is identical to the problem in a job for which he is applying and you ask him: 'What would you do (in that situation)?' Of course, you can use other words to phrase your question. You can go deeper into the response by asking further questions, and although not all answers will demonstrate a full contextual understanding, you should be able to reach some conclusions from the responses. In one interview I gave the candidate for a head of department post the situation of an employee failing to keep administrative records up to date and asked what he would do. He had not experienced this particular problem before, but his answer was: 'Send him to the boss!' From such a reaction it was possible to understand his likely approach to conflict situations a little better than just relying on the history of previous jobs.

Open Questions

You should use these liberally in the interview to elicit facts, opinions and feelings. You may want the interviewee to talk about a particular job-related issue, in which case you might ask questions like:

> 'What views do you have about this?'
> 'What action could be taken?'

You may also want to open up opinions and feelings:

> 'What are your feelings about the way you were treated?'
> 'What is your opinion about our equal opportunities policy?'

Closed Questions

If you were to use closed questions throughout the interview, the respondent would hardly speak, being limited to 'yes', 'no' or short statement answers. You can use them, but only to elicit information which is important and not on the *curriculum vitae* or form:

> 'Do you support our policies on retirement?'
> 'Having seen our company, are you still interested in the job?'

Searching Questions

These are generally used to extend the information and to delve deeper into a subject:

> 'But how would you implement that?'
> 'What other information is available?'
> 'Why did you decide on that course of action?'
> 'What other courses were open to you?'

As in the negotiating situation, you might use these questions to challenge beliefs, assumptions, even facts, but do *not* do it in a threatening way or give the impression that you are trying to win an intellectual contest. You may also use these questions to encourage the interviewee to keep talking by asking:

> 'And following that, what happened?'
> 'Really?'

Searching or probing-type questions are sometimes designed to go beyond the mere acquisition of in-depth information about the job and related skills and capabilities. They may be designed to seek information on personality and the way the interviewee relates to other people. These questions may secure information of more depth about motivations, aspirations and perceptions, which may all help to make wiser selection and development decisions. They are essential to appraisal interviews where appropriate decisions have to be made about development activities to support job performance. In job interviews it is generally thought that the higher the level of the post, the more important it is to go into this depth. If you are in this situation you might ask questions like:

> 'What is the most important feature of this job to you?'
> 'What do you expect to be doing in five years' time?'
> 'Which of your previous bosses has been the most influential on your career?'
> 'Why?'

It is easy to see the utility of such a line of questioning, but it is not clever to simply dream up questions like these and not know what to do with the answers. You have to be clear about how you will interpret the information you acquire and what bearing it is likely to have on your decision-making.

Searching questions may also be 'difficult' questions, pursuing matters which either the interviewer is uncomfortable with, or the interviewee does not wish to elaborate on. However, you have to address such matters and you may have to employ one searching question after another, often asking the same thing but using different words, until you get the information you want:

> 'What were the circumstances for your leaving the company after three months?'
> 'Why did they not listen to your ideas?'
> 'How could the company have influenced you to stay?'

Leading Questions

We recommend you steer clear from these in interviews. They may have the answer in the question, and they can be quite threatening, especially if the respondent wants a job and he does not concur with your obvious views:

> 'You would concede that whoever is appointed to this post needs to give the shop stewards a good shake-up, wouldn't you?'

Other Considerations

There are two other considerations you should be aware of, and these tend to arise in situations where the interviewer is unskilled or in panel interviews which often have inexperienced people on them. They relate to *question combination* and *question clarity*.

In the first, the interviewer has not thought out his ideas sufficiently to convert them into single and simple questions. So he asks two or more questions at one go and as you can imagine this is highly confusing for the respondent.

> 'What would you do in that situation, bearing in mind the levels of experience of the staff involved and the company policy on marginal performance, and what experiences have you had of dealing with that in your former employment?'

The second situation relates to ambiguous or unclear questions. If you get vague answers, it could be because you have asked vague questions. Keep your language simple and practise your questions. Better still, write them down and try them out on a colleague. Some interviewees are so nervous that they are embarrassed to ask for clarification if they do not understand a question; they think it makes them appear dull. The answer given under those circumstances does neither the interviewer nor the interviewee any good, and more often than not, it is the interviewer's fault.

SUMMARY

- Give the interviewee time to respond.
- Ask for clarification where necessary.
- Use 'What would you do?' questions to examine problem-solving capacity.
- Use open questions to obtain facts and open up opinions and feelings.
- Use closed questions sparingly.
- Use searching questions to delve deeper into a subject.
- Use searching questions to gain information on motivations, aspirations and perceptions.
- Be clear how you will interpret the answers to your questions.
- Avoid leading questions which can be threatening.
- Ask one question at a time.
- Make your questions simple and clear.

Pressure Tactics

Applying pressure is a tactic which is sometimes used for a particular purpose. The interviewer, for example, may adopt a hostile attitude and even question the candidate's credibility. There may be a case for using this tactic when selecting people for jobs which involve close relations with customers and where there is a need to be able to withstand unreasonable pressure.

Another pressure tactic is to keep firing questions at the interviewee, giving him little time to answer and interrupting him frequently. This is done to see how he stands up to stress. Again it may be decided that the particular job is highly stressful and could only be undertaken by someone who could withstand such pressure.

Yet one more tactic I once observed was where the panel interviewers placed two chairs in the room. One was a high-backed executive-type chair and the other a humble dining room chair, much smaller in comparison. Each candidate had to choose where to sit when he entered the room. I never managed to find out what interpretation was put on the interviewees' choices, but when I spoke to them, most had difficulty in deciding where to sit, several issues going through their minds at once.

If you do set up a situation like this or use other pressure tactics, you must be able to justify it and know how to interpret what you observe. Unfortunately we get the impression some employers are doing this to follow the vogue for more unconventional ways of interviewing and have not grasped what they are doing. Unless the circumstances genuinely dictate the application of such methods, we find them questionable and best avoided.

SUMMARY

Summary of the Key Points of Good Interviewing:

- Define the purpose and write it down.
- List the key areas to be covered.
- Prepare the important questions for each area.
- Do your homework: read the necessary documents.
- Select a good location, free from interruptions and distractions.
- Arrange the furniture to facilitate interaction.
- Make the interviewee feel at ease.
- Explain the purpose and the agenda.

- Ask questions which give him scope to talk.
- Make your questions clear and simple, even if they are searching.
- Listen and show you are listening.
- Take notes and use them in your review.

You should now be in a position to conduct an effective interview. Although it takes time to develop the skills of listening and questioning, and to apply them appropriately, by getting the basics right, you will have a considerable effect on the quality of your interviewing. The next time you are in an interviewing situation, try using the Interviewing Checklist we have provided in Figure 7.3. It is not meant as an exhaustive guide to the effective interview, but it may help to jog your memory about one or two of the features which are important to successful interviews. It looks at the preparation, the conditions for the interview, and then reviews what happened in the first few minutes. You then review progress about half-way through (it does not have to be exact) followed by a brief assessment at the end.

Finally, ensure you review the process. Things do not always go according to plan and you can learn from your mistakes (as well as your successes): people start to get irritated and show their frustration; they get upset that they were not given the opportunity to express their opinions; the interviewer has been spoken to rudely; there has been an angry exchange; the problem seems even worse than before the interview. 'At such a time, conscientious interviewers are bound to ask themselves: "What happened? Was it my fault that things went wrong? What could I have done differently?" ' (Molyneaux and Lane, 1982 : vii).

Interview Structure

There are three basic types of interview: the *structured, unstructured* and *semistructured* interviews. We like to call them 'straight down the line', 'anything goes' and 'loose–tight' interviews.

Straight Down the Line

The structured interview is not dissimilar to the questionnaire. It is carefully worded and is useful when a number of areas have to be covered and in-depth answers are not required. It is not entirely satisfying to the respondent

Figure 7.3
Interview Checklist

CHECKLIST

Some time before the interview:
- ■   Have I defined and written down the purpose?   ☐
- ■   Have I listed the key areas to be covered?   ☐
- ■   Have I formulated the key questions in each area?   ☐
- ■   Have I planned my time?   ☐

Immediately before the interview:
- ■   Is the temperature right?   ☐
- ■   Is the telephone diverted?   ☐
- ■   Is there a 'Do Not Disturb' sign on the door?   ☐
- ■   Is the furniture arranged as I want it?   ☐
- ■   Have I got all necessary documents?   ☐
- ■   Have I got a list of key issues to be explored?   ☐

After five minutes:
- ■   Have I developed a good rapport?   ☐
- ■   Have I explained the central purpose of the interview?   ☐
- ■   Have I outlined how the interview will proceed?   ☐

About half-way through:
- ■   Is the interview progressing at the right pace?   ☐
- ■   Am I summarising regularly to ensure accuracy?   ☐
- ■   Am I using open questions?   ☐
- ■   Am I probing where necessary?   ☐
- ■   Am I making the interview interesting?   ☐

After the interview:
- ■   Do I know how to evaluate the responses?   ☐
- ■   Did I ask all the key questions?   ☐
- ■   Am I satisfied with all the information I acquired?   ☐

Stott, K. and Walker, A., *Making Management Work*. © 1992 Simon & Schuster (Asia) Pte Ltd.

in that the opportunity is not present to develop answers. It is doubtful whether in many cases an interview is needed since the format is so similar to a questionnaire, and the use of the latter would be more economical. The only real advantages are that clarification can be given and a response is virtually guaranteed. In job interviews also, the intention may be simply to meet the candidate and the interview is nothing more than a compulsory ritual.

Simple questions are asked and the attempt is made to derive very simple items of information, such as that about the skill level of the applicant. There is generally a great deal of standardisation, perhaps to the extent of having listed a set of questions which are addressed in precisely the same way to all applicants. It does have the advantage of avoiding discrimination, although it is very limiting in the extent of information it can gather.

It is the practice sometimes to use this type of interview to gather data on characteristics and qualities. You may wish, for example, to draw some conclusions on an applicant's motivation level or degree of integrity. From the answers to the prescribed questions, you may make some inferences about these qualities.

Anything Goes

The unstructured variety can take some considerable time to conduct but can be satisfying for the respondent, since he can talk freely about anything associated with the issue in question. It also takes a great deal of skill to conduct this kind of interview, but the data collected may not emerge through any other structure. A small group of professionals, for example, were being interviewed about the redesign of the working day, but by using the unstructured format, they were able to comment on the attitude of the employer toward them; that they were being taken advantage of and generally cheated through a reallocation of time. These fears and perceptions of motives had a significant bearing on what the employer could hope to do, and the information therefore was of great utility.

There is considerable freedom to let the conversation take you in directions which were not planned, but which you feel may be productive. It is flexible and somewhat spontaneous, very much like a normal conversation between friends. It can of course get out of hand, and the digressions may be ill-advised, leading nowhere and doing nothing more than wasting a good deal of time. This is the price that has to be paid for a type of interview which can yield information of great value.

You do not tie the respondent down either in time or scope. You give him plenty of time to answer and let him respond in whichever way he chooses. You have to use open questions well, the sort which are short to ask and long to answer:

> 'What are your reasons for applying for this job?'
> 'How do you feel your past experience in supervision will help you in this management post?'

If the respondent diverts the conversation into an area which he obviously wishes to discuss, you would generally let him.

Apart from open questions, the use of more searching questions is widely practised, for example, the 'What would you do?' type. If you are interviewing someone for a job (a management-level post is a good example), you may want to find out how the interviewee would respond to a particular type of problem. This sort of question then would be useful in offering insights on the candidate's preferred way of handling things.

The more important a post is in terms of relating to other people, whether to those inside the organisation or to clients outside it, the more important it is to match the questioning to the depth of information required. You will use the 'searching' questions mentioned earlier and attempt to derive a comprehensive profile of the person you are interviewing.

Loose–Tight

The semi-structured interview offers the advantages of both these forms. The questions are usually worded very carefully and arranged in a sequence (tight). Because of this, in the case of an interview which is designed to acquire data (such as a research interview) the analysis of the information gained is reasonably straightforward and it is possible to repeat the process. If the nature of responses is taking the interview in a different direction to that expected, it is flexible enough to be adaptive and to pursue the new course if this seems productive (loose). Again, skill is required in knowing the questions to ask, when to ask them and whether to go along with a deviation from the planned route.

In this structure, you prepare several questions which cover your key areas, those about which you must gather information. Within this framework, though, there is scope to move away from the path and discuss issues which are important to the other party and which you consider to have relevance.

Because this *loose–tight* interview offers the best of both worlds, we feel it has considerable utility in a wide number of interview situations. It saves more time than the unstructured type of interview, yet the information acquired is usually of comparable depth. The interviewer must possess the skill to keep the conversation reasonably on course, and this can make it slightly less satisfying for the interviewee.

Organisation of Interviews

There are many different ways of organising interviews and each has its advantages and disadvantages. We look briefly at several of these below: *one-to-one* interviews, *panel* interviews, *co-ordinated sets* of interviews and *group* interviews.

One-to-One Interview

This is usually the most comfortable for the interviewee, especially if the interviewer makes him feel relaxed and able to talk freely. The problems usually relate to little control over interviewer bias and the inability to compensate for skill deficiency in the interviewer. If you do not ask the right questions and fail to spot key issues which should be pursued, there is no one else there to do it for you. On the other hand, making the atmosphere as friendly as possible can often offset the disadvantages by encouraging the interviewee to talk freely and candidly.

Panel Interview

This type of interview is being used more and more. Sometimes just two people make up the panel. They more usually comprise three or more people, and the intention is to include those who can make a valid input into the process. In some cases it may be the senior personnel with whom the successful candidate would be working; in others it may be technical specialists who can ask appropriate specialised-knowledge questions. Unfortunately we see too many interviews where panels comprise people who are there for political reasons; they are present because of their position and have little to contribute. They may even have very little influence on any decision. Panel interviews can become unwieldy, and in the absence of good chairmanship, can easily lose direction and focus.

The demands on panels of interviewers are often overlooked. They are usually unplanned, and the chairman may allow each member a certain amount of time or, say, one question each. If the questions are of low quality (and they often are), the process may be a great waste of resources and opportunity. If an important decision is to be made, it is probably not wise to rely on this process.

Where the composition of panels is not based on political considerations they seem to be fairly successful, and this is especially so where some time and effort is given to preparing for the interview. If you are in charge of a panel of interviewers, however small, gather them together for a meeting in advance of the interview session, and adopt a co-ordinated approach. Decide who is going to ask which type of question, who is going to observe the candidate, who is going to cover each major topic (like experience and career aspirations), and so on. The considerations will obviously vary according to the type and level of interview.

The stress on the interviewee can be considerable in the panel interview, and the more members there are, the worse it is. We see few advantages in employing very formal procedures. If you must have a number of people present at the interview you might consider everyone, panel members and interviewee, sitting on easy chairs, fairly close together and in a circular arrangement. This will be less threatening to the interviewee.

Immediately after the interview, the panel members can discuss their main findings and reach some preliminary conclusions, although any decision would not be reached until everyone has been interviewed. Beware of the problem of impressions becoming distorted over the time scale of a series of interviews. If you have been conducting panel interviews for three hours, your impressions may become more favourable as you get towards the last candidate. On the other hand, you may become so tired that you try to get through the final interviews as quickly as possible, or at least fail to give the same degree of attention to the later candidates. We have met interviewers who have said: 'We didn't really need to go through the rest of the candidates, we knew he was our man the moment he walked in!' This is not the best approach to adopt and it is obviously going to lead to a certain amount of bias against the remaining interviewees.

On a positive note, where a panel reaches consensus on the right person for the job, it has probably been more searching and critical than an individual interviewer could be, and the result is arguably the most appropriate in the circumstances. This of course assumes that panel members can contribute freely and are not constrained by a dominant chairman or over-influential member.

Co-ordinated Sets of Interviews

This is an approach which has impressed us in those organisations which use it effectively. It combines the advantages of the 'one-to-one' and panel interviews, but avoids the trauma associated with the latter and the lack of critical scrutiny which may occur in the former. Each interviewee goes through a series of one-to-one (or small panel) interviews, maybe three or four, and each interviewer has a particular brief to follow. One may ask questions which relate to the relevance of the candidate's career history, another may assess his managerial ability by asking 'What would you do?' questions, and yet another may make personality assessments. It requires a good deal of preparation, because each interviewer has to be clear what his role is and how the information gained feeds into the total picture. After each set of interviews, the panel meets to assemble the data and reach some conclusions, usually against a set of criteria previously determined. The structure of each one-to-one interview could be different but is more likely to be of the 'loose–tight' variety.

There is still the problem which the one-to-one situation presents and this is best offset by having small panels. We suggest that by having two interviewers in each 'set', this will go some way to ensuring that the objectives are met. Another advantage of arranging it this way is that one interviewer can do most of the writing whilst the other asks questions and makes prolonged eye contact with the interviewee.

You could adopt this system even on a small scale and you may find it more helpful than the simple one-to-one interview. It gives a few more of your key staff an opportunity to meet prospective employees and it is no more time-consuming than the panel interview, since interviews run concurrently and candidates simply move round at the end of a given period.

Group Interview

We have noticed some organisations increasingly using this method for some positions. Several candidates are interviewed at the same time, either by one interviewer or a panel. In some cases they may be used to save time, or more usually, the explanation is given that social behaviours are being observed along with such attributes as the capacity to be assertive and speak with effect in a group.

We have used them with success in a research project, not only to save on time in gathering data, but also to enable the interviewees to feed off each other and to stimulate each other's responses. If you decide to use them for any other reason, think carefully first why you want to put candidates in a group and whether this sort of exposure is necessary or desirable. Relevant data does not simply emerge; you have to know what you are looking for before the interview. In situations like job interviews we have found them to be scenes for competitive and in some cases argumentative behaviour . Furthermore, it is often the loudest voice which wins, and that in itself may present a highly misleading picture.

SUMMARY

- One-to-one interviews usually encourage open responses.
- The contribution of each interviewer in a panel interview needs to be planned.
- Panel interviews can be threatening unless a 'friendly' setting is arranged.
- Co-ordinated sets of interviews have to be planned meticulously.
- Group interviews can be used effectively for information-gathering purposes.
- A thorough review is needed soon after any type of interview.

What to Cover in Selection Interviews

In a selection interview, there are some key areas which must be covered, although the extent you will devote to each will vary depending on the nature of the job and the experience of the candidate. Generally, you will need to consider *qualifications, work background, aspirations* and *non-work activities*.

Qualifications

Some jobs are more dependent on qualifications than others. Before the interview you will already have assessed the relevance of the applicant's education background and there may be little need to dwell on this unduly, especially if he has appropriate qualifications. For young interviewees you will obviously be interested in what they have done at school. For more mature applicants, there is often too much attention given to what, after all, is ancient history. People do change and it is what has happened recently which should have the most impact. Should someone who failed to make university when he left school but who acquired a degree through part-time study be treated as inferior to someone who reached degree level through the conventional route? He still made it, and it may have taken more tenacity along the road. You must therefore examine your assumptions very carefully about training and qualifications.

Work Background

The most recent job is also the most important. You can then work backwards from there. It is very difficult to read anything significant into what may have happened fifteen years ago. If someone has spent a long or a short time in a job, do not jump to conclusions; ask him the reasons.

Aspirations

We believe in spending more time discussing this aspect with the applicant because it is forward-looking. It examines what he expects to get out of the job, and what the job can get out of him! Past experience of course may be relevant, sometimes essential, but just because someone has done a similar set of tasks before does not automatically mean he is the best person. You also have to examine potential and motivation. By asking the right questions you should be able to delve into areas which will reveal the level of challenge he will gain and whether there is a match between person and job.

Non-job Activities

You may or may not consider these important. You may feel that someone who eats and sleeps the job is going to give you the commitment necessary. On the other hand, you may see a more balanced personality in the candidate who knows how and when to relax, and who has discovered how to achieve a balance between physical and intellectual activity.

Finally, you have to evaluate the information you acquire. 'An important duty in selecting a new employee is interpreting the applicant's answers, attitudes and reactions. You must look for clues to the applicant's *personality, motivation, work history,* and successes and failures' (Halloran, 1986 : 114).

SUMMARY

- Do not spend too much time asking about qualifications.
- Examine relevant aspects of the work background.
- Focus on the future, and match aspirations, skills and abilities to the job.
- Know why you want to ask about non-work activities.
- Decide in advance how you will evaluate responses.

Gathering Information

We now turn our attention to interviews which are not part of the selection process but more concerned with the gathering of information. They may involve acquiring data which can be used for market 'intelligence', or for problem-solving within the organisation. Some of the observations we make apply to particular circumstances, others seem to have universal applicability.

Different Perspectives

Suppose you want to deal with a problem in your organisation or subunit, and the only way to get the information you require is to talk to people. If the problem is sufficiently important you will need to plan these 'conversations' in advance, deciding precisely what information you need. You will of course be interviewing them although you may not call the meeting an interview as such. Nevertheless, the skills we have outlined above will come into play and you will have to demonstrate the same level of competence as you would if you were interviewing someone for an important job.

If the truth about an issue is to be discovered, it is important to recognise that different perspectives will yield different responses. In learning more about an organisation (or a part of it), for example, interviewing the chief executive or top person in the unit will only present one view of the situation. The truth is more likely to emerge from a multi-perspective investigation, achieved by interviewing at all levels in the organisation.

The issue then of whom to interview is a serious one. Having decided, it is probably advisable to maintain a structure for all interviews but be flexible enough to 'follow the hare'. By allowing respondents to talk freely, the quality of data obtained may rise. Respondents reveal more if they are not limited to 'on-line' responses.

Confidentiality

If confidentiality has been promised, then it must be upheld whatever the circumstances. You may, for example, interview an employee about a behaviour problem and you may have decided it is in everyone's best interests not to 'broadcast' the problem. By keeping the matter temporarily between the two of you, you may be able to exchange views in a more candid way than would otherwise be possible. If, after agreeing confidentiality, an interviewer betrays a trust, it will be difficult for anyone to confide in him in the future. Furthermore, a promise of confidentiality is more likely to yield data of utility.

Write a Summary

As soon as possible after the interview write a summary. This must be done whilst it is fresh in the mind, otherwise considerable distortion can take place, even where the discussion has been well recorded in writing. A concise but comprehensive summary is required and, of course, it must be accurate. If possible it is helpful to show the summary to the respondent to verify the content.

Finally, where you have gathered information about a problem, do not try to interpret the data immediately. Let the subconscious work on it for a short while (not too long) and in that way, the analysis and interpretation will be more meaningful.

SUMMARY

- Different perspectives usually yield different responses.
- Maintain confidentiality.
- Write a summary soon after 'information-gathering' interviews.
- Where appropriate, let the subconscious work on the data before reaching conclusions.

Avoid These. . .

Wragg (1984 : 194) looks in particular at interviews which involve research – the gathering of information which will later be analysed – and identifies five stereotypes which are best avoided if interviews are to be conducted well. Whilst they are probably most relevant to data-gathering exercises, there are some points of relevance to interviewers involved in the selection process, and you are well advised to avoid becoming one of these:

The ESN Squirrel   This person collects incredible amounts of data but has not thought out what to do with it. He has not clarified the purpose of his interview, which gives him considerably more information than he really needs. Decide in advance what information you need and collect that first.

The Ego-Tripper   He has decided before the interview just what findings he wants and so he will turn the interview in such a way as to confirm his expectations. Data which does not support his case is usually discarded. Many interviewers are like this and switch off the moment anything is said with which they do not agree. You have to keep an open mind when interviewing and not be bound by your own preconceptions.

The Optimist   He tries to do too much, not realising that interviews take a great deal of time to conduct. They also have to be planned and evaluated. This whole process takes more than the hour or so which an interview itself might last. Unaware of this, he tries to fit too many sessions into a tight schedule and as a result only deals with superficial issues. Sometimes, interviews for managerial jobs are arranged in such a way that there is little time for discussion amongst the interviewers immediately after the interview. This review phase is vital to the success of the interview and you have to be realistic about the time schedule.

The Amateur Therapist   This is the person who gets deflected from the main task. He lets other issues such as the respondent's emotional problems infringe on the main point of the interview. Do not pretend to be a therapist and do try to avoid giving people advice; they may not take too kindly to it, especially if you have no right to give it. Furthermore, as much as some people would like to share their problem, the message is – don't! If you do, you will not only become distracted from the purpose of the interview, but you will end up with a lot more work and several more headaches!

The Guillotine   He arranges a very tight schedule and is determined to complete it no matter what. He has no time to listen to answers and is only able to work at a superficial level. If an interview is worth doing, it is worth doing properly. If you do not have time to listen, then do not hold the interview.

And do not be like the individual who uses the
time when the interviewee is talking, not to listen,
but to think what he is going to say when it is his
turn to speak!

These may ring true for you even in the selection process. Between us, we
have experienced interviews which have allowed an absolute maximum of ten
minutes for a senior post; they decided they were going to interview all the
shortlisted candidates in under half a day, even if it killed them! We have also
experienced interviews where decisions have been taken in advance, and the
things you say which challenge the validity of those decisions are met with
deaf ears; and interviews which cover a vast array of peripheral issues, but
never seem to touch on the main point.

To relate what we have covered in this chapter to a practical situation we
have provided a case study below which you should examine carefully and
attempt to identify points of good and bad practice. It is a true case. Before
reading it we suggest you look back briefly at the summary boxes in this
chapter to refresh your memory about the main points. Then read the case
study and write down any observations you make which relate to the issues
of effective and poor practice outlined in the chapter.

The Training Manager

Richard was the training manager of a large banking organisation. He was
highly thought of by senior management and the quality of his work was
outstanding. He had a deep level of commitment to the job and would often
inconvenience himself and his family in order to promote relatively innovative programmes of training. Previous incumbents had been less accommodating in their attitudes and their departures had generally been welcomed
by senior management. Richard had managed to change several things in his
three years with the organisation and his approach to training and development was admired not only by those superiors who were familiar with his
work but also by several rival organisations. The perception was that performance had really improved through training, although this was more an
intuitive reaction amongst his superiors than the result of objective analysis.
Apart from his work Richard was a friendly sort of person who got on well
with members of senior management and office cleaners alike. He had
pushed for improvements to the training function on several occasions but
the bank had considered them impossible to implement for various reasons.

It came as a bolt out of the blue when Richard's resignation letter arrived
on the desk of the chairman and chief executive officer, who immediately
telephoned the Director of Personnel and Administration, Richard's imme-

diate boss, and asked him to interview Richard at the earliest opportunity. He considered there may still have been time to change his mind.

The interview was too long to record in full here, but we include extracts from different phases. These give the general picture of what happened and also draw attention to some of the key points of interviewing. George has been the Director of Personnel and Administration for six months, responsible for publications, public relations and training, in addition to the two areas mentioned in his job title. He is directly accountable to the chief executive officer.

The interview takes place in George's palatial office. He welcomes Richard warmly, sits on his executive chair behind his large desk which is stacked high with documents, and invites Richard to sit on the opposite side of the desk on a similar executive-type chair.

GEORGE: Well Richard, I don't think either of us are in any doubt why we are having this chat. The boss is taken aback and it has come as a bit of a shock to me as well. I thought you were happy here. Your salary is good compared with the other banks and we work well as a team. I'm really surprised. Why have you decided to part company with us?

RICHARD: An opportunity came up through a friend in a multinational, so I thought I would give it a go. I haven't worked outside the banking sector before. It will probably look good on the old CV.

GEORGE: So they're offering you more money?

RICHARD: No, slightly less actually, but the conditions are slightly better.

GEORGE: You mean holidays and bonuses?

RICHARD: No, I meant working conditions.

GEORGE: How are they different then from this job?

RICHARD: I think senior management are more supportive of training, so I think my ideas will get listened to.

GEORGE: If I hear you right, what you are saying is that you are not happy with the support you get. How do you really feel about your work here?

(At this point, George's secretary walks in with coffee. They go through the pleasantries of offering sugar and biscuits, and there is a minute's pause before Richard starts his reply.)

RICHARD: To tell you the truth, I'm completely disillusioned. I know there's a job to be done but my hands are always tied. I feel professionally impotent. I have tried constantly to promote ideas about improving training, but I invariably get the same answer: it can't be done at the moment. If senior management's attitude were reasonable, I could accept it, but it isn't. I've given sound reasons why we should make some fundamental changes but I have come to the conclusion that senior management is just not interested in training. I know you will say I'm wrong, but it has done nothing to show that it really believes in the benefits of a successful training programme.

GEORGE: OK Richard, so you are extremely disappointed with our attitude. Tell me again about the ideas which have been rejected and which you obviously feel strongly about.

RICHARD: I've been saying for some time that staff are very unhappy and there is low morale because training is outside company time. They see it as a punishment. I think I would too. I don't think senior management is aware of the effects of having such low morale in the workforce. Anyway, I resent the fact that no move has been made towards a compromise. Not even a minute of normal company time can be used for training purposes.

GEORGE: From the company's point of view, we are very lean on staff at the moment, as you know, and it is just impossible to take people away from their jobs. But I understand what you are saying about morale.

RICHARD: The point is they have to attend training. You know what happens if they don't.

GEORGE: OK, so you feel the importance of training may be linked to the time it is held and to morale. What other ideas did you promote?

RICHARD: Appraisal was one. I could never understand how senior management could dismiss it so easily. I wanted to link appraisal with training and development, so at least there would be a formalised link between the job and my function. The only reaction I got from the top was that the workers would get upset if we introduced appraisal. I think many of them are upset enough already about having to give up evenings and weekends. The other point was about the location. Being stuck away in the basement gives a very strong message to everyone about how important training is seen. Some companies even have training centres which are completely separate. I wasn't asking for anything extravagant; just a few rooms, nicely decorated and furnished, and with some windows so that we could see daylight!

GEORGE: I have written down the three main points about training during work time, appraisal and the location of the training department, and I'd like to discuss those with the chief. If I'm right, you are saying that the real problem is an attitudinal one, that senior management needs to be more convinced about the value of training?

RICHARD: Absolutely right.

GEORGE: What is the position with your new job?

RICHARD: I've received a verbal offer over a drink from the Head of Personnel.

GEORGE: I want you to know that we value your work highly Richard and we want you to stay. I can't simply agree to your ideas being implemented, but I will talk to the chief and ask that the training function be seriously reviewed. In the meantime, I want to ask whether you will reconsider your decision and that we should meet in two days' time to see if there is any way of resolving these differences. How do you feel about that?

RICHARD: That's OK. I'm still fairly keen to go but I'm glad I've had the opportunity to let you know what I think.

GEORGE: Thank you for being so open with me.

We put the extracts together so that they read coherently. Obviously that was not the full interview and in the original, Richard was able to expand on his major grievances and also talk about some other concerns. You will probably have identified a number of positive things which happened and also some minus points. Overall, George did not conduct the interview too badly, although some of the things he did and said could be criticised.

Preparing

George was obviously pressured into an interview before he was ready. All the same, he should have done a bit of homework first. He could have planned the interview in just a few minutes and improved the whole process as a result. A rough plan may have looked like this:

> Purpose: To ascertain whether there is any way we can keep Richard.
> Key areas: Why is he leaving?
>   What would persuade Richard to stay?

The more time George has, the more detailed his plan could be, including the listing of major questions. Obviously, he would not read them out in the interview, but just refer to his brief occasionally. The final question is probably the key to success in meeting the ultimate purpose. It would not necessarily be tackled by asking him bluntly what his demands were, but trying to find out what was really important to him, both in specific and general terms. This needed careful thought *before* the interview.

The Setting

Using his office was reasonable enough, but George set things up rather formally when a more informal arrangement would have been better. The atmosphere was somewhat charged at the beginning, not helped by the physical barriers of the large desk and stacks of documents. At least they sat at the same height. Richard was definitely not at ease. It would have been more appropriate to sit on easy chairs near the coffee table.

The interruption could not have come at a worse time. Just as a key issue had been broached, in walked the secretary. In fact, the interruption should not have come at all. It was right to have refreshments, but George should have arranged for them to be brought in right at the beginning, before the interview started.

The Early Part of the Interview

George greets Richard warmly, a good point, but then gets the interview off to a bad start by jumping to conclusions. He assumes salary is the reason and may be tempting providence by referring to good teamwork! Then he comes in 'cold' with the question 'Why?' It was no surprise that Richard was not very forthcoming; in the original, this unproductive exchange lasted for over five minutes.

Clarifying the Purpose and Stating the Agenda

George said that they both knew why they were there. They did not! The purpose may have been for George to ask what the reasons were for the resignation. It could also have been: to give Richard a 'roasting' for being disloyal; to persuade him to stay; to get some ideas about a successor; to obtain views on how the department might progress; to wish him well in his new job; to offer a payrise; to discuss differences so that they could agree terms for Richard to withdraw his resignation. George therefore needs to outline the purpose and the agenda for discussion. In an interview like this it may be realistic to cover only the issue of why Richard has chosen to leave and then to consider the other matters at a subsequent meeting. Nevertheless, this needs explaining at the beginning.

Watching for Cues

Some of the words which were spoken were not important. It was the feeling of irritation and frustration which lay behind the words which had to be explored. George may have noticed that Richard was shifting his position in the chair frequently while he was answering the early questions. A perceptive interviewer would know that the real answer for his resignation lay behind the words.

Searching and Probing

George starts to make progress when he 'reflects' upon Richard's first statement about senior management not being supportive. Nearly ten minutes had passed at this point in the original interview and George sensed the time was right to ask about Richard's feelings. The question was well timed, since Richard opened up and outlined what had been frustrating him. His irritation was quite apparent.

From there on the interview is conducted adequately, although one or two opportunities to probe may have been missed. He may, for example, have ascertained what was really important to Richard, since this may have been a lever to tempt him to stay. Through failing to identify Richard's priority,

George would go to the chief with three issues which had been raised, but no knowledge of which was the most important. Nevertheless, George used several open questions which elicited detailed replies from Richard, and generally avoided the short-response type of question. He might have understood matters more from Richard's point of view had he constructed more searching questions. He might, for example, have asked: 'If you were in my shoes now, what actions would you take with regard to the work of training?' The response may have indicated the areas in which there was the greatest depth of feeling.

An 'exit' interview like this may also be an opportunity to use 'doubt-forming' questions, although you have to handle these with caution and great sensitivity. If, for example, you really want to keep the employee, and the circumstances are right in the interview, you might ask: 'You have thought through everything and are absolutely sure it will work out?' However, if there is a grace period before the final decision, this can be dangerous, because a firm 'yes' may end the whole affair there and then.

The Conclusion

George finished on a positive note by stating his intention and suggesting a further meeting. He also did well by thanking Richard at the end. However, a summary was needed of the discussion, so that they could both be clear about what had been said. This would avert the possibility of any misunderstandings in the future.

Conclusion

In this chapter we have looked at the actions you can take to make your interviews effective and the skills required. Setting the right environment heightens your chances of making the event successful, whilst adequate preparation is essential. The skills of listening and questioning are central, and the former must be supported by sound observation of visual clues. We have examined different structures and looked at some of the advantages and disadvantages of the different ways in which interviews might be organised. Whilst many of our examples have related to employment interviews, most of the material in this chapter has relevance to a wider range of interview situations. Most managers are involved to varying extent in these and it makes sense therefore that skill is developed in making these 'face-to-face' events meaningful, purposeful and productive.

References

Halloran, J. (1986) *Personnel and Human Resource Management*, Prentice Hall : Englewood Cliffs.

Molyneaux, D. and Lane, V. (1982) *Effective Interviewing*, Allyn and Bacon : Boston.

Wragg, E. (1984) 'Conducting and analysing interviews', in Bell, J., Bush, T., Fox, A., Goodey, J. and Goulding, S. (eds.), *Conducting Small-Scale Investigations in Educational Management*, Harper and Row : London.

Chapter 8

Developing Staff

Effective managers today are acutely aware of the importance of providing their staff with the opportunity to develop. They realise that if employees are not given the opportunity to grow, both personally and professionally, they are unlikely to remain motivated and productive. You may have heard statements such as 'George used to be among the best we had, he was really going places – but he just doesn't seem to have improved himself at all. The quality of his work has really slipped.' In many cases employees such as George have simply not been given enough, or the right type of, development opportunities.

A survey of 1000 senior executives from United States corporations indicated that 77 per cent believed 'the developmental job opportunities available (for) attracting, retaining and motivating a sufficient number of people who could help with leadership challenge was less than adequate' (Kotter, 1990 : 10). Many staff development programmes fail their organisations because they have been shabbily planned and are generally unsystematic.

This chapter discusses the type of **staff development** opportunities which may be organised for employees to aid their development and increase organisational effectiveness. It also suggests one possible model for building a coherent programme. The first half of the chapter provides some necessary background information about staff development. The later section concentrates on the 'how-to' of developing an appropriate programme.

As a starting point for this chapter, try to complete the form in Application Task 8.1. It is designed to get you thinking about staff development as it exists in your organisation before you begin reading. Give some thought to the two questions in the task and write in some brief answers.

Training and Development

For our purposes in this chapter, staff development will be regarded as anything the manager does that develops his employees either professionally or personally, for his or the organisation's benefit. We further define staff development as a carefully planned, systematic and integrated process which aims at increasing the effectiveness of individuals, subunits and the entire organisation.

APPLICATION TASK 8.1

NEEDS AND METHODS

1. What needs should you consider when designing a staff develop-
    ment programme?

2. What methods of staff development do you currently use with your
    staff?

Stott, K. and Walker, A., *Making Management Work.* © 1992 Simon & Schuster (Asia) Pte Ltd.

The term *staff development* is used to describe both employee training and
individual development (we include education within these headings). Both
these forms of staff development are important for maximising organisational potential. To begin our discussion let us briefly examine the differences between training and development.

Training

Training is the process of teaching or exposing an employee to a skill or
knowledge which enhances his competence to perform a task more effectively, and so contributes to the realisation of the group's goals. It is intended
to increase productivity and provide staff with the appropriate skills to ensure

they do their specific jobs effectively for the organisation. Training proposes to develop and utilise the human resources of the organisation for the overall benefit and improvement of the organisation.

If, for example, a department purchases a new software package to update its record-keeping system, relevant staff need to be trained in its use. Training is needed almost immediately for the employees and should not be a long, drawn-out process. The training must be planned and aimed at making the employee proficient in the use of the new system. Once they have mastered the skills and knowledge necessary, the need for the specific training is ended. Training therefore aims to impart technical knowledge and skills for a definite organisational purpose.

Development

Development concentrates on the growth of the whole person, i.e. the expansion of individual ability to allow full utilisation of individual capacity. It aims to provide an employee with the opportunity to apply knowledge and experience to a range of situations, or to the resolution of new or different problems.

The components of a staff development programme must be planned. They should be ongoing and not be stop/start like many training components. Both employees and managers need to be continually developed throughout their working lives. Staff development and training aims to improve the personal and professional skills of employees and meet the overall needs of the organisation.

Although some human resource management writers (e.g. Sikula, 1981) have suggested that training is designed for non-managers and development for managerial personnel, we believe both approaches are necessary for the two groups. Technical managerial skills need to be updated through focused training. Non-managers in today's workforce need to develop as individuals if they are to remain motivated and productive. For example, managers may attend a time management workshop, which trains them for a specific purpose, as part of a staff development programme. The differences between training and development are summarised in Figure 8.1.

Why Have a Staff Development Programme?

An appropriately developed and implemented programme can benefit all *employees* (including managers) and consequently the *organisation* in a number of ways. These are discussed below.

Figure 8.1
Staff Development

TRAINING	DEVELOPMENT
Functional improvement	Individual development
Shorter programmes	Ongoing programme
More immediate	Long-range development
Systematically planned	Systematically planned
Learn for a definite, specific purpose	Promotes overall growth Learn for general purpose
To perform current job more effectively	Considers needs and growth potential of individuals
FOR IMPARTING SKILLS, KNOWLEDGE AND TECHNIQUES TOWARDS BETTER PERFORMANCE DIRECTLY IN JOB	GROWTH OF WHOLE PERSON TO FULL OVERALL CAPACITY

Employees

Staff development through training and development should meet the individual needs of employees. Different methods should be used to help them do their jobs more effectively and enable them to keep up-to-date with current trends and methods. If individual needs are met, employees will be more willing to accept and even initiate change. Job satisfaction is more likely to be present if they are continually learning and extending their experiences. Staff development is also necessary to prepare employees for different or increased responsibility and to identify and prepare those ready for promotion.

Staff development can increase the employees' performance on the job. This often leads to improved operational productivity and greater job satisfaction. It also keeps staff up-to-date with advances in their specific areas of specialisation, whether managerial or technical. Workers become more aware of their own role in the company and more committed to organisational goals.

The Organisation

Effective staff development must also meet the needs of the organisation, i.e. those needs identified as being productive for the organisation (or subunit) as a whole. By meeting these needs the organisation's capacity to predict and cope with changing circumstances in terms of organisation, strategy, and management are enhanced. Staff development should also allow the organisation to be more effective, produce better results and make management jobs easier.

The organisation also benefits through improved teamwork and a more flexible environment. If workers are continuously learning and developing they are, in a sense, constantly changing. This can result in an organisational climate which is more receptive to change and innovation. The benefits are outlined in Figure 8.2. After looking at these do Application Task 8.2 which asks you to relate the benefits to your own organisational situation.

Figure 8.2
Benefits to the Employee and the Organisation

THE EMPLOYEE	THE ORGANISATION
Makes more productive	Improves effectiveness
Keeps up-to-date	Improves quality of output
Broadens experience	Facilitates change
Increases satisfaction	Simplifies management
Increases self-awareness	Improves teamwork
Motivates/reduces stress	Increases productivity
Encourages	Ties individual and organisational
Identifies/prepares for	goals together
advancement	
Promotes personal growth	

Methods of Staff Development

Dunphy and Stace (1990 : 127) found that innovative Australian companies: 'placed a strong emphasis on developing the workforce through personal development, career management and cultural management.' The companies concentrated on developing both individuals and teams, promoted from the inside, instituted wide-ranging development programmes and encouraged intrinsic rewards.

APPLICATION TASK 8.2

View the above chart and ask yourself: Does my organisation presently have a staff development programme in place which provides these benefits?

YES ☐   NO ☐

Now list your own ideas of how a staff development programme could benefit your organisation as it stands at present. Be as specific to your own organisation as you can. Make your ideas as practical as possible, e.g. 'my staff seem to have trouble keeping up with current developments in their field.' 'I need systematic ways of ensuring they remain up-to-date.'

There are various methods for training and developing staff. These can be labelled as formal and informal methods. Formal methods tend to be associated (but not exclusively) with training, and informal with development. Both are equally important and need careful planning. Training and developing staff should be seen as much more than sending workers on a few disparate courses outside the organisation, where they are 'taught' what to do. As Winston Churchill once remarked 'I cannot stand being taught – but I enjoy learning.'

Where possible, staff development should be conducted 'on-the-job'. It has been recognised for many years that approximately 90 per cent of all learning comes through on-the-job methods (Scoville, 1969).

The following are some suggested formal and informal methods for staff development, most of which can be conducted at the work site. Once again it should be emphasised that all these methods need to be planned for by management.

Formal Staff Development

Observation

Incidental or planned observation of work as it is being done. Most work environments present ideal opportunities for workers and managers to learn and develop through observation.

Demonstration and Practice

More experienced workers or supervisors can consciously demonstrate a particular skill and then have their less experienced colleague practise the skill.

On-Site Withdrawal

An area is established separate from the actual work site but within the confines of the overall site. Different types of training can be carried out in this area. Skills acquired can then be practised or sharpened in the real work environment. Alternatively, specialised skills can be simulated for safer practice if necessary.

Apprenticeship

A learner or beginner is attached to an experienced worker who takes responsibility for training the new worker in a specific job.

In-House Courses or Workshops

Relevant skills and knowledge are taught by organisational or 'imported' staff to a group of workers from the company.

'Outside' Courses

Employees are sent to courses run by specialised organisations outside the company. Here employees mix with peers from other organisations. These can either be for training or developmental purposes.

Team Meetings

Workers formally meet as teams to discuss ways to increase productivity or solve specific problems.

Supervision

Supervision of staff is also a training and development method. The supervisor is constantly attempting to update the skills and productivity of subordinates.

Classroom

Some aspects of the job may be better learned in a classroom environment either on-site or off the premises. Classroom methods include demonstration and simulation but may also utilise case studies, role plays, lectures, conferences and audio–visual presentations.

Informal Staff Development

Mentor/Protégé

Managers often progress up the promotion ladder through having a mentor who guides their development and teaches them the 'tricks of the trade'. Although mentor/protégé relationships have traditionally been formed on a personal basis, an increasing number of private companies (such as AT&T) and public sector organisations have implemented formalised mentoring programmes.

Job-Swapping

Allowing staff to swap jobs for a set period promotes the infusion of new ideas and allows managers to develop a broader, whole-organisation perspective. Managers may also be temporarily placed in more senior positions for short periods of time – 'King-for-a-day'.

Committee Membership

Allow employees to serve on various teams or committees even if they are not empowered members. This encourages development through exposure to problem-solving and decision-making strategies.

Reflection Time

Provide time for workers, especially managers, to simply sit and reflect on what they are doing. A middle manager from a large private company recently told us that she put an hour aside each day just to reflect on the major aspects of her job and how she could improve her own and her section's effectiveness. She believed her most innovative ideas stemmed from this time. The manager has since encouraged her management team members to do the same.

Professional Organisations

You should encourage (and support) staff to become members of relevant professional organisations. Membership of such bodies enhances awareness and development.

Counselling

Counselling is when the superior makes himself available to a subordinate to discuss personal aspirations, problems and hopes. This can be included in a developmental appraisal scheme.

Developmental Supervision

Supervision to assist the development of an employee is a powerful developmental tool. This concept is discussed more fully in the next chapter, Adaptive Supervision.

The effectiveness of informal staff development may be encouraged by establishing the following conditions:

1. By creating an atmosphere or climate which stimulates interest in professional or personal growth and promotes the desire to become more competent.
2. By encouraging voluntary participation in interest groups, informal discussions and in decision-making.
3. Establishing employee reward systems which promote risk-taking and innovation.

At this stage it may be useful for you to stop and consider the methods you currently employ for staff development and any other methods which may be appropriate for your staff.

APPLICATION TASK 8.3

SOME METHODS OR FORMS

Go through the lists and tick those methods which you currently employ. Then go through the list again and check those which may be appropriate. When you have done this, write yourself a note on why a particular method would be useful and whom it would benefit. Please feel free to add any other methods: our list is not definitive.

FORMAL METHODS	Using now	Could use	How could it be useful
Observation	☐	☐	
Demonstration and practice	☐	☐	
On-site withdrawal	☐	☐	
Apprenticeship	☐	☐	
In-house courses	☐	☐	
Outside courses	☐	☐	
Team meetings	☐	☐	
Supervision	☐	☐	
Classroom	☐	☐	

INFORMAL METHODS	Using now	Could use	How could it be useful
Mentor/Protégé	☐	☐	
Job-swapping	☐	☐	
Committee membership	☐	☐	
Reflection time	☐	☐	
Professional organisations	☐	☐	
Counselling	☐	☐	
Developmental supervision	☐	☐	

Stott, K. and Walker, A., *Making Management Work.* © 1992 Simon & Schuster (Asia) Pte Ltd.

Identifying Needs

Before any staff development programme can be planned, the needs of the organisation, subunits and individual employees must be identified and considered. It is essential that those who will be involved in the programme have some input in its formation. Different needs can be identified in a number of ways.

A needs analysis can be conducted to gather information about needs. This can take the form of an employee survey, either specifically developed for the organisation or adapted from an existing instrument. Informal observation of employees can also add valuable information.

Needs identification does not have to be scientific and structured when dealing with individual employees. Individual interviews, group discussions or informal chats are valuable for collecting and identifying needs data. When attempting to identify subunit or overall organisational needs, performance figures, supervision or individual reports, and department reviews can be analysed.

Figure 8.3 presents a detailed list of possible methods for determining training needs.

Figure 8.3
List of Methods for Determining Needs

- Work activity analysis
- Employee behaviour analysis
- Appraisal mechanism
- 'On-the-move' supervision
- Special committees
- Predetermined checklists
- Conferencing
- Counselling employees
- Interest questionnaires
- Staff interviews
- Problem box
- Role-playing
- Simulation
- Staff workshops

- Organisational analysis
- Equipment analysis
- Brainstorming
- Team supervision
- Standardised checklists
- Comparisons of output
- External consultants
- Assessment centres
- Informal contact with employees
- Informal observation
- Organisational research
- Self-analysis
- Skills inventories

Sources of information for gathering needs data can come from diverse sources ranging from employee grievances to yearly reports. Despite the range of needs identification methods available most small organisations will probably find the methods listed in Figure 8.4 adequate for their needs.

Figure 8.4
Possible Methods for Determining Needs

THOSE INVOLVED IN THE PROGRAMME SHOULD HAVE SOME INPUT IN ITS FORMATION

Possible methods for determining needs:

Employee survey (adapted or developed)

One-to-one interviews

Group discussion

Informal discussion

Performance results

Supervision outcomes

Individual/departmental reviews

For staff development to be effective and to produce the desired organisational results the programme must be meticulously planned. The following example is only one way in which you may go about designing a programme. You can, of course, adjust the process to suit your own organisation's needs or mode of operation. Just a reminder; for any programme to be successful it must address the needs of the individual, the subunit and the organisation as a whole. Those involved in the programme should have some input into its formation.

Staff Development Model – How to Do It

It is our experience that staff development is commonly neglected by many, if not most, managers and organisations. Whether or not your organisation has a department which covers such matters or a systematic scheme, we believe that you have a responsibility to concern yourself with the development of your staff. After all, you know them, you work with them, and you understand the nature of their jobs. It makes sense that you should have a real involvement in the way they are trained and developed. We would even go so far as to say that if you neglect the professional and personal development needs of your staff, you may be neglecting a critical component of the manager's job.

In larger organisations staff development programmes are managed usually by the personnel department, but smaller organisations may not have a single employee concerned with this aspect of the organisation. It is just as essential, however, for these organisations to have a coherent system of developing employees and the model below applies to those who are starting a system from scratch or trying to improve an existing haphazard system.

Brainstorm

The first stage of developing a programme must be a conscious recognition on your behalf of the need for such a programme. You must believe that staff development and training is important for yourself and your employees. You should also communicate this to all staff members through *words*, *actions* and *rewards*. Simply telling staff is not enough. Take the case of a manager in a small graphic design firm. He knew that staff needed developing in certain areas, so circulated a 'policy statement' attesting to his strong belief in such a programme. However, when staff approached him for permission to attend a course or work on a specific innovative project, he simply replied: 'Impossible, you can't be spared for that long – can't you do the course on the weekend?'

Most of us have probably suffered such inconsistencies. How much more meaningful would the manager's words have been if he had backed his words with actions and rewards? Words alone mean very little. Not surprisingly the manager's staff found his commitment to improvement 'all talk'.

In this first stage you should get a few of your key colleagues together and brainstorm what general needs exist for training and development in the organisation or subunit you lead. You must try to reach consensus on these general needs. A policy statement can be developed for circulation. It should be brief and limited to a number of key points. A sample statement is shown in Figure 8.5.

Figure 8.5
An Example of a Staff Development Policy Statement

1.	We all believe in keeping up-to-date through appropriate training.
2.	We encourage all staff to develop their own particular talents.
3.	We shall try to support and reward involvement in staff development activities.
4.	Methods of staff development will match the needs of the organisation, the job and the person.

When you have decided on the general needs and aims of the policy you must get down to specifics – what is actually needed.

SUMMARY

Brainstorm:

- Identify general needs.
- Try to reach consensus.
- Develop a policy statement.
- Communicate support: words, actions, deeds.

Identify

You know by now that training and development must cater to specific organisational or individual needs. Your job now is to identify those needs. You can do this in a number of ways.

The needs identification process can begin with an analysis of your organisational staff development needs. You could give the organisational analysis questionnaire shown in Figure 8.6 to a few of your staff. It will only take one minute to fill in, but may be very useful. It will not be conclusive, but you will get a 'feel' for whether developmental opportunities are really being provided.

Figure 8.6
Organisational Analysis Questionnaire

ORGANISATIONAL ANALYSIS QUESTIONNAIRE: STAFF DEVELOPMENT

Strongly agree   : 1
Agree   : 2
Disagree   : 3
Strongly disagree : 4

1.	Your job makes the best use of your particular skills and abilities.	1	2	3	4
2.	You feel the organisation supplies you with appropriate opportunities to keep up-to-date.	1	2	3	4
3.	You are permitted to do as much as you can to help the organisation reach its targets.	1	2	3	4
4.	Adequate training opportunities are provided for you by your bosses.	1	2	3	4
5.	Your boss wants you to improve yourself.	1	2	3	4
6.	When you leave work you feel you have done a good day's work.	1	2	3	4

Stott, K. and Walker, A., *Making Management Work.* © 1992 Simon & Schuster (Asia) Pte Ltd.

Statements such as those given in the example above will provide some idea of how employees perceive the organisation's attitude to staff development and begin to give some insight into areas of general need. You should combine this data with concrete information such as productivity reports and output figures.

A method for more specifically identifying needs is to do a job inventory. It may be beneficial if you could complete Application Task 8.4 with a group of colleagues, perhaps your management team.

APPLICATION TASK 8.4

JOB INVENTORY EXERCISE

1.   Attach some large pieces of paper to a wall and appoint a scribe. As a group, discuss and record the essential elements (tasks or actions) of a particular job (for example, you may do this exercise with a group of supervisors). Write every contribution down, whether you agree or not. Now transfer what is on the flipchart paper to the small form.

2.   For each task or action, circle the number corresponding to its importance for the job you have focused on.

3.   Next, circle the number which indicates how much time you spend on a particular action or task.

Importance:	Not important	: 1	Time:	(compared to other tasks)	
	Slightly important	: 2		Spend no time	: 0
	Moderately important	: 3		Little time	: 1
	Very important	: 4		Less time	: 2
	Extremely important	: 5		Same time	: 3
				More time	: 4
				Much more time	: 5

TASK	IMPORTANCE					AMOUNT OF TIME					
1.	1	2	3	4	5	0	1	2	3	4	5
2.	1	2	3	4	5	0	1	2	3	4	5
3.	1	2	3	4	5	0	1	2	3	4	5
4.	1	2	3	4	5	0	1	2	3	4	5
5.	1	2	3	4	5	0	1	2	3	4	5
6.	1	2	3	4	5	0	1	2	3	4	5
7.	1	2	3	4	5	0	1	2	3	4	5
8.	1	2	3	4	5	0	1	2	3	4	5

9.	1	2	3	4	5	0	1	2	3	4	5
10.	1	2	3	4	5	0	1	2	3	4	5
11.	1	2	3	4	5	0	1	2	3	4	5
12.	1	2	3	4	5	0	1	2	3	4	5
13.	1	2	3	4	5	0	1	2	3	4	5
14.	1	2	3	4	5	0	1	2	3	4	5
15.	1	2	3	4	5	0	1	2	3	4	5
16.	1	2	3	4	5	0	1	2	3	4	5

Stott, K. and Walker, A., *Making Management Work*. © 1992 Simon & Schuster (Asia) Pte Ltd.

By doing this application task you should be able to identify the important aspects of the job and how much time is spent on them. If some vital aspects are being neglected, it may be because of inadequate training or because development opportunities are not provided. You can then specifically target these areas of need.

Individual or personal needs must also be ascertained. You can do this a number of ways. One useful method is to conduct a type of behavioural analysis. Let us stick with the example of the supervisor. You should know your supervisor fairly well through both observation and interaction.

Behaviour Analysis

To conduct a behaviour analysis you would write down a few key areas of the supervisor's job. You might, for example, put 'dealing with technicians' or, 'checking documentation'. Let us take the first one: dealing with technicians. You can make some sort of assessment of how the supervisor relates to other people by thinking of the best 'indicator' and the worst one (high to low). You can then enter some intermediate ones in the middle boxes. The form can then be used with all supervisors. Figure 8.7 shows an example of the form for dealing with technicians.

If the supervisor is rated towards the lower end of the scale this probably indicates that he needs some training in handling employees and needs to develop better people management skills. You can double-check your findings and discuss them further with the supervisor at a developmental appraisal interview. We have provided a blank Behaviour Analysis Form in Figure 8.8 so you can try it with one of your employees. Incidentally, it is good to use the instrument like this because you can write them with your situation in mind, so they are relevant to you. Secondly, your staff may prefer to look at something which is graphic rather than forms with which they are all too familiar.

When you have identified organisational and personal needs you should decide on which methods best suit your purpose.

SUMMARY

Identify:

- Specific needs: individual; organisational.
- Question employees.
- Utilise 'hard' data.

Plan

The planning phase involves matching identified needs to methods of staff development. You may also want to prioritise various components if resource restrictions prevent you from immediate implementation. You should be clear about what is really important. One plan can be developed to meet organisational needs and one for individual needs.

Try to fill in Application Task 8.5 for your organisation (you can leave the last two columns blank for now). Be realistic – do not forget our warning earlier from the graphics company. You have to implement it. So check that you can carry it out so that your staff can have confidence in you in the future. Feel free to adapt the form for your purposes.

Then fill in the Individual Staff Development Plan in Application Task 8.6 for your employees. Remember, be as realistic as possible.

As long as your staff development rationale is clear and needs have been properly identified, your plans only need to be brief. For further information on planning see Chapter 4.

SUMMARY

Plan:

- Consider resources.
- Match methods to needs.

Figure 8.7
Behaviour Analysis: Dealing With Technicians

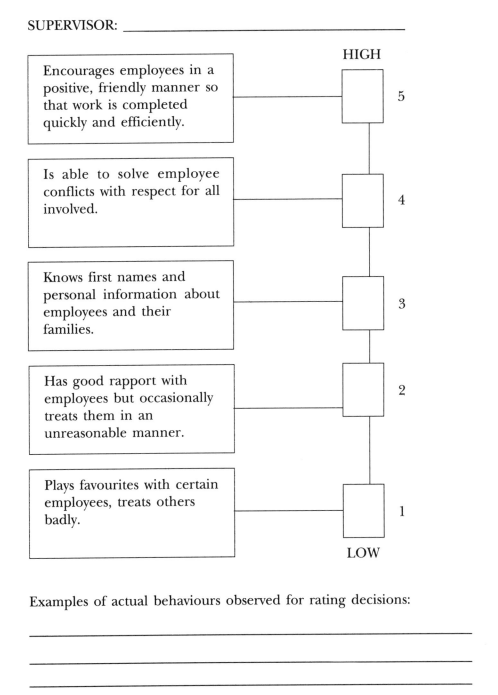

SUPERVISOR: _____

HIGH

Encourages employees in a positive, friendly manner so that work is completed quickly and efficiently.   5

Is able to solve employee conflicts with respect for all involved.   4

Knows first names and personal information about employees and their families.   3

Has good rapport with employees but occasionally treats them in an unreasonable manner.   2

Plays favourites with certain employees, treats others badly.   1

LOW

Examples of actual behaviours observed for rating decisions:

_____

_____

_____

Figure 8.8
Behaviour Analysis Form

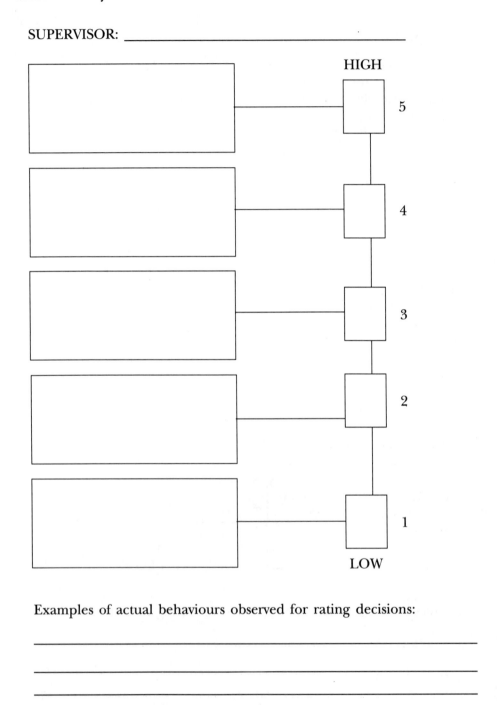

SUPERVISOR: _____

Examples of actual behaviours observed for rating decisions:

_____

_____

_____

ORGANISATIONAL STAFF DEVELOPMENT PLAN

ORGANISATIONAL NEEDS	METHOD(S)	REASON	PRIORITY	TIME	CRITERIA OF EFFECTIVENESS
1.					
2.					
3.					
4.					
5.					
6.					

Stott, K. and Walker, A., *Making Management Work.* © 1992 Simon & Schuster (Asia) Pte Ltd.

INDIVIDUAL STAFF DEVELOPMENT PLAN

INDIVIDUAL NEEDS	METHOD(S)	REASON	PRIORITY	TIME	CRITERIA OF EFFECTIVENESS
1.					
2.					
3.					
4.					
5.					
6.					

Stott, K. and Walker, A., *Making Management Work.* © 1992 Simon & Schuster (Asia) Pte Ltd.

Implement

The time has now come to implement your plan. As mentioned previously, your plan's success will be enhanced if you back up your words with support, actions and rewards. Implement the plan and systematically monitor its progress. Be prepared to adjust methods, timeframes or priorities if required.

SUMMARY

Implement:

* Support.
* Be flexible.

Review

The final phase is to evaluate the effectiveness of your plan. You should do this on two fronts. First, evaluate its effectiveness on an ongoing basis to ensure it runs smoothly. Second, evaluate the entire programme at the end of a specific time, say, one year. While deciding whether it has been successful or not you should be continually looking for ways to improve the plan and its effectiveness. The most important question to ask is: *Has the plan met the identified needs?* If it has, its success should be obvious both in terms of worker satisfaction and increased productivity.

It seems amazing to us when we hear of people being sent on expensive courses, but with no obvious benefits. If you cannot spot the improvement (this may take time of course) you have to question whether you are engaged in the right activities. Below is a simple form or questionnaire you can use to evaluate your own programme.

You should also use this final phase to reassess needs and begin planning for the next period.

Although the evaluation is useful, it is very limited in telling you about the real improvements you want to see. Some companies have tried to evaluate the impact of their staff development programme by asking colleagues, customers and so forth whether they have witnessed any improvement in performance, and this has sometimes taken place as much as two years after the development activity.

Figure 8.9
Staff Development Review Questionnaire

1. How would you rate the programme? (Tick one)

    Unsatisfactory ___   Satisfactory ___   Good ___   Outstanding ___

    Please explain your rating:

    _____

    _____

2. Were your expectations? (Tick one)

    Exceeded? ___   Matched? ___   Not Met? ___

3. Rate the value (1 – Very Beneficial, 2 – Beneficial, 3 – Not Beneficial)
    of the following elements of your staff development programme.
    (Insert own methods.)

    Method 1 _____   Method 2 _____
    Method 3 _____   Method 4 _____
    Method 5 _____   Method 6 _____

4. Do you feel your technical skills were improved by the
    programme? (Tick one)

    Very Much ___   A Little ___   Not at All ___

5. Do you feel the programme allowed you to grow in areas you feel are
    important to you? (Tick one)

    Very Much ___   A Little ___   Not at All ___

6. What suggestions do you have for improving the programme?

    _____

    _____

    _____

    _____

7. Please add any additional comments.

    _____

    _____

    _____

    _____

Stott, K. and Walker, A., *Making Management Work.* © 1992 Simon & Schuster (Asia) Pte Ltd.

SUMMARY

Review:

- On an ongoing basis.
- At end of a specific period.
- Ask: Has the plan met the needs?

Figure 8.10
Designing a Staff Development Programme

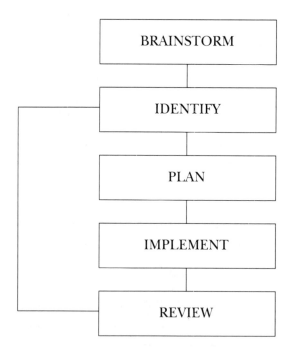

Figure 8.10 summarises the suggested model for developing a staff development programme. Treat this as an outline and adjust it to your own situation.

Now that we have discussed and you have thought about a number of aspects of developing staff, let us try to pull some of the discussion together into a number of practical guidelines that you should consider when establishing or reshaping a staff development programme. These are simply guidelines: it is your job as a manager to incorporate what you need into your organisation's programme.

Guidelines for Improving Staff Development

Involve Participants/Joint Decision-Making

For any staff development programme to be effective those involved in the programme must have an input into its structure and content. Most employees can help identify needs, select methods and decide how outcomes can be assessed.

Conduct 'On-Site'

Staff development is best conducted at the place of work. Learning that takes place in the work place is more likely to be retained and utilised than that taking place elsewhere. Of course, this is not always possible, especially in relation to long-term developmental courses. If staff development does take place away from the organisation, information should be disseminated to colleagues as appropriate and as soon as possible.

Make It Continuous, Tied to Organisational Goals

Staff development should be an ongoing process, not simply a collection of diffuse training courses. The staff development programme must be tied to organisational goals. It must be useful and relevant to all employees.

Promote a Positive Attitude

Staff development will only be effective if management promotes it as a positive activity and builds a climate that encourages self-improvement and risk-taking.

Make It Job-Related/Activity-Oriented

A staff development programme must be related to the jobs of employees and be based on the principles of adult learning. It should be experientially based for greater learning.

Provide Support

Management must provide both moral and material resources for a staff development programme to be effective. If management does not provide the necessary support, employees may feel that the programme is regarded as unimportant. If, for example, you wanted to introduce a formal mentoring programme you would have to commit considerable resources to provide a reasonable chance of success.

Plan Carefully

Staff development must be carefully planned. Employees will rarely develop by accident; needs are met through careful planning.

Ensure Organisation, Subunit and Individual Staff Development Needs Are Met

An effective staff development programme attempts to meet the needs, not only of the organisation as a whole, but also those of subunits and individual employees. Different employees, depending on their stage of development or expertise, will have different needs which will need to be catered for through various methods. When employees have their staff development needs met, they are more likely to achieve both subunit and organisational goals.

Monitor Results

Monitor outputs of the staff development programme to ensure it is meeting the desired needs and achieving set goals.

Make It Non-Threatening/Non-Judgemental

Staff development should not be a stressful experience for employees. Remember it is meant to help them and the organisation reach full potential. Staff, either individually or as a group, are unlikely to be open about their needs and weaknesses if they feel they are being judged. Adults are more predisposed towards learning and developing if they do not feel threatened. When monitoring the programme do not fall into the trap of comparing employees – it is not an appraisal exercise. Simply determine whether the programme is moving the way you planned it.

SUMMARY

Some Guidelines for Improving Staff Development:

- Involve participants/joint decision-making.
- Where possible conduct 'on-site'.
- Make it continuous, tied to organisational goals.

- Promote positive attitude.
- Ensure job-related/activity-oriented.
- Provide support.
- Plan carefully.
- Ensure organisational, subunit and individual needs are considered.
- Monitor results.
- Make non-threatening and non-judgemental.

Do Not Forget – They Are All Adults

Managers responsible for planning and implementing staff development programmes and activities also need to consider what research and practice tell us about how adults learn. If the unique needs of adult learners are not taken into account, staff development programmes may have far less chance of being successful. Here are some points you may want to keep in mind (summarised from Knox, 1986).

- Adults must be convinced that what they are doing is worth-while.
- Adults have a wide variety of experiences – they must feel that this is important by being allowed to share their points of view.
- Adults want genuine input into what will be involved in any programme. If they have this they will be motivated.
- Adult learners, like everyone else, like to be rewarded or acknowledged for their strengths and contributions.
- Adult learners have a fear of failure or of being judged. They learn best in informal/non-threatening situations.
- Adult learners tend to be motivated by the pleasure of doing as much as by any material rewards.
- Adult learners must believe in their own ability and worth if they are to learn. They must feel respected and trusted.

So you are now aware of some of the theory relevant to staff development. However, the best staff development programmes often include elements of a manager's personal experience; that is, experiences the staff development planner has had that he feels made a real impact on helping him make a genuine improvement in how he did his job.

In Application Task 8.7, try to cast your mind back through your career and identify those experiences which you feel made you better in your job and also those experiences which you feel made little or no impact to your job effectiveness. Then, try to translate those experiences into five practical points which may help guide your own staff development programme.

APPLICATION TASK 8.7

WHAT MAKES AN IMPACT?

1. List some experiences that you feel made you better in your job:

2. State why you think these experiences made such an impact:

3. List some experiences that you feel made no difference to increasing your competence as a manager:

4.   State why you think these had so little impact:

How can you translate what you wrote to a staff development programme? List what you consider to be the five most useful elements you
would include in a staff development programme for your organisation,
for example, a supportive infrastructure or a wide range of training
methods.

Element One:

Element Two:

Element Three:

Element Four:

Element Five:

By now you should have done at least some thinking and reflective note-taking about staff development in general and in your organisation in particular. Now let us try and apply some of that knowledge to a problem case. Read the case and try to answer the accompanying questions. It may even be useful for you to discuss your perceptions with a colleague.

Case Study: Steven Low

Steven Low has been working in the same small company as a middle manager for twenty-one years. He is generally liked by both superiors and subordinates and is considered to be a 'reliable person'. Mr Low is very traditional in the sense that he believes his seniority exempts him from having to attend further courses or be advised by his boss, who happens to be ten years his junior.

Steven refuses to admit that the less than effective performance in his unit may be his fault and blames it on 'the lazy youth of today'. You have heard from a colleague that he does not want to go on a management skills course because he believes he is too old and it would be embarrassing.

You, as his boss, realise that you must do something about Mr Low, as his attitude is beginning to affect the attitude of other middle managers. You wonder whether the staff development programme you inherited from your predecessor could be to blame. It basically comprised a few workshops which everyone attended and sending middle managers to available courses at outside agencies. It is time for you to consider the joint, and perhaps related, problems of Mr Low and how the organisation approaches the development and training of employees.

Discussion questions:

1. What is the problem?
2. What would you do about Mr Low?
3. What would you do about the staff development programme to help employees such as Mr Low?

The problem may be that Mr Low is a product of the past staff development programme. If this is so your eventual solution is to work on the programme itself. This, however, will not solve Steven's problem in the shorter term. We suggest that he is afraid of putting himself in an embarrassing situation. He probably feels sensitive about the age difference between you and him. The best way to deal with Steven may be to talk to him alone and allow him some input into his own development. Allow him to approach it slowly while stressing the importance of continuous development for all staff. Perhaps you could make him responsible for the development of a group of young employees. The long-term solution of course is to build a staff development programme that identifies and then addresses organisational *and* individual needs, like those of Steven.

Conclusion

This chapter has attempted to provide some basic background information about developing staff. We tried to communicate the idea that you as a manager must take responsibility for the development and training of your staff, regardless of what the larger organisation is doing. It is essential that you construct a coherent staff development programme that meets both organisational and individual needs. If you do this and periodically update the programme the organisation will benefit.

References

Dunphy, D. and Stace, D. (1990) *Under New Management: Australian Organisations in Transition*, McGraw-Hill : Sydney.

Knox, M. (1986) *Helping Adults Learn*, Jossey–Bass : San Francisco.

Kotter, J. (1990) *A Force for Change: How Leadership Differs from Management*, The Free Press : New York.

Scoville, J. (1969) 'A theory of jobs and training', *Industrial Relations*, **9,** 1, pp. 36–53.

Sikula, A. (1981) *Personnel Administration and Human Resource Management*, Wiley : California.

Chapter 9

Adaptive Supervision

'What do you mean it didn't go out?' screamed the boss. 'We spent two full weeks and over $70,000 to get that project completed, and you're telling me it was delivered to the wrong address. Are you telling me our whole success depends on the drivers of our delivery vehicles?'

The answer to the boss's last question is definitely 'yes'. Any organisation is only effective as long as its employees do their jobs properly. It does not matter how many managerial processes you set up, ultimately people have to do the job, and in the specialised, complex and diverse roles demanded in today's organisations, employees cannot be watched all the time. **Supervision** has always been a vital component of any manager's job and its importance has not diminished as organisations have become more complex. We believe effective supervision is the responsibility of every manager, regardless of their position in the organisation. All managers are, even if by default, supervisors.

> The largest number of managers are supervisors or first line managers, with a range of titles like foreman, office manager, ward sister, sergeant, chief clerk, superintendent, charge hand, leading seaman, head steward, floor manager, leading chef. In any organisation most employees report to their supervisor, who is responsible for assigning tasks to them, overseeing their work, making sure it is done satisfactorily and dealing with complaints and queries. (Torrington, 1989 : 36)

If supervision is so important to the manager, what does it mean? To the layman, it usually implies someone carefully watching a group of workers ensuring they stick to their jobs and do not make mistakes. What we mean by supervision is substantially different: it involves the manager in setting up the conditions in which a subordinate *can* do a good job and ensuring he is effective in the job. You may be thinking that you do this all the time in your managerial capacity. The fact is, supervision is generally practised badly and, in some cases, avoided. As you read on, you will begin to understand the important role which skilfully employed supervision plays in facilitating work effectiveness.

Before we begin our discussion, we would like you to consider the following two questions to start you thinking about supervision:

1.   Is it necessary to have more knowledge about a subject than the employees you are supervising? Explain your answer.
2.   What are the most pressing supervisory problems for you?

We have asked these questions of many managers and condensed some of their answers below.

1.   Do you do the same work as the people you supervise?

A skilful supervisor can usually supervise effectively regardless of whether he has knowledge of the subordinate's field of expertise. It is useful to have some knowledge and this may well enhance credibility, but it must be remembered that the purpose of the supervisory process is aimed at improving job performance by helping the employee become more self-directed. Essentially, effective supervision transcends the boundaries of expertise and specialisation. We are not denying that expertise is important for managers, but we do not believe that in today's organisations any one person can have all the expertise necessary. Managers as supervisors, however, must still ensure that staff get the job done.

2.   What are the most pressing supervisory problems?

- Finding the time to supervise all employees properly.
- Maintaining co-operative attitudes among employees.
- Convincing employees and myself of the value of supervision.
- Convincing employees that developmental supervision is non-judgemental.
- Getting employees to become self-critical.
- Giving feedback about job performance without appearing threatening.
- Motivating people to do good work.
- Getting employees, particularly older colleagues, to participate co-operatively in a judgemental situation.
- Convincing employees that certain data collected is not going to be used for judgemental purposes.
- Convincing oneself of the value of developmental supervision.
- Being able to separate developmental and judgemental supervision in my own mind.

Were your answers similar to those of these managers? We can draw from these perceptions that managers do not necessarily need to have the same specialised knowledge in all areas as employees. This is something that often stops them from supervising effectively.

We can also see that all managers face supervisory problems and that meeting supervisory responsibilities is not easy. We now look at supervision therefore and consider how some of these problems can be addressed.

Supervision

Supervision forms part of many people's jobs already. Generally it is seen as simply involving the monitoring of routine tasks where performance is easily measurable. Supervising the work of employees with more complex roles is an aspect of organisational life which we believe has mostly been unsystematic and less than satisfactory in its administration.

It has been shown, however, that skilled supervision can have a significant impact on performance. This is particularly true in the supervision of those with management and supervisory roles themselves. However, it is not simply a matter of watching a subordinate and telling him what he is doing wrong. It is a structured process of enhancing work performance with the aim of ultimately fulfilling organisational targets, whether maximising profits or offering a quality service. It matters that it is done well.

In this chapter we do not aim to cover the process and purpose of supervision in any detail – there is already an abundance of supervisory literature available. Nor do we attempt a comprehensive discussion of the subskills necessary for supervision. Many of these skills, such as motivating, interviewing, target-setting and negotiating are covered in other chapters. We will however expose you to a systematic approach to the topic which we have labelled *adaptive supervision*. We use the word *adaptive* because we believe the system can be adapted both for your particular organisation *and* for your individual employees. It relates to all levels of management, not simply lower or junior levels. Supervision is perhaps one of the most difficult parts of your job; you have to accept that you, regardless of your level, are responsible to your boss for your organisation or subunit (Video Arts, 1984).

We begin by discussing the different types of supervision necessary in any organisation, the responsibilities of the supervisor, and, briefly, the rationale behind adaptive supervision. The remainder of the chapter sets out the adaptive supervision system.

Judgemental and Developmental Supervision

You are responsible for the supervision of your employees. Typically, this requires both a judgemental and a developmental approach. *Judgemental* supervision basically involves you in making a value judgement about the worth, value, or competence of an employee in a certain situation or across a number of situations in his job. *Developmental* supervision, on the other hand, aims at improving the employee's work ability through a non-threatening approach. It focuses on an employee attempting to identify his own weaknesses and developing (with your help) strategies for improving performance in the work place. What may be included in the two types of supervision will be discussed later.

It is very difficult for employees to differentiate between these two types of supervision. Before they can be convinced of the difference, you must have the distinction between the two modes clear in your own mind and be able to communicate this. You must be able to separate evaluative and developmental behaviour.

A supervisor in a private company informed one of his immediate subordinates that he wanted to watch how she briefed her staff on a new sales strategy. The supervisor's purpose, or so he said, was simply to watch the briefing and then talk to his subordinate about how it went and then let her identify how she could improve her performance next time. At the end of the session however, he sat down with her and rattled off a list of points where she had gone wrong and what to do next time. When he had finished, he left, believing he had helped his subordinate to develop her skills. She must have felt, however, as if she had just received a school report card and performed miserably. Her confidence was dented and she did not feel she had been treated like a professional. She knew she could have done better and had some ideas she wanted to discuss with her boss, but he did not give her a chance. How could she develop if she was simply told what she had done wrong?

In our example, the manager believed he was helping his subordinate to develop, but she felt as if she was on trial. The senior manager did not see the difference between helping his staff to develop, ultimately for his organisation's benefit, and stating in black and white terms what was good or bad.

So the first thing you need to do as a supervisor is to differentiate between developmental and judgemental behaviour. This will help you, even at a subconscious level, to communicate the difference to your employees.

To help in this you should complete Application Task 9.1. Some of the statements are judgemental and others descriptive. Descriptive statements are based on facts which allow the supervisee to identify for themselves where and how they need to improve and develop. Judgemental statements reflect the supervisor's perception of what is good or bad. These are often based on unfounded assumptions.

APPLICATION TASK 9.1

DESCRIPTIVE OR JUDGEMENTAL?

Test yourself: Can you spot the difference between developmental and judgemental statements? Read each statement and identify whether you think the statement is D (descriptive) or J (judgemental). You should also circle the words which influenced you in making your decision.

Descriptive or Judgemental

1. Employees do not like to be watched.
2. No one wanted to be first to answer the boss's question.
3. The boss did not ask any questions.
4. The boss was too tough on Richard.
5. What Mrs Jensen said made Kim feel useless.
6. The manager does not move around enough.
7. That was not the best way to deal with the secretary.
8. The boss talked to ten different customers in one morning.
9. Mary was confused by the accountant's reply.
10. The legal expert asked five factual recall questions.
11. David was day-dreaming as usual during the sales meeting.
12. Nobody learnt anything from the presentation.
13. The boss spent time helping those who needed help.
14. Jane left her office without asking permission.
15. The managing director was in a bad mood during the meeting.

All the statements in Application Task 9.1 were judgemental except numbers 3, 8, 10 and 14, which were descriptive and based on fact. Look at question 2; it appears straightforward enough, but how do you know no one wanted to answer the boss? Perhaps no one could answer?

Supervisory Responsibilities

The main purpose of supervision is to safeguard and improve the work undertaken by employees. It is the process of facilitating the growth of the employee for organisational benefit. This is best done through giving him clear feedback about performance and then encouraging and helping the employee to use the feedback to become more effective in the job.

We believe supervisors in any organisation have three main responsibilities. First, you are responsible for the quality and/or quantity of output for your organisation or subunit. Second, you are responsible for the development of your staff, that is, helping them to develop both personally and professionally so they can reach their maximum potential. Finally, you are responsible for motivating your employees: for building their commitment to their job and the organisation's goals (Sergiovanni, 1987). A supervisor who ignores any of these points risks having to deal with an unbalanced and ineffective team.

Shin (1986) provides three basic rules for the supervisor which support our position:

RULE ONE   : Make your subordinate want to do well.
RULE TWO   : Give your subordinate the need to do well.
RULE THREE: Use criticism as a constructive tool.

You should aim to fulfil these responsibilities and must exercise leadership in supervisory practices. Some of your more practical responsibilities encapsulated in these three main points are displayed in Application Task 9.2. The list is not definitive.

To meet these and other responsibilities, and to encourage more effective work behaviours, you need a system which attempts to meet the needs of all your employees.

Adaptive Supervision

One of your most important managerial functions is to supervise the members of your organisation or unit. As we have seen, supervision includes both judgemental and developmental elements. But is it enough for you to simply implement a system of supervision which caters for all your employees using the same method? Before we proceed, answer the questions posed in Application Task 9.3. Tick the appropriate box.

APPLICATION TASK 9.2

MAJOR RESPONSIBILITIES OF THE SUPERVISOR

QUALITY   DEVELOPMENT   MOTIVATION

Write an 'M' if you believe the particular responsibility involves motivating your employees, a 'D' if it involves development, or a 'Q' if it involves quality control. Each point may involve more than one aspect of your major responsibilities. You can add to the list.

The supervisor aims to help employees to:

1. Better understand their jobs.

2. Select and use resources.

3. Interpret and cope with problems.

4. Develop leadership skills.

5. Promote productive work relationships.

6. Become better managers.

7. Develop a climate for motivating their subordinates.

8. Become effective team members.

9. Understand organisational goals.

10. Become more productive.

11. Reflect upon their practice.

12. Refine their behaviours.

13. Communicate with others.

14. Widen their work perspective.

15. Grow as individuals.

16. Do their jobs more effectively.

Stott, K. and Walker, A., *Making Management Work*. © 1992 Simon & Schuster (Asia) Pte Ltd.

APPLICATION TASK 9.3

THINKING ABOUT EMPLOYEES

	YES	NO
1. Do all your employees learn to do their job better the same way?	☐	☐
2. Do you believe all people in your organisation have the same skills and knowledge?	☐	☐
3. Do all your employees learn at the same rate?	☐	☐
4. Are all your employees at the same stage of development in their job?	☐	☐
5. Do all your employees do the same job?	☐	☐
6. Do you motivate all your employees the same way?	☐	☐
7. Are all your employees happy to work alone?	☐	☐
8. Do all your employees think at the same level?	☐	☐
9. Are all your employees driven by the same wants and desires?	☐	☐

The questions should all have been answered with a 'no'. It would be very difficult to answer 'yes', even if you have a very small staff. Your answers to the questions provide the basic rationale for *adaptive supervision*. No two people develop, grow or learn in the same way; no two people are the same, and this is the basis of our supervision model: *people are different* and should be looked after differently.

Professionals and researchers from the world of education have devoted much time to developing supervisory practices which attempt to meet the needs of different individuals (Glickman, 1981; Glatthorn, 1984; Sergiovanni 1987). They acknowledge that all people progress through common growth stages and that this progression is usually orderly and sequential. The rate of progression, however, and the number of stages an employee progresses through, are dependent on the individual.

We concur with the rationale presented by the above authors but have expanded the system to bring it more in line with contexts in a wider range of organisations. Adaptive supervision aims to balance developmental and judgemental supervision within the one system. The system acknowledges that both approaches are equally important to you and your organisation.

Adaptive supervision acknowledges that different employees develop and learn best through different means. It provides three *options* which can be used with employees to further their individual development, depending on how they best learn, develop and interact with people. Of course, we see personal development as ultimately leading to organisational benefit. Adaptive supervision also suggests three approaches to judgemental supervision which are *mandatory* and common to all employees: these allow you to keep your eye on how your organisation or subunit is performing as a complete unit.

The diagram in Figure 9.1 presents the various components of adaptive supervision. Each employee would have his developmental needs met through participating in one of the *developmental options*. All employees would be judged on the quality of their work through participation in all three of the *judgemental mandates*.

Figure 9.1
The Adaptive Supervision System

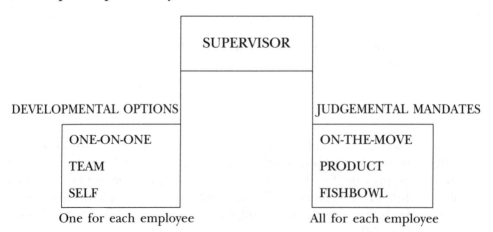

We now take a brief look at both the developmental options and evaluative mandates. The three developmental options available are: *one-on-one*, *team* and *self-supervision*.

The Developmental Options

One-on-One

One-on-one supervision (usually called *clinical supervision*) is an in-depth process designed to improve job performance by meeting with an employee and planning, say, a work schedule, observing part of the job, analysing the data gathered, and giving the employee feedback about the observation. The process can be repeated a number of times during a year. One-on-one is excellent for upgrading specific skills and suitable for those employees who like their learning and development directed by someone else. If, for example, an employee needs to become familiar with a new sales technique, you can observe him in action actually presenting the technique to a group and then help him identify where he could do better. This would involve something similar to the process in Figure 9.2.

Figure 9.2
One-On-One Supervision

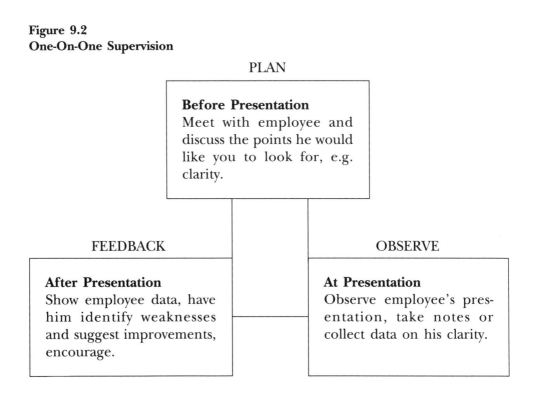

PLAN

Before Presentation
Meet with employee and discuss the points he would like you to look for, e.g. clarity.

FEEDBACK

After Presentation
Show employee data, have him identify weaknesses and suggest improvements, encourage.

OBSERVE

At Presentation
Observe employee's presentation, take notes or collect data on his clarity.

You need to remember that one-on-one supervision is developmental. During the planning phase you should not simply tell the employee what you will be looking for. You should ask him where he feels he would like help. During the observation phase try as much as possible to concentrate on the area identified during the planning phase (if you cannot be at the presentation you could have it videoed and view it later). When you take notes or collect other (possibly quantitative) data, try to make it as descriptive and neutral as possible. When looking for clarity of presentation, for example, you may count how many times others ask for a particular point to be explained again.

After the observation you may want to go over the data you have collected and try to put it in a more easily communicable form for the employee. During the feedback stage simply show the employee the data you have collected and get him to identify weaknesses and suggest how he can improve. You can, of course, offer positive suggestions and answer any questions which the employee may have.

One-on-one supervision will not suit all employees but may be useful to some on a regular basis and others when skills need to be learned or upgraded. This type of supervision is very time-consuming and would be impractical to implement with all employees.

Team

Team supervision is a collegial process in which two (or a small group of) employees agree to work together for their own professional growth. This is particularly appropriate for those working at managerial level. They can observe each other's work and give each other feedback. They may also collaborate in any number of professional activities.

Team supervision follows a certain system:

1. Teams Formed

Subordinates form into teams of two or more members, they should have no more than five members. You can have some input into team formation but those involved should also have a say. You may decide you would like a certain member on the team so he can learn from the other members.

2. Areas Identified

Team members identify areas where they would like to develop and specify plans for achieving their goals (decide on methods). Although it is up to you, planning for one year at a time is preferable. Once again you can have input but should not impose your own ideas. Remember, the team members are aiming to develop in areas they feel are necessary. Both you and the team should agree on the areas for development before they proceed. Members are responsible for keeping track of their developmental activities and should be able to explain why they are valuable. To support this phase, a form along the lines of the one shown in Figure 9.3 would help ensure that progress is systematic.

Figure 9.3
Team Directions Agreement Form

Team members: 1. _____

2. _____

3. _____

Unit: _____   Date formed: _____

Agreed areas for development:

Methods of development:

Team feedback session 1: date: _____   Signed: _____

Team feedback session 2: date: _____   Signed: _____

Individual feedback session: 1. _____   2. _____   3. _____

Manager: _____

Team members: 1. _____   2. _____

3. _____

3. Plan Implemented

Team members are then responsible for planning, guiding and working towards their own development. Methods for doing this are limited only by their ingenuity. They can, for example, observe each other in specific settings or meet informally to discuss professional issues. Team members should keep some sort of *growth log* (such as in Figure 9.4) which shows they are thinking about what they are doing and developing as a result of their activities.

Figure 9.4
Example of a Growth Log for One Team Member

Team area of development #1: DEALING WITH PEOPLE		
Team: _____ Member: _____		
Date	Activity/Event	Benefit to me
20/1	Met team, discussed concerns regarding inability to deal with problem employees.	Realised that others have same problems. Realised I need to improve my HR skills.
26/1	Watched Wendy deal with an employee complaint.	Impressed with how she listened to Mr Low even though he was very rude – calmed him down.
3/2	Met with team to share ways of improving our human skills.	Realised that all employees cannot be treated the same way. Got some hints – gave some too.
16/2	Watched video on HR skills.	Very useful, must try them out.

4. Feedback

You should meet with your team at least twice a year to stay in touch with what they are doing. In these meetings they can share their growth logs with you and discuss how they feel their development is progressing. Here you should act as a type of consultant. You should also meet with each team member on an individual basis to discuss developmental concerns and offer advice if necessary (this may form part of the developmental appraisal process which is discussed in Chapter 10). At no stage should any information gleaned from team members be used for judgemental purposes. There must be a high degree of trust in the process.

Team supervision allows a group of employees to work together to develop jointly in specific areas. They draw motivation and assistance from each other. In most cases employees are aware of their development needs and capable of helping each other grow.

Self

There are always some employees who work better on their own. It is not that they are incompetent or do not like other people, they simply prefer or are forced by circumstances to work alone – and do a good job working that way. *Self-supervision* enables the individual to work independently on his developmental growth concerns. The employee carries out an individual plan for development and the supervisor serves as a resource person. A typical format for self-supervision basically follows the target-setting approach discussed in Chapter 11. It would take the following form:

1. Employee identifies own developmental targets and time frame and submits to you.
2. You provide reactions to employee's targets and time frame.
3. You meet with the employee to discuss, review (if necessary) and agree on developmental targets and time frame.
4. Employee proceeds with plan in accordance with time frame and is responsible for collecting own appraisal information. The employee should keep a growth log similar to the example exhibited in the Team Supervision section.
5. You and the subordinate meet to discuss progress and development. Supervisor provides feedback. Targets for the next session discussed (procedure begins again).

We now briefly depart from the supervision system itself and take a look at two of the skills that are crucial for making supervision effective. In every option we have mentioned *giving constructive feedback* as an integral part of the process. The following section gives some advice on effective listening and giving constructive feedback. We believe these skills are vital for effective, meaningful supervision.

Giving Feedback

All the developmental options involve you in providing feedback to the employee. For your feedback to be worthwhile you must *listen* to the employee before you comment or react. You cannot give constructive feedback until you can really listen.

It is not an easy skill to practise effectively because it involves much more than passively keeping quiet. Some advice on actively trying to improve the skill is given by Low, Chong, Leong and Walker (1990) and this is shown in Figure 9.5.

Figure 9.5
Hints on How to Listen Effectively

THE LISTENER SHOULD:

- Clarify what the speaker is saying by asking questions.
- Paraphrase what the speaker says to check for understanding.
- Be receptive both verbally and non-verbally.
- Pay attention, do not interrupt.
- Delay evaluation.
- Do not jump to conclusions.
- Attach values to what is said.
- Be aware of the speaker's feelings.

After you have listened to an employee during a supervision feedback session (for example, during one of the review meetings for self-supervision) you must provide some constructive feedback. Feedback is not just a matter of *what* you say, but of *when* and *how* you say it (Nelson-Jones, 1986). Sergiovanni (1987) provides some useful suggestions for providing feedback:

1. When giving feedback to your employees try to be descriptive rather than judgemental.
2. Be specific; avoid generalisations.
3. Concentrate on things that can actually be changed.

4. Take care to consider your own motives. Be careful not to try and 'show-off' or impress by espousing your own knowledge.
5. Give feedback as close to the time of the actual behaviour as you can.
6. Rely on evidence and especially where the accuracy can be validated.
7. Concentrate on his strengths as well as his weaknesses.

We have so far looked at the developmental options involved in adaptive supervision and will now turn our attention to the judgemental mandates. All managers need to ensure the quality of their product. You also need a picture of the organisation or subunit as a whole. To do this you have to make some judgements about the effectiveness of your employees. The judgemental forms of supervision enable you to reach some conclusions on this aspect of your evaluative role, although it must be re-emphasised that it is separated from the formative options which we have just discussed.

The Judgemental Mandates

On-the-Move

On-the-move supervision is a judgemental form of supervision that involves you in monitoring the work of employees, making brief and perhaps unannounced visits simply to ensure that the employees are carrying out assignments in a professional manner. This monitoring should be performed by a sensitive and trusted supervisor. Many people are critical of such 'drop-in' monitoring, but evidence seems to show that such a process is an effective aspect of a supervisor's role.

The concept of on-the-move supervision was popularised by Peters and Austin (1985 : 378-92) when they found that Management by Wandering Around (MBWA) was a common practice in successful American business firms. On-the-move supervision should be viewed by employees as a positive and understood part of the organisational management. You should ensure that you perform this function in a systematic fashion and that all employees are visited regularly.

When you have conducted a visit you may even want to write a short comment to the employee. For example:

You would have noticed that I dropped in on your meeting this morning and was fairly impressed with what I observed. Your control was good and you seemed to be following the agenda reasonably closely. I was a little concerned that you were not encouraging everyone to participate and seemed to be running out of time. What do you think? Perhaps we could talk about it some time. I accept I was only there for a short time. Anyway, well done Peter.

On-the-move supervision helps you ensure the quality control aspects of your organisation.

Output

Output supervision is another form of judgemental supervision where you collect and appraise employee written records, such as planning documents, marketing figures, financial accounts, and other samples of employee output. This may mean examining a manager's schedules, records of discussions with customers and so forth. This type of supervision is useful for assuring quality control, comparing departments, and for seeing the organisation as a whole rather than as a collection of separate entities. It is very important, in that it will allow you to identify patterns of successes or weaknesses. This view is very important when outside accountability is emphasised. The key purposes are summarised in Figure 9.6.

Figure 9.6
Output Supervision

OUTPUT SUPERVISION

> The collection and appraisal of planning
> documents and other samples of relevant output.

PURPOSES:

- ■ Comparing subunits.
- ■ Quality control.
- ■ See organisation as a whole.
- ■ Show interest, vehicle for encouragement.
- ■ Gauge overall strengths/weaknesses/successes

Although many organisations have quality control mechanisms for the goods they produce, few seem to have built in mechanisms for the quality of decisions, ideas and more qualitative forms of output which can determine the organisation's success or failure.

When using output supervision, you may not be able to collect all documents. In many cases this would be foolhardy to attempt. You can, however, collect samples. This is not only useful for quality control purposes but also shows your employees that you are interested in what they are doing. Once again a short note to provide feedback may be useful.

Fishbowl

Fishbowl supervision is quite simply an observation that is done to judge the quality of the employee's performance in the job. Where, for example, a manager has to hold meetings, it could involve the supervisor in sitting in on one such meeting and to judge the manager's effectiveness in conducting it. You need not conduct this type of observation too often unless a particular employee is having real difficulties or causing problems. Attached supervision may also be useful if you are considering a candidate for a promotional position and need some hard, summative data about his performance.

Both judgemental and developmental forms of supervision are necessary for you to run an effective organisation. Fishbowl supervision aims to meet both individual and organisational supervisory needs.

Figure 9.7 summarises the purposes of the various components of the adaptive supervision system in relation to your responsibilities as a supervisor.

Figure 9.7
Supervisory Roles and Adaptive Supervision

PURPOSE	COMPONENT
MOTIVATION AND DEVELOPMENT	ONE-ON-ONE TEAM SELF
UPGRADING	ONE-ON-ONE
QUALITY CONTROL	ON-THE-MOVE PRODUCT FISHBOWL

Flexibility, Matching and Planning

Flexibility

When you use the adaptive supervision system, you must be prepared to adapt it to your own situation. In other words, you must be flexible. We have tried to show how to adapt certain types of supervision to suit individual employees. But you must decide how you will adapt the system to your own organisation. Variables, such as the size of your staff, their level of expertise, the nature of their jobs, expectations of more senior managers, the organisational culture and how you feel about supervision are all important factors in determining the appropriate balance of supervisory activities. Regardless of any differences we strongly suggest that you keep the developmental and judgemental philosophies separate. They serve very different purposes and this needs to be clear to everyone involved.

Matching

One question you may well be asking when you come to deciding on developmental options for specific employees is 'How can I decide which option would be most beneficial to a particular employee?' This question of course does not arise for the judgemental components. All employees can be supervised using identical methods.

To help you with your matching, we have included a questionnaire in Figure 9.8 which will give you an idea of which developmental component may suit a particular employee. Despite the questionnaire's utility, it is no substitute for your intimate knowledge of your employees. If you are doing your job you will know how they best operate and how they can best develop. Try the questionnaire and combine its findings with your own perceptions. Do not use the instrument as the only method for matching employees to options. You may also find it very useful to simply ask your employees which option they feel would be most beneficial.

When you have completed the questionnaire for several of your workforce, you will notice that it is highly unlikely that any one employee falls into one option category. Certain options could help the employee develop in different ways. However, we believe the questionnaire will give you an initial idea of where the employee could benefit. The higher the score differentiation between boxes, the more likely the option will match. If the scores are close for two or more options you will have to delve deeper to help decide on an

Figure 9.8
Matching Employee with Option Questionnaire

---

1 : Indicates that you *strongly disagree* with the statement.
2 : Indicates that you *disagree* with the statement.
3 : Indicates that you *agree* with the statement.
4 : Indicates that you *strongly agree* with the statement.

1.	Employee likes you to make decisions for him.	1	2	3	4
2.	The employee likes to experiment with new ways of doing things.	1	2	3	4
3.	The employee dislikes challenging and difficult situations.	1	2	3	4
4.	The employee prefers to watch what is going on and comment, rather than taking an active role.	1	2	3	4
5.	Employee definitely needs my help to improve.	1	2	3	4
6.	The employee likes to see how things work and then try them out.	1	2	3	4
7.	Employee will not give up on a task until it is finished.	1	2	3	4
8.	Employee contributes at meetings.	1	2	3	4
9.	Employee needs my help in a number of areas.	1	2	3	4
10.	Employee readily accepts responsibility.	1	2	3	4
11.	Employee tends to see problems as relating to the whole organisation.	1	2	3	4
12.	Employee likes to make decisions in a group.	1	2	3	4
13.	Employee has fallen behind in his skills development.	1	2	3	4
14.	Employee is self-motivated.	1	2	3	4
15.	Employee learns best from feedback after he has been observed in a real situation.	1	2	3	4
16.	Employee can meet target deadlines.	1	2	3	4
17.	Employee has difficulty in solving problems on his own.	1	2	3	4
18.	Employee needs to be motivated to improve performance.	1	2	3	4
19.	Employee likes to be his own boss.	1	2	3	4
20.	Employee always attends social occasions.	1	2	3	4
21.	Employee needs continuous assistance.	1	2	3	4

22.	Employee does not function well in a team, but is competent in his job.	1	2	3	4
23.	Employee performs badly when forced to work alone.	1	2	3	4
24.	Employee has a good grasp of theoretical concepts and can apply these to problems.	1	2	3	4
25.	Employee likes to make his own decisions.	1	2	3	4
26.	Employee likes to work with his supervisor.	1	2	3	4
27.	Employee likes working on group projects.	1	2	3	4
28.	Employee goes out of his way to help new colleagues.	1	2	3	4
29.	Employee is weak in work-related skills.	1	2	3	4
30.	Employee enjoys working with others.	1	2	3	4

When you have completed the questionnaire add the numbers given in each line and record the total in the corresponding box below.

A. 1 + 3 + 5 + 9 + 13 + 15 + 18 + 21 + 26 + 29   =   ☐   Total

B. 4 + 6 + 8 + 12 + 17 + 20 + 23 + 27 + 28 + 30   =   ☐   Total

C. 2 + 7 + 10 + 11 + 14 + 16 + 19 + 22 + 24 + 25   =   ☐   Total

A	B	C

Now write a 1 in the box which has the highest score, a 2 in the middle and a 3 in the lowest score box.

The box which has the highest score provides you with some idea of which developmental option the employee could be developed most effectively through. As we mentioned in the section on matching, you should not rely solely on this questionnaire. You should consult your employee and use your personal and professional knowledge of him.

A = ONE-ON-ONE
B = TEAM
C = SELF

option. It may help you to give the questionnaire to your colleagues and see what their responses are.

Planning

When you have matched your employee to a certain option you need to plan how you will provide the supervision to your whole organisation. Let us use the example of the manager of a restaurant complex in a large shopping centre. The manager has sixteen outlets and a total of twenty-two junior managers under him. He realises he must supervise all the managers (as they must the employees under them). He decides to use the *adaptive supervision* system.

Let us assume he has matched his employees with a particular develop-mental style and will involve all in the judgemental mandates. His basic planning chart for one year may look like that shown in Figure 9.9.

This figure gives an idea of what a yearly *adaptive supervision plan* may entail. For it to work however, you must be flexible. Perhaps some employees will have some one-on-one sessions and also be members of a team. Perhaps someone who is responsible for his own development will act as an advisor to a team, or team membership will be changed every six months. Adapt the system to suit your organisation or subunit.

As well as the above plan you may wish to keep a simple one-page form on each staff member to keep track of what he is doing. An example of such a form is shown in Figure 9.10. Supervision plans, like all other plans, should be constantly reviewed and evaluated.

Conclusion

In this chapter we have suggested a system of supervision which aims to cater for the unavoidable differences among your staff. Employees learn, grow and develop at different rates and in various ways, so different methods of super-vision should be used to aid this development. As a supervisor you are not only responsible for the development of your staff, but also for ensuring the quality of the output. You need some common mechanisms for ensuring staff are doing the job they are expected to do.

We have presented a six-component system of adaptive supervision which, if implemented appropriately, has the capacity to account for both your developmental and judgemental supervisory responsibilities.

Before we leave supervision, let us examine a few supervisory situations which you may encounter. In Application Tasks 9.4 and 9.5, you should reach some conclusions as to the actions you would take.

Figure 9.9
Supervision Schedule

Employees	Development Option	Jan.	Feb.	Mar.	Apr.	May	Jun.	Jul.	Aug.	Sep.	Oct.	Nov.	Dec.
B. Flood G. Nancy S. Lee	TEAM (Team 1)	T	*				*					*	
R. Lun S. Ponsard P. Little B. Singh	TEAM (Team 2)	T	*					*					*
F. Gotez R. Ladlow T. Chung L. Perez	TEAM (Team 3)	T		*					*		*		
M. Harros	SELF	O	*					*					
P. Stead	SELF	O	*					*					
R. Chew	SELF	O	*					*					
H. Mowbray	SELF	O	*				*						
G. Derg	SELF	O		*			*						
M. Hunt	SELF	O		*					*				
I. McCrew	SELF	O		*					*				
J. Dowson	ONE-ON-ONE	A		*		*		*		*			
W. Kalwitz	ONE-ON-ONE	A	*		*		*		*			*	
B. Vale	ONE-ON-ONE	A		*			*			*			*
T. West	ONE-ON-ONE	A		*		*			*		*		

Symbols:

T = Team meets together to set developmental direction and methods for a year.

O = Individual sets targets for development and growth (and methods) for a year.

A = Individuals decide the areas in which they would like the manager to help them develop during the year.

* = TEAM: Team meets with manager to review what they are doing and subsequently to let him know progress towards development and ask for advice or clarification. The manager may also use this slot to meet with individual team members. Manager gives feedback.

* = SELF: Individual meets with manager to discuss targets and methods of development for the year, manager has input. Subsequently they meet to review progress, give feedback and iron out any difficulties.

* = ONE-ON-ONE: Individual and manager meet to focus on exactly what the employee wants to concentrate on and how the manager can help. They set up dates to match situations and methods of observation. Manager then observes and provides developmental feedback.

Stott, K. and Walker, A., *Making Management Work.* © 1992 Simon & Schuster (Asia) Pte Ltd.

Figure 9.10
Staff Supervision Form

Name: _____   Position: _____

Developmental option: ONE-ON-ONE
(circle one)
 	
     TEAM
 	
     SELF

If using team option, name of other team members:
 	
      1. _____
      2. _____
      3. _____

First meeting: Development areas (in priority order)   Date: _____   Signed: _____
Final review session notes: Date: _____   Signed: _____
If one-on-one, dates and topics for observations: Notes on observation Session 1: Session 2: Session 3: Session 4: Session 5:
Judgemental mandates (notes and documentation attached) 'Product dates'   'On-the-move dates'   'Fishbowl dates'
All supporting material should be attached to this form.

Stott, K. and Walker, A., *Making Management Work.* © 1992 Simon & Schuster (Asia) Pte Ltd.

APPLICATION TASK 9.4

SUPERVISORY SITUATION ONE: DO I INTERFERE?

During an 'on-the-move' visit to a junior manager's meeting with four company representatives (for whom he was responsible), the atmosphere was so bad that you considered assuming responsibility for the meeting. It was obvious that the meeting was not productive, very personal in some of the comments and a waste of company time.

1.   Under what circumstances would you do this?

2.   What are your actions, decisions and recommendations?

Stott, K. and Walker, A., *Making Management Work*. © 1992 Simon & Schuster (Asia) Pte Ltd.

APPLICATION TASK 9.5

SUPERVISORY SITUATION TWO: EXPERIENCED EMPLOYEES

You have the responsibility of supervising and developing all your employees. The employees have a wide range of experience, expertise and ability, ranging from juniors with less than two years' experience to those with over twenty. The more senior employees object to the concept and practice of supervision. They say you can simply tell how effective they are by looking at the balance sheet. You agree with them and have enough confidence in their ability to believe that they do not require any sort of 'one-to-one' supervision on a regular basis. But you have a responsibility to ensure that all colleagues are working effectively and that the customer service is of high quality. You cannot ignore the problem.

How can you address it and ensure that these more experienced colleagues are working effectively in their various jobs?

Stott, K. and Walker, A., *Making Management Work*. © 1992 Simon & Schuster (Asia) Pte Ltd.

There are no right or wrong answers to these cases. In Application Task 9.4, you may feel you have to intervene there and then to stop things from getting out of hand. Alternatively, another manager may wait and talk to the junior manager after the meeting is over and try to discuss the situation and possible strategies to stop it from happening again. In short, your solution will very much depend on your situation and your individual style. The inescapable fact, however, is that you must do something about a problem such as this. No manager can ignore his supervisory responsibilities.

All managers, regardless of their position in the organisation cannot afford to trivialise the supervisory responsibilities they have both to their staff and their organisation. You need some system for ensuring that both professional and personal needs are met, ultimately for the organisation's benefit.

Finally, it is worth reminding ourselves of the key features of supervision, best exposed in this simple definition:

Supervision involves the manager in setting up the conditions in which his subordinates can do a good job and in ensuring that they are effective and satisfied in the job.

References

Glatthorn, A. (1984) *Differentiated Supervision*, ASCD : Alexandria, VA.

Glickman, C. (1981) *Developmental Supervision*, ASCD : Alexandria, VA.

Low, G., Chong, K., Leong, W. and Walker, A. (1990) *Developing Executive Skills*, Longman : Singapore.

Nelson-Jones, R. (1986) *Human Relationship Skills: Training and Self-help*, Cassell : London.

Peters, T. and Austin, N. (1985) *A Passion for Excellence: The Leadership Difference*, Random House : New York.

Sergiovanni, T. (1987) *The Principalship: A Reflective Practice Approach*, Allyn and Bacon : Boston.

Shin, G. (1986) *Leadership Development*, 2nd edn, McGraw-Hill : New York.

Torrington, D. (1989) *Effective Management: People and Organisation*, Routledge : London.

Video Arts Ltd (1984) *So You Think You Can Manage*, Video Arts : London.

Chapter 10

Developmental Appraisal

Appraisal should be a positive, constructive method of helping an individual do better.

(Freemantle, 1985 : 14)

This chapter is about a scheme of developmental appraisal which you as a manager can put into operation. It is not intended as a replacement for any formal scheme currently in place and which may be predominantly concerned with performance and be essentially judgemental. We indeed had great difficulty in deciding on an appropriate title, preferring to avoid the label *appraisal* and its associated connotations, since our intention is to focus very firmly on the developmental aspects of employees' work lives. It became apparent however that this could not be separated from any discussion about performance, and that development is inextricably linked to the way in which an individual does his job. We decided therefore to call our scheme **developmental appraisal** since it is part of the appraisal process, but emphasises that part which is sadly neglected in the actual operation of many appraisal schemes: the development needs of employees.

We have not ignored the performance dimension. On the contrary, we refer to performance frequently and even provide some guidelines on how to consider performance in the context of development. The message we want to get across however is that we believe the *formative* process must receive at least as much attention as the *summative*; that organisational performance is most likely to improve through the development of its members. It is on that premise that we recommend and outline a scheme which attempts to identify the key aspects of the job, consider performance, and specify development and growth activities which will effect improvement in performance and lead to increased satisfaction on the part of the employee.

When looking at the appraisal issue, we have observed three situations in organisations. Many have an appraisal scheme; a few of these schemes are well conceived and effective; some have no scheme at all. For the first situation, you will notice we have avoided describing the schemes as poor ones. We simply feel that the focus is overwhelmingly on performance and its assessment (or even judgements about the individual's characteristics) with little recognition given to development needs and actions. Such schemes tend to have detailed objective assessment documents and may operate on a 'secret' basis with such items as 'confidential reports'. It is not our intention to give advice to the organisation on the nature of an appraisal system, but to help you as a manager look at the way in which you can help your subordinates identify their development needs so that they can grow in the job and consequently lift their levels of performance. If you have a formal scheme in place, we suggest you examine how you can use the material from this chapter to complement and enhance your existing scheme. In a large organisation it is unlikely you can tamper with it, since it will have clear instructions for its operation, but you might consider this more informal and developmental-focused scheme as a separate activity. If you do not have any kind of performance appraisal, you might productively use most of the material, including that which relates to performance. In this context, we have attempted to show the way in which performance and development should be considered together, and we have provided guidelines on how you should examine the priorities of the employee's job, examine performance and then identify 'discrepancies': the gaps between what is happening and what should be happening.

Part of this developmental process involves the day-to-day conversations which may last a matter of seconds. Nevertheless, these provide an ideal opportunity for the regular feedback which must form part of any developmental appraisal activity. 'To the Superboss appraisal is second nature. He does it informally on a daily basis as an integral part of his task of managing people' (Freemantle, 1985 : 14). However, it is also useful to schedule some time when the manager and the employee can sit down together and discuss a variety of matters concerned with the employee's development. The need for an ongoing process is highlighted by Pratt (1986 : 82) indicating that staff

> . . . do not respond to a situation which resembles an audience with the Pope or a meeting with a timid solicitor who is about to tell them that auntie has left them nothing in her will. . . Those managers who treat appraisal interviews as an integral and natural part of their job will undoubtedly create a climate in which they succeed.

It is one of the principal means by which staff get considered answers (which, it is thought, they are entitled to receive) to some very natural questions like:

> 'What is expected of me?'
> 'How am I judged?'
> 'How am I getting on?'
> 'How can I do better?'
> 'How can I further my career?'
>
> (Everard, 1986 : 143)

Figure 10.1
Striking the Balance

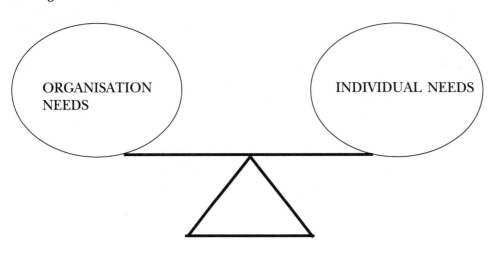

The key purpose of a scheme which answers these questions is to balance the requirements of the organisation against the needs, expectations and contributions of its employees (see Figure 10.1). Implied in this statement are a number of desired outcomes. In considering the benefits to employees, effective systems:

1. Enable them to measure their achievement.
2. Recognise their achievement.
3. Prepare them for advancement.
4. Open up opportunities for personal growth.
5. Clear the air of problems and build their relationship with their manager.

(Everard and Morris, 1985 : 76)

What all this means is that *understanding* is increased and that a positive move is made towards *the effective use of human resources*. As we look to the future, new skills may be required if the job is to be done well. Part of the development process is to match the abilities of employees with the demands of the job. But it is more than that. The employee also expects the organisation to contribute to the pursuit of career goals. These seemingly different dimensions have to be seen together as complementary elements of a coherent developmental process.

Let us look at the benefits outlined by Everard and Morris (1985) and you should now ask yourself what you do as a manager in each of these areas. Try answering the questions in Application Task 10.1.

APPLICATION TASK 10.1

SOME KEY QUESTIONS

1. How do you enable your staff to measure how well they are doing?

2. What strategies do you use to recognise their achievements when they do things well?

3. How do you support them if they desire career advancement?

4. How do you arrange for the right development activities to support effective performance in the job?

5. How do you encourage your staff to air problems and grievances (even about your management)?

Stott, K. and Walker, A., *Making Management Work.* © 1992 Simon & Schuster (Asia) Pte Ltd.

Develop or Stagnate

Before we look briefly at some of the underlying tenets of developmental appraisal, you should complete the short questionnaire A Basic Philosophy.

Questionnaire

A BASIC PHILOSOPHY

	Strongly disagree	Disagree	Agree	Strongly agree
1. My employees are able to improve and want to do so.	☐	☐	☐	☐
2. The organisation is more likely to be high-performing if employees are motivated.	☐	☐	☐	☐
3. I am thoroughly conversant with the skills and abilities of those who work under me.	☐	☐	☐	☐
4. It is important to reach some opinions on the potential of my staff to take on future increased responsibilities.	☐	☐	☐	☐
5. I am aware of the employee skill development needs in my sphere of operation, both immediate and longer term.	☐	☐	☐	☐
6. I should agree work targets and plans with my staff rather than simply impose them.	☐	☐	☐	☐
7. I should devote attention to the personal development expectations and wishes of my staff, even though they may not be directly related to their present jobs.	☐	☐	☐	☐
8. Giving my staff regular feedback on how they are performing is absolutely essential if they are going to improve and develop in their jobs.	☐	☐	☐	☐

You have probably managed to answer 'strongly agree' to at least some of the questions. You may not be able to give that answer to statements 3, 4 and 5, but it is hoped you will make use of the developmental appraisal process to acquire and use the information. All the statements are concerned with what must be seen as a basic philosophy which underpins any commitment to development. The manager needs a sound philosophy of developmental appraisal if the scheme, albeit informal, is to have credibility.

An overriding belief must be that all employees can improve. Not only is there scope for improvement, but most are capable of it. It needs sensitive handling, but the issue has to be addressed. Without employee development it is difficult for the work in the organisation to grow. Through a successful developmental approach, both organisational and employee needs can in many organisations be reconciled.

The second part of the philosophy is concerned with organisation and departmental needs. First, the organisation wants motivated employees. The impact of this on the fulfilment of organisational mission is substantial and often overlooked by managers. Second, the organisation needs to know what its employees can do and what they are capable of learning. This is part of the human resources development process. Are you fully aware of the skills and abilities of each of your staff and the extent of their future potential? Third, having identified future organisational needs and the present abilities available amongst staff (set alongside what they may be capable of) you should be able to pinpoint any discrepancies – the gaps between what is needed and the present skills available.

The final part of the philosophy is concerned with the needs of the employee. Work objectives need to be agreed. With genuine agreement comes commitment, heightening the chances of motivation. The employee also needs regular feedback so that adjustments can be made where necessary. And he needs to know there is a concern with his satisfaction and development.

Working on the premise that many employees display commitment and have a deep concern for their contribution and career path, they need the opportunity to discuss their performance and aspirations with the immediate superior, who is in the best position to influence their development needs and expectations. A discussion therefore:

> . . . provides one occasion on which the individual can make a relevant contribution to the planning of training and other development activities. This should not be limited to asking him what courses he wishes to attend during the forthcoming year (details of which he will not have anyway!), but rather discussing areas of real development which can be approached on a joint basis. (Pratt, 1985 : 4)

SUMMARY

Start with the Premise that Everyone Can Improve.
The Organisation Needs:

- Motivated employees.
- An accurate picture of their abilities and potential.
- An understanding of their development needs.

The Employee Needs:

- Agreed work targets.
- Regular feedback.
- An understanding of how performance is measured.
- Opportunities to discuss development needs.
- Opportunities to discuss personal development and advancement expectations.

Benefits

So what can the developmental component of appraisal do for the organisation and the individual? Many believe that it has a substantial contribution to make to the self-esteem and morale of employees. It is right that good work should be recognised and staff motivated through reinforcement. Unfortunately there may be limited scope in many situations for motivation through career advancement, and esteem may have to be developed in existing roles and in other ways.

It may be suggested that developmental appraisal has a significant part to play in reducing 'people' problems which feature very highly on management training programmes as prime concerns. It can without doubt help create an atmosphere in which key issues take centre-stage and understanding can be elevated between managers and employees. In this way relationships may benefit from the process.

If the system is to be seen as a coherent one, developmental appraisal needs to be related to organisational or subunit review. It is not a separate process, but one where organisational practices and change are logically related to subgroup and individual practices and change. In this context it will almost certainly mean the organisation having to clarify its mission and its strategies for achieving the mission. With an increased understanding of how individuals see their jobs, the organisation is able to plan more appropriately for changes in all dimensions of its operation and ensure that staff development is related to these.

Your staff are more likely to support the scheme if it is seen as a *formative* process and not just a *summative* one of performance. A system which is seen only as being linked threateningly to promotion, pay and to the weeding out of incompetents is unlikely to have much credibility in being concerned with the development of its employees. As Freemantle (1985 : 14) observes: 'appraisals are not witch hunts, nor insurance records, nor pay determinants.'

In specific terms, conducting a process of developmental appraisal might yield the following benefits to employees. The process:

- Enables them to measure how well they are doing.
- Recognises and records their achievements.
- Identifies ways in which they can grow and develop.
- Clears the air of problems and builds up the relationship with the manager.
- Identifies the type of activity which will be most productive in developmental terms.

The benefits also carry over to the organisation, department and the clients. Targets are clarified, practice improved, ideas about good practice are shared and staff morale may improve, with all the attendant benefits which these imply for the organisation's operation.

Purposes

The purposes of developmental appraisal are:

- To encourage staff to work towards the highest levels of performance.
- To provide feedback.
- To change things to support the employee's work and improvement.
- To develop and maintain a climate of trust in which frank discussion can take place.

Changing things may raise the sensitive issue of whether your performance is facilitative or obstructive. How this is approached will be determined by the degree of frankness which you have managed to achieve amongst colleagues. 'A manager who is able to create a climate of openness wherein subordinates feel free to "appraise" her or him will be in a position to enhance her/his own managerial effectiveness' (Rubin and Rose, 1978 : 9). It should be remembered that staff development includes you as manager, and this may also include the improvement of management skills and abilities.

The purpose of developmental appraisal needs to be clearly fixed. Some people see even conventional performance appraisal as a process capable of doing a wide range of jobs, but many of these may be in conflict. It is unlikely that it can improve performance, change behaviour, change relationships, determine pay, determine promotability, and satisfy top management that everything is in order and of sufficient quality. Contrary to opinion, most schemes in the industrial and commercial spheres are not directly related to salary and incentives. Freemantle (1985) too sees pay and promotion as issues to be separated from appraisal, because if a linkage exists, individuals are likely to become defensive and not be prepared to expose their weaknesses, which might be necessary for development to take place. We also see our scheme as an *active* one, like that described in Randell, Packard and Slater (1984 : 9), with an essential feature being 'the assembly and sharing of information, which provides both the individual and organization with a learning experience.' But there are pressures to reward performance and these of course may be desirable. Our developmental scheme has to be separated from such tangible rewards. We see achievement and development as satisfying intrinsic rewards, and we are therefore concerned with openness, trust and the consideration of development in a conducive climate, free from intense competition for scarce rewards and incentives.

The Approach

The system is intended to be a co-operative effort between superior and subordinate. The employee is expected to engage in a process of self-analysis, examining recent past performance, devising plans and objectives for future short-term work and expressing plans and interests in terms of career development or personal job satisfaction.

The manager also has a key role to play. He must help the employee become more self-evaluative about performance (in those circumstances where it is possible) and relate his own managerial role to that of the employee. The perspective is also needed to identify the skills which must be developed and to ensure that realistic advice is given on career expectations and development activities. The manager's central role is further highlighted by Randell *et al.* (1984 : 10): 'how well a manager develops his staff is the final, and perhaps most important, link in the managerial effectiveness of any organization.'

In terms of individual development, the focus is on skills and training, since it is possible to do something about these. It is often tempting to discuss qualities such as resilience and creativity, but these may prove to be elusive concepts, and it is not usually possible to do much about them anyway. It is more constructive, therefore, to emphasise the skills and competencies which need to be developed and can be developed.

The Scheme

The scheme described in this document is one that is structured, systematically assessing the performance demands of the job, identifying development needs (leading if necessary to training and modified assignments), and other activities which promote individual development.

The system described is workable and not unduly time-consuming, since it forms part of a wider informal framework. It has to be recognised however that to do the job properly, some time commitment is necessary, but it has to be perceived as highly productive time, and not a plug-on extra to the 'real' job.

It is intended to be fair and to address the really important issues. It is a standardised format which can be used across the organisation, although it has more scope for use with those employees (e.g. managers and supervisors) who have the capacity to evaluate their own contributions and to determine the sorts of activities which might best reconcile their personal goals and those of the organisation. The materials we have included are also intended to be flexible and easily adapted for use in different contexts. This is an important feature. It is sensible for institutions to work with systems which suit their own ways of working, their distinctive cultures, rather than try to operate an externally imposed, and possibly inappropriate, system.

Although it focuses on careful analysis and disciplined thinking, it is essentially employee-centred, since without the commitment and satisfaction of the individual employee, the organisation cannot reap the benefits.

It is of course not without its problems. How do you respond to the individual who says: 'It is no use to me; I am simply a worker and things are going well'? It is not an easy question to answer, but unless a positive approach is adopted, the individual is faced with

> . . . the prospect of continuing to do the same things in the following year and the years beyond that. The chance to pause and reflect through the appraisal process gives them the opportunity at least to question this ongoing cycle and to consider steps which would bring about change. (Blackburn, 1986 : 52)

This familiar situation is easily transposed to other contexts. People do get into ruts and managers are no exception. They become too busy to reflect on the things they do and to question their practices. If employees are to change their working lives in any way they need a framework within which to do it. Appraisal therefore may be central to making a development system function. It provides open, face-to-face discussion and helps to identify individual strengths and development needs so that any efforts towards improvement are appropriately directed.

Principles

A system of developmental appraisal is based on several principles:

Shared Responsibility

The individual and his manager share the responsibility for improvement in the work place and for future development. It has to be seen as a co-operative effort. It is the case in many appraisal systems that a manager sees his responsibility lying simply with performance improvement, whilst any suggestion of individual development is placed firmly in the employee's court. Both must work together.

Openness

Discussions are open, demonstrating a high level of trust between manager and employee, and conversations focus on specifics wherever possible. You have to be open if you are to make improvements. If, for example, one of your practices is a hindrance to the employee doing his job effectively and he is unable to tell you for fear of the consequences, the job will not be performed optimally. We could tell many anecdotes which demonstrate lack of trust and these generally lead to situations between managers and subordinates where neither group is able to achieve real effectiveness. Furthermore, there are usually relationships problems. It takes a feeling of confidence and security to ask your members whether you have any practices which make their jobs difficult. If you were to do this, would you receive frank and honest replies? Rubin and Rose (1978 : 9) draw attention to some of the benefits of openness:

> Numerous ideas and suggestions come up the ladder and become the stimulus for important improvements and changes which benefit the entire organization. Again, this will happen only when the manager works hard to create a climate of openness and nondefensiveness with his or her subordinates.

Openness is not only about management practice and style. It also encompasses a willingness on the part of the employee to reveal weaknesses and an indication of career or job expectations so that appropriate development activities can be worked out together. 'The Superboss will create a climate of trust and mutual help whereby individuals will readily appraise themselves and discuss methods of improvement' (Freemantle, 1985 : 14).

Specifics

There is little point in talking in generalisations. They mean little to people. You have to give specific examples. If you are dealing openly with an employee's weakness in a communication skill, it is not sufficient to state that he does not listen. You have to draw attention to a specific situation when, say, he asked a question which had already been answered and that you observed his lack of eye contact; you also noticed that certain body language signals suggested he was not paying attention. You have to look for information as specific as this if it is to have utility.

Agreed Work Plans

Achievements are considered against work plans which have been agreed. You need to work collaboratively with employees to devise work plans so that you can achieve clarity and commitment. Target-setting is an invaluable skill and this is dealt with separately in Chapter 11.

Building on Strengths

Development activities are designed to make full use of strengths and attend to deficiencies where appropriate. You have to find out, of course, what your employees' strengths are. We have seen many cases of employees doing jobs which are in total mismatch with their strengths. There was a manager, for example, with a highly analytical mind who dreamt up some very innovative schemes for his organisation. In terms of interpersonal relations and communication skills, he was one of the poorest we have ever seen. The organisation gave him a job which involved dealing with members of the public for much of the time. His irritability had an adverse impact on business. If you recognise strengths then try to use them to advantage.

Follow-Up Mechanisms

There is a mechanism to follow up all agreed development activities. If you say you will do something then do it! Do not make promises which you cannot or are unwilling to keep. The credibility of developmental appraisal lies in demonstrating a concern for development through action.

Shared Commitment

We have already referred to the appraisal process as a shared effort. It requires commitment from both parties. Its success may hinge on motivation and interest, and the skill and interest of the manager in helping the employee to grow or make effective use of strengths. As the employee becomes more involved in the process, with his views on performance and development forming the focus of attention, the more scope there is for individual growth. This is best illustrated in Figure 10.2.

Figure 10.2
Involvement Continuum

MANAGER-DOMINATED   EMPLOYEE-CENTRED

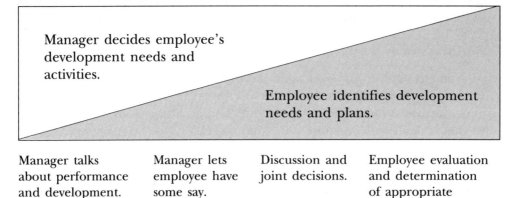

Manager decides employee's development needs and activities.

Employee identifies development needs and plans.

| Manager talks about performance and development. | Manager lets employee have some say. | Discussion and joint decisions. | Employee evaluation and determination of appropriate development activities. |

Where are you on the continuum? See whether you can locate your exact position. You might ask your colleagues to place you where they think you are. You may find some discrepancies! We suggest that the best place to be is towards the right-hand side, but the exact location will depend on the job and the nature of the people under you. For most, the area which allows for discussion and joint decision-making seems to offer the most scope for development and growth, whilst retaining the essential managerial input and support.

It is a key individual responsibility to initiate discussions, consider recent performance, devise development plans and define interests in terms of training and future job assignments and responsibilities. You can help the individual through this process. You can also help to moderate personal impressions of performance. Evidence tends to indicate however that employees are far more critical of themselves than their peers or superiors, and that the appraisal process usually results in the manager providing a more appreciative assessment of the individual's contribution.

We believe many are capable of increased autonomy. The notion of *loose–tight* properties is helpful (Peters and Waterman, 1982). You need to be tight about quality, but you may need to give freedom to act so long as targets are met. If you see your staff as typically hard-working and motivated, you should have no problem in extending such a partnership approach. If, however, you base your assumptions on Theory X (see Chapter 2, Motivating), and see only inherent laziness and incompetence, you may have difficulty in applying developmental appraisal principles.

If you and your employees can work together in a climate of trust and mutual support, there is a powerful force for performance improvement, and the most important thing is that each can gain from the effort in terms of improvement in job performance, personal growth and development.

Problems

The problems which are typical of formal performance appraisal schemes may reappear in even a comparatively informal developmental scheme, and we have tried where possible to avoid these dangers. Some problems, for example, which Everard (1986) found in industry included:

- Too much paperwork.
- Failure to involve employees when introducing a scheme.
- Lack of commitment at the top.
- Failing to follow up on agreed actions.
- Different standards of considering performance.
- The system becoming out of date through little review.
- Lack of training for appraisal.

Halloran (1986) too identified some of these problems and also mentioned excessive demands on managers and personal values as presenting disadvantages. We have recognised the problem of the demands on managers and supervisors, and tried to remove much of the unnecessary documentation. There is a time requirement, though, with which we cannot dispense. Treating employees as individuals with individual development needs and individual expectations requires discussion time and some commitment to follow-up actions. We hope we make a case for this to be considered as highly productive use of managerial time.

Consultation is probably a prerequisite to the successful introduction of even an informal developmental appraisal scheme, for without the involvement of employees, it may be difficult to obtain the commitment required. If it is made too demanding in terms of paperwork and recording procedures, it may be viewed as a burden rather than an opportunity for personal and career development.

If those at the top of the organisation believe in the process, their support should be clearly evident in terms of the follow-up actions. This commitment will inevitably have some effect on the rest of the workforce. Failure to pursue matters which have arisen from the process is potentially one of the most destructive aspects of developmental appraisal. If an employee is persuaded that the scheme represents an opportunity and expects action on certain issues, it is unforgivable to leave the process as a form-filling and friendly chat exercise.

This raises the problem of resources. If training and development needs are identified, the resources have to be made available to meet them, otherwise the appraisal process may be seen as a pointless exercise and commitment may be lost. It is as well therefore to add a time component in any comments on form PAJ about training needs: e.g. 'This member of staff needs to attend a presentation-skills course as a matter of priority. It will be arranged for her to attend a suitable training event before the next developmental appraisal discussion in six-months' time.'

If the involvement of all organisational or subunit members is essential in setting up a system, it is equally important that they have the opportunity to review it so that it does not outlive its usefulness:

> . . . any procedure that is established must be open to change and as soon as it has served its purpose it must be altered. All static procedures can be an enormous constraint on individual and organizational development. An effective human resources management procedure is thus one which has had a facility built into it which can bring it change and development. (Randell *et al.*, 1984 : 11)

Similarly, its successful operation may hinge on the extent to which managers engage in training in the component skills, such as listening, questioning and planning. Resources directed to this activity will indicate quite clearly how seriously senior managers feel about its value to the organisation.

There is one further problem which we should address, although it may be treated in a positive way. It concerns the different levels of experience which individuals bring to the work situation with them and the impact these might have on the process. It is the problem of career stages.

There are some spheres of employment which present difficult arenas in which to discuss career development. Some staff members may be in the later stages of their careers, whilst others are simply not interested in any form of career development for whatever reason. Some employees, particularly those at managerial level, may have enjoyed comparative autonomy and see any form of sharing information about performance and development as an unwelcome infringement on their traditional autonomy. This is a real problem to which there is no quick and easy solution. Similar difficulties occur where the employee disputes the credibility of the manager to conduct such a discussion, either through a mismatch of qualifications, expertise or experience. The answer to this is that the manager is a colleague who has a responsibility to facilitate the development process and to enable relevant matters to be brought into the open so that action can be taken which benefits the organisation. An understanding of this role over time will enhance the relationship between supervisor and employee, and has the potential to lead to outcomes which are productive for all concerned, including the individual employee and the organisation.

Where the discussion focuses on career development, the supervisor must be sensitive to the fact that the needs, expectations and abilities of people change as they go through the different stages of their careers. These changes may have a major effect on interests, values, proficiencies and productivity.

In the early career stage it is probably wise to encourage creativity and innovation whilst the individual gains confidence. Career growth is probably achieved by providing support and guidance when it is required. In mid-career the employee usually has an accurate and realistic assessment of his career goals. If significant career goals have not been achieved, it may be important to help him redefine career aspirations. It may also be necessary to encourage him to update and develop new skills. Those in the later stages may have come reasonably close to achieving the required level of career success and still pursue high levels of performance. They have a wealth of experience and if it can be channelled profitably, it can be used to great effect in helping those employees in the early stages of their careers.

Also, it must not be forgotten that the organisation's environment still presents rapidly changing demands which may lead to the need for the acquisition of new skills by even the most experienced staff. In the case of those who have progressed to the top of the organisation, they may need training in some of the high-profile activities which they must undertake. Public speaking, interviewing and general liaison with those outside the organisation are examples of activities which may have to be developed to reach an adequate level of competence. Similarly, the rate of progress of information technology has placed considerable demands on employees across all levels of many organisations.

The Process

There may be a good case in very small departments or organisational subunits to make the developmental appraisal process totally informal, without the need for planned discussions or anything recorded in writing. It should be said, however, that good documentation makes an important contribution to continuity. The more complete the understanding of an employee's performance and aspirations, the more effective the development plan can be. Some of the documentation can become part of the personnel file, if desired by manager and employee, which may form the basis for future consideration and career development purposes.

This scheme is considered in three distinct phases, although modifications can be made to the documentary items. We believe the discussion is a vital part of the process and is best supported by some preparatory work (mainly form completion) and a commitment to consequent action (by recording intended activities in writing).

- The Developmental Appraisal Employee form (DAE).
- The Discussion.
- The Developmental Appraisal Joint form (DAJ).

DAE

The employee completes this document which summarises his assessment of activities, planned development and objectives. It is shown in Figure 10.3. We have also included a draft memorandum which might be attached to the form. It is shown in Figure 10.4.

Discussion

The discussion between manager and subordinate is directed towards performance improvement, the development of specific plans and consideration of the employee's wishes in terms of professional development and satisfaction.

DAJ

This form is displayed in Figure 10.5. This is the final version of the form, where the information from DAE and the discussion are taken into account, and a document is produced which is agreed by both parties. The manager is responsible for writing the DAJ although there is the opportunity for the employee to add comments. For the next review, a new DAE will be completed by the employee, but the DAJ will be referred to in the subsequent discussion with the supervisor.

The process of developmental appraisal is shown in Figure 10.6 whilst the schedule, which gives approximate time scales between the phases, is shown in Figure 10.7.

We shall now look at each of these in more detail.

Figure 10.3
The Developmental Appraisal Employee Form

DAE FORM

Name	Period covered

REVIEW

> **WORK PROGRESS:** List main assignments and accomplishments during the period.

> **STRENGTHS:** List skills, abilities and knowledge which helped you do the job well.

> **DIFFICULTIES:** Outline any problems which have prevented you from achieving what you intended. How can you overcome them?

> **CONDITIONS:** If you were in your boss's position, what changes would you make to enable you to work more effectively?

> **DEVELOPMENT ACTIVITIES:** List any development activities undertaken and their benefits.

THE NEXT PERIOD

DEVELOPMENT NEEDS: List skills, abilities and knowledge which, if developed, could help you to do your job even better.

TRAINING: List any training activities which you think would help you.

WORK PLANS: List in order of importance your main work assignments in the near term.

DEVELOPMENT: List any tasks or responsibilities which you feel could be built into your current job in order to promote your personal or career development. Which new responsibilities would you like? What would you ideally like to discard?

CAREER: Indicate how you see your career or job developing and outline how you feel the organisation can help you. What do you expect to be doing in three years' time?

JOB DIMENSIONS

This is an attempt to reach agreement with your manager on the key parts of your job. List all the parts of your work which can be considered on a separate basis. Then in the profile section, indicate whether you consider it to be very important, of moderate importance or of little importance to your overall role. You can also make any appropriate clarifying notes.

DIMENSION	Very important	Moderately important	Of little importance	NOTES
	☐	☐	☐	
	☐	☐	☐	
	☐	☐	☐	
	☐	☐	☐	
	☐	☐	☐	

Figure 10.4
A Sample Memorandum

MEMORANDUM

To:

From:

Date:

Date and time for our discussion:　　　　　　　　Place:

DAE DEVELOPMENTAL APPRAISAL EMPLOYEE FORM

Preparation for the discussion:
Before we discuss your work, plans and preferences for the next period,
I would like you to give some thought to several issues which will act as
the basis for discussion.

The purposes of this process are to:

- Reach agreement on what your job should entail.
- Consider how we can develop your potential.
- Agree on work plans for the next period.
- Examine whether the organisation is helping you as best it can.
- Record your preferences for work activities and responsibilities.
- Consider your requirements for training and development.

You can use this form as you wish. You can make notes on it and then
bring it along to the discussion. You may wish to hand it to me in
advance if you feel that is helpful. In any event it is your personal
property and does not have to become part of your personnel file unless
you specifically want it to be. The job profile, however, will be required
so that we can look at what you consider to be the priorities in your
present post.

It is very important that you set some time aside to think carefully about
each of the headings on the form in advance. This is the only way our
discussion can be productive, so that as an organisation we can try to do
our very best for you.

Stott, K. and Walker, A., *Making Management Work.* © 1992 Simon & Schuster (Asia) Pte Ltd.

Figure 10.5
The Developmental Appraisal Joint Form

DAJ FORM

EMPLOYEE	MANAGER	DATE

Summarise strengths and achievements:

Areas agreed for improvement, development and personal growth:

Recommended development activities:

Recommended developmental work experiences as part of the job:

Signatures

Figure 10.6
The Process

Employee completes DAE form.
Considers the job, performance, future plans, expectations and development activities.
Prepares questions.

Manager reviews documents from previous discussions.
Considers expectations and organisation's needs in terms of employee development.

The Discussion.

Consider appropriate targets and activities.
Agree development activities which meet organisational and individual needs.

Manager completes DAJ form.

Employee signs DAJ form and adds comments.

Figure 10.7
The Schedule

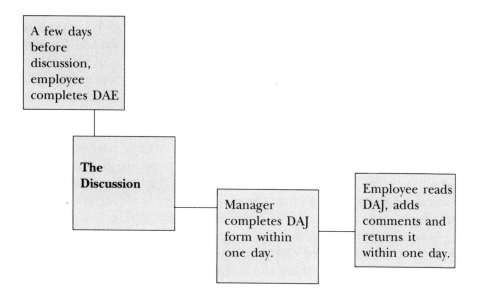

DAE: The Developmental Appraisal Employee Form

Before agreement can be reached on how well a job is being done, it is critical to know precisely what the job is. There are many examples of managers criticising employees for not paying sufficient attention to a certain job dimension, but failing to realise they both have different perceptions of what the job includes and the priority order of job components. For this reason, an analysis of what constitutes the very important and less important parts of the job is included. It forms part of the DAE document and is shown in Figure 10.3.

Elements

The elements of the job are considered and the important parts are determined. It is useful at this stage for the employee to look at his job description to see if it is consistent with what he thinks it actually is.

Profile of the Post

As part of the process of filling in form DAE, employees are asked to list the various parts of the job for which they feel they are responsible. They are also asked to rate each of these parts as very important, of moderate importance or of little importance. This is obviously a useful part of the process for some employees where the job is not restricted to one simple role. A supervisor, for example, may have responsibility for a team of staff, for administrative duties and for dealing with members of the public, and it may be important to sort out the relative importance of these. It is especially critical for senior staff who carry a wide range of key responsibilities, and it often occurs that individual priorities do not match the senior manager's priorities. The developmental appraisal process has to address this issue. A measure of agreement therefore has to be reached between both parties about the degree of importance of each job dimension. The major areas are those parts which are central to the job. They are likely to take up a large part of the employee's time. The 'moderately important' areas are those which are not central, but which nevertheless are important and must be undertaken. 'Of little importance' simply means that the responsibility is a very small one and the involvement is only of marginal nature.

It is important to go through this exercise in order to make sense of the job. In many spheres of employment, it is the norm to see job descriptions which encompass everything the author could think of at the time of writing. The key responsibilities however are generally based on assumptions and an unwritten form of agreement. Under these circumstances, it becomes very difficult to consider how well a job is being done when there is uncertainty about the relative significance of responsibilities.

Targets

Working from these determined major and minor responsibilities, work plans should be drawn up for the period in question. The targets which the individual sets should be challenging but attainable within the time scale. You are advised to refer to the next chapter, Setting Targets, for detailed guidelines on how to formulate appropriate work targets.

Basis for Discussion

Achievements, activities undertaken, personal strengths and areas needing improvement should all be listed as a basis for discussion. Firm evidence to support these statements should be given where possible rather than a reliance on vague impressions and gut feel. There are inevitably circumstances which are beyond the individual's control, and it is a vital part of the process to address these factors which may be inhibiting performance.

Data about Performance

It is best to avoid the unsubstantiated comments of others. Where observation by other people in the organisation is structured and considered in advance by all participants, the information may be used as a valuable input to the appraisal process. Other items which might effectively be considered are reports, written work plans, official documentation and memoranda.

We have mentioned that developmental appraisal is a continuous process, with the formal recording being supported by constant informal interaction between manager and employee. Where information occurs which is relevant to the process, it should be recorded. This may be in the form of events which provide factual sources of information for the formal process. Events may include situations where behaviour can be observed leading up to an event, a description of what actually happened and the results. Dates should also be given. These may form sound bases for evaluation by both parties in the appraisal process.

Assessing Performance

It is performance in the assignments agreed which should be considered and not assignments which the superior has assumed to be major responsibilities. This is why it is so important to agree on the job dimensions so that both parties know precisely which parts of the job are providing the basis for discussion.

Problems in Assessment

Assessments should be based on one responsibility or dimension at a time. It is important for both employees and managers (and particularly the latter) to guard against assuming that, because performance is very high in one area, all other areas are satisfactory. This is not easy, especially when someone is doing a splendid job, and there is a fear that there might be a reaction against exposing areas of weakness.

Managers need to avoid being influenced by the quantity of work undertaken. Although a relationship is often assumed between quality and quantity, it is sometimes the case that efforts may be misdirected and that the content is not consistent with organisational needs. Again, it is recognised that it is not an easy matter to draw attention to quality when such extensive efforts are being put in. We remember a training officer who spent a considerable amount of time writing training manuals for his organisation, and when produced they were extremely heavy volumes. The quality, however, was extremely low and in relation to the main assignment, they were largely peripheral. It was difficult for his manager to draw attention to the inappropriateness of this colleague's efforts.

Another problem is that of being influenced by recent performance and forgetting earlier aspects of work. Achievements may have been high for some time, and then a month or so before the appraisal process, difficulties have been encountered. In this case, the difficulties have to be examined, but the successes over the preceding period must be recognised and commensurate consideration given to them.

Preferences for Development Activities

Potential development activities should be listed alongside the preferences for future work responsibilities. This ensures that a record is kept of the individual's wishes in relation to career development. It does not mean that the organisation should fulfil every wish, but managers need to be aware of the development demands of individuals so that they can be responded to.

The DAE is the major input to the discussion. It will be useful to you to try completing the form for yourself. Like your employees you have development needs as a manager. You may also find it helpful to discuss your completed form with your boss, seeing whether any differences exist in perception about the important parts of your job and whether he shares your views on what would be appropriate development activities to support your job and career.

The Discussion

We see the discussion (even in a general sense) as a key facet in the process of development, best expressed by Randell *et al.* (1984 : 5) as 'a skilfully conducted "conversation with a purpose" between people. This interview, if conducted with the clear and explicit purpose of improving the ability of staff in their existing jobs will maintain and, possibly, increase, their willingness to apply their full abilities to their job.'

Before we go on to consider some issues concerning the discussion, look at the two short case studies below. The conversations are summarised extracts from the dialogue of the full cases. They were from interviews which were intended to put a strong emphasis on the development aspect of appraisal. You will find it helpful to make a few notes after each case about the good or bad points.

Case 1: The Supervisor

Alice is manager at Jenkins Department Store. Pamela is sales supervisor in the hardware department.

ALICE: Well, this should be reasonably short; not too many problems. As you know, I have to decide which are the major parts of your job and how I can arrange for you to improve your performance in them. I am not too concerned about the other things. Incidentally, I think you are doing reasonably well. I have been watching you on and off over the last twelve months and you seemed very pleasant with problem customers but a bit sharp with some of the younger staff. I didn't say anything at the time because I know it takes time for them to find their feet and for you to get to know them better. Oh, and another thing, some of the girls seem to be standing around chatting near the till whilst others seem to be overworked stacking the shelves. Perhaps the work allocation is not too good. Well, as I said earlier, this is not to dwell on the past but to get you to improve. I think you probably need to attend a course on interpersonal skills to help you deal with the junior staff better and then we need to find a course which will help you organise people's time more efficiently. Don't you agree?

PAMELA: I'm not too sure. I always thought I got on well with the younger girls. Anyway, if that's what you think, fair enough. But I am not happy about the work allocation problem. I did not think that was supposed to be my job. You set the schedules and I follow them. My job is to prepare sales reports and to deal with customers, which I think I do very well.

ALICE: I am not disputing the fact that your work is satisfactory. I am just saying that I think you probably need to improve on those few things. Anyway, I shall try and find out what can be done and let you know. As far as the job is concerned, I have always thought it is your responsibility to redeploy staff if we are particularly slack or busy. You only need to go into any store to see it is the sales supervisor's job. Now that that is sorted out, is there anything else you want to ask me?

PAMELA: Two things: I have been a supervisor now for eighteen months and would really like to do a supervisory qualification. I think it would obviously help in my job, but it would also help me if I decide to try for junior management. Also, I have been in the same department throughout this time and I feel it would be good experience to spend some time in other departments. I think it would help my career.

ALICE: I wouldn't waste your time with qualifications. It is experience that matters. I certainly wouldn't be impressed by qualifications if I were hiring people. I am not sure whether the store would be able to give you any support either. As far as moving around departments is concerned, I suppose I could arrange for you to chat with the other supervisors, but you do that socially anyway, don't you? We prefer to keep people in their own departments. It creates more stability. The staff know where they stand and regular customers know who to ask for. I think it's much better that way. If we have to change a supervisor, they tend to come in with new ideas, they want to do things differently and everyone gets upset. Anyway, I wouldn't have any designs on going into management if I were you: too many headaches and less time at home. That's been a good interview. I'm glad we see eye to eye on most things. We'll discuss things again in a year's time. In the meantime, try and improve on the few things I mentioned and everyone will be happy.

Case 2: The Building Society Manager

Mike is the manager of a large town-centre branch and Jim is the area manager.

JIM: I have looked at your form Mike and I notice that you see dealing with customers as a relatively minor part of your job.

MIKE: In relation to the other parts of the job, yes. There are exceptions, of course. If the customer looks like giving us some sizeable business, I like to see him personally, but most of the day-to-day business I leave to the assistant manager.

JIM: OK, I take your point, but it is now company policy to try and make our managers more visible. You've seen it on our advertising campaign: The customer being greeted by the smiling chief with a warm handshake. I know you can't do everything, but can you see any way of being more 'up front' whilst still giving your main attention to the important work?

MIKE: I suppose it would be possible for me to meet each new customer, simply to say 'hello' and introduce myself. Yes, I could easily do that. I also think head office should consider sending in some management support during a 'small loans' campaign so that I can set up a desk near the entrance and meet virtually every customer who comes in. That would be possible if we staggered our campaigns, but I know that poses problems for advertising.

JIM: That's a useful suggestion and I can certainly take it back to head office. Now, I also notice you are not entirely happy with your younger staff.

MIKE: I think the problem is that I am not absolutely sure whether I am identifying the right things when I recruit them. They seem to fulfil all the criteria on paper, but perhaps I am not asking the right questions at the interview. I really feel I need some help with interviewing so that I can find out what people are really like and whether they will do the job for us.

JIM: What sort of help do you think would be useful?

MIKE: It would be good to have a skilful interviewer from head office in to either watch me or preferably to show me how it's done. I also know that the company sends managers on short courses from time to time and I'd like to join an interviewing one as soon as possible.

JIM: If it means you getting better staff, I'm with you all the way, Mike. First of all, I'll speak to the personnel department and see if they can send someone, and I'll also ask them whether they can recommend any programmes. If other managers experience the same problem, it may be worth our while bringing someone in to run an in-house programme. You also mentioned on the form that you wanted to visit another branch.

MIKE: Yes, let me explain. I think I've done reasonably well so far and ideally I would like to move up. But all my experience has been in town branches, small personal accounts and the like. I would like to know more about rural work and agricultural accounts. I know I can find out a little through talking to colleagues occasionally, but I understand the customers are entirely different and you need first-hand experience to understand the business. What I had in mind was to spend a week in one of those branches and let my assistant take over here. There should be no problem, because he should be in line for his own branch soon and he has already handled everything once or twice when I have been away sick.

JIM: If you come into my job, I think you are right; it is useful to know something about the different types of work, especially if you get a wide area. OK, I'll speak to the big boss about that and I shall support you so long as there is agreement that you are on the way up. By the way, Mike, you must also think about one or two other things where you have no experience if you want to open up your career with the company. We can discuss these over lunch sometime.

MIKE: Thanks, and in the meantime, I'll make sure I set up a system where I can personally meet all new account holders and loan applicants.

JIM: That's good. You've got a pleasant personality and perhaps you should be out front a bit more. Within the next seven days, I shall discuss with the personnel department the possibility of sending someone in next time you interview; I shall ask for advice on an appropriate interviewing skills course; and I shall speak to Mr Clark about your wishes to spend some time in a rural branch. I'll write and let you know the outcome of each.

In Case 1, you may argue that no discussion about development could be quite as bad as that; but some are, and may be even worse! To start off with, Alice was not really discussing, she was delivering a monologue. Pamela did not get the chance to talk for even half the time. It was typically one-way communication. It was meant to be a formative process but it was highly judgemental. You probably noticed that Alice came straight in with criticisms without even discussing the situation. Furthermore, they were complete surprises; there had obviously been no informal feedback or discussion about performance during the year. She had failed to agree with Pamela what the really important parts of the job were and was simply accepting her own assumptions to be the true version. As a result, it was difficult to reach any conclusions on what might be appropriate development activities to support the job. Pamela had some ideas but was probably confused about her role, so it would be difficult for her to know what was best in terms of development. Her preferences were clearly explained but clearly rejected by an unreasonable and opinionated manager. It was very unlikely that Alice would have any effect on the improvement of her staff and she was doing little for her organisation in helping to develop talent for the future. There are several other criticisms you may have raised. Apart from her attitude, she appeared to have no questioning skills, but this was hardly surprising since she was not interested in the answers anyway. She may have had listening skills but did not give them much chance to be put into operation.

In short, Alice did little to improve performance in the key tasks, to improve the relationships between herself and the supervisor and between the supervisor and the sales staff, or to improve the opportunities for Pamela to develop her career. How do you think Pamela felt after that discussion, the only structured one in the year to look at her development prospects?

Case 2 presents an entirely different picture and one about which you probably managed to make a number of positive notes. Although we condensed the account of the full discussion, you would have seen that the area manager attempted to clarify what the job was and to reach some mutual understanding of the key parts. He left the manager in no doubt that it was company policy to become more visible and contact with customers therefore was a vital part of the job. He allowed Mike to do most of the talking and this led to a more productive outcome. Jim was obviously listening since he responded to each statement of Mike's. He did not have to agree necessarily, but he demonstrated his interest in what was being said. Despite the fact that they were working in a highly results-oriented business, Jim showed an equal concern for Mike's career ambitions, maybe realising that it was part of his job to nurture talent for the good of the company, rather than try to buy in expertise from outside. He agreed to take certain measures and of course the strength of the process would be determined by his consequent actions. He summarised these intended actions at the end of the discussion and indicated a clear time scale which demonstrated a firm commitment to act. It was a friendly discussion and it was apparent it was the sort of non-judgemental interview in which Mike felt able to discuss his shortcomings and open up about his career plans.

In short, Jim enabled performance to be improved, people to work together more effectively, and career and personal development plans to be considered seriously.

The discussion is an exchange between manager and employee (who may of course be another manager), conducted on a counselling basis, and designed to enhance job performance and employee satisfaction through a process of development promotion.

As a result of the discussion, some conclusions should be reached on:

- Improving performance.
- Improving the way people work together.
- Improving the opportunities for career development.

Discussions are most useful when they are based on specific information; in some systems, they may be called *performance events*. These events may reflect skills, abilities and personal qualities which go into the individual's performance. Objectivity is paramount so that vague impressions do not cloud judgement. The employee needs to know quite clearly which criteria are being used to consider effectiveness, and one of the features of a good system is for both parties to clarify these criteria.

The discussion should generate ideas for capitalising on strengths and for producing plans for making improvements. It is healthy to focus on strengths and celebrate successes, but weaknesses have to be recognised, especially where these limit the achievement of success. Weaknesses which inhibit people's prospects for career development particularly need identifying, and the benefits will be felt by both the individual and the organisation.

Counselling is an important part of most discussions. In many cases the manager is able to help the employee grow and develop, preparing him to take on increased responsibilities. In this respect the manager is expected to maintain an ongoing dialogue with the employee, provide encouragement and recognise achievements. Exploring the scope for development is the central feature of our developmental appraisal scheme. The individual may feel that his talents are not being fully utilised. It could be that others have responsibilities for which they are not suited. Part of the magic of successful organisations is achieving a fit between abilities and aspirations. An employee may, for example, wish to acquire new skills or assume new responsibilities because he sees these as being advantageous to the pursuit of a particular career path. It has to be recognised that, apart from the employee's satisfaction, the organisation may benefit through the enthusiasm generated by the individual for a new responsibility. It can lead to new ideas, different ways of looking at familiar problems and to a new impetus in some aspects of the organisation's activities. Even without these immediate gains, the organisation may benefit through the experience gained by the individual, and this represents a more patient perspective on development than that which is often witnessed.

There should be a working towards agreement on plans and targets. These should be clearly related to the goals of the organisation or subunit, and the manager is obviously the right person to identify such congruence (or its absence). The link between individual targets, subunit goals and overall organisational aims and missions needs to be clearly demonstrated.

An outcome of the process is likely to be a number of actions for the employee. But if it is the two-way process which is intended, there should also be a list of actions for you as the manager. Examples of actions which you might take include modifying job responsibilities, providing opportunities for training and allocating resources. There should also be mutually agreed review mechanisms so that progress towards achieving any plans can be assessed.

In an environment which is becoming increasingly complex and uncertain, a condition which many organisations are facing, it is inappropriate that work and development plans should be static documents. There may be alterations to the job description and changes in environmental factors which necessitate revisions to the work plan. The developmental appraisal process therefore is best seen as a continuous rather than a once-a-year affair.

Because it is ongoing, there should be no surprises in the discussion. What this means is that the manager should not be in a position to raise items of concern or criticism for the first time. Difficulties and shortcomings should have been dealt with as they occurred and not left for the structured discussion. Indeed, failing to act at the right time could destroy the potential positive effects of the system. The discussion, therefore, must be seen as an occasion where successes, intentions, problems and needs are reconsidered.

SUMMARY

Purposes of the Discussion:

- To obtain a joint understanding between the manager and the employee of the important and less significant responsibilities of the job. This will ensure that efforts are appropriately directed. It will also lead to the development of realistic job expectations.
- To discover how to improve work place and related practices.
- To summarise the regular informal feedback which has taken place on a day-to-day basis.
- To identify training and development needs.
- To plan progress, set targets, discover ways of achieving them and implement actions.
- To give 'a pat on the back' where it is deserved.

Preparing for the Discussion

The employee should think about:

- The job.
- His or her future career intentions.
- Reasons for doing well or not so well.
- Preferred development activities.

In addition to completing the DAE form in preparation for the discussion, it is helpful for the employee to reflect on the above points and then write a list of questions which may be raised.

The written material should be prepared several days in advance of the discussion, as the benefits will best be derived from a process which has involved careful thought and preparation. As his manager, you need time to look at this DAE alongside the previous period's documentation to see if the information agreed upon has taken effect. Things may have changed for very good reasons, but this needs exploring during the discussion. The process therefore involves establishing plans, putting them into effect and then analysing the difference between planned and actual events. This is probably best done with adequate documentation.

You should prepare some thoughts on the following:

- An analysis of the employee's job.
- Plans for improvement and personal development.

You can reflect on the ways in which the employee carried out assignments, on his present skills, his level of motivation, whether responsibilities were interpreted appropriately and whether the job environment was a factor contributing to performance. Questions which may be asked are: How has the employee responded to the present assignments? How does the employee appear to regard the present job challenge? Does this reflect a change from the way the job was seen at an earlier date? What skills does he need to develop to the next career stage?

In assessing the extent to which recommendations and agreements have been fulfilled by the employee, you should reflect on the help you have given to assist the employee in improving performance and engaging in relevant development activities.

Last but not least, the discussion must also be seen as an opportunity to record appreciation for a job well done. It can be a tremendous source of encouragement, so do not neglect it!

An Effective Discussion

. . . help the employee feel that the interview is a constructive, co-operative one by placing primary emphasis on development and growth.
(Halloran, 1986 : 173)

Before we look in detail at some of the points which help to make an effective discussion, you should complete the questionnaire Discussing Development with Employees, which will help you gain a preliminary impression of your present skill level in this context. You may never have conducted an appraisal interview as such. That does not matter; simply think of times when you have sat down and talked with one of your staff about anything to do with the job, performance, career plans, development opportunities or any other related issue. The questionnaire covers preparation and the discussion itself, including both the content and the way the discussion is set up.

Questionnaire

DISCUSSING DEVELOPMENT WITH EMPLOYEES

Tick the appropriate box for each statement:

	Usually	Sometimes	Never
1. I tend to ask open questions.	☐	☐	☐
2. If I make observations about performance, I describe actual events rather than generalisations.	☐	☐	☐
3. I try to find something good to say about the employee early in the discussion.	☐	☐	☐
4. I try to get the employee to raise issues of concern about performance.	☐	☐	☐
5. I give praise when something has been done well.	☐	☐	☐
6. In reaching conclusions on how well an employee is doing the job, I try to get him to tell me rather than the other way round.	☐	☐	☐
7. I give feedback soon after something has happened.	☐	☐	☐
8. I try to temper employees' career and job expectations with realism where necessary.	☐	☐	☐
9. Whenever I am to discuss an important matter with an employee, I try to give it some thought in advance.	☐	☐	☐
10. I try to be as specific as possible about my observations.	☐	☐	☐
11. Whenever I make a point, I ask for the employee's reaction.	☐	☐	☐
12. I avoid discussing personal characteristics and qualities such as 'tenacity' and 'co-operation'.	☐	☐	☐
13. When there has been agreement about a course of action, I write it down.	☐	☐	☐
14. If I agree to do something during the discussion, I can be relied on to keep my word.	☐	☐	☐

	Usually	Sometimes	Never
15. I listen attentively when the other person is talking.	☐	☐	☐
16. I avoid interrupting him unless there is something I do not understand.	☐	☐	☐
17. I set aside sufficient time so that all important matters can be discussed thoroughly.	☐	☐	☐
18. I ensure I clear my mind of other pressing matters before holding a discussion with an employee.	☐	☐	☐
19. I avoid sitting behind a desk and choose a more informal arrangement instead.	☐	☐	☐
20. I ensure there are no interruptions from the telephone or personal callers.	☐	☐	☐
21. I do my best to make the other person feel at ease before discussing important matters.	☐	☐	☐
22. I clear the air of relationship problems before the discussion.	☐	☐	☐
23. I ask the other person whether he is satisfied with the outcome of our discussion.	☐	☐	☐
24. I summarise what we have discussed and agreed.	☐	☐	☐
25. I am willing to accept criticism from an employee and to try to improve if appropriate.	☐	☐	☐
26. I avoid making promises which I may not be able to keep.	☐	☐	☐
27. I face up to difficult issues which are relevant, such as performance weaknesses.	☐	☐	☐
28. I am prepared to make constructive criticism, but I link it to development plans.	☐	☐	☐
29. I use questions in such a way that the employee comes up with the solutions to problems.	☐	☐	☐
30. I finish on a positive note and try to ensure that both of us are happy with the outcome.	☐	☐	☐

Score 2 points for each tick under 'usually' and 1 point for each tick under 'sometimes'. Managers who have a concern for their employees and are fairly open in their relationships tend to score at least 30 points. If you have scored above half, look at the statements where you answered 'never' and consider where you need to improve (the next section will help you). If you scored less than 30, you will need to build up your discussion skills and to examine your attitude to employees.

Stott, K. and Walker, A., *Making Management Work.* © 1992 Simon & Schuster (Asia) Pte Ltd.

After completing the questionnaire, you should have some idea of how well you manage discussions about work with your employees. A number of issues were raised in the statements and these are explained in the section below which will help in preparing for and conducting an effective discussion about development and its relation to performance.

Emphasise the Positive

People are more likely to improve if given positive reinforcement. Try to find the good points even in poor performance areas and build on those. It is not helpful to focus on what has not been achieved, but to try and improve on what has been accomplished. This does not mean a blind eye has to be turned to weakness and failure; to do this would be an injustice to both the employee and the organisation. The most effective way of tackling the issue is within a supportive framework and avoiding the finger of accusation.

We like to think of our developmental appraisal system as an opportunity for giving praise where it is due. Are you only good at telling people when they have done something wrong or do you make a point of using those encouraging words 'well done' when even small things have been done well? Do not reserve this just for the discussion however, but give praise on a frequent basis.

Involve the Employee

The employee should be very much involved in the process of self-evaluation, establishing work plans and providing feedback. This will ensure there is commitment to plans. In this way, the individual 'owns' the method. The self-evaluation can also be conducted on a small group basis, but whichever way, the system should not be threatening and should offer sufficient scope for personal growth. 'Self-evaluation squarely locates personal appraisal of one's own behaviour with the personal change and development required to improve performance' (Reynolds, 1987 : 136).

Give Continuous and Immediate Feedback

Feedback is more effective if given on a regular basis and as close to the time of the event commented on as possible. This may be achieved through frequent informal comments and ensuring there is a regular dialogue between manager and employee. Feedback should be timely, whether praise or constructive criticism, so that performance can be improved or self-esteem boosted. It is no good waiting for a formal discussion to talk about performance events. Feedback is at its most effective when given immediately, and a strong supportive relationship, combined with an interest in the progress of the employee's growth, should lead to regular and informal discussions.

Rubin and Rose (1978 : 3) give five 'rules of thumb' for effective feedback. It should be:

1. Descriptive rather than evaluative.
2. Specific rather than general.
3. Directed toward controllable behaviors rather than personality traits or characteristics.
4. Solicited rather than imposed.
5. Close to the event under discussion rather than delayed for several months.

Be Realistic

A meaningful assessment should be given of the employee's aspirations, goals and career plans. You may encourage ambition, but it should be within the bounds of reality. Small-scale successes are more important than continual failures. The same applies to the central part of our scheme – the developmental aspect. You may wish to agree with an enthusiastic employee that a whole agenda of development activities is necessary, but you have to consider the appropriateness of each and whether it is possible to carry it out. Our advice is to identify the key development activities, ensure those are put into action and then build on them during subsequent periods.

Plan the Discussion

The session should be scheduled in advance, with time for preparation and adequate time for the discussion itself. We have provided some pointers separately below about the time involved and the importance of a good location. These need to be planned in advance, not five minutes before the discussion, and make sure you have everything you need for your meeting.

Be Specific

Use documented evidence wherever possible. If any points are presented, ensure that the employee has the opportunity to respond. In fact, it is a good idea to get frequent reactions. When you have made a point or suggested a course of action, encourage the employee to give his point of view by asking: 'How do you feel about that?' Then reach some agreement on it before moving on to the next point, otherwise it may become a distracting factor.

Focus on Targets and Facts

The whole developmental appraisal process is intended to be a positive experience. Concentrate therefore on guidance and counselling in relation to performance and individual development. Weaknesses should form only a very minor part of the discussion. If you are looking at performance, avoid the temptation to talk about personal characteristics. Facts about job behaviour and actual performance are more important. Obscure assessments about such qualities as 'co-operation', 'leadership' and 'tenacity' are usually meaningless to employees.

Practise Joint Problem-Solving

In considering problems about performance or areas which need to be improved through appropriate development, make the discussion a joint problem-solving effort. Focus on the problem and not on the personalities involved. Try also to weigh up alternative solutions.

Write Things Down

Documentation may help in implementing agreed plans. It demonstrates to the employee that the issues discussed are being treated seriously and where there is agreement about development activities, the written evidence will make a firm commitment to implementation more likely. It also forms the basis of the next review process.

Avoid Certainty

It is difficult to be absolutely certain about most things, so statements that imply certainty should be avoided. At the same time, there should be certainty about your efforts to pursue matters which are concerned with the individual's development and which are likely to have an impact on the organisation's effective operation.

Listen

You should be prepared to listen and to let the employee outline his views. There will obviously be some input from you as a manager, but it should be very carefully considered and not take up more than, say, a quarter of the discussion time.

We have referred to the importance of listening skills several times in this book. We cannot over-emphasise the necessity for you to adopt and develop these skills. How good a listener are you now? Do you just rely on natural ability or do you positively use strategies to ensure you absorb what is being said and demonstrate that you are being attentive? Complete the short questionnaire How Well Do I Listen? for a provisional assessment of your present listening skills.

Questionnaire

HOW WELL DO I LISTEN?

Consider each of the statements and tick the appropriate box. Indicate what you normally do and not what you think should happen.

	Very often	Some-times	Never
1. I look at the other person's eyes most of the time when he is talking.	☐	☐	☐
2. I make brief notes as he is talking so that I can remember the key points.	☐	☐	☐
3. I summarise the important things the other person has said to show I have understood.	☐	☐	☐
4. I make supportive remarks and gestures (like smiling and nodding) whilst he is talking.	☐	☐	☐
5. If something is said about which I am not clear, I ask a question straightaway.	☐	☐	☐
6. I try to show interest in the other person and what he is saying.	☐	☐	☐
7. I keep concentrating even when I find I have little interest in what is being said.	☐	☐	☐
8. I avoid thinking about what my response will be until the other person has finished speaking.	☐	☐	☐

Score 5 points for each 'very often' box ticked, and 3 points for 'sometimes'.

25–40	You are probably a very attentive and encouraging listener.
20–25	You probably have some good listening habits but need to improve some skills.
Below 20	You need to practise your listening skills. For a start, look at those statements where you answered 'never' and attempt to do something about those. Whatever your score, you can always improve so that all these skills become second nature. You should try to make improvements in those areas above where you scored lowly.

Be Open

If progress is to be made, it may be necessary that people become open to criticism. In the case of the manager, a willingness to accept criticism and respond to it demonstrates a maturity which can only enhance relationships and act as a basis for improvement.

Use the form we have provided as a guide to the discussion and do not feel you have to stick to a rigid agenda. It may be helpful to sit in such a way that he can see everything you write. This will make the process more open and will enhance the intended friendliness and informality.

Avoid Interruptions

Ensure you set aside sufficient time to conduct your discussion in one session, otherwise the impact is lost and old ground may have to be covered again, especially if there is a long gap between meetings.

Give Sufficient Time

Allow adequate time to discuss the really important issues. You may have important things to discuss from the organisation's point of view but the employee also has priorities and these should not be cut short because sufficient time is not available. We suggest that a minimum of one hour is necessary for a productive discussion, although some managers take longer. We like the idea of one executive we spoke to who always arranged his interviews to start one hour before the end of the working day. If the discussion had not finished and if it was sufficiently important to the employee, then he would willingly agree to stay on until the employee was happy that he had been given full opportunity to say everything he wanted to say.

Choose the Right Time

For the manager above, the right time was 4 p.m., but there may be other considerations and constraints for you. It is not a good idea to hold a developmental discussion when you are under extreme pressure with your mind on other things, either work or domestic, or when you are not in the right frame of mind. Employees easily sense when you are in a bad mood for instance, and that is likely to provoke responses which may be less than open.

Choose the Right Place

Choose somewhere that is reasonably quiet and preferably with comfortable seating. If it is not possible at the place of work to find such a location, consider holding your meeting away from the work place, either in a lounge or somewhere else which provides a pleasant and relaxing environment.

There should be *no* interruptions which may mean finding a room without a telephone and away from any other form of disturbance.

Set the Right Atmosphere

Perhaps you may have experienced this kind of manager before: He sits behind his large desk in his high-back chair, glares over the top of his glasses at you and studies papers bound in a file which you are not allowed to see. This is hardly the best way to put the employee at ease! Try coming out from behind your desk and sit *with* rather than *against* the employee. Talk about a few general things first if you like in order to break the ice and make the employee feel that this is his opportunity to raise issues; the meeting has been set up for his benefit. With this in mind, you might ask the employee: 'What do you expect to get out of this session together?' You can discuss the response and then lay out your objectives.

You may have a problem creating the right atmosphere if there is some animosity or tension present. You really have to address this right at the beginning if you are going to make the discussion productive. Resentment and ill-feeling will not make for an open discussion.

Review the Process

At the end of the process it is crucial to consider how the employee may feel:

- Is self-esteem increased?
- Does he feel he has been listened to carefully?
- Has he received answers to questions?
- Has he seen it as a joint effort with the supervisor?
- Has he a clear idea of future direction?

The answers to these questions may best be obtained by asking him! At least ask the question: 'To what extent has this been helpful to you?'

SUMMARY

An Effective Discussion: Summary of Key Points:

- Emphasise the positive.
  People are more likely to improve if given positive reinforcement. Try to find the positive aspects even in poor-performance areas and build on those.
- Involve the employee in self-evaluation.
  The employee will give greater commitment if involved in the process.

- Give continuous and immediate feedback.
  There should be regular informal discussions. Sincerity is an important component in the help and motivation process. There should be no surprises.
- Be realistic.
  Set attainable targets and career plans.
- Plan the discussion.
  It will not plan itself! If it is to be a worthwhile use of time, it needs thinking about.
- Be specific.
  Use actual evidence wherever possible when discussing performance.
- Focus on targets and facts.
  Forget generalisations and concentrate on attainable goals.
- Practise joint problem-solving.
  Focus on the problem, not the individual, and make it a joint attack.
- Write things down.
  This shows you are interested and you need some verification of agreements.
- Avoid certainty.
  Do not make certain promises about career and development ambitions where there is any doubt.
- Listen.
  The employee can provide far more valuable information than the manager expects.
- Be open.
  Relationships can only be enhanced if there is real openness and trust.
- Avoid interruptions.
  Complete the discussion in one session.
- Give sufficient time.
  If you are going to do the process and the employee justice, you need at least an hour.
- Choose the right time.
  When your mind (and the employee's) is free of other pressing matters is the right time.
- Choose the right place.
  Find somewhere comfortable and quiet where you will not be interrupted by telephone or callers.
- Set the right atmosphere.
  Make the employee feel at ease and comfortable with your approach.
- Review the process.
  Ask him whether it has fulfilled his expectations.

Evaluating the Discussion

The manager should reflect on the discussion and consider what was accomplished for the good of the organisation or subunit and the employee. In particular, the following questions might be asked:

- What new items of information were discovered?
- What can be done to help the employee in the job?
- How much self-evaluation was there?
- What can be done about differences of opinion?
- What can be done to support the employee in terms of both organisation and personal goals?

Earlier we suggested you try completing the form so that you could experience first hand how it works. You could now take it a step further by conducting a discussion. To fully understand the possibilities of such a development scheme, you may find it helpful to seek the co-operation of one of your staff who should first complete a DAE form. If you prefer, you could discuss the issues with one of your management colleagues. This may help you to structure the conversation in such a way that you get the employee to engage in self-evaluation leading to the identification of appropriate development plans.

As manager, you should think carefully about the way in which development needs and plans are approached during any discussion. Are they real or imagined? Do they tie in with work targets and organisational objectives? Are the organisation's future needs considered? Are career goals considered?

DAJ: The Joint Analysis Form

This contains a statement about the employee's strengths and achievements. It also shows areas for development, the specific activities involved and changes in job responsibility which will act as developmental work experiences.

It is a thoroughly positive document, quite short (to avoid unnecessary paperwork) and focusing on specifics. Whereas the DAE form required an analysis of the job and some statement about performance in it so that an appropriate development programme could be formulated, this form looks to the future and considers only that programme. In particular it asks both the manager and employee jointly to examine those parts of the job which need to be improved and developed. At the same time, it asks for a statement of development intentions in relation to personal goals. The skilful manager may of course relate these to organisational benefits. It may not be necessary, for example, for the subordinate to follow a course in supervisory studies, but by doing so, he may be groomed for a supervisory or junior management position in the future. By engaging in this form of development, he is more likely to be satisfied with his work and his organisation.

The form then asks for two types of development activities: those which may be pursued outside the job and those within it, possibly by discarding some duties and taking on others which act as productive work experiences.

Conclusion

The process does not guarantee a perfect matching of personal development and career wishes, and organisational needs. It is often difficult to provide the opportunities to enable everyone to engage in the development activities they require or to modify their job descriptions for whatever reason. Resources may be just too much of a constraint. The system however may provide the best opportunity to develop mutually agreed work plans and to give the individual's future development wishes the structured and detailed attention they deserve.

In this chapter, we have presented an actual scheme as well as guidelines for you as manager. We have tried to meet a tall order. We have attempted to redress the balance in schemes which operate on a 'historic' basis only and which dwell simply on assessments (some of them questionable) of past performance. We have done this by presenting a scheme which places the emphasis firmly on development. At the same time, we recognise that you cannot make coherent decisions about development unless you derive information on performance, and so for those readers with no scheme at all in place, we have provided one which is capable in most situations of considering performance, targets and development.

If we have given the impression that we are less than enthusiastic about some of the weird and wonderful assessment mechanisms around, using such instruments as rating scales and so forth, it merely reflects our distaste for pretending that everything can be turned into numbers. It may simply be an easy way out of considering complex issues. We still need to be convinced that such judgements do anything to transform performance into the realms of excellence. We believe our scheme (not intended as an all-embracing performance appraisal system) can at least go some way to stimulating the motivation needed to move along the path to excellence.

The scheme gives you a framework within which you can consider and discuss employee development. You do not have to use our forms. You could even use a blank sheet of A4 paper. We do urge you, however, to follow our guidelines on conducting effective discussions and to develop your skills for this process.

And do not be like the manager who told us he had no time for such discussions; he and his team were too busy on the job. By investing your time in your workforce, its development and its satisfaction, you can expect the sorts of achievements typical of Freemantle's (1985) 'Superboss'.

Finally, you will have gathered that we have recognised the need to develop a good relationship between manager and employee. We accept things can go wrong, but we hope not quite so badly as in the story shown in Figure 10.8!

Figure 10.8

Poor Work Appraisal, so Man Strips and Goes on Rampage

A SPRAY painter stripped naked and went on the rampage, smashing his head against the windscreens of four cars outside his work-place in Jurong.

Police said the painter was angered by his supervisors' negative appraisal of his work performance.

He was also said to have been offered a S$35 increment instead of the regular jump of S$50.

He reportedly came out of a meeting with the supervisors on Friday last week fuming and shouting.

He damaged some glass panels in the premises in Gul Street 4 before stripping off his clothes.

His brother and some colleagues tried to calm him down, but he ran out to a carpark.

There he smashed his head against the windscreens of four cars, breaking them.

Although bleeding badly, he also butted his head against the door of a police car which arrived, police said.

Police officers subdued him and sent him to hospital.

Source: *Straits Times*, 9 March 1991

References

Blackburn, K. (1986) 'Teacher appraisal', in Marland, M.(ed.), *School Management Skills*, Heinemann : London.

Everard, K. and Morris, G. (1985) *Effective School Management*, Harper and Row : London.

Everard, K. (1986) *Developing Management in Schools*, Blackwell : Oxford.

Freemantle, D. (1985) *Superboss: The A-Z of Managing People Successfully*, Gower : London.

Halloran, J. (1986) *Personnel and Human Resource Management*, Prentice Hall : Englewood Cliffs.

Peters, T. and Waterman, R. (1982) *In Search of Excellence,* Harper and Row : New York.

Pratt, K. (1986) *Effective Staff Appraisal: A Practical Guide,* Van Nostrand Reinhold : England.

Randell, G., Packard, P. and Slater, J. (1984) *Staff Appraisal: A First Step to Effective Leadership,* Institute of Personnel Management : London.

Reynolds, D. (1987) 'Teacher appraisal and development: a review of the key issues', *School Organization,* **7**, 2, pp. 129–137.

Rubin, I. and Rose, E. (1978) *Performance Appraisal,* McGraw-Hill : New York.

The Straits Times, Saturday 9 March 1991, Singapore.

Chapter 11

Setting Targets

Jack Edwards wasn't quite sure what to do. Five weeks previously he had been made head of the marketing division in a medium-sized private company, and had found things in a real mess. Some key employees were dissatisfied because they seemed to have no idea what was expected of them or what they were accountable for. Their job responsibilities appeared to have been changed from day to day and they had no idea where they were going. A number of employees openly complained about having no input into decision-making. Morale was very low.

Jack Edwards is not alone in the problems he faces. You may well be able to identify with him on a number of points. Many organisations or subunits are faced with similar problems; problems which restrict or even damage their optimal performance. Such typical problems are quite recognisable and manifest themselves in ways such as:

1. Employees not knowing what is expected of them.
2. Employees being unsure of what they are accountable for.
3. Employees who are not focused on their job.
4. Management failing to communicate the organisation's direction.
5. Employees complaining about not having any input into organisational decision-making and so losing the motivation to work to the best of their ability.

You can work towards overcoming some of these problems if you are prepared to involve your employees in decisions about how they will achieve certain **targets**, and by giving them responsibility for ensuring they are achieved.

We believe that target management can help you increase your organisation's performance and productivity through involving your employees in setting work targets, and by ensuring that they are focused and accountable for what has to be done. The focus is driven by the overall goals of your organisation. This chapter aims to explain the process of setting targets and to explain some of its strengths and shortcomings. We also try to identify the practical value of target-setting and we provide some practice in writing specific target statements.

410

We have labelled this process *target management* because we believe the term *target* conjures up a more powerful image than that provided by such terms as *goals* and *objectives*. Imagine a target such as that used in archery. The purpose is absolutely clear: the participant has to hit the very centre and any other result is simply less than perfect.

Before we look at the steps of the target-setting approach, it will be useful for you to try writing some organisational target statements. You should do this in Application Task 11.1.

APPLICATION TASK 11.1

Write three target statements for your organisation. Identify three concrete targets you would like it to achieve by the end of the year. You will be able to refer to these statements later in the chapter.

Target Statement 1:

Target Statement 2:

Target Statement 3:

The Simple Steps of Target Management

Target management is derived from a traditional Management By Objectives (MBO) approach as first presented by Peter Drucker in 1954, but it differs in several ways. MBO fell into disfavour in some spheres in the 1980s. It may have been due to the fact that it had become over-complicated and that organisations tended to rely too heavily on the process. We have attempted to condense and simplify the process to make it more practical. The number of steps have been reduced in order to facilitate understanding and implementation. Although it is aimed at junior and middle management, it can nevertheless be utilised at senior levels also. The basic tenets and rationale behind MBO are retained.

Target management basically involves superior and subordinate meeting together to set targets for personal development and organisation benefit. It clarifies what is expected of people and holds them accountable for the outcomes. The focus is on results rather than specific activities or processes.

Your organisation probably has broad organisational goals (they may of course have different names such as aims or objectives). These usually come from the direction or mission of the organisation. They are the starting point for practical target management. There should be room within these goals for flexibility of implementation, that is, how the goals will actually be achieved.

Before proceeding it will help to consider the broad goals of your own organisation or subunit. Some overall goals may simply be:

- To achieve a dominant position in the industry.
- To increase our share of the overseas market.
- To ensure that the prices remain competitive while keeping quality at a high level.
- For employees to become actively involved in finding ways of increasing productivity.

In Application Task 11.2, you should identify the goals of either your organisation as a whole, or your department.

These goals are the starting point for setting practical targets. They need to be combined with the actual job description of employees. To provide a firm basis for target-setting, you should complete Application Task 11.3 which asks you to consider the specific job requirements of just one of your employees, and to use the information to go through the target process.

The target-setting process follows four basic steps. It is presented in Figure 11.1.

APPLICATION TASK 11.2

ORGANISATIONAL GOALS

In the spaces below, summarise the goals of your organisation or subunit.

1.

2.

3.

4.

APPLICATION TASK 11.3

JOB DESCRIPTION

Name: _____

Major job responsibilities:

Other job responsibilities:

Figure 11.1
Steps for Target Management

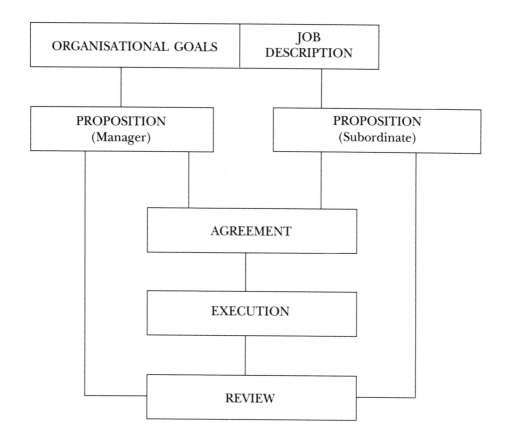

Proposition

The initial stage involves you as the manager and your employee in working separately first of all to arrive at some realistic targets. These targets must be guided by the overall organisational goals and the predetermined job description of the employee. You set a type of framework in which your staff member can set targets. You may also make suggestions for the specific target statements. Your framework should specify which organisational goals you will be targeting. The employee also develops his own target statements, which he believes are attainable and fit in with the overall aims of the organisation and his job description. When this has been done, the resultant initial target statements for the employee may look like this: (in our example, the subordinate is a canteen supervisor in a large catering operation).

- ■ Organisational goal: For employees to become actively involved in finding ways of increasing productivity.
- ■ Framework: At an executive meeting it was decided that one way to meet the organisational goal was to produce a newsletter.
- ■ Manager: To develop and issue a four-page quarterly newsletter encouraging staff to suggest methods for increasing organisational productivity. The newsletter will begin in January 1992 and not involve more than thirty hours preparation time and not cost more than $2,500 per issue.
- ■ Supervisor: To oversee and issue a two-page biannual newsletter so that staff can share their ideas on how to increase productivity on the job. The first issue will come out before March 1992 and will involve forty hours of preparation time. Each issue will be produced for under $1,000.

As you can see, both target statements come from the one general goal. They aim to help the organisation achieve a particular goal through a newsletter but differ in the details. In reality of course the target statements may differ much more.

At this stage you will find it useful to write a few similar target statements for the employee you identified earlier. You can do this in Application Task 11.4.

If you want to make this thoroughly realistic, you could also ask the employee in question to write a target statement related to the same goal. You can then use this to go to the next stage of the process which involves reaching a common level of agreement.

Agreement

Target statements having been prepared, try to come to some agreement with the employee on what the final target statement will entail. These statements are often referred to as *key result areas*. The targets must be realistic, tied to organisational goals, and be within the boundaries of the job description. They must also be attainable. At this point you must be flexible and resist the temptation to simply tell the employee what to do. The employee is the one who has to reach the target and must therefore be committed to it. On the other hand, your job as a manager is to ensure that organisational goals are being met.

This, of course, is the focus most goal-based models emphasise. However, as well as a vehicle for organisational improvement, the target-setting process is a method for developing staff. Targets should challenge the employee and

APPLICATION TASK 11.4

PROPOSITIONS

Choose one of the broad organisational goals you listed (in Application Task 11.2) and write some targets (we will look at how to do this systematically later). You should write down at least one statement which is consistent with the goal (organisational or subunit) identified.

Organisational Goal:

Your Target Statements:

Stott, K. and Walker, A., *Making Management Work.* © 1992 Simon & Schuster (Asia) Pte Ltd.

assist in his development. This often has the beneficial effect of motivating the employee.

Now comes the difficult part. Once you have both agreed on the target you should leave the employee to decide on the *how*. The employee will be held responsible for reaching the target. He should be given responsibility therefore for the means by which this will be done. Returning to the earlier example of the newsletter, the final, agreed target may have been:

> To develop and issue a four-page employee newsletter three times a year to provide staff with the opportunity to contribute ideas about how the organisation can increase its productivity. The first edition will be distributed by February 1992 and will not involve more than thirty hours preparation time. Each issue after the first will be produced at a cost of not more than $2,000.

The supervisor should still have the freedom to decide on layout, format, type of printing, where to print, etc., as long as he can meet the target. For him to be able to do this, you must ensure that he has access to necessary resources and authority.

Now return to your own target-setting exercise and try to reach some agreement with your employee (make up the agreement if you are doing it on your own). Complete Application Task 11.5.

The agreement form becomes a type of contract where the employee agrees to meet the target and you agree to provide the necessary resources (you will also have checked that your organisation is structurally capable of supporting and reaching the target). It also ensures that you both fully understand what is expected and that the employee will be accountable for target completion – as long as you keep your part of the bargain.

Execution

The next stage of the process involves the employee in working to achieve the target. During the execution of the agreed task resist the temptation to become too heavily involved or to continually 'check-up' on the delegate. You should however be available to offer advice and support if necessary.

Do not fall into the trap which recently caught the senior manager in one large public sector organisation. The manager believed in a target-setting approach and progressed through the initial stages with a reasonable degree of efficiency. When the time came, however, for his middle manager to work towards the target, he could not stop interfering. He always seemed to be in the middle manager's office asking 'How is it going?' or 'Staying on task?' Furthermore, he could not restrain himself from continually offering advice:

APPLICATION TASK 11.5

AGREEMENT

Write down the target you and your employee agreed upon below, and list the resources you may have to provide.

Agreed Target:

Necessary Resources:

Signed:

Manager: _____

Employee: _____

Dates of review: _____

_____

_____

Stott, K. and Walker, A., *Making Management Work*. © 1992 Simon & Schuster (Asia) Pte Ltd.

'I certainly wouldn't do it that way' or 'That won't work, will it?' Eventually, his subordinate gave up trying to complete the task himself and did everything the manager suggested. He lost confidence to complete the task satisfactorily and the senior manager virtually finished up doing the job himself! This episode ensured that the process would lack credibility in any subsequent target-setting exercises.

Much of what we advocate here is consistent with effective delegation practice and you may wish to read Chapter 17 in conjunction with this section which proposes that employees should be given sufficient scope to work towards mutually agreed targets without undue interference.

At this stage in our example, the supervisor would be working on the 'nitty-gritty' of conceptualising the newsletter – soliciting ideas, working on layouts, and getting costing estimates. When the target has been set, simply step back and monitor the employee only at previously agreed review dates to check progress and be available for consultation. Step in only if things really start to get out of hand. If this happens of course you must take over, since you are ultimately accountable for the end result.

Review

The formal review or appraisal comes at the time when the target is meant to be reached. At this stage you sit down with the employee and consider the degree of success. If the target was realistic and you have monitored at agreed points and supplied the necessary resources, the target will probably have been met. If it has not, you have reason to ask why not, since the employee had an input into almost every decision. In the worst scenario, you may have a case for employing sanctions. If the employee has done a good job, this is the time to comment on success and perhaps reward him.

You can also use this time to set new targets and iron out any difficulties in the process. The supervisor in our example produced an excellent newsletter – it looked good and some of the employees' suggestions were useful. He was proud of the job he did and felt important. He made improvements for the next issue, following his review discussion with the boss. Best of all, he produced the first issue for $300 less than the agreed budget and indicated he would need less time to complete the process in future.

For a target management system to work, those involved should be skilled in the process and committed to seeing it through. In Figure 11.2 we review the process of target-setting and identify the key practical points.

We see target-setting as consistent with our general approach throughout the book: that if work goals can be considered alongside personal goals, needs and preferences, there is more chance of commitment and effective performance. This of course is a major benefit and one which is identified in our list of advantages below. It would be wrong however to ignore some of the problems which might surface, and we therefore identify some of the ways in which the approach can falter.

Figure 11.2
Key Practical Points

IN A GOOD TARGET MANAGEMENT PROGRAMME:

- Employees must have a clear job description.
- Individual performance must be tied to organisational goals.
- Management must provide sufficient resources for targets to be attained.
- Target-setting is best used as a developmental process as well as a system for achieving organisational goals.
- The system should contain both rewards and sanctions for achievement or non-achievement of targets.
- Sufficient time must be provided.
- Once targets have been set the employee should be responsible for the 'how'.
- The system should be flexible and allow for crisis situations.
- Progress towards target attainment should be reviewed only at agreed-upon points and the manager should be available for consultation.
- Employees must be held accountable for target attainment.

Advantages

Better Managing

You are forced to think about results, not simply activities or work. To ensure targets are realistic, target management requires you to think of the way employees will accomplish results through the organisation. You have to consider capital, material and human resource needs (Koontz and Weihrich, 1989).

Personal Commitment

Target management encourages your employees to commit themselves to their goals. They no longer see themselves as just doing work, following instructions and waiting for guidance. They are more likely to view themselves as individuals with clearly defined purposes through setting targets and having an important input into decisions. This generally promotes a greater feeling of commitment.

Agreement on What Is Expected

Obviously, target management will provide all parties, including yourself, with a better understanding of what is required and expected.

Better Management of Time

When you use target management, you are forced to separate the important from the routine. Effort is directed towards previously determined targets/results, and the less significant parts of the job are relegated in importance.

Fewer Surprises

Nobody in management likes too many surprises. Target management requires that both you and your subordinates look beyond today and plan for the future. This course of action helps minimise the number of surprises faced by all organisational members. The monitoring and feedback mechanisms built into target management help to identify problems at the earliest possible time so that appropriate action can be taken.

Motivation

By using target management, you actually provide employees with some ownership of what they are doing and how they do it. This generally motivates staff to want to perform better. Staff are also motivated by seeing their targets achieved. Success breeds success.

Communication and Co-ordination

Employees have a better idea of what you are planning and where they are heading (you will also know more about them). The target management process has built-in discussion and participatory decision-making. Employees better understand how they fit into the overall structure, direction and mission of the organisation.

Morale and Satisfaction

Involvement in target-setting provides success and involvement for subordinates. This in turn improves morale and provides greater job satisfaction.

Increases Participation

The joint approach to the setting of targets sends a strong message to your employees that their opinions are valued. They are therefore more likely to be willing to participate in decision-making.

Problems (or Why Target Management Sometimes Fails)

Too Time-Consuming

If you go through the process properly, it can be very time-consuming, especially in the beginning and if you have a large staff. You need to be prepared for this and set aside that extra time when you first begin the programme.

Excessive Paperwork

If you are not careful, target management can generate mountains of paperwork. Try to keep this to a minimum. Keep forms and agreement documents to a minimum and do not demand unnecessarily lengthy reports on progress.

Difficulty in Setting Measurable Targets

You are not alone if you experience difficulties in setting measurable, attainable targets. If you cannot, the entire process may collapse through lack of success. Targets which are set too high will probably not be reached, so employees are unlikely to enjoy much satisfaction. Targets which are not set high enough will become tedious and fail to offer sufficient challenge. Most people have difficulty in setting and developing appropriate targets. We shall deal with this problem a little later.

Operational Crisis

Target management effectiveness can be hampered by the inevitable operational crisis which, if allowed, can divert the energies of people away from the targets. You must try to be flexible.

Omitting Periodic Review

If you omit periodic review, motivation and the cross-checking mechanism can suffer. Targets which are allowed to drift can become impotent, useless, or even distractive. Employees need the opportunity to clarify certain points, and you need to be sure everything is on track.

Focus on Easily Measurable Results

Your employees (and even you, yourself) may be tempted to focus on results which are easily attainable or easily measurable. If this happens, your organisation or subunit may not grow or develop as it could.

Failure to Set Guidelines

Guidelines must be set and expectations must be clearly understood and agreed. If this is not done targets may not be as focused as they should be.

These advantages and possible problems are summarised in Figure 11.3.

Figure 11.3
Target Management: The Good And The Bad

ADVANTAGES	PROBLEMS (or why it can fail)
■ Clear expectations. ■ Better managing. ■ Fewer surprises. ■ Motivating. ■ Better communication and co-ordination. ■ Encourages better time management. ■ Improves morale and satisfaction. ■ Encourages greater participation. ■ Encourages greater personal commitment.	■ Too much paperwork. ■ Too time-consuming. ■ No regular review. ■ No guidelines. ■ Targets imposed. ■ Temptation to set easily-reached or measured targets. ■ Targets not measurable. ■ Fails in crisis.

We have already mentioned target statements several times and you may have tried to write a few when we were establishing the relationship between targets and organisational goals in the earlier part of the chapter. We now address this practical issue which often gives rise to concern: the writing of realistic, verifiable targets.

Guidelines for Writing Specific Target Statements

To start this section look at the two statements below and try to identify which is the better, more specific target statement. Keep in mind that these targets should be set using the approach explained at the beginning of the chapter.

1. The unit will increase its productivity;

OR

2. The unit will increase its output by 7 per cent by 30 November of this year, without increasing the cost of its operation and maintaining its current quality level. The unit head will oversee the increase in productivity.

Of course you selected statement 2. Look at the differences. Statement 1 tells us that the unit will increase its productivity. However, it does not tell us when or by how much, nor is it clear whether the unit can sacrifice cost or quality in its quest for the improved productivity or who is responsible. Think what the manager who set this target may get – even if the unit gives him a 0.5 per cent increase in productivity next year and product quality suffers he can hardly complain. In reality, no statement of intent can be quite so vague as this, but some targets are expressed in a way that leaves them open to interpretation.

In contrast, look at statement 2. It has clarity and is easy to understand. It is clear to all involved that productivity should increase by 7 per cent by the end of November; that cost should not increase; that quality should not suffer and that the unit head is responsible. It provides something concrete to aim at, and success can be judged relatively easily. It includes all the attributes of a good target statement. Figure 11.4 summarises the important criteria of a clear statement.

Figure 11.4
What Does a Good Target Statement Include?

- It uses an action word (will).
- It states the person responsible (the unit manager).
- It specifies cost in terms of time and money (cost and quality).
- It specifies a completion date (30 November).
- It specifies a measurable end result (7 per cent increase).

As you can see, a good target states the *what, when, who* and *maximum cost.* However, it avoids feasibility and the *how.* The action plan developed for the target will deal with the how and test the feasibility.

The requirements for a good target statement can of course be even more detailed and specific. The more exact you can make the target the less the likelihood of misunderstanding, confusion or avoidance of responsibility.

For target statements to be measurable they must be stated in concrete and explicit terms. It is preferable if the target outcomes can be quantified. This is not always possible however, and qualitative outcomes may be necessary. When you have written a target statement you should test it using the checklist we have provided in Figure 11.5 to see if it includes the essential elements of a good target statement.

Figure 11.5
A Target Statement Checklist

Not every target statement need explicitly meet the requirements set out below in the actual statement. Some supporting information may be attached. Every aspect however must be understood by all parties involved. The first five points are critical for a target statement to be effective.

	Yes	No
1. Does it state what is to be done?	☐	☐
2. Does it state what the target hopes to achieve?	☐	☐
3. Does it state who has the responsibility for doing it?	☐	☐
4. Does it state when it is to be completed?	☐	☐
5. Does it give details of the resources necessary for its accomplishment?	☐	☐
6. Does it contain a succinct statement explaining the approach to be employed?	☐	☐
7. Does it state who is to co-ordinate different parts of the overall target?	☐	☐
8. Does it include a statement of the justification for accomplishing the target?	☐	☐

You will find it helpful to write some of your own target statements. You could of course use the statements you wrote earlier in the chapter.

APPLICATION TASK 11.6

WHAT'S WRONG?

Identify what is wrong with the following statements. Use the spaces following each statement. When you have done this read our ideas below.

1.　The catering manager should ensure that there is a wider choice of maincourse dishes for the lunch-time period.

2.　The supervisor is to develop a system which gives all workers an equal amount of time off during the day for breaks.

3.　Mike will head a team which will be responsible for implementing the newly developed training programme designed to upgrade computer skills of all twenty-three secretarial employees. The plan is to be implemented by 3 June 1992 and stay within a budget of $30,000.

1. In the first statement, the person responsible was identified as was the period involved, but very little else. It is not specified how many main dishes should be provided, nor the time frame for improvement.

2. As in the first statement, there is no time frame given, nor does it specify what resources the supervisor would have at his disposal. It is not stated how much time each worker should get off during the day or why this needs to be equalised.

3. The third statement states who is responsible, the resources available, a deadline, and what the target hopes to achieve. This statement is the clearest of the three.

Stott, K. and Walker, A., *Making Management Work.* © 1992 Simon & Schuster (Asia) Pte Ltd.

You will have gathered that managers often make assumptions about peoples' understanding and this inevitably leads to lack of clarity in defining targets. You really need to see the process as one which must be dealt with systematically, so that no doubts can exist about what should be achieved. Despite this, it is all too easy to make errors of judgement when writing such statements – this is true both for you and your staff. Bechtel (1980) provides us with a list of some common weaknesses. You need to watch out for these.

Some weaknesses common in target statements:

1. Targets are set too low to truly challenge employee capabilities.
2. Employees overestimate their own capabilities and set inappropriate or unworkable targets.
3. Targets do not reflect the responsibilities of employees who write them.
4. Targets are concerned with how to do something rather than what actually has to be done.
5. Employees are unsure who has responsibility for achieving the target.
6. Targets reflect an employee's perception of what the leader wants, rather than what can actually be achieved.
7. Targets that are found to be irrelevant, unfeasible, or unworkable are not dropped or rethought.
8. Target completion dates are too optimistic.
9. The justification for a target is not substantiated or understood.
10. The approach designed to achieve the target is weak.

Conclusion

In summary, *target management* is a participative process which should involve all managerial and supervisory staff in setting targets. It is based on a very positive philosophy about people and what makes them work. It assumes that employees want to be involved in making decisions and in how to achieve their targets. Employees who are permitted input into target-setting and planning are more likely to be committed to achieving the targets than those who are not. Target management aims to take advantage of people's natural willingness to learn, achieve and work. It has the added benefit of focusing and formalising both personal and organisational targets and direction. It can be introduced at almost any level of the organisational hierarchy.

References

Bechtel, D. (1980) 'Dhabi fehru: an MBO activity', in Pfeiffer, J. and Jones, E., *A Handbook of Structured Experiences for Human Relations Training Volume VII*, University Associates : San Diego.
Drucker, P. (1954) *The Practice of Management*, Harper and Row : New York.
Koontz, H. and Weihrich, H. (1989) *Management*, 9th edn, McGraw-Hill : Singapore.

Chapter 12

Dealing with Conflict

Conflict is inevitable in all facets of life. The more people you have in your charge the greater the number of conflicts you are likely to face. As a manager you are responsible for organising others towards achievement of the organisation's goals. Along the way you will be faced with disagreements between:

- You and your employees.
- Individual employees.
- Groups of employees.
- You and your peers.
- You and your boss.
- You and labour unions.
- You and your competitors or even clients.

You may also encounter conflict within yourself and will certainly face it in your private life. 'Conflict is a natural part of human existence. It is surely a companion of life, death, and taxes' (Lindelow and Scott, 1989 : 338).

Conflict *will* play an influential and recurring role in your job as a manager. To be effective you must be able to deal with different types of conflicts and attempt to transform them from destructive to constructive experiences. You need to understand what causes conflict and that it can be allowed to either assist or hinder your organisation. To deal effectively with conflict you must develop certain skills.

In this chapter we shall attempt to differentiate between the possible positive and negative outcomes of conflict. We shall discuss the types of conflicts you may face as a manager and identify their possible sources or causes. We shall then examine some possible strategies for dealing with conflict.

Conflict: Is It All Bad?

When most people think of conflict, it conjures up negative images of bitter fights, prolonged arguments and unpleasant exchanges. We would be foolish to totally disregard these perceptions. Much of the conflict as it presently occurs *is* destructive and, if allowed to continue unabated, can damage organisational unity and effectiveness. Not all conflict, however, is destructive; it can be productive and a very valuable source of creativity.

Robbins (1991 : 450) states: 'Behavioural scientists and an increasing number of practicioners now accept that the goal of effective management is not to eliminate conflict. Rather, it is to create the right intensity of conflict so as to reap its functional benefits.'

When people discuss conflict they often picture what is called a lose–lose or win–lose situation. We believe managers should attempt to deal with conflicts so they arrive at a constructive win–win situation. There are four situations which can result from conflict:

- Lose–lose: Both parties feel they have lost out in resolving the conflict. Animosity often results.
- Lose–win: One party is unassertive and lets the other win despite the cost to himself.
- Win–lose: One party forces a solution on another, leaving one party feeling defeated and dejected.
- Win–win: Both parties feel they have won. This can result from a compromise but is even more likely from collaboration. If conflicts can be solved with win–win outcomes they are likely to produce positive outcomes.

Our discussion of conflict then is based on the premise that not all conflict is or has to be destructive or result in a loss. If you as the manager can effectively harness conflict it can often result in positive outcomes. What are the conditions which determine whether conflict becomes a detrimental or a beneficial force? It can be destructive when it:

1. Prevents your organisation from achieving what is really important.
2. Hinders co-operative action.
3. Creates employee dissatisfaction.
4. Accentuates differences between co-workers.
5. Demotivates and demoralises people.
6. Causes irresponsible behaviour.
7. Interferes with the decision-making process.
8. Produces distrust, suspicion and ill-will.
9. Damages productivity.

It can be constructive when it:

1. Encourages trust.

2. Produces creative solutions.
3. Opens discussions.
4. Aids individual and group development.
5. Increases self-esteem.
6. Improves communication.
7. Increases involvement and interest in a problem.
8. Increases productivity.
9. Exposes a stagnant system.
10. Causes re-evaluation of outdated procedures.
11. Allows 'built-up' negative emotions to surface.

In simple terms, too much conflict produces negative feelings between individuals or groups which can result in destructive organisational consequences. Too little conflict on the other hand can inhibit open, innovative discussion of a problem and result in organisational mediocrity or even stagnation. This is illustrated in Figure 12.1.

As we discuss various strategies for dealing with conflict it will become clearer how it can be transformed into a positive force. We see conflict as a vital source of energy. What you must do is attempt to harness this energy for the benefit of your organisation. Low (1990 : 56) provides some tips for negotiating this transformation process.

Figure 12.1
Organisational Performance and Conflict

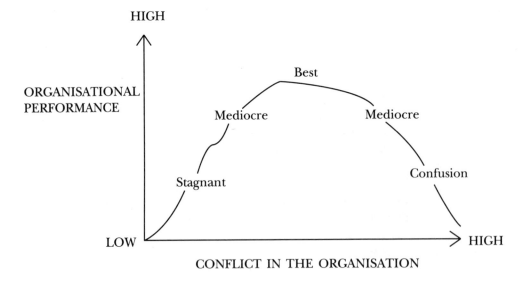

Transforming conflict:

- *Listen* to non-verbal as well as verbal messages. Accept that people are different and have different perceptions. Appreciate these differences and put them to work for you.
- *Don't assume* you know – ask more questions, seek further information.
- *Be open* – try not to judge immediately. Get out of your usual mode of thinking, your 'prefabricated system of thought'.
- *Work* on collaborative problem-solving, do not become too set in your ways.
- *Be self-critical* – see your own weaknesses. Avoid playing psychological games.

The secret then for you as a manager is to be able to deal with and transform destructive conflict into constructive conflict. To do this you need to be aware of the types and causes of such conflict.

Types of Conflict

You will be called upon to deal with a number of different types of conflict. We classify the three main types as *self-conflicts*, *people conflicts* and *team conflicts*.

Self-Conflicts

These types of conflict are intrapersonal: conflicts relevant to making individual decisions. Sashkin and Morris (1984) discuss three types of self-conflict.

1. Approach–approach, where you are forced to choose between a number of favourable alternatives.
2. Approach–avoidance conflict, which occurs when the same target has both favourable and unfavourable outcomes.
3. Avoidance–avoidance conflict which presents a situation where all the available alternatives are negative.

All managers must deal with these types, which are often stressful and frustrating. Such conflicts can affect your organisation peripherally but are not as damaging as people or team clashes. As a manager your prime role is to lead and manage others. Self-conflicts are mainly destructive if they frustrate you to the extent that they affect your relationship with others.

People Conflicts

People or interpersonal conflicts have the potential to be the most destructive to the organisation. If not dealt with they have the tendency to be long-lasting and to 'get out of hand'. These types of conflicts *must* be dealt with. Most of this chapter will be devoted to this issue.

Team Conflicts

There are two types of team conflicts. These can be labelled *in-team* conflicts and *between-team* conflicts. The first type is almost identical to people conflicts and usually pits individual team members against each other. Between-team conflicts refer to conflict between different work teams, whether permanent or temporary. This type of conflict can also be very destructive to your organisation.

These are very general classifications of the types of conflicts you may face. Now we look at the causes of conflict, which may give us some clues about the types of managerial action which can be taken.

Conflict Initiators

Conflict manifests itself in numerous forms. It can be an open, ugly face-to-face slanging match or an employee quietly withdrawing his co-operation. First, it is necessary to have an understanding of what may have caused it. Below we present a list of what can be considered major conflict initiators:

- Combative rather than collaborative attitude.
- Personality clash.
- Differences in goals.
- Poor orientation to conflict.
- Inadequately defined goals.
- Poor confrontation skills.
- Bad timing.
- Unclear areas of personal responsibility.
- Environmental stress.
- Inadequate listening skills.
- Poor use of language.
- Threatening bodily and verbal communication.
- Competition for inadequate resources.
- Role incompatibility.
- Failing to obey rules.

- Lack of openness.
- Lack of co-operation.
- Differences over which methods should be used.
- Poor problem-solving skills.
- Poor managerial skills.
- Lack of relevant information.

The list of possible causes shown above is not intended to be definitive. Rather than try to discuss specific conflict initiators, we will present some broader categories which we believe to be the major causes of conflict which you may face.

These can be grouped under organisational or structural, and people-initiated conflicts.

Organisationally Initiated Conflict

These are usually caused by organisational inadequacies in relation to structure, co-ordination, communication, and ill-defined role definitions and interdependencies.

Unclear Roles and Interdependencies

If job roles and expectations are inadequately defined or ambiguous, conflict often results. If, for example, an employee is chastised for not completing a task which he did not know he was responsible for, negative feelings will result. Conflict can also result if a number of employees who are dependent on each other are unsure of who should be doing what. Imagine you had just completed a fairly involved task and discover that a colleague has been working on an identical project; you would feel as if you had wasted your time and would still perhaps attempt to promote your work as the acceptable solution, thus bringing you into a conflict situation with your peer.

If employees' roles are interdependent (and they usually are) conflict can again be present. When employees depend on each other for task completion, the chances of conflict multiply.

Another form of role conflict can occur even when role definitions are quite clear. A manager was asked to compile a report on the managerial effectiveness of the organisation. His immediate supervisor had very definite ideas of how she wanted the report compiled. Unfortunately, the overall division head also had some very firm ideas about the report which were quite different from those of the supervisor. When he completed the report neither manager was happy with it and told him so. He resented this and felt obliged to justify himself. In doing so, argument, resentment and ill-feeling surfaced in an unpleasant situation.

Co-ordination and Control

Conflict can also result from unnecessarily complex co-ordination or control mechanisms. Conflicts such as these occur when employees with different roles are dependent on each other. Problems often arise from the all too common professional/administrator battle for control. One such situation involved the acquisition of training aids, such as video recorders, in a training organisation. To obtain such equipment staff had to:

1. Go to the secretary's office to obtain a form.
2. Fill in the complex form (time, date, equipment, place).
3. Have the department head sign the form (walk to or mail to his office).
4. Wait for the signed form.
5. Take the completed form to the appropriate location.
6. Sign the form in the presence of the technician.
7. Wait for a duplicate copy to be mailed to him.
8. Hope the equipment turned up!

All trainers objected to this procedure as a waste of time, adding that it made them feel irresponsible. The administration on the other hand insisted they needed the mechanisms to keep track of equipment – conflict resulted. The conflict was exacerbated when inadequate equipment was delivered and the technicians claimed 'they were doing their best under the circumstances'.

The conflict could have been easily avoided by careful consideration of the co-ordination mechanism implemented and by a loosening of administrative control.

Limited Resources

All organisational resources are limited to a certain extent. If your organisation has abundant resources it is quite simple to ensure that everyone has what is needed. When resources are limited however, people or teams are forced to compete for what is available. If this is not dealt with diplomatically conflict is likely to result as individuals and groups identify inequities in allocation and purport to take retributive action.

Latitude and Decision-Making

How much latitude employees are granted in completing a task and how much they are involved in decision-making can also affect the level of conflict.

If employees are given freedom to pursue their jobs as they see fit, conflict is probably more likely to eventuate. The trade-off here is that more freedom and less structure can often lead to greater creativity: *constructive conflict.* The degree of flexibility of course depends on the type of job required by the organisation. In highly competitive organic organisations, flexibility is essential to stay in touch with advances. In more mechanistic organisations, such as an engine-assembly plant, little flexibility is required.

How often and how much employees are involved in decision-making also affects the level of conflict. Robbins (1991) found that the rate of conflict multiplied as participation in decision-making increased. He also pointed out, however, that, although the number of conflicts increased, the number of major incidents of conflict actually went down. Apparently the opportunity to discuss and express dissatisfaction in an open forum prevented minor conflicts from expanding. In other words, the participative format allowed employees to openly work out conflicts. As we saw in Chapter 6 on Solving Problems and Making Decisions, better quality, more creative decisions arise from participative decision-making. Controlled conflict is an integral part of this creative process.

Communication

Lack of communication between manager and worker or between departments or divisions can also lead to conflict. Unclear goals, unstated expectations, lack of trust and hidden agendas can all initiate unrest and division within the organisation. Inadequate organisational communication mechanisms can lead to over-competitiveness among teams or a duplication of work.

SUMMARY

Organisationally Initiated Conflicts Result From:

- Unclear goals and interdependencies.
- Co-ordination and control.
- Limited resources.
- Latitude and decision-making.
- Communication.

People-Initiated Conflict

Organisationally initiated causes of conflict can often be controlled by the manager; people or human conflicts are more difficult to control. Schmidt and Tannenbaum (1972) believe that four types of issues commonly cause conflicts:

1. Disagreement over facts: Where people are aware of the facts but interpret them in different ways.
2. Disagreement over goals: Where employees disagree over the direction of the organisation and the targets they are expected to achieve.
3. Disagreement over methods: How things are actually to be done.
4. Disagreement over values: Basic differences about what is right and wrong.

We have grouped the major causes of people conflicts somewhat differently but our categories encompass the general causes listed above.

We mentioned at the beginning of the chapter that if you wish to deal with conflict effectively you must be aware of what causes it to surface. To make the remainder of this chapter more meaningful you should complete Application Task 12.1. It is designed to provide you with the opportunity to reflect upon conflict situations that you face in your work place.

You should now have some conflict situations in mind to which you can attach your subsequent reading. Consider whether a different strategy for dealing with the conflicts may have been more appropriate. We will now discuss some general causes of people-initiated conflicts.

Conflicts between people are often caused by personality clashes and differing value systems. These factors usually cannot be permanently altered but resultant conflicts must still be dealt with. Read the people-based causes of conflict below and see if you can relate them to your organisation.

Misunderstandings

Many conflicts arise from misunderstanding between two or more people. Conflict results when a person misunderstands what is expected. This usually comes about through a lack of communication. Managers often assume that their employees *know* what is expected of them and do not bother to fully explain requirements. Then, when the employee works on a task which is not what the manager wanted, conflict results. Misunderstanding can also occur during events such as appraisal interviews. A misplaced word or phrase from the manager can upset a sensitive employee and lead to a conflict situation. The same situation can result between two employees who misunderstand each other, either in a personal or work sense. Many people are easily insulted; care must be taken when communicating with such employees.

APPLICATION TASK 12.1

PEOPLE CONFLICT: MY WORK PLACE

1. In the first column, PEOPLE, list a number of your employees or other people at work with whom you have regular contact.
2. In the second column, DESCRIPTION, write a very brief description of a conflict you have been involved in with the person. If you have not had any conflicts leave the space blank. (Here you may wish to ask yourself why there have been no conflicts.)
3. In the third column, CAUSE, write what you thought was the cause of the conflict.
4. In the final column, SATISFACTION, simply write 'yes' if you believe the conflict was dealt with satisfactorily, and a 'no' if you were not satisfied with the outcome. There is no need to write your solution unless you think this would be helpful to you. An example of just one incident is shown below for guidance.

PEOPLE	DESCRIPTION	CAUSE	SATISFACTION
Tom Moors	Stormed into office yelling he was unhappy with the support he got. 'What are you going to do about it?'	One employee has been giving Tom a lot of problems — disagreeing with everything he does. Tom does not handle this too well, gets abusive. Does not believe I support him.	NO

PEOPLE	DESCRIPTION	CAUSE	SATISFACTION

Emotions

Emotional conflicts are caused by people's personal feelings about someone else, rather than any particular event or issue. These types of conflicts can also arise from misunderstandings. Emotions tend to last longer than any particular conflict-initiating event. If, for example, two managers are competing for a promotion and one gets it, apparently by discrediting the opposition, the rejected party is unlikely to forget the incident. Even if the manager who missed out goes on to another promotion and is not disadvantaged financially or professionally, he will not forget what he believes the other person has done.

One important point to note here is that if people believe they have been unfairly treated, their perceptions are very real. As a manager you will be called upon to solve conflicts even when you know the apparent cause of the event to be untrue.

Emotionally induced conflicts can eat away at organisational effectiveness if not dealt with. Such conflicts often continue between people or teams even after the original causes of the disagreement have been forgotten.

Viewpoints

These conflicts arise out of a divergence in viewpoints between people. They may be relatively unimportant or vital to organisational harmony. A simple example would be a department which has been allocated one car-parking space and must decide who should get it. Two managers may believe that their deputy should get the space. A more complicated example may be two senior managers who disagree about the best location for a new plant.

Values

Differences in values or fundamental beliefs often cause conflicts. People's values are reflections of their personality and what they believe. Values often lie behind conflict situations which appear to be initiated by other factors.

Conflicts based on values are thus difficult to deal with. Take the example of two senior executives when planning a recruiting drive for a new crop of junior managers. One manager might believe in hiring a substantial number of minority candidates because he believes it is part of the company's role to promote equality through affirmative action, even if some of the candidates are not of the same quality as others being considered. The other manager may believe that the positions should be based solely on merit if the company is to maintain its competitive position. Conflicting values such as these can infect an organisation and often lead to other types of conflict.

SUMMARY

People-Initiated Conflicts Result From:

- Misunderstandings.
- Emotions.
- Viewpoints.
- Values.

Dealing with Conflicts

Before we examine some strategies for dealing with conflict, let us remember the old saying 'prevention is better than cure'. There are a number of actions you can take to minimise the damage caused by conflicts before they occur:

1. Be 'on your toes':
    Be aware of what is happening in your organisation. Recognise conflicts while they are in their early stages and attempt to turn them around before they get out of hand. Do not allow a situation to develop which employees may perceive as unjust. Respond quickly to events that may damage organisational unity.
2. Share decisions:
    Encourage shared or collective judgements in as many situations as you can. Do not leave too many decisions to one individual.
3. Build a culture of trust and openness:
    Employ strategies to establish a climate where employees are not afraid to discuss their differences and feelings.

SUMMARY

Prevent Conflicts:

*   Be on your toes.
*   Share decisions.
*   Be open and trusting.

Unfortunately, no amount of measures can prevent all conflict situations. You also need to employ practical strategies for dealing with conflicts as they arise.

People Conflicts

We have seen that there are different types of conflict, and that conflicts can be caused by a number of factors. In this section we will discuss some techniques for dealing with conflict.

Robbins (1991) tells us that a person's response to a conflict situation will generally fall into five categories: *competing, accommodating, avoiding, compromising* and *collaborating*. Thomas (1975) places these responses on two dimensions, reflecting varying degrees of assertiveness and co-operativeness. An assertive response to conflict refers to the extent to which someone tries to satisfy his own concerns. Co-operativeness refers to the extent to which an individual attempts to satisfy the other person's concerns. This is best illustrated on the grid shown in Figure 12.2.

We suggest managers will be placed in situations at different times which will require them to utilise all of the five strategies in one form or another.

Figure 12.2
Responding to Conflict Situations

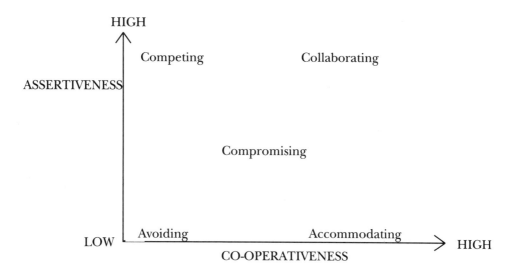

Source: Adapted from Thomas (1975).

Before you read about the various strategies for dealing with conflict, complete the questionnaire Dealing with Conflict: My Way.

We will now discuss each of the major strategies for dealing with conflict. As you read through, ask yourself the following questions:

1. Do I use any one strategy too often?
2. Do I use certain strategies even when they may not be applicable?
3. Do I need to train myself to use a combination of strategies?

Questionnaire

DEALING WITH CONFLICT: MY WAY

The statements below present some descriptions of various ways of dealing with conflicts. Read each statement carefully. Using the scale below (1 to 5) indicate the extent to which you agree or disagree with each statement as a way of responding to conflict.

Strongly agree	5
Agree	4
I am not sure whether I agree or disagree	3
Disagree	2
Strongly disagree	1

1. Letting employees have their own way makes them content. ☐

2. We can work out problems together. ☐

3. The most powerful will always win the argument. ☐

4. If you give a little so will I. ☐

5. Conflicts will go away if you avoid them. ☐

6. When an employee screams at you, let them have their way; they must really want it. ☐

7. Problems should be solved by know-how and discussion, not by voting. ☐

8. If an employee cannot agree with you, he must be made to do what you want anyway. ☐

9. It is better to get part of what you want than nothing at all. ☐

10. If someone argues with me, I'm not interested in them. ☐

11. Letting employees do what they want will make them work better. ☐

12. We must keep digging until we solve the problem. ☐

13. Forcing employees to work together reaffirms my control. ☐

14. Everybody is happy with a fair solution. ☐

15. Nothing is important enough to fight over. ☐

16. Employees will react positively if you always let them do things their own way. ☐

17. Problems may take time to solve but it is worth it. ☐

18. My position gives me the right to make others do things my way. ☐

19. If we both make concessions the outcome will be fair. ☐

20. Stay away from argumentative employees – they are not worth it. ☐

(Adapted from Watson, Vallee and Mulford, 1981 : 107)

Transfer your scores into the corresponding boxes. The number of the statement is above the box. Total your scores in the appropriate boxes and then transfer them to the graph. The higher the score for each conflict strategy the greater the probability that you will utilise the strategy when responding to conflict situations. The lower your total score the less frequently you tend to use this strategy.

	5		10		15		20		Total
Avoiding	☐	+	☐	+	☐	+	☐	=	☐
	1		6		11		16		Total
Accommodating	☐	+	☐	+	☐	+	☐	=	☐
	3		8		13		18		Total
Competing	☐	+	☐	+	☐	+	☐	=	☐
	4		9		14		19		Total
Compromising	☐	+	☐	+	☐	+	☐	=	☐
	2		7		12		17		Total
Collaborating	☐	+	☐	+	☐	+	☐	=	☐

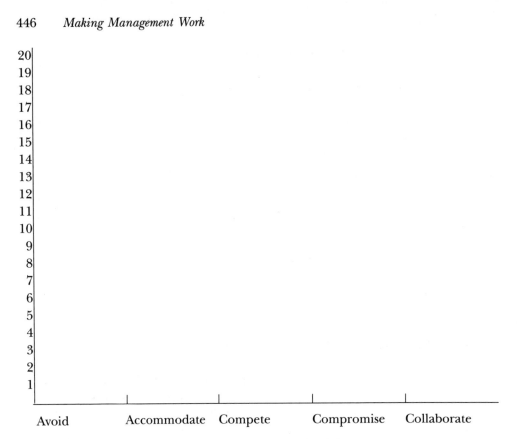

Stott, K. and Walker, A., *Making Management Work.* © 1992 Simon & Schuster (Asia) Pte Ltd.

Avoiding

For many people the most natural response to a conflict situation is to avoid it in some way. Not many of us enjoy stress and unpleasant situations. Is avoiding a conflict always wrong? Surprisingly, the answer is 'no'. There are times when it can be an effective short-term strategy. But beware, there are also many incidences when it can lead to more serious conflicts. There are a number of ways that you can avoid it.

Postpone It

You can postpone a problem until a later date. Although we do not recommend this approach in all situations, it has its place as a short-term strategy. If you feel you do not have enough information to fully analyse a situation, you may be wise to temporarily avoid the incident until you have more facts. Sometimes launching straight into reactive conflict strategies can be destructive, especially if you overreact to an emotional, personal outburst.

Ignore It

In certain situations it may be advisable to totally ignore a conflict. You can do this if you feel one person is attempting to broaden or initiate conflicts for his own purposes.

In Figure 12.3 is the actual letter received by one manager. We have replaced the names with initials. You will note that the author was not prepared to identify him or herself but was quite willing to vent an array of criticisms.

> How would you feel if you received this letter?
> How would you react?

The manager could not believe it when he opened the anonymous letter. He knew his staff well and trusted them. The slurs against himself and some of his employees seemed totally unfounded. Since the writer did not identify him/herself the manager chose to ignore the letter. He believed acting on the letter would have initiated more conflicts than it would have solved.

Isolate Them/Fire Them

If you have done all in your power to resolve a conflict between two parties and failed at every turn, you may have to resort to more drastic options. One option may be to isolate the two parties from each other so they do not have to work together. If this still does not work you can consider using the ultimate avoidance option: move one to a completely different unit or fire one (or both).

Withhold It

When two conflicting parties cannot reconcile their differences a less drastic option is for them to withhold their feelings from each other: control themselves.

The last two avoidance responses should only be used in drastic situations. Any avoidance strategy should be carefully considered before being applied. If you avoid conflict on a regular basis you risk frustrating others and allowing destructive consequences to simmer and explode. Avoidance strategies should mainly be viewed as stop-gap measures.

Figure 12.3
The Letter

Mr C.

23/8/89

Dear Mr C.

I represent a group of workers from Advanced Workshop #3. We are very disappointed in your behaviour as our boss. You preach one thing and then do another. There seems to be favouritism for some of your staff, especially for a certain group. You seem to favour Mr Z. and his gang of two namely Mr N. and Mr U.

We do not think Mr Z. should be our supervisor. We understand he thinks he is dynamic. We all think otherwise. The greather (sic.) the darkness how little the man!

He is a young punk and should show us more respect. When he organised one training session from an outside trainer he treated us like little children and was autocratic in his style. We want him removed immediately.

Another person who belongs to his group and thinks he knows a lot is Mr U. He had the cheek to tell one of us that we should not interrupt you in meetings. He makes decisions on his own when it is not his place.

Mr N., another of Mr Z.'s gang, is the quiet man in the group but works behind the scenes. We understand that he worked behind the scenes in his last job and is doing so now. What do you do inted to do (sic.)?

Come one Mr C., be fair. We understand that you favour certain staff members. What about us. Please don't insult us. Remember you are much younger than us and should show us respect. Please don't say anything about our beliefs. Hope this is some food for thought for you.

Thank you
A staff member

When to use avoidance strategies:

1. If you do not fully understand the cause or details of the conflict.
2. If, after a number of attempts, two conflicting parties cannot reconcile their differences.
3. If the relationship between the competing parties is not strong enough to absorb overt conflict.
4. If one person attempts to place you or others in a conflict situation for his own purposes.
5. When your stake in a conflict is low but the situation may damage working relationships.
6. If you face severe time constraints.

You will find it helpful to think of one conflict situation you have faced at work (or believe you are likely to face) which you believe would be best dealt with using this strategy. Devise a brief rationale (Why?) for your decision. You are advised to do this for each of the five strategies and the forms are shown in Application Tasks 12.2, 12.3, 12.4, 12.5 and 12.7.

APPLICATION TASK 12.2

WHEN CAN I USE THIS STRATEGY (AVOIDING)?

Situation: AVOIDING

Why?

Stott, K. and Walker, A., *Making Management Work*. © 1992 Simon & Schuster (Asia) Pte Ltd.

Accommodating

Accommodating involves you in attempting to satisfy another party's concerns while neglecting your own. The philosophy behind this strategy appears to be self-sacrifice or keeping the other party happy at all costs.

This approach can be useful in some situations. An over-reliance on it can be destructive however. Some managers use this strategy when dealing with their boss or when dealing with powerful worker leaders. Others are accommodating because they believe that the key to successful management is maintaining cordial relationships.

As with *avoiding*, continued use of this response can be detrimental to you and your organisation. If you always 'give way', you may be sacrificing critical analysis of work situations, lose your self-respect, be taken advantage of by others and become known as a 'push-over'.

When to use accommodating strategies :

1. If an argument is in 'full flight'.
2. When trying to win someone over.
3. When dealing with an influential boss or other actor.
4. When the issue is more important to the other party and must be resolved quickly.
5. When strong working relationships are more important than other considerations.

APPLICATION TASK 12.3

WHEN CAN I USE THIS STRATEGY (ACCOMMODATING)?

Situation: ACCOMMODATING

Why?

Competing

Competing or forcing is the opposite response to *accommodating*. You consider only your own concerns and ignore those of the other party. This is sometimes done through force, using an official position: 'I'm in charge here, we'll do it as I say ... NO ARGUMENT.' If you respond to a conflict in this way, you probably regard conflicts as win–lose situations, and you must win.

Managers who deal with conflict through force can be manipulative and will often surround themselves with staff who share their preferences or biases. If this response is used too frequently it can promote destructive consequences such as challenges to authority, loss of initiative and suppressed animosity.

As with the other strategies, however, the use of force does have its place in conflict management. It can settle disputes quickly. It is also often necessary when two groups are diametrically opposed on the basis of values, interests or personalities. If conflicting parties will not budge from their positions, forcing them into a solution may be the only alternative.

When to use competing strategies:

1. If a quick, tidy decision is vital.
2. If the conflicting parties will not budge from their position.
3. When conflicting parties will not even discuss an issue.
4. When you feel compelled to maintain a strong position.
5. When your relationship with the other person is unimportant.

APPLICATION TASK 12.4

WHEN CAN I USE THIS STRATEGY (COMPETING)?

Situation: COMPETING

Why?

Compromising

Compromising, which can include arbitration, negotiation and bargaining, is an attempt to provide both conflicting parties with a somewhat satisfactory result. Both parties are asked to make certain sacrifices in exchange for some concessions from the other – for the common good. Each party wins some things and loses others. This technique is very widely used by managers in a variety of situations.

Compromise can be achieved either through a problem-solving process or through the use of a third-party arbitrator. Compromise can also involve negotiation. Chapter 14 gives detailed information on this process. Managers often find themselves taking the role of the mediator: facilitating and clarifying communication between the two conflicting parties; or of the arbitrator: making a decision after familiarising themselves with both sides of the argument. If the manager is himself one of the conflicting parties he may call for a third party to arbitrate.

It is useful for you to be aware of what is involved in arbitration. You will almost certainly have cause to use it. The system summarised in Figure 12.4 is adapted in part from Torrington (1982).

When you arbitrate a dispute you must be seen as independent. Both parties must believe that you will make a decision which is fair and unbiased. You must also ensure that you have the authority to make a decision. You should see both conflicting parties as having some type of a complaint against each other. It may be useful to see one as the complainant and the other as the respondent, but in reality it may be difficult to see the difference (Torrington, 1982).

Anticipate

Expectations

When taking the role of the arbitrator you have to first consider what the conflicting parties expect the process to produce. Realise that both will view the conflict from different perspectives. These will be based on individual values, insecurities, understandings and priorities.

The conflicting parties will expect you to be impartial and just in your decision. You must come as close to being fair as is possible. This will be especially important if, for example, you are arbitrating a dispute between a worker and his supervisor. You should also be aware that those involved will be concerned that your decision may cause them to look bad in front of their peers, i.e. 'a loss of face'. It is important that you remain as objective as possible. Predicting what may happen and being aware of what people may expect can help you do this.

Figure 12.4
Arbitration: A System for the Manager

ANTICIPATE	
	Expectations
	Preparation
	Targeting
	Location
MEETING	
	Define
	Positions
	Clarification
	Summarising
DECISION	
	Agreement
	Justification

Preparation

Before the actual arbitration meeting you should familiarise yourself with as many of the details of the case as possible. This may be difficult if you step into the middle of an argument and must arbitrate immediately. Once again, try to stay as objective as possible.

Targeting

If possible, before you meet with the conflicting parties you should set yourself a desirable outcome target. In most cases this will involve trying to reach a solution that will be acceptable to both parties. Try to do this without biasing your final decision.

Location

You should also consider the location for the meeting. Ideally you should plan it on 'neutral ground'. We suggest an informal, calm setting away from the office if possible. Try to refrain from placing physical barriers such as desks in front of the conflicting parties as these can hinder open communication. Finally, take care where you place yourself. Make sure you take a 'middle' position. You must not be seen by either party as being closer in any way to the 'opponent'.

We realise that not all conflict situations will present you with the luxury of following the above-mentioned steps thoroughly or systematically. At times you will have to react almost on the spot. The rational steps should however give you some framework for thinking about compromise. When you have anticipated all that you can, proceed to the meeting phase.

Meeting

Define

At the beginning of the meeting it is your task to set a calm, rational tone. Make it quite clear to both parties that you have the authority to make a decision. Give a brief introduction communicating your understanding of the conflict and set the agenda for the rest of the meeting. 'First Bruce will present his side of the case and then Joan will have a chance to present her views. I would appreciate it if you could both refrain from interrupting each other during this time. Then ...'

Positions

When the 'rules' and tone have been established, the arbitrator asks one of the conflicting parties to present his side of the issue. He should be allowed to do so with as little interruption as possible. It may however be necessary for you to clarify some issues during this time, especially if the speaker is shying away from committing himself or seems to be omitting certain details.

When the first party (often the complainant) has finished, you should summarise and recapitulate the main points. The speaker should be given the opportunity to confirm, expand or clarify certain points to ensure your understanding of his position.

The second party is then given the opportunity to present his side of the issue. Exactly the same format should be used for both parties and recapitulation should follow.

Clarification

Your job now is to specify the issues which divide the two parties. Points of agreement can be eliminated leaving disagreements on which to focus the rest of the discussion.

> The points of disagreement are what have to be tackled and they also have to be brought into focus, filtering out the irrelevancies, platitudes and generalities so as to direct action at what lies at the heart of the conflict.... (Torrington, 1982 : 176)

The arbitrator should get both parties to agree with his diagnosis of what separates them. You then begin questioning both parties about their positions in an attempt to get them to see where their differences lie. Try to do this in as non-judgemental a way as possible. It is possible that during this discussion one or both parties will resolve the problem on their own.

Summarising

Following the discussion it is up to you as arbitrator to summarise how you see the case. You provide your interpretations and even some suggestions for resolving the conflict. You do this by summarising what transpired during the meeting and by comparing the various differences of opinion or conflicts of interest. You suggest possible alternatives which usually involve both parties conceding in some areas while gaining in others. You make a real attempt to get those involved to agree to one of your alternatives. You may allow some bargaining or negotiation. You may have to halt your meeting at some stage and reconvene a number of times if agreement is not reached.

Decision

The Agreement

If you managed to get the conflicting parties to agree on a mutually satisfactory solution, this stage is easy: you go over the decision again to make sure it is understood. If, however, they could not come to any agreement, it is your job to institute a solution and inform those in conflict that they should abide by your decision. Hopefully it will not come to this. Often, at some stage in the process, they will be able to come to an agreement on their own.

Justification

When the agreement (imposed or self-decided) has been reached you should either verbally or in writing justify the decision. This will involve reiterating the decision and its rationale.

Arbitration can be time-consuming and stressful but it can be a very satisfactory strategy for allowing employees to have real input into solving their own conflicts.

Although various forms or methods of compromise are often used, they do entail risks. Firstly, great skill and patience is necessary in overseeing a compromise because of the insecurities of the conflicting parties. Secondly, if you use this response too frequently, you may be perceived as being more interested in making everybody somewhat happy than in solving problems. Compromise for the sake of compromise is not the aim.

When to use compromising strategies:

1. If a conflict goes on for an unreasonable period of time.
2. When other employees begin to take sides in a conflict.
3. When an employee's performance on the job is affected by the conflict.
4. When conflicting parties may be willing to meet half-way.
5. When issues are critical and very complex.
6. When conflicting parties request a third-party solution.
7. When both parties have equal power and need a good working relationship.

APPLICATION TASK 12.5

WHEN CAN I USE THIS STRATEGY (COMPROMISING)?

Situation: COMPROMISING

Why?

Stott, K. and Walker, A., *Making Management Work.* © 1992 Simon & Schuster (Asia) Pte Ltd.

Collaboration

Collaboration views conflicts as problem-solving situations. Conflicting parties confront the situation and attempt to resolve it through collaborative or creative problem-solving. We prefer to see collaboration as the latter – creative problem-solving – and believe this to be a powerful strategy for turning destructive conflict into constructive outcomes.

This process encourages those in conflict to channel their energies into a creative problem-solving process, rather than into fighting with each other. Both or all parties play a constructive role. This is designed to produce a win–win situation. While this method is not applicable in all situations, we believe if it is correctly approached, it can be beneficial both to the individuals involved and the organisation as a whole. Whetten and Cameron (1984 : 409) outline these benefits:

- It encourages collaboration and trust while acknowledging the value of assertiveness.
- It encourages employees to focus their disputes on problems and issues rather than personalities.
- It cultivates skills of self-governance: effective problem solvers tend to be less dependent on others.

Schmidt and Tannenbaum (1972 : 134) offer some excellent guidelines for effective, creative problem-solving. It may also be useful for you to refer to Chapter 6, Solving Problems and Making Decisions.

- Accept and welcome conflicts in your organisation. Look on them as challenges and valuable resources.
- Refrain from quick judgements: Listen and attempt to understand people and their conflicts.
- Do not deny the feelings of the parties in conflict.
- Attempt to clarify the nature of the conflict.
- Make sure everyone understands who will be making the decision (individual or group).
- Suggest ground rules and procedures for resolving conflicts in a collaborative process.
- Ensure there are adequate, open and understood communication channels for disputing parties to utilise.
- Encourage the separation of ideas from the employees who propose them.

There are numerous proposals available for dealing with conflict through collaborative problem-solving. Most encapsulate similar suggestions to those offered by Schmidt and Tannenbaum.

We would suggest you use the following steps as a framework for collaborative problem-solving. We have not gone into great detail but aim to provide a flexible outline scheme within which you can work. It is shown in Figure 12.5.

Figure 12.5
A Collaborative Problem-Solving Outline

Admit a conflict exists
Confront the problem/conflict
Brainstorm possible options/alternatives
Select an option/reach agreement
Look to the future

Admit a Conflict Exists

The first step in solving any problem is for both parties to admit that a conflict actually exists. This appears obvious but in many cases people will hide feelings, letting them build up until they explode. It is very important that you as the manager and all parties involved admit that there is a problem.

Those concerned must also agree that the conflict needs to be dealt with, and that a collaborative approach is the best way to proceed. This must be operationalised by the conflicting parties agreeing on a time and place to meet to begin the discussion.

SUMMARY

- Admit the conflict exists.
- Agree it needs to be dealt with.
- Agree to collaborate on a solution.
- Agree on a time and place to meet.

Confront the Problem

This is the stage that begins the face-to-face meeting. It involves 'clarifying and exploring the issues, the nature and strength of the participants, and their current feelings' (Johnson and Johnson, 1991 : 322).

The first phase involves one party explaining his position and then listening to the other's views. Each person in turn should explain why he feels that way and what the other person has done to 'annoy' him. Both parties should listen to the other's points. It is important here to confine the discussion to the actions and issues involved rather than personalities.

> BE CALM, OPEN, FLEXIBLE AND CLEAR

The fact that the conflict is to be solved in a collaborative fashion should be re-emphasised (a win–win outcome). The conflict should be discussed in the most specific way possible, dealing with small issues in an incremental fashion.

You should make a determined effort to understand the other's position and points of view: stay flexible. This stage involves a willingness to see strengths in the other party's position as well as weaknesses in your own. You should feel free to question the other to clarify any points. Once again, concentrate on actions, issues and specifics, not personal biases.

The key result in this step should be that you make a real effort to understand the other's point of view. Only then can a win–win situation eventuate.

SUMMARY

- Confront the problem.
- Explain your own position and feelings.
- Listen to the other's position and feelings.
- Concentrate on actions and issues.
- Re-emphasise collaborative approach.
- Deal with specifics.
- Try to understand the other party's position.
- Clarify 'cloudy' points.
- Be flexible.
- Suppress anger.

Brainstorm Possible Options/Alternatives

This step involves the generation of alternatives. Johnson and Johnson (1991 : 324) offer some sound advice for inventing options for the mutual benefit of both parties:

1. Focus on needs and goals, not positions.
2. Clarify differences before seeking similarities.
3. Empower the other person by:
    (a) Staying flexible in your choice of which option is best;
    (b) Giving him or her clear choices.
4. Avoid the obstacles to creative thinking.
5. Invent a number of options to choose from.

Remember, you are looking for solutions which meet the needs of both parties. You are in fact telling the other party that you value his thinking and believe that together you can be doubly creative when dealing with the conflict. If you want to refresh your memory on 'brainstorming' refer to Chapter 6.

SUMMARY

- Brainstorm options.
- Clarify differences.
- Work together/be flexible.
- Focus on needs and goals.
- Avoid 'narrow' thinking.
- Show you value the other party's thinking.
- Develop a number of options.
- Do not be judgemental.

Select Option/Reach Agreement

By now the conflicting parties should have a list of possible alternatives for dealing with their conflict. It is a good idea to base selection of alternatives on some kind of objective criteria. The various alternatives should be evaluated through a combination of human and organisational considerations.

Firstly, they must be seen as fair by both parties (this does not necessarily mean a compromise). Secondly, they should not be harmful or detrimental to others in the organisation. Thirdly, they should be efficient and effective on an organisational level and, fourthly, have organisational, not personal, advantage. If this does not work, you can flip a coin. The final agreement, or option selected, must be one that has a high probability of working (practical) and not merely present a temporary solution.

When a solution has been agreed on, you should consciously agree on the course it will take, ironing out the details. Agree that the conflict has come to an end.

SUMMARY

- Select option/reach agreement.
- Use objective criteria:
  - Fairness.
  - Harmless to others.
  - Organisational effectiveness.
  - Organisational advantage.
- Is it practical?
- Agree on solution.
- Agree conflict is resolved.

You may gain some practice in selecting the right option by completing Application Task 12.6. It simply asks you to identify a conflict situation with which you are familiar through your managerial work, to generate some solutions and then assess them against the criteria we have just listed.

Look to the Future

The final stage is an attempt to utilise the positive feelings which were (hopefully) generated through the collaborative process for preventing future destructive conflict. The solution selected will not work on its own. If not approached in the correct collaborative spirit it may regress once again into a conflict.

When you have selected an option, talk and come to agreement about implementation, and what you will do if things do not go according to plan. Discuss how you will act in the future to prevent yourselves getting in the same predicament again. Discuss future activities and steps you might take to

APPLICATION TASK 12.6

SELECTING AN APPROPRIATE OPTION

1. In the box below write a problem you have experienced in your job that placed two or more parties in a conflict situation. Think about what caused the conflict.
2. Take ten minutes to generate as many solutions as you can, without judging their various merits or otherwise. Be creative. Use the appropriate box.
3. Evaluate your options using the criteria discussed above. Ask yourself: Would this solution result in a win–lose or win–win solution?
4. Select the alternative you believe meets the criteria and would have the highest probability of resulting in a win–win situation.

CONFLICT SITUATION:	
ALTERNATIVES:	JUDGEMENT:
CRITERIA: Fair Practical Organisationally effective	Non-detrimental to others Both parties win Organisationally advantageous

Stott, K. and Walker, A., *Making Management Work.* © 1992 Simon & Schuster (Asia) Pte Ltd.

ensure that your relationship stays on an even keel. Try to understand what makes the other person angry so you can avoid such actions in the future. Make collaboration an ongoing part of the relationship.

SUMMARY

- Look to the future.
- Discuss strategies if implementation goes off course.
- Discuss how you will deal with conflict in the future.
- Discuss what makes you angry and argumentative.
- Discuss how you can understand the other person better.
- Agree to continue working collaboratively.

If you think the preceding framework can be of use to you, try it out. We have reproduced the main points in the form of a checklist (see Figure 12.6). Remember it is only an outline and will need to be adjusted. Every conflict situation is unique. You can use this checklist as a guide when solving problems collaboratively.

Conflict often stems from communication problems. It involves delving into a conflict situation in an attempt to identify the concerns and fears of those involved and then to find solutions which satisfy both sets of concerns. This can take a number of forms. It may, for example, involve trying to understand any differences of opinion and learning from these differences.

Collaboration, despite its obvious advantages for settling conflicts, is not always the best strategy. If, for example, a conflict is based on divergent values, collaboration can actually polarise differences and is highly unlikely to alter basic beliefs. Robbins (1991) states that forcing two people with vastly different value systems to collaborate risks deepening the differences and perhaps even intensifying the conflict.

We believe, however, that a collaborative problem-solving approach can be very effective between manager and employee, and employee and employee. In the latter circumstance, you may be called upon to act as a facilitator for resolving a conflict situation.

Figure 12.7 outlines roles which each actor in a conflict might take. Let us assume you are the 'conflict facilitator'. Note that facilitation is different from the role of arbitrator which we discussed earlier. The facilitator *does not* make the final decision for the conflicting parties. Rather, he brings the

Figure 12.6
A Framework for Collaborative Problem-Solving

Admit the conflict exists:

- Agree it needs to be dealt with. ☐

- Agree to collaborate on a solution. ☐

- Agree on a time and place to meet. ☐

Confront the Problem:

- Explain own position and feelings. ☐

- Listen to other's position and feelings. ☐

- Concentrate on actions and issues. ☐

- Re-emphasise collaborative approach. ☐

- Deal with specifics. ☐

- Try to understand the other party's position. ☐

- Clarify 'cloudy' points. ☐

- Be flexible. ☐

- Suppress anger. ☐

Brainstorm options:

- Clarify differences. ☐

- Work together/be flexible. ☐

- Focus on needs and goals. ☐

- Avoid 'narrow' thinking. ☐

- Show you value the other party's thinking. ☐

- Develop a number of options. ☐

- Do not be judgemental. ☐

Select option/reach agreement:

- Use objective criteria:

  Fair.

  Harmless to others.

  Organisationally effective.

  Organisationally advantageous.

- Is it practical?

- Agree on solution.

- Agree conflict is resolved.

Look to the future.

- Discuss strategies if implementation goes off course.

- Discuss how you will deal with conflict in the future.

- Discuss what makes you angry and argumentative.

- Discuss how you can understand the other person better.

- Agree to continue working collaboratively.

Stott, K. and Walker, A., *Making Management Work.* © 1992 Simon & Schuster (Asia) Pte Ltd.

conflicting parties together in an attempt to make a collaborative decision.

Facilitating is also different from negotiation where the manager listens to both parties and tries to convince them to modify their behaviour. A mediator, on the other hand, helps those in conflict to reach a mutually beneficial compromise. Another role you can take in dealing with conflict is to delegate by encouraging the conflicting parties to work through their own conflict.

In Figure 12.7, you are the facilitator; the complainant is an employee who believes he has been wronged in some way or who is in substantial disagreement with another. The respondent is the other employee involved in the conflict. He has either initiated the conflict or is at least a key party. The points provide a framework which we believe is a useful guide for each of the roles in collaborative problem-solving. You will notice that many of the points reflect the steps suggested in the collaborative problem-solving framework.

Figure 12.7
Manager-as-Facilitator-of-Conflict Situations

FACILITATOR

1. Treat the conflict seriously.
2. Do not deny feelings.
3. Break down issues.
4. Assist both parties to see the 'big picture'.
5. Do not take sides.
6. Emphasise the possible consequences of the conflict to the organisation.
7. Keep discussion fair and impersonal.
8. Keep conflict and comments in perspective.
9. Assist both parties in generating alternative solutions.
10. Help both parties make decisions.

COMPLAINANT

1. Avoid personal attacks.
2. Do not deny it is your problem.
3. Openly describe your problem.
4. State how you believe you have been wronged.
5. Ensure respondent understands how you feel.
6. Invite questions from the respondent.
7. Concentrate on specific issues.
8. Concentrate on common ground.
9. Generate alternative solutions.
10. Agree on decision which satisfies both you and respondent.

RESPONDENT

1. Allow complainant to express feelings.
2. Reinforce collaborative approach.
3. Exhibit interest in other person's problem.
4. Avoid being judgemental.
5. Search for additional, deeper information.
6. Make descriptive not evaluative statements (and questions).
7. Concentrate on specific issues.
8. Agree with the aspects that you can.
9. Generate alternatives.
10. Agree on decision which satisfies both you and the complainant.

The steps in the figure are designed to provide you with some basic guidelines for facilitating creative problem-solving as a method for dealing with conflict. Another collaborative approach is to create joint targets.

Creating Joint Targets

This strategy involves directing conflicting parties towards the attainment of a common target. Like all strategies this is not always appropriate. Lindelow and Scott (1989 : 347) provide some cautions when considering creating joint targets:

1. Such targets are difficult to create.
2. 'Phantom' targets will fool no one.
3. The trust necessary to work together is often absent.
4. The strategy may be ineffective if conflict grows from personal behavioural differences.

The rationale behind joint targets, however, is sound. It proposes that you set a target and makes conflicting parties responsible for its achievement. The basic philosophy is that employees who must work together on a project will have to settle their differences for the benefit of the team.

Collaborative strategies offer the most productive promise for conflict situations. 'Only problem solving is clearly related to positive outcomes in a wide range of (conflict) circumstances' (Sashkin and Morris, 1984 : 327). It is also the most effective strategy for transforming destructive conflict into constructive, creative outcomes.

APPLICATION TASK 12.7

WHEN CAN I USE THIS STRATEGY (COLLABORATING)?

Situation: COLLABORATING

Why?

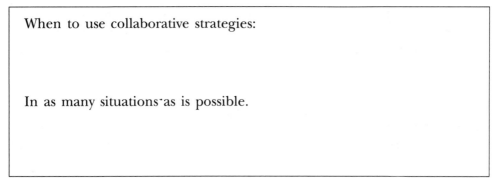

When to use collaborative strategies:

In as many situations·as is possible.

One or Another

All the strategies discussed for dealing with people conflicts are useful in their own way. We have summarised when they may be appropriate at the end of each section, but these are only suggestions. You will decide when they are appropriate because you should know your own staff best.

Figure 12.8 summarises the five approaches, all of which have a place in dealing with interpersonal conflict in your organisation.

A Little about Intergroup Conflict

Conflict does not only occur between individuals. It also occurs between groups: management and workers, males and females, production and marketing, project team and project team. Intergroup conflict can have a number of effects. Once again this can be positive or negative.

When two groups are in conflict, the individuals who comprise the membership tend to forget any personal conflicts and join ranks for the good of the team. This phenomenon is common when nations become involved in external conflicts. Political affiliations and biases are often 'put aside' for the good of the common cause. It becomes 'them against us' not 'you against me'. Groups tend to become more agreeable to autocratic leadership or even dictatorship. Conformity within the group is demanded.

Groups involved in conflict tend to see the opposing party as the enemy. They begin to believe everything they do as 'right' and everything the other group does as 'wrong'. This often leads to a *groupthink* situation. Intergroup competition, like individual conflict, can have the accompanying benefits of increased creativity and commitment, but, also like interpersonal conflict, if not dealt with appropriately it can be destructive.

Probably the best way to deal with intergroup conflict is to avoid win–lose situations. In such cases, groups who perceive themselves as losers almost

Figure 12.8
Dealing with Conflict: A Summary

STRATEGY	OUTCOME	RESPONSE	BEHIND IT	END PRODUCT
Avoiding	Lose-lose	Not interested	Avoid the conflict and hope it goes away	If used too often interpersonal problems are unlikely to be resolved; stop-gap at best
Accommo-dating	Lose-win	Anything you want	Employee relationships must be maintained at all costs	May be seen as a 'push-over' and as having no conviction; can be taken advantage of
Competing	Win-lose	Do as I say	I am the expert and the boss, I know best, might is right	Seen as a dictator; other party feels humiliated; difficult to get co-operation or commitment
Com-promising	Win some, lose some	Give and take	If everybody can be a little flexible and bend we can work this out	People tend to look for easy way out; can start with more than they want; can lead to mediocrity
Collabo-rating	Win-win	Do it together	If we can work together we can solve the problem with the best possible solution	Problem is more likely to be resolved with a creative solution; both parties more likely to be committed to it

Stott, K. and Walker, A., *Making Management Work.* © 1992 Simon & Schuster (Asia) Pte Ltd.

inevitably attribute their loss to something or someone else (for example, the arbitrator) and animosity results. Like individual conflicts it is best to try and employ a collaborative problem-solving approach, one that gets groups to work together on a conflict situation and to understand the feeling and position of the other group.

When we discussed the possible causes of conflict we saw that not all problems were initiated by people. Many had their root cause in the organisational structure. We will now examine some simple strategies for dealing with these causes, many of which can initiate or exacerbate people conflict.

Dealing with Organisationally Initiated Conflict

Role conflict can be reduced by clearly defining the role that each employee is expected to fulfil. Additionally, it is important that the relationships or interdependencies between roles be similarly clarified and defined. It is not enough to simply ensure that each worker knows what he is responsible for. Very few, if any, employees work in isolation, they depend on and must work with others. Areas of possible overlap must first be identified and roles within these areas specified.

Sashkin and Morris (1984) believe that organisationally initiated conflicts can be reduced by either increasing or decreasing employee interdependencies. Increasing interdependencies can be achieved by improved co-ordination and communication: making sure groups of employees know what is going on and how they need to work together. Reduced interdependencies can be achieved through an approach called *buffering*; that is, separating, either mechanically, physically or administratively, certain groups of workers.

A vital component in reducing the likelihood of organisationally induced conflict is to ensure that channels of communication are open. Employees and managers alike must know what is expected and what is happening. Such a system serves dual purposes. It makes sure that managers are aware what workers are doing, thus allowing them to identify conflicts in their early stages when they are easier to deal with. More importantly, it promotes open discussion of problems or conflicts as they arise and promotes collaborative problem-solving.

When Conflict Has Been 'Resolved'

We believe that the strategies discussed for dealing with conflict can help you when faced with such situations. Remember, no one strategy can claim to be *the ideal way* to deal with conflict. There is no sure-fire way of predicting what the outcome of a particular conflict will be, regardless of the strategy employed. You should be aware that the aftermath of conflict is often very uncomfortable. This is especially, but not exclusively, true if one party believes he has 'lost out' or been treated unfairly. Even when a compromise has been reached some animosity can linger.

Your job as a manager is to attempt to build an atmosphere which makes all involved want to get on with the job. To do this you can:

1. Ensure everyone involved (winners and losers) is treated in the same way: *No Favouritism.*
2. Encourage teamwork.
3. Be prepared to counsel people and maintain an open, honest environment.
4. Focus on general tasks rather than individuals.

You will recognise that these suggestions are similar to those mentioned at the beginning of the chapter regarding 'preventive' measures. After a conflict it is your role to get things back to normal as soon as possible, so disruption to productivity is minimised.

Conclusion

Conflict is a natural part of any environment. In this respect your organisation is no different from a corner bar, a family home or a school classroom. In all these settings, conflict will surface. In all situations conflict must be dealt with, whoever is involved, whether the barman, the mother or father, or the teacher. In your organisation it is your job to deal with and attempt to resolve conflict.

In this chapter we have stated that conflict need not be negative. We have also demonstrated how the skilled manager can turn potentially destructive conflicts into constructive outcomes that lead to increased adaptability, creativity and, ultimately, improved productivity.

To be able to deal with conflict, you need to be aware of the types and possible causes, and be comfortable with the various techniques for dealing with it. No one strategy is applicable in all conflict situations. To handle conflicts effectively you have to vary your actions according to what will work best in a particular situation. Even if you do this, be prepared to fail in some of your efforts. Human beings are too unpredictable for you to succeed all the time.

We suggest that the most positive option for dealing with conflict is the *collaborative approach,* one where people work together on settling their conflicts in a co-operative win–win way.

References

Johnson, D. and Johnson, F. (1991) *Joining Together: Group Theory and Group Skills*, Prentice-Hall : Englewood Cliffs.

Lindelow, J. and Scott, J. (1989) 'Managing conflict', in Smith, S. and Piele, P. (eds.), *School Leadership: Handbook for Excellence*, pp. 338–355, ERIC : Oregon.

Low, G. (1990) 'Conflict management simulation', in Low, G., Chong, C., Leong, W. and Walker, A. (eds.), *Developing Executive Skills*, pp. 51–74, Longman : Singapore.

Robbins, S. (1991) *Organizational Behaviour: Concepts, Controversies and Applications*, Prentice Hall : Englewood Cliffs.

Sashkin, M. and Morris, W. (1984) *Organisational Behaviour*, Reston : Virginia.

Schmidt, W. and Tannenbaum, R. (1972) 'Management of differences', in Burke, W. and Hornstein, H. (eds.), *The Social Technology of Organisation Development*, pp. 127–140, University Associates : La Jolla.

Thomas, K. (1975) 'Conflict and conflict management', in Dunnette, M. (ed.), *The Handbook of Industrial and Organisational Psychology*, vol. II, Rand McNally : Chicago.

Torrington, D. (1982) *Face to Face in Management*, Prentice Hall : London.

Watson, H., Vallee, J. and Mulford, W. (1981) *Structured Experiences and Group Development*, Curriculum Development Centre : Canberra.

Whetten, D. and Cameron, K. (1984) *Developing Management Skills*, Scott Foresman : Illinois.

Chapter 13

Influencing

Influence

'Influence entails actually securing the consent of others to work with you in accomplishing an objective' (Whetten and Cameron, 1984 : 266). It is widely accepted that informal sources of power can have an enormous impact in organisational life. Whilst many management texts explain the theoretical basis of this aspect of power, few actually show the skills involved and how it can be used successfully in determining people's behaviour. This chapter explains the different strategies of **influence** which are often used and shows how some may be more effective than others in certain situations.

As a starting point for this chapter, complete Application Task 13.1, which asks you to consider a situation where you had to influence someone.

APPLICATION TASK 13.1

INFLUENCING STRATEGIES

This exercise is designed to help you review how you behave in trying to influence colleagues. It will help you to determine your dominant strategies. Think about an occasion when you needed to influence someone because you wanted some help or something done. You may not have had formal power, so using influence was the only way of gaining compliance. On the other hand, you may have had the authority, but chose not to use it.

1.   Outline the situation in which you tried to influence a subordinate or peer:

2.   What did you want him or her to do?

3.   What outcome did you plan?

4.   How did you go about influencing him or her?

5.   Were you successful?

Many have their own way of trying to get what they want and, regardless of whether they are successful or not, believe that there is only one way to influence people. We have worked with a number of managers, for example, who are adamant that, so long as you give good, sound reasons for your request, people will comply with your wishes. In many cases, that may work, but they tend to measure their success in terms of whether the other person says 'yes' or 'no'. This, of course, is not always the best indicator of having achieved the intended outcome. Look at this example:

> *John told his management colleague (of the same status) he needed the final version of the report they were preparing together in time for a rearranged meeting with the boss the following morning. Martin replied that he was still waiting for some feedback from his staff, and besides, he had some friends coming round that evening – he would not have time. John was well known for his impatience and temper, and he was not slow to show it when things were not going his way. Martin gave in to avoid an embarrassing and unpleasant scene: 'OK, if you want it that much, you can have it.' John may have thought he was successful in being able to determine Martin's behaviour. He did after all get him to agree to comply with his wishes. Or did he? The next morning, Martin turned up with a few pieces of paper, handwritten, plenty of deletions and insertions, and with half of the information missing!*

There are even those who do not see any influencing activity going on, let alone recognise its importance. In truth, there is a great deal of influencing going on throughout all organisations. People want to gain things, persuade colleagues to help them, give them more work, and a host of other outcomes. The fact is though, that some seem to be better at it than others. Regardless of whether they have formal authority or not, they have the knack of getting what they want. They have developed a highly valued skill: that of determining others' behaviour.

Those who are less successful probably choose the wrong strategies. Kipnis, Schmidt, Swaffin–Smith and Wilkinson (1984) attribute this in part to habit, lack of forethought, or a wrong understanding of whether the other person is willing to comply. They also believe that people can learn to choose appropriate strategies through training and self-examination. People who are effective influencers are flexible and are able to select the optimum strategy for any situation. Even for those who have the formal power to order people what to do, the ability to exercise a variety of influencing strategies seems to have greater potential for gaining co-operation and commitment from subordinate colleagues.

Generally speaking, the reasons for using influence fall into five categories:

1. To obtain help with the job.

2.   To give people work to do.
3.   To get something from someone.
4.   To improve performance.
5.   To initiate change.

As you can imagine, the strategies may vary depending not only on the purpose of using influence, but also on the target person's status in the organisation in relation to your own. You may, for example, get away with shouting at a junior colleague because he did not do what you expected, but if you try that with the boss, you may find yourself in hot water! There are some strategies of course which may be effective irrespective of status. You can explain your reasons for wanting something to any colleague, superior, subordinate or peer. The point we are making though is that a single strategy, such as giving logical reasons, may not be successful in every situation.

Kipnis, Schmidt and Wilkinson (1980) demonstrated through their research that specific tactics or strategies may be associated with combinations of the reason for using influence, the target of influence, and the amount of resistance shown. They showed that influence is more complex than simply choosing a strategy you like and then using it for all circumstances.

Leavitt (1978) identifies the factors of self, the other person and the interaction as the key considerations. We shall be looking at the first one in some detail as we encourage you to analyse your own preferences in terms of strategies usually employed. We also consider the other person in terms of status and his projected willingness to comply, although implicit in this is an understanding of factors such as experience, personality and attitudes.

At this stage, you will find it useful to find out the behaviours you prefer to use. By completing the questionnaire Preferred Styles you will gain a picture of your strategy preferences and influencing style.

Questionnaire

PREFERRED STYLES

For each statement below, you are asked to indicate the extent to which it is true of you. Try to give answers which truly represent your typical behaviour rather than how you think you should behave. Circle the appropriate number for each statement.

This never applies to me	:	0
This rarely applies to me	:	1
This is me very occasionally	:	2
This is me some of the time	:	3

This is me most of the time　:　5
This is me all the time　　:　6

1. If I want something done where I cannot force the　0 1 2 3 5 6
   issue, I try to make my colleague feel important.
2. I like to check up on my subordinates with　0 1 2 3 5 6
   surprise visits.
3. If I am trying to make a change, I write a well-　0 1 2 3 5 6
   reasoned justification.
4. Before meetings, I like to make sure I have some　0 1 2 3 5 6
   support for my ideas.
5. I am prepared to take away one of my staff's　0 1 2 3 5 6
   preferred duties to get what I want.
6. I like to be able to give something in return when　0 1 2 3 5 6
   a subordinate is asked to do something extra.
7. If I do not get my way with a colleague, I take the　0 1 2 3 5 6
   matter to the boss.
8. I give people orders: it makes life simpler.　0 1 2 3 5 6
9. I like to be seen as a friendly person and I try to　0 1 2 3 5 6
   get what I want by being friendly and acting
   humbly.
10. I believe that sound logical arguments should win　0 1 2 3 5 6
    the day.
11. I like to use meetings to raise matters formally.　0 1 2 3 5 6
12. If a subordinate does not comply with my wishes,　0 1 2 3 5 6
    I will make life difficult for him or her.
13. I will remind colleagues of things I have done for　0 1 2 3 5 6
    them when I want something done now.
14. I hint that the boss supports my stance when I　0 1 2 3 5 6
    want a colleague to comply with my wishes.
15. I give strict time deadlines when I ask for a　0 1 2 3 5 6
    colleague's co-operation.
16. I say something complimentary to a colleague　0 1 2 3 5 6
    before requesting something.
17. I make sure I assemble all relevant facts and　0 1 2 3 5 6
    information before trying to persuade others to
    do something.
18. I like to have a word with colleagues who I know　0 1 2 3 5 6
    are on my side before raising an issue at a meeting.
19. I am prepared to put the word around about a　0 1 2 3 5 6
    colleague who is unco-operative.
20. I am prepared to make personal sacrifices if　0 1 2 3 5 6
    someone will comply with my wishes.
21. If a colleague will not 'toe the line', I will ask the　0 1 2 3 5 6
    boss to step in.

22. I keep nagging colleagues until they do what I want.   0 1 2 3 5 6
23. I wait for the right time before approaching someone about something.   0 1 2 3 5 6
24. Before asking a colleague for help, I explain the reasons carefully.   0 1 2 3 5 6
25. I like to mention that others are in agreement with me when I make a request. 0 1 2 3 5 6
26. If I do not get my way, I threaten my non-co-operation in the future.   0 1 2 3 5 6
27. If a colleague will agree to do something, I offer to provide adequate training. 0 1 2 3 5 6
28. I will ask the boss to have a quiet word with a colleague if necessary.   0 1 2 3 5 6
29. I get a few people to support me if I am asking the boss for something.   0 1 2 3 5 6
30. If I want people to do things, I mention their experience and abilities, and generally make them feel important. 0 1 2 3 5 6
31. I write a detailed rationale for my boss if I want to implement a plan.   0 1 2 3 5 6
32. I am prepared to ask my boss for a response to a request by a particular date. 0 1 2 3 5 6
33. I will offer to do something extra for the boss if he or she will meet my demands. 0 1 2 3 5 6
34. I threaten to speak to someone higher if I fail to achieve my objective.   0 1 2 3 5 6
35. I am prepared to go over my boss's head.   0 1 2 3 5 6
36. I make myself a nuisance by continually pestering until I get what I want.   0 1 2 3 5 6
37. I request that my boss takes a matter higher if he or she is unable to deal with it. 0 1 2 3 5 6
38. I sympathise with the difficulties which my request will cause.   0 1 2 3 5 6
39. I use unemotional language and straightforward logic to support my case.   0 1 2 3 5 6
40. I ask colleagues if they will support my request to the boss.   0 1 2 3 5 6
41. I will offer to help with other work if colleagues will do what I want.   0 1 2 3 5 6
42. If a subordinate will not comply, I may hint at possible loss of promotion or career prospects. 0 1 2 3 5 6

You will be able to categorise your preferences later after we have explained the strategies and the associated behaviours. We shall also explain some of the advantages and disadvantages of using each of the strategies. We give examples of behaviours which people actually employ. We have drawn on the excellent work of Kipnis *et al.* (1980, 1984) and on our own work with senior and middle managers. The strategies are arranged in seven categories, namely, *friendliness, bargaining, reasoning, assertiveness, upward referral, coalition* and *sanctions*. At the end of each section we have summarised some behaviours which are characteristic of that strategy. Please note that we are not advocating the use of these behaviours, but simply showing what you might encounter in any given influencing situation.

Influencing People: Behaviour Strategies

Friendliness

This involves getting people to see you as a 'good guy'. If you use this strategy you smile, are friendly and choose the right time to raise a matter. If, for example, you sense that the other person has got something on his mind or is pressed for time, you wait until you know you can make your request with more confidence of success. Interpersonal skills and sensitivity to others' moods and feelings are critical. You can display these through sympathetic comments, such as: 'I know everyone wants you to do things, but if you could just do this for me, I'd be grateful.'

You can also make the job sound important or acknowledge the other person's skills or abilities. This works very well for some who may strive to be recognised. Getting the message across that the person is really needed may also be important.

If overused, people become suspicious of motives. It may even be described as 'creeping' by some, especially if it is used to extremes with superiors. We watched with amusement one manager, in a group meeting with the boss, tell him what an excellent job he had done of building up the organisation and how wonderful people outside thought he was. Our guess is that the boss found it as sickening as we did. So if you are going to 'butter people up' do not be too obvious about it; try instead to use more subtle tactics. A simple comment like: 'That sounds like a useful idea' probably has more impact than a paean of praise! Remember though, even the seemingly innocuous comment or behaviour can be taken the wrong way. 'Cheerful exuberance may be interpreted as overbearing; congratulation may be construed as being unctuous; an attempt not to embarrass may be regarded as coldness' (Torrington, Weightman and Johns, 1989 : 259).

SUMMARY

- Making colleagues feel important.
- Acting humbly and acknowledging others' expertise.
- Behaving in a friendly manner.
- Giving colleagues 'pats on the back'.
- Making the task sound important.
- Requesting things politely.
- Waiting for the right time before raising matters.
- Sympathising with problems.

Bargaining

This strategy, referred to as *reciprocity* in the Whetten and Cameron (1984) framework, is about negotiation: 'If you will do this, I may be able to provide this.' It is based on exchange principles and deals. Concessions and compromises may be made. For example: 'I need that report rewritten with the new figures, but I accept you are up to your eyeballs, so you could have an extra week.'

People may be reminded of past favours: 'Fred, could I use your company car on Friday? Remember I lent you mine when your's was in for servicing? Mine is in for a new clutch now.'

You can trade with time, expertise, effort and resources. You may want a colleague to work over the weekend but offer to give him a couple of days off during the week as compensation. You may trade his expertise in tax affairs for your ability in graphic design. You may also offer some financial inducement in return for extra effort in making the project a high-quality job. You may want to retain a talented subordinate's services and discuss changes in responsibilities which are in line with his career aspirations.

All these examples are based on the principle of giving something away and getting something in return. Chapter 14 on Negotiating goes into detail about effective bargaining strategies, but one central element involves trying to obtain something which is important to you and giving away something which is not so important to yourself but possibly of value to the other person. For this strategy to be successful therefore, you must receive at least as much as you concede. It seems on occasions that the more politically aware may achieve success if they are able to identify opinion leaders and strike bargains with those. At the very least, the strategy demands a degree of empathy: 'managers need to think themselves into the position of the person with whom they are talking, to see the topic as clearly as possible from the other point of view in order to make the most of the exchange' (Torrington *et al.*, 1989 : 260).

There are of course problems with this strategy. People can become accustomed to exchange – they expect something every time they are asked to help:

> . . . it engenders a highly instrumental view of work. The target person begins to expect that every request is open for negotiation and every completed assignment will generate a reward of equal value. In the extreme form this approach undercuts organizational commitment, as members take on a highly calculative orientation and downplay the value of working together to achieve organizational goals, regardless of personal gain. (Whetten and Cameron, 1984 : 270)

The theme is also taken up by Torrington *et al.* (1989 : 255) in describing the process of 'accumulating credits':

> . . . to do favours to others, so that there is a scattering of IOUs that can be called in, the bread upon the waters of the Bible. The problems with this type of dealing are first that the 'rewards' offered may have to increase to maintain their value, but also that the exchanges depend on *both* parties being able to reward the other. Offering approval loses its value if approval is not wanted, so that bargaining works best when the parties to the bargain are roughly equal in their power to reward each other.

People can even get greedy and start inflating their demands. This in turn can sour relationships. There is also the problem that some people seem to do well out of exchange processes and others invariably end up as 'losers'. This leads to resentment and a distrust of the strategy.

The strategy seems relatively harmless when compared with the more intimidating strategies (such as 'sanctions') but it should nevertheless be used discriminately. There are many occasions where a straightforward request is more legitimate, but exchange is offered because of the insecurity of the influence user.

SUMMARY

- Offering rewards.
- Reminding of past favours.

- • Making personal sacrifices.
- • Offering help.
- • Offering changes of responsibilities or duties.

Reasoning

Facts, information and data are used to support arguments. 'It makes sense' is a frequent statement. It does not involve impulsive actions but carefully prepared and logical arguments. This strategy abandons all notions of emotional appeals and relies on objective information. Ideas must be well planned and counter-arguments anticipated. It is not a productive strategy if there is inadequate preparation.

It is of course very attractive to many managers. Acceptance by the target person can mean an internalised commitment, necessary for elevated performance. You do not have to watch people as closely and, in theory, the scope is present for initiative and creativity. There seems to be a greater possibility of success in the absence of threat or implied threat. In other words, if you as manager are not in a position to resort to punitive strategies, you are more likely to obtain a committed response if agreement is given.

Many managers believe that if they have a winning argument, the other person is seen as unreasonable, and maybe obstructive, if he does not go along with it. We accept this is true to a certain extent. There are many situations where it is right to be rational and where this is the most persuasive factor. But an outright reliance on sound reason and logic may be over-optimistic.

In this regard there are two major considerations. The reason for using influence may itself not be reasonable. There may be motives other than purely 'rational' ones. You may, for example, require a benefit or want to change something, and it is difficult to defend in rational terms, although you may use contrived reasons. The second consideration relates to the target person. A manager who relies almost exclusively on this strategy may make the wrong assumption that everyone is rational. People do not always respond to logical arguments. It may, for example, make sound sense for all employees in a particular organisation to forego the pleasure of a pay increase for the company's economic good; it would affect them beneficially in the long run. To use this as the sole strategy of influence may, however, be extremely optimistic in this situation.

On the same theme, Whetten and Cameron (1984) draw our attention to the need to be politically aware, that people's motives are not always rationally based and that objective merits of arguments are not always supported. There needs to be an awareness of political undercurrents and a skill to handle them successfully. 'The well-meaning but politically naive seldom make major contributions in organisations' (Whetten and Cameron, 1984 : 266).

The same authors also identify the strength of the strategy lying not only in the manager's knowledge of the subject, but also in his personal characteristics and whether they are attractive to the target person (Whetten and Cameron, 1984 : 268).

Despite the criticisms, we see reason as a strategy in which managers should develop a high degree of competence. It does have high potential for success but it may have to be used in conjunction with other strategies. It leaves you as the manager less open to the criticisms associated with the micropolitical ploys of other strategies and helps you to be seen as a 'thinking' manager, one who carefully considers the consequences of actions before attempting to influence people's behaviour.

SUMMARY

- Providing a detailed justification.
- Giving supporting information.
- Explaining the reasons.
- Using logic.

Assertiveness

This strategy involves a direct approach. The expression *assertiveness* may be a little misleading because many associate it with the skill which is often featured on management programmes. This is part of it, but in this context, it embraces a much wider range of behaviours, some of which might even be described as *aggressive*.

The assertiveness strategy manifests itself in various ways such as firmness and referring to rules and regulations. You may for example want help with your work, so you just give a direct order: 'Please distribute these papers to your staff for me, Bill.' If you sense there may be some resistance, you may say something like: 'It was laid down at the last meeting that department heads were responsible for briefing staff on the new procedures, so please do it.' You also add a time deadline which makes it even more assertive: 'Give me your staffing requirements by Thursday noon.'

You may check up on your subordinates to make sure they are doing their jobs well. You may also check up on peers and superiors to see whether they are making progress with actions you agreed with them. In the latter case you would probably do it quite politely, but nevertheless, it is checking up and as such is part of an assertiveness strategy. 'I was wondering how far you have got with my office furniture problem? You said you would look into it for me.'

Closely related to checking up is the process of nagging, a strategy with which many people are quite familiar! This means constantly reminding others of agreements and commitments. The intention is to ensure things get done, but it can backfire, and you have to be aware of the danger of someone saying: 'Just get off my back will you!'

Some of the assertiveness behaviours are appropriate in certain situations. If, for example, there is a good case and if it does not cause antagonism, then the strategy is acceptable. Not all the behaviours, however, which come under this heading, are like this. Raising your voice and displaying your anger are behaviours to use with great caution. In some cases, it demonstrates that the manager has lost self-control, especially where he starts shouting and making sure other people can hear. There are occasions when it might be useful, but use this type of behaviour sparingly.

Generally, the person who uses this as a strategy is very determined to get what he wants and is prepared to compromise working relationships to achieve it. This is where its weakness lies. You may obtain token compliance but it is difficult to get real commitment.

SUMMARY

- Checking up on subordinates.
- Giving orders.
- Shouting and speaking so others can hear.
- Giving strict time deadlines.
- Nagging.
- Quoting the rules and regulations.
- Reminding people repeatedly.
- Displaying anger.

Upward Referral

This means using the hierarchy to support demands, either with formal or informal requests. Before speaking to a colleague of the same level about a change you want to make, for instance, you may check up that it would receive the support of the boss. In this example, it is tied in very closely with the next strategy of *coalition*. On most occasions, however, it seems to be used as a secondary strategy. If someone will not comply with your wishes, you refer the matter to the boss. The latter of course has the authority to support your stance and may choose to do so. You have to consider the consequences of adopting this strategy very seriously.

If it is used frequently, it can undermine relationships. It may be seen as going over people's heads. It is very dangerous if you are trying to influence a superior. He may react badly and find some way of exacting revenge. If you use it as a form of influence on subordinates, you may be seen as a weak manager by both subordinates and superiors. This strategy should be used with great discretion. Substantial support, however, can be generated through this affiliation if used informally.

SUMMARY

- Speaking to the boss and asking for pressure.
- Mentioning the boss's wishes.
- Referring the matter upwards.

Coalition

This involves using other people to support your stance. It is a political strategy which requires time, effort and skill to be developed. Some managers are very adept at it and understand the political dynamics involved. They know who is worth forming an alliance with and who is not. If you choose to use this strategy you must know who is in the best position to support you. A lot of effort can be wasted in generating support from ineffectual quarters.

One of the most effective settings for the strategy is in meetings where matters are formally recorded. By raising an issue (sometimes without warning or under another guise) you may lessen the power of a superior if it receives strong support from other members. You can of course reduce the chances of failure by obtaining support informally before the meeting. If decisions are reached and endorsed, it becomes very difficult for the boss to overturn them.

There is a very obvious danger. It may be seen as conspiracy or 'ganging up'. Again you have to consider the sort of working relationships you want. One middle manager we knew was very clever at political 'mapping'. He knew the opinion leaders and he always made sure he arrived for lunch at precisely the same time as the boss. He would mention informally his interesting, if unrealistic ideas and would generally gain support. He would also interact socially with the key resource allocators. In meetings he would often say: 'I know that the boss would support me in proposing this course of action.' This was undoubtedly true, but he was despised by most of his colleagues and certainly got no satisfaction from his relationships with other managers.

This is a very powerful strategy and can put you in a strong influencing position if you choose the right people with whom to form alliances. We feel that it has more potential if used to influence subordinates. If you can identify those who help to create and sustain opinions, and then make them the targets of your influence, you may enjoy considerable success in negotiating very difficult influencing situations.

SUMMARY

- Obtaining the support of colleagues.
- Using formal meetings to state requests.

Sanctions

This involves the use of unpleasant 'sticks' to make a forceful statement. It may be a withdrawal of privileges or simply talking about people behind their backs. One of the things you can do is to remove someone from a responsibility which he enjoys. You may also start watching his work more closely which acts as a form of control. In other words, he loses his freedom to operate without interference.

These are situations in which you are trying to influence a subordinate, but this punitive form of influence may also be used with those above you. You may, for example, indicate (probably indirectly) that your boss will not receive the same level of co-operation he enjoys from you at present. You may indicate that you will do everything which you have to, and no more. Similarly, you may hint at the possibility of taking the issue over his head to his boss.

The strategy certainly falls in the category of *fear of retribution* (Whetten and Cameron, 1984 : 268) and may be open as in personal threats, or indirect, as in intimidation which has an implied threat. Examples which the authors give include criticising a report written by a colleague, systematically ignoring someone during a meeting and giving managers impossible tasks.

You can see the immense dangers in this strategy. Whilst the user may achieve his desired outcome, it almost always has adverse consequences in terms of personal relationships and future levels of co-operation. You will see from this list of behaviours that the word 'threaten' is used or implied several times, which may make this a strategy to use only sparingly. In fact, Whetten and Cameron (1984 : 269) draw attention to this very problem:

> . . . threatened sanctions must be sufficiently severe that disobedience is unthinkable. When it is used repeatedly, this approach produces resentment and alienation that frequently generate overt or covert opposition. Consequently, it should be used extensively only when the ongoing commitment of the target person is not critical, opposition is acceptable (the other can be replaced if necessary), and extensive surveillance is possible. Because these conditions tend to stifle initiative and innovative behavior, even when individual compliance is obtained, organizational performance will likely suffer because affected individuals have little incentive to bring emerging problems resulting from changing conditions to the attention of their supervisors.

SUMMARY

- Stopping privileges.
- Cutting off areas of job satisfaction.
- Threatening to spread rumours.
- Introducing controls.
- Threatening not to co-operate.
- Threatening to make a report to the boss.
- Working to rule.
- Distorting information.

Influencing People: Behaviour

Having looked at each of the strategies, which behaviours do you use? Your versatility may best be analysed by thinking of situations in which you have used behaviours from each category. Complete Application Task 13.2.

APPLICATION TASK 13.2

STRATEGIES AND BEHAVIOURS

Under each of the headings below give one example (more if it helps) of the behaviour you used with a brief description of the situation in which you used it.

1. Friendliness:

2. Bargaining:

3. Reasoning:

4. Assertiveness:

5.   Upward Referral:

6.   Coalition:

7.   Sanctions:

Stott, K. and Walker, A., *Making Management Work.* © 1992 Simon & Schuster (Asia) Pte Ltd.

If you managed to complete all the spaces, you are probably capable of using a range of strategies. Whether you are able to select them appropriately is a different matter.

The questions to ask yourself in determining whether an influencing strategy is appropriately selected and employed are:

1.   Was the target person(s) willing to comply?
2.   Was there a willing commitment to compliance?
3.   Is a good relationship maintained between me and the target person?

The first question simply refers to the initial response. Compliance may be evident from the positive response, but it is not confirmed until there is commitment. The third question is an important one. You can often intimidate or coerce subordinates (even peers, and occasionally superiors, for that matter) into actions they would rather resist, but the effects on relationships may be damaging. That is a serious consideration in the light of the fact that you have to continue working with these people.

You can now examine your particular preferences in terms of influencing strategies. Refer to the questionnaire you completed earlier and enter your scores on the scoring chart.

Questionnaire

INFLUENCING STRATEGIES: SCORING CHART

Earlier you completed a questionnaire entitled Preferred Styles. Please enter your scores for each statement on the grid below.

Assertive	Friendliness	Reasoning	Coalition	Sanctions	Bargaining	Referral
2	1	3	4	5	6	7
8	9	10	11	12	13	14
15	16	17	18	19	20	21
22	23	24	25	26	27	28
32	30	31	29	34	33	35
36	38	39	40	42	41	37
Total						

Show your scores by filling in the bar chart below. Shade in the area below your lines. This will give you a picture of your preferred strategies in relation to others.

This gives you a picture of what you prefer to do. Managers we have worked with tend to have one or two dominant strategies. They may score highly on some of the others, but generally the charts have one or two 'peaks'. This is quite natural. You may have a strong preference for being friendly and avoid a more political-type strategy like joining forces with others. At the same time there is a danger in over-reliance on a single strategy across a range of situations. The important thing is that you recognise your preferences and that you identify situations which may need your less preferred strategies. You may indeed have to develop some skill in applying appropriate strategies for the occasion.

It will help you to now tackle Application Task 13.3 which asks you to select appropriate strategies for several different situations. It relates the chosen strategy to the purpose of your influencing attempt and to the status of the target person. You should then justify your strategy selection. There are no specifically correct answers, but obviously some strategies have more potential for success than others, and this should be evident from your reasoning.

Whetten and Cameron (1984 : 270) identify some of the reactions which might occur if a particular type of strategy is being overused:

> . . . managers frequently get into a rut and habitually use only their favorite or most convenient influence strategy and implement it insensitively. When this occurs, a predictable pattern of employee complaints emerges. If these complaints focus on the violation of rights or the apparent insecurity of the manager, coercion or intimidation are probably being overused. If they focus on unfairness, dashed expectations, or the boss's shifting moods, the problem generally stems from the excessive or ineffective use of bargaining and ingratiation. If the subordinates' complaints center on differences of opinion and conflicting perceptions or priorities, the manager is probably using the rational approach excessively or inappropriately.

Some strategies however are probably more widely applicable than others. They can be used successfully on a regular basis, especially if you develop a high level of skill in using them. Friendliness, reasoning and bargaining, for example, all seem to have potential for success. Some of the others have to be used sparingly. Issuing threats and applying some of the assertive-type behaviours, such as raising the voice, may undermine relationships and cause resentment. We are not saying they should not be used, but that you select them with caution and that you should be aware of the possible consequences.

APPLICATION TASK 13.3

REASONS, TARGETS AND STRATEGIES

Consider the following situations and for each one indicate the reason for using influence, the target, the strategy or strategies you would use and then explain the reason for your choice.

SITUATION	Reason for using influence	Target	Strategies Chosen	Reason
1. You want to ask one of your subordinates to organise a special event.				
2. You want the boss to cut down the agenda at your section meetings because they are too long and trivial.				
3. You want to alter the procedure for completing requisitions and ordering goods.				
4. You want to leave work early next week to attend a distant cousin's wedding and you need permission.				
5. You want one of your subordinates to help you organise the next staff party.				
6. You want the old lady cleaner to improve the cleanliness of the toilets.				
7. You want your boss to say a few words at an important event you have organised.				

Stott, K. and Walker, A., *Making Management Work*. © 1992 Simon & Schuster (Asia) Pte Ltd.

Kipnis *et al.* (1984) looked at the relative use of different strategies. When managers tried to influence superiors, the rank order was:

1. Reason.
2. Coalition.
3. Friendliness.
4. Bargaining.
5. Assertiveness.
6. Higher authority.

When they tried to influence subordinates, the rank order was:

1. Reason.
2. Assertiveness.
3. Friendliness.
4. Coalition.
5. Bargaining.
6. Higher authority.
7. Sanctions.

The use of reason and friendliness is high on both lists and the main difference is that assertiveness is used with subordinates, whilst the more political strategy of coalition is used to influence superiors. These seem to be the strategies in which skill should be developed, although much will depend on your situation. The more reasons you have for using influence, for example, the more strategies you are likely to have to use. Inflexibility will diminish your chances of reaching successful outcomes.

The problematic strategies of sanctions and higher authority are used infrequently by most managers. They are employed of course, but they apply more to situations where the manager has low expectations of success.

Another variable may be the culture of the organisation in which you work. We have experienced some organisations which support the strategies of friendliness and reason, whilst others have supported bargaining types of strategies. One organisation we have worked in supports intimidation-type strategies, including aspects of sanctions and assertiveness.

This has serious implications for the manager. If you do not encourage the free flow of ideas from your subordinates, and if your bosses do not support openness from you, many managers will become *bystanders* (the term is explained later) and cease to adopt influencing strategies themselves. This type of organisation may be neat and tidy to run, with everyone doing what he is told, but it is unlikely to support an organisation that wants to be dynamic. This may be a disturbing imposition for those organisations which need to grow and develop.

The point is also made by Torrington *et al.* (1989 : 252) that competition in the climate may militate against some strategies and favour instead political-type strategies.

Working Into the Evening

Some of the issues we identified in looking at influencing strategies are raised in the following episodes which illustrate different strategies being applied. These are a little over-simplified in order to highlight the strategy and its associated behaviours. In many situations a combination of strategies may be used. Look at the following case:

> *Ian is training manager for a medium-sized printing company. He shares Julia, his secretary, with the production manager. He wanted Julia to work overtime one evening, because he had been instructed to conduct an important senior manage- ment training session the following day. At the last minute like this, he knew it would mean considerable inconvenience for Julia who has family and social commitments. She had a right to refuse of course, since her contractual hours are 8.30 – 5.00. Although she is generally helpful, she is quite a forthright person and on a few occasions she has refused to stay on late. Ian has managed in the past to get secretarial help from the agency, but Julia knows the job and having agency staff in only doubles Ian's work.*

Situation 1

> *The moment Ian came in after lunch he knew something was wrong. Not her usual chirpy self, she just smiled politely at his harmless innuendo. She was used to it. This was not like Julia who usually had a thing or two to say in return. Ian, knowing that he really needed her to stay on late, decided he should wait before raising the matter.*
>
> *A short while later, he suggested they have tea together in the staff canteen. Having spent a few minutes talking about Julia's son and her interest in aerobics, Ian said that an important assignment had come up and that Julia's help was essential that evening. He told her she was the only one who could do the job properly and he would appreciate it if she could change her domestic arrangements and help him out. He sympathised with the fact that it would be inconvenient and told her how his own family felt about it when he had to work late into the evening. Without Julia's expertise in preparing the necessary mate- rials, the session could be a flop.*

Before reading on, complete the following boxes:

What is the strategy used?

What are the advantages from Julia's point of view?

What are the drawbacks?

Ian has obviously adopted a friendly approach. He makes Julia feel indispensable and that she is required for an important project. She may feel flattered that he has to wait for the right time to ask her to work overtime. At the same time, she may feel that Ian is always 'sweet-talking' her and if he does it too often, she may not believe the work is any more important than normal.

Situation 2

Ian sits down beside Julia's desk and bemoans the fact that he will have to stay late that evening to prepare for an executive 'special' he has been instructed to do. He then asks Julia whether she will also stay late to help him. In return, if she needs some time off during the next couple of weeks, he offers to do his best to arrange it. He also says he will mention her name at the presentation to show she has given up her time.

What is the strategy used?

What are the advantages from Julia's point of view?

What are the drawbacks?

Ian draws attention to the personal sacrifice he is making, trades some time with Julia and offers the reward of having her name mentioned in a favourable light to the top people. All these are characteristic of a bargaining strategy. They may be quite persuasive if Julia sees true value in compensatory time off or in gaining recognition. The danger is that she might come to expect something in exchange every time Ian wants work done.

Situation 3

Ian tells Julia the training department is well resourced, evidence that top management thinks highly of the work. He adds that they are also left to organise things the way they want, which has considerable advantages to everybody. 'It makes sense then that we do a good job of the training session tomorrow, especially if we want anything in the near future. And being able to respond like this at short notice always looks good when we are negotiating our pay.'

What is the strategy used?

What are the advantages from Julia's point of view?

What are the drawbacks?

Ian is simply explaining that it is logical they do a good job. He has the evidence to back up his arguments. His department is well resourced in comparison to some of the others and they are allowed to get on with things without too much interference. Both he and Julia probably want this state of affairs to continue and so it makes sense to stay beyond criticism. Whether these rational arguments will persuade Julia to work late that evening, we do not know. She may be very responsive to well thought-out reasoning, but on the other hand she may not. If she did not get on well with Ian, she might use this as an opportunity to ensure his materials were not of the highest quality. We are also assuming that the rationale Ian has presented is a genuine one. His reasons for wanting to put on a good show may be a little more personal than we think.

Situation 4

Julia tells Ian she is sorry, but she cannot possibly stay behind that evening as she has a badminton match. Ian pleads with her but she still politely refuses. Ian is obviously becoming frustrated and starts to raise his voice. 'So your badminton match is more important than the work of the department. I haven't asked you to help out like this for weeks, but the first time an important presentation comes up and I really need you, you've got a badminton match. What is it that pays you the money so you can play badminton? I know it is outside your normal working time, but I've always been reasonable with you about time off when you have had to go to your children's school. I think it's time some people got their priorities right!'

What is the strategy used?

What are the advantages from Julia's point of view?

What are the drawbacks?

Ian has adopted the direct approach of assertiveness. He has become irritated by Julia's resistance, especially since she is giving what he thinks is a trivial excuse as the reason for not staying on. He has not accepted that Julia's social life is important to her. In terms of priorities she has probably got it right in her own mind. She is not very happy about his insinuations and may have a few things to say in return to his mild emotional outburst. She may of course also give him the response he wants to hear. This sort of behaviour can damage working relationships and people can become immune to the strategy, rendering it ineffective.

Situation 5

When Ian first asked, Julia refused point blank to stay that evening. He mentioned it once or twice more (assertiveness) but still met with the same reply.

In the end he decided to mention it to his boss, who telephoned Julia and said that in special circumstances like these, good employees were expected to support their departmental heads.

What is the strategy used?

What are the advantages from Julia's point of view?

What are the drawbacks?

Ian has asked his boss to exert some pressure, knowing it will have more impact than he has achieved. On the one hand, Julia may feel flattered that someone higher up is taking the trouble to persuade her, but on the other hand, she may resent the fact that Ian has 'reported' her resistance to a higher authority, showing her to be an unreasonable employee. It seems unlikely she will think very highly of Ian after an incident like this, and she may even make an attempt to put the record straight. What is probably more important is that Ian may be seen from above as a manager who cannot handle his own simple problems.

Situation 6

Ian had a word with the production manager mentioning the importance of the presentation. He made sure he was in the office when he asked Julia to stay on. He explained to her it was important from the department's point of view, and the production manager reinforced Ian's comments. In fact, Ian's colleague said that the former secretary would always stay behind for something important like this.

What is the strategy used?

What are the advantages from Julia's point of view?

What are the drawbacks?

Ian has generated some support for his stance before even approaching the subject with Julia. By forming a coalition, he may exert more pressure on her, but she may feel intimidated by this apparent 'ganging up'. She can still refuse but it is a bit more difficult when several people are trying to sway her. This is probably not the best situation to apply this strategy as it demonstrates a weakness in the manager. If he was trying to influence the course of a major issue, the forming of an alliance may have been a useful and productive strategy.

Situation 7

When Julia refuses Ian's request that she stay to work late, Ian tries to apply pressure. 'I am simply asking you for help with this important assignment. After all, I make life pleasant for you here. I let you get on with your work. I don't ask you to handle some of the trivial administrative chores I get. I could just pass everything over to you. And I'm very lenient about extended breaks. Some of the other secretaries don't enjoy the same conditions. I don't really want to start checking up on the way you spend your time and such like. I just hope you will see your way to change your mind about tonight.'

What is the strategy used?

What are the advantages from Julia's point of view?

What are the drawbacks?

Behind Ian's remarks are some very clear threats about the way Julia's work might be monitored, obviously part of a 'sanctions' strategy. He hopes that she will value the conditions she enjoys enough to give in to his request. She may indeed see some value in acceding to Ian's demand, but at what cost to their relationship if he has to imply threats? It is this aspect which provides the greatest danger. If goodwill has existed in the past, it is likely to be replaced by distrust and antagonism if sanctions are enforced or threatened.

Successful Influencing

Where does all this leave you as a manager? What type of manager are you? Do you use whatever strategy you feel like at the time? Do you use just one or two for all situations? Do you avoid using any strategy in some situations for fear of failure? Kipnis *et al.* (1984) identified three types of manager:

- Shotgun managers.
- Tactician managers.
- Bystander managers.

Shotgun Managers

Shotgun managers use strategies indiscriminately and are often unsuccessful in achieving desired outcomes. They are usually inexperienced and with high expectations. Generally they do not consider the impact of their influencing attempts on the target people and as a result their personal relationships with employees are shaky. They may of course be very ambitious and fail to see the need to establish strong working relationships and extended commitment. Their thinking therefore is short term.

Tactician Managers

Tactician managers rely very much on reason and are very deliberate. They do their homework, thinking carefully about their arguments in advance, and they tend to be effective in getting their way. Their work is typical of that in organisations where complex work is managed. The key to their influencing success is that they are *flexible* in their use of strategies.

Bystander Managers

Bystander managers, in contrast, only see the helplessness of their situation and seldom try to influence others, either for personal or organisational objectives. They express their dissatisfaction with their ability to work effectively. They tend to be those managers who direct routine operations and see themselves as having little organisational power.

Flexible, Selective and Rational

Why do managers often choose the wrong strategies? Firstly, preferred strategies tend to become habitual, even if inappropriate. Secondly, they may fail to think things through before attempting to influence. Thirdly, they may misjudge whether someone is willing to comply.

It is likely to be productive in most organisations to follow the example of the *tactician manager* and learn to be:

- Flexible in the use of strategies.
- Selective in the right one for the situation.
- Strong on rational strategy.

Earlier we mentioned that the reasons for using influence should have some bearing on the strategy employed. If you want to obtain something from your boss (it may be a personal benefit) the friendliness strategy has the most potential for success. You may behave in a friendly way, be extremely polite and be sympathetic to his problems. These are some of the behaviours which are likely to lead to your desired outcome. If, on the other hand, you are trying to persuade him to change something and to accept your ideas, this strategy is not so valid. It is better to use the strategy of reason, thinking out your ideas clearly and presenting them in the form of logical arguments.

The same principles apply to your influencing of subordinates. If you want to obtain a benefit in some way, it is probably best to use the friendliness strategy, whilst if you intend to change something or promote your ideas, the rational strategy is likely to be the most effective.

If you want to obtain help with your job, whether from a superior, subordinate or peer, the friendliness strategy probably gives the best chance of success, whereas the assertiveness strategy (employing appropriate behaviours) is most likely right for giving people legitimate work to do.

Getting benefits from people, improving performance and initiating change, apart from the preferred strategies mentioned above, may all require a mix of strategies depending on other factors. Effective managers who need to influence for these reasons are more likely to use a variety of strategies, whereas unsuccessful influencers adhere rigidly to single strategies.

SUMMARY

- Be flexible.
- Select the appropriate strategy.
- Build up skill in rational strategy.
- Use friendliness to obtain benefits.
- Use reason to change things and promote ideas.

A Problem Case

Until now the company has had a single-page newsletter which it sends round to employees from time to time to give them what the chief executive considers to be important items of information. In a casual conversation, he has discovered that these sheets seldom get read and indeed a spot check revealed large numbers of them in waste paper baskets within minutes of distribution. The girls in the typing pool described them as 'boring rubbish'.

In an effort to improve communication the chief executive decided that a different type of newsletter was needed, one which had some human interest stories about employees and to which they could relate. At the same time he would attempt to convey his company information in a more readable form.

The company did not have a publicity department and did not want to go to the expense of producing something externally. The head of personnel, Les, was asked to take care of the project and start producing a monthly internal publication within three months.

Les knew it was a highly demanding assignment and one which would place a considerable burden on the member of his team who would take the task on. It seemed obvious from the start that Shirley was the right person to ask in view of her 'journalistic' skills and general commitment to the organisation. The problem was that Shirley was often asked to do things because of the quality of her work and the willingness to co-operate. The fact was though that there was no one else who had the skills or who could develop them in the time available. Furthermore, Les saw this as a prestigious project and one which could reflect well on his department.

He knew that Shirley would be less than enthusiastic about extending an already overstretched workload but he saw it as an important task and he would have to ensure she did it no matter what.

Shirley as usual was in the middle of a busy week and under pressure. She felt that others did not pull their weight and she was determined not to take on any more work. She knew that her family life was suffering and she had resolved to speak to Les in the near future about making her workload lighter.

When Les met Shirley he came straight to the point. He told her he wanted her to take on the responsibility for producing the in-house magazine and to fit it into her existing schedule. He said he had spoken to others in the department and they all felt she was eminently capable of doing it. Shirley politely refused, explaining carefully the demands on her time and how her home life was being affected by the sheer volume of work. Les responded by saying that it would not go down well with the 'big chief' if he discovered she was unwilling to do something which was important for the company. Shirley replied by saying that if he did not like it he could lump it and that she was more than willing to hand in her resignation.

> What strategies did Les use to try and influence Shirley?

> Were they appropriate for the situation?

It is easy to understand Les's problem. For one reason or another, the assignment was important to him and Shirley was the obvious choice. We do not know what options were available in terms of work redistribution but it was clear that he did not do his homework before meeting Shirley. He did not have much information and he had not thought out his strategy sufficiently. Whilst his initial direct approach may have been appropriate with the right person in the right situation, his follow-up attempt at influencing was less than successful and yielded the opposite result to that he wanted.

What strategies would you advise Les to have used and what specific things could he have said to heighten his chances of persuading Shirley to accept the assignment?

Conclusion

It is necessary to recognise your dominant and preferred strategies, and to identify the situations in which they are appropriate. You may have to develop skill in implementing other strategies, but you should do this in such a way that you minimise the chances of resistance and resentment to the attempt.

In this chapter, we have looked at a framework of seven strategies of influencing other people. We have drawn attention to the need to consider whether the person whose behaviour you are trying to determine is your junior, senior or peer in status terms; what the reason is for using influence; and whether you expect any resistance.

We have looked at the advantages and disadvantages of each strategy and suggested that you evaluate the effectiveness of your selection by considering the target person's willingness to comply, his commitment to the agreement and whether you have managed to achieve intended outcomes without impairing personal relationships.

We have examined some of the employee reactions in conditions where single strategies are overused. We have suggested that the strategies of friendliness and reason have the most potential for securing commitment which is willingly given by the target person. Other strategies may be successful in certain situations, but some may only erode trust and lead to a compliance which has no accompanying commitment. The effects on relationships can be harmful. The most dangerous strategies are those where coercion and intimidation are present, and these might include assertiveness, sanctions, upward referral and coalition. Organisation and subunit cultures which support and promote these strategies may be problematic, especially if the free flow of ideas is required in a dynamic setting.

Finally, we have supported the view that the *tactician* manager's example is the best to follow.

It is our experience that effective managers are flexible and are able to identify and use the most appropriate strategy in a given situation. The tactician profile best exemplifies this approach. Such managers use the whole spectrum of influence strategies to a moderate extent, but they rely most on reason, a strategy that appears to have the greatest utility in organizational life. (Kipnis *et al.*, 1984 : 66)

References

Kipnis, D., Schmidt, S., Swaffin–Smith, C. and Wilkinson, I. (1984) 'Patterns of managerial influence: shotgun managers, tacticians and bystanders', *Organizational Dynamics,* Winter, pp. 58–67.

Kipnis, D., Schmidt, S. and Wilkinson, I. (1980) 'Intraorganizational influence tactics: explorations in getting one's way', *Journal of Applied Psychology,* **65**, 4, pp. 440–452.

Leavitt, H. (1978) *Managerial Psychology,* University of Chicago Press : Chicago.

Torrington, D., Weightman, J. and Johns, K. (1989) *Effective Management: People and Organisation,* Prentice Hall : England.

Whetten, D. and Cameron, K. (1984) *Developing Management Skills,* Scott Foresman : Illinois.

Chapter 14

Negotiating

'It's time for bed now' said I.

'Dad, I want to watch "The Good Life" and it only lasts for half an hour,' said my daughter.

'But you've got school tomorrow and you are always in a rush in the mornings,' said I insistently.

'No, I promise to get up early, and if you let me watch, I could probably colour in that poster you wanted me to do for the tennis club dinner.'

Needless to say, she managed to watch 'The Good Life' and my poster got finished. What my young daughter was doing was to give me an elementary lesson in the art of **negotiating**. We reached an agreeable solution to our initial difference of opinion, because she watched television and I was happy to have a tedious job done for me.

We all negotiate. In fact, we do it most of the time. Maybe it is the choice of food when we go out for a meal, selecting our annual holiday venue or the day-to-day business of persuading the children to go to sleep. Our skill levels vary though, and some people are more successful than others. Generally, in the more mundane affairs of everyday life, our negotiation episodes are not all that critical; it does not matter too much if we fail to agree. Occasionally, however, we might encounter a situation where the outcome does seem very important to us. We may be buying a new car, for example, and want to get the best deal we can. In this case obtaining the maximum discount might be important. Similarly, if we want a pay rise, an improvement in working conditions or an increase in status, the outcome may be seen as quite significant.

Negotiation skills can be developed and you can improve your performance in a short space of time by working at the component skills. We believe that negotiation is important to you. The outcomes are far more beneficial than some of the alternative ways of dealing with differences (such as giving orders or arranging for someone else to settle the matter) which may lead to dissatisfaction, resentment and non-commitment.

In this chapter, we shall look at the way in which negotiation works, the order of play and other methods which might be used to solve differences of views. We shall then consider the preparation which is required to negotiate effectively. Finally, we shall propose a way of putting negotiation into practice and highlight the constituent skills. By putting these lessons into practice, we do not guarantee that you will get 50 per cent discount on your next car, but we are confident that your dealings with colleagues will yield more satisfying outcomes for both parties and that good working relationships will be maintained even in the midst of severe differences.

As a start, use the questionnaire What Sort of Negotiator Am I? to make a preliminary assessment of your negotiation skills. The statements are not about what you think you *should* do but about what you *actually* do. Be honest with yourself as you answer the statements, since this will help you to learn as you work your way through the chapter. Do not be too disappointed if you do not score highly: it is only a rough guide to illustrate some of the key features and weaknesses of how we negotiate.

Questionnaire

WHAT SORT OF NEGOTIATOR AM I?

This is a questionnaire about how you normally behave in negotiation. Do not look at the scoring key until you have answered all the statements. Tick under 'yes' or 'no'.

When you are negotiating with someone, you:	Yes	No
1. Say what your demands are early in the conversation.	☐	☐
2. Feel a sense of satisfaction if you can defeat the other person's case completely.	☐	☐
3. Listen to arguments before you indicate the weaknesses.	☐	☐
4. Refuse to budge from your original position.	☐	☐
5. Suggest solutions after discussing the problem.	☐	☐
6. Issue open or veiled threats if he will not let you win.	☐	☐
7. Have a good idea of what his main arguments will be.	☐	☐
8. State your absolute and final position at the beginning to save time.	☐	☐
9. Like to find a solution that makes him as happy as yourself.	☐	☐
10. Avoid planning it in case it reduces flexibility.	☐	☐
11. Prioritise your issues, demands or requests.	☐	☐

	Yes	No
12. Let the order of items occur naturally during discussion.	☐	☐
13. Know exactly what will be an acceptable outcome for you.	☐	☐
14. Concede ground on the important things to you to demonstrate flexibility.	☐	☐
15. Have already acquired relevant facts and information in advance.	☐	☐
16. Have incentives and benefits which you offer at the beginning to show goodwill.	☐	☐
17. Pinpoint the weaknesses in the other person's arguments.	☐	☐
18. Are so adept, you can conduct it without any prior thought or preparation.	☐	☐
19. Summarise what he says from time to time.	☐	☐
20. Listen to his case and then come straight in with 'take it or leave it' offers.	☐	☐
21. Jot down a few notes as he talks.	☐	☐
22. Take his 'no' as a 'no' and end the discussion immediately.	☐	☐
23. Find a pleasant setting with comfortable seating.	☐	☐
24. Ask simple 'yes/no' questions to put him on the spot.	☐	☐
25. Treat the problem as the common enemy and avoid personal attacks.	☐	☐
26. Give him a cold stare to drive home your advantage when he makes concessions.	☐	☐
27. Use humour to break the tension.	☐	☐
28. Often get emotional and raise your voice to show your depth of feeling.	☐	☐
29. Use probing questions to find out more and keep him talking.	☐	☐
30. Rely on your memory when you reach agreement and avoid putting it in writing.	☐	☐

Now score as follows:

For every *odd*-numbered statement answered with a '*yes*', score 2 points.

For every *even*-numbered statement answered with a '*no*', score 2 points.

45–60	You are probably highly competent in negotiation and understand the benefits of working towards agreement which both of you can be happy with.
30–45	You generally employ good practices, but have some weaknesses which need to be remedied. Look at the answers on which you did not score and relate these to the appropriate text as you read the chapter.
20–30	You probably know something of the principles but have a number of weaknesses which will inevitably let you down. See if there are any common themes such as lack of preparation or an unwillingness to listen to the other point of view, and then try to formulate some remedial strategies as you read the appropriate sections in this chapter.
Less than 20	Don't worry! It is possible to improve. Start with the fundamental processes of negotiation by getting the structure right and then develop the essential skills of listening, questioning and discussing, so that you can increase your competence in moving towards mutually satisfying agreements.

Stott, K. and Walker, A., *Making Management Work*. © 1992 Simon & Schuster (Asia) Pte Ltd.

The Way Negotiation Works

The sequence of negotiation is best thought of in three stages and these are shown in Figure 14.1.

Figure 14.1
The Order of Play

Stage 1	**PROBLEM** Two or more differing standpoints about an issue.
Stage 2	**EXCHANGE** Views and cases stated. Attempts to resolve differences to mutual satisfaction.
Stage 3	**AGREEMENT** Everyone is happy with the outcome.

Stage 1: Problem

The problem: Two people or groups have different standpoints about a course of action. This, of course, is the basis of negotiation. If there is no difference of perspective, no disagreement, then there is no need to employ the negotiating process. You can simply agree. The word is used very loosely in some circles. You may hear a manager say: 'I like to negotiate all working arrangement changes with my staff.' They may not disagree however, and what he means is that he wishes to *discuss* changes. If, after discussion, there is some obvious difference of opinion about what should be done, then negotiation processes can be put into action, but there has to be willingness by both parties to seek a solution together.

There are many examples of problems, some of them far more critical than a child's bedtime arrangements. You may have to work your way through a different perspective on job responsibilities with one of your employees, or there may be disagreement about working hours or conditions. In the performance appraisal process, you might have interpreted an employee's behaviour as tardy whilst he thought his enthusiasm was exemplary. This sort of situation may be the ideal setting for negotiation if a mutually satisfying outcome is required. There are situations however where the matter is non-negotiable. Where a principle is involved for example, one party may refuse even to consider the matter.

Stage 2: Exchange

There is an exchange of views. The parties involved examine the areas where they agree and disagree. The areas of agreement are settled; they then try to resolve their differences or accommodate them.

This is the strength of negotiation. A wiser decision can emerge through listening to each other's views and discussing the respective cases. Whilst on the surface it may seem as though there is wide disagreement, it may be possible through discussion to discover common points of agreement; then it is possible to identify the areas of concern. The way in which these areas are dealt with will be covered later.

Stage 3: Agreement

The two parties reach agreement about what should be done. Both people or groups are happy with the outcome. This is the key word in negotiation: *agreement.* If both sides can feel they have derived something positive out of the episode, they will be committed to the outcome and relatively satisfied. Contrast this with the feelings which accrue when someone simply tells you what to do and you strongly disagree. In negotiation, whilst you may not get the perfect result, you can often be reasonably happy that both you and the other party are not only satisfied with the outcome but are also departing on good terms with one another. Some ways of settling differences do not have that advantage.

You Do Not Have to Negotiate

Earlier we said that you do not have to negotiate to solve problems. The situation determines when it is right to negotiate and when it is right to effect other action. The thing which distinguishes negotiation from other methods is securing agreement. In other words, everyone wins. If there is no disagreement, there is no need for negotiation. Where there are differences, some managers still opt for processes other than negotiated settlements. What are some of the strategies you can use to get people to comply with your side of things?

Firstly, you may be able to *instruct* the person to do what you require by giving a direct order. This is one-way communication. As the manager, you probably have the authority to resolve your differences by simply using your 'muscle'. What do you think are the likely effects of that? This may be a form of influencing behaviour which has unsatisfactory consequences over time. Using directive strategies at the wrong time can have harmful effects on relationships and lead to dysfunctional work behaviour outcomes.

Secondly, you can *consult*. You recognise that there is a difference of view. Do not fall into the trap of confusing this process with negotiation, as so many managers do. You still reach the decision yourself and you can ignore the other party's views. The other person is asked about something – it does not mean reaching agreement and it is not negotiation. The other party may resent his views not being acted on.

Finally, you can *opt out* and get someone else, a third person who may be impartial, to make the decision. You could still end up with a winner and a loser, and there is no common agreement.

We have already stated that one side can refuse to negotiate. There are also some fundamental problems which might make negotiation difficult or even impossible. If you have nothing to bargain with, no resources and no power, you are hardly in a position to negotiate. At the same time you may possess a degree of power not derived from any position of authority, but which is not recognised as being important by the other side. The other party may then fail to negotiate, often to its cost.

We witnessed an example of this with interest. Some foreign workers in a public sector organisation felt that their salaries had fallen way below the levels in their home countries. At the time of reorganisation, they attempted to negotiate improved terms, only to be told that they were not in a position to negotiate. They could only ask and then the employer would issue a response. What the employer failed to recognise was that they had power by virtue of that fact that they did an important and essential job, and there was no one else with the qualifications or experience to take their place within a short space of time. Many of them in fact left and the organisation faced insurmountable difficulties in trying to fulfil its obligations. There was no two-way communication, no agreement and both sides probably lost as a result.

Towards Agreement

So, as we can see, negotiation is separated from these other processes in that the goal is that of securing agreement, and hopefully a degree of commitment. Let us look briefly at the three stages we identified earlier and raise a few further issues which we need to consider when we attempt to improve negotiation skills. These are shown in Figure 14.2.

Different Standpoints

People have different motives or interests. These determine the way they look at things. It is important to find out what they are. Look at the following situation:

> *Sally is one of several senior clerical assistants working in the open-plan administrative office. She has asked the senior administrative officer whether she can have her desk moved near to the office entrance since, she claims, it is claustrophobic and she needs to be near the door. For the boss's part, this would not be helpful as it would interrupt the work flow and take her away from those with whom she needs to communicate most.*

What are the possible hidden interests? Do you just accept what Sally says? Do you, on the other hand, refuse her request out of hand, since it would interfere with work? If you take things at face value, it may put you in a disadvantageous position during negotiations. We do not know whether Sally's claim was true. It would be worth investigating, however, the nature of her relationships with her co-workers and whether she wished to be more visible to senior staff when they came into the office. You may have thought of other possible hidden interests.

Figure 14.2
Towards Agreement

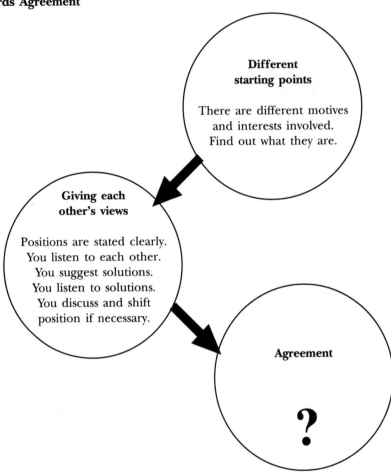

Giving Each Other's Views

The participants in the negotiation process must:

- State their position clearly.
- Listen to the other person's case.
- Suggest solutions.
- Listen to the other person's potential solutions.
- Discuss suggestions and perhaps be prepared to shift position if appropriate.

All the key elements are included in this framework. It involves *stating, listening, suggesting* and *shifting*. Each of these is important in its own way and will be covered in more detail later. At this stage, it is helpful to recognise that your case must be stated clearly, that you must show skill as a listener, that your suggestions must demonstrate a sensitivity to the situation (what might work and what definitely will not), and that you must have your ground mapped out in advance, so that when time comes to shift your stance, you do it in such a way that you concede the minimum ground.

When we enter negotiation to resolve differences, we have a reasonable idea of what we can expect to get out of it. First of all, we have a target – the top prize. We know that it may not be possible to achieve it, but it would be the perfect outcome. It has nevertheless to be within the bounds of realism. Our realistic expectations are usually less. If we are buying a new car, for example, the perfect outcome might be to obtain a 15 per cent discount, but realistically we know that anything over 8 per cent would be acceptable. Expectations may become modified during the process and trade-offs may be made. We might modify our expectations by conceding there is fairly heavy demand for that brand of car and thus accepting less discount. We might also trade off some of the expected discount for a radio to be installed or for a service contract.

The approach to the negotiation is that you try to persuade the other party to modify his expectations to fit in with yours. Whilst your expectations are a priority, you also consider what the other person can get out of it, otherwise there will be disagreement and resentment.

We know what our threshold limit (the absolute minimum we will accept) is, but it is vital to have an idea of the other party's threshold. If we are way out, he will lose interest. Using the example above, you can often obtain discount when you go to buy a car. The salesman has clear guidelines on the maximum discount he can offer, and if you are to get the best deal, it is more than useful to know what this 'threshold limit' is. There is little or no basis for an agreement if the threshold limits do not overlap. This is shown in Figure 14.3.

The Agreement

It is obviously ideal if both parties can leave the negotiation completely satisfied with the outcome, having achieved perfect agreement. It is not easy however to resolve differences totally. More often than not, we agree to accommodate them. This is still reaching agreement and represents a positive outcome. We shall be looking later at optimising agreements so that each side derives the maximum benefit available.

Figure 14.3
No Overlap

If the threshold limits do not overlap, there is no basis for agreement.

Example: You go to buy a new car and price is the key factor. Your ideal would be to obtain 15 per cent discount but the absolute minimum you would accept is 10 per cent. The salesman on the other hand would prefer not to discount the car at all in order to maximise his profits, but he has the authority to give up to 8 per cent. As you can see, the threshold limits do not overlap, so unless one or both sides move the threshold limit, it will be difficult to secure an agreement.

You	IDEAL	15%
	THRESHOLD	10%

Salesman	THRESHOLD	8%
	IDEAL	0

At this stage it will be helpful for you to complete Application Task 14.1. This will help you to relate the information we have provided so far to your job. You are asked to think of an occasion recently in your job when you had to negotiate. It may have been when you had to discuss something with a subordinate or it might have been when you had to negotiate a problem with your immediate boss. Similarly, you may have attempted to resolve a difference with someone in the organisation at the same level as yourself. Try to

APPLICATION TASK 14.1

THE NEGOTIATION SEQUENCE

Think of a recent incidence in your work where you had to engage in negotiation.

1.   Describe the two different views about the problem:

2.   Summarise what happened in the negotiation:

3.   What was the outcome? Were differences resolved or accommodated?

4.   What were the factors which contributed to either the succcess or failure of your negotiation?

Stott, K. and Walker, A., *Making Management Work.* © 1992 Simon & Schuster (Asia) Pte Ltd.

recall what the different standpoints were and what actually happened. How did the discussion start? Was there a clear explanation of perspectives to each other? Were possible solutions discussed and was either side willing to move ground? Then you should try to remember whether the outcome was successful in resolving the differences. If it was, then you should analyse the factors which contributed to success. On the other hand, if the negotiation got nowhere, perhaps you can identify the point at which the discussion broke down and try to assess why.

If it is possible, take the opportunity to watch two people negotiating. Observe them and see how they deal with the following:

- Are the cases stated separately?
- Are they clear about what they want to achieve?
- Have they thought about arguments in advance?
- How do they use 'carrots' or inducements?
- Do they control the conceding of ground?
- Is agreement reached, and if so, how?

By watching people do this, you will not only learn to be critical of the way negotiation is conducted, but you will also improve the way you do things.

Preparing to Negotiate

To be successful in securing agreement, you must think about:

1. What you want to achieve.
2. The best way to achieve it.

Preparation is undoubtedly the key to effective negotiation. Unless a number of issues are thought through in advance, your performance in the negotiation episode is likely to be less than satisfactory. You will need to think about your stand on the problem and why you have adopted a particular view. You will also have to consider the other party's view and possible supporting arguments. This may mean doing some intelligent guesswork or, in more serious cases, carrying out some research so that your facts and figures are accurate. You will also need to know how much movement you can make away from your ideal position and the solutions which offer the most potential for a settlement. By thinking these things through, you will heighten your chances of a successful outcome for yourself.

The Agenda

It is helpful to know and agree with the other person what is to be discussed and the order in which things are discussed. This latter point is quite important. The order of items may be useful for the following reasons:

1.   You will not omit important things. You have to ensure that the items which are important to you are on the agenda. You may, for example, be meeting your boss to discuss your pay and upgrading. Experience of another area of work may be important to you; you need to agree in advance that this item will be discussed.
2.   If there are several items, it may be that some have to be agreed before the rest can be discussed. It is pointless to include some items late in the agenda, since the earlier ones may hinge on them.
3.   The two of you may want different orders of items on the agenda. The other person may therefore have different priorities, which helps you to see his angle on the situation.

   The above refers to formal or semi-formal negotiations. Sometimes we may be in the position of negotiating something which is relatively minor and this may even be done as we pass a colleague in the office or carpark. In these situations, there will not be a written and agreed agenda, but it is important that both sides are clear about the matter being discussed and the outcome. You must still know what you want to achieve and you must ensure that the other person understands what is going on. If it is felt he has been taken advantage of, you may run into problems later.

Preparing the Case

The Target

This is the main thing you want to achieve, but you accept it may take a long time to get there. Your target and threshold limit will be set at realistic levels in accordance with this. We have introduced two expressions so far which require explanation: the *target* is your ideal outcome and the *threshold limit* is the very least you are prepared to obtain from the negotiation. A third term, the *acceptable area*, describes what you consider to be the realistic outcome to the negotiation. These are shown in Figure 14.4 and outlined below:

Figure 14.4
The Target

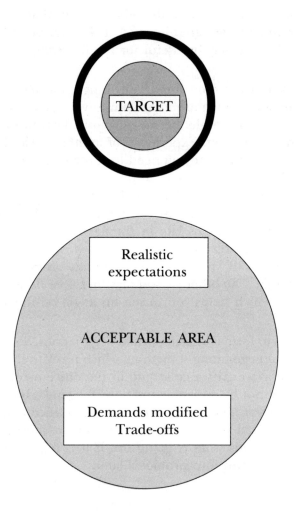

- The target (top prize):
  This represents the perfect outcome. The target itself, however, has to be realistic, otherwise there is no basis for discussion, let alone agreement. The target represents the starting point for the party concerned and by setting it unrealistically high, he might cause the other party to lose interest
  immediately.

- The acceptable area:
  This is the area you are prepared to end up in. In most negotiations this is the probable outcome area. Obviously the closer you can get to the target, the better, so it is best not to concede too much ground in the early stages of negotiation.
- The threshold limit:
  This represents the very least you expect to achieve. You need to be clear about this before negotiating because you will be extremely dissatisfied if you accept anything below this limit and may regret it at a later stage. If you are discussing a large issue, you may break it down into bite-sized chunks. Failure on one part will not prevent your reaching agreement on others necessarily.

These three expressions are summarised in Figure 14.5.

Figure 14.5
Where We Can End Up

| THE TARGET | This is the 'top prize': the best. |

| THE ACCEPTABLE AREA | This is the area we expect to end up in. |

| THE THRESHOLD LIMIT | The very least we expect to achieve. |

Specific Goals

This is what you actually want to achieve. The issue may be broken down into smaller items. You can make further subdivisions, and each will have a target and threshold limit.

The Other Side's Case

It puts you in a better position if you understand how the other person sees things. In this way, you will anticipate arguments and suggestions, and have your responses prepared. You do not know for sure, of course, so you should keep an open mind.

At this stage you have completed your preliminary preparation. You have decided mutually what is to be discussed. You have clarified what you want and you have some idea of what you can realistically expect. You also have some information on the other party's agenda preferences, so you might have some clue about his views on the issue under discussion. Now you need to firm up your case ready for the negotiation.

Strengthening Your Case

You now know what you want and you have a reasonable idea of what the other party wants. You begin to prepare your case.

Assemble Arguments

You obtain accurate facts and you assemble your arguments. In an important negotiation it cannot be over-emphasised how important it is to ensure that all data is accurate. In fact, if the other person has not done his homework, his arguments can collapse with insufficient or inaccurate information. Having knowledge which the other person does not have is an invaluable source of power. Even acquiring knowledge which the other party possesses, but wants to keep concealed, can strengthen your position. If, for example, you have discovered that his company is struggling to win orders at the present time, you know that gives you more control over the situation than if he has full order books. Do not lose sight of the fact, however, that this is *negotiation*, that you are looking for agreement and a mutually satisfying outcome. It is not war nor an attempt to tear the other person's position apart. You want the sort of agreement with which he is happy as well as you and one to which he can commit himself.

Play on Strengths

You play on your own strengths. You pick out the key points of your case and you emphasise these. At this point, it is worth referring to the power you already possess apart from the power of position. This may increase the fundamental strength of your arguments right from the beginning and you should use this to advantage. As an example, refer specifically to a situation where the nature of your contribution is directly relevant to the negotiation.

You may, for example, be negotiating with your boss for improved conditions or an increase in pay. We have arranged the informal sources of power available to you in three categories: *indispensability, link in the chain* and *key job.*

- Indispensability:
  This indicates that no one else can do the job. You may not be totally indispensable of course, but the organisation or subunit would face considerable difficulties in filling your role. It may be better to explain this condition as one in which there is no one else readily available to take over your work.
- Link in the chain:
  Other people depend so substantially on your contribution, that you are a critical 'link in the chain'. If you are not there the whole process breaks down. Obviously as a manager you will try to avert this highly dysfunctional condition, but if you are in this critical position, you enjoy a considerable amount of power.
- Key job:
  This simply means that your contribution is central to the department or the company's work. It may have elements of the other two conditions but it is seen essentially as a job which is crucial to the success of the organisation or subunit.

All these put you in a position of considerable strength, and although we suggest you do not go to extremes in promoting them (by linking them with threats, for instance) you should nevertheless make the other person aware, preferably in a subtle way, that your contribution is vital.

Play on Weaknesses

You play on the other party's weaknesses. This is not done in a destructive way but it is an attempt to shift the focus away from the weaker arguments and on to your strong points.

Cast Doubts

You hint at the possible unfortunate effects of following a particular course of action. This must be done sparingly or it may sound like a threat, which is dangerous in any negotiation. It does, though, serve the purpose of planting thoughts in the other person's mind, and some people employ this tactic quite skilfully. We know of one manager, for example, who was discussing a subordinate's request for a pay increase and stated that he had purposely avoided sending him to work in a particular section which would have been good for his experience. He stated that he would, of course, reach agreement on an increase and make appropriate recommendations to senior management. Everyone knew that the section in question was the worst place in the organisation to work. The seeds of doubt had been sown in the employee's mind and that somewhat weakened his resolve to push for the sort of increase he originally demanded.

Use Benefits

You use 'carrots' – inducements or benefits. This again has to be handled skilfully. Many who are unfamiliar with negotiation principles offer inducements which might be important to themselves but which do not feature prominently in the other party's list of benefits. Extra money, for example, may be very important to the manager but, to the subordinate, it may not be as important as, say, a change of title, which would enhance his status.

Hold Back Information

You control the revealing of information: do not put all your cards on the table at the beginning. This would put you in an extremely weak position. If, for example, you go to buy a new car and tell the salesman that you do not want to waste time by arguing, that you will not accept anything less than 10 per cent discount, you have nothing left with which to bargain. You have given everything away immediately. If he then says the most he can offer is 7 per cent, you will either walk out or accept and feel quite dissatisfied about the outcome, assuming your original proposition was an honest one.

Rehearse

You think it through very carefully. You rehearse mentally what is likely to happen. What are the arguments the other party will use? How can you counter them? What are his threshold limits likely to be? The more important the negotiation, the more important it is to go through it in your own mind.

SUMMARY

Preparing:

- Define your targets and threshold limits.
- Define specific goals.
- Think things through from the other point of view.

> •   Strengthen your case by:
>   obtaining facts;
>   assessing your power;
>   identifying weaknesses in the other person's case;
>   assembling benefits;
>   controlling the way you reveal information;
>   rehearsing your arguments.

We now look at a case in preparing effectively for a negotiation meeting. Imagine you are the manager in the following situation. A brief, duplicating some of the information, is included for the senior technician, so that you can see the problem from his perspective. This is the best way to try and look at differences. Read the information carefully and then in Application Task 14.2 plan for the subsequent negotiation between these two people.

Manager's Brief

You have acknowledged for some time that your department is somewhat behind the times. The department is concerned with servicing electrical appliances and half of your staff spend most of their time 'on the road'. The stock control system is done manually and relies to a large extent on the diligence of the servicing staff in filling in the appropriate cards when they remove spare parts from stores. When they are in a hurry however, they frequently do not bother to deal with the paperwork and this leads to arguments amongst the technicians when no parts are available.

Your senior technician has recently completed a part-time course in supervisory studies and is obviously keen to move up the promotion ladder. As part of his course he completed a project on computerised stock control and came up with a good scheme for ensuring that most of the paperwork was cut out and that there was always an adequate supply of spare parts. Basically it involved self-adhesive labels being put on all parts with an appropriate code and when the technicians went into the stores to remove parts, all they had to do was to remove the label and stick it on a sheet near the stores exit. At the end of each day one of the store operators would simply enter the data into the computer.

The senior technician gave you all this information during his course and you agreed that it was a more effective way of doing things. You agreed to purchase a computer and to implement the system. You now want him to train the stores staff in the use of the computer and to hold a meeting with technicians to outline the system and its advantages. The senior technician is not happy that stores staff should have the responsibility for this and in the past he has never enjoyed much co-operation from the other technicians in keeping the system working. He does not see it as his job therefore to give training or to persuade his colleagues to make it work. At the very least, you feel he has a responsibility as senior technician to outline the system to them and to show the stores staff how to input data. Ideally you would like him to spend a few hours each week for the next couple of months ensuring the stores staff do everything correctly.

Senior Technician

He is good at his job and very hard-working. In the past he has been constantly frustrated by colleagues' attitude to stock control and there have been several occasions when he has had to deal with angry customers who cannot get appliances repaired because the stores have run out of parts.

He recently attended a course in supervisory studies and completed a successful project on computerised stock control. He devised a simple system for improving matters in the department and you were very supportive and agreed to buy a cheap personal computer to get the scheme off the ground. He felt that, in order to implement the scheme successfully, you should persuade the technicians to play their part and that expert help should be brought in for part of the day to input the data into the computer and to check the print-out for stock levels. He himself has a full-time job to do with customers and he does not see it as his responsibility to either train staff to use the computer (since he does not feel they are competent anyway) or to persuade his colleagues to abide by the new system. If absolutely necessary, he might be prepared to outline the system to them and to hold a short workshop with the stores staff to show them the basic computer operation.

Before reading on, you should now attempt Application Task 14.2 which asks you to consider the important points from each side's perspective.

There is definitely a basis for agreement, since the manager will be happy with some basic training for the stores staff and an information-giving meeting with the technicians. There are probably several answers to the benefits question, but the clue may lie in the fact that the senior supervisor wishes to progress in his career and the manager may be able to link some career development benefit to the training of staff in computerised stock control.

How Negotiation Proceeds

> . . . it is much more helpful to view negotiation as a joint exploration of the situation in which potential adversaries find themselves, and as a joint attempt to find mutually satisfactory solutions. (Lowe and Pollard, 1989 : 121)

APPLICATION TASK 14.2

Think of the preparation points for each of the two people involved. The exact details of the case are not too important, but you need to develop a clear idea of the respective goals and the areas which have potential for agreement. Answer the following questions:

1.   What is the manager's main goal?

2.   What is the manager's target?

3.   What is the manager's threshold limit?

4.   What is the senior technician's case?

5.   What is the senior technician's target?

6.   What is the senior technician's threshold limit?

7.   What inducements or benefits can you offer?

Stott, K. and Walker, A., *Making Management Work*. © 1992 Simon & Schuster (Asia) Pte Ltd.

There are several explanations in the literature of the processes involved and we have outlined in Figure 14.6 the elements of what we consider to be a simple and workable framework which will give you a useful guide whenever you negotiate. It comprises six stages and these are outlined below.

Figure 14.6
What Happens In Negotiation

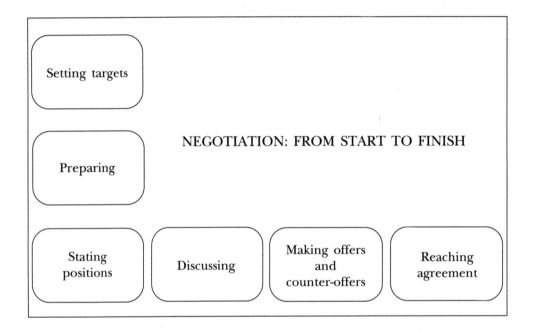

Setting Targets

You have to be clear about what you want from the negotiation and you have to express this in fairly accurate terms. It is insufficient to set targets which are vague and ill-defined, since these make the bargaining phase of negotiation difficult to sustain through lack of specificity. You will also need to formulate some preliminary ideas about your 'threshold limit' and your 'acceptable area'. In other words, you should decide where the cut-off point is and what sort of outcome would be reasonably satisfactory.

You must at this point identify those items on which no movement is possible for you. For example, if you are buying a car, you may have decided on a particular model which meets all your criteria, and a different model, even at a greater discount, is non-negotiable. At the same time, you should list the areas on which concessions may be given, but this should be done only to get something in return.

Set your ideal target fairly high but within the bounds of realism and try to gain as much as you can without giving too much away. You will need a good deal of flexibility, but the margins within which you can operate will have been defined in advance.

SUMMARY

- Set clear targets and threshold limits.
- Identify items on which you will not move and those on which you can afford concessions.
- Be realistic and flexible.

Preparing

We have already given some pointers to effective preparation. It simply needs reinforcing that you must acquire all relevant information and that it must be accurate. If, for example, you are negotiating a price with one of your customers for your product, you need to know what relevant competitors are charging. Without this data, you are in a weak position, because your customer will probably know what other suppliers' prices are. You must also try to understand things from the other party's point of view, since this will determine the strategies you use during negotiation. You also need to prioritise your targets if several issues are involved. If, for example, you are negotiating your work activities with your boss for the next twelve months, you need to know in advance what is most important to you: is it a change in status, a change of responsibilities or a pay rise? Finally, you also need to rehearse your approach to the negotiation. What are the strengths of your arguments and the weaknesses of the other party's views? What sort of 'carrots' can you dangle in front of him and which arguments are likely to be most persuasive? What is really important to him? The answers to these questions will help you adopt the approach which is likely to be the most productive for the circumstances.

We have emphasised the importance of putting yourself 'in the other person's shoes'. Try rehearsing his arguments and this will help you to understand the nature of the disagreement better. It will also help you to develop some arguments which are effective counters to his line of thinking.

SUMMARY

- Obtain appropriate data.
- Find out what is important to the other person.
- Put yourself in his shoes.

Stating Cases

Although there is usually some preamble in most situations, it is important to state your position early in the episode. This is usually an expression of your target or ideal outcome. Do not forget that in your preparation, you have set this at a realistic level, otherwise it may be difficult for the negotiation process to continue. You may say something like: 'As you know, I would like all the secretarial staff to be able to use word processors within the next twelve months. Although we shall send them for training, I thought it would be useful for you to run one workshop support session each month for them.' At this stage, the response may be accommodating in part or resistant to the idea. You have to gauge the feelings and thus modify your approach. It is possible that the meeting will not continue beyond this point, as one party may say: 'Let me think about this for a while.' It then gives you the opportunity to plan for the next meeting since you understand the position of the other party a little better.

You should note that this phase involves listening to the other person's case. Some managers fail to do this adequately and they miss out on an excellent opportunity to gain the advantages of understanding the other party's position. We advised you earlier not to lay all your cards on the table too early, but if you get the other person to speak freely at this stage, he may do precisely that, which of course strengthens your position.

You should also seek clarification. Even at this stage, it is a two-way process. By skilful questioning you may be able to pinpoint weaknesses. Make sure you understand his position fully by asking open questions, which demand answers beyond a mere 'yes' or 'no'. Do not start giving your point of view yet, but ask why he feels a particular way and how he arrived at a certain conclusion.

SUMMARY

- State your case clearly.
- Listen to his case.
- Seek clarification.

Discussion

There is now a period of discussing the relative positions, outlining the advantages and disadvantages of each other's cases and using data in support. Various strategies are used in this phase. You may, for example, decide that it is best to be thoroughly rational, demonstrating the wisdom of your argument. You may decide however that other strategies are more productive. You must decide what works best for you. You will also use this phase to test the ground for various preferred outcomes.

The first thing you must do is to decide on those issues where you agree. Do not forget that negotiation is about resolving differences, not about discussing agreement. You need to get the items which represent common ground out of the way. You can then spend your time and effort on the more contentious items.

During this period of discussion, you should listen intently and weigh the other person's arguments up. You will not make any firm offers or statements at this time since you are not totally aware of the other party's stance. You will tend to use conditional clauses, such as: 'If I were to consider this, perhaps you might consider doing that.' By playing this game, you do not commit yourself to anything, but you find out what the reaction would be and whether there is any chance of concession on a particular issue. When you are satisfied you have sized up the situation and that there is a basis for agreement, you can then enter the bargaining phase where you make firm offers.

In this phase you are engaging in joint problem-solving. It is best to think of yourselves as being on the same side, rather than as opponents. You should focus on the problem and see this as the common enemy. This moves you away from personality difficulties and on to the fundamental cause of the difference. For this to work of course, you both have to adopt this attitude. You are both searching for solutions which will be acceptable to both parties.

You may have to think laterally and creatively. Whilst the main topic under discussion may be that of price, you may ascertain that speed of delivery is an important consideration to your customer, so you can build that into the list of negotiation topics. So instead of just discussing price alone, you may be able to gain concessions from the other party by agreeing to a faster delivery time.

If you think about it carefully in advance, there may be a number of alternative solutions, some of which demand greater concessions from you than others. Obviously it makes sense to go for the solutions which derive maximum benefit for you and to leave those which involve bigger concessions till the end.

SUMMARY

- Identify areas of agreement.
- Weigh the situation up with tentative questions.
- Focus on the problem and not the individual.
- Think creatively and suggest solutions.
- Try for agreement on the small concession items for you.

Making Offers and Counter-Offers

If you have done the exploratory work well, you should be making the sorts of offers which come close to being accepted. It should be difficult for the other party to refuse outright. You might preface such offer questions with: 'Now, how does this sound to you...?' Even when the response is negative, that may still not be the end of the matter, and the skilled negotiator looks for signals which tell him that the other party is prepared to make concessions on other related issues. We shall be considering such 'signals' when we look at the skills involved in negotiation a little later.

We have used the word 'argument' but we use it here in a positive sense. It is not helpful for you to get drawn into an acrimonious exchange, so you must learn to keep cool during negotiation and not weaken your position by losing self-control. Try to behave normally and make your approach constructive. Remember, you want an agreement, otherwise you would not be using the negotiation process. The last thing you want is for a breakdown to occur, which could lead to some tension in relationships.

The most successful type of deal in negotiation is where you give something away which is not important (or expensive) to you, but receive something in return which you consider very important. If it is not important to the other party, so much the better, because he will feel good about the fact that he has not conceded very much. Naturally, this leads to a happier outcome for both parties. A firm of architects was offered a contract to design an office extension. The firm had good cashflow and was not too interested in 'staged' payments. The client was not so financially viable, so delayed payment was more important to him. A deal was struck which resulted in the architects firm receiving a promise of contracts for two further extensions to the company's offices in exchange for delayed payment for the job. This outcome satisfied both parties. The cash was not so important to the architects, but it was important to have a commitment to further work. The client on the other hand was happy to develop a relationship with this firm but the ability to delay his payment for the job was important.

Whenever we are dealing with the subject of negotiation, we are frequently told by managers that they experience deadlock. We have already hinted above at the importance of moving gradually to the offer and counter-offer phase, that you do not just jump in with the sort of insensitive offer which leads the other party to say 'no' without reservation. All the same, some negotiations do seem to end in stalemate, but it is our experience that some managers do not know the difference between genuine stalemate and the sort of situation where one party is actually saying: 'I do not agree with what you have said . . . so far!' It is this last phrase (not necessarily using these words) which signals a willingness to continue the process, but perhaps searching in a different direction for the solution. One thing you can do as a manager is to search for the issues, however minor, which are forming the obstacle to an agreement. This may mean breaking down the issue into smaller parts, and this sort of fragmentation can yield beneficial results as you identify the items on which you agree and disagree. By resolving these you can then reassemble the issue and hopefully move towards an agreement.

Despite all this, there are still issues on which you may be so far apart that it seems impossible to find a solution. If you do agree to disagree, do it amicably and bear in mind that you probably have to work with the other person for some time. There is no need to destroy human relationships. Sometimes, when the other person seems obstinate or unwilling to match your flexibility, the temptation is to use threats or to start using the muscle of your authority (if it exists in that situation). We feel this approach should be used with great caution and sparingly. There may be times when it is appropriate to adopt other approaches, but you have to consider carefully the advantages and drawbacks, and also the longer-term implications. At all costs, avoid losing your temper and making personal remarks which are injurious to relationships.

SUMMARY

- Make offers.
- Watch for signals.
- Exercise self-control.
- Gain things which are important to you and make concessions on those things which are not.
- If you agree to disagree, do it amicably: there is always another day.

Agreement

When you have reached this point, you should now review precisely what you have agreed, otherwise misunderstandings could occur. And memory has a habit of playing tricks on us! It is important to write down the agreed points and ensure that you both agree to the agreement! This may sound like a laborious way of dealing with the less important matters, but it will help to ensure there are no repercussions later if one party misinterprets the negotiation outcome.

At this point we wish to draw on some work by Dean Pruitt (1983) which goes beyond the notion of compromise and accommodation, and focuses on the sorts of agreements which yield high benefit to *both* parties. These are called *integrative agreements* since they integrate both sides' interests.

Whilst there are some situations which have little potential for this type of outcome, there are many situations which you face as a manager where there is scope for gaining an integrative agreement. There are three good reasons for you to try to achieve this:

1. It may not be possible to reconcile differences any other way, since expectations may be very high, both for you and the other person.
2. The agreement is likely to last and will probably avoid the pains of renegotiation.
3. It will reinforce relationships.

How do you achieve integrative agreements? Pruitt identifies five methods which we summarise below by outlining what you can do as a manager.

Expanding the Pie

You can increase the resources. Two of your staff want the desk near the window, for example. You may be able to rearrange the furniture so that both desks offer a view through the window. You do not have to investigate *why* they want this location, so it may be a quick form of problem resolution, needing little information requirement.

Non-Specific Compensation

You may agree to what the other person wants and receive something which is unrelated, but still important to you. You may agree to work on a contract through the weekend, for example, in return for two seats in the company's private box at the opera. You need to know what is important to the other person and what concessions mean to him.

Log-Rolling

This is about priorities and the situation in which you have different priorities amongst a range of issues. You give way on your low-priority items in order to obtain concessions from the other party on your important issues. You want your supplier to provide quick delivery, for example, because an important customer is waiting. The supplier can arrange for this through overtime working, but that will inevitably lift his costs. You agree therefore to pay a higher price for fast delivery, knowing that you can either pass the cost on or at least retain a valued customer. An accurate assessment needs to be made of the respective priorities. In this simple example, delivery time was critical to you and cost not so important, whereas for the supplier, price was important and delivery time an issue that could be resolved without too much difficulty.

Cost-Cutting

You get what you want and the other person's costs are minimised. Your boss wants you to work through the weekend with your colleague on an important contract. It involves you in sitting down together, analysing information and devising a plan. The cost to you is that you will be away from your family. The problem may be offset in part by the company arranging for you, your family and your colleague to spend the weekend in a country hotel so that you can work, and at the same time be with your family.

Bridging

In this method you do not get your demands but your underlying interests are satisfied. You and your colleague manager have been delegated to organise the company's annual dinner. You cannot agree on the venue. Your colleague (head of finance) wants to patronise a hotel he knows which offers a large discount for company functions, whilst you prefer the one which offers a wide choice of menu. The initial question is probably: 'Shall we choose Hotel A or Hotel B?' This question needs to be asked in a different way in order to arrive at a more creative solution: 'Where can we hold a function where we can obtain a good discount and enjoy a wide menu choice?' The intention is to attempt to satisfy the key interests of both sides. In the process you may have to discard some low-priority interests.

   This particular way of solving a problem emphasises the need to identify relevant interests. You may have to go beyond the more obvious interests however and delve into the other party's motives. A cry for esteem or recognition for example can manifest itself in various ways, and we are more likely to spot the symptoms than the real motivational forces which underlie the apparent sets of behaviours.

SUMMARY

- Write down.what you have agreed.
- Ensure you both understand.
- Try to achieve agreements which last and which yield high benefit to you both.
- Consider whether you can expand resources.
- Look for unrelated exchanges which may be attractive.
- Examine priorities of both sides.
- Reframe questions so that both major interests are taken into account.

Some Negotiation Skills

> You will need to use negotiating skills when you have to resolve differences. Your aim in a negotiating session is to reach an agreement that serves the best interests of both parties and encourages the development of a long-term relationship based on trust and respect. (Hind, 1989 : 189)

We have already drawn attention to several skills which might be necessary in pursuit of this aim. Earlier, for example, we mentioned the need to listen carefully, to communicate your expectations clearly and to observe. You must be able to listen for verbal signals which will indicate the other party's position and his willingness to shift on certain issues, and you must be able to read body language signals. The congruence or incongruence of body language with the verbal expressions can either confirm or contradict what is being said.

Listening

We are of the opinion that some managers need to spend more time on developing this skill than any other. In appraisal meetings, for example, they are likely to do most of the talking, even though the intention is for them to listen to the employee. Even when they are quiet, they are not really listening, but planning their next comment whilst hearing 'noise' in the background. The saying 'there are those who listen, and those who wait to speak' seems very true to us.

Listening is a skill and requires a great deal of concentration. There is a set of strategies you can employ which will help you improve your listening technique. One is to give a reflective summary when the other person has finished speaking: 'So what you are telling me Mike is that you would be prepared to take less of a salary increase this year if we could give you some experience in marketing.' You do not have to summarise or paraphrase every sentence of course, but it is useful to indicate you have been listening and also to use the opportunity to clarify your own understanding. You can do this by asking questions, which can be either clarifying-type questions or those of the more probing type.

It is also useful for you to write short notes as you listen, simply identifying the main points. This will help you to review what has been said at a later stage with a greater degree of accuracy. The other person may contradict something he said earlier and you will then spot this more easily.

SUMMARY

- Concentrate.
- Use reflective summaries.
- Take notes.

Body Language

There are two considerations with respect to body language: your own gestures which will either support or contradict what you are saying, and secondly, your ability to read the other person's body language. You can use your body language to get the message across to the other person that you are open to his suggestions and in a receptive frame of mind. You would face him (preferably without a table between you) and you would generally employ gestures which have your palms facing upwards. You would tend to look him in the eye most of the time. When he says things that you want to hear, such as when he is shifting his position nearer to yours and making appropriate concessions, you should smile and nod in agreement. This is a very persuasive form of encouragement. Try to avoid turning away from the other person and putting barriers up, such as folding your arms and placing a large desk between you.

SUMMARY

- Use supportive gestures.
- Make eye contact.
- Avoid barriers.
- Watch for incongruence in the other person's body language.

Your Speech

Avoid beating about the bush when it comes to stating your position. Be quite assertive and do not feel embarrassed about your stance, which should be a reasonable one anyway. As in all forms of verbal communication, you should avoid speaking monotonously and aim to make your tone interesting. This can increase the supportive feeling in the meeting. If you have finished what you are saying, do not feel you have to fill in any periods of silence which may occur. Simply because someone continues to stare at you does not mean you have to talk.

We said earlier that you should keep a check on your emotions and the same goes for speech. You may become irritated about something and the temptation is to raise your voice or become over-excited. Try however to remain calm, since emotive outbursts can be an unnecessary distraction during negotiation meetings.

SUMMARY

- Get to the point.
- Use variation of tone.
- Do not feel embarrassed by silence.
- Do not raise your voice.

Spotting Signals

We raised the problem of one party saying 'no' and that being interpreted as the end of discussion on that point. Sometimes, though, we miss the signals which are being sent that it is not really the end, but the cue to change tack and to find another avenue for agreement. Apart from the contradictions between spoken word and body language, what the other person actually says can give the message that negotiation should continue. Complete Application Task 14.3.

APPLICATION TASK 14.3

Without looking at our suggested interpretations, see whether you can identify what the person might actually be saying. In other words, see if you can spot the signals.

Write your suggested interpretation below each statement:

1. 'I'm sorry, I would find it far too difficult to put on that number of training sessions.'

2. 'I'm not willing to compromise on our design package.'

3. 'Oh no, we don't usually serve meals at that time of day.'

4. 'I could not possibly cut down my costs on materials.'

5. 'This is not the right time to discuss your promotion.'

Stott, K. and Walker, A., *Making Management Work*. © 1992 Simon & Schuster (Asia) Pte Ltd.

Did you spot the clues? You will notice that in each of the examples, you were getting a negative response, but it was not an outright and unconditional 'no'. He was leaving a little gap through which you could squeeze. Here are a few possible interpretations of what those people might have been saying in the negotiation:

1. I'm sorry, I would find it far too difficult to put on that number of training sessions.
   I would find it difficult but I could still do it if I got something in return.

2. I'm not willing to compromise on our design package.
   I would compromise on something else.

3. Oh no, we don't usually serve meals at that time of day.
   We don't usually do it but we could if the price or the size of order was right.

4. I could not possibly cut down my costs on materials.
   I could possibly cut my costs on labour or something else though.

5. This is not the right time to discuss your promotion.
   We can discuss it at some other time. This is the right time to discuss something else.

SUMMARY

- Listen for the signals and use them.

Questioning

We have mentioned the need to use questioning technique several times and have indicated the importance of using questions of the more searching variety. Questions are used in the phase where cases are stated in order to clarify positions and seek additional information. This enhances the preparation for bargaining. They are used to their best advantage however in the discussion and bargaining phases. You will use them to question facts which are not proven and to challenge particular beliefs and assumptions. You will look for inconsistencies in lines of argument and you will use them to support concessions.

Open questions are the most productive in terms of expanding the information available to you. They use the question words beginning with 'W' and 'How'. Here are some examples:

- What do you think we should do about the operatives?
- Why can you not agree to delivery in two weeks?
- When can you supply the main parts?
- How do you propose to persuade the supervisors?
- Where would you relocate the sales department to?
- Who do you suppose would take responsibility for completion?

When you are negotiating, try to use these sorts of questions and less of the closed questions. You will find you are then able to elicit much more information. It will be useful for you to think of something either at work or at home that you will have to negotiate in the very near future. Try to formulate some open questions which will help you to acquire the information you need.

Questions can be used in support of the other person as he appears to be making concessions, perhaps to persuade him to continue talking, and they can also be used to highlight the weaknesses in the other party's argument.

With these aims in mind, you can use the following types of questions in some circumstances (but not all the time). Leading questions should attempt to elicit the response you want. This tends to be of the 'closed' variety but it is a tactic which can be successful if used with discretion. An example would be: 'You would agree that it would be for the good of everyone concerned if you were to lead those training sessions, wouldn't you?' Only use these occasionally because they can be threatening.

Doubt-forming questions raise doubts in the other person's mind. It may cause him to rethink and may affect his confidence in his line of argument. You do not use this type of question to raise disagreement but to give the impression that you are being helpful. 'You are absolutely sure you want me to raise the matter with the managing director at this time?' could cause some doubt, and 'Would you like me to record that in writing?' may cause a rethink about the validity of the facts and opinions expressed.

Binding questions are again a useful tactic, although they are closed questions and you have to be fairly sure that if you want a 'yes' in reply, that is what you actually get. They act as a summary of progress and as a confirming mechanism. We have called them 'binding' questions for two reasons: firstly, they 'bind' things together in a summary, and secondly, they 'bind' the respondent to the answer. An example would be: 'I can safely say then that we have agreed to review the overtime situation, right?'

SUMMARY

- Use open questions widely to elicit information.
- Use leading questions only sparingly.
- Use doubt-forming questions as a positive tactic to force a re-think.
- Use binding questions with discretion.

Influencing

This tends to be a neglected subject in negotiation skills. You will find it helpful to read Chapter 13, Influencing, as this will give you some guidelines on the use of different strategies. We consider the development of influencing skills important for the manager. The choice of strategies can have a considerable impact on the outcome of negotiation, because the strategies should vary according to the situation. This is suggested by Kipnis and Schmidt (1983 : 317): '. . . the choice of tactics will vary according to the objectives involved, the relative power of the contending parties, and their general expectations of the willingness of each other to comply.'

There are several choices available ranging from *rational* strategies which are characterised by well-reasoned arguments prepared in advance and supported by accurate data, through to *ingratiation* strategies where you behave in a friendly way and perhaps make the other person feel important. It is our belief that you are more likely to progress by becoming first of all adept at employing rational strategies and that you should attempt to reason with appropriate information and listen to reason.

Whichever strategy is chosen, we must alert you to the danger of using persuasive (in some cases, bullying) tactics which are designed to force concessions. Some people become highly assertive and may use personality characteristics to obtain the responses they want. These tactics will almost certainly make it more difficult for you to secure agreements that reconcile both parties' interests. These sorts of accommodating agreements are arrived at through a process which includes flexibility, a willingness to consider mutually beneficial alternative solutions, and an attitude of friendliness and concern for the other person's benefits. Strategies which involve rigidity of stance, a hostile attitude or the desire to win at all costs do little to promote the search for 'integrative agreements' (Pruitt, 1983).

On the other hand, the use of one of the more contentious strategies, such as *assertiveness* or *coalition* (joining forces with others) may have the right effect if employed at the appropriate time. They may be used, for example, where the other party is obviously intransigent or when you want to indicate an area on which you will not move under any circumstances because of the principles involved. Signifying your high-priority area may be a useful way of influencing the other person's subsequent behaviour.

SUMMARY

- Develop skill in using sound reasoning which is well prepared.
- Be aware of other strategies and their use.
- Consider the drawbacks of persuasive and coercive tactics.
- Avoid strategies which involve rigidity, hostility or competitiveness.
- Use contentious strategies with discretion.

Miscellaneous Tactics

Supporting comments can help to push the other person along your road. They also show you are fully attentive and interested in what he is saying. You might say things like: 'Yes, that could be a crucial view when we come to look at restructuring' and 'Yes, I didn't really think of that, but you have a very strong point.'

Putting it off is a delaying tactic. There may be no sign of an agreement and you feel there is scope for discussing the matter later. You can say: 'OK, let's come back to that later.'

The *redirected question* is a tactic which is used very adeptly by many politicians. They either do not know the answer or they simply just do not want to answer. You can play for time by answering a question with a question. You have been asked whether you are going to recommend departmental upgradings or not. You might redirect the question by asking: 'Let me ask you this: what would be the reaction in the rest of the department if only a few gained advancement?' The problem with this type of question is that you are probably perceived as evading the issue (which you are) and this may make productive negotiation very difficult. We are not saying you have to answer all questions, but this particular tactic is best used sparingly when you need time to consider your response.

Those who are experienced negotiators have an array of tactics to call on and we do not intend to cover these in detail in this text, but you should be aware that you can use the following to advantage. The right location can often enhance your chances of success in negotiating, especially if you choose a pleasant and relaxing atmosphere. That is why many professional negotiators conduct a good deal of their business in restaurants, bars and hotels. The seating arrangements can also influence the receptivity to ideas. We have mentioned the drawbacks of placing barriers between you and the other person. It is often wise to use comfortable furniture and combine this with pleasant surroundings.

Apart from the physical environment, the use of tactics, such as *humour*, appropriately timed, can often enhance negotiation and soften a tense atmosphere. You may be able to think of other tactics you employ which help to swing things in your favour.

One final tactic is that of *timing*. You can get things hopelessly wrong. It is difficult, for example, to negotiate a pay increase when the company has severe financial problems, the boss is working twenty-five hours a day and your colleagues are receiving redundancy notices one by one. As a manager, you have to learn to choose not only the right time for negotiation but also the right time to raise certain issues within the negotiation itself.

SUMMARY

- Use supportive comments.
- 'Putting it off' can lead to later agreement.
- Use redirected questions sparingly.
- The right environment can have beneficial effects.
- Use humour to break the tension.
- Consider your timing.

Style

We decided to mention the issue of the manager's style in negotiation because we consider it to be a skill which should be developed. Some styles are appropriate for certain situations, whereas others may be totally inappropriate. In the same way that we said the effective manager can vary his leadership style depending on the circumstances, the same amount of flexibility should be applied to negotiation. There the similarity ends, because the styles we refer to here are not concerned with the degree of participation of the other party, but with the manager's attitude and approach to the meeting. The skill therefore now focuses not on what you say but how you conduct the negotiation. So you should consider how you present your side of the argument and your approach to dealing with the case from the other side. The style will either help or hinder a successful outcome.

The variation in style may be related to the preferred influencing strategies of those involved in negotiation. Some try to combine a number of strategies and go in with all guns blazing; some are purely rational; and yet others are quite reactive, doing little to determine the course of the negotiation episode (Kipnis and Schmidt, 1983).

Consider the situations we have outlined in Application Task 14.4, Negotiation Style, and see if you can identify which you think to be the most appropriate.

APPLICATION TASK 14.4

NEGOTIATION STYLE

Look at each of the situations below and circle what you consider to be the most appropriate style. If you can think of another style which would be even more appropriate, then write it in at the side.

1. You negotiate a loan with the finance department to buy a new car.

   Friendly and receptive.   Earnest and rational.   Forthright and assertive.

2. Your son wants to borrow your GTI to go to a party. The last time he drove your car it came back with a smashed door mirror.

   Friendly and receptive.   Earnest and rational.   Forthright and assertive.

3. You meet one of the office staff who has been taking longer lunch breaks than she has been entitled to.

   Friendly and receptive.   Earnest and rational.   Forthright and assertive.

4. You meet an architect to discuss the completion date for plans for an extension to the company's offices.

   Friendly and receptive.   Earnest and rational.   Forthright and assertive.

5. You meet your colleague in the carpark and discuss the best date for the office Christmas party.

   Friendly and receptive.   Earnest and rational.   Forthright and assertive.

6. You see the person who cleans your office about your floor not being swept properly.	Friendly and receptive.	Earnest and rational.	Forthright and assertive.
7. You discuss with your young children what arrangements they would like for their birthday parties this year.	Friendly and receptive.	Earnest and rational.	Forthright and assertive.
8. You see your boss about your long-overdue promotion.	Friendly and receptive.	Earnest and rational.	Forthright and assertive.
9. You meet a client to discuss a delay in delivery date due to unforeseen circumstances.	Friendly and receptive.	Earnest and rational.	Forthright and assertive.
10. You meet the church teenagers' group to discuss collecting for the jumble sale.	Friendly and receptive.	Earnest and rational.	Forthright and assertive.

Stott, K. and Walker, A., *Making Management Work.* © 1992 Simon & Schuster (Asia) Pte Ltd.

You probably found it not too difficult to indicate the appropriate styles, although you may have felt one or two of the situations fell between two options, and may have depended on the nature of the relationship between the people. In general, though, you probably felt that the out-of-work situations called for a more friendly approach (with the exception of number 2, which involved lending the car) whilst the work-related situations demanded either a serious or an assertive approach. The latter may be a better style where there is marginal performance (as in the cleaner's case), but it is true to say the two can be combined.

Conclusion

In this chapter, we have looked at the 'order of play', how a negotiation is structured, the way in which preparation might lead to more effective negotiation, and some of the essential skills involved, including those of listening and questioning. Negotiating is an effective way of managing differences and we cannot over-emphasise the benefits of using an approach which promotes the happiness of both sides with the outcome. If there is one lesson above all others which we would stress, it is that you should see the problem of different perspectives as the enemy to be attacked, avoiding all personal attacks and ill-feeling, and look for an agreement which genuinely 'integrates' the interests of both parties: it is this process of reaching agreement which forms the true strength of negotiation.

References

Hind, D. (1989) *Transferable Personal Skills for BTEC,* Business Education Publishers : Sunderland.

Kipnis, D. and Schmidt, S. (1983) 'An influence perspective on bargaining within organizations', in Bazerman, M. and Lewicki, R. (eds.), *Negotiating in Organizations,* Sage : Beverly Hills.

Lowe, T. and Pollard, I. (1989) 'Negotiation skills', in Riches, C. and Morgan, C. (eds.), *Human Resource Management in Education,* Open University Press : Bristol.

Pruitt, D. (1983) 'Achieving integrative agreements', in Bazerman, M. and Lewicki, R. (eds.), *Negotiating in Organizations,* Sage : Beverly Hills.

Chapter 15

Managing Time

Time is the most valuable resource available to any manager. It does not matter what kind of job you have. It makes no difference whether you are a junior, middle or senior manager, you are responsible for managing yourself and your time. Most definitions of management state that it is getting things done through other people. Despite this, you cannot effectively organise other people until you can organise yourself. 'Time is the scarcest resource, and unless it is managed, nothing else can be managed' (Drucker, 1966). Managing yourself and your own responsibilities involves organising your time and what you use it for.

Once time is gone you cannot get it back. When you hear people talk about time management, they are usually referring to 'tips' they have picked up on special courses through reading gems of advice, such as: 'I must learn to say NO.' Whereas we believe such items of practical advice can be useful (we have included a number in this chapter), they are not enough by themselves to develop high-level time management skills. As Taylor (1989 : 19) points out:

> (Managers) shy away from more complicated suggestions such as 'get organised' or 'delegate' or 'design your own work' because these are time consuming in themselves. And time is a thing they haven't got.

To develop higher-level time management skills you must have a definite system or plan which reduces the time you spend on minor or unimportant tasks, and so increase the time you spend on actions which are really important to you both personally and professionally. The increasingly complex nature of your job in today's organisations demands more than ever that you consciously consider and plan how you can best use your time to produce maximum results.

Stewart (1986 : 194) distinguishes between the effective and the efficient use of time: 'To improve (effective time usage) managers must decide what they personally ought to be doing. To improve the second (efficient time usage) they can learn to organise their time better.' You need therefore to carefully and systematically identify what is important to you at both a personal and professional level. You should do this before you attempt to implement any practical strategies for better utilising your time.

In this chapter we present and describe an approach which can help you to control and maximise your time usage. You are asked to consider your goals and analyse how you presently spend your time. We also challenge you to reduce factors which often invade your time and provide some practical suggestions for combatting them. Finally, you will be asked to develop a customised plan which *you* can implement to manage your time on a continuing basis, not just for the week after you read this chapter!

Before we begin our discussion, complete the questionnaire Managing Time: Details to Consider. It will provide you with some idea of how you manage your time. You can then consider the points listed and keep them in mind as you read the chapter.

Questionnaire

MANAGING TIME: DETAILS TO CONSIDER

	Yes	No
1. I have a great memory, I never write things down.	☐	☐
2. I never throw anything away, I never know if I will need it at a later date.	☐	☐
3. I don't seem to be able to finish a telephone conversation, they go on and on.	☐	☐
4. I get very little time to exercise, I'm simply too busy.	☐	☐
5. I always make time for my employees. My door is open no matter what is happening.	☐	☐
6. I don't ask my staff to do any difficult tasks, after all I can do them much better myself.	☐	☐
7. When I chair a meeting I make sure everybody gets a say. I don't mind if they run over time.	☐	☐
8. I keep a calendar to keep track of where I should be and for how long.	☐	☐
9. I often leave tasks to the last minute. I work much better when I'm under pressure.	☐	☐

	Yes	**No**
10. I put some time aside every week when I can think about important aspects of my job.	☐	☐
11. You can almost see the top of my desk. It is covered with all the projects I am presently working on.	☐	☐
12. I pride myself on my work. I never leave any task until it is perfect.	☐	☐
13. I like to put off making decisions; it gives more time to think about what I will do. I certainly don't want to make a mistake by rushing.	☐	☐
14. I am so busy I rarely have time to go out with family or friends. This is the price of success.	☐	☐
15. If I don't particularly like a task I tend to put it off.	☐	☐
16. I often have so much to do that I do nothing at all.	☐	☐
17. I spend a lot of time walking around aimlessly and taking long coffee breaks.	☐	☐
18. I try to handle each piece of correspondence only once.	☐	☐
19. I set deadlines for myself and stick to those deadlines.	☐	☐
20. I have time to relax and spend time with my family and friends.	☐	☐

Scoring Key:

If you answered 'yes' to numbers 8, 9, 10, 18, 19 and 20 and 'no' to the remaining points, you are probably managing your time fairly well. If you answered 'no' to the numbers listed above or 'yes' to any of the remaining points, you are more than likely wasting a considerable amount of your time.

Managing Time

Managing involves working with and organising people. The major part of your day is probably spent, one way or another, in interacting with and organising employees. Before you can expect to organise other people you must be able to organise yourself and your own time. On how many occasions have you heard someone say 'I can't, I simply haven't got the time?' How many times have you said this yourself? You must be able to manage *your* time if you want to produce the best results possible from both yourself and your employees.

Effective time management has some very persuasive claims to make. It can:

- Simplify your life.
- Reduce stress.
- Increase effectiveness.
- Increase efficiency.
- Increase job satisfaction.
- Increase personal and organisational productivity.
- Create more 'personal time' for you to use.

Time saved through thoughtful time management can be used for reflecting on what is really important in the job as well as for increased leisure.

The Five A's

Time management is actually common sense. The trick is to identify and channel what you already know into some type of framework which will stand the test of time. We believe you can manage your time better by using a scheme we have labelled the The Five A's and which is shown in Figure 15.1. Following the scheme will make you more aware of what you are presently doing and encourage more effective and efficient time usage. The different stages of the scheme incorporate the key aspects of time management.

Awareness

This first stage asks you to consider what is really important to you in both a personal and professional sense. It encourages you to set concrete goals which reflect these factors. We also ask you to consider other factors associated with how you spend your time: your habits, behaviours, ways of communicating and job responsibilities.

Figure 15.1
The Five A's; A Scheme for Managing Time Better

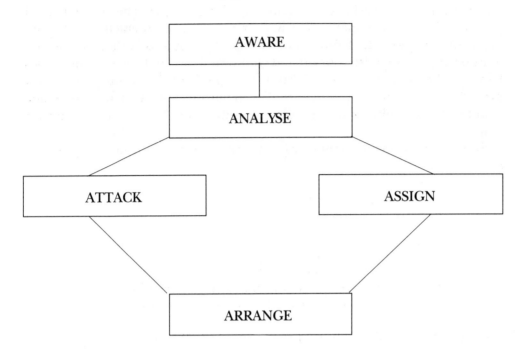

Analysis

If you are to improve your time usage you must delve into the details of how you presently spend your time, or risk wasting it. By analysing what you actually do, you can identify what you need to alter to make better use of it.

Attack

An analysis of your time usage will undoubtedly expose many things that waste your time. These 'time thieves' need to be eliminated if you are to concentrate on the things that are really important to you.

Assignment

While eliminating 'time thieves' you need to assign priorities to the tasks you still have to do. This needs to be carried out on a regular basis.

Arrangement

The final stage involves arranging your time in a purposeful fashion: thinking about how to improve those 'little' skills on a permanent basis so that you actually retain control of your time. This requires some thoughtful planning.

Working through the five A's, if applied correctly, can certainly assist considerably in the more productive utilisation of available time. We now look in detail at each of the five stages.

Aware

Before you can improve your time management skills it is essential that you are aware of a number of things about yourself. First, you need to consciously clarify your own personal and professional goals (or key result areas): where you are going and where you want to be. It is useful to write these goals down to remind yourself of their importance. An awareness of individual goals or key result areas is crucial because they should form the base from which most of your actions originate.

Secondly, you also need to be aware of your habits, behaviours, personality, personal and professional responsibilities, values and patterns of communication. An awareness of these points should help you realise why and when you do things and what factors influence your behaviour. Actions are what consume time and need to be controlled therefore if you are to effectively manage time.

Huffstutter and Smith (1989) believe effective time management stems from two forms of control: self-control and job control. Self-control arises from a knowledge of yourself: your strengths, weaknesses, personality type, and whether you see things as a whole or as smaller details. 'Self knowledge plus self discipline equals maturity, and maturity boosts one's potential for effective management of time' (Huffstutter and Smith, 1989 : 317).

Job control requires a knowledge of your job: that is, of the organisation and your role within it. You must be aware of the organisation's major purpose since your values as a manager will be measured in terms of this. A knowledge of the primary purpose helps you define and clarify your role and areas of responsibility.

By setting goals and targets you are actually defining what is important to you. Think about the type of person you want to be. Which direction do you want your career to go? What do you want your organisation to achieve? As emphasised in Chapter 11, Setting Targets, it is vital that you know where you are going. To use an old but accurate analogy, without direction you will be like a ship's captain in a storm when the navigation system is broken. You will be unsure of where you are going or how you will get there.

It is not an easy task to identify your goals accurately. Usually you will have some idea of what they entail, but you must consciously 'dig' them out of your mind. The following points may help you to define and set goals.

Importance/Priorities

Separate personal, professional (career or business) and family goals. They will require some balancing. If you plan to promote a new product item throughout the continent, teach your children to swim and learn to sailboard all at the same time, think again. All your goals are important, but you must decide which are the more important for the immediate future. The relative importance of goals will change as certain targets are achieved or priorities change. Although this chapter deals primarily with organising your time at work, it is impossible to do this if you fail to take into account your 'outside' needs and goals.

Past Experience

Think about the things you have done or those that have happened to you that have made you feel 'good': when you felt you had really achieved something. You probably felt elated when you were promoted to your present position, for example, or when you made an important sale. On a personal level, the purchase of a new house or an enjoyable holiday with a friend may have given considerable pleasure. The things that give you a sense of satisfaction are probably the basis for what is important to you.

Realistic

Make sure the goals you set are realistic. If you are 146cm tall, and want to become a centre in a professional basketball team you are probably overestimating what you can achieve. We do not intend to counsel against ambition or setting lofty goals for yourself, it is merely a caution against setting unrealistic goals.

Limited

While some goals may be realistic, others may be set too low to challenge you. Sometimes seemingly impossible goals can be reached through sheer persistence and dedication.

Specific

Make sure your goals are reasonably specific and include some form of a deadline. Think about *how* you will achieve your goals and plan for this.

Written

Put your goals in writing. You are only fooling yourself if you believe you can form and retain often spurious goals in your head. Remember, we are not necessarily referring to your goals for next week or even next month. Initially we are talking in terms of years or even life goals. Additionally, by making yourself record your goals, you are forcing yourself to be reflective about what you believe. Goals written on paper often look completely different from those which are simply thought about.

We emphasise the setting of goals because, if done correctly, it will reflect your values and assumptions and what you believe is important. This should guide how you spend your time. You will organise your time so you can concentrate on working towards these goals.

Application Task 15.1 enables you to start this process off. It encourages you to think about the process of setting, prioritising and then actively working towards your defined goals.

The goals and priorities you have just developed are not 'set in stone'. You will need to review and update them as circumstances change and goals are achieved. Be prepared for obstacles and setbacks which may occur. We have not dealt with how to turn these goals into manageable targets. This is covered in Chapter 11, Setting Targets, and is specifically related to the matching process between organisational goals and individual work targets.

You also need to be aware of other factors which influence how you use your time. These are your *behaviours, habits* and *ways of communicating.* If you have always communicated with your employees verbally, for example, this can affect how you use your time. You may well be telling ten different people the same thing ten times. Perhaps a memo would suffice on some occasions.

It is difficult to change these typical ways of doing things, but it can be done. Take some time to reflect upon the three factors of habits, behaviours and methods of communicating and list some of the most obvious in Application Task 15.2. When you have done this make some suggestions as to how the identified points may influence how you use your time.

Other factors which influence your use of time are your actual job responsibilities. These are often separated from what you believe are important. There are usually some requirements associated with our jobs which we do not particularly like and cannot avoid. In many cases they are not high on our lists in terms of importance, but they are often unavoidable.

We have to learn to balance what we consider important in our jobs with duties which are imposed. First though, we need some clarity about our responsibilities. Managers who work in complex environments, in particular, do not always enjoy clear job definitions. While this may facilitate organisational flexibility, some awareness of responsibilities is essential. It may be worth asking several questions which might help clarify in your own mind what the key parts of your job are. Note that we avoid referring to job descriptions which are often removed from reality.

APPLICATION TASK 15.1

DO IT NOW: YOUR GOALS

1. On a piece of paper, generate a list of what you would like to achieve in the next two to three years: your personal goals, professional (business and career) goals and family goals. At this stage, write as many goals as you wish.
2. Put your list aside for some time (a couple of days if possible). Return to the list and make any adjustments or refinements. Now prioritise your goals within each of the three areas. (If you are not sure how to prioritise, it is covered later in the chapter.) Select the five statements in each area which reflect what are really important to you. Write these, in priority order, in the form provided below: Do It Now: My Goals.
3. Carefully look at each of the goals you have recorded and think about which are the most important *overall*. Prioritise the entire list and number them from 'one' onwards. If you are not comfortable with being this precise at this stage, you can group them using these relative categories:

    I : Very Important
    II : Important
    III : Not as Important
4. Set some tentative deadlines (*When by?*). Some of these may be relatively short term, others may involve two years: It is up to you to decide.
5. List a few very brief ideas about *how* you may go about achieving your goals. What can you do to work towards their attainment? An example of the process is shown below.

Example:

OVERALL PRIORITY	AREA PRIORITY	GOAL	WHEN BY?	HOW?
3	2	To win the division award for most yearly sales.	June 1993	Contact two new prospects each week. Retain close contact with clients, increase orders.

PERSONAL

OVERALL PRIORITY	AREA PRIORITY	GOAL	WHEN BY?	HOW?
	One			
	Two			
	Three			
	Four			
	Five			

PROFESSIONAL

	One			
	Two			
	Three			
	Four			
	Five			

FAMILY

	One			
	Two			
	Three			
	Four			
	Five			

APPLICATION TASK 15.2

INFLUENCES ON TIME USAGE, OTHER FACTORS

An example of a preferred way of working is shown below, with an assessment of its impact on the manager's time.

Example:

DESCRIPTION	INFLUENCE ON TIME USAGE
Door is always open to employees for any reason.	*Always being interrupted. Never seem to be able to work on a project for a long period of time. Concentration broken.*
1. 2. 3.	**HABITS**
1. 2. 3.	**BEHAVIOURS**
1. 2. 3.	**WAYS OF COMMUNICATING**

Stott, K. and Walker, A., *Making Management Work*. © 1992 Simon & Schuster (Asia) Pte Ltd.

- Who am I responsible for?
- How am I responsible for them?
- Do I control my own resources and budget?
- What are my major areas of activity?
- What administrative functions and routines am I in charge of?
- Am I responsible for dealing with people outside the organisation?
- Am I expected to be innovative?
- What authority do I have?
- What are my employees responsible for?
- What are my colleagues responsible for?
- What is the mission of the organisation I work for?
- Are there any unstated expectations in my job?

This is not a definitive list, but answers to such questions can help you become more aware of and delineate *your* responsibilities. Use a piece of paper to answer these questions and to generate your own questions. Try to develop an initial list of your job responsibilities.

In this section we have tried to increase your awareness of a number of factors which should influence how you spend your time. An awareness of where you want to be and what is expected of you forms the basis for beginning to organise your time.

Analyse

When you have clarified and recorded your goals you should move onto a more practical analysis of how you actually use your time. *Before you can control your time you must know how you are using it.* This is of course a simple statement, but it is a surprising fact that most managers cannot tell you in any detail how they spend an average day or week.

It is essential that you know how you spend your time. It is just as important, once you know what you are doing, to analyse your time usage. Break your day up and look at it. Ask yourself questions such as: How much time do I spend in meetings? How long do I spend doing other people's jobs?

Your first step is to find out exactly what you are doing at present. There are a number of ways of doing this.

Shadowing

Have someone follow you around for a set period of time – a week is the ideal but this is usually not possible. Even asking someone to spend half a day with you can be revealing. Ask the person to observe and record everything you do in at least the following detail:

Time: How long you spend on a particular activity.
Activity: Record what you were actually doing.
Involved: Refers to the people you interacted with during the time period and activity.

You can include more detail if you wish, but these three areas should be adequate to begin with.

Diary/Self-Observation

This method involves shadowing yourself. You can either use a form similar to Joe's Day, as described later, or develop a more manageable format. This may involve recording your actions at five, ten, fifteen or thirty-minute intervals. Your form may be similar to the one set out in Figure 15.2.

Figure 15.2
Self-Observation Form

MONDAY	
TIME	**ACTIVITY**
8.30–9.00	_____
9.00–9.30	_____
9.30–10.00	_____
10.00–10.30	_____
10.30–11.00	_____
11.00–11.30	_____
11.30–12.00	_____
12.00–12.30	_____
12.30–1.00	_____
1.00–1.30	_____
1.30–2.00	_____
2.00–2.30	_____
2.30–3.00	_____
3.00–3.30	_____
3.30–4.00	_____
4.00–4.30	_____
4.30–5.00	_____

5.00–5.30	_____
5.30–6.00	_____
Work at home:	_____

Another method, suggested by Stevens (1984), utilises a type of grid. He recommends that you design a grid and write a list of your normal duties along the top and time intervals down the side. Time intervals can be five, ten or twenty minutes. During the day you simply tick the appropriate squares. We would suggest this method may be more useful if done after an initial, more thorough recording of what actually happens.

The type of activity log you decide to use is up to you. What is important is that you identify what you *actually* do in your job. We suggest that you track your time for a period of a few days at least three times a year. Try to make a habit of recording your activities. If you do this you will become more aware of what you are doing and keep on top of those important (goal-related) tasks you want to do.

After you have completed your observation, move onto the analysis stage. If you want to make the remainder of this section more meaningful, conduct a 'mini time log' for one day. We suggest you include as much detail as possible, recording each activity and its duration. Joe's Day (in Figure 15.3) is an example of such a log.

Figure 15.3
Joe's Day

Day/Date: Tuesday, 23 March

TIME	ACTIVITY	INVOLVED
8.00–8.11	Cup of coffee, catch up on newspaper.	Self
8.11–8.14	Phone call from Marketing, need figures on stock availability.	Ted Danson
8.14–8.20	Searching secretary's office to find files.	Self
8.20–8.23	George (secretary) arrives, asked to find files.	George
8.23–8.26	Tim drops in to confirm meeting time.	Tim
8.26–8.30	Finish explaining to George what he wants.	George
8.30–8.32	Phone call from home.	Wife

8.32–8.46	Work on unit triennial report for B. of D's.	Self
8.46–8.48	Call from Marketing – reminder of files.	Ted D.
8.48–8.53	Hurry up George for files – send to Marketing.	George
8.53–8.59	Continue work on triennial report.	Self
8.59–9.17	Judy drops in, invitation to BBQ.	Judy
9.17–9.19	Call from bank to inquire about an LOC.	Bank Worker
9.19–9.24	Jose joins Judy and suggests Yacht Club for BBQ.	Judy, Jose
9.24–9.31	Continue work on triennial report.	Self
9.31–9.37	Call from Rosita (Boss) about change in schedule.	Rosita
9.37–9.51	Review unit plans for next year.	Self
9.51–9.53	Call from transport regarding updating company car.	Marcus
9.53–10.00	Flip through brochures of cars available.	Self
10.00–10.04	Zenon drops in to check on holiday leave and complains about bossy supervisor. Meeting arranged for afternoon.	Zenon
10.04–10.22	Coffee break.	Others
10.22–10.31	Prepare agenda for meeting.	Self
10.31–10.50	Walk to meeting and stop to chat to workers.	Others
10.50–10.55	Wait for everyone to arrive at meeting.	Others
10.55–12.02	Conduct meeting on improved unit plans for next year.	Others
12.02–1.35	Lunch.	
1.35–1.50	Walk around unit chatting to various workers.	Others
1.50–2.00	Prepare for appraisal meeting with Leonard.	Self
2.00–2.07	Leonard arrives, appraisal process begins.	Leonard
2.07–2.11	Call from supplier regarding late delivery.	Cal
2.11–2.14	Call Ruth to tell her about delivery.	Ruth
2.14–2.22	Continue discussion with Leonard.	Leonard
2.22–2.25	Call from the floor that Zenon and his supervisor are yelling at each other.	Others

2.25–2.30	Ask Leonard to come back tomorrow, go to floor.	Leonard
2.30–2.54	Talk to Zenon and supervisor to help work out their problem. Arrange to meet again.	Zenon and Supervisor
2.54–3.05	Sign letters for George and dictate a memo.	George
3.05–3.09	Call from son asking for a loan.	Randy
3.09–3.17	Finish dictating memos, sign some cheques.	George
3.17–3.45	Coffee break.	Others
3.45–4.16	Work on unit figures for next year with supervisors.	Supervisors
4.16–4.18	Call from June saying she is going home sick.	June
4.18–4.26	Continue with meeting.	Supervisors
4.26–4.29	Call from home, pick up beer on way home.	Daughter
4.29–4.37	Bob calls in to talk about promotion exercise. Call off rest of meeting until tomorrow.	Bob Supervisors
4.37–4.50	Discuss promotions with Bob.	Bob
4.50–4.52	Call from Rosita to meet her tomorrow.	Rosita
4.52–5.02	Pack bag: next years figures, triennial report and tennis gear. HOME	

When conducting a time analysis, Shinn (1986 : 196) suggests you ask the following questions regarding your day's (or week's) activities.

1. Which of my constructive activities took most of my time?
2. Which of my non-constructive activities took most of my time?
3. Which of my constructive activities were not worth the time I spent on them?
4. Which of my activities were worth more time than I spent on them?
5. Which were my busiest times of the day?

We recommend that, in addition to asking these important questions, you conduct a more systematic analysis. Such an analysis, based on the example of Joe's activities, is shown in Figure 15.4.

Figure 15.4
Joe's Day; After Analysis

CATEGORY	NUMBER OF ACTS	DURATION (MINUTES)	% TOTAL TIME
PROFESSIONAL	7	139	27.5%
CRISIS	5	41	8.1%
ROUTINE	25	165	32.6%
INDIVIDUAL	11	161	31.8%

Joe went through each of his activities and placed them in one of the following categories.

Professional (P): Those activities which involve the professional aspects of the job, e.g. long-range planning, writing influential reports or developing staff.

Crisis (C): Activities which have to be done immediately. Problems which arise within the unit, such as interpersonal conflict or crisis decisions.

Routine (R): Activities which basically deal with routine administrative matters such as correspondence, phone calls and 'on-the-move' supervision.

Individual (I): Any activities which are personal: phone calls from home or coffee breaks.

Next to each activity Joe wrote either P, C, R or I. He totalled the duration and number of activities in each category.

It is fairly obvious that Joe is not spending much of his time on the really important parts of his job. Routine and personal activities account for far too much of his working day. If you want even more detailed information regarding your own activities, it is possible to conduct a deeper analysis identifying such details as the number and duration of telephone calls, formal and informal meetings, interpersonal contacts or who initiated contacts. Joe could also have analysed who he spent most of his time with.

If your work day looks something like Joe's, you are not alone. Numerous studies have discovered that the typical manager's day is characterised by variety, brevity and fragmentation or discontinuity (Mintzberg, 1973). In practical terms you probably have difficulty in finding solid 'chunks' of time to complete those really important tasks. You are too busy (or feel you are) dealing with constant interruptions such as phone calls, 'drop-in' visitors or handling interpersonal conflicts. Many managers and organisations seem to equate 'business' with productivity, and as a sign that someone is a hard worker. This is not accurate. If someone is constantly running around and under intense pressure, it is highly likely he is not managing his time properly.

If you fit the model of the typical manager, you spend most of your day reacting to the actions of others, rather than setting your own agenda and working on what is important. You probably waste substantial time on the less important tasks.

To manage time more productively, you need to learn how to complete *crisis* and *routine* tasks efficiently, so that you have time to do your *professional* activities effectively (Sexton and Switzer, 1978). Additionally, you need to control your personal time during the work day.

Through your analysis you need to assign priorities to what you do and identify and attack those activities or actions which waste your valuable time.

Assign

When you have mapped your time usage you should consider your actions in a number of categories:

- Controllable/initiation.
- Importance.
- Urgency.
- Delegatable.

Controllable/Initiation

Ask yourself: How many of my activities do I have control over? Which activities have to be completed as part of my job? If you are spending too much time on activities not directly related to your job, or activities someone else should or could be doing, you may be wasting your time.

How many of your activities did you initiate yourself? How many were initiated by others? Refer to your own time log and select any of the activities you recorded. Rate yourself on your *control* over an activity on a scale of 0–6. Zero (0) would indicate that you had no control over the activity, three (3) would indicate that you had some control and six (6) that you had complete control. Using this scale, you can then assess the degree of control you had for each of the activities on your personal time log.

Now do the same for *initiation*. Zero (0) would indicate you played no part in initiating the action, three (3) would indicate you were somewhat involved in initiating the action, and six (6) that you initiated the activity on your own. You can of course use the intermediate numbers. To illustrate this complete Application Task 15.3.

APPLICATION TASK 15.3

CONTROL AND INITIATION

Place a cross on the appropriate axes *control* and *initiation*. If you rated the activity as high on the control axis and high also on the initiation axis, the activity is probably very important to you. You were a major force in initiating the action and had considerable control over its direction.

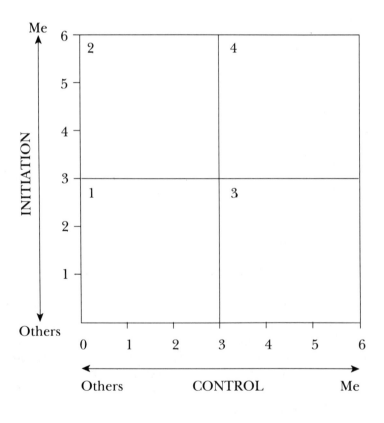

This is of course an example of just one activity. If you go through this process with a day or a week's activities, you will probably discover that many of your actions fall in sector 1. Having too many activities in this sector indicates that you may be reacting to other demands rather than controlling your own time. Of course, there will be activities over which you have little control or say, but must carry out – this is a fact of the work place. In many instances however, you may be allowing others to control your time with actions they have initiated and which you do not have to do. Take for example a colleague who visits your office every Monday morning for half an hour to talk about the weekend football game. He has initiated a discussion during your time and by allowing it to continue you have surrendered control of that half an hour.

Your task then is to work out how you can spend more time on activities in sector 4. You cannot disregard all unpleasant responsibilities, but you can gain much stronger control over many situations. You can talk about the football during your break time.

Considering control and initiation also involves identifying *proactive* and *reactive* tasks.

> The active positive tasks are the ones you must do to achieve the *objectives* of your job. The reactive tasks are all the junk that lands on your desk every day and has to be dealt with to keep things running. (Video Arts, 1984 : 22)

The labels used are unimportant. What is important is that you categorise tasks and concentrate on controlling your own time and working towards what is important.

Importance

You should also rate your activities as being 'very important' to 'not important'. Importance refers to the consequences of decisions or activities. If you are spending too much time on activities which are unimportant in relation to your goals and major responsibilities, you are probably wasting your time. *Pareto's Law*, sometimes labelled the *80/20 rule*, tells us that only 20 per cent of a manager's time creates results, whereas 80 per cent of time tends to be spent on unstructured 'little things' (MacKenzie, 1972). The importance of an activity is related to your professional, career or business goals. Very important tasks should be given your immediate and undivided attention.

Urgency

Consider whether the action is urgent. Do you really have to do it now? Urgency refers to time pressure to complete the task. Would it be more effective to do it at another time?

It is vital that you distinguish between *urgent* tasks and *important* tasks. Urgent tasks can often be unimportant but have a tendency to push really important tasks into the background. Unless urgent or 'crisis' tasks need your immediate attention you should not spend too much time on them. There is the danger that important tasks could be pushed into the background. These important tasks are those activities which are tied to your identified *key results areas*. Urgent tasks are often initiated by others – you should attempt to control the amount of time you spend on them.

You need to consider also the order in which tasks should be done. This is called *prioritising*. Both the urgency and importance of the task need to be accounted for. One way to do this is presented in Application Task 15.4.

If a task is *very important and very urgent*, you must do it immediately. It cannot wait and is congruent with what you believe is important.

Example: Your biggest customer wants a detailed list two days from now of the new items you have available. He wants you to note how the new lines could be useful to him. If you can convince him of this, his orders could significantly increase, pushing you into the promotion stakes.

If a task is *very important but not urgent*, you have time to work on it. You can even delegate parts of it to start the process. Be careful not to put these tasks off for too long. Remember, they are important to achieving your overall goals.

Example: Your report, which is due to be submitted to the board of directors in two months time, could significantly increase the size and influence of your unit and your position in the organisation.

If a task is *very urgent but not important*, you can deal with it in two ways. Do it now but do not spend too much time on it – get it out of the way quickly. Alternatively, delegate it to someone else.

Example: The boss wants a list of low-stock items within the next hour. It is a simple administrative chore.

If a task is *neither important nor urgent* ask yourself whether you should even be doing it. These tasks should either be shelved, ignored or delegated.

Example: Your assistant wants to know which car he can let the new salesman take, the blue or the red one.

Considering the importance and urgency of a task allows you to prioritise your actions by assigning them in order of importance to you and your organisation. Obviously, tasks which are both very important and very urgent should be your first priority.

MacKay (1989 : 96) suggests that you need to follow up your prioritisation

APPLICATION TASK 15.4

IMPORTANCE AND URGENCY

Consider some of the tasks from your activity log. Ask yourself how important and urgent they are? Rate the tasks on these dimensions on the corresponding axis. This will give you some idea of the priority of the task. (This will be explained more fully a little later.)

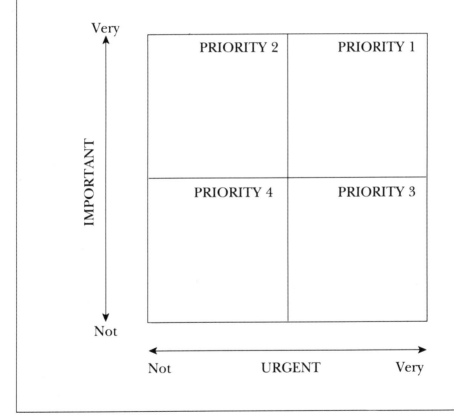

Stott, K. and Walker, A., *Making Management Work*. © 1992 Simon & Schuster (Asia) Pte Ltd.

by asking whether the priority is *feasible, suitable* and *acceptable*. Feasibility refers to the likelihood that you will be able to achieve what you set out to do, considering constraints and possible consequences. Suitability asks whether the achievement of the task will promote or assist your productivity at work. Acceptability questions whether the action has your approval: is it too risky? These three 'tests' challenge your priority for practicability, further strengthening the prioritising process.

Delegatable

Ask yourself whether you have to perform the action or could someone else do it just as well. If you can delegate a task for your own, the organisation's or an employee's benefit, why spend time on it yourself? Delegation is discussed in detail in Chapter 17.

At this stage you may want to return to the time log you developed earlier in the chapter and consider your actions in the light of controllability, initiation, importance, urgency and delegatability. When you do this, you will almost certainly identify some activities which uselessly steal your time. We call these actions or activities *time thieves*. They need to be attacked and eliminated.

Attack

Many things steal our valuable time. A knowledge and awareness of such factors is a vital step in eliminating them. You should be aware that time thieves may be hidden beneath the sterile tasks listed in your activity log.

In Application Task 15.5 is a list of some of the major time thieves. Place a tick next to the ones which you feel waste your time.

When you have identified activities or behaviours which unnecessarily waste your time you must work towards eliminating them.

There are two types of time thieves you need to attack. The first, we call *outside thieves*: unwanted or long telephone calls and visitors, unstructured meetings, interpersonal conflicts and idle talk. The second type comes from *inside*: an inability to say no, indecision, procrastination, guilt, inability to prioritise or plan, and poor delegation skills. You have probably encountered both types.

We surveyed a large group of middle managers to discover what they considered to be their biggest 'time thieves'. We asked them to identify their ten activities or actions which wasted their precious time. Here is the list they arrived at.

- Too much time on the telephone.
- Poor delegation skills.
- Poor 'meetings' skills.

APPLICATION TASK 15.5

MY COMMON TIME THIEVES

Putting things off.	☐	Indecision.	☐
Worry.	☐	Poorly run meetings.	☐
Lack of confidence.	☐	Lack of delegation.	☐
Unscheduled meetings.	☐	Fatigue.	☐
Guilt.	☐	Perfectionism.	☐
Idle talk.	☐	Unclear goals.	☐
Lack of direction.	☐	Poor control.	☐
Inadequate planning.	☐	Poor writing skills.	☐
Time on the telephone.	☐	Doing others' work.	☐
Not listening.	☐	Not using 'prime time'.	☐
No written goals.	☐	Unclear communication.	☐
Depending on written notes.	☐	Long lunches.	☐
Not using set forms.	☐	Not using time-saving devices.	☐
Constant checking of staff.	☐	No routine.	☐
Not setting deadlines.	☐	Cannot say 'no'.	☐

- Interruptions by visitors.
- Procrastination.
- Too much paperwork.
- Inability to say 'no'.
- Poor communication.
- Poor office organisation.
- Perfectionism.

A scheme for delegating effectively is presented in Chapter 17 and the conduct of productive meetings is discussed in Chapter 16. We will concentrate on how to attack the eight remaining time thieves.

Thief 1: Inability to Say 'No'

Most of us have difficulty in saying 'no'. It is natural that we like to help others; we certainly do not want to offend anyone. You may avoid saying 'no', since becoming involved in many projects makes you feel important and needed. Saying 'yes' may make you feel busy or liked by others. Beware! If you accept any task at any time, people will begin to take an affirmative answer for granted.

> **Attack strategies:** Prioritise your actions and tasks. Consider every request on the basis of its importance to you and the organisation. If it is not important, or not one of your responsibilities, give a courteous 'no'. If someone is asking you to do part of his job, you are not doing him any favours by saying 'yes'.
>
> Try to train yourself to say 'no' in stages. Begin by saying 'no' to small requests. These, after all, are probably the items which steal most of your time. Then build up to saying 'no' to more substantial requests. The major question to ask yourself when someone asks you to do something is: Is it congruent with my goals and responsibilities or could someone else do it?

SUMMARY

Saying 'No':

- Prioritise your actions.
- Say 'no' if it is not important.
- Say 'no' if it is not your job.
- Begin by saying 'no' to small requests.
- Ask: 'Could someone else do it?'

Thief 2: Too Much Time on the Telephone

How much time do you spend on the telephone? How much time do you need to spend on the telephone? Most of us spend more time than we need. Some of the main reasons for this are:

- Talking for too long.
- Engaging in unstructured conversations.
- Being unable to terminate conversations.
- Accepting all calls.
- Not using the secretary properly/ no secretary.

Attack strategies: The first action to take is to separate idle chat from purposeful discussion. An initial 'Good to hear from you, how are the kids?' is acceptable but do not let it go on for too long. When you are making the call, plan in writing what you want to discuss. Stick to these items and try not to get sidetracked.

Many managers cannot finish a conversation. If you initiate the call, perhaps you could begin with something like: 'Afternoon Jenny, I'm a bit rushed so...'. If you receive a call which drags on, use an expression such as: ' Before we finish up...'.

The final two strategies are interrelated. If you answer your own phone or have the telephonic equivalent of an 'open-door policy', you are probably wasting time. Instruct your secretary (if you have one) to 'buffer' or 'limit' your calls. Have all calls screened, limiting the ones you accept to those which are important. To do this you may have to establish some system of prioritisation with your secretary. If you do not have a secretary you may consider taking your phone off the hook or redirecting calls when you need to concentrate. You will find it difficult to work on any in-depth task if you allow the phone to control your day.

SUMMARY

Too Long on the Telephone:

- Separate chat from important discussion.
- When calling, plan what you want to say.
- Learn to terminate a conversation.
- Have your calls screened.
- Take your telephone off the hook.

Thief 3: Interruptions by Too Many Visitors

'Just thought I'd drop in to say hello. I can't seem to work today. Could I trouble you for a cup of coffee?' It has happened to us and it has almost certainly happened to you, usually when you are in the middle of something really important. Sometimes it is your own fault. Many managers adhere to what is labelled the open-door policy. They tell their staff to come and see them whenever they have a problem or 'just to have a chat'. What they are actually saying is: My time is unimportant – come and take it.

Even if you do not have an open-door policy you are probably constantly interrupted by visitors for a variety of reasons. Many managers have no plans to avoid these disruptions. Others are unable to terminate a conversation and are afraid of being rude.

Attack strategies:
1. Establish and communicate to employees when you are available. Institute a 'limited' open-door policy, perhaps Wednesday afternoon from 2 p.m. to 5 p.m. Even then, encourage visitors only if they have something important they need to discuss. This includes personal problems. Give yourself those vital blocks of time for working on important tasks.
2. Establish with your secretary a screening process whereby only those who really need to see you are admitted. Without a secretary, insist on people making appointments if they want to meet with you.
3. If unwanted visitors do get into your office, stand up to talk to them – or sit on your desk. 'I'm fairly busy at the moment Hal!' Set limits, and move them on as soon as possible. Try not to be rude, but you must be firm. If you have a choice, meet in someone else's office – it's easier to leave. These strategies can also be applied to a 'disruptive' boss.
4. Try to be ruthless with your time but gracious with people; after all, you must still work with them and unwanted animosity could culminate in your wasting a great deal more time. If an employee does come into your office, consider using the following strategy:

    -   Try not to feel annoyed.
    -   Listen carefully.
    -   Do not interrupt.
    -   Get to the point and say 'no' if necessary.
    -   Go back on task following interruptions.

SUMMARY

Interruptions:

- Restrict the time when you can be seen.
- Inform people when you will be available.
- Establish a screening process.
- Do not make unwanted visitors feel welcome.
- Control interruptions but be courteous.

Thief 4: A Disorganised Office

Having a disorganised office and desk is almost certainly an indication that *you* are not organised. Try the following short questionnaire. If you answer 'yes' to any of the following questions you probably need to reorganise your office. Simply answer 'yes' or 'no'.

Questionnaire

DO I WORK IN AN ORGANISED OFFICE?

	Yes	No
1. Does it take you more than five minutes to locate something on your desk?	☐	☐
2. Do you constantly have trouble finding a particular item on your desk?	☐	☐
3. Do you have stacks of files sitting on your desk for long periods?	☐	☐
4. Do you usually read and even keep all the junk mail that you receive?	☐	☐
5. Do you ever go through the papers on your desk and find things you had forgotten?	☐	☐
6. Do you find it difficult to find that certain file in your filing cabinet when you need it?	☐	☐
7. Do you have to get up from your desk every time you need something for your work?	☐	☐

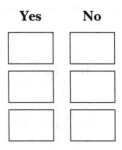

	Yes	No
8. Do you have papers on your desk that have been there for over a week?		
9. Do you feel everything would improve if you had a bigger desk/office?		
10. Do you just leave papers on your desk without indicating when they have to be dealt with?		

If you answered 'yes' to more than half of the items you probably have a disorganised office which results in your wasting time. Even if you had one 'yes' you should think about how you can improve that particular aspect. If you answered 'no' to all the questions there is a good chance that you have an organised office and time wastage is minimised.

Perhaps you have not seen the top of your desk for quite some time. Some managers waste considerable amounts of time searching for 'misplaced' files. Perhaps you have to get up frequently to locate items you consistently use. We have been into some offices which look like the result of a natural disaster. If your office approximates this description, the chances are that you are wasting time.

Your desk itself should be tidy and you should know where everything is. If you are away from your office as you read this, a good test is to draw the surface of your desk, putting all items in their correct location. If you can do this without too much trouble, you probably have a reasonably tidy desk. If you cannot remember where things go, or what is on your desk at this moment, perhaps you need to give it some attention.

Attack strategies:
1. Have as little on your desk as possible. Only allocate space to the items you constantly use, for example, telephone, in and out trays and pens. By doing this you will have space to work on the project at hand. Only have your current task on your desk. Do not let piles of paper mount up – these will only take up valuable space and can also be distracting.
2. Try to have everything you need within easy reach: files, project folders, computer terminal, calculator – anything you use or need on a regular basis.
3. Designate a place for everything and keep it there. This helps prevent those frustrating moments when you cannot find what you want, just when you need it most.

4. Have a workable filing system. How you do this is up to you: numerical, colour-coded, alphabetical. File regularly and throw away redundant items. You may find you could reduce the weight in your filing cabinet by half if you went through it now and discarded out-of-date items.

These are only a few strategies; others can be found in the many texts on time management. There is no one best way to organise your office. The best advice is probably to try out a number of arrangements until you find the one which suits you. Even then, keep experimenting until you identify an arrangement which supports your work and reduces distractions.

SUMMARY

Disorganised Office:

* Only have what you need on the desk.
* Have necessities within easy reach.
* Have a designated place for everything.
* Have a workable filing system.
* Discover what suits you.

Thief 4: Procrastination

We are all familiar with this thief. It is most prevalent when we have something really important or unpleasant to do, or a major decision to make. It rarely strikes us when we have low-priority or routine tasks at hand.

Procrastination manifests itself in idle conversations, going through mail for a second time, filing papers or tidying the desk. Procrastination eats away at our time regularly. How many times have you thought: 'I'll start that task tomorrow, I don't have time now?'

Attack strategies:

1. Lakein (1989) offers the best advice for overcoming procrastination. If you are faced with a daunting or unpleasant task, just do a little at a time. Break it up into small pieces and attack them one at a time. Even if you only have ten minutes, start the task: chip away at it. Lakein calls this the 'swiss cheese' method. He also suggests that you reward yourself when you complete subtasks.

2.   Do not put low-priority work before high-priority tasks. It is easy to do the less important tasks first. After all, they make you feel busy and allow you to justify avoiding the vital tasks.

3.   Teach yourself to '*do it now*'. If you do not want to do the task, make yourself. Do it now and get it out of the way. Try to substitute a '*do it now*' attitude for the procrastination habit.

4.   Recording and remembering your goals will also help defeat procrastination. An adherence to these will focus your actions on what is important.

5.   Set times to begin your work, not just for when you will finish. Try to stick to these 'startlines' like you do to deadlines.

SUMMARY

Procrastination:

- Do a little of the task at a time.
- Do important tasks first.
- *DO IT NOW* .
- Remind yourself of your goals.
- Set and stick to deadlines.

Thief 5: Perfectionism

Before we deal with perfectionism, you will find it useful to complete the questionnaire Am I a Perfectionist?

We all derive satisfaction from a job well done. Some managers however are so consumed by having to complete a job perfectly that they needlessly waste time. If you expect and demand perfection in everything, you risk never being satisfied with the end results. You will either end up doing everything yourself, because you believe you are the only person capable of such perfection, or you will alienate and frustrate employees and colleagues alike, because their outputs will 'never be good enough'.

Questionnaire

AM I A PERFECTIONIST?

Circle the number which best describes you.

This does not describe me   :   1

It describes me at times   :   2

This describes me perfectly   :   3

1. If I want a job done properly I must do it myself.	1	2	3
2. I set myself very high expectations and never give up until I reach them.	1	2	3
3. I usually do more than three drafts of a letter.	1	2	3
4. I will extend my deadlines if I am not satisfied with the job: I do this often.	1	2	3
5. I am always correcting others at work and at home.	1	2	3
6. When I reread work I have done I am rarely satisfied with it.	1	2	3
7. I often get 'stuck' on small details when working on a task.	1	2	3
8. I am afraid of making a mistake – I don't like it and neither do others.	1	2	3
9. My employees say that I am always hard to please – I want it done perfectly.	1	2	3
10. I don't like to ask others for help.	1	2	3
11. I don't delegate too much because I still spend too much time supervising the work.	1	2	3
12. If I don't believe I can do a really good job, I don't attempt it.	1	2	3

Total your score and place it in the box. If your score is over 24 you may be too much of a perfectionist. In other words, you are hung up on getting everything exactly right all the time. Few tasks are ever exactly as you would like. You must learn to accept this or you may be wasting too much of your time.

Total

If you tend towards over-perfectionism you will shy away from correct delegation, believing no one can do the job without close supervision. You may also shy away from requesting assistance because of a fear of making mistakes. Perhaps you will have a tendency to constantly extend deadlines to permit you to 'just make sure those final details are exactly right'.

If you are always reorganising files, searching for the perfect system, do you have time left for the more important work? One manager considered himself an expert in detecting even the most minor mistakes in any piece of writing: small grammatical and typographical errors, even the quality of print. There were rumours that he even corrected the graffiti in the bathrooms! He was thorough, but seemed to spend so much time searching for mistakes that he achieved little else.

Attack strategies: Prioritise your work! Do not spend time trying to perfect low-priority tasks. Ask yourself: does the time commitment justify the quality of the output?

It is permissible to concentrate on some details, but not when it prevents you from seeing the 'big picture': what you are there for. Ensure you are aware of your priorities. Do not become so distracted by trivia and detail that you ignore what is really important in your job. To be effective, speed is often as vital as accuracy. Prioritise your actions, trust others to complete tasks and concentrate on what is really important.

SUMMARY

Perfectionism:

- Prioritise your work.
- Do not spend time on low-priority tasks.
- Keep your eye on the 'big picture'.
- Do not be distracted by trivia.
- Trust others to do a job.

Thief 7: Too Much 'Paperwork'

If you fit the profile of the typical manager, even in the age of computers, you are constantly dealing with paperwork: reports, memos, letters, fliers, leave forms..., the list is almost endless. What do you do with the paper that arrives on your desk each day? Do you pile it up and hope it will go away? Or do you file everything – just in case you might need it?

As well as receiving paper, managers are notorious for generating it. We know of a school principal who always communicated with his deputy and department heads by memos, sometimes up to twenty a day. The deputy's office was just next door! Taylor (1989) suggests some reasons why we write so much:

1. To cover ourselves if something goes wrong.
2. To increase our visibility.
3. To impress the boss.
4. To justify our existence.
5. For enjoyment.

Do you write for some of these reasons? If so you may be guilty of producing useless paperwork without good reason. Too much paperwork then is a two-pronged problem: we get too much and we often produce too much.

Attack strategies: When you receive your mail, or any incoming paper, set aside a time each day for dealing with it. Sit at your desk with the rubbish bin at your side. Then go through it. First, skim what you have received and *immediately* do one of the following.

1. Throw it away.
2. Delegate it.
3. Do it.
4. File it (a) long term;
        (b) for further action.

It is probably true that 80 per cent of mail can be dealt with immediately. When you have finished your sorting, the rubbish bin should be fairly full. When you decide to delegate the handling of certain items, write the person's name on it and hand it over straight away. If you must do it yourself think about the best way to proceed. Do not write a reply unless you have to and use the phone whenever possible: it is much quicker than writing.

It is important that you try to handle each piece of paper only once. You can usually throw it away once it has been dealt with. Some of the paper you receive will need to be filed. Some you can file permanently or semi-permanently, but take care when deciding to do this. Ask yourself how long it should be filed for. Note expiration dates on what you file so you are aware when it can be discarded. Ensure your files are labelled appropriately and afford easy access. Go through files at set intervals (every six months or so) and throw away anything you do not need. You may be surprised to discover you missed a few deadlines for replies: probably no one has bothered and it has not had any adverse effect.

Other items will need to be kept close at hand for follow-up action. It is a good idea to have these files near your desk and, if necessary, to organise them into task or project folders.

Do not produce more paper than is absolutely necessary. Verbal communication is much less time-consuming and is often suitable for minor tasks. When you do have to write, keep it simple. Use form letters and get straight to the point. To begin organising your paperwork, look around your office and classify your 'paper' according to the categories listed earlier. You will be surprised how much cleaner your office will be when you finish.

SUMMARY

Too Much Paper:

- Set aside time each day to deal with mail.
- Prioritise and categorise your 'paper'.
- Do not write a reply unless it is necessary.
- Use the phone whenever you can.
- Handle each paper only once.
- Communicate verbally.
- When you must write, keep it simple and to the point.

Thief 8: Poor Communication

Another factor which wastes your time may be inadequate communication within your organisation. If employees do not know what is expected of them they will either be continually harassing you to find out what they should be doing or, worse still, not doing what is expected. We often communicate with subordinates using the wrong medium. Writing memos to someone in the next office is probably quite inappropriate for example, unless it is absolutely necessary to have written evidence. Your job as a manager is to streamline communication structures so you do not waste time telling people the same things over and over again.

Attack strategies: Think about what you have to communicate and decide which medium is most suitable: meeting, telephone, bulletin board, memo, etc. Match the level of the communication to those involved and the complexity of the task. Take care not to over-communicate. If you are asking an employee to carry out a specific task, provide only the information he will require to do the job. Read the memo in Figure 15.5 from a manager to one of her employees. Is it an example of over-communication?

Figure 15.5

Memo 7/6/91

To: Bob

From: June

Would you please proceed to the DINLOW warehouse located on the corner of Douglas and Jeffrey Streets to collect several cartons of multi-purpose, irridescent PD86913 marking tape for use by the employees on the second level. The tape comes in five colours: blue, red, green, black and purple. Please pick up the above-mentioned items between 15.00 and 17.00. I have made appropriate arrangements with Mr William Lew for you to collect the PD86913's from the DINLOW warehouse between these hours. Mr Lew is the supervisor and his office is third from the left on the right-hand side of the second warehouse annex nearest to Douglas Street. I believe the complex is well signed and Mr Lew will be at the warehouse between 15.00 and 17.00. He will ask you to sign a sheet attesting to the collection of the PD86913's when you arrive. When you have collected the PD86913's please bring them back here.

How could June have communicated more effectively? She could have reduced almost all the detail she provided. Bob probably did not need 80 per cent of it. In fact, June probably could have simply telephoned Bob to tell him what to do. If she had to write a memo, a much simpler form would have been more appropriate and saved her a great deal of time. You would find it useful to try rewriting the note, including only the essential information.

Ensure lines of communication are established and understood by employees. You should be able to feed information into the system quickly and simply and know it will reach its destination in an understandable form. Only write or meet if you have to brief on a group basis. Use 'language' which is common and understandable by everyone.

SUMMARY

Poor Communication:

- Decide which medium is most suitable.
- Match communication to task complexity.
- Do not 'over-communicate'.
- Ensure lines of communication are open.
- Use understandable language.

There are many other time thieves and suggestions for overcoming them. We have dealt only with what we consider the most significant ones. You must be aware of what wastes your time. To do this, return to the list of time thieves you identified from My Common Time Thieves and select the three 'thieves' which you believe waste most of your time: those which prevent you from getting on with the job. By doing this you are prioritising your time by planning. Use Application Task 15.6 to identify those time thieves and plan for their elimination.

APPLICATION TASK 15.6

ATTACKING 'TIME THIEVES'

TIME THIEF NUMBER 1 _____

1.   What will I do to help solve the problem?

2.   How can others help me solve the problem?

3.   Develop a brief 'attack plan' for dealing with the problem. Set a
     deadline for overcoming it.

TIME THIEF NUMBER 2 _____

1.   What will I do to help solve the problem?

2.   How can others help me solve the problem?

3.   Develop a brief 'attack plan' for dealing with the problem. Set a deadline for overcoming it.

TIME THIEF NUMBER 3 _____

1.   What will I do to help solve the problem?

2.   How can others help me solve the problem?

3.   Develop a brief 'attack plan' for dealing with the problem. Set a deadline for overcoming it.

Stott, K. and Walker, A., *Making Management Work.* © 1992 Simon & Schuster (Asia) Pte Ltd.

When you identify your 'thieves' and think about how to eliminate (or at least reduce) them, you are on the way to having more time for those important tasks. You should now be ready to arrange your time on a more permanent basis.

Arrange

Any number of time management 'tips' become irrelevant if you do not arrange your time. More than likely you will quickly regress to your old habits. By this stage you should be aware of where you are going (goals), have analysed how you presently spend your time, assigned priorities to your actions and begun to plan how to eliminate time thieves. We will now attempt to tie these stages into a system for arranging and managing your time.

The key to planning your time is deciding what you want and need to do and then deciding when to do it. We suggest you use two types of planners: A Yearly Planner and a Week/Day Planner.

A Yearly Planner

This type of planner may be placed on your wall or made portable enough to carry with you. On the planner you should record a number of things. We suggest a colour-coded system. You may, for example, want to use green dots to indicate your holidays: something to look forward to! Use a red 'warning dot' to signal when any major reports or presentations are due: regular yearly or biannual reports, or promotion exercises. You can also block in regular meetings you must attend and preplanned business trips.

By recording all these dates (and times) you will know approximately how much time you have available. You may be surprised at how little is left. Of course, you will need to update the planner fairly regularly.

If you decide to use such a planner you may wish to consider displaying a duplicate outside your secretary's office to inform staff of your schedule. If you decide to do this, add the times when you will be available to them for appointments. This serves the dual purposes of keeping them informed of what you are doing and subtly letting them know when you are and are not available. Make sure you keep both planners up to date. If this is impractical, perhaps you could put a staff calendar up a month at a time.

A Week/Day Planner

A planner such as the one shown in Figure 15.6 gives you a more detailed system for planning your work. Decide what needs to be done during the week and then prioritise your actions. Before you do this however, transfer relevant information from the yearly planner. So before you schedule the week's events your planner may already be somewhat full. At this stage it may look like the planner in Figure 15.7.

Figure 15.6
Week/Day Planner (Form)

Date:			Week	Name:

	Mon.	Tue.	Wed.	Thu.	Fri.
9.00					
9.30					
10.00					
10.30					
11.00					
11.30					
12.00					
12.30	L	U	N	C	H
13.00					
13.30					
14.00					
14.30					
15.00					
15.30					
16.00					
16.30					
17.00					
17.30					
18.00					

Out of work hours:

Sat.

Sun.

Work Tasks	Correspondence	Appointments	Others

Tasks to be completed or started this week:

1.   By when: To whom:

2.   By when: To whom:

3.   By when: To whom:

Notes: (carry to next week)

Stott, K. and Walker, A., *Making Management Work*. © 1992 Simon & Schuster (Asia) Pte Ltd.

Figure 15.7
Week/Day Planner (Form)

Date: *17/4/92*				Week *10*	Name: *Judy Lafore*

	Mon.	Tue.	Wed.	Thu.	Fri.
9.00 9.30 10.00	*Plan week*	*in/out tray* *Self time*	*in/out tray*	*in/out tray* *Self time*	
10.30 11.00 11.30 12.00		*Self time*	*Weekly production meeting*	*Self time*	*Trip to Riverside*
12.30 13.00	L	U	N	C	H
13.30 14.00 14.30 15.00		*Walk around*	*Self time*	*Staff Appointments*	*Reflection Time*
15.30 16.00 16.30 17.00 17.30 18.00	*Open door for staff*			*Walk around*	

Out of work hours:	Sat.
Tape Gremlins II, 8.30 Ch 9 (Tue.) *Squash with Lorine, Th. 7.30 Slurp Gym.*	*Dinner at Malas* Sun.

Work Tasks	Correspondence	Appointments	Others
Phone (in/out)			

Tasks to be completed or started this week:

1.   By when: To whom:

2.   By when: To whom:

3.   By when: To whom:

Notes: (carry to next week)

Stott, K. and Walker, A., *Making Management Work*. © 1992 Simon & Schuster (Asia) Pte Ltd.

Next, write a list of everything else you know you have to do during the week. Your list may look something like this:

- Appraisal meeting with Andrea.
- Continue with request for increased staff complement.
- Tour floor each day.
- Check with Gayle on progress of negotiation with insurers.
- Check maintenance schedule for machines on second level.
- Speak to Mike regarding lighting in offices.
- Get three quotes for supplies for next year.
- Check on status of Fairchild orders.
- Ask Shirley to lunch regarding her leaving.
- Write follow-up letters to Marcia and Fred Crank.
- Set up meeting with boss.
- Phone all district managers: prepare for meeting on 12th.
- Think about new staff development policy.
- Fax: Longines regarding replacement workers.
- Anita's birthday 4 p.m. Thursday.

When you have as complete a list as possible, you must *prioritise*. You must prioritise your tasks and activities. Go through each task and prioritise it using the system explained in the *assign* section. Is the task important? Is the task urgent? Either prioritise the tasks numerically or place them in three categories: very important, important, not so important. Do the same for urgency. Then, slot your tasks into the vacant spaces on your Week/Day Planner. We suggest you be fairly generous when allocating time or you may fall behind. If you think something may take twenty minutes, allocate thirty and if you finish early, it is a bonus.

When 'filling slots', do not just place tasks anywhere. Remember you are planning and scheduling your priorities, not simply writing down what has to be done. Think carefully. Put your very important tasks, those which require careful reflection, into the slots you have reserved for yourself, 'self-time'. List letters and phone calls in the appropriate boxes. Perhaps these can be scheduled in the 'in-out tray' time or in those spare moments between activities. If they are really important set aside special scheduled time.

Similarly, list your appointments or other routine tasks in the appropriate boxes along the bottom of the planner. Then allocate time in accordance with their importance and urgency. Employee appointments can be scheduled in the appropriate time slot, the one set aside for staff colleague 'drop-ins'. Advertise such times and firmly discourage these types of visits at any other times. If employees do not use this time, it can be utilised for routine tasks such as filing: tasks which do not suffer if interrupted. This time is a bonus.

You should also utilise the planner to schedule your personal life. Work is not everything. Remember, your life must be a balance between work, personal, family and health-related goals.

Try to leave some time each day for unexpected activities or crises, but not too much. Crises will arise and you must be prepared to drop what you are doing and deal with them – this is part of your job. This requires that you be *flexible*. Try your best to adhere to planned activities but do not get frustrated, upset or 'stressed-out' if unanticipated events interfere with your plans. The fact that you plan carefully however should reduce the number of crises you face. Take five minutes each morning to go over or adjust your priorities for the day. Review and remind yourself of the purpose of the priorities.

By planning and scheduling by priorities (which are tied to your goals and responsibilities) you are making a very positive statement about the importance of your time.

Throughout the entire planning process, keep your goals or *key result areas* and primary purpose firmly in view. These should be the major force driving how you use your time.

An added advantage of planning your time as we suggest is that you can analyse your Week/Day and Yearly planners at regular intervals. This allows you to stay on top of time thieves. Take a short period of time at the end of each day to record any extra tasks you did during the day which had not been planned for. Keep your planners for a month or six weeks and then analyse their content as you did your time log. If, for example, you find you are beginning to spend too much time on the phone, it may be time to consciously renew your attack on the problem.

Energy Cycle

Some managers and management writers suggest you identify when you work best. For you, is it in the morning, afternoon or night? They suggest you isolate these times and, if possible, schedule your most important tasks during the time when you seem to work most effectively. Perhaps you can try this yourself.

Arranging your time is vital for continued efficient and effective time management. You cannot simply start at this stage however. Unless you identify what is really important to you and analyse your time usage in the light of your goals, the *arrange* stage will have very little power. Put your goals in a prominent position, refer to them, and update them as circumstances change. Adjust your time usage accordingly. Your goals also guide your assignment of priorities and focus your actions so you can eliminate activities that waste your time. The arrange stage then is the culmination of considerable 'lead-up' reflection and action. It includes elements uncovered in all the preceding stages.

Conclusion

Alan Lakein (1989) suggests ten time management secrets which work for him:

- Start with the most important parts of large projects; often it is unnecessary to do the rest.
- Keep pushing and be persistent when you are 'on a winner'.
- Handle each piece of paper only once.
- Clear the desk and put the most important item in the middle.
- Have a place for everything.
- Save trivia for one three-hour session each month.
- Give yourself special rewards when you do something important.
- Realise some time will be beyond your control; don't fret about it.
- Write replies to letters as soon as you receive them.
- Continually ask yourself: 'What is the best use of my time right now?'

In this chapter we have presented a practical system for more effective and efficient time utilisation. We have stressed the importance of setting goals and becoming aware of other factors which can influence your time usage. We emphasised the analysis of your current time expenditure to provide a knowledge of where your minutes go. We also suggested methods for prioritising what you do and some strategies for overcoming some of the most common time thieves. Finally, we suggested a system for arranging and planning your time that you can implement on a permanent basis.

SUMMARY

Managing Your Time:

- Decide on what is really important to you and write it down.
- Develop an awareness of your behaviours, habits and methods of communication.
- Know what you are responsible for in your job, and what you are not responsible for.

- Find out how you are actually spending your time.
- Look closely at how you use your time.
- Sort your tasks and actions in terms of what is really important to you.
- Consider how much time you have to complete a task.
- Identify actions which waste your time and consciously try to eliminate them.
- Organise and plan your time in accordance with what is really important to you.
- Monitor your time usage on an ongoing basis.

Since you have got this far, you have invested a considerable amount of time just reading the chapter. We have attempted to provide a realistic scheme for managing your time. It is now up to you to implement it if you find it worthwhile. Be aware that this may require a substantial extra time commitment in the initial stages, but you should reap the benefits before too long.

We conclude with an exerpt from *The Unorganised Manager, From Damnation to Salvation*. Do not be a manager like Richard.

St Peter: You are the most unorganised person I know. Why don't you ever plan anything?

Richard: I do...Well, I haven't got time for planning.

St Peter: Without planning, you'll never have time for anything.

Richard: Look, I can't sit around planning what to do. I have to get on and do it. I'm harassed, overworked and I haven't got the time...

(Video Arts, 1984 : 20)

References

Drucker, P. (1966) *The Effective Executive*, Harper and Row : New York.
Huffstutter, S. and Smith, S. (1989) 'Managing time and stress', in Smith, S. and Piele, P. (eds.), *School Leadership: Handbook for Excellence*, ERIC : Oregon.
Lakein, A. (1989) *How to Get Control of Your Time and Life*, NAL : New York.
MacKay, I (1989) *35 Checklists for Human Resource Development*, Gower : England.

MacKenzie, R. (1972) *The Time Trap: How to Get More Done in Less Time*, McGraw-Hill : New York.

Mintzberg, H. (1973) *The Nature of Managerial Work*, Harper and Row : New York.

Mintzberg, H. (1975) 'The managers job: folklore and fact', *Harvard Business Review*, July–August.

Sexton, M. and Switzer, K. (1978) 'The time management ladder', *Educational Leadership*, **35**, 6, pp. 482–83 and 485–86.

Shinn, G. (1986) *Leadership Development*, 2nd edn, McGraw-Hill : New York.

Stevens, L. (1984) 'Administrative techniques: the principal's time', *NASSP Bulletin*, **68**, 468, pp. 59–63.

Stewart, R. (1986) *The Reality of Management*, Pan : London.

Taylor, H. (1989) *Time Management*, Eagle Trading : Malaysia.

Video Arts (1984) *So You Think You Can Manage?*, Methuen : London.

Chapter 16

Running Productive Meetings

Meetings, Meetings!

It is sometimes said that the best meeting is a committee of three with two absent.
(Welsh, 1980 : 69)

Meetings are a regular source of complaint in most organisations. Many people seem to think that if they can string two words together coherently, they are capable of running meetings, and that is where the problem starts, because meetings are thought to be forums for talking when, in many cases, they should be about action – doing things.

How often have we heard the cry that everything is talked about, but nothing ever happens. If this is your organisation, department or section, then you will find it difficult to convince your employees that meetings serve any purpose other than that of using up valuable time.

The aims of this chapter then are:

- To examine the reasons why some meetings are more successful than others.
- To identify the behaviour which best contributes to the effectiveness of meetings.
- To consider what can be done to make organisation meetings more effective.

After a brief look at the all too familiar shortcomings of meetings, we examine some guidelines for conducting effective and productive meetings. In particular, we consider what you should do before, during and after the event. Good preparation and appropriate follow-up action are essential, as is your behaviour during the meeting itself. We then look at some matters related to setting up the right conditions, including the issues of membership and the physical setting. Finally, we provide some guidelines which will help you improve the meetings for which you are responsible.

It will be useful at this stage to gain a rough impression of your present level of ability in running meetings. If you actually organise and lead them, however infrequently, complete the questionnaire How Well Do I Run Meetings?

Questionnaire

HOW WELL DO I RUN MEETINGS?

When you hold a meeting: **Yes**   **No**

1. Are you always sure it is the best way of dealing
   with matters?   ☐   ☐

2. Are you convinced you are using expensive employee
   time wisely?   ☐   ☐

3. Do you always state the purpose simply and clearly?   ☐   ☐

4. Do you always brief members in advance?   ☐   ☐

5. Do you prioritise your agenda?   ☐   ☐

6. Do you allocate appropriate amounts of time to each
   agenda item?   ☐   ☐

7. Do you explain each agenda item and what is to be
   done at the meeting?   ☐   ☐

8. Do you encourage people to state their views?   ☐   ☐

9. Do you show that you value members' contributions?   ☐   ☐

10. Do you stop compulsive talkers from dominating the
    meeting?   ☐   ☐

11. Do you keep the discussion on the matter in hand?   ☐   ☐

12. Do you make regular summaries of the discussion?   ☐   ☐

13. Do you keep to time, both for agenda items and
    the meeting?   ☐   ☐

14. Do you repeat the main points and decisions at the
    end of the meeting?   ☐   ☐

15. Do you write down decisions, actions and people
    involved?   ☐   ☐

16. Do you identify the purpose of subsequent meetings?   ☐   ☐

	Yes	**No**
17. Do you summarise the meeting's business in the minutes?	☐	☐
18. Do you inform other interested people about what went on?	☐	☐
19. Do you monitor agreed actions to ensure they stay on course?	☐	☐
20. Do you consider who should really attend and who should not?	☐	☐
21. Do you try to keep the meeting size as small as possible?	☐	☐
22. Do you arrange it at a time when people can concentrate easily?	☐	☐
23. Do you try to keep your meetings as short as possible?	☐	☐
24. Do you choose a location which is free from interruptions and distractions?	☐	☐
25. Do you arrange the furniture in the way you want it?	☐	☐

You should have answered 'yes' to at least some of the questions. The relevance of each of the twenty-five questions will be explained as you read through the chapter.

We were recently with the chief executive of a public sector organisation and he claimed proudly that he believed in a completely participative style of management, showing us the agenda of his last staff meeting. It had thirty-seven items on it! He maintained that by involving staff in all decisions, they could never complain about being left out. We doubt whether his colleagues shared his enthusiasm for the four-hour epics which could hardly be described as productive use of expensive professional time. As a manager, you have a great responsibility to ensure that precious time is not being wasted.

Of course, not all meetings are about decisions or consequent action. They may be arranged to give information, but the question arises as to whether this could be dealt with in another way. If it involves straightforward dissemination with little discussion, a note sent to all interested parties would probably do the job more economically. If, however, comment is required or if there could be misunderstanding, then a meeting is appropriate. Similarly, if it is important that employees listen to a certain person because he has the status, knowledge or information, then that may be another good reason to bring people together. Below are some important functions which meetings might serve:

Testing out the Quality of Decisions

Although many criticisms have been raised about meetings, they can be excellent vehicles for testing out ideas and developing creative solutions to problems. By encouraging members to engage in constructive criticism, only quality ideas will survive and you will avoid the disappointments caused by failing to put decisions to the test of critical scrutiny. You have to be careful here though. Some people have great skill in taking ideas apart and finding the faults in them. This is a good thing but it can also turn into a destructive exercise and cause many upsets.

Getting a Message Across to a Group of Employees

Meetings are also suitable for conveying a message to a group of employees, but they should be used for this purpose only sparingly. You have to think carefully before taking many people away from their jobs and generally disrupting the progress of work. But if you want to say something important, it may be better to hold a meeting rather than let the 'rumour mongers' go to work.

Building Up Team Cohesion Within the Organisation or Department

Many talk about the team-building attributes of meetings as a form of justification for the inadequate gatherings for which they are responsible. They do help to build teams, but only if they are run well so that members are working together cohesively towards a common goal and are enjoying success in their efforts.

Tied in with the different purposes are the different types of meetings. Any single organisation may have board meetings, production meetings, daily, weekly or monthly meetings, sales meetings, staff meetings, advisory meetings and special project meetings, not to mention committees and, in some organisations, quality circles. The list is seemingly endless. Although different imperatives may exist, the fundamental principles are similar.

It also has to be recognised that some meetings are more formal than others, involving rigid rules and procedures. In this chapter, we are concerned primarily with those meetings which are organised and led by you and which are conducted in comparative informality, but many of the points we make may well relate to behaviour possible in more formal sessions.

You should now consider your own experiences of good and bad meetings. You will probably know intuitively if they have been of any use, but it will be helpful for you to analyse the factors which have led to them being effective or a waste of time. By completing Application Task 16.1, Thinking about Meetings, you should reach some initial conclusions on the influencing factors, including the behaviours adopted by participants. You should also find some consistency between what went on at the meeting and its outcomes: generally, good meetings achieve things and poor ones do not.

Having thought about several issues related to effective and ineffective meetings, ask yourself the following questions:

- What are the factors most likely to make meetings successful?
- What are the factors most likely to make meetings a waste of people's time?
- What behaviour contributes to the success of meetings?
- What behaviour makes meetings ineffective?

We shall be looking at the first and third questions a little later. First we examine some of the reasons for managers using expressions like 'a waste of time' and 'ineffective'.

Poor Meetings

If you talk to managers about poor meetings, the same complaints can be heard time and time again. These are some of the common reasons given for meetings failing to achieve very much.

There Is No Clear Reason for Bringing People Together

Have you ever been to a meeting where there is nothing to discuss of any significance but the meeting takes place anyway because it is on the regular schedule? Your answer may well be: 'Yes, every week!' You may even be the person who organises these 'events'. We sometimes hold meetings because people get used to the idea and they seem to enjoy them. Many become accustomed to the idea of attending meetings because they are probably an escape from real work. Even those temporary havens from reality wear thin, though. If you insist on getting your people together for reasons of *esprit de corps*, bear in mind there are far more interesting ways of conducting social gatherings than sitting round a table in the company's meeting room.

They Make Even the Simplest Things Complicated

It is amazing how often meetings manage to make life more complex than it really is. The reason is simple. Meetings were never designed for dealing with trivial affairs which could easily be handled by one person. So when you put several people together to discuss whether the cleaner should be given

APPLICATION TASK 16.1

THINKING ABOUT MEETINGS

Think about two meetings in which you have recently been involved at work. You may have been in charge or you may have been a participant. One of the meetings should have been, in your opinion, a successful one, and the other a poor one. Answer the questions below.

THE SUCCESSFUL MEETING | THE POOR MEETING

What was the meeting's purpose?

What was the meeting's purpose?

What made it a good meeting?

What made it a poor meeting?

What did you and others do to help?

What did you and others do to hinder?

Did you contribute and, if so, how? (Asked, volunteered, etc.)

Did you contribute and, if so, how? (Asked, volunteered, etc.)

What were the outcomes?

What were the outcomes?

a red brush or a blue one, do not be surprised when someone talks for fifteen minutes about the cost savings of buying yellow plastic-coated ones!

They Invariably Last Far Too Long

How often have you attended a meeting which has finished early? If the answer is 'frequently' then it may be that the convenor is well organised or perhaps there was nothing to discuss and the meeting should never have been held anyway. But where productive issues are raised, meetings are generally managed in such a way that trivial matters get more time than they deserve and the really important things are cut short.

They Provide the Stage for Those Who Love the Sound of Their Own Voices

You can hear the moans: 'Oh no, here he goes again!' The chairman has probably made the mistake of asking if anyone has an opinion. That is the cue for the professional opinion expert to air his views, usually at length. He leaves the meeting satisfied that he has exercised his larynx, the chairman believes there has been involvement and participation, and everyone else is frustrated. Even worse, the talker and the chairman may be the same individual.

We have attended meetings which chairmen have used as forums to promote their own strongly held views, given others little opportunity to speak (and did not listen to them even when they got the chance) and then recorded in the minutes the decisions which the committee had 'agreed' on. Sometimes they bore little resemblance to what had actually been said at the meetings. There were enough crossword puzzles completed and letters written at these meetings to fill a book!

Members Avoid Making Decisions When Procrastination Will Do

Another common fault in meetings is to put decisions off. If the purpose was to reach a decision, then that is what should happen before the end of the meeting. Decisions tend to be avoided because the issues become complicated. The chairman may have failed to keep control of discussions and draw contributions together so that the issue remains clear and reasonably simple in everyone's mind.

They Seldom Result in Any Plans for Action

How often do you leave a meeting and the only thing which has been decided is when the next meeting will be held? There are many occasions when members should leave with something to *do*. There should be plans of action.

So these are poor meetings, ones with which we are all too familiar. However, meetings can be highly beneficial if run well. In the next section, we shall look at ways in which you can plan an effective meeting, engage in purposeful discussion, and end up with clear decisions and action plans.

Effective Meetings

Preparation

Decide first of all whether you really want a meeting or whether you could deal with matters in a more economical way. The best question to ask yourself is: 'What would happen if we didn't have the meeting?' If the meeting is sufficiently important, you should have a fairly convincing answer.

Secondly, you need to consider the purpose (which may well be related to your reason for deciding on a meeting). Is it to give advice, to generate some ideas or to make a decision? From this purpose, you should be able to devise your criteria of success. If the meeting is intended to thrash an issue out and then reach a decision, the criterion of effectiveness will be whether a decision is made based on relevant discussion and the weighing-up of options.

Explain to employees what the purpose of the meeting is. Write to them in advance stating in one sentence what the meeting hopes to achieve. Then you can use a paragraph to elaborate on the issue. Tell them what you expect of them, for example that they should read any attached documents, speak to their colleagues to gather views, be prepared to discuss the issue at the meeting and finally reach a decision on one of the options available. Figure 16.1 presents an example of such an advance notice that might be distributed to participants.

Ensure that each individual has prepared for the meeting. If it is an important issue you do not want people voicing opinions when they have neither read the necessary materials nor gathered the views of others. We were in one meeting where the chairman, an aggressive no-nonsense man, asked a committee member to leave the meeting and only return when he had read the discussion papers. Although it did not enhance the chairperson's relationship with the individual concerned, it meant that everyone was prepared for subsequent meetings, or they went on sick leave!

SUMMARY

- Decide if a meeting is necessary.
- Define the purpose.
- Write to those attending informing them of the purpose and what they should do.

Figure 16.1
Advance Notice

Policy Committee Meeting on 31 March 09.00 – 10.00

The purpose of this meeting is to reach a decision on whether to introduce a flexitime scheme for secretarial staff.

Recruitment difficulties have led the company to look into the possibility of attracting qualified staff who have family commitments. A major stumbling block is our office hours. There appear to be three options:

- Tolerate the present difficulties.
- Introduce a flexible scheme for those with family commitments.
- Introduce flexitime working for all.

Enclosed is a five-page discussion document which examines the relative advantages and disadvantages.

You are required to:

- Read the document and be prepared to offer opinions.
- Seek the general views of secretarial staff in your department.
- Be prepared to reach a decision by the end of the meeting.

The Agenda

Put an agenda together and give as much thought to the order as you do to the content. There are some things which must be discussed before others, so they must be aired first. The temptation is to think of everything and put it all down on the agenda. Remember our democratic chief executive and his thirty-seven items? We doubt whether he managed to do any prioritisation. It is best to include as few items as is realistically possible: treat it as a virtue to have short agendas. Sometimes you may have only one issue to discuss. It is still worth calling a meeting if it genuinely needs discussion.

You must ensure you have adequate time to discuss the important things and give less time to those items of little significance. What about the urgent things which inevitably crop up at the last minute, though? It is a good idea to get those out of the way so that you can focus your mind on the important issues. Give urgent items only a short amount of time and reach a decision quickly.

The agenda shown in Figure 16.2 is an example of failing to plan adequately. It had been circulated in advance.

Figure 16.2
An Unplanned Agenda

Meeting on 24 January, 10.00   Exec. Room

Agenda

1.   Staff canteen.

2.   Staffing position for 1 April.

3.   Visit of industrialists from Kenya.

4.   Revision of business strategies for next year.

5.   AOB.

At least the agenda was reasonably short (but not the meeting). The key item was number 4 which was central to the company's operation. An explanation of each item would have shown that some were of little importance, whereas the item relating to company direction and the impact which changing employment patterns were having in the area was critical to survival and success.

The item should never have been put so far down the agenda. Secondly, it needed to be supported with a statement and appropriate documents. Thirdly, members should have been given some preparation to do for such an important issue.

At the start of the meeting, the chairman said he had a lunch engagement at 12.00 and would have to leave at 11.30 sharp. The condition of the staff canteen seemed to be close to everyone's heart. If the chairman had made it clear on the agenda, the issue was about furniture replacement and the desirability of having unitary construction pieces instead of conventional tables and chairs. As it was, the discussion digressed into quality of food served, to the problem of drink machines breaking down and eventually on to staggered lunch breaks to ease the space congestion problem. At 11.00, the chairman moved on to the second item and reached the key item at

11.25, saying that, since it was so important, it could be deferred to the next meeting.

It is usually up to the chairman to set the agenda and priorities, although in some work settings, prioritisation can be dealt with at the beginning of the meeting amongst those present. A useful idea is to set a certain amount of time for each item and stick to it. Put the urgent items first and give them little time. Then allot sufficient time to the really important things. Let us look at the above agenda. The staff canteen was urgent because new furniture had to be ordered immediately to get the invoice through within the financial year. The staffing position item was simply a review of who was leaving the company and about the present response to advertisements. The foreign visitors item was merely a notification that it would take place and that members would be joining the party for lunch. It was worth putting on the agenda in case there were any questions of clarification but it was not important if it was not discussed. The new agenda might look like that shown in Figure 16.3.

Figure 16.3
A Well-Constructed Agenda

1. Canteen furniture – decision on unitary construction or traditional items.

    (5 minutes)

2. Strategies – there are indications our markets will change substantially next year in view of local population movement. Action plans to be drawn up to review strategy options available.

    (60 minutes)

3. Staffing position – to identify any potential problems with regard to recruitment.   (15 minutes)

4. Foreign visitors.   (5 minutes)

5. AOB.   (5 minutes)

> ## *SUMMARY*
>
> - Ensure the agenda contains only essential items.
> - Deal with urgent items first and give them little time.
> - Allocate most time to important items.
> - Prioritise the agenda, ensuring important items take precedence.

Conducting the Meeting

Purpose

Right at the beginning of the meeting, ensure that no one can be in any doubt as to why he is there. State the purpose. It should already appear on the agenda, but reinforce the message.

Interaction

The meeting is a time for interaction and exchange, not a monologue from the chairman (or anyone else for that matter). Similarly, it is not for closed discussions between the chairman and individual members. The active meeting is about 'a crossflow of discussion and debate, with the Chairman occasionally guiding, mediating, probing, stimulating and summarising, but mostly letting the others thrash out ideas. However, the meeting must be a contention of ideas, not people' (Video Arts, 1984 : 59). From this, it is clear that skilled chairmanship is essential.

The Chairman

The chairman has to exercise his skills even in the most informal settings. To start with you should recognise the need to employ strategies to get members involved. You should refer to them by name and ask for their comments and opinions. It is also best to ask those of junior status to 'chip in' first so that they are not intimidated by the contrasting views of senior personnel.

Being in charge is not easy. You often have to bite your tongue, knowing you have strong views and wanting others to be aware of them too! It is probably helpful to see the chairman as:

... the servant of the group, rather than as its master. His role then

becomes that of assisting the group toward the best conclusion or decision in the most efficient manner possible: to interpret and clarify; to
move the discussion forward; and to bring it to a resolution that everyone understands and accepts as being the will of the meeting, even if
the individuals do not necessarily agree with it. (Video Arts, 1984 : 60)

So apart from promoting participation, you should exercise control, ensuring
that one person at a time speaks (not to be interrupted by others), that
discussion stays on line and that personal disputes do not emerge. You have
to deal tactfully, but firmly, with vociferous individuals, those who try to hide
away, those who pretend to know it all, those who live in the past and those
who can only identify the faults of others and never their own.

Tack (1986 : 150) identifies seven types of people who, without skilful
chairmanship, are unlikely to do much to improve the quality of meetings.
He calls them: the *compulsive talker*, the *silent listener*, the *reminiscent member*,
the *team bigot*, the *timid member*, the *overbearing member* and the *blamer*. As
chairman, you have to focus their contributions and bring them into the
discussion at the appropriate moment. The reminiscer, for example, can be
very negative, dwelling on the 'good old days'. At the same time, he has
experience which you can draw on, and so long as you point him in the
direction of the future, he can make a useful contribution.

The one who seems to do all the talking (if the chairman lets him) is a
particular problem and we shall look at this briefly below. But one more type
we would add to the list, and which we consider the second-biggest potential
problem in meetings, is what we call the *digressor*, the one who meanders away
from the subject with consummate ease. In this situation you must be determined in your efforts to 'stay on line'.

Staying on Line

When the meeting is under way, we have emphasised the importance of
keeping control and ensuring discussions stay on line. If someone deviates
from the subject, interrupt and politely ask the person to stick to the matter
in hand. This can be done in a pleasant way: 'Peter, let me stop you there
a moment. I know you have some interesting views on flying saucers, but if
I could take you back to the central issue of staff morale, could you elaborate
a little on what you were saying about the effects of bonus schemes?'

The Perpetual Talker

A similar approach needs to be adopted with the perpetual talker, only you
have to be a little firmer: 'Jane, just hold on one moment please. I want to
bring Robert in here on this point as we only have limited time.'

If you use people's names and actually ask them for contributions, it makes it more difficult for those who like the sound of their voices to dominate the meeting. Avoid if possible saying 'Has anyone got views on this?' Your lime-light-seeker will respond even if he has nothing to say.

The chairman therefore has to prevent any single individual or group of individuals from taking over the meeting, and that includes himself! Because he is chairman that does not confer the right to talk more than anyone else.

Regular Summaries

Make regular summaries so that you retain your own understanding of what is being said and also to simplify matters for others. If you are not sure what someone means, ask for clarification. It is probably not your fault that you do not understand: it is more likely that the speaker has not assembled his ideas properly or is not voicing them articulately.

Discussion Stages in Problem-Solving Meetings

Margerison (1974 : 148), in looking at the way 'problem-solving' business meetings might be managed, identifies six main stages and draws attention to the important problem of people working at different stages at the same time. One person may, for example, be proposing a course of action, another weighing up options, and yet another trying to identify the real problem. You can see the ·difficulties here as almost three separate discussions are taking place. Little progress is possible.

What implications does this have for you as chairman? 'The essential thing is to know how to recognize when people are talking at different stages of the problem, and when members are mentally distant from one another. The manager must be able to do this and be able to guide people to concentrate on one area at a time.' Margerison (1974 : 148) then gives the guideline: 'When people are discussing at different stages, seek to return the conversation to the stage at which the difference first emerged.'

A systematic approach to such meetings will help to concentrate discussions on the correct stage. Firstly, the purpose has to be defined, followed by a diagnosis of the problem. Ideas are then generated and developed. Options are weighed in terms of their capacity to solve the problem and their acceptability to those involved. A decision is reached on the optimum solution and details about tasks, time, personnel and resources are identified. These issues are taken up in detail in Chapter 4, Planning Team Action.

Keep to Time

Stick very closely to the time you have allotted to each item. If you run over time, other items may have to be neglected. There are occasions however when you have to be flexible because of the nature of the discussion, but there is a difference between this and poor time management.

Reinforce Main Points and Decisions

At appropriate points, in addition to your regular clarifications and summaries, reiterate the main points and state the decisions which have been taken and the conclusions which have been reached. If it has been agreed that someone is to take action on something, then repeat what the action is, who will do it and the time deadline set.

At the end of the meeting, go over the main points yet again. This is an opportunity to summarise your summaries! After this there should be no misunderstanding. State the main points, including all conclusions and decisions, and specify the actions to be taken along with the names and time scales. If there is no secretary present, you can even use this as the writing of your minutes, which will save you a job later on.

Write It Down

Having repeated, summarised and reinforced, you need to ensure that everything is recorded in writing. In one of the meetings we described earlier, several of us were asked to contact two industrial colleagues for some information. At the next meeting, there was some dispute about who was supposed to make the contact and no one was aware it was supposed to be done in time for this next meeting. Furthermore, it was not exactly clear what information was required.

An example of what a simple record of the actions to be taken might look like is shown in Figure 16.4.

Figure 16.4
Record of Actions

Bob to contact our printers and find out why the last batch of leaflets was delivered late. He has authority to obtain quotation from another printer if necessary. To be done within three days and report back to the next management meeting.

Peter to discuss with senior staff in the typing pool possible changes in hardware and report back at the next meeting the general feelings.

Mary, Richard and Jane to look at the draft plan for relocating the finance office and produce a one-page report on the advantages and disadvantages of the two options. This to be done in time for the next meeting.

Ideas

Ideas are the lifeblood of many meetings. Such gatherings may indeed be arranged for the express purpose of finding creative solutions to problems. Your experiences at some meetings however may have told you that people are not always receptive to ideas, especially if they are thought up by other members. You may be familiar with some of the tricks some chairmen get up to in order to avoid change and the work which sometimes necessarily accompanies good ideas. If you want to suffocate ideas before they get a chance to breathe, you can:

- Quickly divert attention to another subject.
- Mention resource constraints and the present economic difficulties.
- State it is dangerous to try out ideas which are untested.
- End the agenda item.
- Suggest it is not really serious or practicable.
- Hint that something similar has been tried before and did not work.
- Identify the similarity to another idea.
- State what a good idea it is and still ignore it.
- Ridicule the individual who suggested it.
- Suggest changes so that it is modified out of recognition.
- Mention that the boss will not like it for some reason.
- Indicate that the originator is not fully conversant with the situation.
- Defer its discussion to another meeting and then omit it from the agenda.
- Give the originator so much work that he forgets about advancing ideas.

Of course, we are not suggesting for one moment that you adopt the above behaviours! Sadly, these tactics are often used. We have to recognise that meetings are unlikely to be effective if new ideas are not promoted and seriously discussed. If you chair a meeting try to ensure that participation is meaningful and supported. This means encouraging people to contribute and valuing their ideas and suggestions. You may still reject and discard ideas, but members must feel they have been treated seriously.

At the End of the Meeting

The purpose of the next meeting should be stated and when it is to be. It should be a direct consequence of what has taken place at the present meeting and not just an extension because you ran out of time.

Before you draw the meeting to a close, ensure you have achieved the purpose for which the meeting was called. If it was the intention to reach a decision, then make sure you have actually decided something and that everyone is sure what that decision is.

SUMMARY

Key Points in Conducting the Meeting:

- State the purpose of the meeting at the beginning.
- Encourage interaction.
- Refer to people by name when asking for views.
- Keep the meeting under control.
- Keep discussions on line and contributions to the point.
- Stop any one person or group from dominating discussions.
- Give regular summaries to facilitate understanding.
- Ask for clarification where necessary.
- Adopt a systematic approach in problem-solving meetings.
- Ensure members are discussing the same stage of the process.
- Actively encourage people to generate ideas in problem-solving situations.
- Keep to time, both for agenda items and the meeting as a whole.
- Repeat main arguments and reinforce decisions.
- At the end, summarise the main points of the whole meeting.
- Record the main items of information in writing.
- State the purpose of the next meeting and when it will be.

After the Meeting

Inform Others

So you have done all this and the meeting is over. Your job does not end there though. If you have kept your membership small, you will need to inform others who are concerned with the issues discussed. Send them some notes of what has taken place, but try to avoid distributing the rather daunting-looking sets of minutes which people file away without reading. In the same way you summarised all the main points covered during the meeting, now do the same on paper. Highlight the decisions taken and state briefly the implications. You can also outline the main arguments, but avoid excessive and irrelevant detail.

There are some pieces of information which it is advisable to include. The data serves as a record for future meetings. Include:

- Date of meeting.
- Names of those present.
- Agenda items:
  Main arguments;
  Decisions;
  Actions;
  Names of people involved.
- Length of meeting (and possibly time given to each item).
- Date, time and place of next meeting.

It is also advisable to underline or type in bold the important pieces of information, namely, the decisions reached and the actions to be taken.

There is no set way of dealing with this, but whatever method you adopt, you should make it as easy as possible for the reader to assimilate the important information. In Figure 16.5 is an extract from the minutes taken at a meeting of senior partners in a firm of management consultants. Although the discussion on the agenda item was fairly extensive, they captured the main points for this document which was circulated to their colleagues in the practice.

Figure 16.5
Extract from Minutes

Agenda item 2: Choice of project
We received two contract offers for projects at about the same time. We cannot accept both. A decision had to be reached on which one we should proceed with.

Main arguments:	Taylors are regular clients. They have given us fairly regular, but small, business in the past. If we refuse this one, they may employ another firm. PMW are new to us but the contract is worth five times the Taylor contract. This may be too much to turn down.
Decision:	Accept the PMW job. By widening the client base, we may open up scope for expansion. There may also be the opportunity for repeat business from PMW. Explain the situation to Taylors.
Actions:	John Dowson to meet PMW by 10 April to discuss details. He will prepare a project plan for the next meeting. Peter Williams to meet Taylors by the same date and explain the situation personally. He will try to negotiate a deferred contract.

Monitoring

Your remaining job is concerned with monitoring. It is not good practice to delegate actions during a meeting and then forget about them until they are due. You should monitor so that you know the people concerned are getting on with the tasks and the next meeting therefore will have all the information necessary. There is no need to overdo this part of the process, but simply to keep a watchful eye and to let your colleagues know you are concerned with and interested in what is going on.

SUMMARY

To make meetings in the organisation successful:

- Inform others of what took place.
- Highlight the decisions taken.
- Monitor agreed actions.
- Tell your employees clearly what the purpose is.
- Make sure everyone has done his or her homework.
- Prepare an agenda with items in the right order.
- Prescribe a certain amount of time for each item, and stick to it.
- Only let people talk if they have something useful and relevant to say.
- Do not invite everyone just because they have always attended.
- Make sure you achieve the purpose of the meeting.
- Make action plans and name people who are to do things.

Setting the Right Conditions

Who Should Attend?

When you next run a meeting, take a look at the members. Why are they there? Why is it those people in particular? What do they bring to the meeting with them in terms of knowledge, experience, abilities and so forth? Are there people there who have little to offer, but attend because they have always done so or because of their position in the organisation?

You are probably aware of this happening in several situations: the colleague who has always attended so it becomes a right; the individual who insists on participating because of status. These are not easy to deal with, but the composition of the group needs looking at, and where action is possible, you should do your best to reduce the size of your meetings to include only those who have a real contribution to make. That may mean the membership changes from time to time, and that can be healthy if the right people are involved.

In attempting, then, to make your meetings more manageable, the following factors should be considered:

1. Why is each person there?

    ■   Does he have control of relevant resources?
    ■   Does he know something which is related to the topic under discussion?
    ■   Does he have special skills which can be utilised?
    ■   Does he know appropriate people?
        (You should be able to answer 'yes' to one of these questions.)

2. Is the employee's position or status in the organisation influential in any way? In other words, can his presence help the business of the meeting because he is important, or, if he were not there, would the meeting's potential outcomes be hindered?

3. Are there considerations such as hidden interests or hurt feelings which should determine the meeting's membership? We often fail to take action that we know is right for fear of hurting someone's feelings. The purpose of the meeting should come first. Whilst we have to consider the effects of our actions on human relationships, successful task completion is of prime importance and it may be necessary to take an unpopular decision to improve the longer-term effectiveness of your meetings.

SUMMARY

- Consider members' contributions in terms of resource control, knowledge, skills and contacts.
- Consider membership also in terms of position, status, influence and developmental needs.
- Take actions where possible to reduce the numbers present so that only essential people are included.

How Large Should the Group Be?

Generally speaking, meetings have too many people at them. A greater degree of selectivity is needed if meetings are to become more productive. We all tend to assume that people have to be there because of their position or because of historical precedent. To be truly effective however we have to dispense with outdated notions and move towards practices which are enabling mechanisms – to ensure meetings really work.

One of the factors which might be considered is the complexity of the task. It is likely that problems with numerous dimensions require the contributions of a larger number of people. Bear in mind though that meetings become more unmanageable as the number increases, making the process counter-productive. Even if you do need more people to be involved, they do not necessarily have to be at every meeting. You may indeed call individuals in for specific items at scheduled times. This ensures that their time is not wasted sitting through items which are irrelevant to them, and that the business of the meeting is not impeded by the presence of too many people.

Another factor is the amount of participation which is expected of members. Are some there for the weekly snooze or are they in attendance to make a valuable input which could not be made in any way other than by attendance at the meeting? Ideally, each person should have something to bring, information or the results of tasks, and they should generally leave with specific things to do.

Most committees have an average of eight members; this is really too large and considerably reduces the effectiveness of the group in achieving tasks. Different studies have produced different 'ideal' numbers, but there is a general level of agreement that the smaller the group, the better the quality of work. For us, a meeting size of five or six has generally led to effective meetings, but a lot depends not only on the respective contributions in terms of expertise, but also the behaviour of individuals. This issue is taken up in detail in Chapter 5, Developing Team Roles. If the membership is much greater, there is less participation time, an increased chance of conflicts and subdivisions, and generally more people to listen to. 'The value and success of a committee meeting are seriously threatened if too many people are present. Between four and seven is generally ideal, ten is tolerable and twelve is the outside limit' (Video Arts, 1984 : 57).

SUMMARY

- Consider inviting relevant people to the part of the meeting which concerns them.

- Each person should generally have something to bring and leave with something to do.
- Keep the group as small as possible.

At What Time Should the Meeting Be Held?

The time at which the group meets can have a considerable impact on the meeting's quality. There are problems if the meeting is held very early or very late. People being inconvenienced can make concentration difficult. This is particularly true of meetings held after work or near to the close of the day when people are anxious to leave and are relatively tired. Under these circumstances, it is hardly surprising that hasty and poor-quality decisions are made. Think of the time when you have been anxious to leave a meeting for one reason or another. You have probably been willing to go along with almost any decision to expedite a speedy conclusion.

SUMMARY

- Hold the meeting at a time when people can easily concentrate.
- Inconveniencing people can lead to poor-quality decisions.

How Long Should the Meeting Be?

The length of a meeting can have a similar effect. People begin to get irritated, easily distracted and intensely bored. It is best to set a time limit in order to maintain concentration. If the business is unfinished, then reconvene on another occasion. There is nothing particularly courageous about soldiering on to the bitter end.

The use of frequent breaks is a useful strategy. Far from interrupting the concentration, it actually intensifies it, as people have time to reflect on the information and get things in perspective. They feel refreshed after a drinks break and the work is likely to be considerably sharper.

Breaks enable people to physically move which in itself can relieve anxiety and indifference. Where an extended break is just not possible, the simple act of standing up for a few minutes can have a beneficial impact. When you are in charge you can tell everyone there will be a two-minute break before the next item and members can stretch their legs. If you stand up yourself, you will probably find others do the same.

In organisation meetings the manager should become adept at reading the non-verbal signals that say people have had enough. Fidgeting and lack of eye contact, for example, are easy cues to spot. A verbal signal may be evident when people's tempers become easily frayed.

SUMMARY

- Take frequent short breaks.
- Get members to stand up and walk round for a few minutes.
- Watch for signals of irritation.
- Set strict time limits for the meeting.

Where Should the Meeting Be Held?

Like the time of day at which a meeting is held, it is best not to underestimate the effect which the choice of location has on a meeting. If it is held away from the work place in a pleasant environment this gives a very strong message to participants about their importance and the importance of the task. Another benefit is the absence of interruptions which are often unavoidable if the meeting is held on organisation territory. Noise, telephones and well-meaning visitors only serve to make the effective conduct of the meeting difficult.

Being realistic it is unlikely that you can hold regular meetings away from work. Generally you have to make the best use of what you have. Whatever the choice of location, the room should be well lighted with adequate ventilation. There should be no physical distractions and the seating should be comfortable. Do not accept conditions which could best be described as intolerable. If the meeting is important to you (and it should be) do something about your environment. If there is a telephone in the room, then take it off the hook or unplug it. If there are roadworks outside, close the window.

SUMMARY

The Location Should:

• Be well lighted.
• Have a comfortable working temperature.
• Have no physical distractions.
• Provide comfortable seating arranged suitably.

Seating Arrangements

Seating arrangements affect the flow of communication between people. It is best therefore not to accept the arrangement as it is in the room when you enter it but to move chairs and tables according to the purpose of the group meeting. It is worth spending a few minutes on this. If you want people to interact freely and without inhibition, a circular arrangement of chairs without tables is appropriate, assuming that you do not want your colleagues to write a great deal. If writing is involved then the same arrangement but with tables serves the purpose well. Ensure that senior employees do not sit together, because, even in an informal arrangement of furniture like this, it can be quite threatening for less experienced colleagues and you will not elicit the sort of contribution you want.

Small working groups will probably have a table round which everyone sits. It is worth finding a round table, as the shape has been shown through research to have a considerable impact on communication flow.

Where a formal presentation is being made to the employees, an appropriate arrangement would be a horseshoe shape or semi-circle for the audience with the speaker at a separate position in front. Visual aids can then be positioned next to the speaker. This ensures that the focus is appropriately located. Several different seating arrangements are shown in Figure 16.6.

SUMMARY

• Spend a few minutes rearranging the furniture if necessary.
• Some seating arrangements facilitate interaction.

Figure 16.6
What Seating Arrangement?

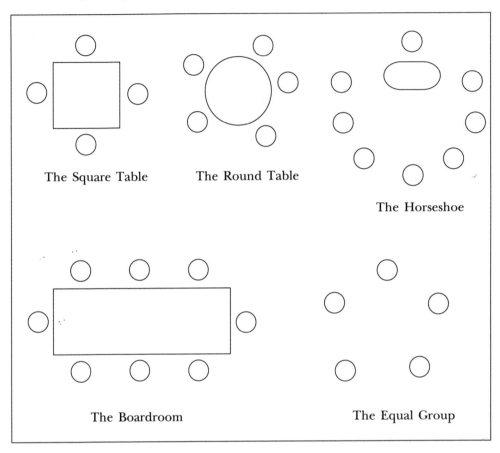

The Square Table   The Round Table

The Horseshoe

The Boardroom   The Equal Group

Improving Meetings: A Checklist

Figure 16.7 gives you a checklist of the action points listed throughout this chapter. The conduct of meetings is considered in three phases – before, during and after – all equally important if you are going to make them successful.

Before you conduct your next meeting, however simple it is, think about its improvement in advance by completing Application Task 16.2, Preparing for Your Next Meeting. By doing this you will ensure it is highly focused and that your agenda items have been appropriately prioritised.

Figure 16.7
Improving Meetings: A Checklist

BEFORE THE MEETING

1. Decide if a meeting is really necessary. ☐

2. Write down the purpose. ☐

3. List the intended outcomes. ☐

4. Put essential items on the agenda. ☐

5. Arrange the items in priority order and logical sequence. ☐

6. Allocate time to each item. ☐

7. Get all relevant information to hand. ☐

8. Send relevant preparatory documents to members. ☐

THE MEETING

9. Tell participants what it is about – simply. ☐

10. Invite specific contributions. ☐

11. Keep the discussion on line. ☐

12. Give regular summaries. ☐

13. Stick to the time for each item. ☐

14. At the end of each item, summarise decisions and actions. ☐

15. At end of meeting, summarise main points. ☐

16. Identify individuals, the actions and time scales. ☐

17. State purpose of next meeting and when it will be. ☐

AFTER THE MEETING

18. Let others know what happened. ☐

19. Highlight decisions made and actions to be taken. ☐

20. Monitor agreed actions. ☐

APPLICATION TASK 16.2

PREPARING FOR YOUR NEXT MEETING

Consider the next meeting you are scheduled to run. Prepare for it by completing the boxes below and then use this as a memory aid.

What is the purpose of the meeting?

What is the intended outcome?

Now plan the agenda below. First of all, write down your agenda items in the first column. Then use the second column to explain briefly why the item is included. The third column should be used to indicate the order of priority. The last column is for allotting the time for each item. Do not forget to give the most time to important items and the least time to the unimportant ones, even though they may be urgent.

AGENDA ITEM	RATIONALE FOR INCLUSION	PRIORITY	TIME

Stott, K. and Walker, A., *Making Management Work.* © 1992 Simon & Schuster (Asia) Pte Ltd.

Conclusion

In this chapter, we have tried to cover the key issues of running effective meetings and to encourage you to consider the way you do things. Preparation is central to ensuring success and at least as much time should be spent on this phase as the meeting itself. The time and effort spent in preparing the agenda, prioritising items and allocating time, and in preparing relevant materials, will help to ensure that the event fulfils its purpose. Similarly, conducting the meeting so that discussion is focused and so that members are actively encouraged to contribute will make it possible to conduct business efficiently and for members to feel a real sense of involvement in the process. Actions taken after the meeting are also important in making sure that others are kept informed and that agreed actions are actually going according to plan. Finally, setting the right conditions for meetings should not be overlooked. The impact of noise, interruptions, discomfort and just too many people present can reduce the potential effectiveness.

By trying to improve your preparation, conduct, follow-up action and meeting conditions, you will be going some considerable way to making your meetings worth the organisational time they consume.

References

Margerison, C. (1974) *Managerial Problem Solving,* McGraw-Hill : England.
Tack, A. (1986) *The High Quality Manager,* Gower : England.
Video Arts (1984) *So You Think You Can Manage?,* Methuen : London.
Welsh, A. (1980) *The Skills of Management,* Gower : England.

Chapter 17

Delegation

The best executive is the one who has sense enough to pick good men to do what he wants done and then the self restraint to keep from meddling with them while they are doing it.

(Theodore Roosevelt)

Delegation is a major part of the management process: getting things done through other people. Unfortunately it is a skill which is generally poorly practised and most managers find difficulty in going through the process with confidence. As a result many suffer the far-reaching consequences of attempting to do everything themselves.

With the complexity of tasks which senior and middle managers now face, delegation is the only way that things can get done properly with the organisation reaching its potential. Additionally, it is self-deceit to believe that one person can do everything. Just think of the many managerial tasks which are not receiving the attention they deserve.

Delegation is about giving employees the authority and resources to carry out a task. It involves motivating them. The manager though is still accountable, and it is unrealistic therefore, to believe that dishing out work and then forgetting about it is remotely associated with delegation. Unfortunately many people cannot see the difference.

In this chapter we shall explain what delegation is, and what it is not. We shall examine some of the general tenets of effective delegation and then attempt to relate some of the principles discussed to actual practice in your organisation.

Before you begin reading the chapter answer the questions in Application Task 17.1, Do I Delegate Enough?, to give yourself some idea about whether you need to delegate more.

APPLICATION TASK 17.1

DO I DELEGATE ENOUGH?

	True	Not true
1. I don't delegate because I can do the job more quickly myself.	☐	☐
2. Tasks pile up when I have to go on trips.	☐	☐
3. I'm really busy and have no time to think.	☐	☐
4. I always seem to be taking work home.	☐	☐
5. I don't delegate because my staff might learn as much as me; I could be replaced.	☐	☐
6. I don't want to just give away all my hard-earned experience.	☐	☐
7. I have to keep putting off important tasks because I am too busy to complete them.	☐	☐
8. My employees complain that they are not given any responsibility or say in decisions.	☐	☐
9. I know I need to spend more time planning but simply cannot find the time.	☐	☐
10. My employees never seem to get any better at what they are doing – no improvement or growth.	☐	☐

If you answered 'True' to any one of these questions you probably need to delegate more.

Stott, K. and Walker, A., *Making Management Work*. © 1992 Simon & Schuster (Asia) Pte Ltd.

What Is Delegation?

> Delegation: Telling him results required and giving him the authority –
> 'Do it your way and ask for help if required'. (Adair, 1988 : 152)

Delegation can be simply defined as a manager granting a subordinate the authority to act and make decisions on his behalf. It is more than simply 'getting work done through others', although this is certainly part of it. As both our initial definitions show, delegating is about giving an employee the *authority* to carry out a task and *discretion* on how the task will be completed. At the same time you retain ultimate *accountability* for the task; after all, you are the manager. There are different levels of delegation. We shall look at these in a moment.

Delegation is not simply 'giving out work', 'abdicating your responsibility' or 'giving orders and instructions'. Let us look at the difference.

When we discuss delegation we are referring to *effective delegation*. Many managers believe they are delegating when they are actually abdicating or simply telling employees what to do. We believe that ineffective delegation is the same as not delegating at all. Backing out or merely giving orders can have a detrimental effect on your own standing and organisational effectiveness. Figures 17.1 and 17.2 show the distinction between delegating and 'dishing out' work, and between delegation and abdication. If you do not delegate effectively you risk the following consequences:

- Unfocused employees, unsure of organisational direction.
- Uninvolved, uninterested employees.
- Losing touch with what is happening.
- Spending more time on co-ordination and supervision.
- Wasting organisational resources.
- Lower-quality decisions.

Giving out Work

When you give out work, strict instructions or give orders, you are directing, not delegating. You give the task and tell the person exactly how to do it and then check up on him frequently to make sure he is doing what he is told.

Abdicating

When you abdicate you do the opposite. You give up any responsibility for the job. You throw the task at the employee and tell him to do it and not bother you: 'Give it to me when it's finished, and don't mess up.'

Figure 17.1
Drawing the Distinction 1

DRAWING THE DISTINCTION 1.

When the manager delegates, the delegate:

Plans the way of doing things;
Decides what to do;
Controls resources;
Is monitored only at agreed points;
Gets helpful suggestions, but is not ordered.

When the manager merely dishes out work, the employee:
Is closely watched;
Has to refer all decisions to the superior.

Figure 17.2
Drawing the Distinction 2

DRAWING THE DISTINCTION 2.

When the manager delegates he:

Makes necessary resources available;
Checks performance at agreed points;
Is available to provide help and advice;
Makes tasks challenging.

When the manager abdicates tasks, the employee:

Is inadequately briefed;
Can suffer stress when faced with difficult problems;
Is inadequately trained;
Does not get help until it is too late.

Consider the following examples of how to approach delegating a task:

1. Bruce Dowson informs an employee to let all outlets know about a new line of stationery which will soon be available. He sends a message: 'take care of this, let me know when it's done.'
2. Bruce Dowson tells an employee that he needs to inform all product distributors that a new line of stationery will soon be available. Bruce sends a memo and some written material to the employee stating: 'Photocopy the production and sales information (make *sure* it is clear) and send two copies to all our outlets by Thursday next week.'
3. Bruce Dowson explains to an employee what needs to be done (informing all outlets about the new line of stationery) and asks him to work out the best way to do it and to get back to him in a week's time. When the employee has a plan, he discusses it with Bruce.

In the first example Bruce leaves his employee completely on his own. The employee must either 'sink or swim'. He does not even have a time frame. If the employee does something wrong, Bruce will not even know about it until after the fact. In Example 2, Bruce treats his employee as an unthinking, incapable machine. He offers no scope for development or initiative. The job will get done, but not benefit the employee or, in the long run, the organisation.

In the final example, Bruce at least offers his subordinate the opportunity to be creatively involved. The employee may decide to do it exactly as Bruce would, but the climate of trust and respect generated by the process will pay dividends. Think about how you would have 'delegated' a similar task.

There are a number of different levels of delegation you can use depending on the task and the level of competence of the employee. Carr (1989 : 115–16) lists five levels:

Complete Delegation

This is used with the very competent worker whom you know well. It can also be used for relatively minor or clerical tasks. You tell the employee the *task* you want completed and *when* it should be completed. The *how* is up to the delegate. You make yourself available for consultation if required.

Substantial Delegation

At this level of delegation you explain the task to the employee and set the final deadline. You also set firm dates when you can meet to discuss the delegate's progress towards task completion. The employee still has freedom on how to approach the task but keeps you informed at the agreed intervals. Do not overrule the employee's approach and decisions unless you really have to.

Limited Delegation

Explain the task to your employee and ask him to think about how he might approach it. The delegate then presents his recommendation to you. You either accept, modify or reject his proposal and then set the time frames for completion and progress discussions.

The final two levels are *minimal delegation* and *no delegation*. They basically involve the manager in telling the employees what to do and how to do it, or in not delegating at all.

Now let us examine the positive potential of effective delegation.

What Can Delegation Do for Me?

Despite the plethora of excuses for ineffective delegation, deep down, you know that you must delegate. Let us remind ourselves of the major benefits of delegation.

1.   *Delegation Frees Your Time*

Delegation allows you to concentrate on those aspects of the job that are really important, those which contribute to the organisation's primary purpose. It increases your efficiency as well as your effectiveness by getting work done with fewer personal resources.

2.   *Delegation Can Be Used for Developing Staff*

Delegation is an excellent vehicle for developing your staff. By delegating to your employees, you are helping them and subsequently the organisation.

Cameron and Whetten (1984 : 355) present these additional benefits of delegation:

3.   *Delegation Demonstrates Trust and Confidence*

By delegating effectively you are showing your staff that you trust them and have confidence in their ability. 'Delegation, the entrusting of authority to someone to act as your deputy, is a major expression of trust and a means of creating responsibility' (Adair, 1988 : 136).

4.   Delegation Increases the Quality of Decisions

Better decisions eventuate because those individuals involved in making the decisions (employees) through delegation are often more acquainted with the problem than you are.

5.   Delegation Produces Commitment, Motivation and Morale

Delegation gives employees some ownership of the task. Since successful delegation often gives latitude in the *how* of task completion, employees feel more committed to its achievement. When they complete a task successfully they feel satisfied and good about themselves.

SUMMARY

Benefits of Delegation:

- Delegation frees your time.
- Delegation can be used for developing staff.
- Delegation demonstrates trust and confidence.
- Delegation produces high-quality decisions.
- Delegation produces commitment, motivation and morale.

It is difficult to think of any stronger arguments for effective delegation than these.

Effective delegation also has the potential to enhance your career prospects. You will ultimately be judged on how well your unit contributed to organisational goals and targets, how well you related to your employees, and how those in your organisation performed. You will get little recognition for having done everything yourself.

Delegation can also increase your standing and power as a manager. If you trust your employees they will reciprocate and be committed to you. This can often be reflected in increased productivity.

Delegation then benefits you, your employees, your subunit and your overall organisation.

'I Couldn't Possibly Delegate'

In our experience most managers find it difficult to delegate. The reasons for this are varied. Some managers are afraid to delegate; they worry that their employees will not like them. If you think like this, reconsider. Even if this were true the dangers of not delegating effectively are much more serious.

Three factors prevent effective delegation. The first can stem from your own assumptions about your employees. The second factor relates to your human fears (we all have them). The third is your individual perception of what your role entails (Cameron and Whetten, 1984 : 359).

Your Assumptions

To begin to understand how your assumptions affect if and how you delegate, complete Application Task 17.2, My Assumptions.

If your dominant assumptions correspond with Theory X you will need to examine your role as a delegator seriously and consciously follow a delegation plan. If you lean towards Theory Y, do not be complacent: effective delegation is not easy. 'The case for delegation is easy to make. Consequently people rush into delegating without effective planning' (Rees, 1988 : 84).

Let us look at some of the most common *assumptive* excuses managers make for not delegating effectively to their subordinates.

> 'They are not up to it.'
> 'They do not like extra work.'
> 'They are happy enough doing what they are doing.'
> 'They are paid well to do their own jobs.'
> 'They can do it when they become managers.'

'They Are Not Up to It!'

'Most employees do not really have the ability. It is better not to trust them with the work.' Effective managers know that to be really successful they must take risks. They also realise that even if an employee does not have the skills now, they can be trained, often through delegation, to complete a task. This, in the long term, can save time and increase productivity and motivation, and help you to identify the developmental needs of employees.

'They Do Not Like Extra Work!'

'They are only junior employees and they are not enthusiastic about additional responsibilities. They see them as chores. They will complain that I am the one who is paid to do the job.' If you use this excuse you may need to

APPLICATION TASK 17.2

MY ASSUMPTIONS

You have 10 points to allocate to each pair of statements. For example, you have 10 points to distribute between (a) and (b) in question 1. Read the statements carefully and allocate the points to reflect the strength of your beliefs in the statement. If you believe strongly in part (a) of question 1 and only somewhat in part (b) you may allocate 7 and 3 respectively (the scores for each pair *must* equal 10). Respond honestly; there are no right or wrong answers.

1. (a) Employees will do as little work as they can get away with.

          10

    (b) Employees avoid work because it is uninteresting and means nothing to them.

2. (c) If you keep employees informed about their jobs, they will be more motivated and responsible.

          10

    (d) If you give employees more information than they need to do their job they will misuse it.

3. (e) Employees' suggestions are of little value to the organisation or you.

          10

    (f) Getting employees' ideas is good for them and helps the organisation. Their ideas are valuable.

4. (g) On the whole, employees have very little creativity.

          10

    (h) Employees are creative if given the chance to be.

5. (i)   Employees will improve on the job if given
         responsibility.

         ☐

         | 10

   (j)   Employees will not perform well if they are
         not punished for their mistakes.

         ☐

6. (k)   Employees want to know the whole story: the bad
         as well as the good.

         ☐

         | 10

   (l)   Employees only want to hear the good news.

         ☐

7. (m)   Managers should never admit when they are
         wrong.

         ☐

         | 10

   (n)   Managers lose nothing by admitting when they
         are wrong or make a mistake.

         ☐

8. (o)   Employees are more interested in money and
         conditions than in responsibility and
         recognition.

         ☐

         | 10

   (p)   If employees are challenged by interesting
         work and given responsibility they are less likely
         to be concerned about money and conditions.

         ☐

9. (q)   If allowed, employees will set high standards for
         themselves.

         ☐

         | 10

   (r)   If allowed, employees will set themselves very
         low standards.

         ☐

10. (s) The more freedom an employee has in the job
         the more controls you need to implement.

         ☐

         | 10

   (t)   The more freedom an employee has in the job
         the fewer controls are necessary.

         ☐

(Based on McGregor's Theory X and Theory Y)

Scoring:

Total the scores for the following letters:

a + d + e + g + j + l + m + o + r + s = ☐ Theory X

b + c + f + h + i + k + n + p + q + t = ☐ Theory Y

Transfer your totals to the graph below.

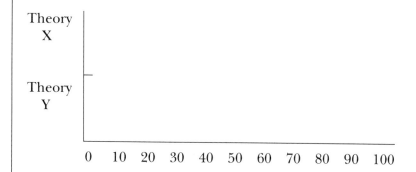

Theory X

Theory Y

0   10   20   30   40   50   60   70   80   90   100

If your Theory X score is dominant you are probably less likely to be naturally disposed towards effective delegation. You assume that your employees are extrinsically motivated and need to be pushed to work. If your Theory Y score is dominant, you believe your employees want responsibility and you are more predisposed towards delegating tasks. If you want more information on Theories X and Y, refer to Chapter 2, Motivating.

Stott, K. and Walker, A., *Making Management Work*. © 1992 Simon & Schuster (Asia) Pte Ltd.

examine your managerial assumptions about why people work. Of course there may be some employees who fit the above description, but on the whole most probably enjoy and need challenge and responsibility to develop. Most people want to learn and progress in their chosen careers and are willing to work to gain experience.

'They Are Happy Enough Doing What They Are Doing!'

'They are not interested in development, nor are they ambitious, so there is no need for the experience of delegated authority and created responsibilities.' Experienced managers realise that most staff members are interested in development. Often they may appear uninterested because they have never been given the opportunity to improve and develop. If employees have not been given such opportunities they can become disinterested and lose their motivation and ambitions.

'They Are Paid Well to Do Their Jobs!'

'Why should I spend time training and developing them. Don't we have a department for doing that? Anyway, they were hired to do a job and should be able to do it without my help.' This excuse can inhibit effective delegation. Managers who think this way may be in the wrong profession. As we have stressed throughout the book, one of the major responsibilities of the manager is to achieve organisational goals through working with and developing his employees. Those who do not develop staff through delegation may soon find themselves, at best, heading stagnant, unproductive organisations or, at worst, out of a job.

'They Can Do It When They Become Managers, Not Before!'

This attitude smacks of elitism. Managers who believe this should think back to how they got into their present positions. In most cases it will probably be because a superior trusted them enough to delegate meaningful tasks to them. Of course, there are tasks that you cannot delegate. Your job is to decide what can and cannot be delegated.

Human Fears

> 'If they make a mistake I will be blamed'.
> 'If they can do better than me I am dispensable'.
> 'I might lose the recognition I now enjoy'.

'If It Goes Wrong, I'll Get the Blame!'

'I let Stanlow do a job two years ago and he blew it. I could have been in big trouble.' Fears such as these can cause you to become fanatical about control and more concerned about your image and position than your employees. 'This inclination towards self-preservation may take the form of denying responsibilities for errors, demeaning subordinates who make mistakes, or refusing to delegate any but trivial tasks' (Cameron and Whetten, 1984 : 362).

'I Don't Want Them Getting Ideas!'

'Things are okay at the moment. I've got them under control. They may become disenchanted with the simple life if I give them responsibility. And what if they start to think they could do my job? This would make me dispensable, especially if they can actually do some things better than me. After all, I am supposed to be best at everything.' These fears can be a real source of anxiety and insecurity.

Effective managers realise that they cannot possibly be doing the best job possible if they do it all themselves. Organisations today are far too complex. Successful managers also realise that it is part of their job to develop and promote capable staff for the benefit of the organisation. If an employee can do something better than you and if you recognise and utilise this, you will be more valuable to the organisation as a whole. This should be recognised.

Some managers also fear that if they delegate meaningful tasks, they may lose some of the recognition they get as a leader. In reality they probably stand to gain more reward if their entire team can work effectively.

Individual Beliefs

> 'I can do a better job of it.'
> 'I can do it more quickly myself.'
> 'I like to be busy.'
> 'I should work longer and harder than them.'

'I Can Do a Better Job of It!'

'If you want the job done properly, do it yourself.' Most of us work to this principle because it simplifies life for us. We do not have to become involved in the precarious process of applying interpersonal skills; asking people to do things is a difficult job. It is easier to believe that we can do the job better. Really effective managers know this is not true. They recognise the fact that others can often do the job just as well, if not better, than they can. Remember, it is only our perception that we can always do a better job.

'I Can Do It More Quickly Myself!'

'Why should I get someone else to do it when I can do it myself in half the time?' This could be accurate. You may very well be able to do it more quickly. This, however, is not the only consideration. Recall the main reasons for delegating: to free your time for the important aspects of your job and as a means for developing staff. A time investment when starting to delegate a task can pay dividends in the future: you develop an employee through delegation so he can eventually do the job himself, thus freeing your time.

'I Like to Be Busy!'

'I feel good if I've rushed around all day; that's what I'm paid for.' Many managers like to do busy work; it makes them feel important. It also provides them with an excuse to avoid the more difficult and important tasks they must face. Think what you are really there for. Is it to do tasks others can easily complete or should be doing anyway?

Some managers think they have to work longer and harder than everybody else. They believe this makes people respect them. Working longer does not mean working 'smarter': effective delegation does.

You have probably heard all these excuses at some time or another. In fact, if you think carefully, you have probably used similar excuses yourself. Now let us forget the excuses and examine some ways through which you can increase your delegation skills.

Increasing Delegation

The skilful manager will be concerned about the performance of the organisation, subunit or area of responsibility. Is it doing everything it is supposed to be doing? Is it reaching optimum levels of performance? He will also realise that the effective use of human resources is a prerequisite to successful management. The leader who does everything is unlikely to have an organisation which succeeds on all counts. When considering delegation, you as a manager should ask yourself a number of critical questions:

- Am I really using the abilities of my staff?
- Could someone else do the task and benefit as a result?
- Do I think I am indispensable?
- I know I am busy on critical tasks. Could someone else do this task?

First of all, you need to know what the abilities of your staff are; some form of inventory is needed. You should then consider the identified abilities when delegating tasks.

'Could Someone Else Do the Job?'

It is worth asking this question for each task you decide to delegate. You must accept that others may do things differently or not as quickly as you would, but they are capable and it may be a real benefit to employees in terms of development to have the experience of taking on a responsibility. Take care however not to delegate only the menial tasks. If you do this, delegation will not be viewed in terms of development or effective human resource utilisation, but simply as a means of getting rid of meaningless chores.

'Am I Really Indispensable?'

Fear and suspicion can be destructive. We can become so insular in our approach that we ignore the development needs of not only our employees but also the organisation. A mature manager is able to accept that we are all dispensable in some way – sad but true.

'Could Someone Else Do This Task?'

The effective manager knows that there are some critical tasks that command his total attention. Rather than let the unimportant things interrupt the vital activities of planning, motivation, monitoring and so forth, it is worth asking ourselves whether someone else could take on the work.

Successful delegation then is a balance of passing authority to do a task to free your own valuable managerial time and to develop your employees. To do this you must know which tasks you can delegate and which you cannot.

If at all possible, plan ahead: avoid last-minute crises. Plan which tasks you will delegate well in advance. Do not wait and delegate those tasks which occur at the last minute. The delegate needs time to plan his course of action. Having to deal with only crisis situations will not encourage reflective or thorough action.

At this stage it will be useful for you to think about what parts of your job you can delegate and those you cannot. It is also worthwhile to prioritise the tasks you can delegate. This will provide you with a good starting point. Complete Application Task 17.3.

APPLICATION TASK 17.3

WHAT TO DELEGATE?

Part 1.

1.1 Identify in as much detail as you can what is involved in your job. Be sure to list the important tasks as well as the routine, day-to-day activities.

1.2 Examine your list and think about which tasks can be delegated and which cannot (simply place a 'tick' next to those you can and a 'cross' next to those you cannot). While doing this it might help you to ask yourself the following questions:

- Which tasks keep repeating themselves?
- Which details take the largest part of my time?

- What aspects do I neglect?
- What small decisions do I make all the time?
- Which tasks allow for some decision-making?
- Which tasks will help your staff develop?
- Which tasks do not require your level of competence?
- Which tasks might some employees be more capable in than you?

TASKS:

Part 2.

2.1 You now have a list of worthwhile tasks you believe you can delegate. You will now be asked to further develop the list by prioritising the tasks.

2.2 Consider each of the tasks which you decided you could delegate. Keep in mind the importance of the task, when it needs to be completed by, and how it can have developmental benefit for your staff. For more detail on prioritising see Chapter 15, Managing Time.

2.3 When you have completed your initial prioritisation, write your 'top' five priorities in the spaces provided below. Then check why you have rated them highly. Write a brief rationale for each.

TASK	RATIONALE
1.	
2.	
3.	
4.	
5.	

Stott, K. and Walker, A., *Making Management Work.* © 1992 Simon & Schuster (Asia) Pte Ltd.

You should now have a list of tasks which you believe you can delegate. Make sure they are not all meaningless, trivial tasks. Remember, one of the main reasons for delegating is to develop your staff. Although it is difficult to generalise, there are certain tasks which you should not delegate:

1.   Performance appraisal.
2.   Setting organisational direction.
3.   Disciplining employees.
4.   Motivating employees.
5.   Communicating with employees.
6.   Building a team.

Successful Delegation

Successful delegation may be thought to be synonymous with development. If you make development the main focus of delegation you will probably find that the other benefits will automatically follow. You should realise however that implementing successful delegation may take considerable time when you first begin, but it will almost certainly pay off over the long term.

Inman (1983 : 43), probably drawing on the early work of Henri Fayol, suggests seven guidelines or principles for the effective delegation of responsibility and authority.

1. *Principle of delegation by results expected.* Enough authority should be delegated to ensure that the task can be completed successfully.

2. *The authority-level principle.* The delegate should be permitted to make decisions within the parameters set by the delegated authority, without having to ask permission of his boss.

3. *Principle of unity of command.* It is preferable for the delegate to have a reporting relationship with only one superior. This reduces the likelihood of conflict.

4. *The principle of absoluteness of responsibility.* The delegate is responsible to his superior for the completion of the task. The superior *is* still responsible to the overall organisation for his subordinate's activities.

5. *Principles of parity and responsibility.* The responsibility of the delegate cannot be greater than the authority he has been granted. Nor can it be less.

6. *Principle of functional definition.* The greater the clarity of the subunit's role, role descriptions and function, the greater the possibility that it will work towards the achievement of organisational goals and targets.

7. *The scalar principle.* The clearer the lines of authority in an organisation, the more effective the lines of communication will be. Hence, the easier it is to delegate real authority.

These principles are embedded in the scheme presented in the next section.

Getting Delegation Right: A Scheme for Successful Delegation

For delegation to be successful there are a number of central tenets or steps which the manager should follow. These are displayed in Figure 17.3.

Let us look at these points in a little more detail. You should go through this or a similar process for each task you wish to delegate. If you follow the plan it should eventually become automatic and so improve your delegation on a permanent basis.

Before we discuss the scheme, it will be valuable for you to select one task to keep in the back of your mind as you read through this section. Complete Application Task 17.4.

Figure 17.3
A Scheme for Successful Delegation

PREPARE
SELECT
MEET
CONTRACT
MONITOR
REVIEW

APPLICATION TASK 17.4

Select the specific task that you want to delegate. Make sure *you* understand what is involved in the task and what outcome its completion should bring to the individual and/or organisation.

1. Think of a task in your area of responsibility which is important to your organisation which you can delegate. Perhaps you could use one of the tasks you decided you could delegate in Application Task 17.3.
2. Consider the following points:

    ■ Is it menial or will it provide *challenge?*
    ■ Is it really my task or is it *legitimate* to delegate it?
    ■ Is it simply a time-consuming chore or a real *development opportunity* for one of my staff?

    The answer should be the latter in each case.

Write the task in just a few words below:

Keep this task in mind as you read through the different steps.

Stott, K. and Walker, A., *Making Management Work.* © 1992 Simon & Schuster (Asia) Pte Ltd.

Prepare

When you have selected the task it is essential that you prepare for 'handing over' to an employee. There are a number of points you need to consider.

Your first step is to decide on the objectives for your task: what it is expected to achieve. You must be clear in your own mind about the expected outcomes, the criteria by which success will be judged. Ensure these are realistic. You must know how successful task completion will be measured. Identify the specific aspects of each task if it is complicated.

Carefully consider how much time you anticipate the task will take, or when it must be completed by. Give a reasonable time scale. It may vary depending on the task and existing skills of the employee. It may be that the employee is inexperienced and requires some help in the early stages, so time must be given to ease him into it. Learning what is involved takes time. Setting deadlines which are over-optimistic or unreasonable can interfere with effective task completion and damage morale. Conversely, allowing too long for a task can also be counter-productive.

Prepare some guidelines as to what resources will be needed by the delegate to complete the task. Here you may have to set some realistic parameters. Resources include money, personnel, equipment, etc.

Consider the standards you expect for task completion. Also balance the developmental value of the task for the delegate with the cost-effectiveness of the task. A reasonable level must be struck. It is pointless to sacrifice an important task for the sake of a minor opportunity for development.

Prepare a tentative monitoring schedule to discuss progress and performance with the delegate as he works on the task. Once again, you need to balance delegate freedom and outcome considerations.

Finally, think about the support you will need to offer the delegate. It is pointless delegating a task but not supporting the person. Remember, in order to complete the task successfully, the employee will probably need more authority than he normally has. You must decide how much authority he will require to complete the task. When you have considered all these points, it is a good idea to prepare a *task brief* which succinctly lists the basic details. This is useful when you first meet to discuss the task with the employee. One example of a task brief is shown in Figure 17.4.

Figure 17.4
One Example of a 'Task Brief'

Objective: To design a new product brochure.

Suggested time frame: Completed by 1 June 1992.

Suggested monitoring dates: 12 January 1992;
                              10 March 1992;
                              10 May 1992.

Resources available: Budget $5,000;
                       Two Assistants.

Authority needed: Use of design computers;
                    Two assistants;
                    Photographers.

Specific outcomes: Colour;
                     Clear, easily readable benefits;
                     Attractive to wide range of clients.

When you have considered all these points and prepared your task brief, you are ready to decide who to delegate to. Before you do this take note of one important caution: it is vital that you do not consider what you have prepared to be 'written in stone'. One of the main tenets of delegation is that it develops employees through involving them in how a task should be completed. If you are too inflexible, and do not allow them input, you risk ineffective delegation by simply 'giving out work'.

SUMMARY

Prepare; Ask Yourself:

- What are the objectives of the task?
- What are the expected outcomes of the task?
- How will success be measured?
- What standards do you expect for task completion?
- What specific aspects are involved in the task?
- How much time should the task take?
- What resources will be required for task completion?
- What support will I need to provide?
- How much authority will be required?
- Will it take more than one person to complete the task?
- Have I prepared a task brief?

- AM I PREPARED TO BE FLEXIBLE WHEN I MEET WITH THE DELEGATE?

Before you move onto the next stage, consider the task you selected to delegate at the beginning of this section and complete Application Task 17.5. This will help you formulate a task brief which may act as the basis for discussion.

Select

Think of the most appropriate person to delegate the task to. When deciding this, do not just assume it has to be the employee who is the best at everything, the one you always trust. This person may not need the responsibility in terms of development. He may be sick of having everything dumped on his desk. Obviously there has to be a match between person and task, but look for those who might benefit from the experience. This may be an inexperienced employee or someone just starting on the managerial ladder who needs the equivalent of job-rotation opportunities: the experience in an unfamiliar area.

When deciding who to delegate to, consider two aspects. First ask yourself: Who could do this task (who is ready for delegation)? And, second: Who could benefit in a developmental sense from doing this task? Implicit behind both of these questions is the assumption that delegating the task will also benefit you and the organisation.

APPLICATION TASK 17.5

MY 'TASK BRIEF'

1. Use the task you selected in Application Task 17.2 (or select another task).
2. Prepare a task brief for delegating the task (feel free to design a different form if you wish). Although this form does not include all the points you have been asked to consider during the 'prepare stage' we suggest you think about these as well.

TASK BRIEF FORM

Objective:

Suggested time frame:

Suggested monitoring dates:

Resources available:

Authority needed:

Specific outcomes:

Who Could Do This Task, and Why?

When asking yourself this question there are a number of points to consider. Are there, for example, some employees who you feel need to be given greater responsibility, or who you feel need to be challenged in some way? Delegation can also be used to prepare or 'test out' someone who you think may be ready for promotion: can you delegate the task to an employee in this category? You may also wish to consider employees' potential and confidence in a particular area.

Employees in this category may be best suited to the more complex or urgent tasks. Here experience and competence may have to take precedence over developmental needs.

Who Could Benefit Developmentally from Doing This Task?

As with the previous question, selecting a staff member requires an intimate knowledge of your staff. This type of information may be gathered during developmental appraisal or supervision. The former is also an excellent avenue for discussing delegation.

Identify staff whom you believe lack confidence or have a weakness in a specific area. Can they benefit? Of course, if you select an employee who fits this category, make sure you do not initially choose too difficult or complex a task. Start him off slowly. It will not develop the staff member if he is forced into a situation where he is likely to fail. If you choose an employee for this reason you must be prepared to spend a little more time with him in the initial stages.

Also consider employees who have weaknesses in a specific skill area which can be improved through completing a task under your guidance. Here it may be best to begin delegating a relatively 'low-demand' task and work your way up.

Other points outside these areas also need to be considered. For example, if the task you are going to delegate requires someone who can communicate with workers in another department, this will need to be taken into account.

It is not possible to supply a complete list of what you should think about when selecting who to delegate to. Different tasks will have their own complexities, problems and requirements. What is important is that you match the complexity or special requirements of the task with the needs, abilities and potential of the employee.

In an ideal situation, work could always be delegated for developmental purposes, but this is not always possible. If you aim, however, to delegate tasks which provide the delegate with a variety of new experiences, job satisfaction and motivation, you will be on the right track.

SUMMARY

Select; Ask Yourself:

- Who could do this task?
- Who could benefit developmentally from doing this task?
- Who needs more responsibility?
- Who needs to be challenged?
- Who can do the task right now?
- Who has a weakness which could be helped by doing this task?
- Who needs a boost in confidence?
- Who may be ready for promotion?
- Who needs developing in a specific skill area?
- Who can get on with other employees?
- Is the job urgent?

- ARE THERE OTHER CONSIDERATIONS?

If you were asked to select a delegate for the task you identified at the beginning of the section, who would you choose? Why would you choose this person?

Meet

In this stage you meet with the person you have decided to delegate to. This is where you use the *task brief* we discussed earlier. Discuss the job and expectations. Talk in general terms and focus on the development benefits to the individual. Allow the employee to help structure the delegated task. Ensure that you both understand what is involved in the task.

Give authority for the whole task: it will be more productive for the employee to understand that he is accountable to the manager for not just part of the task. This may also avoid the situation of apportioning blame elsewhere when tasks are not completed or somehow go wrong.

Always hand over the task brief face-to-face. Also provide any other material which may be useful to the delegate. Provide a very careful explanation of what you are looking for. Encourage the employee to ask questions and make suggestions at any time during the discussion. A firm understanding is essential for successful task completion. Remember, the meeting phase is meant to be participative.

Carefully explain the objectives of the task and be sure the employee is convinced of its usefulness and necessity. It is also a good idea to explain to the delegate why you selected him and not someone else. Concentrate on the benefits you see both him and the organisation deriving from the task. Explain the time frame you have developed and if necessary how much time he needs to be released from other duties to complete the task.

Discuss the authority you will be delegating with the task and how much freedom of action he will have. Let the delegate know that you will be available for advice and guidance (as well as at agreed monitoring points).

This stage should mainly be regarded as a discussion between you and the delegate. The delegate should be fully involved in the *how* of the task: how the task will be approached and how the outcomes can be attained? He is the one who is expected to complete the task successfully so he must have the major say into how it will be done. He must have the opportunity to question you to clarify any issue, from resources to authority available. Encourage a two-way exchange of ideas.

If the task is fairly major the delegate should be permitted to go away and refine plans and ideas and meet with you at a later date to finalise what he intends to do. In some instances you may have to meet a number of times before a plan is agreed upon and a *contract* drawn up.

SUMMARY

Meet; Ask Yourself:

- Have we discussed task expectations/objectives?
- Is he aware of the justification for the task?
- Have we discussed desired outcomes?
- Have we discussed standards of performance?
- Have we discussed time frames?
- Does the delegate understand all of the above?
- Is the delegate aware of available resources?
- Does the delegate understand how much authority he has?
- Did I use a task brief sheet?
- Did we meet face-to-face?
- Did I provide adequate opportunity for the delegate to question me for clarification?
- Did I tell the delegate why I chose him?
- Do we need to meet again?

- **HAVE I PROVIDED THE OPPORTUNITY FOR THE DELEGATE TO DECIDE THE 'HOW TO' OF THE TASK?**

Following the meeting (or meetings) stage, you and the delegate must come to a mutual agreement on the task. We suggest you do this in the form of a *contract*.

The Contract

The delegation process involves both manager and employee reaching agreement on a number of points. This can be called a delegation contract.

For successful delegation to take place, there must be firm agreement between the manager and the subordinate to whom the work is delegated. There must be agreement in a number of important areas. These are basically a summary of the points agreed on during the preceding meeting. You will notice that our *contract* does not include an open agreement of *how* the task will be carried out. You can easily add this if you believe the task is important enough to warrant your having to know what is going to be done in detail, or if you believe the delegate needs to be more closely monitored because of his inexperience. Items which need to be agreed upon are:

The Precise Nature of the Delegated Task

In other words, the terms of reference and details of the task must be clearly delineated. Employees (or delegates) must be clear about what is expected of them and the scope of the task: what they are expected to cover. Careful consideration by the manager and a firm agreement between the two parties at this stage can avoid confusion, frustration and resentment later on. There should also be agreement on the resources available.

The Required Outcomes

You, as manager, must carefully outline what you expect the employee to achieve. Although you should have expectations carefully prepared before you delegate the task, you should leave some room for negotiation when you discuss the task with the employee.

How the Employee's Success Will Be Judged

The criteria for successful task completion must be clearly defined and understood. If this is not done you risk the employee thinking the task has been completed satisfactorily when you are less than happy with the performance.

How Much Time Is Allowed

Some type of time scale and some definite deadlines must be built into the task definition. This is essential if the employee is to complete the task within an acceptable time period. Monitoring points should also be agreed upon at this stage.

The Amount of Authority Needed

Many tasks cannot be delegated unless they are accompanied by a certain degree of authority. Even the ability to call a meeting to discuss initiatives or make recommendations requires some authority. The extent of authority must be made clear at the outset and communicated to other employees likely to be involved or affected. Repeated referrals to the manager signifies a weakness in the delegation process and possibly a lack of confidence in the delegate.

Agreed Monitoring Points

Agree on a number of points during the task implementation when you will meet with the delegate to monitor his progress. Do not continually ask 'Done that yet?' or 'Are you sure you're keeping on track?' We will discuss the monitoring process in more detail in the next section.

Agree and Then Trust

When agreement has been reached you should trust the employee to get on with it and only involve yourself at agreed monitoring points and when the delegate needs help.

SUMMARY

The Contract; Both Parties Must Agree Upon:

- The nature and scope of the task.
- Expected outcomes.
- How the subordinate will be judged.
- How much time is allowed.
- The amount of authority needed.

At this stage complete Application Task 17.6. It is designed to simulate the process of a 'contract-setting' approach.

APPLICATION TASK 17.6

A CONTRACT

Now you have some idea of what is involved in effective delegation, it may be useful for you to try and translate some of that knowledge into a 'contract' relevant to a specific task. Select a task from your own work situation which could be delegated (or use the task you have been following during this section). Develop a 'contract' for the task that both you and the delegate can agree with. In a practical situation you would meet with the employee involved and discuss the various aspects. If you can do this here, good. If you cannot, try and simulate the exercise.

Specify task:

What is it?

What is the intended outcome?

Deadline for task completion?

Criteria success will be judged by?

Preparation:

Support that will be available?

Resources that will be available?

What preparation is required?

The delegate:

Existing skills to be utilised?

Expected benefits in developmental terms?

Authority:

Authority agreed upon for period of task completion?

Monitoring:

How will progress be monitored?

Dates for monitoring meetings?

Signed   Date: _____

Manager: _____   Employee: _____

Stott, K. and Walker, A., *Making Management Work.* © 1992 Simon & Schuster (Asia) Pte Ltd.

When the contract has been signed the delegate implements the plan for task completion. As you know, your job does not end here.

Monitor

Whilst unnecessary interference must not take place, progress needs to be monitored for the benefit of both parties. Where this procedure is mutually agreed, it may be seen as a supportive mechanism rather than an intrusion into the domain of the delegate.

We have seen that delegation is not dishing out work: the manager cannot simply issue the job and wait for it to be done. Nor is it an abdication of accountability. Remember, even when you delegate, you are still accountable for the work of your subordinates.

Only Monitor at Agreed Points

When you have delegated the task you should monitor the delegate only at previously agreed-upon points in the task-implementation process. The delegate should be aware that he is responsible for completing the task. You should also keep him informed on any policies or changes which may affect what he is working on. Be consistent when you are monitoring. During this stage you must do more than simply monitor task progress.

Be Available

There is still an attachment to the task and the person doing it. The initiative for contact, however, should come from the delegate. If he requires help and advice, you must be available.

Give Help and Advice When Needed

The employee may wish to have freedom to make decisions, but at the same time, support may be needed in various ways, including encouragement and genuine interest.

Provide Adequate Resources to Achieve the Task

This must be carefully thought out at the beginning. It is no good expecting a satisfactory job to be completed without the necessary resources, whether financial, material, temporal or human. Even when decided at the outset, you may have to 'find' extra resources during the implementation of the plan.

SUMMARY

Monitor:

- Only monitor at agreed points.
- Be available.
- Give help and support when needed.
- Give adequate resources to achieve the task.
- Provide encouragement.

You monitor, then, both to assist and develop the employee and to ensure that the task is 'on track'. After you have delegated a task you should neither supervise too closely nor simply leave the delegate to his own devices.

Review

You should also evaluate the success of the task, the performance of the employee, and your performance as a delegator.

The Task

Were desired outcomes attained? The first thing you must evaluate is how successfully the task was completed. This should be relatively easy if you were careful in the early stages to set reachable targets and agree on desired outcomes. If the task met or exceeded the agreed criteria it was successful. If it did not, you will need to delve a little deeper. Did you explain the task properly? Did you monitor regularly? Did you gain the commitment of the employee? Or did the employee not live up to his part of the agreement. If he did not, you may decide to monitor a little more closely next time. Remember, the delegate agreed to complete the task. He is responsible to you just as you are responsible to your boss.

If unintentional mistakes were made, look at them logically. Look at how the work was approached rather than at personalities. Review the methods used without being too critical. Try constructive criticism.

The Delegate

Review how the delegate responded to the challenge. Consider how he approached the work. Was the commitment and judgement there? Most importantly, review the task and delegation process to ascertain its effectiveness as a developmental tool. Did the delegate learn through completing the task? Were certain skills upgraded? Was a weakness addressed? If the employee feels good about completing the task and was successful, development has probably resulted. Ask not only how this has helped the individual but also how it has or will help you and the organisation.

You/The Process

Consider how you approached the delegation. Were you comfortable with accepting the ultimate responsibility for the task? Did you follow the steps of successful delegation or did you slide back into your old ways? You should be able to see the value of delegation to yourself in the extra time you have at your disposal and in more competent, motivated employees.

SUMMARY

Review; Action Points:

- The task: Was it completed successfully in terms of its original objectives/desired outcomes and against the set criteria?

- The delegate: Did he develop through the delegated task? Did he feel as if he was successful? Did it address weaknesses or sharpen skills?

- You/the process: Were you comfortable with your performance as a delegator? Did you and the organisation benefit in any way?

- **WHAT WOULD YOU DO DIFFERENTLY NEXT TIME TO IMPROVE DELEGATION?**

You have now been through a system for successful delegation. While it may appear somewhat complicated and involved at this stage, you will find that it becomes easier the more times you do it. Once you are used to delegating effectively and begin to see the benefits to your staff, to your organisation and to yourself, it will become almost automatic. All you need to do then is go through the stages from time to time to remind yourself of what is important.

Finally, it is a good idea to keep track of the details of your delegated tasks. Throughout our discussion we have been talking as if you only delegate to one person. This, of course, is not realistic. In practice you will delegate to several or many employees and their various tasks will be at different stages. You can monitor this aspect by recording who is doing what and when on a fairly simple form. One such form is shown in Figure 17.5.

Figure 17.5
Delegated-Tasks Record Form

TASK	EXPECTED RESULTS	DELEGATE	COMPLETION	CHECKPOINTS
1.				
PROGRESS NOTES			OUTCOMES	
2.				
PROGRESS NOTES			OUTCOMES	
3.				

Stott, K. and Walker, A., *Making Management Work.* © 1992 Simon & Schuster (Asia) Pte Ltd.

Before we conclude the chapter try to apply some of what you have read by analysing the case below: Barbara Chelford.

Case Study: Barbara Chelford

Barbara Chelford, the personnel officer for Southhead Catering Company, Central Division, is responsible for all recruitment and training within the Central Division. She is responsible for recruiting five new chefs for a planned expansion project. Barbara has eleven staff members in her division who, in her opinion, are already working very hard. Barbara is also very committed to introducing an extensive and innovative training programme for all junior managers which is taking most of her time. She knows she will not be able to handle the recruitment of the required staff herself and knows someone else from her division will have to do it. She does not consider this a problem as she trusts her staff and believes they can do the job with very little supervision. Her main problem is whom to ask. Realising that she will need some time to decide, and to prepare herself for the briefing, she decides to spend the morning on the task.

Barbara begins to assess her subordinates in relation to their experience, interests, ability, and current workloads. She asks herself: 'Who will do the best job with the least amount of fuss? Who can I spare from other tasks for the exercise?' After pondering the questions for an hour or so, she realises that Edward, one of her oldest staff members could definitely do the job. He has a lot of experience and always does a good job. Although he has not worked on recruitment before, she is sure he can work out what to do with very little advice. Anyway, he has been struggling with his routine duties and seems to have trouble keeping up with more dynamic, younger staff members.

Barbara prepares some briefing notes for Edward, setting out step by step what he must do and decides to allow him two months to hire the 'right' people. She sees Edward the next day and takes twenty minutes to explain the task to him in minute detail. Edward agrees to do the task and Barbara says he should let her know when the new chefs have been hired. She excuses Edward and gets back to work secure in the knowledge that she will have the new personnel within two months. She writes her boss a memo to this effect and gets back to her training programme.

Questions

1. What things did Barbara do which indicated good delegation practice?
2. What things did Barbara do which were questionable?
3. What could Barbara have considered and done to improve the whole process?
4. Do you think Edward will successfully complete the task?

This case study is about a middle manager. The principles apply equally at all levels in the organisation. Think about what you are doing which could be considered:

■ Good practice.
■ Ineffective practice.

Conclusion

Delegation is an often-neglected managerial skill even though the benefits are obvious. So next time those tasks start piling up on your desk, ask yourself: 'Do I have to do all this?' Remember, by delegating you are not only making your own job easier, you are also developing and motivating your staff. Plan to delegate and you will find yourself with more time to pursue those really important tasks – the ones which are vital to your job – and with a team of staff which is more capable and satisfied.

References

Adair, J. (1988) *Effective Leadership*, Pan : London.

Cameron, D. and Whetten, K. (1984) *Developing Management Skills*, Scott Foresman : Illinois.

Carr, C. (1989) *New Manager's Survival Guide*, Wiley : New York.

Inman, M. (1983) *Organisation and Management*, Financial Training Publications : London.

Rees, W. (1988) *The Skills of Management*, Routledge : London.

Chapter 18

Writing Reports

. . . in perfecting the art of report writing, you will at the same time be improving your performance as a manager, project leader, researcher or investigator as the case may be. For the report is an essential part of the work. It is not simply a chore at the end of an investigation. On the contrary, the production of a report may in some cases be the main purpose of the work.

(Sussams, 1983 : 1)

Most managers are involved in writing reports. It is not their favourite occupation.

To anyone who has had to prepare a report, it should come as no surprise that many people look forward to writing reports with all the enthusiasm they reserve for an attack of appendicitis. Because writing is painful, they try to avoid it. When they can't avoid it, they postpone it, evidently hoping that if they ignore the task long enough it will go away like a psychosomatic pain. (Gallagher, 1969 : 6)

Reports are written for various reasons. They may explain some work that you have done in your area. They may give the results of something. They may explain an investigation which has taken place. They may propose changes. *Modern Business Reports* (1987 : 55) identifies three main types:

- ■ The Data Report.
- ■ The Analytical Report.
- ■ The Recommendation Report.

The *data report* may examine a problem or give information about a project. It is factual and the data you are conveying has to be clearly presented. *Progress reports*, *sales reports* and *research documents* all fall into this category.

The *analytical report* goes one step further and analyses the data. Sales figures, for example, may be presented, but then they are interpreted with explanations of why certain events occurred. The analysis is very important and should lead to some conclusions. You may even discuss possible options for future action. A performance appraisal report is an example of an analytical report.

The *recommendation report* provides the answer to the question: 'What should we do?' You may be recommending a policy change or that an employee receives a salary increase. There is a host of issues on which recommendations can be made. The recommendation is the key part of the report and you are expected to be firm and clear; you do not hedge your bets. You would not say, for example, 'The department should consider replacing a few of the computers if money becomes available.' It is better to say: 'Three new computers should be purchased by the end of March.' You have to make it clear to the recipient precisely what you want him to do.

Sussams (1983 : 1) identifies two other outcomes which may be quite important to you as the author:

> The first is that the form and quality of the report is an indication, indeed, as will be shown, a determinant, of the quality of the work discussed in the report. The second is that the author of the report will be judged, to some extent, on the quality of his written work. Promotion may actually depend on it. To put this another way: unless you do the work thoroughly you will not be able to write a satisfactory report and if you do not write a satisfactory report you may well be deemed to be incompetent.

Sometimes, reports are very formal and take a good deal of time to write. If, for example, you have been conducting an investigation into an organisational problem for the last six months, you are likely to write a very detailed and formal report for the boss. This does not mean it has to be long. At the other extreme, reports may be quite informal and be similar to a memorandum.

You may write reports on a regular basis, such as a weekly report on the unit's figures or a quarterly report on the department's work. In some cases, the structure for these will have become established: you always do them in the same way. Other reports may be 'one off' documents and you have to plan these from scratch.

Whatever type of report you have to write, there are some common principles which must be applied. You must keep these in mind despite the fact that you may be using different formats and styles to those suggested in this chapter. Generally, we shall be referring to the more structured type of report because this offers a solid basis on which you can construct less formal reports. It is also very coherent and shows you how to 'tell a story'. If you learn to think in this way, you can be assured that all your documents will get the message across and provide the right amount of information.

We shall be asking you some questions in the chapter about your own report writing. You will find it useful to have a report which you have recently written to hand. If you do not have one, then you should obtain one from your organisation. You can still learn to improve your skills by analysing someone else's report writing.

What is your present standard of report writing? Unfortunately, you are probably not the right person to answer that question! If you can obtain the help of someone who normally receives your reports, or a colleague who is prepared to read even just one, you should ask him to complete the questionnaire How Good Is My Report Writing? Failing that, complete the questionnaire yourself and you can obtain some preliminary impressions of your skill in presenting information coherently.

There are fifteen items. Some of these may be inapplicable depending on the type of your report. If it is one which makes recommendations, then all the questions are relevant. If it is simply a factual report, presenting, say, statistical data, only questions 1–9 may be relevant.

Questionnaire

HOW GOOD IS MY REPORT WRITING?

	Yes	No	NA
1. Before you even start reading, does the report look inviting as you flick through the pages?	☐	☐	☐
2. Is the language used easy to understand at the first reading?	☐	☐	☐
3. Are both sentences and paragraphs fairly short?	☐	☐	☐
4. Are there plenty of subheadings?	☐	☐	☐
5. Is the purpose clearly stated at the beginning?	☐	☐	☐
6. Does it specify precisely what the report is about?	☐	☐	☐
7. Is there a summary in less than one page at the beginning?	☐	☐	☐
8. Are facts and findings given 'straight' and without opinions?	☐	☐	☐
9. Does it answer all the important questions?	☐	☐	☐
10. Is the problem stated clearly?	☐	☐	☐
11. Is there an analysis of the findings?	☐	☐	☐

	Yes	**No**	**NA**

12. Is there a section which outlines the conclusions reached? ☐ ☐ ☐

13. Are the recommendations straight to the point? ☐ ☐ ☐

14. Are the implications of the recommendations identified? ☐ ☐ ☐

15. Do any illustrations which are used aid your understanding? ☐ ☐ ☐

Stott, K. and Walker, A., *Making Management Work.* © 1992 Simon & Schuster (Asia) Pte Ltd.

Obviously, the more 'yes's' you have the better, but it is conceivable that even the most experienced manager could truthfully answer 'no' to many of the questions. Report writing is a skill which can be developed and some of the components can be acquired fairly quickly. By following the guidance in this chapter, you should be able to say 'yes' to every question for every report you write.

Report Preparation

Like much of what we have said in this book, preparation is the key to effective report writing. You will have done your background work, read appropriate documents, assembled information and reached some tentative conclusions about any proposals you might wish to make. Before you actually write the report you need to consider several points. These relate to the purpose, the information you need to give, the way you interpret it, and the conclusions you will draw.

Purpose

Decide on the purpose of your report. Is it:

- To describe a situation?
- To recommend changes?
- To give facts?
- To record progress?

This will determine the way in which the report is presented.

Information

Decide on the information you need, acquire it and then put it together. Include only the information which is relevant to the report's purpose. Some managers are not very selective when they gather information. They collect anything which is remotely connected with the subject in question and then try to deal with it later. At worst, it breaks their hearts to discard anything, so they put everything in the report's appendices. This is not the best way to go about things. Decide in advance precisely what information you need and include that. Even then, you will still find information which is not directly relevant. You should put it aside. You do not want anything which might confuse matters.

Assimilate the Information

Think about the information you have collected. Give yourself time to assimilate data: do not be too hasty in reaching conclusions. There are times when you will collect data which is complex and you need time to consider it carefully. It is best not to rush into making interpretations.

Preliminary Outcomes

Prepare some arguments and think about conclusions and the recommendations you might make. These are not final, and when you come to actually write your report, you may well change your mind. This is because as you present your findings and then discuss them, you may arrive at new insights. Nevertheless, it is a good idea to have some provisional thoughts on outcomes and this will help to focus your report.

SUMMARY

Preparing:

- Decide on the purpose.
- Decide what information you need.
- Acquire it.
- Keep the relevant information and sort it.
- Assimilate the information.
- Think through some arguments and discussion points.
- Think about tentative conclusions and recommendations.

As you are thinking about your next report, you will find it helpful to spend just a few minutes completing the form Preliminary Ideas in Application Task 18.1. This will help you clarify your purpose and to include appropriate information. We have also shown a sample of a completed form in Figure 18.1. At this stage it is not meant to be perfect and comprehensive; just a few simple notes will do to ensure you travel in the right direction.

APPLICATION TASK 18.1

PRELIMINARY IDEAS

Think about a report you must write soon. Make a few notes below each heading.

1. State the purpose and intention of the report:

2. What information is essential?

3. What line of argument will you follow?

4. What are your thoughts at this stage about recommendations or proposals?

Figure 18.1
Preliminary Ideas Sample

> Sample

> Preliminary ideas

> State the purpose and intention of the report:

> *To explain to senior management problems with getting admin. work done and to persuade them to do something about it.*

> What information is essential?

> *Data about actual clerical hours. Data from managers about number of hours needed. Jobs not done. Managers wasting their time on admin.*

> What line of argument will you follow?

> *Performance in the dept. is suffering. Expensive management time is wasted on trivia. Customers inconvenienced.*

> What are your thoughts at this stage about recommendations or proposals?

> *Three more admin. staff needed in the dept. Offset by increased profits in medium term.*

Stott, K. and Walker, A., *Making Management Work*. © 1992 Simon & Schuster (Asia) Pte Ltd.

Getting the Message Across

Layout

Tell a Story

This should be coherent, logical and well sequenced. The best advice we can give you is learn to tell a good story! If the report is disjointed and one section not relating to the next, it will not be easy to read and definitely *not* compulsive reading. We are not suggesting that you write miniature novels in a literary style, but you will find it advantageous to develop a 'storyline'.

Put the End at the Front

Put the end at the front; that is, put the main conclusions and recommendations at the beginning so that the busy reader can decide whether he is sufficiently interested to read on. You must 'hit' the reader with the crucial points right away. This can be done in the *executive summary*, which for many managers is the only part of the report to be read! This makes it all the more important that the key messages are placed near the beginning. In the consultant's report at the end of this chapter, he chose to have a separate section near the beginning for his major conclusions and recommendations. This was so he could gain the greatest impact.

> Remember, you are writing for busy people. They want to discover the essence of your topic quickly so that they will know if it is worthwhile for them to spend time reading it. They don't want suspense. They don't need to read a logical argument or a compilation of supporting facts *before* they reach your central point. (*Modern Business Reports*, 1987 : 1)

Where you have bad news for the recipient however, you may decide to delay your recommendations a little by outlining a few of the problems of the situation first. If the manager who commissioned the report set up an inventory system a few years ago and you have found it to be an unworkable disaster, it may be best to break it to him gently!

These points are about the structure of the report and we shall be looking at this in some detail later. Now we want to consider the visual appearance.

Visual Appearance

If you have one of your own recently written reports handy, take a look at a few pages. What does it look like: something very attractive and encouraging to read, or a document to be avoided because it looks tedious and 'heavy'? Do not underestimate the impact of your page layout. It is very important. How you set out your material on page can either have a favourable impact or can deter the reader from going any further. Look at the two pages in Figure 18.2 and see the advantage of one over the other of getting the information across easily.

Figure 18.2
Page Layout

The first one reminds us of the old-fashioned textbooks. Given any choice in the matter, you would not go anywhere near them. The manager who receives a report which looks like that probably feels the same way. It either looks like many other documents he receives or it compares unfavourably. Long, uninterrupted paragraphs without subtitles not only make reading difficult, but also make the appearance discouraging.

The second page is entirely different. There is less to read (a good point) because the writer has probably managed to condense his ideas into shorter passages and then convey information through his titles. It looks inviting. The sections and subsections help you to understand how the ideas are broken up. It does the work for you. You do not have to start working out how one idea is related to another; it is done visually. It is not compulsory to have diagrams. Breaking up the text is sufficient. Graphics and other visual aids however definitely enhance appearance and we suggest you look at ways of incorporating them if they are relevant. If they do not make a contribution to the understanding of the message at that point however, do not use them.

Graphics

Graphics definitely help to break down the complexity of some items of information. They may also help to reinforce key points. If they are out of context however, they can make the meaning more difficult to comprehend. Keep your graphics as simple as possible. The following aids are usually appropriate for management reports:

- Pie charts: Give a good picture of how the whole pie is broken up.
- Bar charts: Show relative sizes.
- Graphs: Show trends.
- Tables: Arrange statistical data.
- Organisation charts: Show intended relationships between positions, groups or individuals.

There are many other forms of illustrating information, including flow-charts, maps and scattergrams, but whatever you choose to use, ensure it enhances understanding of your message.

Spacing

It is best to use plenty of space, leaving adequate margins so that the recipient can write notes. Use one-and-a-half or double spacing as this is far easier to read, and use only one side of the paper. Although it is not absolutely necessary, we prefer to start main sections on a new page.

We maintain that you can convey the same information on the second page as the one on the left in Figure 18.2. You do not need any more paper! In fact, we are advocates of reducing the amount of paper. This can be done by developing skills in writing concisely and deciding what is important and what is not. This brings together several skills and one is concerned with writing style and its clarity. We shall look at this in our next section.

Look at your report:

- Does it read like a story, with a middle and an end?
- Are the important parts near the front?
- Does the page layout look attractive and inviting?
- Are illustrations used appropriately?

Style

We all have different styles of writing. This is a good thing. Imagine what it would be like if all novelists wrote in the same style! Despite our differences, some seem to have more attractive styles than others. We look enviously at some authors who have the gift of making everything they write eminently readable. Most of us are not that fortunate. Nevertheless, we can do something about our style. After all, we do change it for different situations. For example, if you look at a job application you have made in the past and then compare it with a letter to a close relative, you will almost certainly detect at least some difference in style. The style will depend very much on the situation and your own preferences. Whatever way you write, however, there are some fundamental principles which make reading easier and which facilitate the process of getting the message across.

To show two extremes of style, we have provided examples from management consultancy reports in Figures 18.3 and 18.4. The first was for a multinational company and written for its top management. The second was for a large public sector organisation. They were both looking at the same issue. Both are fine examples of report writing. The first has a rather clipped and 'matter of fact' style. The second in contrast is flowing and uses words in a creative way. Both writers are experts in their craft.

Figure 18.3
Sample A of Management Consultancy Report

2.2   Members of both organisations have a positive attitude towards the merger and are committed to its future success.

2.3   The new management structure should consist of the Chief Executive and a management group of three, Directors for Resources, Operations and Corporate Responsibility.

2.4   The Director for Resources will be responsible for Resources, Administration and Development.

2.5   Operations should be the responsibility of Regional Directors with Co-ordinators for CAPs and Enterprise Agencies, reporting to the Director, Operations.

You will notice that Figure 18.3 comprises recommendations, and they are in the second section of the report. The author decided that this was the part the client was waiting for, so why keep him waiting? It was a final report. Figure 18.4 is from an 'interim' report, a description of work in progress on the consultancy.

Figure 18.4
Sample B of Management Consultancy Report

> Reorganisation involving closure and merger is never comfortable; for every person who gains, there are those who suffer a vivid and unforgettable personal trauma. Whilst most of us try to manage in organisations at the level of the rational and logical, the emotional and gut reaction is never far from the surface.
>
> It would be quite unforgivable not to record the sadness and disillusionment expressed by some of those interviewed, when they reviewed the present situation in which they found themselves in relation to past experience or hopes. Little can be done with such a depth of feeling at the rational level save to understand how it arises. What must be said is that the frustration felt by some has a disproportionate effect. The ghosts of the past have to be laid if the organisation is to continue to develop the quality of its provision.

Note the skilful use of language which creates images in the mind. Despite the fact that we give you guidelines in this chapter, they are not 'rules' and there are times when you can deviate from established procedures to create the sort of effect so well conveyed in the passage in Figure 18.4. We get the feeling that many business reports are just that bit too formal and some are even a few years out of date (herein contained, thereafter)! There are many circumstances where it is better to be more conversational to avoid obscuring what you are trying to say by using over-formal expressions.

Short Words

Your reports should be readable, preferably using short words which are easy to understand. Most of us fall into the trap of using long words when there is a simpler alternative. Perhaps we feel that using complicated words make us look clever. If you look at some academic journals, there are a lot of clever people around, if you use that criterion. For us, though, the best managers, writers and researchers are the ones who can simplify their ideas. They know what they are talking about and they do their best to ensure *we* know what they are talking about, unlike some writers who do not seem to want you to understand a single sentence! It is a sign of maturity that one can clarify his thinking and then present his ideas using words that everyone can understand.

We accept that there are certain jargon words which you may have to use out of necessity. Most of the time, however, you could possibly be using simpler language. A useful test is to take an idea which you have to present in writing to your colleagues in the near future. Read it to someone at home (not your two-year-old child, obviously) who is not familiar with your work. If he or she can understand, you have probably done a good job.

Short Sentences

The use of short, simple sentences is more effective than elaborate prose. This needs lots of time and practice. The writing of an important report is the time to practise, because it is worth the investment of time and effort to get it right. When you have written the report, go through it and see if you can break up your sentences into smaller ones.

Short sentences do convey ideas more easily. When you look at the *fog index* section below, you will see how confusing it is when the sentences become excessively long. You do not have to be short and abrupt of course. The style in the consultant's report at the end of the chapter is like this, but it was done for a purpose. You can have a more flowing style, but still try to avoid including too many ideas in one sentence.

Short Paragraphs

We have already explained how short paragraphs improve the visual appearance and improve message transmission. You can go through the same management report you have written and then try to reduce the size of the paragraphs. You will often find you can do this without too much trouble, because as soon as there is a break in the idea, you can start a new paragraph. Do not worry if your paragraph is only two or three lines long. That does not matter so long as you are improving your chances of getting the message across accurately. In a report, once your paragraph has reached seven or eight lines, you ought to look for a way of breaking it up sensibly.

Try to put the main idea of the paragraph in the first sentence. This creates the impact for the rest of the paragraph and complies with the principle we outlined earlier of putting the end at the front.

Journalists are experts at putting these principles into practice. Newspapers have to be easy to read (even the serious ones) or they do not sell. Look at a newspaper and examine the words used, the sentence lengths and also the paragraph sizes. You do not have to write in journalistic style, but you may improve your report writing by following the same basic principles.

Short Reports

Newspapers also keep the length of articles relatively short. They have to allocate advertising space, otherwise they may reduce income! You do not have to worry about that in your reports, but you are well advised to keep your reports as short as possible. One of my former bosses used to say to me quite regularly: 'Write me a report on your recommendations! On one side of A4 please.' What he was saying was that he did not want to read anything longer. We can understand that sentiment. There are some managers who go so far as to say that if you cannot summarise your ideas in one page, you have not clarified your thinking sufficiently. They may have a point.

Most of the important reports you write will exceed one page. This is inevitable in view of the information you have to provide. Bear in mind however that quantity is not the same as quality. Some management students we have worked with seem to link the two. The thicker it is, the more work has been put in! That is what they would like you to believe. We would also add that there is more work for the reader! Wherever possible, keep your reports short and sweet, by pruning them and leaving only the essential information concisely written. If you do this with your next few reports, you will find that it becomes increasingly easier to write succinct reports first time round. You will always need to have a final read through of course, but you will not need to do quite so much remedial work.

Lists and Subheadings

You will notice in this book we have frequently used subheadings and lists to separate ideas to make the key points easier to identify. It is possible to keep lists of items in traditional paragraphs but that does not give the same visual appearance and it generally makes the passage more difficult to read. Arranging vertical lists actually does the work for the reader, because that is what he is trying to do mentally when a number of points are made in a paragraph. Look at the following and decide which is the clearer, the first version or the second:

VERSION 1
The general manager has reviewed the work of the marketing division and concluded that there are advantages in splitting up some of the functions. These advantages are increased autonomy to the regions, a reduction in administrative overheads, more innovative responses to the market and a reduction in the number of staff needed at head office.

VERSION 2

In his review of the marketing division, the general manager has identified the following benefits from splitting up some of the functions:

1.   Increased regional autonomy.
2.   Reduced administration costs.
3.   More innovative responses.
4.   Less head office staff.

Subheadings are particularly important for the report writer. The document is not so daunting to the reader if he can see it is broken up into coherent sections. This will also help the attention span to be maintained. Furthermore, he may only be interested in one issue, and if he cannot find it quickly, he may not bother to read the document at all.

In the above example, you can then use subheadings to explain each of the points on the list:

1. Increased Regional Autonomy

There is evidence to suggest that relatively minor decisions are being referred to head office. This will affect our competitiveness if we cannot respond quickly to market demands. Regional managers should therefore be able to do the following without permission:

1.   Recruit sales staff.
2.   Approve orders to an upper limit.

At this point we shall draw a few of these features together. Look at the passage in Application Task 18.2 and see if you can improve its readability by splitting it up, giving it a better visual shape and drawing out headings.

Try doing the exercise before you look at just one possible solution below. You should find that you have made the passage less daunting than the above example. It should have a better visual appearance and the subheadings should cover the main topics. If you want to refer therefore to the issue of overtime, you should be able to find the appropriate part without having to search through the whole piece of writing. If you really wanted to improve it of course, you could change some of the words and alter the way the ideas are expressed. In the example in Figure 18.5, we have not changed the words, but tried to improve the passage through the use of subheadings and shorter sentences and paragraphs, and where possible, we have tried to list ideas.

APPLICATION TASK 18.2

Apply the following four processes to improve the passage:

1. Reduce the length of the sentences.
2. Split it up into more than one paragraph.
3. Create lists.
4. Write appropriate subheadings.

Interviews were held with the managing director, the three workshop supervisors and the sales manager, and most of the questions were open-ended and the interviews were not limited in time, which allowed respondents to speak freely about their feelings and opinions. The managing director felt that he gave his supervisors a good deal of authority to run the workshops as they wished and that he was a good delegator but they couldn't operate on their own because they kept running to him every time a problem occurred, and that was his impression. The supervisors felt he was a poor delegator always interfering in their work and demanding to know everything that was going on and he even chastised them if they made small decisions without asking his permission. The other major source of complaint was about decision-making, the supervisors claiming that it was too slow and holding up their work, not participative and was generally based on inadequate information. The managing director claimed that he had to make decisions quickly because he was under pressure from customers, suppliers and the bank and participation did not work because no one was interested anyway. The issue of overtime came up in the three interviews with supervisors who said that when overtime was allocated they were never consulted, it occurred without warning and the rates had not been reviewed in two years.

Stott. K. and Walker. A., *Making Management Work.* © 1992 Simon & Schuster (Asia) Pte Ltd.

Third Person

In report writing, it is common practice to use the third-person singular:

> not 'I interviewed the managing director;
> but 'The managing director was interviewed.'

The reason for this is that it depersonalises your work and makes it sound more objective. There are some moves to reverse this process, but by and large managers still prefer reports written without the pronouns 'I' and 'we'.

Figure 18.5
An Improved Report

Interviews

Interviews were held with the managing director, the three workshop supervisors and the sales manager. Most of the questions were open-ended. The interviews were not limited in time. The respondents had time therefore to speak freely about their feelings and opinions.

Delegation

The managing director felt that he gave his supervisors a good deal of authority to run the workshops as they wished. He felt he was a good delegator. His impression was they couldn't operate on their own because they kept running to him every time a problem occurred.

The supervisors felt he was a poor delegator. He was always:
    (a) interfering in their work;
    (b) demanding to know everything that was going on;
    (c) chastising them if they made even small decisions without asking his permission.

Decision-making

The other major source of complaint was about decision-making. The supervisors claimed:
    (a) it was too slow and held up their work;
    (b) it was not participative;
    (c) it was generally based on inadequate information.

The managing director claimed that he had to make decisions quickly because he was under pressure from customers, suppliers and the bank. He also claimed participation did not work because no one was interested anyway.

Overtime

The issue of overtime came up in the three interviews with supervisors. The following complaints were made:
    (a) they were never consulted when it was allocated;
    (b) it occurred without warning;
    (c) the rates had not been reviewed in two years.

On the other hand, there are some persuasive arguments for making reports more 'human' and showing that they are written by people for people and usually about people. You have to consider your own style preference and that of your organisation. Whichever you choose to use, be consistent and stick with it throughout the report.

The Fog Index

This is a way of measuring just how clear your writing is. Most of us think we write clearly but that is because we have become too close to our own style, and we have learnt to understand it. Other people may not find it quite so easy to read. That is where the *fog index* comes in. Although it does not account for your actual choice of words and whether they are appropriate to the situation or not, it does cover two important factors which have a major impact on understanding: word length and sentence length. By calculating this index, you may assess how clearly you are putting across your message. The calculation process is shown in Figure 18.6.

Figure 18.6
The Fog Index

STEP 1
Count the number of words in the passage. Count the number of sentences. Then divide the number of words by the number of sentences.

STEP 2
Count the number of words with three syllables or more (you can discount necessary technical terms or names).

STEP 3
Divide the number of words with three or more syllables by the total number of words in the passage. Then multiply by 100.

STEP 4
Add the result of Step 1 to the result of Step 3.
This gives you the FOG INDEX.

Under 30   Probably gets the message over

30 – 40   Not easy to read

Over 40   Gobbledegook

Read the passage below which is taken from a management report:

Because of the excessively high level of unemployment in this particular area, and indeed in the region, it is desirable to consider the possibility of creating an industrial park in the vicinity of the coastline near enough to the port to allow for adequate accessibility to those facilities, although it has to be recognised that this would necessitate cutting through large amounts of agricultural land. This, of course, may not be politically acceptable and there is bound to be strong opposition from environmental lobbies and other pressure groups, particularly the owner occupiers in the area. Nevertheless, unemployment is a distressing problem and the need to attract industry will almost certainly mean taking some hard decisions, although every effort should be made to preserve existing amenities and to protect residents as far as possible through landscaping, otherwise the areas which currently attract tourism will become less popular and that will affect the livelihoods of many which can not be offset even with the introduction of new industrial operations. The whole issue will have to be presented in a persuasive way to the local population, because strong opposition could affect the regional development programme and have a considerable impact on the region's economy which would prevent the opportunity to make inroads into the unemployment problem insofar as prospective manufacturing industries have time and time again shown they are sceptical about establishing operations in areas where local support is not forthcoming.

How clear is that extract to you? You may have some idea of the message, but you probably found some parts confusing. The last sentence in particular loses the reader because there are so many ideas. Now calculate the fog index.

The same information is contained in the passage below:

Something must be done about the high level of unemployment in the area. An industrial park should be set up and it should be near the coast with easy access to the port. This will mean losing some agricultural land and there is bound to be strong opposition. Since local support is needed to attract new businesses, residents must be convinced that the scheme is right. This may be done by keeping amenities and making sure the area remains visually attractive. This is also vital from the tourism point of view. Tourists provide a source of living for many locals.

Do you find that easier to read and assimilate? You should do, because it uses shorter words and shorter sentences. It also takes the key ideas and condenses them. Now calculate the fog index for this passage.

We purposely took an extreme example of a badly written report passage to illustrate a point. Not all reports are quite as bad as that, but we have seen many examples of documents which are worse! Try deciphering the instructions in income tax forms or the content of legal documents. Many of these contain genuine 'gobbledegook'. It is so easy to let your management reports become like that. You start using long words where shorter ones will do; writing sentences which never end; before you know it, the whole thing is unintelligible. You are probably aware of one of the best pieces of advice given to a manager: KISS – Keep It Simple Stupid. And that is particularly true of management reports.

You should have arrived at the following Fog Index figures: 83 for the wordy passage and 24 for the simpler one. You may be skilful enough to write even better than the second example, but so long as you can keep the index below 30, you are writing clearly enough.

You should now take a piece of your own writing and calculate your Fog Index. Ideally it should be a management report or a document which you have written for colleagues at work. If you do not have these, then one page of an assignment or other piece of writing would do. It is quite sufficient to base the assessment on one page, as that is a good guide to the rest of the content. Take a random page though rather than one which may be uncharacteristic!

Having understood the features of the index, you should be able to have some impact on your writing immediately. In Application Task 18.3 you are asked to make sense of a wordy passage that it is difficult to understand.

APPLICATION TASK 18.3

REDUCE THE FOG INDEX

Rewrite the passage below and reduce the Fog Index to 30 or less:

When the board met earlier in the month there was a demand that the decision had to be reached by 11.00 on 24 March as consultants from the local authority's management unit were meeting with potential contractors on 25 March and would obviously require a firm commitment as to whether the company wanted to be involved in the project. With a general tightening of the economy, the company cannot afford to withhold its commitment to projects which may not be very profitable because of local authority spending controls, because there would be the imminent danger of redundancy for a large proportion, maybe even a quarter, of the employees, if the company were not able to secure contracts with foreign clients, although they invariably offer substantially higher profits. New equipment would be necessary if the company were to commit itself to this project with the local authority, but it would at least make provision for increased security of job tenure for some time.

Stott, K. and Walker, A., *Making Management Work*. © 1992 Simon & Schuster (Asia) Pte Ltd.

You probably gathered that the ideas were fairly simple, but the passage tried to make them sound difficult! This is a common phenomenon in management reports. You probably took out the key ideas and just wrote them out in simple sentences, but in a logical sequence. When you have done the exercise, you can look at the version below. It is not the 'right' answer but just one way of keeping simple things simple!

> *The contract with the local authority is not as profitable as a contract with foreign clients. It also means buying new equipment. Despite this, it offers job security for workers in the short term. The company has to decide if it wishes to be involved. In its meeting earlier this month, the board was told that the decision must be reached by 11.00 on 24 March. This would be taken to the meeting with the local authority the next day.*

The index for the first passage is 73. We hope you at least managed to improve on that! The second passage's index has been reduced to 23.

Imprecise Expressions

Avoid using meaningless expressions like 'many' and 'good'. Always avoid emotive expressions which lack precision, such as 'an enormous drop in revenue'. What does 'enormous' mean? It is better to say that 'revenue fell by 20 per cent last year.' Aim therefore for conciseness by preempting the questions an intelligent reader would ask. If, for example, you are saying: 'The administrative unit should have a substantial increase in the number of staff', the reader would probably ask what 'substantial' means. In other words, he wants to know precisely how many (especially if he has to pay for them!) It is better therefore to write: 'there should be between four to six additional staff in the administrative unit.' You might then give the reasons for your figures.

Unadorned Facts

Focus on facts, pure and unadulterated. They should be presented simply and clearly without adornment. Then you can interpret and colour them with your own views, but this should be done in a rational way rather than using it as an opportunity to give vent to your emotional feelings about the subject. The reader therefore should be able to look first at the facts which have been presented impartially, and perhaps interpret them in his own way before reading your discussion.

Look at the following passage:

> *The department suffered a desperate turnover in staff last year. This affected performance enormously. It was most likely due to the fact that so many employees*

are in the younger age bracket and they leave to get married or have children.

First of all, it has departed from the facts and started interpreting reasons. The reader should be allowed to read the facts and make what he will of them before the author imposes his analysis on the matter. The fact in this passage is that there was a turnover of staff in the department last year. Did you spot the other weaknesses? What is a 'desperate' turnover? Did performance improve or decline? That has not been stated. How enormous is 'enormous'? How many employees are in the 'younger age bracket'? What is the 'younger age bracket'? We are not suggesting that the length of the report, or the passage for that matter, be increased; just that facts replace the woolly statements which are there at the moment. Instead of 'desperate', say how many staff left; state how performance was affected; and explain what is meant by 'young'. It could, for example, be employees in the 20–30 age group.

All this of course should come in your section on facts. If you entitle one section 'Findings' or 'Results', you should keep the section solely for that purpose, and not get drawn into a discussion on the possible reasons for things turning out as they did. Save that information for later.

Jargon

Think about your readers. What do they know? Are they familiar with the jargon or are you mistakenly assuming they understand all the acronyms and technical terms which trip off the tongue? This should affect the language you use and the overall presentation. If you are writing a report for one of your bosses who is entirely familiar with your work and an expert in the field, it is in order to use specialist language. A hospital doctor, for example, writing a report for a senior consultant, could use medical terms which no one outside the profession could understand. If, however, you are writing the report for someone who is not familiar with the language, you must omit jargon or explain it.

SUMMARY

Getting the Message Across:

- Use a style you are comfortable with, making it readable.
- Use short words.
- Use short sentences.

- Use short paragraphs.
- Write short, concise reports.
- Avoid unnecessary information.
- Use lists and subheadings, and break into coherent sections.
- Avoid imprecise expressions.
- Present unadorned facts, not drama.
- Avoid jargon where appropriate, and make it understandable.

Writing the Report

You are now ready to write an effective report. Even just applying the points outlined above can help to transform unintelligible reports into documents of managerial utility. Now we need to look at the way in which the 'story' unfolds, and give the report a framework which will help to ensure coherence.

There are several items of information which you must cover. Although they do not apply to all types of report, they are generally relevant to most of the 'management-type' reports which managers are expected to write. As a guide, you must tell your reader:

- The original intention of your report.
- What you actually did.
- What you found out.
- What you made of your discoveries.
- The conclusions you reached.
- Your recommendations.

In this list we have used language everyone can understand. In other texts, you may find those items under the headings of parameters and terms of reference, methodology, findings, analysis and interpretation, conclusions, and recommendations. Whichever words you use, they mean very much the same, and provide the structure within which you can reveal your story. Some experts on report writing offer the good advice:

'Tell 'em what you are going to tell 'em'.
'Tell 'em'.
'Tell 'em what you told 'em'.

This is a useful way of thinking about your writing in three phases. Outline what you are going to cover in the report. In other words, provide a summary of the *key* points. Then write the report (this will cover the bulk of the document). At the end, go over the main points again. This may sound repetitive and tedious. What you are trying to do however, is to reinforce the messages you want to get across. You are not repeating word for word, but re-presenting your major points in a slightly different way.

You will find the structure we suggest covers this three-stage format, but goes into more detail about what to put in the middle, the main body of the report.

There is no one set way of structuring a report. The example we give at the end of the chapter deviates slightly from the framework we give below, but nevertheless the impact is present and it is quite coherent. We have found however that most management reports fit neatly into our simple framework. In the outline shown in Figure 18.7, we have not mentioned the title page, table of contents, appendices and bibliography. We shall cover these briefly in our more detailed explanation of report structure later.

The Summary

This, you will note, comes at the beginning, although it is the last thing you write! Some people call it the *executive summary*. About 200 words or less should be sufficient to explain succinctly the purpose of the report, what you discovered, the conclusions you reached and the key recommendations. A well-written summary can whet the appetite and encourage the reader to look at more of the report.

If you have been asked to make recommendations, you should use this opportunity to emphasise them. That way, they are going to be mentioned three times in the report in varying forms, and that should reinforce the message.

Devote some time and effort to writing your summary. As managers who both write and receive reports (notice we did not say 'read'), we feel it is probably the most important part. If it is skilfully written, makes sense and outlines some persuasive recommendations, we are more likely to be influenced to treat the rest of the report seriously.

SUMMARY

- Devote time to writing your summary.
- Write it in less than one page.
- Include the purpose, main findings, conclusions and recommendations.

Figure 18.7
Report Outline

REPORT OUTLINE	
SUMMARY	Emphasise major conclusions and recommendations.
INTRODUCTION	
Terms of reference.	Delimit the report.
Relevant situational details.	Set the scene for the reader.
Statement of problem.	
Background to problem.	Give the bird's eye view.
Methods of collecting information.	
MAIN BODY	
Facts and findings.	Presented straightforwardly.
Discussion.	Analysis of findings, putting them in perspective.
CONCLUSIONS	Arrived at logically from the reasoning in the discussion.
RECOMMENDATIONS	Made in specific terms. Include implications (resources, reactions, etc.)
FINAL COMMENTS	Reinforce major recommendations and benfits.

Stott, K. and Walker, A., *Making Management Work.* © 1992 Simon & Schuster (Asia) Pte Ltd.

Introduction

Terms of Reference

You need to clarify the purpose. Why have you written it? 'This is a report to ...' You should fill in the missing space. It could be to inform the managing director about new market opportunities, to make recommendations about overtime rates, or a host of other things.

You should then outline the scope of your report. Explain why you limited your investigation to a certain time period or to a particular group of employees. Also explain briefly what is not covered in order to preempt any suggestions that you failed to examine a particular aspect of the problem. You are laying out your boundaries.

You also need to indicate for whom it is written. Some people may read it and it is not prepared for them: they will need to know who the intended recipient is.

Relevant Situational Details

Set the scene for what is about to follow. Give a few brief details of your organisation or department which will help the reader understand the context. You have to be careful to include only information which is important. Do not forget, for every additional sentence, there may be a commensurate decrease in understanding. If you are dealing with a problem in a small area of work, you may write a few lines about how that work fits into the whole business. You may also wish to give a few historical background details. This is generally acceptable so long as you do not distract from the key purpose of the report. As a rule of thumb, ask yourself what questions the reader is most likely to raise as he goes through the report. Answer these and forget the others. Suppose, for example, you are writing a report recommending the installation of some new personal computers. As you think things through from the reader's point of view, you decide you would like to know what the current level of usage is, how long the present machines have been in operation and the sorts of jobs they are used for. These are the questions you should answer so that the reader has the relevant information about the situation.

Statement of Problem

In our chapter on Solving Problems and Making Decisions we emphasised the need to identify the *real* problem rather than the symptoms. If, for example, you go into a company and notice that there is much litter on the floor and the reception is very untidy, you might well say there is a litter problem. In fact, it is more likely a symptom of a problem. Without all the details it is impossible to say precisely what the problem is (it may be something to do with attitudes or morale, for instance), but you have to search for the real problem if you are to cure it. Treating symptoms has only a short-term effect. So you must now state what that real problem is, assuming that your report deals with such an issue. And you should demonstrate that you have identified the root problem and are not making recommendations about the treatment of symptoms.

Try to state the problem dispassionately and without judgement. You would not say: 'Our performance over the last quarter has been dreadful'; or 'The marketing people have not been doing their jobs very well.' You would be making judgements before you have even given any facts. It would be better to say: 'There was a 15 per cent drop in sales over the last quarter.'

It is always tempting to start introducing your own opinions when outlining the problem. This is because you probably have some notion about the possible cause. At this stage, however, you are only interested in an objective statement of what the problem is.

Now comes some difficult advice: Look at the problem from the perspectives of other interested parties. How does it affect other managers, employees, customers and suppliers? Similarly, when you look at potential solutions, you should also consider the possible impact on the same groups.

Background to Problem

The background to the problem is not quite the same as setting the scene, although the two may be related. Imagine you could have a picture of the issue from a few miles above it. You would be able to see all the relevant forces on it. You have to do this for the reader: give him a bird's eye view. But do it succinctly. We hear managers say: 'But it is a very complex issue; it needs a vast amount of background.' Complex it may be, but it does not alter the fact that the recipient may not read it. You have to be selective and only include that material which is of critical relevance. Then you have to condense the amount of information to something which can be easily read.

Charles, the hospital's catering manager, was asked to write a report for the hospital general manager about the problem of catering. Surveys of patients had revealed that the food was perceived as being of low standard and not hot enough by the time it was served. As background to the problem, Charles had to explain about the number of beds served, how far the kitchen was from the wards, the transportation equipment currently in operation and the number of staff who relayed food from kitchen to ward. All this information was necessary to put the problem in perspective.

Methods of Collecting Information

Explain briefly how you investigated the problem (e.g. interviewed someone, inspected official records, etc.). In doing this, just answer the obvious questions your reader might ask. You do not have to go into extensive detail about the duration of interviews, the structure of questionnaires and so forth. If the method really has high relevance to the report, you could always include important documents in the appendices.

SUMMARY

- Outline the purpose and scope of the report.
- State for whom it is written.
- Give relevant details of the situation.
- Explain the problem clearly.
- Give background information to the problem.
- Explain briefly how you collected information or 'evidence'.

The Main Body

Facts and Findings

This is the opportunity to show to the reader precisely what you found out. Present the unadorned facts. These can be quite revealing. When some managers write reports, they discover things which quite clearly contradict established thinking, and they take great pleasure in presenting the facts as they stand. I once did that with a consultancy: the organisation had a matrix structure and believed that a vast amount of interdepartmental activity was taking place. My findings showed that less than 10 per cent of the work involved people from different departments! The facts in that case provided a powerful statement on their own.

Present your findings, but do not overdo it. You may have acquired a vast amount of data but you will swamp the reader if you present it all, so you may have to do some drastic pruning. Only include relevant facts. We outlined the problem earlier of getting too close to your work, so much so that you find it heartbreaking to discard anything. Unfortunately for you (but fortunately for the reader) you have to be ruthless and only use what is important. Failing to do that will cloud the issue.

Whenever possible, use visual aids such as charts, graphs and tables. If they are simple like pie charts, they are easier to take in than wordy explanations. If there are many figures, summarise them before putting them in graphic form. The more comprehensive data can be put in an appendix. Sometimes you may not be sure whether to include a visual aid in the main text. Two things you can do:

- Ask yourself whether it is critically relevant.
- Ask someone to look at it for ten seconds and then explain what it means. If it is simple enough they will be able to do this.

When we state our findings as part of a consultancy, we like to say something positive first, even if we have seen a very negative picture. The client likes to feel that you have not merely found the faults but also observed some good points. This does not mean you avoid the truth. It simply shows you are able to see both weak and strong aspects.

Discussion

This is the part where you analyse the facts and interpret them. In your analysis, you wish to draw attention to particularly interesting results, perhaps unexpected ones. You will highlight discrepancies, the gaps between what you were expecting to find and what you actually found. You will identify patterns or trends. You will discuss the results which are very important and perhaps disregard those which are of no importance. At the same time, you will discuss possible reasons for results turning out as they did and give explanations where necessary. You may, for example, draw attention to the fact that the sales figures were very low during January and February. You can then go on to explain the possible or probable reasons. You may say, for instance, that the war in the Middle East deterred people from travelling which in turn had an impact on your business.

Whilst the summary may be the most important part of the report from a presentation point of view, you will probably spend a great deal of time on the discussion. This is really the substance, the meat of your report. Generally, most managers can write a passable report which gives facts and figures, and then presents some recommendations which may or may not be related to the findings. This goes on all the time, because they often have their recommendations firmly laid out even before they do any research work. Everything else then has to fit in with those. You have to be different. You have to be analytical and to use your interpretation of data to inform your recommendations. In other words, your writing has to be more coherent.

It is true that many managers experience great difficulty in analysing their findings. One activity which helps in this regard is to sit down with another manager and tell him about your findings. Ask him to fire questions at you and as you answer, note down the main points. You will probably find that at the end of the exercise, you have sufficient material to be able to do an effective interpretation.

If you are unable to discuss your work with anyone, then try for a start simply asking the question 'Why?'

'Why are the subordinates always failing to meet deadlines?'
'Why did the sales figures dip during that period?'
'Why did most of the staff say they would prefer not to be relocated?'

It is also helpful to try and convert information to pictures. It is very easy to do this with things like figures, because you can draw graphs and charts. Even with other items of data, you may be able to represent them graphically which will aid your understanding of relationships. You may, for example, have interviewed a few people to gather opinions on a matter. Rather than simply work with the straight written record of what each person said, you can summarise the main points under predetermined headings and put the opinions of each interviewee in a separate box. Although it is a very simple process, it certainly helps when it comes to analysis and interpretation.

SUMMARY

- Present relevant facts and findings.
- Do not colour them with your own opinions.
- Use graphics to simplify information where appropriate.
- Analyse and interpret your data.

Conclusions

These will emerge from the analysis of the facts and the discussion. Any conclusions you reach will not come direct from the results or findings but as a logical outcome of the analysis and discussion. If you have reasoned the case well in the discussion, the reader should be taken along with you into the conclusions and would almost be able to tell what they are before reading.

You may also have considered some possible options for recommendations by this stage. After due consideration you may 'conclude' that some are workable and others are not. In this section you might explain the advantages or benefits of particular courses of action. This leads the reader nicely into the recommendations you will make, because you will have shown by now that some recommendations are just not viable whilst others have high potential. Your reader should now have a fairly good idea of what you are going to say in your next section.

SUMMARY

- Reach conclusions from your reasoning during the discussion.
- Present relative advantages of various options.

Recommendations

If these do not relate closely to your conclusions, you are hardly likely to convince anyone to implement your recommendations. They should be a natural and logical consequence of everything which has been written before. These are the end of a story, one which makes sense. The readers should be satisfied therefore that they have read a convincing and coherent storyline.

Recommendations should be absolutely clear. They stand little chance of success if they are vague. It is not a good idea, for example, to write: 'It is recommended that we consider the possibility of taking on more ancillary staff, assuming we remain in a state of growth.' It is difficult to believe anyone could take any action on a recommendation like that. How many ancillary staff should be employed? When are they needed? And is the writer trying to shirk responsibility if things go wrong by referring to growth? Be precise and ensure that you are realistic, and that you explain briefly why you have chosen that course of action. It is a good idea to type the recommendation statement in bold or italic characters (or underline) and then give a few lines of explanation. An example is shown in Figure 18.8.

Figure 18.8
A Recommendation

Recommendation 1.   *Two additional clerical assistants ought to be employed immediately.*

The present staff are considerably overloaded. There is a four-day wait for typing. Photocopying and other essential jobs are being unreasonably delayed.

You must also explain the implications of your recommendations so that an informed decision can be made. Now you are showing that you have thought about everything possible in advance. You have anticipated problems and worked out costings and resource implications. You have attempted to answer the important questions the reader might ask. You cannot be reasonably expected to get it all right of course, but you must demonstrate you have made every effort to cover the key issues. In the example from Figure 18.8, you would explain the costs of hiring two additional staff, but set these against the benefits.

SUMMARY

- Show how your recommendations are a consequence of your conclusions.
- Make them specific with clear guidelines for action.
- Make them realistic and workable.
- State time scales and personnel involved.
- Outline cost implications, if appropriate.

Final Remarks

We like to put a small section in at the end just to refresh the reader's memory about the principal recommendations and benefits. It is simply an attempt to reinforce the main message and to remove any lingering doubts about the wisdom of what has been said. Where this is not an issue, you may not need this section.

SUMMARY

- Tie the report together with a brief statement.
- Reinforce your key message.

We said at the beginning of this chapter that you have to learn to tell a good story. If you follow this format, it will help you do just that. You will explain what the point of the story is and then set the scene. You will go on to outline the problem with some supporting information. Then you will write about what you found when you entered the 'forest' and what you made of it. Finally, you will reach some conclusions, possibly followed by some advice about how to make a better story!

So far in this section, we have looked at the main parts of the report. We now want to consider briefly a few other parts which go to make the finished product. These are the *title page,* the *table of contents, appendices* and *bibliography.*

Title Page

Depending on the nature of the report, you may or may not decide to have a title page. In the example at the end of the chapter (Figure 18.11), the consultant chose to have a front page which gave the title of the project, for whom it was written, his name and company, and the date.

Contents

We always feel this is useful to have in a report, as it helps the reader to locate the·section he wants immediately. It can be quite frustrating searching through the entire document to look for a particular subsection when it could easily be listed by its page number on the contents page.

Appendices

For some report writers, these are very useful waste disposal dumping grounds. If they cannot think of what to do with some information they have acquired, they put it in the appendix. This is not the best use for this section. An appendix is meant for useful information which supports the main text. The keen reader will probably want to refer to it. The reason it is not in the main part of the report is that it is not central (in its full form) and that it possibly takes some time to assimilate.

Tables, charts and other documents sometimes have information which is very important and which should be included in the body of the report. The best way of dealing with this is to put it in summary form and then put it in the main text. You may, for example, have a table with lots of figures and it would take several minutes to decipher it. In this case, try to prepare a summary table. It may look something like the one in Figure 18.9.

Figure 18.9
Summary Table

Products sold in the first quarter:

	PRODUCT A	PRODUCT B	PRODUCT C
January	234	87	112
February	155	80	96
March	180	81	101

Figures represent units sold

Bibliography

This is not a common feature of most management reports, although it is possible you have drawn on information sources such as journal articles, books and magazines. If you have, you must provide the references, and a suitable system for doing this appears in the reference sections of this book.

Writing Your Next Report

We find it useful when we have a report to write to have a sheet of paper handy with our main headings. When we think of anything relevant, we just make a note in the relevant section. When it is time to write the actual report, we have a number of points ready to guide our thinking. We do not have to use them all of course, but it provides a very useful 'crib sheet' and because it is on one piece of paper, it is easier to see how the points in each section might be related.

In Figure 18.10 we have provided one of these sheets for you to use when you write your next report. You could put the title at the top and leave it in a handy place so that when you think of anything which is relevant, you could jot a few notes down. You would then find these helpful when you come to the real thing.

Figure 18.10
A Report Notes Form

Title:

Terms of reference:

Situation:

Problem:

Problem background:

Ways of obtaining data:

Facts and findings:

Discussion:

Provisional recommendations:

Stott, K. and Walker, A., *Making Management Work.* © 1992 Simon & Schuster (Asia) Pte Ltd.

This form is to be used *before* you start writing the report proper. That is why we have not put a conclusions section in. You cannot reach conclusions until you have obtained findings and discussed them.

Important reports may well require far more space than that on the form. In that case, use a separate sheet of A4 paper for each heading. If it is a lengthy investigation, you may need several sheets for the discussion section. Put the papers in a ring binder (or simply staple them together) and make relevant notes as before. You will find this more helpful than going straight into the report. Writing those first few words is never easy, but if you have notes laid out in a roughly logical sequence, it will be so much easier.

When It Is Finished

Accuracy

When you have finished writing your report your job is not finished. If you are given an important document to write, never aim to complete it just before the deadline for submission. Depending on the nature of the report, it may take up to several days to knock into shape.

You must show that you are meticulous about accuracy, both of the information and in the presentation. A report which has false data lacks credibility and so does the author! If someone demonstrates that the facts are inaccurate in a meeting, your report will at least lose its impact and may even be discarded.

Spelling mistakes and typographical errors may not be quite so serious but they are very distracting for the reader, and they call your professionalism into question. If you know you have a spelling weakness, get someone else to check the report or do a spell check on the word processor. It is not good enough to blame the secretary's inadequacies for mistakes in an important report. You have to check it yourself.

Discard the Unnecessary

This is now the time to cut the 'waffle'! If you have any irrelevant information there, take it out. Ask yourself again: 'What is really important?' You may have to be quite severe, but it is worth it in the end when you produce a clear, highly focused document. We have a system of what we call *red-penning* each other's work, which we read very critically. We then strike out unnecessary words, sentences, whole paragraphs and even sections. We may find that we can express the contents of a paragraph in a single sentence and get the meaning across more clearly. The red pen in this case is a very useful instrument!

Put to the Test

This is exactly what we do when we read each other's writing. But if you really want to put your report writing to the test, let someone read it who is not familiar with your work, and ask him to mark those parts which are not absolutely clear the first time he reads them. You should not expect someone to read a sentence three times to grasp its meaning.

If parts of the report are unclear, they have to be rewritten. This need not take too long and sometimes the change of the odd word here and there will do the trick. There are occasions however when you have to accept that a whole section has to be completely rewritten.

> . . . at this point you have to take another distancing step – this time right away from what you have written. You now have to become the EDITOR.
>
> As the editor you are concerned with accuracy and completeness. You are editing with the reader in mind. You are cutting the waffle. You are instructing the author to rewrite anything that is not absolutely clear and lucid. And, after the author has rewritten it, if you are not satisfied you will coldly order the author to draft that piece again – and again! Gradually, between the two of you, AUTHOR and EDITOR, a final draft will appear. (NEBSS, 1987)

This will help to ensure that the approach is thoroughly rigorous and that the final version for submission meets all the criteria we have previously identified.

SUMMARY

When It Is Finished:

- Check for accuracy.
- Cut the waffle.
- Put to the test and rewrite where meaning is unclear.

The Consultant's Report

There are many ways of writing reports and we have suggested in this chapter just one format which works. Naturally, you will have your own style which will differ from that of other managers. We would not recommend that you copy the style of the report we have included in Figure 18.11. We have put it in to show you what one professionally commissioned management report looks like.

It was written by a consultant who was instructed to review the management structure of his client organisation. The chief executive was a 'no-nonsense' man. He was also impatient and wanted the consultant to get straight to the point. This was reflected in the crisp, direct style of the report which fulfils all of the criteria we have outlined in this chapter. In this case the consultant decided to put his conclusions and recommendations near the beginning, knowing that this was the information his client wanted. If the client did not like what he read in this section, he probably would not bother to read the rest. This section then in particular had to be concise and to convey his ideas accurately. He chose to number his sections and subsections, and this made it easier for the client to refer to a particular paragraph. You do not have to do it like this necessarily.

We have condensed the report and included the first part of each subsection. This gives the general picture and shows the coherent way in which it is presented.

Conclusion

In this chapter we have examined some of the preparatory activities which must take place before a report is written, and some of the techniques for getting information across to the reader accurately. We have suggested a structure for management report writing which we believe creates the right sort of impact and which enables you to write a coherent story. We have tried to ask questions which will challenge you to look at your report writing critically.

Next time you write a report, when it is finished, see whether you have converted the principles into practice by using the checklist shown in Figure 18.12, The Finished Report: A Checklist, to test its quality.

Figure 18.11
The Consultant's Report

Alpha Electronics
Management Structure Consultancy

Report prepared by:
Calvin Howe

Harbury Consultants
Chelmsford

June 1991

CONTENTS

1. SUMMARY   1

2. CONCLUSIONS AND RECOMMENDATIONS   2

3. INTRODUCTION   3
    3.1 Terms of reference
    3.2 Procedures

4. THE STUDY   4
    4.1 Nature of information acquired
    4.2 Key findings

5. NEW MANAGEMENT STRUCTURE   5
    5.1 Key features
    5.2 Specific details

6. OPERATING THE NEW STRUCTURE   7
    6.1 Communication
    6.2 Resource allocation
    6.3 Management development opportunities

7. CONCLUDING REMARKS   8

1.   SUMMARY

1.1 This report recommends and outlines a new management structure for Alpha Electronics.

1.2 A detailed examination of the company's environment was made and interviews conducted with a cross-section of the company's workforce.

1.3 Findings showed that the company is operating in a dynamic and highly competitive environment. The present structure however is not flexible enough to respond to the changes which are demanded.

1.4 Many managers face uncertain conditions and are unsure of their roles.

1.5 The newly designed structure accommodates resource constraints and creates more flexibility. It supports the need for co-operation across departments.

1.6 By implementing this structure, it is expected the company will be able to meet client demands more rapidly and effectively.

1

2.   CONCLUSIONS AND RECOMMENDATIONS

2.1 The company's open management style has encouraged initiatives and many developments to take place.

2.2 High standards of excellence are evident throughout the organisation and these must be supported.

2.3 Central values are shared by many key staff. They have a positive attitude to impending changes in the management structure and are committed to the company's success.

2.4 The new management structure accounts for the need for increased interdepartmental work.

2.5 It is based on the current functional arrangement but with an overlay of integrating devices.

2.6 The number of managers will be reduced. This will help to contain costs and make co-ordination easier.

2.7 Reward systems and resource allocation processes should be reviewed to achieve congruence with the new structure.

2

3. INTRODUCTION

3.1 Terms of reference

3.1.1 On instructions from the client, the chief executive of Alpha Electronics, an examination has been made of the existing management structure and recommendations made for improvements.

3.1.2 Only issues relating to the structure have been addressed. Other systems and processes have not been considered.

3.2 Procedures

3.2.1 The company's external environment was examined by talking to experts in the field and detailing the activities of rival companies.

3.2.2 Interviews were held with a cross-section of employees to ascertain readiness for change and their understanding of their roles.

3

4. THE STUDY

4.1 Nature of information acquired

4.1.1 Information was acquired on the way managers saw their future operating conditions, their present responsibilities and the amount of interdepartmental work required.

4.2 Key findings

4.2.1 Interdepartmental projects are becoming increasingly important to meet the complex demands of clients. The present structure does not accommodate this requirement.

4.2.2 Helpful behaviour by some managers and general goodwill is going some way to cope with changing work patterns as they occur.

4.2.3 Some departments are guarding their resources jealously and are reluctant to release staff for special projects. Fortunately, this is not widespread, but it could become highly dysfunctional in the near future.

4

5. NEW MANAGEMENT STRUCTURE

5.1 Key features

5.1.1   The structure is both simple to operate and flexible enough to respond to changing demands.

5.1.2   It is based on a simple functional form with an overlay of integrating devices.

5.1.3   These integrating devices are designed to cope with the expanding interdepartmental activities.

5.2 Specific details

5.2.1   Diagram 5.1 shows the outline structure. Those members in integrating positions are responsible for managing projects.

5.2.2   The co-ordinators may take staff into their project teams through negotiation with divisional heads.

5.2.3   The least expensive integrating devices have been used. These are temporary positions and co-ordinators return to their units when not supervising projects.

5

5.1   Outline structure

6

6. OPERATING THE NEW STRUCTURE

6.1 Communication

6.1.1 Clear delineation of responsibilities could impede the free flow of communication currently enjoyed. There has to be flexibility within the formalised layout.

6.1.2 Staff must become used to frequent small changes in the structure. It may be difficult for them at first, but they will accept it when they see the advantages.

6.2 Resource allocation

6.2.1 Senior co-ordinators report direct to the CE. They receive their budgets from him and do not have to rely on the functional heads.

6.2.2 A system of 'buying in' departmental staff will be installed.

6.3 Management development opportunities.

6.3.1 Younger managers should be encouraged to take on temporary assignments to develop their management skills. Short-term secondments to projects will increase organisational flexibility and lead to career development.

7

7. CONCLUDING REMARKS

7.1 The proposed structure is to enable the company's business to be managed more effectively in a dynamic environment.

7.2 It is designed so that it supports the present level of quality production and at the same time is able to respond quickly to new developments in the market.

7.3 It redistributes power through reporting relationships and resource allocation. The project co-ordinators have a direct line to the CE which should enhance the quality of projects.

7.4 Gratitude is expressed to all those employees of the company who have so willingly co-operated in this consultancy project.

8

Figure 18.12
The Finished Report: A Checklist

Have you:

- Stated the purpose and intention of the report? ☐

- Stated the major details of purpose, findings and recommendations in the summary? ☐

- Ensured all factual statements are accurate? ☐

- Presented your facts uncoloured by your opinions? ☐

- Outlined the scope of your report? ☐

- Indicated for whom it is written? ☐

- Provided some details of the situation? ☐

- Stated the problem clearly? ☐

- Provided important information which has a bearing on the problem? ☐

- Described how you collected your information? ☐

- Analysed your findings and discussed them? ☐

- Answered questions the reader will ask? ☐

- Reached conclusions based on your reasoning? ☐

- Made clear, purposeful and specific recommendations? ☐

- Made recommendations which are a natural consequence of your conclusions? ☐

- Ensured recommendations indicate personnel to take action and a time scale? ☐

- Ensured your recommendations are realistic? ☐

- Included the resource cost implications? ☐

- Identified constraints? ☐

- Written a coherent story? ☐

- Checked it for typographical accuracy? ☐

- Discarded unnecessary information? ☐

- Got someone to test it for understanding? ☐
- Rewritten parts which are unclear? ☐
- Checked it for readability? ☐
- Ensured it looks good? ☐
- Ensured there are adequate margins? ☐
- Given suitable spacing? ☐
- Used illustrations to aid understanding? ☐
- Used short words? ☐
- Used short sentences? ☐
- Used short paragraphs? ☐
- Ensured everything falls under a heading or subheading? ☐
- Given it a title which shows clearly what it is about? ☐

Stott, K. and Walker, A., *Making Management Work.* © 1992 Simon & Schuster (Asia) Pte Ltd.

References

Gallagher, W. (1969) *Report Writing for Management,* Addison-Wesley : Boston.

Modern Business Reports (1987) *Writing Winning Reports and Proposals,* Alexander Hamilton Institute : New York.

NEBSS (1987) *Project Preparation,* Pergamon : Oxford.

Sussams, J. (1983) *How to Write Effective Reports,* Gower : England.

Chapter 19

Making Presentations

. . . the relationship, which I might tentatively venture to aver has not been without a degree of reciprocal utility and even perhaps occasional gratification, is approaching the point of irreversible bifurcation and, to put it briefly, is in the propinquity of its ultimate regrettable termination.

So said Sir Humphrey Appleby in *Yes, Prime Minister*. Sadly, Sir Humphrey is not the only one who has difficulty in expressing himself. How often have you listened to someone who has something important or interesting to say, but who just cannot get his message over? He may have irritating gestures, speak in a monotone voice, never complete his sentences or simply sound incoherent. In contrast you may have listened to a presentation where the speaker is an expert communicator, but when you examine the content, he may have said very little. Politicians the world over for example are very adept at using rhetoric, cliché and exhortation to inspire. We can learn much from such exponents.

Our aim in this chapter is to outline how you can enhance what you have to say through effective **presentation** skills. We start with the premise therefore that you have something worthwhile to say. To begin with, what sorts of situations in the work place give rise to presentations? You present when you:

1.   Inform colleagues about your work.
2.   Update colleagues with information.
3.   Inform interested parties about the work of the organisation.
4.   Attempt to engage in joint problem-solving.
5.   Gain support or acceptance for your ideas.

Some of the situations you might face are departmental meetings where you have to present an idea to a few colleagues, meetings with clients where you have to tell them about your products and talks to groups of your superiors. There are other situations. You may for instance have to speak to hundreds of experts at a convention or conference, or you may have an informal gathering of two or three colleagues in your office. You may from time to time make an inspirational presentation where the emphasis is not so much on what is said as on providing a stimulus for action. The start of a sales drive is a case in point where the sales manager may exhort the team to make extra efforts. All these situations call for effective presentation skills.

This chapter ties in with Chapter 18, Writing Reports. Many of the principles are very much the same, especially those relating to preparation and structure. We shall nevertheless go over these issues and then look at skills which are particular to the oral presentation.

Making Presentations

Not all presentations are formal and organised. Some are comparatively casual. We may, for example, be explaining to a colleague why we are making a particular schedule change, or on the domestic scene, we may be giving our opinions on where the annual family holiday should be.

Presentations are more than just informal discussions. They have a purpose. We are trying to gain something from them. It may be as simple as increased understanding on the part of the other person or it may be more complicated, such as the commitment to an idea. But all presentations are designed to achieve something.

Formal presentations can cause a great deal of consternation. You hold the floor and everyone looks to you in expectation. Although your ideas and the way you arrange your material may make sense and be profitable to all concerned, you may still fail to reach your objectives because of poor presentation. You may, for example, have a stunning idea for saving people's time and effort, but because it is not skilfully presented, it is not well received and is not implemented. Content therefore is not the be all and end all. We have to develop effective presentation skills if we are to get the message across clearly and, in many cases, persuasively. These skills can be learned. You can learn how to gain attention, how to organise your ideas, how to reinforce information and how to deliver the presentation. Giving presentations can be a highly rewarding experience.

> But try to persuade the beginner of that fact, and you are likely to be met with a disbelief that is exceeded only by the victim's contemplative misery. And this is because of the lack of one essential ingredient – *self-confidence.* The great fear is that we shall 'dry' up, be unable to remember the words we once had in mind; our jokes will fall flat on their faces; our audience will sit silent and stony-faced, and, in short, we shall succeed only in making complete and utter fools of ourselves. (Lord, 1982 : 147)

Lack of confidence in giving oral presentations is something which afflicts many managers. Speaking to large groups in particular gives rise to fears which can hamper effectiveness. Like some unfortunate examination candidates, managers often get themselves into such a state that they are unable to perform. They are virtually paralysed. Overcoming such fears however is easier said than done, but you have to take some action to reduce the effects of potentially dysfunctional anxiety, otherwise performance in terms of delivery can suffer badly. Some anxiety of course is helpful, for it goes some way to making the presentation sharp and efficient.

Fear is often associated with the belief that you do not have the competence, the knowledge or the skills. You may believe you will forget your material, become tongue-tied or stumped by difficult questions. The clue to overcoming these beliefs (which may of course be justified) lies in the quality of preparation and we shall be looking at this aspect of the process shortly. The more understanding you have, the more you develop your delivery skills, and the more you rehearse the procedure, the greater confidence you will enjoy. Destructive fear can be turned to productive apprehension. The message is simple: take no chances; get everything right before the presentation and this will increase your confidence for the actual event. You can then have confidence that you have organised your material, that you probably know more than your audience and that they want to enjoy the presentation. In most cases they are supporting you – they want you to do well. If you go into it with that attitude, you are likely to be more positive and to reflect that in the way you relate to the audience.

We want to avoid giving the impression that there is a single presentation method which everyone should adopt. We are not in favour of the sorts of training courses which have everyone doing the same things and which teach people to behave in very much the same way. The outcome is the most important consideration. The criterion of success is: 'Was the message transmitted accurately?' Our aim then is to help you get the message across accurately and, if necessary, persuasively.

We have used the word 'audience' in this chapter as a short form for 'members of the audience'. Our understanding is that an audience comprises individual people with individual differences. This is an important consideration. 'It is necessary for us to understand that each individual in the audience will hear a different message and respond to it in a different way ' (Hasling, 1982 : 116). This makes it all the more essential that you make some attempt to find out what the audience (and the different parts of it) want to hear and whether the message is one which they are willing to receive. This is not to say that you have to accommodate contrasting views, but you must be prepared for blockages to your communication. If you are not going to get people listening to you, there seems to be little point in talking.

In this chapter we consider the three major issues of *preparation, shape* and *delivery.* Preparation is the key to presenting ideas effectively: it is concerned with the *shape* we give to our material and the way in which we *deliver* it. We give a three-stage outline and discuss the points which should be covered in each of those phases. We then examine how presentations should be delivered, giving advice on a number of matters related to speech, movement and other related points which contribute to getting the message across successfully.

You can gain an initial impression of your presentation skills by completing the questionnaire How Well Do You Present? Think about presentations you may have given in the past and answer according to how you normally behave.

Questionnaire

HOW WELL DO YOU PRESENT?

	Yes	No
1. Do you acquire all relevant information for your presentation?	☐	☐
2. Do you always feel knowledgeable?	☐	☐
3. Are you always clear why you have chosen the oral presentation as the means of communication?	☐	☐
4. Do you devise a clear statement of purpose?	☐	☐
5. Do you set targets, objectives or intended outcomes?	☐	☐
6. Are you very selective in assembling your information?	☐	☐
7. Do you find out what your audience's major concerns are?	☐	☐
8. Do you write down in advance what you would like the outcomes to be for the people in the audience?	☐	☐
9. Do you find out about your audience's status or background?	☐	☐
10. Do you find out how much they know already?	☐	☐
11. Do you find out about their attitudes and values?	☐	☐

	Yes	No

12. Do you find out about what they expect to hear? □ □

13. Do you try to see things from their point of view? □ □

14. Do you plan how you are going to establish a good relationship with the audience? □ □

15. Do you find out about the room or area in which your presentation will be held? □ □

16. Do you ensure there are no unnecessary interruptions? □ □

17. If it is possible, do you move seating to suit your arrangements? □ □

18. Do you allocate most of the time to the main body of your presentation? □ □

19. Do you plan what you will cover in your conclusion? □ □

20. Do you indicate a time allocation in your notes? □ □

21. Do you check your materials for accuracy and sequence? □ □

22. Do you prepare cues and prompts? □ □

23. Do you rehearse the presentation with someone listening? □ □

24. Do you memorise an opening statement? □ □

25. Do you plan a closing statement? □ □

26. Do you introduce yourself briefly? □ □

27. Early in the presentation, do you try to convince the audience that it will be of benefit to them to listen? □ □

28. Do you outline what you are going to say? □ □

29. Do you give a 'map' of the presentation early on so that they understand how ideas relate to each other? □ □

30. Do you tell them when they will be able to ask questions? □ □

31. Do you present your key points in logical order? □ □

32. Do you reinforce your message by repeating it? □ □

Yes   No

33. Do you arrange your material according to the purpose of the presentation?

34. Do you demonstrate how ideas are linked together?

35. Do you build an integral question period into the presentation?

36. Do you repeat and re-emphasise your main points at the end?

37. Do you summarise your presentation during the conclusion?

38. Do you thank the audience for their attention?

39. Do you keep your material simple and easily understandable?

40. Do you use authoritative sources to support your arguments?

41. Do you try to behave naturally when giving a presentation?

42. Are you friendly?

43. Do you smile and look at individuals?

44. Do you refer to things with which they are familiar?

45. Do you find out names and associated information in advance?

46. Do you mention people's names?

47. Do you use humour which is non-offensive?

48. Do you wear clothes which are not too distracting?

49. Do you deal effectively with distractions?

50. Do you avoid actions which might be distracting?

51. Do you make eye contact with most of the audience during the course of a presentation?

52. Do you maintain your enthusiasm regardless of other factors?

	Yes	**No**
53. Do you watch for signs of irritation or boredom?	☐	☐
54. Do you vary the speed of your speech?	☐	☐
55. Do you vary the tone of your voice?	☐	☐
56. Do you vary the volume of your voice?	☐	☐
57. Do you avoid meaningless expressions like 'OK'?	☐	☐
58. Do you use natural gestures which harmonise with your words?	☐	☐
59. Do you move occasionally to emphasise a key point?	☐	☐
60. Do you avoid standing behind desks and lecterns?	☐	☐

There is no scoring index but obviously the more 'yes's' you have the better. If you have answered 'no' frequently, see whether they are largely connected with one particular aspect. Questions 1–25 relate to *preparation*, 26–40 to *shape*, and 41–60 to *delivery*. If you detect strong weaknesses in any of these areas, these may be the aspects of presentation skill to work on. This is only a guide and you will see that some of the points relate to more than one area. Finding out about people's names, for example, is relevant to both delivery and preparation. All three considerations are indeed closely linked.

Stott, K. and Walker, A., *Making Management Work.* © 1992 Simon & Schuster (Asia) Pte Ltd.

Preparation

> Failures are divided into two classes –
>> those who thought and never did,
>> and those who did and never thought.
>
> (John Charles Salak)

The best presenters understand the need to be knowledgeable. Their confidence then shows. They actually enjoy receiving questions because they know it is an opportunity to display their understanding of the subject and to help their audience understand it. They can listen to other people's views and are able to compare and contrast them with their own. They do their homework; they are thoroughly prepared. Do you know a presenter who is like this? If you do, is it not true that you have confidence in what he says? Ideally, every presentation you make should demonstrate that you are well prepared and that you are knowledgeable about the subject.

A question which should be addressed early in the proceedings relates closely to this point and is concerned with what Phillips (1982 : 64) calls *propriety*. Are you qualified and the right person to make the presentation? He lists four questions which cover the appropriateness of the presentation as the mode of transmission, whether you should be doing it and the reason for taking the audience's time.

1. Is there a situation that public speech will help correct?
2. Do you have the authority to say what needs to be said?
3. Do you have the knowledge and ability to say it?
4. Can you give your listeners a good reason for paying attention to you when you say it?

If the answers to these questions are 'yes' you can then get on with the business of preparation. Preparing is the initial key to effective presenting. By being clear about what you want to say and how you are going to say it, you are more likely to transmit an accurate message and one that stands a chance of being convincing.

SUMMARY

- Prepare meticulously.
- Acquire the relevant knowledge.
- Ask whether the presentation is the best way of getting the message across.
- Ask yourself whether you are the right person to do it.
- Ask yourself whether there is a very good reason for taking the audience's time.

For an informal presentation, the preparation may take only a matter of seconds, just thinking things through quickly and sorting out the sequence of your ideas. A more formal presentation however is likely to require more extensive preparation and this will involve thinking about several issues. You need to ask a number of questions which might include:

■   What is the purpose of the presentation?
■   What should be included?
■   How should I present it?
■   Who will be in the audience?
■   Where will it be held?
■   How much time do I have?

Purpose

First of all you must be clear about what the purpose is for you. Is it to sell an idea to a group of colleagues or to simply inform them about a new procedure? The purposes of presentations generally fall into two categories: to inform or to persuade. The purpose will obviously affect the delivery.

So the first step is to ask yourself why you are making the presentation. It is usually not an end in itself and must lead to something. It is this 'something' which forms the target. You will therefore have to set goals or objectives which contribute to your reaching the target or fulfilling the purpose. Suppose for example your purpose is to persuade a group of colleagues to change a working practice. You may set out your objectives as follows:

1.   Inform them of the present inadequacies.
2.   Get them to agree that your ideas make sense.
3.   Obtain a commitment to change.

The first objective in this example is to *inform* and this implies that the information must be received accurately and with understanding. You may be able to check whether you have achieved this by opening up the discussion and using questions to ascertain the level of understanding. The second and third objectives are to *persuade*, so you would have to devise appropriate strategies to test whether you have gained the commitment you require. You may, for example, ask direct questions to ascertain the level of agreement or commitment.

From your central purpose, it is helpful to define several targets or intended outcomes which should be a consequence of listening to the presentation. These are simple statements and it should be easy to tell at the end whether you have attained them. The sales manager of a pharmaceutical company, for example, was speaking to a group of general practitioners about a new drug which was being launched. He devised three *intention statements*. These reflected what he wanted to achieve. He set his targets as follows; By the end of the presentation they should:

1. Understand the problems of side effects with currently available drugs.
2. Appreciate the clinical advantages of using our drug.
3. Agree to try out the new drug with one in ten patients suffering from the condition.

You can see from the above how the manager probably structured the main body of his presentation. He drew attention to the problems and difficulties they were facing with repeat visits because of unpleasant side-effects (thus capturing their attention because it related to their own real experiences). Then he gave a well-documented account of the new drug's advantages. Finally, he tried to persuade them that it made sense to try out the drug for both their benefit and the patient's well-being.

By stating his targets or outcomes, he could also gauge his degree of success. For the first one he could draw on the experiences of his audience; he could test the second one through questions which might be asked, and the third may only become clear after he examined sales details.

SUMMARY

- Ascertain the purpose.
- Set objectives.
- Specify intended outcomes in the form of statements.

Content

Think about what should be included. What content is appropriate? What does the audience need to hear? Also think about the most appropriate way to present the content. You have to be quite selective and include only material that is directly relevant.

In the same way that we advocate a 'compact' approach to report-writing, presentations too need to be economical. 'Effective presentational speaking is crisp and terse, direct and simple, designed to give the maximum of information in a minimum of time. People who can do this appear to be credible and reliable, worthy of being leaders' (Phillips, 1982 : 61).

Content relates closely to purpose. Your content will be derived from your interpretation of the purpose. But even then you can get it wrong. You may focus on issues which interest you rather than your audience. You have to consider their expectations. How does your content relate to their concerns? Phillips (1982 : 50) maintains that a worthwhile idea can be identified through its applicability to the concerns of the listeners.

Although we have emphasised your purposes, you must not lose sight of the fact that you are making the presentation for *their* benefit. You have to help the audience understand the message and give them something they can use in their own spheres.

The process of relating content to purpose may be aided by using *outcome statements*. These are concise expressions of what you want your audience to take away with them (and possibly do). They are slightly different from *intention statements* because they refer to the listener and what you want him to say, think or do.

You cannot realistically expect them to absorb everything you say, even if they are looking politely at you! The chances are that they will remember two or three things at the most. It will help to focus your preparation if you determine what these things are and you can do this in short outcome statements. In the example above, the manager wanted his audience of doctors to take the following away, even if they forgot everything else:

1. I am unnecessarily wasting a lot of time seeing patients with side-effects.
2. My patients would be happy with me if I could get rid of the side-effects.
3. My life would be easier if I gradually introduced the new drug.

SUMMARY

- Make the content relevant.
- Consider what the audience wants to hear.
- Be selective.
- Focus on the concerns of your audience.
- Write audience outcome statements.

Your Audience

Think about the members of your audience. What status do they hold? Are they familiar with the jargon you will be using? Will it be necessary to simplify your language and assume they know nothing of your technical terms and acronyms? What do they know about the topic in question? Also consider their attitudes. It may not be the right thing to upset the audience by criticising attitudes and beliefs. We said earlier that you need to be aware of your audience's likely receptivity and the blockages which might be present and which might inhibit the transmission of the message. It is helpful during your preparation to put yourself in the audience's place and see things from their point of view.

Hasling (1982 : 117) draws a number of conclusions from trying to understand the audience. In summary, they are:

- The presenter has to compete for the listener's attention.
- He has to create the motivation to listen. There may be no natural interest.
- The audience may be judgemental about mannerisms and style.
- The selection of examples and supporting materials is crucially important in keeping attention.
- Use of language can make listening easy or difficult.
- The speaker must be audible.
- The presentation should be as short as possible to maintain attention.
- The environment for listening has to be right.

If they are friends or colleagues, there may be little need for preamble or niceties to get them in the right frame of mind. You can obviously be comparatively informal and you may decide that a discussion is more appropriate than a 'straight' presentation.

If your audience comprises people you are meeting for the first time or whom you do not meet regularly, you will have to adopt a different approach. You will almost certainly have to apply strategies to create a rapport in order to increase the chances of acceptance of what you will say. Without that rapport, even the most persuasive arguments may falter.

SUMMARY

- Consider the audience's status.
- Consider their level of knowledge about the subject.
- Consider their attitudes.
- Consider what they expect to hear.
- Understand things from their point of view.
- Plan rapport-building strategies.

The Location

Think about the place in which the presentation will be held. If you have a choice, you can ensure that the ambience is supportive. If, for example, you are trying to win some colleagues' support for your idea, it may be better to meet them over a cup of coffee and using comfortable chairs rather than in the corner of a noisy workshop. If you have no choice of location, you may nevertheless be able to rearrange the furniture so that everyone feels relaxed and comfortable, and is able to see and hear you clearly.

SUMMARY

- Choose a pleasant environment if possible.
- Avoid noisy places.
- Ensure it is free from interruptions.

Seating Arrangements

The effect of seating arrangements has an important impact on the message and this should be considered carefully. If you want to make a formal presentation with little audience interaction, it is acceptable to have people sitting in straight rows. If the numbers permit, a horseshoe arrangement facilitates discussion, but still leaves the speaker as the focal point. The best interaction however occurs when the seating is arranged in a circle so that the speaker is part of the group. This gives an intimate feel although the use of visual aids is difficult.

One more arrangement is worth considering and that is to have groups of people sitting round small tables. This can be used with large numbers. It enables small group discussions to take place but it is important that people do not have their backs to the speaker when he is making the presentation, otherwise attention may wander.

SUMMARY

- Seating arrangement is important.
- Sitting in a circle facilitates interaction.

Time

Plan your time carefully. The main body of the presentation will last the longest, whilst the introduction and conclusion will take up comparatively smaller amounts of time. If you have twenty minutes for the whole presentation, you may divide it up by giving two minutes to the introduction, fifteen minutes to the main body and three minutes for the conclusion. You will need to check that you are sticking fairly closely to these times, otherwise you may not have time to re-emphasise the main points or you may fail to cover your major points in the main body. We advocate indicating your time allocation on cue cards, and information about these is given later.

During the presentation, it is not a good idea to look at your wrist as this can be distracting, so place a watch near your notes or visual aids on the table and you can then glance at the time when you refer to your materials. You do not need to do this if there is a clock at the back of the room.

SUMMARY

- Allow most time for the main body.
- Ensure you allow time for a conclusion.
- Indicate the time allocation in your notes.
- Use a watch near your notes.

Earlier we referred to *intention statements* and *outcome statements*. Now you can try devising these for a presentation situation. In Application Task 19.1, you are asked to consider what you want to achieve in the presentation (intention) and what you would like members of the audience to think or do at the end (outcome). We suggest you undertake the task now before reading on.

There are no 'correct' answers as such, but examples of appropriate *intention statements* would include:

- They should understand the amount of time we waste with our present system.
- They should be convinced that the equipment is easy and flexible to use.
- They should agree to use the equipment for a one-month trial period.

APPLICATION TASK 19.1

Read the statement below. Think about what you would like to achieve in your presentation and then consider what you would like the audience to think or do at the end.

The situation: Traditionally in your office, managers have written all correspondence, memoranda and so forth by hand and then sent it to the pool for typing. Occasionally, you have given dictation. You have reached the conclusion that much time could be saved if managers used portable microcassette recorders and a few of the typists could be trained to do audio work. You have asked for fifteen minutes at the next management meeting to persuade your manager colleagues (all of the same status) to adopt your idea. In your preparation, you formulate statements of intention for you and of outcome for your colleagues.

First, what do you want to achieve? Write up three statements below:

1.

2.

3.

Second, what do you want them to take away? Write up to three 'outcome statements':

1.

2.

3.

Stott, K. and Walker, A., *Making Management Work*. © 1992 Simon & Schuster (Asia) Pte Ltd.

Suitable *outcome statements* would include:

■ Writing everything is very cumbersome. I would prefer to dictate my correspondence.

■ It would be easier to concentrate on more important matters if I could cut down the time spent on writing.

■ Using a microcassette recorder would make my life easier, because I could dictate when and where I liked.

Essential Features

There are several features which must be adhered to if the presentation is to meet its objectives. Some of these are common sense but we often forget them once we start to talk.

Interesting

You alone are responsible for making the presentation interesting. The use of humour and anecdotes are strategies which may help to achieve this. The closer you can relate what you say to the needs, wants and experiences of your audience, the more likely you are to gain their attention. By outlining benefits to them, you are more likely to be interesting. You may for example demonstrate the inadequacies of their present actions and then show how doing things your way will be productive and enjoyable.

To the Point

It must be clearly focused – to the point. It is easy to meander off course, especially when irrelevant questions are asked, but this will only serve to hinder the message's understanding and retention.

Account for Audience's Understanding

The message must be clearly presented, using short words whenever possible and avoiding the unnecessary use of jargon. It should account for the audience's present level of understanding.

Only Essential Information Included

It should be realistic in the time available. Trying to cram too much into too short a space of time will ensure that little is assimilated. Do not be too ambitious. It is better to have less material than too much. Not only will your audience possibly retain what you have said but they may also appreciate finishing a little earlier than planned! Experience shows however that, even when you have condensed your information, you are unlikely to finish before your time is up.

SUMMARY

- Make it interesting.
- Keep to the point.
- Present your material simply and clearly.
- Limit your material to information which is essential.

Getting Ready for the Presentation

In preparing the content of your presentation, you will need to think about the prompts you need during the presentation itself. Do not write it out word for word. If you were to do that, you would lose your place when you look at the audience, or just as bad, you would appear to be reading it. You can become reasonably 'word perfect' by rehearsing several times.

It is best to use words or phrases which act as the headings for you. You can either put these on the overhead projector or use cue cards. You can of course do both and we recommend this, because you can write a few notes on your cards which you do not want the audience to see. You may, for example, want to indicate where you have a humorous anecdote to tell or where you want to show a transparency.

We do not recommend trying to memorise the content. It is really a waste of valuable time. So long as you understand the topic and you have arranged your material coherently, it is quite acceptable to use a few notes. Using small index cards is a good idea because they are inconspicuous. Use plenty of cards, putting separate sections and ideas on separate cards. Then number them so that you put them in the correct order quickly if you drop them or accidentally mix them up. Ideally each card should have a heading or title, and you may wish to use a colour code for headings, subheadings and so forth. Examples of cue cards are shown in Figure 19.1.

Instead of cue cards, you can mount your overhead transparencies and then write your notes on the mounting frames. This method has the advantage that you are seen to be referring to the transparency whilst it is on the projector, but in fact you are looking at your notes. This is less distracting for the audience.

Figure 19.1
Cue Cards

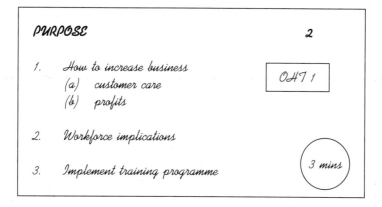

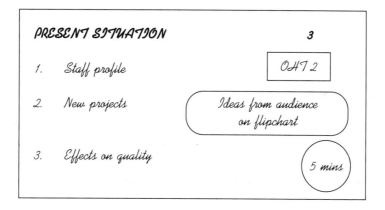

You should rehearse your presentation with a friend or colleague. By talking through the topic using your cards, you will soon identify the weaknesses: a card may not be clear; you are not sure how the transparency fits in; there is too much material in one part. By going through like this (maybe several times) you can iron out the difficulties and give yourself confidence for when it comes to the real thing. Ask your colleague also to interrupt you when something is not perfectly clear. If he does this, you will know that improvement is necessary and you can make notes as you go along. At the end of your rehearsal, ask him for questions. These may provide a clue as to the questions the audience is likely to ask.

Although we advise you not to waste valuable time memorising an entire presentation, it is useful to commit an opening and a closing line to memory. As soon as you come face-to-face with the audience, you should know what your very first statement is. If you have practised it and it sounds natural, it will give you confidence for the rest of the event. Another reason for getting the beginning and ending sorted out is because audiences tend to remember the first and last things you say. It is important therefore that you use these two opportunities accordingly.

SUMMARY

- Use words and phrases as headings.
- Use cue cards and/or visual aids as prompts.
- Rehearse your presentation with a friend or colleague.
- Write down your opening and closing statements and memorise them.

Giving It Shape

Good shape is vital to understanding. It will enable you to create the maximum impact in the shortest possible time. It will also help your audience to follow your story line and to receive the intended message more clearly. A good shape to the presentation also helps you because the ideas are organised coherently.

It is helpful to think of structuring a presentation in three phases:

1. Introduction.
2. Main body.
3. Conclusion.

In our last chapter on Writing Reports we mentioned the maxim which explains structure quite succinctly: 'Tell 'em what you are going to tell 'em; tell 'em; tell 'em what you told 'em.' That is a useful way of planning presentations because the introduction is essentially about explaining what is about to follow, the main body involves presenting the key points simply and clearly, and the conclusion is about repeating and re-emphasising the main points. There is more. The presentation is a form of communication which puts you face-to-face with your audience. Apart from the features which are consistent with writing reports, you also have to develop an understanding with the audience. We now look at the three phases in more detail.

The Introduction

The first thing you should do is to make a few introductory comments. These may be in the form of a welcome or an expression of thanks if members of your audience are there voluntarily. If you are new to the audience, introduce yourself and if the presentation is a longer one, you may have to outline something of your background in order to enhance credibility. This will depend on the type of presentation. For some presentations of course, someone else does the introducing and it is therefore unnecessary to go over the same ground. If you have a team of people with you (they may be experts in particular fields) it is reasonable to introduce them briefly.

Do not spend too long on this phase. We have listened to presentations where the speaker spends an inordinate amount of time explaining how privileged he is to speak to such distinguished people and hopes that he can say something of interest. He probably cannot, which explains why he is wasting too much of his time on preamble! The audience is not interested in apologies, details of traffic conditions or expressions of admiration for the wonderful facilities. It wants the speaker to get on with it. Whatever you do, avoid apologies. They make it sound as if you have nothing of value to say and that the audience is doing you a favour by being there. So do not say that you will take as little of their valuable time as possible. That is a very negative statement. Similarly, do not start by explaining that you are not very accomplished or that you do not know very much. You want your audience to have confidence in you. These sorts of opening statements could only destroy it.

You now have a choice. You can explain the purpose and what you hope to achieve. If you are trying to sell an idea, you can outline the principal benefits to the audience. But instead of going straight into the purpose, you may have planned an effective 'opener', a statement or question which captures the imagination. The audience sits up and listens. You may say something like: 'If you adopt the proposals I am going to make today, your departments will get better results and your staff will enjoy higher morale.' If you do choose to make a statement like that, you have to ensure it is true, of course.

Other speakers use statements which border on the controversial but which have that familiar ring of truth about them. If it is well planned, the presenter may say something which the audience wishes he would say. We were making a presentation to a large group of managers about 'meetings' and we started with the statement: 'Most of the meetings in our organisations are a waste of time: they waste our time and they waste the organisation's time. They cost our organisations an awful lot of money.' This was greeted with applause and smiles of familiarity. We went on of course to explain how meetings could be made productive.

Starting with an outline of benefits helps to personalise the presentation and stimulate interest from the start. That is what people are interested in – the benefits to them. This will also secure their attention from the start. They must be made to feel that it is worthwhile to listen because they will gain something from it. Whichever approach you decide to use, you have to convey the importance of your topic.

You do not have to begin with benefits if you do not want to. Some speakers start with an interesting anecdote which leads neatly into the main body of the presentation. It is also quite business-like to explain that you want your audience to listen to your ideas on improving public relations and to accept the new strategies which you will propose. Nevertheless, they must be convinced that listening is going to be of value to them. Phillips (1982 : 80) lists some possible 'good reasons' for listening. You can offer one of these to your audience:

1. What you ask them to know, believe, or do will make their job easier.
2. What you ask them to know, believe, or do will clarify some confusion.
3. What you ask them to know, believe, or do will mean more money, advancement on the job, security, or employee benefits for them.
4. What you ask them to know, believe, or do will make their life more pleasant.
5. What you ask them to know, believe, or do will help them defend themselves against forces that would hurt them.

At some stage in the introduction, whatever strategy you choose to use, you must incorporate a statement of the purpose. It should be expressed as simply as possible. It can usually be done in one sentence. You need to formulate this sentence in advance so that you state with clarity what you intend to do.

Next, outline what you are going to say and the structure you will use. This acts as the *executive summary*. It not only outlines the key points, but also presents a framework for the presentation which will aid their understanding. It is almost like giving the main headings and subheadings, but leaving the content under each blank. It is also useful to let them know whether they will have the opportunity to ask some questions at the end or whether you would like them to interrupt as you go along.

SUMMARY

- Introduce yourself briefly.
- Avoid apologies and meaningless remarks about trivia.

- Use a planned 'opener' or a statement about purpose.
- Convince them that listening will be good for them.
- Outline what you are going to say and set it in a framework.
- Tell them whether they can ask questions.

The Main Body

The main body is where you present your key points, arranged logically and as simply as possible. The audience's attention is probably at its lowest during this phase. Make it easy therefore for your listeners to remember what you have said. You can do this by using subheadings in order to compartmentalise the audience's thinking. You are doing essentially what you would do in a written report.

If you want your audience to remember your key points, do not try to cover too much. Repetition is a useful tool. It is sometimes wise to have just one or two points and to reinforce them by explaining them in different ways. You can do this by paraphrasing, by giving different examples, by providing different items of supporting evidence and by citing other sources. Especially when the speaker is trying to persuade the audience about something, impartial supporting evidence may be necessary to avert suspicion about motives.

It is a good idea wherever possible to support your arguments by using authoritative sources. In addition to presenting supporting evidence, you need to support what you are saying with sound reasoning. It should be intelligent and make sense to the audience. 'Effective speakers are able to justify their opinion, present examples to illustrate their points, and relate what they say to material that is familiar to the audience' (Phillips, 198 : 50).

There are various ways of structuring the main body of your presentation and it largely depends on the purpose and the time available as to which one you use. For the presentation of ideas or information, it may be best first to highlight your key points and then provide the supporting arguments. If, however, you are trying to solve a problem jointly (despite the fact that you may be the only one who has thought about it) you will outline preferred solutions and the possible outcomes.

Whatever arrangement you use, you should do it to ensure you create the best effect. The 'order of play' therefore is important from an impact point of view. You may describe a series of events from a historical perspective, the sequence in which they occurred. On other occasions, you may categorise your topic so that you can talk about 'compartments'. The arrangement must be coherent and help the audience's understanding. If we are making a presentation about a management topic, we often use the *category arrangement* alongside the *pros* and *cons* pattern. So we look at the relative advantages and disadvantages. This is a useful arrangement of information when you are making a presentation about the options available to solve a problem. The *geographical* pattern is useful where the presentation is about physical areas. You may, for example, be comparing performance in different branches of the organisation, so you deal with each one of them in turn. The *build-up pattern* is very useful where there is opposition to your views. You start off with ideas which are universally acceptable and move towards the controversial position. In other words, you are 'building up' to the central issue.

The form Preparing the Outline displayed in Figure 19.2 shows the way in which you can prepare your main headings. It gives an initial shape to your presentation. Next time you have to make a presentation, try using this form to guide your thinking. In Figure 19.3, An Outline Presentation 1, we have given an example of how the order of topics was laid out for an actual event, a presentation by a team of consultants to a senior management group. You will notice that they indicated the times they allotted to each of the three phases. This acted as a guide during the actual presentation. In Figure 19.4, An Outline Presentation 2, we show the presentation outline of the manager in the earlier example who was trying to persuade his traditional colleagues to dispense with quills and ink, and adopt more sophisticated means to deal with their paperwork. He too gave times to each of the phases and also broke down the time for the main body. This was because he wanted to ensure he gave sufficient time to the demonstration of the equipment.

You can of course modify the forms to meet your requirements and you can incorporate items such as *intention statements* and *outcome statements.* You should however always have a statement of purpose which will be central to the presentation, and a list of the key points.

In Report Writing we advocate putting the important matters at the beginning. These would include key findings and recommendations, but we also warn against doing this in some situations. The same applies to presentations. You cannot put your key point first if it involves bad news. 'I am going to explain to you how you will all lose your jobs within the next two years' is hardly the best way to start your presentation. This sort of information has to be built up to. Similarly, you may know there is some opposition to your ideas, and by coming straight to the point, those who disagree may not listen to the rest of your presentation. It is better therefore to start off with a more impartial approach, with a weighing up of the advantages and disadvantages, and then to move towards a statement of your position.

Linking ideas can be a problem in many presentations and you have to develop ways of taking the audience from one point to the next. You need to do this for them so that they can understand how everything fits together. You can do it by using transitional phrases (Hasling, 1982 : 100) which indicate how ideas are joined together and their relationship. You may use ex-

Figure 19.2
Preparing the Outline

<table>
<tr><td colspan="2" align="center">OUTLINE</td></tr>
<tr><td>Title of presentation:</td><td>Total time:</td></tr>
<tr><td colspan="2">Purpose:</td></tr>
<tr><td colspan="2">For whom:</td></tr>
</table>

Introduction

First statement:

Purpose:

Outline:

Main body

Main headings and ideas:

Conclusion

Points for re-emphasis:

Figure 19.3
An Outline Presentation 1

OUTLINE

Title of presentation: *Senior management review*	Total time: *20 mins*

Purpose: *Information on review findings*

For whom: *Senior executives*

Introduction

First statement: *High gains made in quality development*

Purpose: *Information on strengths and weaknesses*

Outline: *Statement of review findings*
Implications for company performance | 2 |

Main body

Main headings and ideas:

Findings:
1.   *Strong on quality promotion.*
   (a)   new products
   (b)   support for maintenance operations
   (c)   resources for quality development
2.   *Marketing fairly effective*
   (a)   external links
   (b)   support for research
3.   *Weak on employee morale*
   (a)   signs and symptoms
   (b)   work conditions

Implications
1.   *Performance and quality may be affected*
2.   *Staff turnover* | 15 |

Conclusion

Points for re-emphasis:
Performance may suffer unless attitude to workforce improves | 3 |

Stott, K. and Walker, A., *Making Management Work.* © 1992 Simon & Schuster (Asia) Pte Ltd.

Figure 19.4
An Outline Presentation 2

OUTLINE

Title of presentation: *Introducing microcassette recorders*	Total time: *25mins*

Purpose: *To persuade colleagues to try using them*

For whom: *Management colleagues*

Introduction

First statement: *Your job made easier by reducing writing*

Purpose: *To show the benefits of using recorders*

Outline: *Explanation of time wasted presently*
Advantages of using the recorders
Proposal

     2

Main body

Main headings and ideas:

1. *Time wasted*
 (a) *unproductive*
 (b) *time saved for important tasks*

     5

2. *Advantages*
 (a) *easy to use (demonstration)*
 (b) *can be used at home, in car*

     10

3. *Proposal*
 Try out for a period of one month

     5

Conclusion

Points for re-emphasis:
More time for important tasks and meeting your staff
Makes life less tedious

     3

---

pressions such as: 'From this, it is possible to see that . . .' and 'Closely related to that is . . .' You may also achieve the same purpose by altering your voice inflection. Whichever method you adopt, you have to clearly indicate how the ideas are linked so that the audience does not have to spend time puzzling out why you have introduced a new idea and how it relates to the previous one. You have to make it easy for them so that understanding is maintained.

Encouraging people to ask questions is important in most presentation situations since it gives them an opportunity to participate. There are several things you can do to make this form of interaction as productive as possible. First, repeat the question or paraphrase it so that everyone knows what the question was. It is often people sitting at the front who ask questions and those sitting behind them cannot hear what the question was. Then speak to everyone. You are giving the answer to the whole audience, not to an individual. Answer it directly if you can. If you cannot, say so. Give short, clear answers. Make even silly questions sound worthwhile – your audience will appreciate your tact. Be assertive about the person who likes to hog the questioning and politely draw questions from others.

We feel it best not to finish with questions but to see the period as an integral part of the whole presentation. If the audience senses a 'break' between the main part and questions (especially if they are at the end), they may well lose attention. Ensure you have thought about possible questions in advance and that you have any information which may be required with you. If you have done your homework properly, you will welcome questions and will have thought about the sorts of challenges you might receive.

You can have a short concluding section at the end of this question and answer period which draws the section together and which may even incorporate some of the points made by the audience during the discussion time.

SUMMARY

- Present key points logically and simply.
- Use repetition to reinforce.
- Use the arrangement of information for maximum impact.
- Use a structure which is appropriate for the type of information.
- Show how ideas are linked together.
- Make the question period an integral part of the presentation.

The Conclusion

The conclusion is not something to be plugged onto the end of your presentation to give it a 'nice' finish. It is of crucial importance. Its content is more likely to be remembered than that of the main body. Remember we said earlier that audiences remember the first and last things which are said. It must be seen therefore as an opportunity to repeat your main points and to emphasise them. It also enables you to draw everything together into a coherent whole so that the audience is entirely clear about what has gone on beforehand. This final part of the presentation also gives you the chance to ensure people leave the meeting with positive feelings. You must plan your final statement. Do not leave it to chance, but write a final statement which has impact and which will leave the audience with an important idea to take away.

You can use this phase to answer any final questions which people may have and, in some presentation situations, it is an opportunity to either gain commitment or to take action.

Finally, it is useful to thank the audience and to say that you have enjoyed the opportunity to share ideas with them and to receive their comments. If this is not the case, then simply thank them.

SUMMARY

- Plan your final statement.
- Repeat the main points and re-emphasise them.
- Relate these to your outcome statements.
- Draw ideas together into a summary.
- Thank the audience.

Delivery

Be Natural

We would encourage you to be natural, to be yourself. This sounds like common sense, but a few of the business presentations we have observed have shown the presenters trying to behave like professional actors. Everything seems to be stage-managed. There may be false smiles and gestures, and words that sound a little less than natural speech. We find this a source of distraction.

On the other hand, you must be professional, but this is different from putting on a false act. You should be prepared, know what you are talking about and make the presentation crisp and clear. Do it in a natural way, though, one with which both you and your audience feels comfortable. The words should sound like yours, the gestures should be a natural accompaniment to your speech and the clothes you wear should look like your own!

SUMMARY

- Be natural.
- Adopt a professional approach.

Set the Tone

During the introduction, you establish a relationship with your audience. This, of course, does not apply if you are talking to people you work with every day, but it certainly applies if you are addressing a group of customers or senior executives who seldom meet you. First impressions count: during this phase they will either like you or they will be switched off. Look too serious or aggressive, and your listeners will become resistant to your message. If people like you, they are more likely to listen to your message, so the first few minutes are vitally important. If you show the members of your audience that you like them, they will probably reciprocate your feelings.

The early part of the presentation sets the tone for the rest of the presentation, so the verbal and non-verbal communication has to be right. Smile at people and maintain eye contact without threatening them. Try to look at all the audience rather than just a few individuals, however supportive they might be in their facial expressions. In terms of verbal communication, it is helpful to ask questions and use their answers to inform other parts of your presentation.

SUMMARY

- Establish a good relationship early.
- Adopt a friendly approach.
- Smile and look at people.

Maintaining Interest

Maintain interest by referring to things with which they are familiar. This is good advice if you are losing their attention. By mentioning a name, a department or an event in which they were involved, you will recapture interest. You can do this easily if you are presenting to colleagues, but for other audiences, you will have to do some homework in advance to acquire relevant information. This all relates to knowing your audience.

SUMMARY

- Refer to things with which they are familiar.
- Obtain relevant interesting information in advance.

Knowing Your Audience

Relating familiar experiences to support what you are saying is part of knowing your audience and being able to relate to them. If you are speaking to 500 people, you cannot be expected to know very many of them. If, however, you are speaking to five people, you should get to know their names right at the beginning. Write them down and keep a little seating plan to hand so that you know who everyone is. During your presentation, you can say things like: 'As Mr Jones said to me before this talk . . .' or 'Miss Lee has raised an important issue about advertising problems.' Even with larger audiences, you can personalise your presentation by knowing a few names. If someone asks a question, ask for their name and write it down discreetly. You can then refer to that person as you answer the question. Do it in a positive way though so that they feel they have made a valuable contribution to the discussion.

If you include personal anecdotes, these often help to illuminate the message and gain the audience's interest. Ensure that they are to the point and that you can relate them succinctly. Sometimes the listeners will be able to support what you are saying with examples from their own experiences.

SUMMARY

- In small groups, refer to people by name.
- In larger groups, refer to the names of people who ask questions.

Humour

The presentations which stick in our minds all had humour in them. Sometimes it is used as an ice-breaker with a joke at the beginning. This is acceptable so long as it is in context. Some can use humour and some cannot. There is nothing worse than telling a funny story and for your audience to sit there with straight faces. You know yourself whether you are good at using humour. If you are, then use it by all means.

Do not use humour in a destructive way, as a means of taking revenge on people or the organisation. Try to make it non-offensive and of universal appeal. Avoid 'in-jokes' which are only understood by a few people in the audience.

SUMMARY

- Use humour appropriately.
- Make it non-offensive.
- Avoid 'in-jokes'.

Dress

If you are presenting your ideas to a small group of colleagues, you obviously will not dress up for the occasion. If you are making a presentation outside your immediate circle, you will have to think about appropriate dress. It is best not to wear clothes which could distract the audience: they would draw attention away from your message. Being too casual could also lower some people's opinion of you. You have to decide what is right for the situation.

SUMMARY

- Wear what is right for the occasion.
- Avoid distracting colours and styles.

Avoiding Interruptions

You should try to ensure that you do not get interrupted. The right location for the presentation will help in this regard, but you may have to take additional measures such as placing a sign outside the room explaining there is a session in progress or informing a secretary not to put any messages through.

Despite taking these actions, you will probably find you still face interruptions. As a good presenter should, you start on time but find that one or two people are not as punctual as you. If you are unable to do anything about the room arrangement, they may walk in from the front, across the screen and in full view of everyone. (We get the feeling some people do it on purpose!) This is distracting for you and the audience. Although some presenters advise continuing regardless, we feel the message is lost during the interruption. It is better to stop, allow the person to sit down and then continue with what you were saying. Try to be polite and avoid embarrassing them. You will be better thought of by the audience for showing your tolerance.

A far greater distraction is the private conversation or whispering which sometimes goes on. If you look at the people concerned as you continue your presentation, they may get the message that they are attracting attention. It needs to be dealt with politely however, especially where the audience is new to you. You will probably find your own way of dealing with the situation, which may involve pausing or mentioning a few names. Bear in mind that an intolerant remark may sour your relationship with the rest of the audience. They will appreciate it if you are tactful and they may even do something about the interruption themselves.

SUMMARY

- Take actions to avoid unnecessary interruptions.
- Pause for latecomers and avoid embarrassing them.
- Deal tactfully with people who hold private conversations.

Avoiding Distractions

During one presentation a member of the audience rose from his seat, walked to the front and took a drink from the speaker's glass of water. Afterwards, he explained that he had become so frustrated by the presenter stopping regularly to drink that he could not restrain himself. He was not only getting distracted but he was also becoming thirsty!

It is not just drinking water (especially when the audience does not have any) which annoys people. There are many other habits which can take the attention away from the message. Shaking keys, fastening and unfastening your jacket button, talking to the ceiling and fiddling around for transparencies which are in the wrong order all contribute to reducing the effectiveness of your presentation.

SUMMARY

- Avoid any actions which distract your audience.

Look at the Audience

It is natural to make more regular eye contact with those members of the audience who use supportive gestures. They look back at you, smile and nod in agreement. This is very helpful to you because it gives approval to what you are saying. So you look at these people all the more. They give you confidence. However, you have to make an effort to make eye contact with other members of your audience, otherwise they may feel it is not for them. Even if they stare back at you with a frown, you have to consciously avoid any doubts about your message. Continue to show enthusiasm and confidence rather than be distracted by unsupportive expressions.

This does not mean you should ignore everything you see. On the contrary, your audience will give you some valuable messages. Watch for signals that people are becoming restless. They may stop looking at you or start whispering. They may start reading things or looking round the room. This tends to happen if the presentation is due to end at a particular time and questions are still being asked. Those who are not involved may be getting bored. Rather than try the patience of some of the audience, it is better to finish the presentation and then stay around for a while to talk to those who are genuinely interested.

Be aware of signals and expressions, but do not read too much into them, otherwise you may be misinterpreting the information. We have noticed some listeners prefer to close their eyes. It does not mean they are sleeping. In fact, some are listening more intently than others with their gaze directed at the speaker. The supportive people who smile at you may or may not be listening. It is very difficult to tell unless you ask them questions. They are helpful in that they give you confidence but you cannot be certain that your message is reaching its mark simply through the facial expressions.

SUMMARY

- Look at more than just a few individuals.
- Show enthusiasm even though you may be faced with unsupportive expressions and gestures.
- Look for signs of irritation and boredom.

Using Your Voice

You should vary your speed of speech, ensuring at all times that you speak clearly so that each word can be understood. Sometimes you may wish to speak quickly (not as fast as normal conversational speech), whilst at others you will speak slowly, dwelling on, and thereby emphasising, certain words and phrases. You can apply even greater emphasis with the occasional use of pauses either immediately before or after an important statement.

The tone of your voice must vary. Especially when we are nervous, we tend to speak in a monotone. It is useful practice to exaggerate your tone variation to increase the interest in your voice. As you get more confident, the variation will come in a more natural way. It is a fact though that most presenters are more monotonous than they think and this exaggeration therefore helps to offset the tendency. The other extreme however can be just as bad as a monotone. This is where the speaker has a regular 'musical line' which is repeated over and over again, regardless of the words. It is like a musical phrase which goes up and down at certain intervals. This can be quite distracting.

If you have done your preparation thoroughly, you will be confident and that will usually be reflected by your speaking louder. Those who are not too sure of their material tend to speak more quietly. Although we advise you to speak so that people at the back of the audience can hear you, you should apply some variation to your volume. The main complaint is often that presenters speak too softly and put a strain on the hearing. Speaking loudly may be the lesser of the two evils, but it can also be a source of distraction. We attended a presentation by an enthusiastic young man who was promoting a higher degree course for managers from the business world. There were twenty people in the audience and the presentation was in a small conference room. He spoke as if he had an audience of 200 in a conference hall and never varied the volume from start to finish. It was very difficult to listen to the message because of the physical discomfort. If you watch your audience, you will soon observe if they are having difficulty in hearing you.

SUMMARY

- Vary the speed of your speech.
- Vary your tone, but keep it natural.
- Speak loudly, but vary the volume.

Words

The same person in the above example also punctuated each sentence with a regular supply of 'OK's' and 'Yeh's'. These became so distracting that the two people sitting in front of us started a counting competition to see how many more of these 'non-words' he would use! If you listen to yourself with a tape recorder, you may find you are using more than your fair share of such expressions. Do not become too conscious of them, otherwise they can distract you and take your attention away from what you are saying, but at the same time, you should try to eliminate them gradually.

Just as bad as the 'non-words' above are those words which cannot be understood. Use simple words wherever possible and make it easy for the listener. If you are talking to a group of technical experts who can understand the jargon, then you can use the jargon words which are familiar to them. If your audience comprises people who are not experts, then you have to use a completely different language.

SUMMARY

- Gradually eliminate 'non-words' from your natural speech.
- Use words which make listening easier for the audience.

Gestures

Avoid waving your arms about in wild gestures like some of the more ostentatious orchestral conductors. The hand and arm gestures you use should be supportive to what you say and look natural rather than a response to a script cue. Equally bad though is standing like a tailor's dummy with no movement at all. This looks just as unnatural, especially if your arms appear to be glued to your sides.

> ### SUMMARY
>
> • Use natural gestures which are supportive to your speech.

Presenter's Position

Movement can be useful to emphasise key points. If you move closer to the audience, you attract attention and create emphasis. There is an increased feeling of closeness. It is a good tactic when used at the right time to reinforce a message.

Many presenters stand behind items of furniture, mainly desks and lecterns. We prefer to come away from furniture and become more 'part' of the audience. So we stand in front of the desk rather than behind it. If we are showing transparencies, we stand away from the projector and ensure there is nothing between us and the audience. If you are not confident enough to do this, initially try standing at the side of the desk or table on which you can place your materials.

> ### SUMMARY
>
> • Use movement to emphasise key points.
> • Avoid standing behind furniture.

Types of Presenter

Each time we see a presentation, we can usually put the speaker into one of the categories below. Sometimes people belong to more than one category. If you can identify with any in the typology below, try to eliminate the inappropriate behaviour. Give your audience the impression you are comfortable with your situation and that you want to develop a rapport with them. Speakers who are less than perfect may say it in different ways, but they are really making the statements below:

■ 'I'm sorry – this is not worth listening to ...' He says this by apologising for his lack of knowledge and promising to waste as little of the audience's time as possible.

- 'I'm nervous and not enjoying this, so don't blame me.' By not enjoying it, he is virtually ensuring the audience will not enjoy it either. He is one of those for whom the ordeal is as welcome as an income tax demand, and he makes sure everyone knows.

- 'I'm bursting with energy and I'm going to expend it all during this presentation.' This person is a little more than keyed up. Not only do too many words come out too fast, but this presenter has usually lost any idea of sensitivity to the audience and their signals.

- 'I'm rather fond of dancing.' This person may do something which resembles a square tango whilst trying to talk intelligently. A friend of ours takes two steps forward, dips the knees, then two steps backwards and dips the knees again. We are often too hypnotised by the aesthetic movement to listen to what he is saying!

- 'I'd rather be a film star.' This person dresses, speaks, moves and even looks like a film star. He regularly sweeps his hair back with his hand. He may appear good, but he is so unnatural that few listen to his message.

- 'I have so much to say, I don't know where to start.' There is so much important information swimming around in his head, he cannot make up his mind how he should begin. Often his notes and visual aids are mixed up because he has not prepared. No one disputes his knowledge but he seldom conveys any of it effectively to his audience.

Visual Aids

There is a whole array of visual aids which can be used and some of them are highly sophisticated. If you have access to these, you may use them to enhance your presentation. They have to be relevant however, and not be simply an attempt to impress the audience with elaborate displays of technology. There are many sources of information about visual aids and you are advised to refer to these if you want to develop advanced materials.

We like to use the humble overhead projector. We use it as much for ourselves as for the audience. At times when the memory fails, it provides the appropriate clues about what comes next and therefore gives confidence. However, we only put our main headings and subheadings on the transparencies. These are helpful to the audience who can then understand the way we have arranged our various topics. Of course we use the overhead projector in other ways, such as the display of information which is more understandable visually than orally. Understanding is usually increased if people can look at an aid while you talk.

If you use a projector, a whiteboard or flipchart, try to support your presentation throughout. When you outline the structure of what you are going to say right at the beginning of the presentation, for example, present this visually so that they have a 'map' of your talk. This makes it possible for them to put your points into context. Similarly, when you summarise everything at the end and emphasise the key points, you can again do this visually. This will help to reinforce the message.

Most visual aids are prepared in advance and you should ensure they are done well. Even black writing on a clear background has to be checked. Make sure everything is properly laid out and that there are no spelling mistakes. Get someone else to proofread your visuals, because even a simple error can be a major source of distraction.

There are times when you will not want to prepare the aid in advance because you consider it important that the audience watch you construct it at the time. You may wish for instance to draw attention to some key words and it is helpful if the audience watches you write these words on the flipchart. You can explain each one immediately after writing it. You are more likely to use this technique if there is audience participation. You may ask them for some ideas about an issue and then summarise them on the flipchart. This can be useful in the right circumstances because the audience sees its contribution being 'written' into the presentation.

Even the simplest aids can be effective. You need to follow a few basic guidelines which will help to transmit the message rather than impede it. Firstly, write as little as possible: single words or phrases rather than sentences. Secondly, write large enough for the people who are furthest away from the visual aid to be able to see clearly. Many presenters type transparencies, but it may be quite sufficient to write them by hand so long as you are neat and clear. Sometimes, hand-written materials make a welcome change from the normal typed ones and can therefore create more impact. There are some situations however where it may be frowned upon and seen as a sign of unprofessionalism. You have to weigh up the situation, but if you are in any doubt, it is probably safer to use a graphics application. Thirdly, use dark colours. It can be quite frustrating for those far away from the screen to squeeze their eyes trying to read something written in light green or pink.

When you use visual aids, make sure you show them only when you are referring to those points. If you have an overhead projector, switch it off when you have finished with the transparency. You can then get your audience to look at you. When you show a transparency, a quick look to see what the next heading or point is may be in order, but turn back to face your audience immediately. Never stand talking to the screen. If you have several points on one transparency, it is useful to reveal just one point at a time. This will help your audience's attention to focus on that single point. Our experience is that, if you show the whole transparency, the avid note-takers will be writing everything whilst you are trying to get them to concentrate on the first word or phrase.

If you put visuals up, you want people to see them, so do not stand in front of them. It is also not a good idea to sit unless you are presenting to a small group of colleagues. Generally it creates more impact if you stand and if you have a screen or flipchart in use, make sure you stand to one side, not obscuring the screen or chart.

Next time you make a presentation and choose to use visual aids, refer to the Visual Aid Checklist in Figure 19.5 to ensure they are appropriately prepared.

SUMMARY

- Ask if the visual aid is really an aid and not a distraction.
- Use aids as prompts to yourself.
- Only show headings or simple supporting material, not excessive details.
- Provide a visual map of the presentation.
- Check all aids before using.
- Ensure they are in order.
- Make writing large enough for people at the back to see.
- Use bold colours.
- Do not obscure the aid.
- Remove it immediately when you have finished referring to it.

Conclusion

In this chapter we have looked at three key aspects of presentations: preparation, shape and delivery. How you structure what you say can affect the impact on the audience and their understanding of the message you are trying to convey. It will also determine whether it becomes instantly forgettable or well and truly imprinted on the mind.

Applying an appropriate structure is only part of the story, though. You have to be able to deliver your message using your resources to best advantage. Your voice, hands, dress and a number of other factors all combine to create an impression on your audience. If the delivery is natural and support-

**Figure 19.5
A Visual Aid Checklist**

VISUAL AIDS

1. Will the aids really help the audience's understanding? ☐

2. Are they directly relevant to what I am saying? ☐

3. Do they contain only essential information? ☐

4. Do they give the audience a 'map' of the presentation? ☐

5. Have you checked for spelling mistakes? ☐

6. Have you checked that you understand each aid yourself? ☐

7. Have you ensured they are in the right order? ☐

8. Have you got all the materials you need, such as flipchart pens which work? ☐

9. Is the writing large enough for everyone to see easily? ☐

10. Have you used bold colours? ☐

Stott, K. and Walker, A., *Making Management Work.* © 1992 Simon & Schuster (Asia) Pte Ltd.

ive, the audience is more likely to be receptive to what is being said.

Like so many of the skills in management, preparation is the key to successful execution. Unless you think about the purpose of the presentation, the content and the way in which you are going to transmit your information, success may be hit or miss. We have found that even the most accomplished presenters spend considerably more time preparing than the presentation itself takes. It is only through practice and preparation that a high level of competence can be achieved.

References

Hasling, J. (1982) *The Message, the Speaker, the Audience,* McGraw-Hill : New York.
Lord, G. (1982) *It's My Business to Know,* McGraw-Hill : England.
Phillips, G. (1982) *Communicating in Organizations,* Macmillan : New York.

Conclusion

We have two key purposes in mind in the writing of this book: first, to provide managers and those in training for management with a basic, but sound, conceptual background in some of what we consider to be the essential management skills; and second to provide opportunities for real and simulated application of these skills, to encourage a deeper (diagnostic) understanding of what practical management entails – a discovery of how it relates to the real situation.

We do not claim to have covered all the necessary skills and practices of management, but selected those we believe to be important across a range of circumstances. We have also addressed some issues which, if not dealt with appropriately, can have far-reaching consequences for the organisation's or subunit's work and its capacity to operate at a high level of effectiveness. Such issues are often neglected in management texts because they may be seen to be either too broad or too specialised to consider alongside the more commonly accepted features of people management training.

Developing management skills and abilities is an ongoing, cyclical process; it involves several phases, all closely woven together. An understanding of relevant conceptual material is first necessary, alongside an examination of personal assumptions, preferences and actual behaviours. These can then be considered in relation to present practice in the job. At this stage, being prepared to accept that there is room for improvement or that there are better ways of doing things may be essential to development. The final phase therefore considers the applicability of learning to modified practice in the job. In this way the practice of management becomes informed by appropriate theory and careful reflection.

We have attempted to provide knowledge and the opportunity to apply it in simulated and 'real' situations. It is not realistically possible of course to develop expertise overnight, but an attempt to grasp the fundamental principles underlying the various topics and a serious approach to the application tasks should lead to improved performance within a relatively short space of time. Like the skilled sports performer, however, the continued practice and application of skills, supported by a process of reflection, is the only way for the manager to achieve competence.

As we have stressed throughout the text, you need to adapt what you have learnt to suit the conditions under which you work. Realise that in today's organisations you work under considerable constraints (for example, in making decisions) from policies, organisational aims, politics and, often, a rapidly mutating environment. Set yourself realistic targets both in mastering management skills and in utilising them to alter the present state of affairs. Use and adapt your skills to assist others in dealing with change.

The concepts and propositions presented therefore should not be regarded as unalterable blueprints. They are suggestions for action and should be regarded as broad frameworks that provide you with ideas on how you can improve your management skills and performance. We have of course attempted to make our suggestions as pragmatic as possible, but it must be emphasised that thought must precede action, especially where changes to ways of doing things can have a considerable impact on people's lives.

There is no one 'best' way to approach management problems or situations. We have therefore shied away from suggesting absolute solutions in any area. You may have noticed however that a number of general themes emerge throughout the book. These obviously reflect our philosophies of how management, in a general sense, should be approached.

The dominant themes revolve around *teams* and *people*. We are convinced that your success as a manager ultimately depends on how you lead, manage and deal with your employees, both individually and as a team. As Torrington (1989 : 225) succinctly states: 'The nucleus of the organisation is the working team of individuals, each of whom have different aspirations, skills and needs.'

In almost every chapter we emphasise that managers in today's complex environments can no longer simply tell or order people what to do. You must work through them, gain their commitment, involve them in planning and making decisions, motivate and guide them, rather than simply push and coerce them in the desired direction. If you do not work with your employees, you may still get the job done; we accept this. We have seen managers behaving in such ways on occasions too numerous to mention. Our impression is that the situation becomes management *versus* employees. The notion of working *together* is replaced by bullying, distrust, suspicion and a general feeling of dissatisfaction amongst the workforce. If the organisation, department, division or section is to get anywhere, we see the greatest scope lying in the situation where the manager establishes a partnership with those for whom he holds responsibility.

The second thrust also relates to people, but this time groups of people: the team. Many problems in today's complex milieu cannot be effectively handled by only one person. A team approach to problem-solving, planning and developing is strongly advocated. Your job then becomes one of team builder and developer; a leader who can mould individual talents, strengths and aspirations together into a productive team. To do this you must balance task, individual and group needs within the framework of organisational direction and requirements.

The third theme is closely related to the first two; much of our material strongly promotes the development of employees as a means for organisational improvement. We believe that most employees have the desire and ability to develop and improve themselves and their performance in the work place. The benefit of this naturally flows to the organisation in terms of worker satisfaction and increased output and productivity. We suggest throughout the book that one of the prime foci of your role is the improvement of your staff through continued development. Development opportunities exist in many of the activities that you, your employees and your work teams face. Your job is to identify these opportunities and fuse the developmental aspects with the desired organisational outcomes. Development can be fostered through employee participation in making decisions, setting targets, planning, meetings and supervision; as well as through the more formal mechanisms such as the developmental appraisal process and structured staff development.

At the beginning of the book we stated that you need not read all the chapters in sequence, or even necessarily refer to all sections. However, even the reading of just a small proportion of the materials will show how the seemingly diverse topics are related and how common themes emerge. Different management skills cannot be viewed independently. It is not realistic, for example, to discuss the development of an effective management team without having at least a basic understanding of motivation, decision-making, target-setting, effective meetings and a number of other related issues. The skills you develop are dependent on each other. To be a complete manager necessitates a willingness to work for development across a whole range of skills. In the same way that the Olympic sprinter must develop his arm as well as his leg muscles, all-round development seems to have greatest potential for the manager who wants to run an effective race.

The themes we have identified encapsulate the basic thrust of the chapters. Not everything, of course, can be so easily categorised. The book tries to allow and encourage the manager in you to develop. It presents the opportunity to identify and diagnose your own needs, and those of your organisation, and then to progress with those in mind. The skills, schemes and actions discussed will not on their own solve your problems. They are not intended to. But they have the potential to provide conditions in which you, your staff and your area of responsibility can all grow and develop.

The more reflective and skilled you become, the greater your ability to deal with problems as they arise. Organisations change and people change within and outside their organisations' increasingly permeable boundaries; they change as their needs, aspirations and preferences change. The effective manager continues to learn and grow also, so he can cope with his changing circumstances and responsibilities. To some, this book may be a beginning, to others a refresher. Whatever the use to which it is put, and whatever the management context in which the material might be applied, we hope it has helped you in some way to becoming a more competent and confident manager.

References

Torrington, D. (1989) *Effective Management: People and Organisation*, Routledge : London.

The Authors

Kenneth Stott is Lecturer in Management Studies at Nanyang Technological University in Singapore. He has worked with managers at all levels, and his broad management, consultancy, research and teaching experience has been gained in the United Kingdom and Singapore. His publications cover a wide range of management topics.

Allan Walker is Senior Lecturer at Northern Territory University in Australia. A specialist in programmes for senior managers from the education service, he gained his own management experience in Australia before completing doctoral studies in the USA. He has researched and published in a number of management areas.

INDEX

A

absoluteness of responsibility, 638
acceptable area, 517, 518, 519, 526
accountability, 623
achievement (motivating factor), 65, 86, 93
action-centred leadership, 31-35
Adams, J. Stacy, 71
adaptive process, 204
adaptive supervision *see* supervision
advancement (motivating factor), 89, 93
affiliation (motivating factor), 65
agenda, 517, 600-602
alternatives, generation of, 234, 237
      also see brainstorming techniques
analytical report, 657
analytical thinking, 239-241
anything-goes structure, 287-288
appraisal, developmental *see* developmental appraisal
apprenticeship, 311
approach vs avoidance conflicts, 433
arbitration *see* negotiation
assertiveness (influence strategy), 483-484, 491-493, 497
assess *see* review
authority delegation, 623, 648
authority-level principle, 638
Autocratic Method, 224
avoidance vs approach conflicts, 433

B

balanced teams, developing, 187-191
bar charts, 666
bargaining, 480-482, 491-493, 496
      also see negotiation
behaviour analysis, 321-322
behavioural approach (influencing strategies), 479-499
behavioural approach (leadership style), 20-23
behavioural role (of teams), 163, 182, 184
Belbin, Meredith, 164
between-team conflicts, 434

binding questions, 539
body language, 275-276, 534-535
bounded rationality, 206
brainstorming techniques, 145-147, 237-238, 317, 460
also see alternatives (generation of)
Bridges, Edward, 216-218
bridging, 533
briefing, 151, 160
build-up pattern, 723-724
bystander managers, 500

C
category arrangement, 723-724
causes vs symptoms, 208-209, 682
Chairman, the (a team role), 169-170, 189, 192
chairman (role at meetings), 603-604
checkpoints, progress, 126, 139, 151, 160, 651
Clean Sheet Method, 146
clinical supervision, 345-346
closed questions, 281, 539
coalition (influence strategy), 485-486, 491-493, 499
collaborative approach (to settling conflicts), 471
commitment, shared, 373-374
commitment of employees, 1, 75, 429
committees, 612
communication
        lack of c., 438, 580-582
organisational c., 437
Company Worker, the (a team role), 175-176, 195
compensations, non-specific, 532
complete delegation, 625
Completer, the (a team role), 179-180, 197-198
conflicts
        accommodating c., 450
        avoidance vs approach c., 433
        avoiding c., 446-449
        between-team c., 434
        collaborative approach to c., 459
        compromising (a c.-solving strategy), 452-456
        c. handling techniques, 442-471
        c. initiators, 434-435, 438-441
        c. made constructive, 433, 471

c. not always bad, 430-432
dealing with c., 10, 430-472
emotional c., 440
intergroup c., 468
organisationally initiated c., 435-437, 470
people-initiated c., 437-441
role c., 470
types of c., 433-434
use of force (to settle c.), 451
conformity, 199-200
      also see groupthink
consensus, 126, 149
Consensus Method, 225, 230
consideration (leadership function), 20, 22
Consultancy Method, 225, 229, 230
contingency approach (leadership style), 20, 23, 36
contingency planning, 149, 156, 160
control, 33-35, 139, 153-154
      also see evaluation
coordinated sets of interviews, 290-291
cost vs consequences (in decision-making), 242
cost-benefit analysis, 241
cost-cutting, 533
cost-effectiveness analysis, 241
counselling, 394
counter-offers, 530-531
courage (leadership quality), 18-19
creativity
      c. in decision-making, 234-237, 254
      team c., 112, 145
crisis, operational, 423
crisis decisions, 204, 254
cue cards, 718

D
data report, 657
deadlines, 647
decisions, types of, 203-204, 251, 254
decision implementation, 245
decision-making, 8, 113, 126, 202-256
      d. in planning team action, 126, 148, 160
      d. process, 206-251

d. rationality, 206
d. styles, 224-230
participative vs directive d., 36-38
when to involve others, 216-223
Decision Tree Approach, 222
deep decisions, 204
also see decisions, types of
delaying tactic, 541
delegation, 11, 52, 568, 621-656
benefits of d., 626-627
complete d., 625
d. by results principle, 638
d. contracts, 647, 649
d. inhibitors, 628-634
d. sequence, 638-653
d. vs abdication, 623
d. vs directing, 623
d. vs staff development, 644-645
increased d., 634-635
levels of d., 625-626
limited d., 626
principles for effective d., 638
substantial d., 625-626
development, staff *see* staff development
developmental appraisal, 9, 362-409
benefits of d., 368-369
d. process, 377-408
principles of d., 372-375
problems of d., 375-377
purposes of d., 369-370
Developmental Appraisal Employee form (DAE), 378, 379-381, 385
Developmental Appraisal Joint form (DAJ), 378, 383, 406-407
developmental options, 344, 345-351
directive (leadership style), 38
discharging of task, 126, 152, 161
discipline, need for, 155
discrepancy
d. performance, 156, 161
rectifying of d., 153-154
discussions, open
at meetings, 605
conditions for successful d., 395-406
in planning team action, 126, 144, 159-160

in staff development process, 388-406
distractions, 278, 403
documentation, 401, 606
doubt-forming questions, 539

E
effectiveness vs efficiency, 1
in time management, 546
80/20 Rule, 565
Elite Group Method, 225
environmental conditions (as a motivator), 89-90
Equity Theory of Motivation, 71
evaluation see review
execution of task, 418-420
executive summary, 664, 680, 722
Expectancy Theory of Motivation, 69-71

F
facilitating, 452, 465, 466
false assumptions, 279
feedback soliciting, 157, 161, 346, 348, 349, 350, 399-400
Final Say Method, 224
fishbowl supervision, 353
flexibility (in leadership), 44, 354
flexitime, 85
fog index, 674
follow-up mechanisms, 373
also see review
formative process, 362, 369
friendliness (influence strategy), 479-480, 491-493, 495
functional definition principle, 638
functional role (of teams), 163

G
geographical pattern, 723-724
goals *see* targets
graphs, 666
graphics, 666
groups vs teams, 111
group interview, 291

groupthink, 231, 468
growth log, 348

H
halo effect, 279
Herzberg (Frederick) 2-Factor Theory of Needs, 32, 61-63
human skills (leadership function), 20, 22, 155

I
implementation, 126, 152, 161
indicators, progress, 126, 139, 151
influencing, 52, 473-504
        strategies, 475-499, 540-541
information gathering *see* review
information management, 661
ingratiation strategies (influencing), 540
initiating structure (leadership function), 20, 22
innovative process (in decision-making), 204
Innovator, the (a team role), 172-173, 193
inside time thieves, 568
        also see time thieves
in-team conflicts, 434
integrative agreements, 532
integrity (leadership quality), 18, 19
intention statements, 712, 714, 724
interviews,
        conducting i., 272-278
        confidentiality in i., 294
        data inquiring i., 294
        employment i., 292
        hindrances to successful i., 278-279
        identifying key topics before i., 268
        interpreting visual clues at i., 275-276
        i. pitfalls, 295-297
        i. structure, 285-288
        organisation of i., 289-292
        planning i., 265-272
        purpose of i., 261
        questioning techniques at i., 265, 267, 280-283
        the environment for effective i., 265-266
        time allotment at i., 268, 274-275

interviewing, 257-304
>   practices, 261-264
>   skills and ethics, 265, 272-278
investigation, 234-242
involvement (as a motivator), 85-86
isolation analysis, 211-216

J
jargon, 678, 712, 717, 736
job control, 551
job enlargement (as a motivator), 85
job enrichment (as a motivator), 85, 93
job-swapping (staff development programme), 312
joint problem-solving, 401
judgemental mandates, 344, 351-353

K
key result areas, 416, 551, 588

L
Lawler, Edward, 69
leadership, 4, 6, 14-53
>   action-centred l., 31-35
>   balanced l., 106, 110
>   definition of l., 15-16
>   l. activities, 33-35
>   l. analysis form, 27
>   l. qualities, 17
>   l. styles, 20-23, 36-38, 39-44
>   l. vs management, 14-15
>   shifting-l., 19-20
leadership theories, 17-23
>   ongoing research on l., 52-53
leading questions, 282, 539
limited delegation, 626
limited rationality, 206
listening skills, 275, 276-277, 350, 401, 534-535
log-rolling, 533
loose-tight structure, 288, 374-375
lose-lose situation, 431
lose-win situation, 431

M

maintenance factors (Herzberg Theory), 62-63

Majority Rules Method, 225

management, definition of, 2, 15

Management by Objectives (Drucker), 412

managers

        as motivators, 76

        as team leaders, 118

        as technical experts, 1, 19-20

        complex role of, 1, 140

        types of, 500-501

Managerial Grid, 20-21

managing, people *see* people management

managing, time *see* time management

managing information, 661

marginal analysis, 241

Maslow (Abraham) Hierarchy of Needs, 32, 58-61

maturity, components of, 22-23

McClelland (David) Theory of Needs, 65

McGregor's X and Y Theory, 72-74, 375, 628

mediating, 452, 465

meetings

        choice of location, 614

        conditions for effective m., 610-617

        conducting m., 603-608

        digressions, 604

        effective m., 599

        follow-up action, 608-610

        functions of m., 595-596

        length of m., 613

        m. preparation, 599

        minutes, 609

        role of chairman, 603-604

        running productive m., 11, 592-620

        seating arrangements, 614

        unproductive m., 596-599

minutes, 609

money (as a motivator), 91

monitoring, 126, 139, 153, 651

motivating, 7, 55-98, 422

        motivation factors (Herzberg Theory), 62-63

        motivation theories, 58-63, 69-75

        practical framework of m., 57-92

rationale behind m., 56
motivators, types of, 62-63, 85-91
Motivator-Evaluator, the (a team role), 113, 174, 194-195

N
needs
      group n., 32
      hierarchy of n., 58-63
      identifying n., 78, 315-316
      individual n., 32, 155, 367
      individual vs organisation n., 364, 367, 420
      theories of n., 32, 58-63
      types of n., 56, 58-61
negotiating, 10, 505-545
negotiation
      an influence strategy *see* bargaining
      n. sequence, 508-510, 511-516, 526-534
      n. skills, 534-542
      n. style, 541-542, 542-544
      n. tactics, 541-542
      n. vs facilitating, 465
      preparing for n., 516-523, 527-528

O
objectives *see* targets
on-the-move supervision, 351-352
one-to-one interview, 289
one-to-one supervision, 345-346
on-site withdrawal (staff development programmes), 311
open-evaluation, 146
openness, organisational, 372, 388, 403
open questions, 281, 539
operational crisis, 423
opt-out leader, 41
organisation charts, 666
organisationally initiated conflicts, 435-437
Ouchi's Z Theory, 74-75
outcome statements, 712, 714, 717, 724
output supervision, 352
outside time thieves, 568 *also see* time thieves

P

panel interview, 289-290

paperwork, excessive, 375, 423, 578-579

Pareto's Law, 565

participation (as a motivator), 85-86

participative (leadership style), 36, 38

participative decision-making, 216-221, 231, 254, 329, 422, 437

people conflicts, 434

people-initiated conflicts, 437

people management, 12, 15, 744
    also see leadership and teams

perfectionism, 576-577

performance events, 393

performance markers, 126, 139, 151, 160, 647

personal forces, 56

pie charts, 666

plan execution, 418-419

planning
    a managerial activity, 33-35, 139, 357

short-term p., 139

Plant, the (a team role), 172-173

politicking, 116

Porter, Lyman, 69

power (motivating factor), 65

presentations, 702-741
    arrangement of information, 723-724
    the audience, 713, 731, 734
    choice of location, 714
    delivery, 705, 729-738
    functions of p., 703, 710-711
    preparing p., 705, 708-717
    p. structure, 717, 720-729
    question and answer session, 728
    seating arrangement, 714
    time allotment, 714, 717
    types of p., 703
    types of presenters, 737-738
    use of cue cards, 718
    use of humour and anecdotes, 717, 718, 731, 732
    use of visual aids, 738-739

pressure tactics, 265, 284-285

principles of parity and responsibility, 638

prioritising, 145, 159, 552, 566-568, 587

proactive vs reactive tasks, 565
problems
      early detection, 210
      joint p.-solving, 401, 529
      p. confrontation, 459
      p. identification skills, 207-210
      p.-solving, 207, 211-212
            also see decision-making
procrastination, 575-576
progress checkpoints, 126, 139, 151, 160, 651
promotion (as a motivator), 89, 93
pros and cons pattern, 723-724
pull forces, 56
pulling together, 104-105, 110
push forces, 56

Q
Quality of Working Life (QWL), 85
questions
      quality of q. 267
      types of q., 280-282, 539-540
questioning technique, 538-539

R
rational strategies, 540
rationality in decision-making, 206, 254
reactive vs proactive tasks, 565
reasoning (influence strategy), 482-483, 491-493, 496
reciprocity (influence strategy), 480-482, 491-493, 496
recognition (as a motivator), 86-87
recommendation report, 658
redirected question, 541
relationships, quality, 103-104, 108
relationship behaviour, 22
reports
      layout tips, 663-666
      outline of r., 681-690
      purposes of r., 660
      types of r., 657
      use of visual aids, 666
      writing style, 667-674

writing techniques, 11, 657-701

research, 126, 143, 159

resources, limited, 436, 651

Resource Investigator, the (a team role), 178-179, 196-197

responsibility (as a motivator), 88-89, 93

responsibility, shared, 372

responsibilities, assignment of, 126, 150-151

review

        follow-up action, 326, 652-654

        formal vs informal r., 250

        managerial function, 33-35

        role in planning team action, 126, 139, 153-154, 157, 161

        role in staff appraisal, 420-421

reward (as a motivator), 86-87, 93, 157

risk-taking, 88, 89

role-modelling, 246

role preferences, 181, 187

rules and regulations leader, 39

S

sanctions (influence strategy), 486-487, 491-493, 499

scalar principle, 638

searching questions, 281-282

selective process (in decision-making), 204

self-

        conflicts, 433

        control, 551

        evaluation, 399

        supervision, 349

7D Scheme for Planning Team Action, 137-158, 159-161

shadowing, 557-558

Shaper, the (a team role), 170-171, 189, 193

sharing leader, 40-41

shifting-leadership approach, 19-20

shotgun managers, 500

signals, body *see* body language

Simon, Herbert, 207

situational elements (impact on leadership), 20, 21-22

Situational Leadership Theory, 21, 22

skills (not in-born), 3

solo (autocratic) leader, 39

staff development, 305-335

a managerial function, 9, 144, 155, 317, 361, 370
guidelines for improving s., 329-331
s. vs delegation, 644-645
s. vs staff training, 305-308
staff development programmes
benefits of s., 307-309
developmental supervision, 313
also see supervision, adaptive
formal vs informal methods, 311-314
on-the-job s., 311
planning and developing s., 317-329
types of s., 309-314
staff involvement *see* participative
staff training, 305-308
standard decisions, 203, 251, 254
straight-down-the-line structure, 285-287
strengths and weaknesses analysis, 122
substantial delegation, 625-626
summary *see* executive summary
summative process, 362, 369
supervision, adaptive, 9, 313, 336, 341-361
developmental options, 344, 345-351
judgemental mandates, 344, 351-353
supervision, judgemental vs developmental, 339
supervision styles, 338, 345-353
supervisory responsibilities, 341
support (as a motivator), 89-90
sweet-talking leader, 39-40
symptoms vs real causes, 208-209, 682

tables, use of (in presentations), 666
tactician managers, 500, 504
targets
individual vs organisation t., 412, 420-421, 744
joint t., 467
realistic t., 400, 552
shared t., 102-103, 108
specific t., 552
written down vs verbal t., 552-553
target management, 411, 412
also see target-setting
target-setting, 10, 126, 151, 410-429, 551-557

advantages of t., 421-423

t. problems, 423-424

t. process, 415-421

target statements, 425-428

weaknesses in t., 428

task

proactive vs reactive t., 565

t. behaviour, 22

t. brief, 641, 643, 645

t. communication and definiton, 126, 140, 141-142, 159

t. division, 126, 150-151, 160

t. execution, 418-420

t. implementation, 126, 152

t. initiation, 565

urgent vs important t., 566

team

appropriateness of t. members, 187-191, 198-200

developing t. balance, 187-191

phases of t. development, 115-124

planning t. action, 7, 137-161

t.-building strategies, 102-106

t. characteristics chart, 107-108

t. cohesion, 104-105, 110, 155

t. condition assessment form, 131-135

t. conflicts, 434

t. creativity, 112, 145

t. development, 5, 99-201, 744

t. management, 164-165, 169

t. performance evaluation form, 101

t. supervision, 346-349

teams

t. vs groups, 111

developing balanced t., 187-191

developing effective t., 7, 99-135, 164-165, 169

functions of t., 110-113, 140

team roles

developing t., 8, 163-201

t. preferences, 181, 187

t. supervision, 346-347

t. theory, 165

types of t., 163, 169-180

teamwork

t. inhibitors, 128-129

systematic approach to effective t., 124-126
Teamworker, the (a team role), 177-178, 195-196
3-D Management Style Theory, 21-22
threshold limit, 513, 514, 517, 519, 526
time analysis methods, 557-563
time log, 559
time management, 10, 422, 546-591
      benefits of t., 549
      effective vs efficient t., 546
      t. secrets, 589
time planners, 584-588
time thieves, 11, 550, 568-573
      outside vs inside t., 568
timing (negotiation factor), 542
training, staff, 306-307
Trait Theory, 17
transactional leadership, 52
transformative leadership, 52-53
trust, 88, 89, 93, 222

U
unity of command principle, 638
upward referral, 485, 491-493, 498
urgent vs important tasks, 566

V
visual aids, 666, 738-739
visual clues, reading *see* body language
Vroom, Victor, 69

W
wants *see* needs
win-lose situation, 431, 451
win-win situation, 431

X/Y
X and Y Theory (McGregor), 72-74, 375, 628

Z
Z Theory (Ouchi), 74-75
zone of acceptance, 216, 218